FREEDOM FROM VIOLENCE AND LIES

Essays on Russian Poetry and Music by Simon Karlinsky

Simon Karlinsky, early 1970s
Photograph by Joseph Zimbrolt

Ars Rossica

Series Editor — David M. Bethea
(University of Wisconsin-Madison)

FREEDOM FROM VIOLENCE AND LIES

Essays on Russian
Poetry and Music
by Simon Karlinsky

Edited by
Robert P. Hughes,
Thomas A. Koster,
Richard Taruskin

Boston
2013

Library of Congress Cataloging-in-Publication Data:
A catalog record for this book as available from the Library of Congress.

Copyright © 2013 Academic Studies Press
All rights reserved
ISBN 978-1-61811-810-3

On the cover:
Heinrich Campendonk (1889–1957),
Bayerische Landschaft mit Fuhrwerk (ca. 1918).
Oil on panel.
In Simon Karlinsky's collection, 1946–2009.
© 2012 Artists Rights Society (ARS),
New York / VG Bild-Kunst, Bonn

Published by Academic Studies Press in 2013.
28 Montfern Avenue
Brighton, MA 02135, USA
press@academicstudiespress.com
www.academicstudiespress.com

Contents

Preface 7

I PUSHKIN AND ROMANTICISM

1. Two Pushkin Studies. 14
   - *I.* Pushkin, Chateaubriand, and the Romantic Pose 14
   - *II.* The Amber Beads of Crimea 27
2. Fortunes of an Infanticide 43
3. Pushkin Re-Englished 49
4. A Mystical Musicologist 56
5. Küchelbecker's Trilogy, *Izhorsky*, As an Example of the Romantic Revival of the Medieval Mystery Play 62
6. Misanthropy and Sadism in Lermontov's Plays 77

II MODERNISM, ITS PAST, ITS LEGACY

7. Annensky's Materiality 86
8. Zinaida Gippius and Russian Poetry 97
9. Died and Survived 105
10. Symphonic Structure in Andrei Bely's *Pervoe svidanie* 114
11. The Death and Resurrection of Mikhail Kuzmin 125
12. Nikolai Gumilyov and Théophile Gautier 133
13. An Emerging Reputation Comparable to Pushkin's 145
14. Tsvetaeva in English: A Review Article 154
15. A New Edition of the Poems of Marina Tsvetaeva 167
16. New Information about the Émigré Period of Marina Tsvetaeva (Based on Material from Her Correspondence with Anna Tesková) ... 174
17. Pasternak, Pushkin, and the Ocean in Marina Tsvetaeva's *From the Sea* ... 182
18. "Traveling to Geneva...": On a Less-than-Successful Trip by Marina Tsvetaeva 194
19. Isadora Had a Taste for "Russian Love" 205
20. Surrealism in Twentieth-Century Russian Poetry: Churilin, Zabolotsky, Poplavsky 212
21. Evtushenko and the Underground Poets 229

III POETRY ABROAD

22. In Search of Poplavsky: A Collage 242
23. Morshen, or a Canoe to Eternity.................................267
24. Morshen after *Ekho i zerkalo*...................................291
25. A Hidden Masterpiece: Valery Pereleshin's *Ariel*..................301
26. Russian Culture in Manchuria and the Memoirs of Valery Pereleshin...310

IV ON CHAIKOVSKY

27. A Review of *Tchaikovsky: A Self-Portrait* by Alexandra Orlova.........322
28. Should We Retire Chaikovsky?...................................330
29. Man or Myth? The Retrieval of the True Chaikovsky 339
30. Chaikovsky and the Pantomime of Derision........................346

V ON STRAVINSKY

31. The Composer's Workshop 358
32. The Repatriation of Igor Stravinsky 369
33. Igor Stravinsky and Russian Preliterate Theater 376

VI ON SHOSTAKOVICH

34. "Our Destinies Are Bad" 398
35. Taking Notes for Testimony.....................................408

VII SONG AND DANCE

36. The Uses of Chaliapin..416
37. Russian Comic Opera in the Age of Catherine the Great 423
38. Contralto: Rossini, Gautier and Gumilyov 440
39. A Cultural Educator of Genius 457
40. Opera and Drama in Ravel 475

Index of Names 486

Preface

Simon Karlinsky (1924–2009) was a prolific and provocative scholar of modern Russian literature, music and, latterly, sexual politics. In this volume we republish a selection of his reviews and essays about poetry and music, leaving aside his even more numerous writings on Russian prose fiction, literary history, and cultural phenomena. As there are over 250 publications to his credit, including a number of full-length books, this represents no more than ten to fifteen percent of his published writing.

Karlinsky taught at the University of California, Berkeley for some thirty years. His path to a scholarly career was anything but direct. An only child, he was born 22 September 1924 in the Russian enclave of the Manchurian city of Harbin, where he received his primary education and developed his tastes for music and literature.[1] The family left for the United States in 1938, after the Japanese occupation of Manchuria and the worsening of conditions there. He attended high school and college in Los Angeles before enlisting in the US Army in 1944.[2] Between 1945 and 1951 he served as a Russian interpreter in occupied Berlin, not only for the Army but, after discharge from the Army, for the American military government and the office of the Control Council for Germany.[3] He spent a year (1951–52) in Paris, where he studied musical composition with Arthur Honegger at the École Normale de Musique. Subsequently he returned to Berlin, where from 1952 to 1957 he was employed again as liaison officer and interpreter for the US Berlin Command. During that period he

---

1 Consult herein his essay entitled "Russian Culture in Manchuria and the Memoirs of Valery Pereleshin" for personal reminiscences of life in Harbin at that time, In the 1990s, SK wrote an extended memoir of the first fourteen years of his life. It remains unpublished, and is now preserved among the Simon Karlinsky Papers at the Bancroft Library, University of California, Berkeley.
2 For his life in Los Angeles, see the opening pages of "In Search of Poplavsky: A Collage" in the present volume.
3 An episode from his life in Berlin is recounted in S. Karli [Simon Karlinsky], "My Most Durable Translation," *New Yorker*, 10 October 1959.

continued his studies under Boris Blacher at what was then the Staatliche Hochschule für Musik, and several of his scores were performed. He remained deeply involved in music and dance throughout his life, and the music of Chaikovsky and Stravinsky drew his particular admiration. But he ultimately decided against a composer's career, and he came to regard that phase of his life as a closed book. To one of us, who was pestering him for a peek at his scores, he finally wrote, drolly but emphatically:

> As for my compositions, I'm sure you don't want to see them. As the quotation goes, "that was in another country, and besides, the wench is dead." There was a cantata which Gérard Souzay was to sing in Berlin, but the concert was cancelled. Later on, an American baritone wanted to do it, but that concert was also cancelled. Ergo, one can't fight fate.[4]

And that is when his early love of literature (Russian, French, English, and in time German and Polish) came to the fore. Karlinsky received a BA degree from the University of California, Berkeley in 1960, an MA from Harvard University in 1961, and a PhD in Slavic Languages and Literatures from UC Berkeley in 1964, where he was immediately appointed to the faculty and rapidly rose to the rank of full professor by 1967. He was twice awarded the Guggenheim Fellowship. At Berkeley, he taught with great panache a wide variety of courses and seminars, including advanced language and stylistics, surveys of eighteenth- and nineteenth-century Russian literature, Russian Romanticism, Russian Modernism, and the history of the Russian theater and drama, as well as single-author courses on Pushkin, Gogol, Tolstoi, and Chekhov. He retired in 1991.

Karlinsky's career as a publishing scholar was extraordinary. His first, pioneering book (his revised dissertation, written under the direction of G. P. Struve) was on Marina Tsvetaeva and appeared in 1966. This study was the product of indefatigable research into Tsvetaeva's biography and spectacular close reading of her wildly idiosyncratic poetry. Karlinsky's work became the cornerstone for future Tsvetaeva studies well before her

---

[4] Simon Karlinsky to Richard Taruskin, 28 August 1985, in the editor's possession. The quotation is from Christopher Marlowe's *The Jew of Malta*:
> Friar Barnardine. Thou hast committed—
> Barabas. Fornication? But that
>   Was in another country, and besides
>   The wench is dead.

renown either in the West or in Soviet Russia. He published a second book on Tsvetaeva in 1985, now taking full advantage of the mass of research and analysis inspired by his initial study.

To be reckoned among Karlinsky's most valuable contributions, widely read inside and outside the profession, is his now-standard edition of the selected letters of Anton Chekhov (1973). He collaborated closely on the translations, and his erudite, scintillating introduction and annotations to the letters comprise a virtual critical biography of the writer whom he considered an exemplary human being.

Other volumes under Karlinsky's editorship were signposts in the English-language reception of Russian émigré literature, a phenomenon that he knew at first hand. He coedited a two-volume issue of the journal *TriQuarterly* in 1974 devoted to Russian literature and culture in the West, which was republished in 1977 as *The Bitter Air of Exile: Russian Writers in the West, 1922-1972*. His editorial work was decisive and his contributions therein included introductions, articles, commentary, and translations. The commanding figure for him was Vladimir Nabokov (long before his fame as an English novelist), about whom Karlinsky wrote frequently and discerningly. His edition of the Russian writer's correspondence with the American critic Edmund Wilson, *The Nabokov-Wilson Letters, 1940-1971* (1979; German expanded edition, 1995; revised and expanded, *Dear Bunny, Dear Volodya*, 2001), was widely hailed.

Meanwhile, *The Sexual Labyrinth of Nikolai Gogol* had been published in 1976 and had provoked a storm of controversy over its assertion of the reflection of repressed homosexuality in the writer's life and work. This study signaled a series of articles, reviews, translations, and conference appearances on the role of sexuality in art, homosexual themes, and queer theory that were at the time almost unprecedented in the study of Russian literature and culture. Karlinsky's writings on the subject appeared primarily in the leading gay outlets, but his concerns were echoed across the board. He was particularly active in exploring the hidden and not-so-hidden lives of some Russian cultural figures who happened to be homosexual.[5] He played a leading role in promoting or defending the reputa-

---

[5] For one example among several, see Simon Karlinsky, "Russia's Gay Literature and Culture: The Impact of the October Revolution," in *Hidden from History: Reclaiming the Gay and Lesbian Past*, ed. Martin Bauml Duberman, Martha Vicinus, and George Chauncey, Jr. (New York: New American Library, 1989), 347-64, 552-59.

tions of outstanding gay figures such as the émigré poet Valery Pereleshin and the persecuted Soviet poet Gennady Trifonov, along with Mikhail Kuzmin, Sergei Diaghilev, and Pyotr Chaikovsky. At the same time, he worked to combat what he described in *Christopher Street* as the "self-imposed brainwashing ... in the [American] gay movement" in the 1970s. Subjects that he addressed included the virulently homophobic nature in the practice of Marxist-Leninist ideology, to which a number of Western gay liberationists then subscribed and which, Karlinsky pointed out, had given rise to genocidal terror in the Soviet Union and China.

The author himself considered his *Russian Drama from Its Beginnings to the Age of Pushkin* (1985), a book that grew out of an admired course in the history of the Russian theater, his greatest achievement. It is the result of monumental research and thinking about the origins and early development of the Russian stage. His colleagues lamented the fact that he never produced a follow-up, for he was a rare connoisseur as well of the plays of Gogol, Ostrovsky, Tolstoi, Chekhov, and the Russian Symbolist and Postsymbolist theater.

A steady stream of articles and reviews in such mainstream media as the *New York Times Book Review*, the *TLS*, and the *Nation*, and in the professional journals, addressed a wide gamut of subjects and personalities. Karlinsky's interests ranged from saints' lives and the *Domostroi* to Soviet institutions; from eighteenth-century Russian comic opera to Chaikovsky, Ravel, Diaghilev, Stravinsky, and Shostakovich; from the prose of Gogol, Dostoevsky, Tolstoi, and his revered Chekhov to the novels of Nabokov and Solzhenitsyn. He devoted special attention to Modernist poetry and drama (Gippius, Annensky, Kuzmin, Acmeists, Futurists and Soviet-era poets) and was the enthusiastic champion of such younger émigré poets as Pereleshin and Nikolai Morshen.[6]

Karlinsky had a nuanced command of both Russian and English. He was a master of simultaneous translation, a superb interpreter—and performer—of literary texts. Numerous translations of works by and about

---

[6] For lists of his publications, see the bibliography compiled by Molly Molloy, pp. 4–31 of the Festschrift in his honor, *For SK: In Celebration of the Life and Career of Simon Karlinsky*, ed. Michael S. Flier and Robert P. Hughes (Oakland: Berkeley Slavic Specialties, 1994); and the more selective list accompanying Christopher Putney's entry "Simon Karlinsky" in *Gay and Lesbian Literature*, vol. 2, ed. Tom Pendergast and Sara Pendergast (Detroit: St. James Press, 1998), 201–4.

Russian writers bear his imprint, both acknowledged and silent; his readings of many major texts will endure.

The heyday of Karlinsky's scholarly career coincided with the Cold War and an extended period of stagnation in social, political and cultural life in the Soviet Union, and much of his most valuable work is best understood against that background. His disgust with the restrictive and restricted worldviews, rampant censorship, and hidebound ideologies that were so characteristic of the period (1950s–1980s) is everywhere evident in his published writings.[7]

Karlinsky was in his eighty-fifth year when he died at his home in Kensington, California, on 5 July 2009. He was surrounded in his later years by friends and colleagues, two devoted care-givers, and his beloved companion of thirty-five years, Peter Carleton (whom he was able to marry only in 2008). We offer the present volume as a tribute to the distinguished career of Simon Karlinsky as a teacher and publishing scholar.

The idea for this collection originated in our conversations at and after a conference held in Simon's memory at the University of California, Berkeley in October 2010 ("'Freedom from Violence and Lies': A Conference in Celebration of the Life and Work of Simon Karlinsky").[8] Several of his colleagues translated articles for the present book, and we are grateful to them for this contribution: Joan Grossman, Olga Raevsky-Hughes, Joachim Klein, Liza Knapp, Hugh McLean, Eric Naiman, and Kevin O'Brien. We also extend our appreciation to the helpful staff of the Bancroft Library of the University of California, Berkeley for providing us access to the Simon Karlinsky Papers prior to the complete processing of this collection (BANC MSS 2010/177), to Peter Carleton, to David Frick and Irina Paperno of Berkeley's Department of Slavic Languages and Literatures, to Sharona Vedol, our editor at Academic Studies Press,

---

[7] The reader will occasionally come across a "current," "new," or "recent" reference that pertains to a time when the essay first appeared. We have not endeavored to revise all such language, and as noted, this context is well worth understanding and appreciating.

[8] The title is from Anton Chekhov's letter to Aleksei Pleshcheev, 4 October 1888: "My holy of holies is the human body, health, intelligence, talent, inspiration, love and the most absolute freedom imaginable, freedom from violence and lies, no matter what form the latter two take." *Letters of Anton Chekhov*, translated from the Russian by Michael Henry Heim in collaboration with Simon Karlinsky; selection, commentary, and introduction by Simon Karlinsky (New York: Harper & Row, 1973), 109.

and to the publishers identified herein who granted permission for republication.

The editors have supplied contextualizing postscripts and footnotes (identified as such), and have silently added references and made small corrections as needed. A reader moving continuously through the essays will find some repetition on related topics, but we decided there was value to preserving the integrity of each individual piece and limited our editorial intrusion. We gave much thought to how we should normalize the transliteration of Russian in SK's texts (republished from a wide range of periodicals and miscellanies) and in our footnotes and postscripts. In the end, for Russian names we largely adopted the approach in the *Handbook of Russian Literature*, edited by Victor Terras (New Haven: Yale University Press, 1985), which is close to the systems used in periodicals like the *New York Times Book Review* and the *TLS*. The adjectival endings –*ый* and –*ий* (which appear in many Russian names) are rendered by –*y* in the English text. The soft and hard signs are usually ignored. However, in the patronymic suffixes –*ьевич* and –*ьевна* the initial soft sign is rendered by *i*. The front vowels ё, я and ю are rendered by *yo, ya,* and *yu*, and a stand-alone ы is rendered by *y*. The Cyrillic front vowel e, however, is rendered by *e*, and so the sequence of two front vowels *ee* in Russian remains *ee* in transliteration. Thus the initial *e* of a transliterated word is usually pronounced "ye," and we adjure our non-Russian readers to pronounce the double vowel *ee* as two separate syllables, each involving a diphthong ("ye"-"ye"), and not as the *ee* in *tweet*. For some Russian names where a standard variant has been in wide use for a very long time (e.g., Chaliapin, Diaghilev, Rachmaninoff)—but with Chaikovsky as a notable exception—we have retained that variant. Words and quotations transliterated from Russian as well as Russian citations in the footnotes employ the system used by the Library of Congress (LC), but with diacriticals omitted.

RPH
TAK
RT
September 2012

PUSHKIN AND ROMANTICISM

Two Pushkin Studies

I. Pushkin, Chateaubriand, and the Romantic Pose[1]

The Romantic Pose—I

"*I* dare say it was the French who made boredom fashionable," says the naive Maksim Maksimovich in *Hero of Our Time*. The narrator disabuses him of this notion by informing him that the fashion of being bored had been invented by the English. For Lermontov and his readers in 1840, there was no doubt whatsoever that the Romantic pose of boredom and disillusionment had been invented and popularized singlehandedly by Lord Byron. Byron's phenomenal stranglehold on the literary world of the 1820s and 1830s had done much to obscure in the minds of both the writers and the public the great debt that the English poet owed his immediate predecessor, François-Auguste Chateaubriand. Lev Tolstoi, who had a better historical perspective than most, gives us an example of the Chateaubrianesque Romantic pose in the episode of the courtship of Julie Karagina by Boris Drubetskoi, in *War and Peace*.[2] Julie's pretense of having suffered a mysterious misfortune, of having become disillusioned with people and about her own future, is, despite certain lingering overtones of Karamzinist sentimentality, a rare case of quasi-Byronic affectation in a female character. (It was with the advent of Byron that Byronism became an exclusively male prerogative.) This Byronism *avant la lettre* is historically correct around 1812 if attributed to the vogue of Chateaubriand. Pitilessly, Tolstoi shows the attitude for what it is: a set of emotional mannerisms based on literary sources. Pushkin the prose writer, describing the arrival of Aleksei Berestov in the remote province in which the action of "Mistress as Maid" is set, would obviously have agreed with this view of the Romantic pose, and so would Maksim Maksimovich, although Lermontov himself would probably have had a reservation or

---

[1] Originally published in *California Slavic Studies* 2 (1963): 96–107.
[2] Lev Tolstoi, *War and Peace*, vol. 2, pt. 5, chap. 5.

two. As for Chateaubriand, who thought that he was describing a real phenomenon when he wrote *René*, he lived long enough to denounce most of the descendants of his famous hero as poseurs, and to express regret that he had ever started the trend.[3]

Chateaubriand and Byron

There can be no doubt of the prestige and popularity of Chateaubriand in Russia throughout Pushkin's adult life. Scenes from *Atala* decorate porcelain cups and vases manufactured in Russia in the 1820s.[4] The impact of *René* on Batyushkov is well documented. Chateaubriand and Ballanche were the major French sources of inspiration for Pushkin's close friend, the political philosopher Chaadaev. As early as 1810, Prince P. B. Kozlovsky (who much later was a friend of Pushkin's) wrote to Chateaubriand to inform him that *Atala* and *René* had been translated in Russia and had been "received with unparalleled avidity." He continued, "I have made deliberate inquiries, and was informed that even in Tobolsk the subscription for both works was great, and thus now the poor Siberian, wrapped in his furs, can dream of the beautiful sites where the Meschacebé flows!"[5] And a glance at the letter that Vyazemsky wrote to Chateaubriand in 1839, when, after Pushkin's death, he sent the aged writer a French translation of Pushkin's article "Milton and Chateaubriand's Translation of *Paradise Lost*,"[6] furnishes conclusive proof that Chateaubriand was a major and awesome literary figure to the majority of literate Russians throughout the period of Pushkin's career.

In retrospect, it seems clear that the work of Chateaubriand which had impressed his contemporaries most profoundly, *Le génie du christianisme*, was a labor of synthesis rather than of imagination. (Indeed, his only original contribution was the restoration of religion as a respectable intellectual pursuit.) With amazing thoroughness, he combined and fused the disparate elements which had appeared as early as the last half of the

---

[3] Chateaubriand, *Mémoires d'outre-tombe* (Monaco, 1958), 1:462.
[4] Reproductions are shown in *Literaturnoe nasledstvo*, vols. 33/34 (Moscow, 1939), 653, 657, and 665.
[5] Gleb Struve, *Russkii evropeets* (San Francisco: Delo, 1950), 81.
[6] Reproduced, together with Chateaubriand's indifferent reply, in *Literaturnoe nasledstvo*, vols. 31/32 (Moscow, 1937), 146.

seventeenth century, and which we can now consider to have been signs of the evolving Romantic sensibility. In the three key texts of *Le génie du christianisme*—the diagnostic chapter entitled "Du vague des passions" (part 2, book 2, chapter 9) and the two famed set pieces, *René* and *Atala* (the latter first published separately in 1801), Chateaubriand incorporated such basically antirationalist eighteenth-century trends as the love of tears in the writings of Richardson, Sterne, and Diderot; the taste for ruins and other morbid settings in Walpole and Mrs. Radcliffe; the back-to-nature philosophy of Rousseau and of his German and English followers; and of course the various forms of exoticism: historical, as in Ossian; American, as in Bernardin de Saint-Pierre; and Oriental, as in Beckford. We can complete the Chateaubrianesque recipe by adding Molière's Alceste, solitary and misunderstood, calling on Célimène to follow him into the desert; the vague yearnings and discontent of Goethe's Werther (there is little chance that Chateaubriand knew the German pre-Romantics at the time when he was writing *Le génie*); nor should we forget such seventeenth-century French poets of the "Baroque" school as Saint-Amant and Théophile de Viau, whose favorite themes were meditations on the transience of human glory, a predilection for solitary and melancholy landscapes, and a longing for a happy, sunny, orange-and-lemon-filled Italy. Chateaubriand transmits to the nineteenth century all the diverse attitudes and preoccupations which were considered peculiar and bizarre by the seventeenth century, but were gradually made respectable through the efforts of the eighteenth-century writers. Even with this repertoire, there were still a few themes and *décors* of the later Byronic Romantics that were missing in *Le génie*, and some of these were utilized by Chateaubriand when he published his account of his travels through the Moslem Near East, the Greek Isles, and Spain, *Itinéraire de Paris à Jérusalem*, in 1811, one year before the appearance of the first cantos of *Childe Harold*.

With the advent of Byron's popularity, Chateaubriand was not exactly forgotten, but his contribution to the formulation and synthesis of many of the Byronic themes was often overlooked, much to his later resentment. From about 1820 on, even such an obvious child of Chateaubriand as Lamartine had to consider himself Byronic. According to the description given by Edmond Estève in his huge and useful book,[7] there was some-

---

[7] Edmond Estève, *Byron et le romantisme français* (Paris, 1907).

thing hypnotic about the hold that Byron acquired over the French literary world after the publication of Amédée Pichot's prose renderings of the poet's major works into French in 1819–21. And it is after the appearance of Pichot's version, significantly enough, that Byron became the major center of attention in the Slavic countries as well.

The influence of Byron's verse tales on Pushkin is clear, even if Pushkin read them, as he probably did, with the aid of Pichot's Chateaubrianesque-Ossianic prose paraphrases. Volumes have been written about this influence, and during the lifetime of the greatest Russian poet it was common practice to refer to him (rather unjustly, we might add) as a disciple of Byron. The problem of Chateaubriand's direct influence on Pushkin, besides being complicated by the mere fact of Byron's, has always presented a peculiarly Russian difficulty to any Pushkin scholar who may have wished to examine it. There is a long Russian tradition, going back to the 1840s and still very much in vogue, of dealing with every literary influence primarily in the light of its social and political implications. Now the legend of Lord Bryon, the ardent enemy of kings, the critic of established churches, the martyr who lost his life in the fight for Greek freedom, makes him an eminently suitable literary ancestor for the great Russian poet from the point of view of the nineteenth-century Russian progressive tradition.[8] Chateaubriand, the Catholic apologist of *Le génie du christianisme*, the royalist who turned his back on the earlier philosophic positions expressed in his *Essai ... sur les révolutions ...*, and who, in his capacity as Minister of Foreign Affairs during the Restoration, was instrumental in sending French troops to put down the Spanish rebellion—*this* Chateaubriand is quite unacceptable to the greater part of nineteenth-century Russian opinion, and certainly to present Soviet views, as an influence on Pushkin, and the numerous professions of admiration for Chateaubriand by the poet himself seem to make no difference in the face of the official Pushkin hagiography.

---

[8] A typical expression of this viewpoint can be found in Aleksei Veselovskii, *Bairon* (Moscow: Tipo-lit. A. V. Vasil'eva, 1902). Obviously confusing the later political reputations of the two writers with the content of their writings, Veselovsky (*Bairon*, 62) dismisses Chateaubriand's influence on Byron on the grounds that "the selfishness of Chateaubriand's René is irreconcilable with love of the people.... Rousseau alone had bequeathed to Harold the protest against the false civilization, the delicacy of feeling and understanding of nature."

Nevertheless, the question of the relationship between Pushkin and Chateaubriand was raised at the beginning of the twentieth century by V. V. Sipovsky in his study *Pushkin, Byron and Chateaubriand*.[9] Professor Sipovsky's thesis is that most of Pushkin's so-called Byronism is attributable to the influence of Chateaubriand's *René*, *Atala*, and *Les Natchez*; this conclusion is based on the comparison of those works with Pushkin's *The Prisoner of the Caucasus* and *The Gypsies*. The study contains some excellent insights, but is badly marred by some curious juggling of quotations, which confuses rather than supports the basic thesis. In 1911, A. L. Bem sharply attacked Sipovsky's contentions, charging him with "stacking" quotations and ignoring the social, political, and biographical data involved.[10] V. M. Zhirmunsky's book *Pushkin and Byron*, published in 1924, relies heavily on Bem for its refutation of the Chateaubriand theory of the origin of *The Prisoner of the Caucasus*. Zhirmunsky maintains that *The Corsair*, being a work written in verse, is a more likely ancestor for Pushkin's poem, quite forgetting that in Pichot's prose *The Corsair* often looks amazingly similar to *Atala*. Both Sipovsky and his two adversaries disregard the relationship between Chateaubriand and Byron, which after all existed quite independently of Pushkin;[11] moreover, they seem to be wholly unaware of the chronology of this relationship. Bem's triumphant conclusion, approvingly quoted by Zhirmunsky, that "had there not been a Byron, Pushkin's literary production would have been different, but had there been no Chateaubriand, Pushkin's production would have been the same,"[12] can be easily countered by a third possibility, namely, that had there been no Chateaubriand, Byron's production would have been different.

One is tempted to suspect that both Bem and Zhirmunsky tend to minimize the role of Chateaubriand because of their own commitment to Germanic studies. More recently, one of the most notable Soviet Pushkin

---

[9] Published as a separate study in 1899, it later became a chapter (under the same title) in V. V. Sipovskii, *Pushkin* (St. Petersburg, 1907).

[10] A. L. Bem, "K voprosu o vliianii Shatobriana na Pushkina," *Pushkin i ego sovremenniki*, vol. 15 (1911), 146–63.

[11] While pointedly insulting Chateaubriand the politician in stanza 16 of *The Age of Bronze*, Byron makes clear his respect for Chateaubriand the writer in a footnote to this stanza. Teresa Guicciolli's interesting testimony on Byron's opinion of Chateaubriand is quoted by Estève, *Byron*, 22.

[12] V. M. Zhirmunskii, *Bairon i Pushkin* (Leningrad, 1924), 43.

scholars, B. V. Tomashevsky, has cautiously tried to revive Sipovsky's theory of the origin of *The Prisoner of the Caucasus*.[13] Tomashevsky's account of the Pushkin-Chateaubriand relationship is informative, but it is unfortunately given in the form of an arbitrary reconstruction of Pushkin's changing attitudes toward Chateaubriand, based not on the poet's own testimony (which is available in abundance), but rather on Soviet notions of how a liberal and patriotic Pushkin ought to have felt about various vicissitudes of Chateaubriand's political career under the Restoration and the July Monarchy. This involves Tomashevsky in some strange distortions of causes and results of the Revolution of 1830, in line with the common Russian practice of suppressing historical fact to score a political point.

Pushkin's Opinion of Chateaubriand: Pushkin's Prose

Pushkin's attitude toward Chateaubriand can be seen most clearly in the poet's critical articles. Chateaubriand is mentioned in seven of Pushkin's articles and essays: (1) "André Chénier" (an unfinished draft, dated 1825); (2) "Essay of Reply to Certain Nonliterary Accusations," and its earlier version, "Refutation of Critics" (1830), both of which contain quotations from Chateaubriand; (3) "Review of Reviews" (1831), in which Chateaubriand is listed among the French and English journalists to whom contemporary Russian journalists are unfavorably contrasted; (4) Pushkin's review of A. N. Muravyov's *Journey to the Holy Land* (1832); (5) the article "M. E. Lobanov's Opinions about the Spirit of Literature, Both Foreign and Domestic," which Pushkin published in his magazine *The Contemporary* in 1836; (6) "John Tanner" (*The Contemporary*, 1836); and finally, (7) "Milton and Chateaubriand's Translation of *Paradise Lost*" (*The Contemporary*, 1837). The article on Milton and Chateaubriand, the last of Pushkin's articles published within the poet's lifetime, contained an extended critical appreciation of Chateaubriand as a writer, as well as a defense of *Essai sur la littérature anglaise*, one of the two Chateaubriand texts in which the French writer complains of Byron's ingratitude in not recognizing his literary parentage.

---

[13] B. V. Tomashevskii, *Pushkin i Frantsiia* (Leningrad, 1960). Pushkin's attitude toward Chateaubriand is discussed on pp. 159–61. Sipovsky's role is mentioned in a note on p. 452.

The general picture that emerges is the one of utmost respect and admiration felt by the Russian poet for the founder of French Romanticism. The draft on Chénier and the review of A. N. Muravyov's travel book, respectively, show how thoroughly Pushkin had studied *Le génie du christianisme* (the passage on Chénier quoted by Pushkin occurs in a footnote to an appendix) and *Itinéraire*. It is not that Pushkin was blind to Chateaubriand's literary shortcomings. The Muravyov review contains implied criticism of Chateaubriand's deliberate search for religious experience suitable for expressing in picturesque prose, as well as explicit criticism of Chateaubriand's arbitrary and obstinate fusion of biblical and Homeric imagery. "John Tanner" shows that a good half century before the studies of Joseph Bédier demonstrated the falsity of Chateaubriand's America, Pushkin realized how little the Indian scenes of *Atala* had resembled the life of real American Indians. In the article on Milton and Chateaubriand, Pushkin puts his finger with marvelous perspicacity on Chateaubriand's basic fault, which is the source of all of his other defects: his obvious dislike and mistrust of facts and his preference for abstract ideas not based on any fact.

But with all these literary reservations, there is no mistaking Pushkin's attitude toward the older writer when he says in his essay on Milton and Chateaubriand that Chateaubriand is "the foremost among contemporary French writers, the teacher of the entire generation now writing."[14] There are no objections anywhere in Pushkin to Chateaubriand's ultraconservative political role, which Byron had criticized so vehemently in *The Age of Bronze*. In defending France against Lobanov's charge of impiety (in the article "M. E. Lobanov's Opinions"), Pushkin reverently lists Chateaubriand's name among the past and present French writers noted for their Catholic orthodoxy (Fénelon, Bossuet) and even for mystical fervor (Pascal, Ballanche). The basic thesis of *Le génie du christianisme*—that Christianity was the greatest civilizing force in human history—is completely accepted by Pushkin, *Gavriiliada* and the irreverent epigrams of his youth notwithstanding. The influence of this idea on Pushkin can be traced in his review of the second volume of Polevoi's *History of the Russian People* (1830), in which he writes: "The greatest spiritual and political revolution on our planet was Christianity. It was in this sacred element

---

[14] Pushkin, *Polnoe sobranie sochinenii v desiati tomakh* (Moscow, 1956–58), 7:497.

that the world dissolved and renewed itself."[15] Chateaubriand's ideas on the civilizing role of Christian missionaries (*Le génie*, book 4 of part 4) are vividly reflected in Pushkin's demand that missionaries be sent to the Caucasus in his *Journey to Arzrum*,[16] as well as in the original plan for the unfinished narrative poem now called *Tazit*, written at approximately the same time (1829–30) as the original draft of the *Journey to Arzrum*. As the plan shows,[17] the poem was intended to describe the conversion of a savage mountaineer by either a monk or a missionary. All this had not prevented both Sipovsky and Tomashevsky (who probably knew better) from asserting that the religious side of Chateaubriand was alien and repellent to Pushkin.

This survey of Pushkin's attitude to Chateaubriand can be completed by a brief comment on the unfinished novel *Roslavlev*, in which the lady narrator can think of no higher praise for Madame de Staël than the statement that she was the friend of Byron and of Chateaubriand. A few pages later, a maxim of the favorite writer of the narrator is quoted: "Il n'est de bonheur que dans les voies communes." Pushkin, coyly masquerading as the publisher, identifies this in a footnote as "Chateaubriand's words, it would seem." This slightly distorted quotation from *René* (in Chateaubriand it reads "Il n'y a de bonheur que dans les voies communes") was evidently a favorite of Pushkin's, for he brought it up again in his letter to Krivtsov of 10 February 1831.

Chateaubriand's Influence on Pushkin: Narrative Poems

Pushkin's prose writings of the 1830s set forth the poet's attitude toward Chateaubriand as man and writer. To seek evidence of the nature and extent of Chateaubriand's literary influence on Pushkin, however, one has to go back to his narrative poems of the 1820s. Here the problem of Byron versus Chateaubriand becomes particularly significant, and a satisfactory answer concerning Chateaubriand's impact on the narrative poems of Pushkin would require a thorough examination of the complex interrelationship of all three writers on a scale much broader than that of Sipovsky's essay. Byron comes within the purview of the present study

---

15 Ibid., 7:146.
16 Ibid., 6:648.
17 Ibid., 4:566.

only marginally, yet, if we refuse to delve into the problem of his influence, we are left with only three of Pushkin's verse narratives in connection with which we can speak meaningfully of Chateaubriand's influence. These are *The Prisoner of the Caucasus*, *The Gypsies*, and *Evgeny Onegin*.

While *The Prisoner* is unquestionably a Byronic tale in form (as Pushkin's contemporaries never tired of pointing out), the character of its hero does show affinities with René and with the hypothetical character described in "Du vague des passions," as well as with Byron's Childe Harold (and not, Zhirmunsky notwithstanding, with the hero of *The Corsair*). The liberation of the prisoner by the Circassian girl, the description of Circassian mores and warlike pastimes, the frequent use of native words necessitating footnotes with translations, and even the language that the principals speak, all might well have been patterned on *Atala*, and the general tone of the narration is closer to Chateaubriand's more mellow Romanticism than to the tone of the demonic jingles of *The Corsair*. This does not preclude clear Byronic echoes in some passages, and one is rather astonished to hear the Atala-like heroine turn into Gulnare at the words

> No umoliu ottsa i brata,
> Ne to—naidu kinzhal il' iad.

Sipovsky is often convincing in his parallels between *The Prisoner* and *René*, but he is on much less certain ground when he attempts to link *The Gypsies* with Chateaubriand. Aleko's flight to the gypsies may resemble René's search for peace and freedom among the American Indians, but the basic conception of *The Gypsies* is one of Pushkin's most independent, and, as far as influences are concerned, seems to bypass both Byron and Chateaubriand and to reach back to their common father, Jean-Jacques Rousseau. Sipovsky's attempted parallel between the Indian Chactas and the Old Gypsy shows that he did not read *Atala* with sufficient attention: Chactas was not an "unspoiled savage," for he had spent his youth at the court of Louis XIV, where he had attended performances of Racine's tragedies and had heard Bossuet preach.[18]

---

[18] *Atala*, in Chateaubriand, *Génie du christianisme, ou beautés de la religion chrétienne* (Paris, 1802), vol. 2, pt. 3, 177.

The preoccupation with character and ideology has prevented Sipovsky from noticing the most striking poetic image that links *The Gypsies* with Chateaubriand. The famous interpolated little song about the migratory bird (memorized by generations of Russian school children) is abruptly followed by the comparison of the bird to the solitary wanderer without a nest of his own. These two not particularly original themes, and the sequence in which they are presented, may have been suggested to Pushkin by the lengthy treatise on migratory birds and the ensuing series of comparisons of such birds to homeless and dissatisfied human beings in *Le génie du christianisme* (part 1, book 5, beginning with chapter 7), which have also inspired some of Lamartine's poems. With his unerring taste, Pushkin uses the poetry of the situation and of the description in Chateaubriand, but discards the religious pseudozoology which makes much of part 1 of *Le génie* such ludicrous reading today.

The Romantic Pose—II

> ... Coldness, misanthropy, and strangeness are now included among the toilet articles.[19]
>
> —Bestuzhev-Marlinsky

In discussing the role of Chateaubriand in the genesis and realization of Pushkin's novel in verse, *Evgeny Onegin*, we inevitably enter the field of literary speculation. Onegin as a literary type (that most labored problem in Russian criticism) is undoubtedly of the family of René, one of the numerous literary progeny of Chateaubriand's hero who display to the admiring public "un malheur dont il ne savait pas le nom, ni eux non plus,"[20] or, in Russian, "nedug kotoromu prichinu / Davno by otyskat' pora." The roots of René's *mal* are stated by Chateaubriand very clearly, and they lie in his unfortunate love affair with his own sister Amélie, thought by some critics to have been modeled after Chateaubriand's sister Lucille. This situation also forms the plot of Byron's *Manfred*, and on close examination is found to be present in the first canto of *Childe Harold's Pilgrimage*. It is all a part of that astonishingly frequent pattern of brother-and-sister love

---

[19] A. A. Bestuzhev-Marlinskii to Pushkin, 9 March 1825, in A. A. Bestuzhev-Marlinskii, *Sochineniia v dvukh tomakh* (Moscow, 1958), 2:627.

[20] Chateaubriand, *Mémoires d'outre-tombe*, 2:462.

affairs that we find both in life and in literature at the early stages of the Romantic period—Byron and Augusta Leigh, Alexander I and the Grand Duchess Ekaterina Pavlovna, William and Dorothy Wordsworth, and the heroes of Nikolai Karamzin's "The Isle of Bornholm" all spring to mind. By the 1820s all this was either forgotten or disregarded, but the spiritual attitude that resulted from such singular situations remained in fashion for decades afterward. This very significant aspect of the whole Romantic movement has until now not been explored in literary criticism, at least not with the attention that it deserves.

In untangling the strands of René and Childe Harold in *Evgeny Onegin* one cannot ignore the third literary source. The idea of an inherent inability to feel was probably suggested to Pushkin by the novel *Adolphe*, by Benjamin Constant, a writer essentially alien to the Chateaubriand-Byron trend, although, oddly enough, Pushkin at one time considered *him* the originator of Byronism.[21] What can be said with certainty is that Chateaubriand was very much on Pushkin's mind at the time of writing of *Evgeny Onegin*. The French writer is mentioned in the novel several times, especially in earlier drafts and the passages that were omitted in the final version. One such example is the verse in chapter 2, stanza 29, which now lists Richardson and Rousseau as Tatyana's favorite authors, but originally read "Chateaubriand and Rousseau."[22] The celebrated maxim in the same

---

[21] Pushkin, *Polnoe sobranie sochinenii*, 7:97. That Pushkin could consider Constant a predecessor of Byron provides added proof of his dependence on French sources for information on Byron. The following chronology should explain what happened: *Childe Harold's Pilgrimage*, 1812; *Adolphe*, 1816; Pichot's translation of Byron, 1819–21. In Madame de Staël's circle, to which Constant belonged, Byron was read in the original and at the time of publication.

[22] Quoted by Tomashevskii, *Pushkin i Frantsiia*, 159. In her study of Benjamin Constant's *Adolphe* and Pushkin, Anna Akhmatova published for the first time two earlier versions of stanza 22 of chap. 7 of *Onegin* (*Vremennik Pushkinskoi komissii* [Moscow and Leningrad, 1936]). This stanza is usually associated with Constant's novel, because Pushkin later quoted passages from it in his short article on Vyazemsky's translation of *Adolphe*. The "two or three novels" which Onegin adds in that stanza to the works of the "singer of Giaour and Juan" on his bookshelf, and which to him represent a correct reflection of modern sensibility, are listed in these drafts. They are *Corinne*, by Madame de Staël; *Adolphe*; *René*; *Melmoth the Wanderer*; and the entire output of Sir Walter Scott. The second draft cited by Anna Akhmatova is very close to the final version, but instead of Giaour and Juan it mentions René. As a result of Anna Akhmatova's study, these two earlier versions have been appended to some of the editions of *Evgeny Onegin* published since 1936.

chapter which states, in reference to Tatyana's mother, that habit is a substitute for happiness, is a paraphrase of a passage in *René*, as is revealed by Pushkin himself in a footnote.[23]

One can only marvel at the conviction of Chateaubriand's contemporaries that he was a master at observing and describing nature. His well-known description of the Mississippi in *Atala*, to take a random example, was pieced together from travel accounts of obscure Irish explorers and French Jesuits of the eighteenth century (Chateaubriand never got as far as the Mississippi on his American journey), and embellished with flora and fauna from all over North, Central, and South America; the result is more like the description of a botanical garden than of any river that has ever actually existed. His moral tales of American birds, crocodiles, and two-headed serpents are medieval in tradition and intent. Yet in chapter 4, stanza 26 of *Evgeny Onegin* we find Lensky reading to Olga "an edifying novel, in which the author knows nature better than Chateaubriand." There is a gentle irony in the passage, but it is directed at the unknown author of the edifying novel and at Lensky's naively idealistic mode of courtship, not at Chateaubriand's incompetence as zoologist and botanist. Together with Sainte-Beuve, together with the French reading public of the first half of the nineteenth century, Pushkin seems to have accepted at face value Chateaubriand's not very subtle revival of the medieval tradition of the bestiaries (theology disguised as natural history), and not to have been disturbed by the expression of a view of nature based on Pliny and St. Ambrose in the age of Lamarck and Cuvier.

The omitted stanza 9 of the first chapter of *Onegin*, which is usually printed separately in an appendix or in the editor's notes, is especially pertinent to the problem of Chateaubriand's influence on Pushkin. The original draft of this stanza (which begins "Nas pyl serdechnyi rano muchit ...") mentions the names of Madame de Staël and Chateaubriand and contains an idea that shows Pushkin's debt to the thinking of Chateaubriand:

> My alchem zhizn' uznat' zarane,
> My uznaem ee v romane.
> My vse uznali. Mezhdu tem
> Ne nasladilis' my nichem.

---

[23] Pushkin, *Polnoe sobranie sochinenii*, 5:194, n. 15.

The corresponding passage in "Du vague des passions" reads: "… la multitude de livres qui traitent de l'homme et de ses sentiments, rendent habile sans expérience. On est détrompé sans avoir joui; il reste encore des désirs, et l'on n'a plus d'illusions."[24] The relevance of this passage to the conception of Pushkin's novel is quite clear; it emphasizes in a manner typical of *Evgeny Onegin* the importance of literature in the emotional and intellectual formation of certain types of personality.

The rest of the paragraph in which this passage occurs in Chateaubriand reads: "L'imagination est riche, abondante, et merveilleuse; l'existence pauvre, sèche et désenchantée. On habite avec un cœur plein, un monde vide; et sans avoir usé de rien, on est désabusé de tout."[25] Here, it would seem, one can discern the raw material for *both* Onegin and Tatyana.

For more than a century, much of Russian criticism has persisted in regarding the characters of *Evgeny Onegin* as incarnations of definite Russian social types of the 1820s, observed and faithfully reproduced by Pushkin. Studies by Vladimir Nabokov[26] and Leon Stilman,[27] however, have pointed out the absurdity of mistaking for sociology the literature-oriented and literature-derived ideas in *Evgeny Onegin*. Anyone who considers Onegin's *spleen* to be a result of specific social and political conditions need only read "Du vague des passions" or the passage in *René* which begins "On m'accuse d'avoir des goûts inconstans …"[28] in order to realize that Chateaubriand's book of Catholic apologetics (and its impact on Byron and Constant) is nearer to the roots of that particular mental climate than are any actual evils of serfdom and autocracy.

---

[24] Chateaubriand, *Génie du christianisme*, vol. 1, pt. 2, 158.
[25] Ibid.
[26] Vladimir Nabokov, "Problems in Translation: *Onegin* in English," *Partisan Review* 22, no. 4 (1955): 496–512.
[27] Leon Stilman, "Problemy literaturnykh zhanrov i traditsii v *Evgenii Onegine* Pushkina," in *American Contributions to the Fourth International Congress of Slavicists, Moscow, 1958* ('s-Gravenhage, 1958), 321–67.
[28] Chateaubriand, *Génie du christianisme*, vol. 1, pt. 2, 183.

II. The Amber Beads of Crimea[1]

The Image of Crimea in The Fountain of Bakhchisarai, *by Aleksandr Pushkin, and in* Crimean Sonnets, *by Adam Mickiewicz*

Crimea as Greece

*I*n the fall of 1820, an inquisitive and cultured Russian nobleman undertook an eight-week trip through the Crimean peninsula. His name was Ivan Matveevich Muravyov-Apostol; a member of a collateral branch of the noted Muravyov family, he lived a long and eventful life from 1765 to 1851. At the time of his Crimean voyage he had behind him a distinguished record as an army officer and an eminent career as a classical scholar; had been tutor in classical languages to the Grand Duke Konstantin Pavlovich and his brother Nikolai Pavlovich, the future tsar; had held diplomatic posts at the Russian legations in Hamburg and in Madrid; and had published Russian translations of Horace and Aristophanes. Five years in the future lay the fateful Decembrist uprising in which he was to lose two of his three sons and several of his nephews. Two years before the uprising, in 1823, came the published account of his Crimean journey, under the title *Puteshestvie po Tavride*, which caused the name of Muravyov-Apostol to be remembered in literary history.

Crimea became a tourist attraction immediately after it was incorporated into the Russian Empire in 1783. One of the first tourists to come was Catherine the Great. It was for her sojourn that several rooms in the old palace of the Gireys at Bakhchisarai were redecorated in the current Western European style (the Gireys were the Crimean Khans who were direct descendants and successors of the Golden Horde of Genghis-Khan). By the time of Muravyov-Apostol's voyage, a number of late eighteenth- and early nineteenth-century travelers had published descriptions of Crimea, among them an enterprising Englishwoman named Mrs. Guthrie, whose book entitled *A Tour through the Taurida or Crimea* was highly regarded by Muravyov-Apostol, despite her insistence on hearing "the flute of Theocritus in every Tatar reed-pipe."[2]

---

[1] Originally published in *California Slavic Studies* 2 (1963): 108–20.
[2] I. M. Murav'ev-Apostol, *Puteshestvie po Tavride v 1820 gode* [sic] (St. Petersburg, 1823), 175.

To most of these travelers, Crimea meant first of all the setting of the tragedies of Iphigenia and Mithridates: an ancient Greek colony mentioned many times in classical literature. Muravyov-Apostol was even more classically oriented in his aims than his predecessors had been. Armed with a thorough knowledge of Greek and Latin literatures and with some dubious archaeological hypotheses of his own, he set out to determine the exact locations of various Crimean points of interest mentioned in Strabo, Herodotus, Pliny, and others. But Muravyov-Apostol was also familiar with new developments in the English and German literatures of his time: his book opens with a quotation from Byron, and several more quotations from English, German, and Italian poets are modestly interspersed in the body of the book among the learned references. The classical tastes of the author are not to be doubted when he admits to preferring Vergil to either Shakespeare or Ariosto, yet he is sufficiently a man of his time to have included in his book descriptions of the picturesque ruins at Balaklava, of a dramatic confrontation between an aged Tatar and his daughter, who had run away with a Christian, and, of course, of the principal nonclassical tourist attraction, Bakhchisarai. Such passages are written in Karamzinian Russian prose, intended to touch the reader and, by rather obvious means, to engage his sympathies. Especially telling in this respect is the description of the dangerous crossing of Mount Kikeneiz. These picturesque episodes, rather than the archaeology and geography which are the author's principal concern, brought *Puteshestvie po Tavride* its high reputation among the author's contemporaries. Two great poets, Adam Mickiewicz and Aleksandr Pushkin, were among the enthusiastic readers.

Both of these poets had had their own Crimean vacations. Their itineraries—the standard tourists' tour of the time—paralleled that of Muravyov-Apostol. Pushkin's trip occurred in the summer of 1820, when he spent three happy weeks in Gurzuf with the family of General Raevsky, staying at the same house of the Duc de Richelieu that Muravyov-Apostol was to visit a few months later, and participating in excursions to such points as Bakhchisarai and Mount Kikeneiz. As is often pointed out, it was on this trip and through the Raevskys that Pushkin first came into contact with the poetry of Byron. Pushkin's Crimean impressions were later reflected in a number of short poems and in the most popularly successful work of his earlier period, the narrative poem *The Fountain of Bakhchisarai*.

Even before reading Muravyov-Apostol's book, Pushkin wrote to Vyazemsky, asking him to select suitable passages from it and to reprint them, by way of introduction (together with Vyazemsky's own preface) in the first edition of *The Fountain of Bakhchisarai*. After reading the book at Mikhailovskoe late in 1824, Pushkin composed his often-quoted "letter" to Delvig (actually a sort of literary meditation, obviously intended for publication), in which he compares his own impressions of Crimea with Muravyov-Apostol's and comes to an oddly Proustian conclusion about the ability of human memory to transform past impressions with its magic power. The letter was included by the poet in the third edition of *The Fountain*, along with the Muravyov-Apostol description of Bakhchisarai selected earlier by Vyazemsky.

Adam Mickiewicz was acquainted both with Pushkin's poem and with Muravyov-Apostol's book at the time of his two Crimean excursions in the spring and summer of 1825. In June of that year, the exiled Polish poet left Odessa and, accompanied by Henryk Rzewuski, paid a visit to Count Gustaw Olizar in Gurzuf, the village in which Pushkin and Muravyov-Apostol had spent some time in 1820. About a month and a half later, Mickiewicz returned to Crimea with a larger group of traveling companions, among whom was Rzewuski's sister, the redoubtable femme fatale Karolina Sobańska, with whom the poet was romantically involved and who had been the subject of his earlier love sonnets. This time Mickiewicz made a thorough study of local *Sehenswürdigkeiten*, meanwhile being spied upon by Aleksandr Boshnyak, the same government agent who a year later was to send the authorities a long report about Pushkin's doings at Mikhailovskoe. The result of the poet's impressions made up the celebrated *Crimean Sonnets*.

The most obvious point of contact between the Crimean impressions found in the three authors is in their respective treatments of the legend of the Polish captive of the Khan, which forms the subject of *The Fountain of Bakhchisarai*, is alluded to by Mickiewicz in the sonnet "Grób Potockiej" (Potocka's grave), and is discussed in the book by Muravyov-Apostol. Other profitable comparisons could conceivably be made; for example, the evidently related, awesome passages on Kikeneiz in the sonnet of that name and in Muravyov-Apostol, as contrasted to Pushkin's "letter" to Delvig, in which the poet merely recalls his amusement at the quaint Oriental method of mountain climbing. In the notes to "Grób Potockiej"

Mickiewicz mentions *The Fountain of Bakhchisarai*, as well as Muravyov-Apostol's book, which he calls "uczenie i pięknie napisana" (eruditely and beautifully written). The thorough familiarity of Mickiewicz with the latter book can also be deduced from a phrase in his letter to Joachim Lelewel, written in January of 1827: "Deptałem chmury na Czatyrdahu (podobno Trapezie starożytnym)" (I trod the clouds on Chatyr Dagh [like an ancient Trapezion]).³ This identification of the Crimean mountain mentioned by Strabo is one of the theses that Muravyov-Apostol claimed to have proven during his journey.

Puteshestvie po Tavride was not a primary source for either Pushkin or Mickiewicz.⁴ But reading it alongside their Crimean poetry makes one appreciate more fully their originality and helps one to understand the impact of the Crimean landscape and tradition on the poetic imagination of two contemporary but in many ways profoundly dissimilar poets.

Greece or Italy?

There were four literary traditions that were bound to occur to any poet who contemplated a literary treatment of Crimea in the 1820s. There was, first of all, the classical heritage of the area: the Greek ruins, the use of

---

3   Quoted by Leon Gomolicki in *Dziennik pobytu Adama Mickiewicza w Rosji 1824–1829* [The diary of Adam Mickiewicz's stay in Russia 1824–1829] (Warsaw, 1949), 175. The Crimean place names in quotations from the writings of Mickiewicz and in the titles of his sonnets are given in this study in his own Polish spellings. When quoted from Russian sources, the same place names have been transcribed directly from the Russian. The resulting doublings (e.g., Bagczysaraj and Bakhchisarai, Kykyneis and Kikeneiz, Czatyrdah and Chatyr Dagh) seemed preferable to a uniformity which could have been achieved only by an arbitrary transcription of Russian spellings of Tatar place names into Polish.

4   The book by A. L. Pogodin, cited by Professor Weintraub (Wiktor Weintraub, *The Poetry of Adam Mickiewicz* ['s-Gravenhage, 1954], 107) on the subject of Muravyov-Apostol as a source of *Crimean Sonnets*, was not available to me at the time the present study was written. I relied only on my own comparison of the two texts. Since that time I have had an opportunity to examine the work in question, A. L. Pogodin, *Adam Mitskevich: Ego zhizn' i tvorchestvo* (Moscow, 1912), vol. 1, chap. 14, "Krymskie sonety." The point-by-point comparison of the itineraries of the poet and the traveler in the chapter on the sonnets is certainly valid, but both Pogodin and the Polish critic W. Bruchnalski, whom he quotes, tend to exaggerate the role of Muravyov-Apostol's influence. One need only examine the diction and the tone of the two texts to see that there can be no question of any emotional or stylistic impact of Muravyov-Apostol on the *Crimean Sonnets*.

Crimean settings in such works of later classicism as Gluck's opera *Iphigénie en Tauride* and Racine's *Mithridate*, in which "la scène est à Nymphée, port de mer sur le Bosphore Cimmérien, dans la Taurique Chersonèse." This aspect of Crimea always held great attraction for Pushkin, from his 1820 "Epistle to Chaadaev," about the ruins of the temple of Diana, to one of his later evocations of Crimea in "Onegin's Travels," in which he adds the memory of Mickiewicz to such other sacred traditions of the area as the contest in generosity between Orestes and Pilades and the suicide of Mithridates. Pushkin usually called Crimea by its ancient name of Tauris (*Tavrida* in Russian), while Mickiewicz resolutely stuck to its Tatar name, *Krym*. Not only the shift in poetic fashions within the five years that separate Pushkin's Crimean sojourn from that of Mickiewicz, but also a profound difference in temperament and taste, must account for the fact that Crimea's classical heritage was of such scant interest to Mickiewicz, who, in some of his other poetry, did use classical imagery.

The next two traditions which Crimea would call to mind corresponded to the two schools of nature poetry: that of the warm Mediterranean landscape (usually Italian), with its cypresses, lemon trees, and blue skies; and that of savage, stupendous nature, with stormy seas and towering mountains. Although found in the poetry of many periods, these settings had been neglected by the late seventeenth- and early eighteenth-century classicists, but had been revived by the Preromantics and developed by Romantic poets. Meridional nature was frequently connected with the theme of homesickness, whereas savage nature seems to have been related to the Nordic poetry of ruins and, possibly, of ghosts. Among those of the *Crimean Sonnets* that are not specifically based on Oriental imagery, "Stepy Akermańskie" (The Akkerman steppes) and "Pielgrzym" (The pilgrim) fit neatly into the first category, while "Bajdary" (Baydary), with its savage seacoast, and "Ruiny zamku w Bałakławie" (The ruins of the castle of Balaklava) represent the Romantic poetry of wild and desolate places.

The picturesque aspect of desolation is as rare in Pushkin's Crimean poetry as classical allusions are in that of Mickiewicz. On the other hand, the idyllic, southern poetic tradition represents a common ground on which the styles of the Polish and the Russian poets occasionally coincide. Pushkin thought of Crimea in terms of Italy as readily as in terms of ancient Greece, and, as always, his uncanny ability to take over any existing poetic manner or tradition and make it entirely his own enabled him to create something that appeared fresh and new. A case in point is his description of Crimea in his 1821 poem "Kto videl krai" (also printed under the title "Tavrida" in some editions), unmistakably yet subtly based on one of the best-known poetic evocations of Italy in Western literature, Mignon's song from Goethe's *Wilhelm Meister*.

The closing passages of *The Fountain of Bakhchisarai* contain a lovely description of this blessed, opulent Crimea-Italy; a similar, quasi-Italian landscape occasionally also shows through the usually Orientalized Crimea of the Mickiewicz sonnets. Among the comparable images: (1) there is the poet on horseback on the Crimean seacoast (the very end of *The Fountain* and the sonnet "Bajdary"); (2) "U stóp moich kraina dostatków i krasy" (At my feet a land of plenty and beauty), which opens "Pielgrzym," recalls "Volshebnyi krai, ochei otrada" in Pushkin; (3) the description of the rock of Ayudagh at the end of *The Fountain* is not unlike the first quatrain of the sonnet "Ajudah" (Ayudah); and (4) both poets make lyrical use of the river Salgir, though "Salhiry dziewice" (the maidens of Salhir) seems to be more closely related to "plennitsy beregov Salgira" in the first chapter of *Evgeny Onegin*.[5]

Both poets like to compare features of the Crimean landscape to jewels: the rubies and garnets of the dew in the morning forest in "Ałuszta w dzień" (Alushta by day) ("Jak z różańca Chalifów rubin i granaty" [A ruby and garnets like from the prayer-beads of the caliphs]) and "rubinowe morwy" (ruby-red mulberries) in "Pielgrzym" vividly recall Pushkin's frequent comparisons of grapes to jewels ("iantar' i iakhont vinograda" in *The Fountain*, "iantar' visit na lozakh vinograda" in "Kto videl krai"). But there is a difference in the way this effect is used: in Pushkin the grapes-jewels are Italianate, but in Mickiewicz they are Moslemized:

> Tu z winnicy miłośći niedojrzałe grona
> Wzięto na stół Allaha
>
> (Here from the vineyard of love unripe clusters
> Have been taken for Allah's table);

---

[5] Both Pushkin and Mickiewicz seem to associate the river Salgir with Bakhchisarai, where it does not flow. Bertier de la Garde, in *Pushkin i ego sovremenniki*, vols. 17/18 (St. Petersburg, 1913), explains the inconsistency by the fact that "salgir" in Crimea is also a generic term, meaning any river and not only the one bearing the proper name of Salgir.

and while in Pushkin the evocation of jewelry may occasionally also create a deliberate Oriental effect (the metonymic "iantar'" for Girey's water pipe at the beginning of *The Fountain*, the amber rosaries in the description of the deserted harem), the jewels of Mickiewicz are invariably Oriental: "perełki wschodu" (pearls of the East), "baldachim z brylantów" (baldachin of jewels), and the already-mentioned ruby and garnet rosaries of dew.

It must be pointed out that the emotional use of the southern landscape is diametrically opposite in the two poets: Pushkin sees Crimea from a distance and yearns to return to it, whereas Mickiewicz describes himself as actually present in Crimea and yearning for Lithuania ("Stepy Akermańskie," "Grób Potockiej," "Pielgrzym"). But again the two poets find a meeting ground in the idea that the Crimean landscape is conducive to melancholy recollections of the past. This theme, present in almost all of Pushkin's evocations of Crimea, is strikingly expressed in the comparison of memory with a polyp in the sestet of the sonnet "Cisza morska" (The calm of the sea).

Orient à l'anglaise

The native inhabitants of Crimea, the Crimean Tatars, were Moslems. This single fact brought Crimea into the province of the fourth poetic tradition, which was all the rage in the literary life of the 1820s: that of Oriental, or, more specifically, Near Eastern Moslem exoticism. The fashion seems to have started in England with Beckford; it was brought into Romantic poetry by Landor and Southey after 1800, and was made immensely popular in the second decade of the nineteenth century through such works as Byron's *The Bride of Abydos* and *The Giaour* and Chateaubriand's *Itinéraire de Paris à Jérusalem*. Goethe's *West-östlicher Divan* came in 1811; Pushkin and Mickiewicz popularized the style in the literatures of their respective countries; and French poetry finally capitulated to the Orient in 1829 when Hugo's *Les orientales* was published. The decorative use of Oriental detail and the deliberate evocation of *couleur locale* were in direct contrast to the use of the Moslem world in such earlier works as Racine's *Bajazet* and Voltaire's *Zaïre*, in which exotic details were avoided and the similarity of the Moslem to the European was stressed. The Orientalism of the Romantics presupposed a certain amount of deliberate stylization, based on imitating the styles of Arabian and Persian poets; in this respect, Mickiewicz outdoes not only Pushkin, but also Byron and even Goethe.

Among the works of Pushkin inspired by Crimea we find a two-page beginning of an unfinished humorous poem, a free adaptation of an Oriental *conte* by Sénecé, about the life of the Crimean Tatars, which begins:

> Nedavno bednyi musul'man
> V Iurzufe zhil s det'mi, s zhenoiu …

Inconclusive as it is, this fragment offers an interesting notion of the kind of Crimean *couleur locale* that a poet could produce, were he to rely only on his own observations of the area rather than on its history or on the prevailing literary fashions at the moment of writing. The family described here is obviously Moslem, but there is not a single Romantically exotic detail in their prosaic and humorously described doings. In his letter to Vyazemsky, written in March or April of 1825, Pushkin expresses his attitude toward Oriental stylization in these words:

> Oriental style was a model for me as much as is possible for us sensible and cold Europeans. Incidentally, do you know why I do not like Moore? Because he is much too Oriental. He imitates in a puerile and ugly way the puerility and ugliness of Saadi, Hafiz, and Mahomet. A European, even in his enthusiasm for Oriental luxury, must retain the taste and the vision of a European. That is why Byron is so charming in *The Giaour* and in *The Bride of Abydos*.

And indeed, the Crimea of *The Fountain of Bakhchisarai* is closer to the Oriental tales of Byron than to either any actual Moslem life which the poet could have observed during his trip or authentic Moslem poetry of the kind quoted by Muravyov-Apostol when he speaks of the inscriptions at the palace of the Gireys. Tomashevsky[6] gives a list of exotic words which became common currency in most European languages after Byron used them in his Oriental tales, and which also appear in Pushkin's Crimean tale: harem, eunuch, fakir, sherbet, chibouque. Tomashevsky goes on to explain that Pushkin was far more adventurous with the local Caucasian terms which he introduced in *The Prisoner of the Caucasus*. Nor are there

---

[6] B. V. Tomashevskii, *Stikh i iazyk* (Moscow and Leningrad, 1959), 434.

in *The Fountain* any Orient-inspired figures of speech of the type found in Pushkin's later *Imitations of the Koran*. The Oriental image in *The Fountain of Bakhchisarai* is, in short, a generalized image, such as one would expect at the time in any poetic work dealing with, say, Turkey or Arabia.

In basing the plot of his poem on a local legend, Pushkin takes the middle ground between the version accepted by Mickiewicz and that utilized by Muravyov-Apostol. The Polish poet, for sentimental and patriotic reasons, asserts that Girey's captive was indeed a Potocka, while Muravyov-Apostol argues, with the pedantry of a classical scholar, that a Georgian girl was buried in the tomb.[7] Pushkin has both the Polish heroine *and* the Georgian one. The confrontation of the two is of course the dramatic climax of the poem, but it is characteristic that their respective Polish and Caucasian backgrounds are outlined in general terms, without any attempt to obtain effects through the use of additional contrasting *couleur locale*. The narrative technique of the poem, while clearly Byronic, frequently continues the line of *Ruslan and Lyudmila* and through it can be related to the verse tales of Voltaire and Bogdanovich, so much admired by Pushkin.

Alhambra—Baghdad—Shiraz

During the period just before his stay in southern Russia, Mickiewicz undertook a study of Arabic and Persian poetry.[8] His thorough knowledge of German enabled him to have firsthand access to Goethe's *West-östlicher Divan*, with its evocation of the manner of Hafiz and Saadi; one would

---

[7] The critic Julian Klaczko, in his pious and pompous article "La Crimée poétique" (*Revue contemporaine* 19 [1855]: 314–34, 498–524), claims to give the Muravyov-Apostol version of the legend, while in fact giving a combination of the Pushkin and Mickiewicz versions. Both of these versions contradict that of Muravyov-Apostol. In Pushkin, the Polish girl is simply called Mariya; Mickiewicz calls her Potocka; Muravyov-Apostol says she is neither Polish nor a Potocka. From all this, Klaczko blandly derives "la belle Marie Potocka." Klaczko's amusingly Victorian objection to *The Fountain of Bakhchisarai* is that Pushkin leaves the reader in doubt concerning the exact state of Mariya's virginity.

[8] For a detailed examination of the Orientalist studies and preoccupations of Mickiewicz, the reader is referred to Wacław Lednicki's article "Ex Oriente Lux," in *Semitic and Oriental Studies: A Volume Presented to William Popper*, ed. Walter J. Fischel (Berkeley: University of California Press, 1951). See also W. Weintraub, *Poetry of Adam Mickiewicz*, 101.

be inclined to assume the acquaintance of the author of the *Crimean Sonnets* with Goethe's Oriental volume even without the epigraph: "Wer den Dichter will verstehen ..." On the other hand, there is no evidence of Pushkin's having known or admired the *Divan*. Finally, Mickiewicz had none of Pushkin's aversion to the extremes of Oriental stylization, and thus, although *The Fountain of Bakhchisarai*, the "Turkish" poem in *Journey to Arzrum*, and the *Imitations of the Koran* represent the limit of Pushkin's Orientalism, Mickiewicz was to continue and to develop further the exoticism of the *Crimean Sonnets* in his Arabian *kasydas* (quasidahs) "Szanfary," "Almotenabbi," and "Farys" (Faris). In view of all this it becomes easier to understand that whereas Pushkin used Oriental imagery sparingly and for decorative effect, Mickiewicz made it the substance of his poetry, an integral part of the poetic language he had evolved in the *Crimean Sonnets*. We know that he was a little uneasy about some of his excesses, for he expressed the hope that his friend, the Orientalist Kowalewski, "prynajmniej ponotuje, co by w technicznych mahometańskich wyrazach poodmieniać lub lepiej wyjaśnić należało" (at least I will note what one ought to change, or, better, explain, in technical Mohammedan expressions).[9]

The four opening sonnets have nothing either Oriental or specifically Crimean about them. The first sonnet paints a landscape in terms of the sea; the next three are seascapes. In each case, the scene described is shown to fit and to accentuate the poet's frame of mind. The mood is introspective; the emotions are intensely subjective in the Romantic manner. One realizes how new the manner of Mickiewicz is for his time, and how adequate it is for the expression of his mood, when one compares the sonnet "Żegluga" (Sea voyage) with the inept, pseudoclassical Russian translation of it by the Karamzinist poet Dmitriev, which Vyazemsky chose to publish with his own frequently incorrect prose translations of the sonnets.[10] Thus, "wiem, co to być ptakiem" (I know what it is to be a bird) is rendered by Dmitriev as

>Otnyne tol'ko on uznal
>Zavidnuiu pernatykh doliu.

---

[9] Mickiewicz to J. Kowalewski, 9 (21) June 1827, quoted by Leon Gomolicki, *Dziennik pobytu Adama Mickiewicza*, 190.

[10] P. A. Viazemskii, *Polnoe sobranie sochinenii* (St. Petersburg, 1878), 1:348.

The added adjective "zavidnuiu" is especially typical of a mediocre poet's distrust of the readers and of their powers of perception.

One is suddenly plunged into the Orient in the fifth sonnet, "Widok gór ze stepów Kozłowa" (View of the mountains from the steppes of Kozlov), which describes the impressions of a pilgrim (the poet's representative) upon catching the first glimpse of Crimea's highest summit, the Chatyr Dagh. We have Muravyov-Apostol's matter-of-fact description of this first glimpse: it made him think of Strabo. In his "letter" to Delvig, Pushkin recalls: "'This is the Chatyr Dagh,' the captain said to me. I could not distinguish it and was not particularly curious." The pilgrim in Mickiewicz, however, is immediately transported into a state of mixed awe and excitement. The hyperbolic terms, the profusion of Moslem terminology, more Arabic than Tatar ("diwy" [djinn], "gwiazd karawana" [caravan of stars], "chylat" [honorable article of clothing bestowed by the sultan], "turban"), the images from Arabian mythology, and the awed attitude of the local Crimean inhabitant to whom the pilgrim speaks all show the Oriental stylization of Mickiewicz at its most lavish and set the pattern for three other mountain sonnets: "Czatyrdah" (Chatyr Dagh), "Droga nad przepaścią w Dżehud-Kale" (The road along the precipice at Chufut Kale), and "Góra Kykyneis" (Mount Kikineis). The last two describe precipices. "Góra Kykyneis" is connected thematically with a corresponding passage in Muravyov-Apostol; on the other hand, the traveler's account of his trip to the Karaite fortress (its name is given by Muravyov-Apostol as Dzhukhud-Kale[11]) is most prosaic when compared with the poet's conception. It is ironic that Muravyov-Apostol's guide and interpreter ("Murza") betrays his ignorance of both the Old Testament and the Koran on the very same spot where his Mickiewiczian counterpart discourses learnedly on "chaos" and on the "studnia Al-Kahiru" (spring of Al-Kahir).

The Bakhchisarai group (sonnets 6 through 9) is connected to Pushkin's Crimean tale in source of inspiration and in subject matter. More specific parallels can be drawn between the sonnet "Bagczysaraj" (Bakhchisarai) and the passage in Pushkin that begins "Pokinuv sever nakonets"; the subsequent section, beginning "Ia videl khanskoe kladbishche," corresponds to the sonnet "Mogiły haremu" (The graves of the harem). "Grób Potockiej" is, of course, about one of the heroines of Pushkin's tale, and

---

[11] Murav'ev-Apostol, *Puteshestvie po Tavride*, 125.

the predicament and homesickness of the Polish captive have been understood by the two poets in a similar way, even though Mickiewicz relates her situation to his own, while Pushkin remains sympathetic in a more detached manner. "Grób Potockiej" evokes a Polish girl and a Polish poet, both in Crimea, both thinking of Poland. Therefore, the Oriental manner of Mickiewicz, though still present, becomes muted, veiled: the glance of the fair captive, which burns its traces into the starry sky, or the wonderful

> ... przeszłości chwile
> Ulatując od ciebie jak złote motyle
>
> (... moments of the past,
> Fleeting from you like golden butterflies).

Pushkin's Orient at its most lavish meets the Orient of Mickiewicz in its subdued form at the moment when their subject matter becomes almost identical, and it is here that the two manners show their greatest inner kinship. One may further cite the picture of nocturnal Bakhchisarai (in the sonnet "Bagczysaraj w nocy" [Bakhchisarai by night]) and its very similar counterpart in Pushkin ("nastala noch'"); soon thereafter Pushkin again evokes the Crimean night in even more Oriental terms, using imagery not unlike the comparison of night to an odalisque in the sonnet "Ałuszta w nocy" (Alushta by night).

In all of these related passages the main difference lies in the frame of mind of the poet. Mickiewicz seems to require a more pathetic tone and greater eloquence than does Pushkin; the Oriental tropes and the exotic and rare vocabulary are the external means used to convey the poet's exaltation. To oversimplify the case, one might say that Mickiewicz is impressed and seeks to impress, whereas Pushkin is charmed and seeks to charm. Both states of mind are legitimate in that they both result in fine poetry. However, Mickiewicz is able to achieve an intensity that is in keeping with the rest of the cycle even without resorting to Oriental imagery. There is no such imagery, for example, in "Bajdary" or in "Ajudah." The sonnet "Ruiny zamku w Bałakławie" develops and intensifies the theme of ruins and desolation (also found in "Bagczysaraj"), in a macabre way that is without parallel in the usually sunny poetry of Pushkin. When Mickiewicz writes about the mountains, his own Romantic sensibility motivates his choice of attitude, and here again we have a striking contrast with the idyllic and tranquil poems that Pushkin wrote about the far more awesome Caucasus mountains ("Kavkaz," "Monastyr' na Kazbeke").

Prince Vyazemsky, a critic who was a close friend of both poets and who translated the sonnets of Mickiewicz, was in no way surprised by the Oriental stylization in Pushkin's tale. In his critical appreciation, he complimented the poet on his fresh and vividly conveyed local color.[12] In the sonnets of Mickiewicz, however, Vyazemsky, for all his admiration, felt obliged to point out a "hyperbolic audacity which is akin to insolence in the eyes of our Hyperborean common sense."[13] This contemporary reaction is understandable. The poetry of Pushkin's southern period is, for all its novelty, firmly planted in the eighteenth-century French and Russian tradition. The sonnets of Mickiewicz are nearly independent of the earlier tradition; the Oriental tradition to which the poet here turns genuinely corresponds to his exaltation, to his need for pathos, color, and excitement.

On their Crimean trips, each poet found more or less what he expected: where Pushkin saw only a rusty fountain and crumbling rooms tastelessly redecorated in unsuitable style (see his "letter" to Delvig), Mickiewicz found "Wschód w miniaturze" (the Orient in miniature) (his letter to Lelewel, mentioned above). What Pushkin did with his impressions, and the means for doing it—which he may have borrowed from contemporary literary practice—were new in Russia, but familiar to a reader versed in current literary fashions. *The Fountain of Bakhchisarai* is a historical poem, evoking the vanished Crimea of the Gireys, and its Orientalism is a costume that requires no further explanation. The sonnets of Mickiewicz are an account of the poet's experiences in the actual Crimea of his day, yet they are so elaborately decorated with Arabian-Persian imagery that he had to supply many notes to explain strange Islamic terms and paraphernalia and to smooth over the geographic incongruity of the Turkish "chylat," the Arab "chalif" (caliph), and the Persian "Ptak-Góra" (Bird-Mountain) in the land inhabited by the impoverished and uneducated Crimean Tatars. For, while there is every *poetic* reason for the

---

[12] The article "Razgovor mezhdu izdatelem i klassikom," in Viazemskii, *Polnoe sobranie sochinenii*, 167.
[13] Viazemskii, *Polnoe sobranie sochinenii*, 332.

Orientalism of the sonnets, there is, properly speaking, no *logical* reason for it. Since the landscape is quite similar to that of Greece or Italy, the only excuse is the Moslem religion of the Tatars. But by the same token, a hypothetical Persian poet describing Poland would be justified in speaking of it in terms of Spanish bullfights and Irish shamrocks, likewise on the basis of a religion common to the three countries.

The ultimate difference is that the spirit which we perceive behind the poet's art in *The Fountain of Bakhchisarai* is Apollonian and rational, while the spirit behind the *Crimean Sonnets* is, for all their controlled mastery, Dionysian and explosive. What all this means is that, of the two poets, Mickiewicz is by far the more genuine Romantic.

Pushkin was undoubtedly familiar with the *Crimean Sonnets* and with the Russian translations of them by Vyazemsky, Kozlov, Illichevsky, and others.[14] There is a direct reference to them in Pushkin's "The Sonnet" and we can cite, by way of indirect evidence of Pushkin's close study of the cycle, Wacław Lednicki's very convincing parallel between the last completed stanza of Pushkin's "Autumn" (1833) and the imagery that results from the juxtaposing of "Cisza morska" and "Żegluga."[15] In the poet's canon there is an unfinished poem with Crimean setting and with lovely and strange Oriental imagery: "V prokhlade sladostnoi fontanov." This poem was evidently not written by Pushkin in its final form, but was very believably reconstructed by Shchyogolev in 1911 on the basis of numerous sketches and drafts found among the poet's manuscripts. The sketches presumably originated in 1828 and may have been written under the impact of the *Crimean Sonnets*. Since the 1940s, it has been repeatedly maintained that the poet referred to in the last stanza of this poem is Mickiewicz, and that the entire poem is a fragment of what was to be a critical appreciation of the *Crimean Sonnets*. This opinion, voiced by such Soviet commentators as Mark Zhivov and N. V. Izmailov,[16] is also shared

---

[14] An account of Russian translations of *Crimean Sonnets* which appeared in Pushkin's lifetime is given in Gleb Struve's article "Mickiewicz in Russian Translations and Criticism," in *Adam Mickiewicz in World Literature*, ed. Wacław Lednicki (Berkeley: University of California Press, 1956).

[15] Wacław Lednicki, "Mickiewicz's Stay in Russia and His Friendship with Pushkin," in Lednicki, *Adam Mickiewicz in World Literature*, 55–59.

[16] N. V. Izmailov's special study of this poem and its connection with Mickiewicz is quoted by Tomashevskii, *Stikh i iazyk*, 435. The USSR Academy of Sciences' edition of the complete collected works of Pushkin (Moscow, 1956–58) goes so far as to list the

by Professor Lednicki[17] and by the Polish editors of the 1954 edition of Julian Tuwim's volume of Pushkin translations, *Lutnia Puszkina*.[18] If this supposition is correct, Pushkin reacted to the cycle not only with great admiration, but also with a certain amused irony:

> Poroi vostochnyi krasnobai
> Zdes' razvival svoi tetradi
> I udivlial Bakhchisarai.

In the 1830s, both Pushkin and Mickiewicz turned to more sober and realistic poetry. In "Onegin's Travels," Pushkin looks back upon his Crimean period nostalgically and rather humorously. Mickiewicz has his anti-Romantic moments in *Pan Tadeusz*: the diatribe of Tadeusz, in book 3, against cypresses, lemon trees, and other warm-climate flora is a long way from the loving description of these trees in "Pielgrzym." By then, however, Crimean Orientalism had become a part of the Polish and Russian literary traditions, having been taken over and developed by Słowacki and Lermontov. The brilliantly inaugurated tradition was still alive in the Russian poetry of the twentieth century, when Crimean themes found their expression in poems of Osip Mandelstam and Anna Akhmatova.

* * *

With these two research papers on Pushkin, SK established his scholarly credentials in a decisive way. (They had been written in graduate seminars, and then revised and combined for publication in *California Slavic Studies* at the suggestion of his mentors and the editors of the series, Gleb Struve and Nicholas V. Riasanovsky.) SK's sure-footed deployment of a wide-ranging knowledge of Russian, French and Polish literatures to comparative ends and

---

poem in the alphabetical index under the alternate title "Mickevichu." Yet it must be pointed out that not all Soviet literary scholars subscribe to the theory that this poem refers to Mickiewicz. For example, L. P. Grossman, in his recent study of the genesis of *The Fountain of Bakhchisarai* ("U istokov *Bakhchisaraiskogo fontana*," in *Pushkin: Issledovaniia i materialy* [Moscow and Leningrad, 1960], 3:81), maintains that this poem is a record of the impression the palace at Bakhchisarai made on Pushkin during his visit there in 1820.

17 Lednicki, *Adam Mickiewicz in World Literature*, 21–22.
18 Julian Tuwim, *Lutnia Puszkina* (Warsaw, 1954), 249.

his vivid expository skills were marks of a first-rate literary scholar. This performance surely was a major factor in his appointment to a tenure-track position in the Department of Slavic Languages and Literatures at the University of California, Berkeley immediately upon the receipt of his PhD the following year, and he achieved the rank of full professor in only three years' time. The essays also demonstrated that SK was a Pushkin scholar of note, and he was soon invited to review publications by periodicals catering to professionals in the field and to a wider community of well-educated readers. See, by way of example, his discerning essay on two Pushkin biographies in the *Nation*, 14 April 1969, or his entry on Pushkin for the well-known *Atlantic Brief Lives*. Given the focus of the present volume, it is appropriate to cite the conclusion of that pithy article:

> In his impassioned defense of Pushkin written in 1940, Igor Stravinsky stated: "In justice, his name should be revered on the same plane with those of Dante, Goethe, Shakespeare." Generations of Russians who have returned to Pushkin again and again with reverence and gratitude would vouch for that statement. It is well worth mastering Russian just to be able to read Pushkin.
>
> Or one can simply forget translations or language study and listen to Mozart's G-Minor Quintet or the A-Major Piano Concerto. One will find there better than anywhere else the same polished elegance, the same sunlit clarity, and the same sudden intimations of the tragic aspects of existence that form the most precious essence of Pushkin's poetry.[19]

---

[19] Simon Karlinsky, "Alexander Pushkin," in *Atlantic Brief Lives: A Biographical Companion to the Arts*, ed. Louis Kronenberger (Boston: Little, Brown, 1971), 614–16.

Fortunes of an Infanticide[1]

Few events in modern history have appealed to the imagination of so many poets and playwrights of diverse literary traditions as the overthrow in 1605 of Boris Godunov, a monarch with dubious claims to the Russian throne, by a pretender of lowly birth known to history as the False Dmitry. The pretender claimed to be the youngest son of Ivan the Terrible, miraculously saved from the assassins sent by Boris to kill him fourteen years earlier.

Within a decade after the events in Moscow, there appeared in Spain Lope de Vega's play *El gran duque de Moscovia*, based on a somewhat distorted account of the defeat of Boris and the False Dmitry's short-lived triumph (he was deposed and put to death eleven months after his coronation). An even more distorted but still recognizable version reached England by 1618 in John Fletcher's play *The Loyal Subject*, as was demonstrated by Ervin C. Brody in his comprehensive study of the subject, *The Demetrius Legend and Its Literary Treatment in the Age of the Baroque*. Published in 1972, Brody's book, despite its title, also described the later treatments of the Boris Godunov and False Dmitry theme by German and Russian playwrights of the eighteenth, nineteenth, and twentieth centuries (including its inexplicable popularity during the National Socialist period, when four dramas in German about the False Dmitry appeared in 1937 alone). This book supplemented and augmented the fundamental study published in the Soviet Union in 1936 by the noted Pushkin scholar Mikhail Alekseev, who also examined the dramas, novels, poems, and harlequinades the subject inspired in England, France and Italy.

Since about the middle of the nineteenth century, historians have repeatedly demonstrated that the responsibility of Boris Godunov for the accidental death of the young Tsarevich Dmitry in 1591 was a legend deliberately kept alive by Russian chroniclers to curry favor with the tsars

---

[1] Review of *Boris Godunov: Transposition of a Russian Theme*, by Caryl Emerson (Bloomington: Indiana University Press, 1986). Originally published in *Times Literary Supplement*, 17 July 1987, 762.

who reigned after the overthrow of the False Dmitry. The aim of this calumny was to discredit in the eyes of posterity the two upstart monarchs: Boris Godunov, who did not belong to any of the Russian princely houses of ancient lineage, came to rule first as regent during the reign of Tsar Fyodor (the feeble-minded second son of Ivan the Terrible and the husband of Godunov's sister) and was elected to be tsar after Fyodor's death; and the False Dmitry, who impersonated the prince supposedly murdered as a child on Godunov's orders.

For about a century now, no responsible historian has believed that the real Dmitry was killed instead of falling accidentally on his own dagger during an epileptic seizure, which is what sources dating from the time of his death show. Yet in theaters and opera houses all over the world audiences watch the guilt-ridden Tsar Boris agonizing over the failures of his reign and the misfortunes visited upon his family and his people in retribution for the murder of an innocent child that had enabled him to attain the throne. This is the situation depicted in two major nineteenth-century works, Aleksandr Pushkin's neo-Shakespearean tragedy (1825) and Modest Musorgsky's Dostoevskian opera (two different versions: it was first completed in 1869, and then revised and published in 1874). The opera was based in part on Pushkin's play, but the ultimate source for both the poet and the composer was the tenth volume of the monumental *History of the Russian State* by Nikolai Karamzin (1766–1826).

Caryl Emerson's book is an interdisciplinary and intergeneric study of ways in which the work of a historian is transposed into a work of literature and what happens when history and literature are adapted for the operatic stage. The author herself negotiates, with assurance and elegance, passages from one branch of scholarship to another, being equally sure-footed as a student of history, literature, and music. The dominant presence in her book is neither the historical Boris Godunov, nor Karamzin, Pushkin, or Musorgsky, though the last three are allotted a robust chapter each. It is instead Mikhail Bakhtin (1895–1975), the philosopher, linguist and literary scholar, whose rapidly growing posthumous popularity in English-speaking countries was attested to in 1984 by the appearance of the excellent study of his life and ideas, *Mikhail Bakhtin* by Katerina Clark and Michael Holquist.

Caryl Emerson is one of Bakhtin's principal standard-bearers and popularizers in English. She has translated and edited his influential

Problems of Dostoevsky's Poetics (first published in Russian in 1929) and is also the cotranslator (together with Michael Holquist) of *The Dialogic Imagination*, a collection of four Bakhtin essays. For a number of years now, two Bakhtinian concepts have been in common use among teachers of Russian literature: the polyphonic novel (as in the novels of Dostoevsky, where the views of several characters are given equal weight and validity); and carnivalization, a special form of comedy that occurs when the powerful and powerless characters switch roles, as they did in carnival celebrations and also in novels by Rabelais and Dostoevsky.

These concepts have now moved to fields other than Russian literature, and so have two others which are basic to Emerson's book on Boris Godunov. Central to her approach are Bakhtinian "dialogism" (an artist who creates a work on a theme familiar to the audience is engaging in a dialogue with the artist who used this theme earlier) and "chronotope," a term Bakhtin found in Einstein's relativity theory and applied to literature to indicate that a literary work reflects the notions of time and space that are current in the period in which the writer lived. Chronotope was postulated by Bakhtin in his essay "Forms of Time and of the Chronotope in the Novel," a study of the Greek and Roman romances of the early Christian centuries. Emerson uses it as her main tool for investigating the transition of the theme of Boris and False Dmitry from one medium to another. "Chronotopes can never be abstract," Emerson explains. "Therefore every chronotope inevitably contains an *evaluation*..., inevitably delimits and individualizes the perspective from which the story is told. It constitutes a justification for the unstated causality that joins a series of events into a plausible narrative."

Her most cogent examples are found in the chapter on Karamzin. Before his career as a historian, Nikolai Karamzin was a much-admired writer of Sentimentalist fiction. His transition from the fictional to the historical mode of narration began, according to Emerson, in 1802, with a brief essay, "Historical Reminiscences and Observations on the Way to the Trinity [St. Sergius Monastery]," in which there is a portrait of Boris Godunov as an enlightened monarch who did a great deal of good for his country. Yet some two decades later, in the tenth volume of his *History*, which served as the main source for both Pushkin's and Musorgsky's works, Karamzin showed Boris as a guilt-crazed murderer.

Two historical developments had occurred and changed Karamzin's idea of Godunov in the intervening years. In 1812, Russia was ravaged by the invasion of Napoleon, another parvenu monarch with no dynastic claims to support his right to the throne. Also, in an age when Shakespeare was regarded in both France and Russia as unsuitable for the stage and had to be performed in simplified and "regularized" neoclassical adaptations by Jean François Ducis, Karamzin was a longtime champion of the Bard in his original form. Back in 1787, Karamzin translated *Julius Caesar* from the English original and not from the French of Ducis, as was the custom at the time. Regarded as a willful eccentricity in the 1780s, Karamzin's view that Shakespeare's plays did not need tampering with came to be generally accepted in Russia by the 1820s. As Emerson rightly points out, Godunov the usurper of Karamzin's *History* bears a strong imprint of Napoleon and of Shakespeare's Macbeth and Richard III.

Pushkin, as Emerson sees it, "drew on particular incidents in Karamzin's *History* and entered into a complex dialogue with the whole." It was a case of a poet of the Romantic age rethinking the historical account permeated with the Sentimentalist outlook of Karamzin. Even though there is a section headed "The Shakespeare Connection" in the Pushkin chapter, Emerson underestimates the significance of Pushkin's self-proclaimed intention to sacrifice on the altar of "our father Shakespeare" the neoclassical unities and poetics in which Pushkin had been brought up. The discussion of the neoclassical views on translation and adaptation of foreign plays is handicapped by Emerson's failure (and that of the sources she cites) to realize that the tragedy *Dmitry the Pretender* by Pushkin's eighteenth-century predecessor Aleksandr Sumarokov and Sumarokov's emasculated version of *Hamlet* were conversions of the chronicle accounts and of Shakespeare into Sumarokov's admired neoclassical models, *Le Cid* by Corneille and *Britannicus* by Racine.

The chapter on Musorgsky is perhaps the richest in the book. Drawing on the recent ground-breaking studies of the operatic *Boris* by Robert William Oldani and Richard Taruskin,[2] Emerson finds that the difference

---

[2] Emerson later collaborated with Oldani on a comprehensive study of the opera: Caryl Emerson and Robert William Oldani, *Modest Musorgsky and "Boris Godunov": Myths, Realities, Reconsiderations* (Cambridge: Cambridge University Press, 1994). Taruskin's views of the composer and the opera can be found in Richard Taruskin,

between the 1869 and 1874 versions can best be explained by Musorgsky's evolving concept of what an opera could be, by his withdrawal from Pushkin's model of Boris to that of Karamzin, and by the fact that this music was composed in the age of Dostoevsky rather than that of Pushkin. All these things account for the opera's revisions, rather than the usually cited pressures of government censorship and the operatic conventions of the time. This chapter also contains an extended and illuminating discussion of the operatic libretto as literature and its relationship to drama and prose fiction.

There are some problems in the transcribing and translating of Russian names and texts. The Russian word for Trinity, *Troitsa*, appears throughout in its dative case form, *Troitse*, because that is how it occurred in the title of Karamzin's essay. The adjective *tsarskii* has existed for centuries in Russian with the meaning of "royal." It is wrong to equate it, as Emerson does repeatedly, with "tsarist" (Pushkin's Marina speaks to the False Dmitry about "your tsarist word alone" and we also read of Boris Godunov's "tsarist dignity"). "Tsarist" and its related noun "tsarism" entered Russian usage after the October Revolution, with the meaning of "autocratic" or "despotic." This is the meaning with which it was absorbed into English. It isn't a synonym for "royal," and couldn't have been used in the seventeenth century. Pushkin's chronicler Pimen was sent to the town of Uglich "to perform a certain penance" (*poslushanie*), which Emerson reads as "sent ... on a vague suspicion."

The worst single lapse occurs in the discussion of Pushkin's dedication of *Boris Godunov* to the memory of Nikolai Karamzin. The play was dedicated to Karamzin because "it was inspired by his genius." Caryl Emerson reproduces a garbled version of this dedication from a two-volume collection of Russian plays in English translation, which first appeared in 1961. In that version, the translator confused the two Russian equivalents of "his," *ego* and the self-referential *svoi*, which must pertain to the subject of the sentence. So his translation began: "Alexander Pushkin, inspired by his genius, dedicates this work ..." Instead of eulogizing Karamzin, this translation makes Pushkin brag of being inspired by his

---

Musorgsky: Eight Essays and an Epilogue, foreword by Carol Emerson (Princeton: Princeton University Press, 1993). See also *passim*, Richard Taruskin, *Defining Russia Musically: Historical and Hermeneutical Essays* (Princeton: Princeton University Press, 1997).—Ed.

own genius. Small wonder that Emerson could see this dedication as some kind of parody.

Such blemishes do not diminish the fact that this is an engrossing, many-layered and rewarding book.

* * *

The subjects of dramatic theater, stagecraft and music drama intermingled in this review essay—along with readings of the writings of Aleksandr Pushkin—reflect many of SK's principal interests. It is one in a series of pieces on poetic drama (e.g., plays by Küchelbecker, Lermontov, Kuzmin, Gumilyov and Tsvetaeva) and on the masterworks of the nineteenth-century Russian stage, represented above all by Nikolai Gogol, Aleksandr Sukhovo-Kobylin, Aleksandr Ostrovsky, Lev Tolstoi and Anton Chekhov. SK was particularly delighted by the underground absurdist theater of the Soviet period, which was almost unknown to its contemporaries. For many years he taught popular, highly regarded undergraduate courses on Russian drama and on the life and writings of Chekhov, and he accumulated an immense store of knowledge about the subject. In light of these facts, it is regrettable that he did not write a companion volume to his book on the origins of Russian drama.[3] The several articles on the topic collected in the present volume are partial compensation. The attention devoted in this review to problems of translation is a signal of an ongoing concern in SK's writings about Russian literature and culture.

---

[3] Simon Karlinsky, *Russian Drama from Its Beginnings to the Age of Pushkin* (Berkeley: University of California Press, 1985).

Pushkin Re-Englished[1]

*I*n Aleksandr Pushkin's great novel in verse *Evgeny Onegin*, Tatyana has a dream about a swarm of demons who are made up of bits and pieces of incongruous animal shapes. They point at her with their "tufted tails, fangs, whiskers, blood-stained tongues, horns and bony fingers," and each one shouts, "She's mine! She's mine!" Efim Etkind, the foremost Soviet expert on problems of poetry translation, who now lives in France and whose book on the subject, *L'art en crise*, should be required reading for anyone interested in this topic, once likened the fate of Pushkin's poetry to the plight of Tatyana surrounded by those dream demons.

No literary figure arouses people's proprietary instincts to the extent that Pushkin does. In Russia, he has been claimed as precursor, ally, or spokesman by every political faction, from monarchists to Bolsheviks; by people of every religious persuasion, from fundamentalist Christian to atheist; and by adherents of just about every literary trend from his day to ours. In English-speaking countries, where Pushkin's reputation was not really consolidated until a century after his death in 1837, editions of his work have tended to be accompanied by an outline of the method the translator claims to have devised to overcome Pushkin's notorious untranslatability. This is also the case with the new volume of Pushkin's lyrics, verse tales, and plays put into English by the novelist D. M. Thomas, the author of the best-selling *The White Hotel*.

In the original Russian, the brilliance, virtuosity, and depth of Pushkin's poetry are garbed in a style of extreme simplicity and modesty. Because of this, when one of his poems is divested of his own words it is often turned into an unprepossessing frog, cruelly deprived of whatever made him a prince in his original incarnation. Translators are aware of this. The solutions they have so far tried come in three varieties. The first is to forget meter and rhyme and to render Pushkin's lyric and narrative

---

[1] Review of *The Bronze Horseman: Selected Poetry of Alexander Pushkin*, trans. D. M. Thomas (New York: Viking, 1982). Originally published in *New York Times Book Review*, 26 September 1982, 11, 25–26.

poetry into maximally precise English prose. This method, exemplified by Edmund Wilson's version of *The Bronze Horseman* included in his book *The Triple Thinkers*, satisfies the reader's curiosity about what Pushkin has to say. But it leaves out the verbal music of the text, which in Pushkin's case means that it leaves out the poetry.

The adherents of the second method seek to convey Pushkin's meters through their (very approximate) English equivalents. They try to reproduce his rhyme schemes by facile English rhymes of the "singing-winging-ringing," "love-above" and "passion-fashion" variety, though anything this trite is the very antithesis of Pushkin. Besides, as Andrei Bely demonstrated years ago, the melodic quality of Pushkin's meters derives from his variable pattern of withholding the metrical stress from positions where it would be expected in traditional Russian iambic tetrameter and pentameter.[2] This subtle effect cannot be duplicated in English, which is why the various translations of *Evgeny Onegin* in rhymed English iambic tetrameter (e.g., the recent one by Sir Charles Johnson, undeservedly overpraised by critics, to my mind) produce on a person closely familiar with the original the effect of a Chopin nocturne played in the tempo of a military march.

The third method is a compromise of the first two: The translator settles for vaguely metered prose, arranged on the page to look like verse, thus preserving a semblance of Pushkin's iambic or trochaic pattern while avoiding the filler words and other distortions necessitated by scansion or rhyme. This was the path chosen by Vladimir Nabokov in his well-known translation of *Evgeny Onegin*, a translation that makes sense within his voluminous commentary (for which it is actually a pretext) but no sense at all if considered on its own.[3]

---

[2] The reference is to four technical analyses of Pushkin's verse collected in Andrei Belyi, *Simvolizm* (Moscow: Izd-vo Musaget, 1910). SK greatly admired Bely's prose fiction and his narrative in verse, *The First Rendezvous* (1921). See his review of translations of *The Silver Dove* and *Kotik Letaev*, "Unknown Here, Suppressed There," *New York Times Book Review*, 27 October 1974, 1–2; and his "Symphonic Structure in Andrej Belyj's 'Pervoe svidanie,'" *California Slavic Studies* 6 (1971): 61–70, included in the present volume. See also his entry "Bely, Andrey," in the *Columbia Dictionary of Modern European Literature*, 2nd ed. (New York: Columbia University Press, 1980), 70–71.—Ed.

[3] SK's cagey evaluation of the first edition of this translation appeared in an unsigned review in *Choice* 2, no. 4 (June 1965): 232–33:

> Nabokov's version of Pushkin's novel in verse, despite an iambic metrical pattern, reads like a prose translation. It is remarkable in its fidelity to the nuances of the original, although the translator's excessive scruples at times lead

Until now, Pushkin's English translators have selected one or another of these methods. D. M. Thomas is, as far as I know, the first to have opted for all three at once. That is, some of the poems that were metered and rhymed in Russian do have both meter and rhyme in this translation, while others are provided with a modicum of meter but no rhyme. For the most part, however, Pushkin's verse has been turned into prose, pure and simple, despite the verse-like typography (e.g., the title poem, *The Bronze Horseman*, or the long lyric that begins "Winter. What shall we do in the country?"). But the play *The Stone Guest*, written by Pushkin in blank verse of matchless elegance, has been rendered by Thomas in jangling couplets of rhymed iambic pentameter (with such dubious, un-Pushkinian rhymes as "chance-mischance" and "creature–at your feet for"). This is a procedure that strikes me as being as peculiar as arranging Hamlet's soliloquy in limericks.

---

him into mannerism and archness (e.g., "dulcitude" and "juventude" are used where the Russian says "sweetness" and "youth," merely because Pushkin used the slightly archaic Russian variant of the latter word). The translation, which occupies only a part of the first of four volumes, is really a pretext for publishing a wide array of highly subjective scholarly commentary by Nabokov on Pushkin, *Onegin* and various tangential matters too numerous to cite. His commentary on *Onegin* tells us almost as much about Nabokov as it does about Pushkin. With all that, Nabokov is an informed and imaginative literary scholar as well as a master stylist. He has the additional advantage of being free from the compulsory sociological and political approach that is now imposed on the Pushkin scholarship in the Soviet Union. For all its lack of objectivity and occasional unfairness (Nabokov's blanket dismissal of various lesser Russian poets is seen in proper perspective with the realization that Molière and Corneille are similarly treated by him), his commentary is a valuable contribution to Pushkin studies and can be used with pleasure and profit by scholars and specialists. It is far too special and erudite for the general reader.

It is happy circumstance that this anonymous review—typically judicious—probably remained unknown to Nabokov. Over the years he and SK established a friendly relationship and correspondence, SK published analyses of Nabokov's fiction and wrote several laudatory reviews of his novels (both those translated from the Russian and those written in English). SK's remarkably comprehensive knowledge of Nabokov's biography and writings led to his selection (by the widows of the two writers) to edit and annotate the epistolary exchange between the Russian writer and the American critic Edmund Wilson: *The Nabokov-Wilson Letters: Correspondence between Vladimir Nabokov and Edmund Wilson, 1940–1971*, edited, annotated, and with an introductory essay by Simon Karlinsky (New York: Harper & Row, 1979); *Dear Bunny, Dear Volodya: The Nabokov-Wilson Letters, 1940–1971*, rev. and expanded ed. (Berkeley: University of California Press, 2001).—Ed.

I. Pushkin and Romanticism

Trying to compare Thomas's work to the originals in order to check its accuracy, I soon realized that much of the book was not translated from Pushkin's Russian but rather adapted from two earlier volumes of Pushkin translations into English. The first of these is John Fennell's anthology *Pushkin*, which contains Russian texts "with plain prose translations of each poem."[4] In his acknowledgment section, Thomas admits to having been "much influenced" by Fennell's "lucid prose versions" of Pushkin. But influence seems hardly the right term when we juxtapose the end of the first part of *The Bronze Horseman* as "translated" by Thomas (six lines as compared to Pushkin's eight):

> And he, as though bewitched, as if riveted
> To the marble, cannot get down! Around him
> Is water and nothing else! And, his back turned
> To him, in unshakeable eminence, over
> The angry river, the turbulent Neva, stands
> The Image, with outstretched arm, on his bronze horse,

with Fennell's "plain prose," which runs:

> And he, as though bewitched, as though riveted to the marble, cannot get down! Around him is water and nothing else! And with back turned to him, on unshakeable eminence, over the turbulent Neva, stands the Image with outstretched arm on his bronze horse.

Or consider how much translating Thomas had to do in these three stanzas from "To the Sea," followed by their source in the Fennell book:

> Farewell, free element!
> Before me for the last time
> Your blue waves roll
> And you shine in proud beauty.
>
> . . . .

---

[4] *Pushkin*, introduced, edited, and translated by John Fennell (Baltimore: Penguin Books, 1964).

> One cliff, the sepulchre of glory ...
> There, majestic memories subsided
> Into chill sleep; the memory
> Of Napoleon went out.
>
> . . . .
>
> Your image was stamped on him,
> He was created by your spirit.
> Like you, he was powerful, gloomy, deep;
> Like you, nothing could daunt him.

Farewell, free element! For the last time you roll your blue waves before me and shimmer in your proud beauty.

One cliff, the sepulchre of glory ... There majestic memories subsided into chill sleep: there Napoleon's flame died out.

Your image was stamped upon him, he was created by your spirit: like you, he was powerful, deep, and gloomy; like you, nothing could daunt him.

(The one independent contribution by Thomas is a total misreading, since "there Napoleon's flame died out" should have been "there Napoleon slowly expired," i.e., on St. Helena.) Both "To the Sea" and *The Bronze Horseman* (especially the latter's famous prologue) contain numerous passages based on the Fennell version, either quoted verbatim or rearranged but still recognizable. This also occurs throughout the rest of the book. The lyric "Lines Written at Night during Insomnia," though printed as verse, is repeated in its entirety and almost word for word from the prose version in the Fennell *Pushkin*.

The other source on which Thomas has heavily drawn is *Pushkin Threefold* by Walter Arndt.[5] This volume contains translations in verse, followed by original Russian texts and "linear" (i.e., metrical prose) translations. It is these last that Thomas used, as can be easily seen by comparing his versions of the poems "Young Mare" and "Echo" with those of Arndt. Up to sixty percent of their text is simply taken from Arndt, and the rest

---

[5] *Pushkin Threefold: Narrative, Lyric, Polemic, and Ribald Verse*, trans. Walter Arndt (New York: Dutton, 1972).

is adapted from him. Especially telling is the derivation of the rhymed version of the longest poem in Thomas's book, *The Tale of the Tsar Saltan*, from Arndt's prose rendition of it. The dependence is so strong that we see Thomas repeat even Arndt's few misreadings: the magical transformation of the young prince into a buzzing mosquito (*komar*, mistranslated as "a gnat"); the mosquito's sting causing the prince's slanderous aunt to lose sight in one eye (a point missed by both translators); and the tutor (*diad'ka*) who accompanies the thirty-three ocean-dwelling heroes (both translators misread his function, confusing it with *diadia*, and therefore made him these soldiers' uncle).

A check of the table of contents of D. M. Thomas's Pushkin collection shows that more than three-quarters of the works he selected are also contained in the anthologies of John Fennell or Walter Arndt (or in both). His reliance on the work of these two scholars (barely hinted at in the case of Fennell, unacknowledged in that of Arndt) is so wholesale that in all fairness Thomas ought to have at least named them as his cotranslators. Significantly, it is when Thomas dispenses with the guidance of his two mentors that he comes to miss the meanings of certain poems. Thus, in "Demons," by materializing the demons and making them plainly visible in the third stanza, instead of at the end of the poem, as Pushkin did, Thomas wrecks the whole point of the poem, which is the traveler's doubt as to whether he is seeing the blizzard or something supernatural.

But even apart from the derivative (if that is the right word) character of these translations, there are many other things that are wrong with them. Major cuts have been made with no indications in the text. The central digression in *The Gypsies*, with its oft-anthologized comparison of the protagonist to migratory birds, is left out. The opening section of *The Gabrieliad* is reduced from about a page to two lines, while the same poem's epilogue is cut by about one-third. In the play *Rusalka*, one of the male characters has been turned into a woman. There is a strange monotony of vocabulary: when Pushkin mentions a maiden, a princess, a peasant lass, or a virgin, Thomas has only one word for all of them—girl. Most unfortunate of all, the tone of these translations sounds closest to Pushkin when they repeat passages from the Arndt and Fennell books and least like him whenever Thomas strikes out on his own.

The dust jacket carries glowing endorsements from three literate people for whose judgment I have the highest respect. I am not sure what this means, but my guess would be that the genius of Aleksandr Pushkin comes through, if only in part, even in less-than-competent translations and that the two eminent Pushkin translators who, unbeknownst to themselves, were harnessed to help out with this project must have indeed helped. What I am sure about is that this volume has not brought us any closer to (to quote from one of the endorsements on the dust jacket) "the forever impossible goal of truly translating Pushkin."

* * *

This piece stirred up a "battle royal" (as one of SK's correspondents wrote) even before its appearance. As if to stoke controversy, a preliminary account of a first skirmish was published five days in advance of publication of SK's review, in Edwin McDowell, "Author of *White Hotel*: A New Dispute," *New York Times*, 21 September 1982. (Thomas had brushed off charges in the *Times Literary Supplement* earlier the same year that he had plagiarized Anatoly Kuznetsov's documentary novel *Babi Yar* in his novel *The White Hotel*.) McDowell solicited statements by telephone from Walter Arndt, John Bayley (one of the "three literate people for whose judgment [SK had] the highest respect") and Thomas himself for his report. Thomas's thunderous and lengthy counterattack was published in the *New York Times Book Review* on 24 October 1982. He likened the treatment of his work to a Soviet show trial; rejected allegations of plagiarism despite evidence to the contrary; and, implicitly, derided SK's competence to judge his work. McDowell returned to his position on the sidelines in a second report, published in the *Times* on 12 November 1982, and in it he rehearsed yet another charge that Thomas had pilfered the prior work of Carl Proffer (the scholar, translator, and founder of Ardis Publishers) for Thomas's English version of a long poem by Anna Akhmatova. McDowell had by then discovered the whereabouts of John Fennell of New College, Oxford, who was teaching that term at Stanford University, and extracted from him a letter regarding Thomas's "use" of his work. (The letter was never published, but a copy of it is to be found among the Simon Karlinsky Papers in the Bancroft Library, University of California, Berkeley.) Echoes of "battle" resounded on a diminishing scale for several months thereafter, with interventions in local Berkeley papers, the *St. Louis Post Dispatch*, the London *Sunday Telegraph*, the *Wall Street Journal* and the *TLS*.

A Mystical Musicologist[1]

"There are writers whose fate makes one gasp in astonishment: how could it have happened that the new contemporary readers know neither their names nor their writings?" With these words the Soviet literary scholar Evgeniya Khin began the introductory essay to her 1959 edition of selected stories and novellas by Prince Vladimir Odoevsky.[2] A contemporary and friend of Pushkin, Gogol, and Lermontov, who all regarded him as their peer, Odoevsky (1804–69) was a major figure on the Russian cultural scene between the 1820s and 1860s. His highly original tales of the supernatural, which made him the Russian counterpart of E. T. A. Hoffmann and Edgar Allan Poe, were much appreciated by Russian writers, readers, and critics of the first half of the nineteenth century.

Odoevsky also wrote antiutopias, which in our century have been included in collections of early science fiction, and humorous stories of social satire. His two big novellas, *Princess Mimi* and *Princess Zizi* (the titles come from minor characters in the comedy by Aleksandr Griboedov—another friend of Odoevsky's—called *Gore ot uma* [Woe from wit]), with their sharp analysis of how the minds and characters of upper-class women could be warped by the artificiality of their upbringing, give Odoevsky a modest claim to be the earliest Russian writer with what is today called a feminist consciousness. His one book-length literary work,

---

[1] Review of *The Life, Times and Milieu of V. F. Odoyevsky, 1804–1869*, by Neil Cornwell (London: Athlone, 1986). Originally published in *Times Literary Supplement*, 26 September 1986, 1067. [Odoevsky's fiction figured prominently in SK's graduate seminars in Russian prose of the Romantic period. See his study "A Hollow Shape: The Philosophical Tales of Prince Vladimir Odoevsky," *Studies in Romanticism* 5, no. 3 (1966): 169–82. A biography of Odoevsky comparable to Cornwell's appeared in Russia some five years later: M. A. Tur'ian, "*Strannaia moia sud'ba ...*": *O zhizni Vladimira Fedorovicha Odoevskogo* (Moscow: Kniga, 1991).—Ed.]

[2] V. F. Odoevskii, *Povesti i rasskazy*, ed. and with an introductory essay and annotations by E. Iu. Khin (Moscow: Gos. izd-vo khudozhestvennoi literatury, 1959). A step towards redressing Khin's complaint was the publication, in 1975, of a scholarly Russian edition of *Russian Nights*: V. F. Odoevskii, *Russkie nochi*, ed. B. F. Egorov, E. A. Maimin, and M. I. Medovoi (Leningrad: Izd-vo Nauka, 1975).—Ed.

Russian Nights, available in English translation, is a series of philosophical dialogues interspersed with brief fictional episodes.[3] In it Odoevsky expounds his antirationalist, antiutilitarian outlook derived from such idealist Western predecessors as Emmanuel Swedenborg and Friedrich von Schelling. The philosopher Schelling was for Odoevsky the Christopher Columbus of the nineteenth century who discovered "the hitherto unknown continent"—the human soul, a concept which in our day would be conveyed by "psyche."

Odoevsky's idealistic philosophy, combined with his interest in the occult and the rejection in his dystopian stories of all forms of social engineering based on materialist views or economic theories, turned against him the entire dynasty of radical-utilitarian critics who dominated Russian journals from the 1840s to the end of the century. The outcome was that Odoevsky's fictional writings were little read or studied between the time of his death and the death of Joseph Stalin. This neglect has obscured not only Odoevsky's influence on his younger contemporaries, such as Turgenev and Dostoevsky, but also his considerable contributions to several other areas of Russian culture.

The dialogues in *Russian Nights* and his other philosophical writings give Odoevsky a minor but incontestable place in the history of Russian thought. He was also an important theoretician and practitioner in the field of elementary education. He wrote several children's stories which remain favorites to this day. And, as Neil Cornwell's biography well shows, Odoevsky "gave a vast amount of time and energy" to ameliorating the situation of the urban poor and of homeless or abandoned children, working for their cause quietly and effectively (as Anton Chekhov would do some decades later), rather than taking the path of histrionic confrontation (to which Lev Tolstoi would occasionally resort in his philanthropic ventures).

Vladimir Odoevsky's most durable achievement, apart from his creative writing, was his impact on the development of music and musical taste in his country. A musician and an amateur composer since childhood, Odoevsky was the first important Russian musicologist and music

---

3   V. F. Odoevsky, *Russian Nights*, trans. Olga Koshansky-Olienikov and Ralph E. Matlaw, with an introduction by Dr. Matlaw (New York: E. P. Dutton, 1965); republished by Northwestern University Press in 1997 with an afterword by Neil Cornwell.

critic. As a teenage boy, Odoevsky was introduced to the music of Johann Sebastian Bach. He immediately placed this composer at the center of his musical universe—a full decade before Mendelssohn's performances of the St. Matthew Passion restored to Bach the eminence he now enjoys. Odoevsky demonstrated to his countrymen the greatness of Haydn, Mozart and Beethoven, especially the difficult and supposedly illogical Beethoven of the late quartets. He described repeatedly the sublime beauties of *Don Giovanni*, the only Mozart opera performed with any regularity in Russia at the time, even though he believed, as many nineteenth-century critics did, that the opera should end with the protagonist's descent into hell and that the final ensemble which Mozart wrote should be left out as supposedly redundant and distracting.

Because the opera-going public of St. Petersburg and Moscow loved the art of the Italian bel canto, as exemplified by Rossini's *Tancredi*, Bellini's *Norma*, and *Nabucco* by the young Verdi, to the exclusion of any other kind of opera, Odoevsky fought a prolonged and ultimately successful journalistic battle to vary this repertoire with some productions of Mozart, of Weber and, in the 1860s, of Wagner. His anti-Italian opera crusade may seem absurd now, but in his time it was an important and badly needed undertaking. When the St. Petersburg Opera commissioned Verdi's *La forza del destino* in 1862 and gave it a lavish premiere (for which the composer was imported and paid an exorbitant sum), while allotting skimpy budgets for productions of Mozart and Russian operas by Mikhail Glinka and Aleksandr Serov, Odoevsky was so incensed that he characterized Verdi's new work as a "polka in four acts." Some of the neologisms Odoevsky coined in his efforts to break the bel canto hegemony are still remembered: *vzbellinit'sia*, "to become mad after listening to Bellini," by analogy with *vzbelenit'sia*, "to become enraged after ingesting henbane" (*belena*: the still common phrase "Did you have too much henbane?" is the Russian equivalent of "Have you taken leave of your senses?"); or *verdiatina*, which likens Verdi's music to some kind of edible animal flesh, on the pattern of *teliatina*, "veal," or *kuriatina*, "chicken meat."

As a close associate of every notable Russian composer of his time, Odoevsky was involved in the birth throes of Glinka's *A Life for the Tsar* and *Ruslan and Lyudmila*, Aleksandr Dargomyzhsky's *Rusalka* and Serov's *Judith*. After the premieres of these operas, Odoevsky published analytic essays on them, explaining to his sometimes incredulous compatriots their originality and importance. At the end of his life, Odoevsky met Chaikovsky and Rimsky-Korsakov and heard their early compositions. He died with the knowledge that the future of Russian music was in good hands.

Odoevsky also studied Russian folk music. He pointed out the inappropriateness of harmonizing Russian folk songs in the familiar Western major and minor modes and of reducing their rhythmic complexity to the usual three-four or four-four time of European music. Musorgsky's operas and, in the twentieth century, Stravinsky's *Les noces* bore out the justice of Odoevsky's objections and proposals in this area.

Odoevsky's versatility and the diversity of his interests have proved daunting to literary and cultural historians. The only book-length study of him in Russian is Pavel Sakulin's *From the History of Russian Idealism: Prince V. F. Odoevsky*, published in 1913.[4] A treasure trove of useful information on Odoevsky and his time, the book is only the first volume of an unrealized two-volume work. Its emphasis is on the intellectual trends of the period, with the result that the ostensible protagonist, Vladimir Odoevsky, keeps disappearing from the text for long stretches.

With the revival of interest in Odoevsky in the Soviet Union in post-Stalinist times, there has been a tendency to compartmentalize his writings. The musicologist Grigory Bernandt has edited an important volume of Odoevsky's essays on music[5] and published articles about his contacts with various composers. The pedagogical writings were taken over by Soviet specialists on theories of education. In the 1970s–1980s there appeared a small Soviet pleiad of dedicated Odoevsky literary scholars. Their essays and commentary for new editions of his fiction are usually well informed and perceptive, but these scholars are handicapped by the compulsory requirement to ignore Odoevsky the mystic, the admirer of the medieval alchemists, and the Romantic investigator of the human subconscious and to emphasize the nationalist and the satirist.

Neil Cornwell has been publishing articles on various aspects of Odoevsky since 1975, and has now produced what is surely the most comprehensive study of Odoevsky ever attempted. The book is, above all, a

---

4   P. N. Sakulin, *Iz istorii russkago idealizma: Kniaz' V. F. Odoevskii, myslitel', pisatel'* (Moscow: M. i S. Sabashnikovykh, 1913).
5   V. F. Odoevskii, *Muzykal'no-literaturnoe nasledie*, ed. and with an introductory essay and annotations by G. B. Bernandt (Moscow: Muzykal'noe izd-vo, 1956).

feat of synthesis. The "life, times and milieu" mentioned in the title do not begin to cover the range of information that the book encompasses. The biography of Odoevsky takes up only the first twenty-eight pages. His literary milieu is addressed in the last of the book's six chapters, where his encounters with and/or his influence on thirteen Russian writers, among them Pushkin, Gogol, Dostoevsky, and Lev Tolstoi, are examined.

Between the biography and the milieu we find detailed and well-documented chapters on Odoevsky's literary writings, his philosophy, his involvement in music (including a fascinating subchapter on his personal contacts with Franz Liszt, Hector Berlioz and Richard Wagner) and his role as an educator. In chapter 5, "Odoevsky and Tsarist Society," Cornwell undertakes voluntarily something that Soviet literary scholars are forced to do: deciding whether Prince Odoevsky, a direct descendant of Ryurik, the earliest known ruler of Russia, was "reactionary" or "progressive" within the framework of his society (incidentally, what other form of Russian society existed in the nineteenth century except the "tsarist" one?). At the turn of the twentieth century and during the first decade of Soviet rule, he was mostly seen as a reactionary mystic. His latter-day Soviet champions tailor his views to the requisite "progressive" dimensions—whatever that term may mean in the Soviet Union of the 1980s. Cornwell's unprejudiced examination of the issue convinces at least this reader that placing a figure as complex as Odoevsky on this particular Procrustean bed will add little to our understanding of the man or his writings. The book ends with an exhaustive bibliography of everything ever written by and about Odoevsky.

Sir Isaiah Berlin is undoubtedly right when he says in his foreword that Cornwell's book "is exceedingly well written." The few cavils I can make all stem from the fact that Cornwell has so thoroughly immersed himself in his Russian sources that he occasionally writes in Russian, though using English words. "The first description of tennis [in Russian literature]," says Nabokov's Pnin in the novel that bears his name, "occurs in *Anna Karenina*, Tolstoi's novel, and is related to year 1875." Poor Pnin does not realize that the Russian verb which can mean either "is related to" or "dates from" has no exact counterpart in English. Cornwell similarly cites entries from diaries of Odoevsky's contemporaries, of which he says "relating to the 1840s" and "relating to 1837." When an opponent of Odoevsky's is quoted as saying that "[in music] it is impossible to open anything new," only the reader who knows that the Russian *otkryt'* means both "to open" and "to discover" will understand the phrase.

Another minor barrier for readers who know no Russian is Cornwell's resolute maintenance of the Russian custom of identifying people by the initials of their given name and patronymic followed by the family name. But since English has no patronymic, the initials in A. S. Pushkin or F. M. Dostoevsky are not at all the same thing as the initials in W. H. Auden or E. E. Cummings. A friend of mine who knows no Russian, faced with a book bearing the title *V. F. Odoyevsky*, assumed that it must have been translated from the Russian. And indeed, isn't Aleksandr Pushkin more natural in English than A. S. Pushkin? The same fidelity in transcribing from the Russian led Cornwell to spell familiar German names, such as Wilhelm, Leopold and Elsa as Vil'gel'm, Leopol'd and El'sa. The music critic known to Western musicologists as Hermann Laroche appears in the book as G. A. Larosh.

But these minor objections are, as already stated, cavils: Neil Cornwell has produced a definitive, detailed, and beautifully organized book on Vladimir Odoevsky. There are not too many books in English on other, more famous, Russian nineteenth-century writers that can be compared to Cornwell's in scope and overall achievement. Scholars who have until now regarded Odoevsky as a minor or peripheral figure will have to think again and think hard.

Küchelbecker's Trilogy, *Izhorsky*, As an Example of the Romantic Revival of the Medieval Mystery Play[1]

The Russian émigré critic Georgy Adamovich once observed that the normal state of a flourishing literature is civil war. In periods when literary life is vigorously active, when various different factions are springing up and clashing with one another and a struggle is raging over the desired direction of literary development and over which stream literature will choose to follow—at such times conditions really are reminiscent of warfare. In the history of Russian literature the Romantic age was like that. In periods of decline or stagnation, when literature stops moving forward, literary battles that renew and invigorate verbal art are only the stuff of dreams. However, the impassioned aggressiveness that literary battles sometimes exhibit also has its destructive side: interesting literary phenomena fully worthy of attention are victimized. Writers of a defeated literary school are simply read out of the literature in question, and the history of literature is thus obscured and distorted. Subsequent generations of literary scholars and critics can manage only with difficulty (and sometimes not manage at all) to recapture a true perception of the historical process.

For example, as Sergei Aksakov and Yury Tynyanov pointed out, each in his own period, the victory of the Romantic movement in Russian literature led to the exclusion from the history of literature of the large and important school of neoclassic verse drama of the beginning of the nineteenth century, from which in subsequent decades only Aleksandr Griboedov's *Gore ot uma* (Woe from wit) remained on the surface, like the summit of an enormous iceberg (as Tynyanov put it). From works

---

[1] Translated by Hugh McLean. Originally published as "Trilogiia Kiukhel'bekera *Izhorskii* kak primer romanticheskogo vozrozhdeniia srednevekovoi misterii," in *American Contributions to the Seventh International Congress of Slavists, Warsaw, August 21–27, 1973*, vol. 2, ed. Victor Terras (The Hague: Mouton, 1973), 307–20.

by the same Tynyanov most literary scholars knew that Aleksandr Shakhovskoi's comedy *Lipetskie vody* (The Lipetsk spa) contains a lampoon of Vasily Zhukovsky, which aroused the anger of the "Karamzinians" or "innovators," who then tried to cause the play to flop. However, to this very day it has not been noticed that this comedy, produced in 1815, is written in the literary language of the Pushkin era, whereas Pushkin himself, in poems from 1815, was still writing in the language and style of the Karamzinian poets. Few have noticed the fact that in light and supposedly "content-free" comedies adapted from the French by Shakhovskoi's ally Nikolai Khmelnitsky in 1817, when Pushkin was only beginning *Ruslan and Lyudmila*, you already hear the verse and language of *Count Nulin* and *The Little House at Kolomna* (two comic poems by Pushkin written much later, in 1825 and 1830, respectively). It is seldom pointed out that it is in the writings of the comic dramatists of the second decade of the nineteenth century, and to a greater degree than in the fables of their literary associate Ivan Krylov or, as is usually stated, in the work of Pushkin's immediate predecessors, Zhukovsky and Batyushkov, that the literary language of the Pushkin era, which became the literary language of the whole nineteenth century, was developed. These facts cannot detract from Pushkin's standing as a linguistic innovator. They would be common knowledge if the neoclassical comic dramatists of Shakhovskoi's school had not been expelled from the history of literature by the victory of the Romantics. The superb editions of the authors of this school published in the series "Biblioteka poeta, bol'shaia seriia" (Poet's Library, large scale) in the 1960s[2] struck many literary scholars both in the West and, I am sure, in the Soviet Union, and made them take thought.

However, the victorious Romantics were themselves pushed aside a mere fifteen years later under the pressure of new currents then developing. Here too there again were victims: it is enough to mention Evgeny Baratynsky, who with great sensitivity was "resurrected" and reintroduced into literature by Sergei Andreevsky in the 1890s, or one of the most remarkable Romantic prose writers, Vladimir Odoevsky, who has

---

2   E.g., V. A. Ozerov, *Tragedii i stikhotvoreniia* (1960); A. A. Shakhovskoi, *Komedii; stikhotvoreniia* (1961); *Stikhotvornaia komediia kontsa XVIII–nachala XIX v.* (1964); P. A. Katenin, *Izbrannye proizvedeniia* (1965).

still not been given the recognition he deserves for his contributions to Russian literature, despite the numerous studies and new editions of his works published in the early twentieth century and in the Soviet period. One of the principal losses suffered by Russian literature as a result of the battles leading to the demise of Romanticism was and remains Wilhelm Karlovich Küchelbecker.

To speak of Küchelbecker as a forgotten or little-known writer a half century after the publication of Tynyanov's famous biographical novel would seem paradoxical. Beginning in 1925, the year *Kiukhlia* came out, thanks to the labors of Tynyanov and others, Küchelbecker's diaries were published (1929), as were collections of his lyric poetry, longer poems, and dramatic works, including the capacious two-volume "Biblioteka poeta" edition edited by Nina Korolyova in 1967. Soviet literary scholars and historians have carried out substantial, painstaking work in studying and documenting Küchelbecker's role in the Decembrist uprising. Of the poet's dramatic works, the luckiest in the critical literature has been the tragedy *Argiviane* (The Argives), an exceedingly interesting effort to produce a truly classical ancient Greek tragedy rather than a neoclassical tragedy with a Greek plot according to the French model, which had been followed in Russian literature since the middle of the eighteenth century. However, the authors of studies of *Argiviane* were usually interested exclusively in the political content of this tragedy, leaving aside its literary features—for example, the striking similarity of this work by Küchelbecker to analogous efforts to revive ancient Greek tragedy, complete with choruses and traditional ancient strophic forms, undertaken at the beginning of the twentieth century by the Symbolist poets Vyacheslav Ivanov and Innokenty Annensky.

All the same, despite the great, necessary work carried out during recent decades to bring to light and publish Küchelbecker's literary work and resurrect his human image, for most literary scholars he remains an interesting and attractive historical personality, a phenomenon of literary history, but not a living, beloved poet and dramatist.

For this there are valid reasons. Küchelbecker is not an easy poet. In comparison with the language of his great contemporaries, Pushkin, Baratynsky, and Lermontov, Küchelbecker's language, deliberately complex, frequently archaized, may seem tiresome and heavy. Moreover, he is an exceptionally uneven poet; not all his work is equally successful, and whereas in some of his works readers who make their way through the difficulties of style and syntax are rewarded with suddenly revealed deep thought and incomparable poetic mastery, in other works by the same Küchelbecker behind the poetic verbal thickets are hidden only well-worn commonplaces of Russian and Western European Romanticism and nothing more.

However, the basic reason for the lack of attention paid by the ordinary reader (and the ordinary literary scholar, too) to Küchelbecker as a poet lies in the fact that his talent was most fully and at the same time most vividly displayed in works in large, extended forms. It is hard to imagine what Pushkin's literary reputation would have been if, with regard to *Ruslan and Lyudmila*, *Boris Godunov*, and *Evgeny Onegin*, from the moment they were written there had been a conspiracy of silence on the part of the critics. Despite all Pushkin's genius, critical assessment and interpretations for the reader of these three, his biggest works, which began the moment they appeared and have continued to this very day, have undoubtedly played a tremendous role in making them popular. If you take the works that occupy a similar place in Küchelbecker's corpus, his two most successful narratives in verse, *Agasfer* (The wandering Jew) and *Sirota* (Orphan), and the three-part mystery play, *Izhorsky*, we must admit that neither the critics nor the literary scholars have done anything to bring these outstanding works to the ordinary reader or even to the world of literary scholars. The present article is an attempt to correct this situation at least with respect to *Izhorsky*.

Izhorsky is not only Küchelbecker's greatest achievement as a poet, but a work of exceptional interest with respect to genre, form, and the variety of literary currents and influences evoked in it, and also because of the extremely instructive story of the publication of its text.

In its genre markings *Izhorsky* is the only example in Russian literature of a Romantic mystery play, a genre that played a prominent role in the literatures of Western countries during the age of Romanticism. The Romantic poets were attracted by the mixture of genres and stylistic levels not permitted in the poetics of the preceding classicism. The conventions and artificial limitations of classicism had been observed in the dramatic genres with especial strictness, and therefore liberation from them in drama was an especially stormy process. The universal popularity of Shakespeare helped break down the rules of the stage, but the most decisive example was Goethe's *Faust*. Invoking in this work the medieval tradition of mystery and miracle plays, which permitted the combination on the stage of everyday life with the world of the mystical and supernatural, Goethe liberated the Romantic drama from any worries about what is acceptable or unacceptable for representation on the stage. The example of *Faust* made possible such fundamental achievements of Romantic drama as Byron's *Manfred, Cain,* and *Heaven and Earth,* Shelley's *Prometheus Unbound,* Mickiewicz's *Dziady* (Forefathers), and Zygmunt Krasiński's *Nie-boska komedia* (Undivine comedy). These revived the genre markings of the medieval mysteries and were not necessarily designed for stage production.

Alongside the imposing genre of mysteries, in *Izhorsky* Küchelbecker made use of the more intimate medieval genre of the miracle play, as Goethe had in *Faust*. In miracle plays the plot usually consisted of a struggle between good and bad supernatural forces for the soul of a sinner, which of course ended with the victory of the good ones. This species of miracle play had survived in various literatures after the Middle Ages—for example, in the *Fastnachsspielen* of Hans Sachs and the religious dramas of Calderón, mentioned by Küchelbecker in the preface to the first edition of *Izhorsky* as models he had used for his mystery play. In Russian literature, superb examples of miracle plays of this kind had existed at the turn of the seventeenth to the eighteenth century in the school dramas *O pokaianii greshnogo cheloveka* (About the repentance of a sinner) and *Uspenskaia drama* (The drama of the Assumption) by St. Dmitry of Rostov, a writer who had aroused Küchelbecker's interest. Küchelbecker transposed (into modern Russian) St. Dmitry's spiritual fables and devoted to him one of the last poems he wrote before his death.

Although in its genre and structure *Izhorsky* is a Romantic variant of a mystery or miracle play, the central figure in this imposing literary structure is a character from a Romantic poet's own time. Lev Petrovich Izhorsky should not be regarded as a Russian variant of Faust.[3] Even less valid would it be to regard him as the "one thousand and first parody of Childe Harold," as Vissarion Belinsky did. Both Goethe's *Faust* and Byron's *Manfred* are basically tragedies of *knowledge,* or more accurately,

---

[3] Cf. *Dnevnik V. K. Kiukhel'bekera* (Leningrad, 1929), 198, n. 1, and *Literaturnoe nasledstvo,* vol. 59, 431, n. 8.

tragedies illustrating the inadequacy of a purely Romantic approach to the problems of life. The chief source of the dissatisfaction and rebellion of the Byronic hero, both in *Childe Harold's Pilgrimage* and in *Manfred*, lies in the incestuous love of the hero for his sister, forbidden by society. This same plot forms the basis of Karamzin's "Ostrov Borngol'm" (Bornholm Island) and of Chateaubriand's *René*, which played, as is widely acknowledged, an enormous role in the development of Romanticism. This whole plot theme is entirely lacking in *Izhorsky*. The hero of *Izhorsky* suffers neither from Onegin's spleen nor Pechorin's jaundice. If one insists on indicating literary precedents, Küchelbecker's protagonist is closest of all to the disillusioned, emotionally paralyzed heroes of the prose writers of early French Romanticism, Étienne Sénancour's Obermann and Benjamin Constant's Adolphe.[4] Pushkin's phrase "rano chuvstva v nem ostyli" (feelings in him turned cold early) could apply to Izhorsky as it does to Adolphe, but where in Pushkin Onegin is bored and melancholy, Izhorsky is troubled by the lack of emotional warmth which could facilitate the communion he longs for with other people. The conflict in Izhorsky's soul between his incapacity to feel and his need for normal human relations delivers him into the power of the demons who, without his knowing it, he encounters in the very first scene of the mystery play.

In this crucial first scene of the play (quite impossible to produce with the stage facilities of that time, but quite feasible to film with the aid of helicopters), the action unfolds simultaneously in a troika galloping along the road to Tsarskoe Selo and in the air above that troika. In Küchelbecker's conception this stratification should correspond to the simultaneous representation of heaven, earth, and hell in the art of the Middle Ages. The three chief demons who appear in this scene and into whose power the poet delivers his hero during the first two parts of the trilogy constitute a most interesting and original discovery on Küchel-

---

[4] Which played, as Anna Akhmatova showed, a significant role in the conception of Pushkin's Onegin (Anna Akhmatova, "'Adol'f' Benzhamena Konstana v tvorchestve Pushkina," in *Pushkin: Vremennik Pushkinskoi komissii* [Moscow and Leningrad: Izd-vo Akademii nauk SSSR, 1936]: 91–114). Küchelbecker met Constant in Paris in 1820 and at his invitation gave lectures on the Russian language and Russian literature in the club Athénée, which Constant headed. See also Iurii Tynianov, "Frantsuzskie otnosheniia V. K. Kiukhel'bekera," in *Literaturnoe nasledstvo*, vols. 33/34, 331–78.

becker's part. Up to that time Russian writers had accepted literary adaptations of images taken from Old Slavic mythology or from Russian folk fairy tales. Küchelbecker boldly introduces into his mystery play beings from the everyday peasant folklore of his own time. The chief demons in *Izhorsky* are Kikimora, Shishimora,[5] and a being with which nurses and mamas had long frightened little children, Buka. Deriving these images from the sphere of everyday peasant folklore anticipated, like much in *Izhorsky*, developments in Russian literature of the twentieth century, in particular the use of similar material in the 1907 volume *Posolon'* (Follow the sun) by Aleksei Remizov, a great connoisseur of Russian folklore, or Velimir Khlebnikov's drama *Snezhimochka*, where friendly coexistence is depicted between simple peasants, elemental spirits, goblins, and speaking animals, as in the historical scenes of *Izhorsky*.

Izhorsky's three chief demons are three different hypostases of cosmic evil (which again has parallels in the twentieth century, reminding us of the three-headed dragon, represented by three different actors, in the play *Drakon* [The dragon] by Evgeny Shvarts). The youngest demon, the jolly jokester Kikimora, represents Romantic freedom bordering on playful amorality; he is like a Dostoevskian devil equipped with the slogan "all is permitted." Kikimora's opponent, the more dignified Shishimora, personifies evil in its more traditional aspect. Under his influence in the second part of the trilogy Lev Izhorsky engages in an inhuman and cruel game with the fates of other people, the murder of his only sincere friend, and the betrayal of a woman who loves him. Finally Buka, Kikimora and Shishimora's boss, represents cold, calculating evil, subject to logic, legality, and discipline. Externally the opposite of Kikimora, he is actually his reverse side, and the two of them together lead the hero to ruin. Besides their ethical and metaphysical role in the mystery play, Kikimora and Buka also bear a literary-critical burden. Buka, shown in the form of a huge ape in the costume and wig of the age of Louis XIV, personifies the rigid and inexorable laws in the poetics of neoclassicism which Küchelbecker, formerly an archaist and classicist, now rejects. But equally unacceptable to him is the literary attitude of the extreme Ro-

---

[5] In the twentieth century Kikimora and Shishimora were regarded as beings of the female sex (for example, in the program of Anatoly Lyadov's symphonic poem *Kikimora*), but in Küchelbecker's time they were male, as is also clear in Vladimir Dal's dictionary.

mantics who deny and reject the literary forms represented by Kikimora. This is shown with especial clarity in the second scene of the second act of the third part, where Küchelbecker puts himself on the stage ("the study of a very poorly endowed poet," where *nedostatochnyi* may be understood both in the sense of the poverty of the exiled poet and the modesty of his literary talent). Kikimora offers the author of *Izhorsky* guaranteed success if he will imitate the formulas of the ultra-Romantic school (this scene contains an unambiguous attack on Lermontov's *Hero of Our Time*):

> Diary chefs d'oeuvre: like a skillful anatomist,
> Our phrase-monger lays out his cadaver—
> And cooks from it a black, Spartan soup,
> A nasty soup perhaps, but devilishly tasty.

However, the exiled poet rejects this offer and prefers to go his own way in the hope that posterity will judge him as he deserves.

Both the fantastic and the everyday scenes in *Izhorsky* are strikingly varied and many-layered. In addition to the Russian peasant folklore (which includes river nymphs [*rusalki*], a werewolf, and the peasant magician Vavila, from the last act of the first part), the play contains elemental spirits which go back to the tradition of Western European alchemists (the fire demon, Salamander), and, following the example of the second part of *Faust*, characters from Shakespeare's fantasy comedies, Titania and Ariel. In *Izhorsky*'s realistic scenes we see representatives of Petersburg high society, of provincial landowners (Izhorsky's neighbors, somewhat reminiscent of Evgeny Onegin's neighbors and certain characters from *Dubrovsky*), and also of the lower strata of the Russian population of that time: Izhorsky's peasant serfs, the family of a Black Sea fisherman (Izhorsky's conversation with the old fisherman at the beginning of the third part is possibly inspired by a similar conversation in Byron's *Manfred* between the hero and an Alpine hunter who has rescued him), a stationmaster full of his own dignity, and in the third part Greek rebels and their Turkish oppressors. Among the characters of *Izhorsky* space was found for an extended characterization of Princess Lidiya, the heroine of the first two parts of the mystery play, who in the course of the action is transformed, under the influence of her humiliations and suffering, from a flighty society belle into a self-sacrificing, deeply feeling woman (in this she unexpectedly reminds us of another Lidiya, the heroine of the first two parts of the three-part drama by Sukhovo-Kobylin, in whom just such a metamorphosis takes place[6]). Another added character is the peasant girl Marfutka, who appears only for an instant, concerned with the feeding of her calves. The range of the enormous number of episodic characters extends from real historical figures such as the well-known Greek statesman Count Johannes Kapodistrias and the English writer Edward John Trelawny, a friend of Shelley and Byron, to a demonic owl and a talking hare, which the demon Shishimora compels to commit an act contrary to its leporine nature and which, before submitting, makes a desperate protest.

It is interesting to compare the third part of *Izhorsky* with the famous finale of the second part of Goethe's *Faust*. In Goethe the redemption of Faust takes place entirely on the mystical plane, attained by the appeal of the contrite Gretchen to the Virgin. Izhorsky, saved from the demons by the Good Spirit at the end of the second part, earns forgiveness and redemption with his participation in the liberating struggle for the independence of Greece (here there is an allusion to the death of Byron and the episode with Euphorion in the second part of *Faust*). In accordance with Küchelbecker's freedom-loving ideology, his hero can earn forgiveness for his sins at the price of fighting for the liberation of mankind from oppression and tyranny. However, in the larger scheme of the mystery play political struggle is only the first step toward the salvation of the soul, as Izhorsky explains in his conversation with Kapodistrias. In Goethe's finale the forces of good are represented by an enormous number of characters; in Küchelbecker final redemption is obtained by earthbound, human means. The Good Spirit at the end of the second part is rather the traditional deus ex machina of the neoclassical drama. The promise of the possibility of redemption for the hero of

---

[6] A reference to A. V. Sukhovo-Kobylin's trilogy (*The Wedding of Krechinsky, The Affair, The Death of Tarelkin*), which dates from the 1850s. For more, see Simon Karlinsky, "The Alogical and Absurdist Aspects of Russian Realist Drama (Gogol, Pisemsky, Sukhovo-Kobylin, Kozma Prutkov)," *Comparative Drama* 3 (Fall 1969): 147–55. This essay is yet another example of SK's interest in the history of the Russian theater and of his exploration of unexpected "aspects" of mid-nineteenth-century drama.—Ed.

the mystery play is conveyed in two songs that he hears at the beginning and middle of the third part. Embedded here are two widely known tales of redemption: the biblical parable of the prodigal son, which is sung in the marketplace by blind guitarists; and a song Küchelbecker must have heard in Greece, a modern Greek variant of the story of King Oedipus (which must go back to the version in the *Speculum Magnum*, which is the basis of Thomas Mann's novel *Der Erwählte* [known in English as *The Holy Sinner*]). The decisive factor in Izhorsky's redemption is also not brought about by angels, but by the shades of Vesnin, the friend he murdered, and Lidiya, whom he abandoned. By these means Küchelbecker moves the redemption theme from the abstract, mystical plane to a down-to-earth, vital one.

A factor that sets *Izhorsky* apart from such Western examples of the Romantic mystery play as *Manfred* or *The Undivine Comedy* is the constant presence of humor and Romantic irony. As a contemporary of ours said on a somewhat different occasion, Küchelbecker in this work "makes his way along the crest lying between truth and a caricature of truth."[7] Küchelbecker himself noted in his diary at the time he was working on the third part of the mystery play that

> humor may appear in all kinds of poetry. Tragedy itself does not exclude it; it may even serve as its basis, the element of the tragic fable. In proof I cite Goethe's *Faust* and my *Izhorsky*, which was so poorly understood by our critics. *Izhorsky* is entirely based on humor.[8]

Indeed, although about *Izhorsky* one can speak more or less accurately of the influence of Shakespeare, Goethe, and Byron on this or that particular scene, the fundamental influence that pervades all three parts of this work is the influence of the refined dramatic works of Ludwig Tieck, which are full of humor and irony, especially *Der gestiefelte Kater* (Puss in Boots, 1798) and *Die verkehrte Welt* (The land of upside down, 1799).[9] The influ-

---

[7] Vladimir Nabokov, *Dar* (New York: Izd-vo im. Chekhova, 1952), 225.
[8] V. K. Kiukhel'beker, *Izbrannye proizvedeniia v dvukh tomakh* (Moscow and Leningrad, 1967), 2:751.
[9] Küchelbecker met Tieck in person during his trip abroad in 1820. Tieck's name is mentioned several times in Küchelbecker's letters to his relatives from solitary confinement, which confirm his close knowledge of Tieck's works.

ence of Tieck was discerningly noted by the first reviewer to write about *Izhorsky*, Ivan Kireevsky.[10] It was precisely Romantic irony in Tieck's style that made it possible for Küchelbecker to include in a serious work with deep spiritual content a series of literary parodies and self-parodies, to put himself and his literary opponents on the stage, and to have his heroine, Princess Lidiya, parody the cross-dressing scene from Shakespeare's comedy *Two Gentlemen of Verona* right after the climactic, intensely dramatic scene with Izhorsky, and do all this without falling into stylistic cacophony. It is the presence of humor and irony that gives the whole mystery play peculiar charm and freshness and raises it above the level of several other works of the same genre and time.

Izhorsky was written while Küchelbecker was in solitary confinement, which he served in various fortresses for his participation in the Decembrist uprising and his attempt to shoot Grand Duke Mikhail Pavlovich (the tsar's brother). The work was apparently begun in 1826. In 1827 and 1829 isolated scenes from the first part of the mystery play were published without the author's name in various almanacs and evoked the sympathetic response from Ivan Kireevsky mentioned above. The first part was finished in 1830, when the poet's younger sister, Yuliya Karlovna, began her long efforts, lasting five years, to get permission to publish *Izhorsky* as a separate book, with the help of Aleksandr Pushkin. In 1835 Yuliya Karlovna's efforts were at last successful, and the first two parts of the mystery play were allowed to be published as a book, printed—a curious twist—by the printers of the Third Section of His Imperial Majesty's Own Secretariat (i.e., the secret police). Often prejudiced and unjust in his judgments, Osip Senkovsky took exception to some archaisms in Küchelbecker's vocabulary, but nevertheless acknowledged that *Izhorsky* was a powerful and original work and allowed the possibility that after the appearance of the missing third part it might win a reputation among

---

[10] "Certain scenes from this dramatic fantasy were published last year in *Severnye tsvety* [Northern flowers]. They are remarkable for the combination, rare with us, of depth of feeling with playfulness of imagination. We assign this work to the German school, despite some imitation of Shakespeare, because the Shakespeare here is more the Shakespeare of Tieck, Germanified, than the real Shakespeare ..." I. V. Kireevskii, *Polnoe sobranie sochinenii v dvukh tomakh* (Moscow: Tip. Imp. Moskovskago universiteta, 1911), 2:26 (first published in the almanac *Dennitsa* [Morning star] for the year 1830).

readers equal to that of *Manfred*.[11] Senkovsky's prediction might have been realized if soon after the appearance of his review a completely devastating misfortune had not happened to *Izhorsky*, one that for an entire century determined the fate of this work and of Küchelbecker himself. At the end of 1835, in *Molva*, a supplement to the journal *Teleskop*, there appeared an annihilating review by Belinsky, full of sarcasm and contempt. Belinsky called *Izhorsky* a pathetic attempt at an imitation of Byron and its author a man utterly devoid of any literary or poetic talent.[12]

If you glance through other articles and notes by Belinsky for the year of 1835, it becomes clear that his attitude toward *Izhorsky* could not have been otherwise. Though he had a favorable view of folk poetry, Belinsky was very hostile to any effort to adapt it to artistic literature, as he showed by his contemptuous response to Pyotr Ershov's *Konek-Gorbunok* (The humpback horse, 1834), a fairy tale that has become a classic, and to Pushkin's fairy tales. By that time Belinsky could not abide the fantastic or mystical in any form whatever, which caused him to see in "The Queen of Spades" by the Pushkin he adored a "decline in talent" and to single out among the works of Gogol, with whom he was enraptured, "The Portrait" and "Vii" as works that were in many respects failures. Belinsky could not help being reminded by the high society scenes in the first part of *Izhorsky* of similar scenes in the society tales of Aleksandr Bestuzhev-Marlinsky.[13] Belinsky likewise was inevitably shocked by the following ostentatiously antirational soliloquy by Izhorsky, which sounds up-to-date in our time:

> But the world has changed: day after day.
> Resurrected ancient traditions
> Gain more and more power over us;
> O people, people! Strange creatures you are!
> A passion for the miraculous has arisen on all sides.
> Was it long ago that people cried: "Hell and heaven are nonsense!"?

---

11 Cited from *Dnevnik V. K. Kiukhel'bekera*, 350–51.
12 V. G. Belinskii, *Polnoe sobranie sochinenii* (Moscow, 1953), 1:228–33.
13 For SK's detailed analysis of a travelogue in verse and prose by this contemporary of Pushkin's and Decembrist compatriot of Küchelbecker's, see Simon Karlinsky, "Bestužev-Marlinskij's *Journey to Revel'* and Puškin," in *Puškin Today*, ed. David M. Bethea (Bloomington: Indiana University Press, 1993): 59–72.—Ed.

> They believed neither in God nor in devils.
> Everything was enlightened, even [servants in] the entry hall.
> But now, look at your children,
> You pupils and admirers of Voltaire!
> Of course, superstition is not faith:
> But where, O where is your much-praised success?
> Where is your wisdom? Even to think about it is a joke!

The very genre of mystery play and its whole poetic structure inevitably disgusted the "furious Vissarion," who in that same year, 1835, had read out of Russian poetry not only Vladimir Benediktov, but also Evgeny Baratynsky. If you wanted to, you could find weak places in the poetry of *Izhorsky*; however, Belinsky's review quoted long excerpts from the very best poetic flights Küchelbecker ever achieved—Lidiya's dramatic confrontation with Izhorsky from the second part and Shishimora's striking curse, with its hypnotic refrain, "Tear yourself asunder, rend yourself apart, and hearken!" One concludes that the case here was not a lack of poetic sensitivity, but the critic's organic disgust at the whole poetic system of *Izhorsky*.

Historically speaking, it is possible that Belinsky was right in his way, since he sought to clear the way for *Dead Souls*, *A Hunter's Notes*, and *Poor Folk*. All the same, one cannot help but be struck by the inhuman cruelty shown by this enemy of tsarist oppression and arbitrary power, since he knew who the author of the work he was reviewing was. Nevertheless, in his polemical ardor he nailed down the lid over the head of this particular victim of that oppression and arbitrary power and condemned to literary death a poet who had made his way to the reader at the price of unbelievable effort and suffering. In subsequent decades, as we know, there was no appeal against Belinsky's sentence. Belinsky's article on *Izhorsky* convinced Russian critics for an entire century that its author was a hack without poetic talent. They remembered Pushkin's phrase "both Küchelbeckerish and tiresome," but they stubbornly refused to recall the stanzas Pushkin addressed in "Nineteenth of October" (1825) to his "beloved brother in fate and in service to the muse," where Küchelbecker is proclaimed a poet the equal of Pushkin himself. Literary scholars of the nineteenth century were so thoroughly convinced that Küchelbecker was a literary nonentity that it never entered their minds to pay attention to the strong influence of *Izhorsky* on the poetry of Lermontov.[14]

Despite the rehabilitation of Küchelbecker as an individual in Soviet times and despite the superb (but far from complete) editions of his works, his works still are being studied mainly by historians. In the last decade two major contemporary Russian artists have turned their attention to Küchelbecker's works. Dmitry Shostakovich used several stanzas

---

[14] It is found not only in the high society scenes of Lermontov's *Maskarad* (the corresponding scenes in *Izhorsky* form an intermediary link between *Gore ot uma* and *Maskarad*), but in direct textual echoes. Cf.

> S glazami, polnymi lazurnogo ognia
> [With eyes full of azure fire]
> (Lermontov, p. 467)

(This line is cited in Vladimir Solovyov's *Tri vstrechi* [Three meetings] as a quotation from Lermontov.)

and

> S glazami, polnymi ognia i chuvstva
> [With eyes full of fire and feeling]
> (*Izhorsky*, p. 300)

and also

> A vy, *nadmennye potomki*
> Izvestnoi podlost'iu proslavlennykh ottsov
> Piatoiu rabskoiu popravshie *oblomki*
> Igroiu schastiia obizhennykh *rodov*!
> [And you, proud descendants
> Of fathers famed for their well-known vileness
> Who with slavish heel trampled the remnants
> Of clans injured by the play of fate!]
> (Lermontov, "Smert' poeta"
> [The death of the poet], p. 412)

and

> ... Neuzhel' ne znaiu vas,
> Smeshnye, *gordye* Adamovy *potomki*
> Vas, rod zanoschivyi, kak vechnyi kedr *i lomkii*
> Kak trost' sukhaia, kak zerna lishennyi klas?
> [Can it be that I do not know you
> You ridiculous, proud descendants of Adam
> You, clan haughty as the eternal cedar and brittle
> As a dry twig or empty ear of grain?].
> (*Izhorsky*, p. 307)

All italics are mine. The quotations from Lermontov are from *Sobranie sochinenii v chetyrekh tomakh* (Moscow and Leningrad, 1961, vol. 1; from Kiukhel'beker, from the edition *Izbrannye proizvedeniia v dvukh tomakh* (Moscow and Leningrad, 1967), vol. 2.

from Küchelbecker's poem "Poety" (Poets) in his remarkable Fourteenth Symphony. Vladimir Nabokov, in his extensive commentaries to his translation into English of *Evgeny Onegin*, especially singles out Küchelbecker from among poets contemporary with Pushkin (toward whom, incidentally, Nabokov is too severe), and even ranks him above Baratynsky. In particular, Nabokov considers Küchelbecker's poem "Uchast' russkikh voinov" (The fate of Russian warriors) "a dazzling chef d'oeuvre, the creation of a first-class genius," and about the long poem *Agasfer* he writes: "Despite the strange archaisms, awkward expressions, eccentric ideas, and a series of structural faults, this poem is a major work, which with its harsh tonalities and clumsy originality deserves a special study."[15]

As great artists, Shostakovich and Nabokov sensed the originality and distinction of Küchelbecker's work and called attention to it. It is now the turn of literary scholars and critics.

* * *

Rather than transliterating from the Russian the writer's name (Vil'gel'm Karlovich Kiukhel'beker, 1797–1846), as consistency would demand, we have chosen to call him Wilhelm Küchelbecker. This spelling retains the original German spelling of the name of Pushkin's fellow *lycéen*, the Decembrist revolutionary who was condemned to death and eventually exiled, a thoroughly Russian poet, critic and dramatist. The trilogy *Izhorsky* is treated briefly in SK's important book on the origins of the Russian theater, Simon Karlinsky, *Russian Drama from Its Beginnings to the Age of Pushkin* (Berkeley: University of California Press, 1985); see especially pp. 221–25. The present essay analyzes in greater detail the idiosyncratic style and structure of Küchelbecker's dramatic trilogy, and develops more fully its fascinating lineage and the literary and cultural context of its composition.

---

[15] *Eugene Onegin: A Novel in Verse*, by Aleksandr Pushkin, translated from the Russian, with a commentary, by Vladimir Nabokov (New York, 1964), 2:446 and 3:505.

Misanthropy and Sadism in Lermontov's Plays[1]

Mikhail Lermontov's literary output can be broken down into three periods: the immature, prior to 1834; the transitional, 1834–36; and the period of artistic maturity after 1837. He began writing at the age of fourteen. For the next six years he wrote numerous lyrics, several narrative poems, and three plays. No one would have ever heard of any of these writings were they not by the young Lermontov. They are the work of a juvenile graphomaniac who does not know where imitation stops and plagiarism begins, and who interlards his writings with unaltered or slightly altered passages, mostly from Pushkin, but also from Aleksandr Bestuzhev-Marlinsky, Byron and other poets of the Romantic period. Where the young Pushkin could absorb any number of eighteenth- or nineteenth-century literary influences and then incorporate them into works that were unmistakably his own, the young Lermontov kept producing inferior versions of what Pushkin or Byron or Bestuzhev-Marlinsky had already written and written better.

This derivative method can be illustrated by the first of his melodramas, *Ispantsy* (The Spaniards), written when he was sixteen. It combines elements from Schiller's *Don Carlos*, from Kotzebue and Victor Hugo. The atmosphere is reminiscent of the most obvious French melodrama of horror, descended from Guilbert de Pixérécourt (whose plays had been popular in Russia since the early nineteenth century). *The Spaniards* features a diabolical Jesuit villain, who tortures the naive heroine, and a ranting hero, who stabs the woman he loves rather than let another man possess her. Sponge-like, the play soaks up ingredients from an incongruous array of other literary works. The persecuted old Jew and his beautiful daughter Noemi are Isaac and Rebecca from Scott's *Ivanhoe*; Noemi's bedtime colloquy with her old nurse is simply lifted from Tatyana's conversation with

---

[1] Originally published in *Studies in Russian Literature in Honor of Vsevolod Setchkarev*, ed. Julian W. Connolly and Sonia I. Ketchian (Columbus, IN: Slavica, 1986), 166–74.

her nurse in *Evgeny Onegin*; and the gravediggers are transferred bodily from *Hamlet*. Apart from sympathy for the persecuted Jewish characters, something that was extremely rare in Russian nineteenth-century literature (Lermontov must have taken this attitude from Scott), there is nothing to recommend *The Spaniards* on any literary or dramatic level.

Equally obvious and melodramatic but far more personal are Lermontov's next two plays. The first, written in 1830, bears a German title, *Menschen und Leidenschaften: Ein Trauerspiel* (People and passion: A tragedy) in homage to *Menschenhass und Reue* (Misanthropy and repentance) by Kotzebue and possibly also to *Kabale und Liebe* (Intrigue and love) by Schiller. The play is sixteen-year-old Lermontov's exorcism of the domestic situation which scarred him emotionally throughout his childhood and adolescence: the ugly fight for his custody between his father and his wealthy maternal grandmother. *Menschen und Leidenschaften* is obviously autobiographical, portraying the poet's grandmother, peasant nurse, father, and paternal uncle (of all of whom he was ostensibly fond) as a nest of hypocritical vipers who torment the idealistic young hero—Lermontov's self-portrait—and drive him to suicide. "I am surrounded by such base creatures and everything is done to spite me," the protagonist confides to his best friend, pretty much summing up Lermontov's attitude to his family and to humanity in general. In the 1831 *Strannyi chelovek* (An odd man), a similar plot about a young idealist driven to suicide is replayed. But this time Lermontov's relatives do not appear; the hero is persecuted by the high society in which he moves, and there is a subplot taken from Kotzebue's *Misanthropy and Repentance* about the once faithless, now repentant wife and mother. The suicide of the young male protagonist who is starved for affection and understanding, with which both *Menschen und Leidenschaften* and *An Odd Man* end, must have been the young Lermontov's way of signaling his misery and resentment to the unresponsive world.

It is a somewhat different Lermontov that we meet in the transitional period of 1834–36. His attitudes and ideas did not change during those years (they never did), but he acquired the verbal facility and melodious expressivity which were to give him his high position in the Russian literary pantheon. Important for this evolution were the erotic or pornographic (depending on the commentator's viewpoint) poems he wrote at the age of twenty. Unlike his juvenilia, these stylistically more mature productions do not appear in the academic editions of his writings because of their explicit eroticism. Five of them were, however, published in the West.² Far from being mere literary curiosities, they are an important key to Lermontov's outlook and poetics.

Written while the poet was a cadet at a military academy, these poems are usually called his "Cadet Poems." Russian commentators who do mention them are wont to bracket them together with Pushkin's erotica, both sets of poems supposedly representing the two poets' youthful high-spirited pranks. Actually, their respective notions of what constitutes the erotic could not be more different. Pushkin's erotica are humorous, joyous, and life-affirming.³ Lermontov's are grim, sadistic and censorious. Three of the five "Cadet Poems" deal with rape (gang rape of a peasant girl by a group of cadets, rape of a blind old woman by a drunken young lout, and the rape and beating of a prostitute by a customer who refuses to pay her), narrated with approval for the rapists and contempt for their victims. Two other "Cadet Poems" are about homosexual encounters at the military academy, described in a manner that combines prurience, moralizing censure, and, again, contempt for the participants. These poems exemplify the growth of Lermontov's verbal elegance and lyrical power, qualities that will again and again cause his readers to overlook or accept ideas and subjects that might otherwise have repelled them.⁴

Lermontov's two remaining plays date from the same transitional period as the "Cadet Poems." *Maskarad* (Masquerade), published in 1835, is his best-known play and the only one occasionally performed on the stage. *Dva brata* (The two brothers), which he wrote one year later, is known only to Lermontov scholars. Both are lurid melodramas with strong sadistic overtones. The reason for the popularity of *Masquerade* and the obscurity of *The Two Brothers* is that the former is in verse—Lermontov's verse— and the latter is in prose. Lermontov did not yet know how to write good

---

2   M. Yu. Lermontov, "Piat' eroticheskikh stikhotvorenii," *Russian Literature TriQuarterly*, no. 14 (Winter 1976): 416–29.
3   See Anthony Cross, "Pushkin's Bawdy; or, Notes from the Literary Underground," *Russian Literature TriQuarterly*, no. 10 (Fall 1974): 203–36.
4   William H. Hopkins, "Lermontov's Hussar Poems," *Russian Literature TriQuarterly*, no. 14 (Winter 1976): 36–47, is a good scholarly examination of Lermontov's "Cadet Poems," containing a valuable tabulation of the references to them in Russian criticism. But the author fails to notice the sadistic tone of these poems and the glorification of violence and rape that is central to three of them.

verse at the time of *The Spaniards* (*Menschen und Leidenschaften* and *An Odd Man* were in prose). The emergence of his own poetic voice is evident in a few of his earlier lyrics, such as "The Angel" (1831) and "The Sail" (1832), the famous first line of the latter being actually a quotation from Bestuzhev-Marlinsky. Lermontov's literary craft was further perfected in the "Cadet Poems." Yet when he came to write *Masquerade* he was still insecure enough to borrow the voices of two other poet-playwrights.

More seductively melodious than any other work for the stage by Lermontov, *Masquerade* is even more derivative than his juvenile melodramas. The plot is a Romantic variation on Shakespeare's *Othello*. The protagonist is a demonic ex-gambler named Arbenin, patterned in part on the semicriminal gambler-hero of *Trente ans; ou, La vie d'un joueur* by Victor Ducange, which was premiered in Russia in 1828. It kept playing in the capitals for the next two decades in two competing translations, one by Fyodor Kokoshkin and the other by Rafail Zotov. Part melodramatic gambler and part disillusioned Byronic hero, Arbenin has found peace and fulfillment in his marriage to Nina, an aristocratic young woman much younger than himself.

Their happiness is wrecked by two unrelated plot stratagems. One is the clandestine affair between Nina's friend Baroness Shtral and a young nobleman, which take place at a public masquerade and which Arbenin mistakenly assumes to have involved Nina rather than the baroness. The other concerns a mysterious avenger, who corresponds to Shakespeare's Iago and is determined to bring about Arbenin's downfall. These two plot lines are poorly meshed together. The imbroglio between the baroness, her lover, and Nina is shown as a random chain of accidental circumstances. For the avenger to have caused all these events, as is implied at the end of the play, he would have needed to read the thoughts and predict the actions of Arbenin and of the three other principal characters. Yet he is not depicted as a supernatural being but as an ordinary victim of Arbenin's earlier gambling operations. Like his prototype in *Othello*, Arbenin is manipulated into believing that his wife was unfaithful, murders her (by serving her poisoned ice cream), watches her die in horrible torment, and is then informed that she was innocent.

The language of *Masquerade* was modeled by Lermontov on two works of Russian dramatic literature that appeared in print in the five-year period that preceded the writing of this play. They are the two first parts of

Küchelbecker's *Izhorsky* trilogy, which Lermontov had studied with great attention when they were published in 1830;[5] and Griboedov's *Gore ot uma* (Woe from wit), a censored version of which came out for the first time in 1833. No textual study of the dependence of *Masquerade* on these two works has yet been done, but even a cursory reading reveals constant phraseological borrowings, which Lermontov utilized with a great deal of ingenuity for his own melodramatic purposes.

Lermontov considered *Masquerade* his best play and made determined efforts to secure its production on the stage. But the objections of the censors proved insurmountable. As the history of censorship in Russia and elsewhere has shown again and again, repressive political control invariably brings about the control of the moral content of literary works. The censors of Nicholas I were shocked by the sexual fling of the baroness at a public masquerade, by the cruelty of Arbenin's taunting of his wife as she slowly dies of poison, and by the general idea of a husband murdering his wife out of jealousy. They required that Lermontov provide his play with a happy ending in which the spouses are reconciled, a recommendation almost as asinine as the advice of Nicholas I that Pushkin convert his *Boris Godunov* into a novel in the manner of Sir Walter Scott. In his anxiety to get the play staged, Lermontov prepared two alternate versions, but the censors remained adamant. *Masquerade* was eventually freed from censorship restrictions after the reforms of the 1860s and had a few stage productions in prerevolutionary times.

The single most famous staging of *Masquerade* was the one Vsevolod Meyerhold began preparing in 1911 at the Empress Alexandra Theater in St. Petersburg. Scheduled to open in 1914 so as to commemorate the centenary of Lermontov's birth, the production actually required almost six years of rehearsals and planning. With lavish, elaborate sets and costumes designed by Aleksandr Golovin (known in the West for his contributions to Diaghilev's ballet productions) and music especially composed by Aleksandr Glazunov, this was Meyerhold's most ambitious project prior to his ultra-Modernist postrevolutionary phase. It finally opened on the

---

[5] For some of Lermontov's borrowings from Küchelbecker, see my essay [included in the present collection] "Trilogiia Kiukhel'bekera *Izhorskii* kak primer romanticheskogo vozrozhdeniia srednevekovoi misterii," in *American Contributions to the Seventh International Congress of Slavists, Warsaw, August 21–27, 1973*, vol. 2, ed. Victor Terras (The Hague: Mouton, 1973), 307–20.

eve of the liberal-democratic Revolution of February 1917, and it played for many years after the October Revolution, when it came to be interpreted as an opulent relic of the decay and corruption of prerevolutionary Russia. As was often the case with Meyerhold, his conception of the play departed radically from Lermontov's text, with Arbenin represented as a poet victimized by an uncomprehending society and the anonymous avenger seen as a hired assassin,[6] none of which is even hinted at in the original play.

Masquerade is not the greatest Russian Romantic drama, as Russian commentators sometimes claim it to be, but it may well be one of the better Russian Romantic melodramas, superior to the specimens of that genre that were offered at the time by the temporarily successful Nestor Kukolnik. The suspense and the contrived *coups de théâtre* testify to a certain flair. Above all, the verse texture has the benefit of stylistic borrowings from Griboedov and Küchelbecker, which are combined with the contributions of Lermontov, the Lermontov who was on the verge of becoming a genuinely major poet. He had not quite made that breakthrough when he was writing *Masquerade*, but he was close. A good insight into the importance of this play's verse texture for its enduring high reputation can be gained from juxtaposing it with its companion in prose written one year later, Lermontov's last work in dramatic form, *The Two Brothers*.

A melodrama like everything Lermontov wrote for the stage, *The Two Brothers* tells of the victimization of a woman by the three men in her life. They are the idealistic Yury, whom she once loved, Yury's cynical and sadistic brother Aleksandr, who debauched her, and the dim-witted prince whom Aleksandr had forced her to marry. The heroine is Vera Ligovskaya, who was later to appear in somewhat altered form in Lermontov's unfinished novel *Princess Ligovskaya*. She also appears as Vera in *Hero of Our Time*. Her fate in *The Two Brothers* is a prerequisite for understanding her character in those two later works of prose fiction. The evil Aleksandr and the sensitive Yury may well be derived from the similarly contrasted pair of brothers in Schiller's *The Robbers*. But Aleksandr's ruthless manipulation of Vera's life and person is Lermontov's own idea. Her prolonged torture is a form of spiritual rape, as are the tormenting of Emiliya by the

---

[6] See V. E. Meierkhol'd, *Stat'i pis'ma, rechi, besedy* (Moscow: Iskusstvo, 1968), 1:296–300 and 303–4.

Jesuit villain in *The Spaniards* and the slow, cruel poisoning of Nina in *Masquerade*. Echoing the violent physical rapes described with so much relish in the "Cadet Poems," these scenes add up to a demonstration of Lermontov's strongly sadistic attitude toward women.

The obsessive sadism in Lermontov's plays and erotic poems of 1834–36, traceable biographically to various real and imagined rejections he suffered during that time, is also evident in his verse tales that date from the same period. In these tales—*The Mountain Village of Bastundzhi*, *Hajji Abrek*, and *The Boyar Orsha*—Lermontov first found the melodious fluency that characterizes his later verse narratives, such as *Mtsyri* and *The Demon*. All three describe the terrorizing, murdering, or incarceration of helpless women by cruel males who seek to punish them for loving men of whom the male protagonists disapprove. Anton Chekhov showed a greater insight into this aspect of Lermontov than most Russian critics when he made the morbidly possessive, insecure, and murderous Captain Solyony in *Three Sisters* pattern his personality and behavior after Lermontov.

The literary quality of *The Two Brothers* is about equal to that of *Masquerade*, but because this play lacks *Masquerade*'s seductive verse garb, its handicaps and deficiencies are all the more glaring. Meyerhold, whose love for Lermontov's dramas was, if anything, uncritical, considered *The Two Brothers* Lermontov's "most perfect play." He insisted on staging it in 1915.[7] The production lasted for three performances. It is the only known instance of the staging of a Lermontov play other than *Masquerade*. In his notes to the production, Meyerhold maintained that all Lermontov plays, beginning with *Menschen und Leidenschaften*, belong to his period of maturity. This opinion seems willfully perverse. The really mature period of Lermontov, the one in which his work is not preparation but achievement, begins only in 1837, after he wrote all the plays he was to write. It begins with his brilliant and hysterical invective against the society that allowed Russia's greatest poet, Pushkin, to die in a duel. This poem, for which Nicholas I banished Lermontov to the Caucasus, marks the point at which Lermontov became a brilliant poet and a heroic living legend.

This was the Lermontov who wrote the fine novel *Hero of Our Time*, the moving narrative poem *Mtsyri*, and the lyrics of his last five years,

---

[7] Ibid., 301ff., and K. Rudnitskii, *Rezhisser Meierkhol'd* (Moscow: Nauka, 1969), 179.

lyrics which Russian children still learn by heart as soon as they are taught to read. This consummate poet and novelist is every bit as misanthropic and bilious as the young graphomaniac who wrote *Menschen und Leidenschaften*, but now he knows how to express his negativism in some of the most perfectly crafted and hauntingly melodious lines ever penned in Russian. People could not then and still cannot believe that something as beautiful and musical as those poems can really express such repugnance for the whole of humanity. The continuing national acclaim for Lermontov's poetry proves Marina Tsvetaeva's contention that in verse people will applaud ideas which they would have hated in prose.[8]

Charmed by Lermontov's verbal magic, Vissarion Belinsky mistook his misanthropy for a form of social protest. This view was seized upon by the rest of the nineteenth century. It made the smoldering hatred of Lermontov's poems acceptable by providing it with a plausible raison d'être. In Soviet times, he has been adorned with the same revolutionary tinsel as all other important prerevolutionary writers. This can be done crudely, as in the academic editions of his writings,[9] or, on occasion, with considerable subtlety.[10] Popular lore often brackets Lermontov with Pushkin, as if the two were a pair of matching giants, similar to Tolstoi and Dostoevsky. Osip Mandelstam made a necessary correction when he wrote in *The Noise of Time* that even as a child he never thought of Lermontov as Pushkin's brother or any sort of relative.[11]

---

[8] Marina Tsvetaeva, *Proza* (New York: Chekhov Publishing House, 1953), 244.

[9] Boris Eikhenbaum's biographical essay, appended to vol. 4 of M. Lermontov, *Sobranie sochinenii v chetyrekh tomakh* (Moscow and Leningrad: Izd-vo Akademii nauk SSSR, 1961–62), states that all factual evidence dating from Lermontov's time is unreliable, except for the essays and letters of Belinsky and the statements on Lermontov by Aleksandr Gertsen (4:754). A great Tolstoi scholar who did not live to see the publication of his fine study of *Anna Karenina*, completed thirty years earlier, Eikhenbaum was forced in the last decades of his life to disregard his own research and insights and keep restating officially decreed ideological platitudes.

[10] Emma Gershtein, *Sud'ba Lermontova* (Moscow: Sovetskii Pisatel', 1964), amasses a great deal of fascinating biographical information, but arranges it to support the official image of a saintly and progressive Lermontov, hounded and killed by a reactionary society. The book studiously disregards all contemporary evidence that might show Lermontov's character in any different light and fails to mention any of his actions that do not fit the desired image.

[11] Osip Mandel'shtam, *Sobranie sochinenii* (New York: Inter-Language Literary Associates, 1966), 2:96.

II

MODERNISM,
ITS PAST,
ITS LEGACY

Annensky's Materiality[1]

*H*istorians of Russian literature are wont to assign writers and poets to some definable ideological or aesthetic movement. After his death, Innokenty Annensky was classified as a Symbolist, which is of course essentially correct. But this obscures a good deal, both in his poetry and in his personal relations with other poets of his generation. In Annensky's own literary and critical articles, Symbolism figures as a very expansive and capacious notion. He considered not only Dostoevsky but even Maksim Gorky to be a Symbolist. In his own poetry he set himself apart from the Russian Symbolists. In his revealing poem "Drugomu" (To the other) Annensky writes about Russian Symbolism with understanding and even admiration, but stresses that his poetry is totally different. His personal attitudes toward individual Symbolist poets were complex: toward Balmont he was benevolent, but slightly mocking; toward Vyacheslav Ivanov, amicable; and toward Merezhkovsky and Blok, sharply negative.

Further, the mature poetry of Annensky's last period contained certain features which seemed to be close not to Symbolism, but to the movements derived from it—Acmeism and Cubo-Futurism. Akhmatova considered Annensky to be her teacher. She retained this attitude throughout her long poetic career: from reading in proof his *Kiparisovyi larets* (The cypress chest) in the year of Annensky's death to dedicating a poem written after World War II to his memory. In addition, the young Vladimir Mayakovsky found Annensky both interesting and essential. According to the memoirs of Kornei Chukovsky, Mayakovsky "very carefully studied" and "continually declaimed to himself" Annensky's poems. This note is from 1915; it is supported by the mention of Annensky's name in Mayakovsky's poem "Nadoelo" (It is tiresome) of 1916. And it is true that the "futuristic" aspect of Annensky's poetry becomes

---

[1] Translated by Olga Raevsky-Hughes. Originally published as "Veshchestvennost' Annenskogo" in *Novyi zhurnal*, no. 85 (1966): 69–79.

evident long before the appearance of Futurism itself in such poems as "Kolokol'chiki" (Sleigh bells) or "Kek-uok na tsimbalakh" (Cakewalk on cymbals), in which attention is focused on the verbal texture, on the phonetic aspect of the word, on the precise display of the verbal style—all clearly in counterbalance to the hazy, vaguely magical handling of the word by such poets as Blok or Vyacheslav Ivanov. Such "futuristic" poems of Annensky's are considered to be "jokes" despite their almost consistently tragic themes.

Though it anticipates almost all major movements of Russian poetry in the first half of the twentieth century, Annensky's poetry was formed in the nineteenth. When Annensky is spoken of as a Symbolist, it is usually forgotten that he was considerably older than the major poets of the Silver Age. Annensky is older than Nadson; as a poet he is a contemporary of Vladimir Solovyov, Minsky, and even Fofanov, who, at some point, was listed (also incorrectly) as a forerunner of Symbolism.

Annensky began writing poetry in 1875. Nowadays it is fairly difficult to imagine the Russian poetic culture of the 1870s and 1880s that surrounded the young Annensky. It was a time when Apukhtin and Nadson were considered masters, when Nikolai Dobrolyubov was taken seriously as a poet, and Mme Chumina was highly rated. One has only to leaf through a reader for professional reciters (*Chtets-Deklamator*) from the early twentieth century to sense all this false pathos and false poetry. Had Annensky written *Tikhie pesni* (Quiet songs) and *The Cypress Chest* during the antipoetic 1880s, Mandelstam's Acmeist partisan evaluation of him—which is historically unacceptable—would be comprehensible: "All were asleep while Annensky was awake. The everyday realist writers (*bytoviki*) were snoring."

Those Russian poets who wrote about Annensky tended to emphasize one particular aspect of his poetry and somehow bypassed its essence. In his article, Vladislav Khodasevich compared Annensky with Tolstoi's Ivan Ilich. This is an interesting comparison, but it misses the point, because it is narrowed to this theme only. There is no doubt that the theme of death is central for Annensky, but all his poetry cannot be reduced to endless variations on this theme. Besides the quotations adduced by Khodasevich, the very same Annensky wrote: "I am not afraid of life. With its invigorating noise / It fires one up, it lets thoughts light up."

In his poem "Pamiati Annenskogo" (In memory of Annensky), Gumilyov found more precise and convincing words to convey the nature of Annensky's poetry, more so than in his review of *The Cypress Chest* (see *Pis'ma o russkoi poezii* [Letters on Russian poetry]), which is more or less accurate, but at the same time too concise. One might also point to Marina Tsvetaeva's insightful comparison of Annensky and Bryusov in her lengthy and vicious article about the latter. Speaking of Bryusov's socio-literary activity, she quotes (apparently from a letter to her from Pasternak): "Bryusov was the first, Annensky was not the first," and draws her own conclusion: "Someone unique cannot be the first."

True, Annensky was in a way a unique poet. True, he was first of all a Symbolist poet, perhaps the only true Symbolist in all of Russian poetry. If we accept the prior role of French poetry in this movement, then—in light of the depth of his penetration into the very essence of French Symbolism—this "A" should precede all the "Bs" of Russian Symbolism, if not chronologically (Annensky became a Symbolist only in the twentieth century, after Merezhkovsky, Bryusov, Balmont and Sologub), then by his authenticity, by his ability to respond to French Symbolism's most significant phenomena.

French Symbolism was perceived one-sidedly in Russia. The Russians began with Verlaine (without forgetting the Parnassians), and then came the enthusiasm for Maeterlinck and Verhaeren, who nowadays seem much less interesting. The major poets were nearly overlooked: Baudelaire was mostly reflected in Sologub, although very idiosyncratically; Mallarmé was written about with respect, but was little known; and there was almost no recognition of Rimbaud, nearly until the time of Poplavsky.

It was Annensky who assimilated the prose of Huysmans and the poetry of Baudelaire and Mallarmé as no one else in Russia did. Therefore, Mandelstam's words about Annensky's inability to respond to influences remain incomprehensible. Influence as such is no hindrance to originality, and if in Annensky's translations from Mallarmé we at times do not recognize the source, his original poems demonstrate a deep knowledge of both Mallarmé and Baudelaire.

Annensky's literary genealogy is not limited to French Symbolism. To elicit the sources and influences on Annensky's poetry is just as easy, fascinating and, in the end, fruitless, as to trace the sources of the various poetic styles of Pushkin. Annensky is a poet of wide range, and his style (or styles) often move ahead of or retreat from his own methods of the 1900s, the years when he was working on *The Cypress Chest*. Some traces of the 1880s, the years when he was taking shape as a poet, are perceptible in this collection:

> Forget about the nightingale on the fragrant flowers,
> But do not forget the dawn of love.

This is not as bad as it seems on first reading, but nonetheless these lines inevitably remind one of Nadson. They could have been written by Apollon Maikov (about whose poetry Annensky once wrote a serious article); and in that case, we would have had a Chaikovsky song set to this text. But one has only to turn a page in the collected poems of Annensky, and we find his "Verbnaia nedelia" (Palm Sunday), a remarkable and rare example in Russian poetry of true Surrealism:

> Into the yellow dusk of dead April
> Taking leave of the starry desert
> Palm Sunday was floating away
> On the last, lost snow-bedecked ice floe;
>
> It was floating away in the clouds of incense,
> In the dying of funeral bells,
> Away from the icons with bottomless eyes,
> And from Lazaruses forgotten in a black hole.
>
> The white moon on the wane stood high,
> And for all those whose life is irretrievable,
> Burning tears were flowing over the palms
> Onto a cherub's rosy cheeks.

Excluding the somewhat Blokian ending, nothing similar to this poem with its Baudelairian personification (quite unlike either the allegorical personification in the poetry of the eighteenth-century Russian Baroque, or Tyutchev's struggle between winter and spring) can be found in Russian poetry before Mandelstam's late surrealistic poems (for example, about the "six-digital falsehood" [*shestipalaia nepravda*]) and some pieces by Poplavsky.

Annensky's Symbolism comes both from literature and from life. "As a reward (for humiliation and disappointments) life leaves him a few symbols," he writes about a poet in his *Vtoraia kniga otrazhenii* (Second book of reflections). And in a depressing but precisely depicted situation of one of the poems of *The Cypress Chest*, a wooden doll in the waves of a waterfall becomes a symbol of human life, and additionally enriches the poet with a new understanding of *pity for a thing*. In the poet's critical articles, no less than in his *The Cypress Chest*, symbolistic dream and life are constantly intertwined, and Annensky never lets life (not death, as Khodasevich would have it), even for a moment, disappear from view. This is one of the permanent features of his poetry, and in this is its unique charm.

The chasm between art and real life, the poet as theurgist and mythmaker—these concepts, so typical for the Russian Symbolists, are totally alien to Annensky. A variety of concrete details from everyday reality is necessary for the poet to make his poetry come to life. A late confession from Akhmatova, "Had you known from what trash / Verses grow without shame," was long before anticipated by her teacher Annensky in his article on Gorky's play *Na dne* (The lower depths), where we read: "Poetry, a tenaciously surviving creature, does not distinguish between a stable, a drink, the old or the young, a christening or a funeral. Its forms are infinitely various." None of the Russian Symbolists (perhaps with the exception of Fyodor Sologub) would have dared to underline the substratum of the living reality of all art in such a sharp and crude way. It was only Vladimir Mayakovsky who went beyond Annensky, calling poetry a "capricious old woman," a "nasty piece of rubbish" (*kapriznaia baba; presvolochneishaia shtukovina*)—but then he is Mayakovsky.

Everyday details and, at times, everyday spoken expressions play an enormous role in Annensky's verse. He knows how to convey and reflect a mood as no one else does, a personal mood, the atmosphere of a person's soul, so to speak, precisely, by using an everyday detail presented with complete clarity and precision. At times in his verse such a detail acquires a value of its own. Only Annensky could define *Crime and Punishment* as "a novel of the sultry odor of slaked lime and drying oil, and, even more so, a novel of *ugly oppressive rooms*" (Annensky's italics). Conveying in a critical article the contents of Lermontov's "Vykhozhu odin ia na dorogu" (Alone, I come out onto the road), using images relatively close to the original, Annensky, characteristically, adds: "I slow my step on the crushed stone of the roadway." From here the path leads not only to the Acmeists, but to the poetry of Pasternak as well.

Without attempting to exhaust the topic, we will try to trace this "materiality" in some themes of *The Cypress Chest*. There are no real women in this book (excluding quasi-folkloric stylizations, such as "Milaia" [Darling], and the bourgeois, everyday scenes à la Chekhov). However, throughout the whole book a symbolic feminine figure is present: woman—dream—life, and perhaps at the same time, even death. We will quote again the *Second Book of Reflections*: "Beauty for a poet is either the beauty *of a woman*, or beauty *as a woman*." Despite her insubstantiality, this woman is presented visually. Blok's Strange Woman has "a figure draped in silk," rings and ostrich feathers, but we cannot imagine her face. And Annensky has not only her "tenderly swaying figure," but also "fixed eyes," "a white wreath in a braid in disarray," "you yourself—all atremble—arise!"—and, especially impressive, "a moist glimmer of crimson smiles." We recognize her. We saw her in portraits by painters of the end of the nineteenth century—Gustave Moreau, Franz von Stuck, and Vrubel, with her mysterious, indeed, motionless glance and dark head of hair. She has an affinity with The Blessed Damozel of Dante Gabriel Rossetti's paintings and verse. Her more distant relatives are the passionless Negro women of Baudelaire and Mallarmé.

Annensky has a recognizable connection with the fine arts of his times. His *intérieurs* bring to mind the overripe, banal—and captivating—style of Art Nouveau (or Jugendstil). An affinity with this style is also suggested by such titles as "Struia rezedy v temnom vagone" (A stream of fragrance of mignonette in a dark train car) or "Buddiiskaia messa v Parizhe" (A Buddhist mass in Paris). The poet achieves precise shades of colors with the exactitude of a Postimpressionist. If we trust the calculations of Amédée Ozenfant, the favored colors of French poets, both the Romantics and the Symbolists, were rose and blue. Annensky often uses two colors that were the least in demand by French poets: yellow and various shades of lilac (18% and 7%, according to Ozenfant). In Annensky at every turn there is "yellowness" (recall van Gogh's yellow *Bedroom*), and it has, more often than not, depressing emotional associations: "yellow dusk of dead April," "wet yellow boards," yellow water given to someone from the cross in the Kiev caves, "yellow steam of the Petersburg winter," "yellow and slippery country house." The color of lilac, the color of "Ametisty" (Amethysts) (the title of two Annensky poems) and of "Sirenevaia mgla" (Lilac mist), is less gloomy, rather dreamy.[2]

There is a connection also with Japanese painting, perceived through a Western European prism. Such poems as "Nezhivaia" (Lifeless) and "Ofort" (An etching) are clearly reminiscent of graphics with the Japanese bent fashionable at that time.

Music, whether concert or chamber, plays a limited role in Annensky's poetry. True, he describes both piano and violin performances, a vocal recital, and a symphony orchestra. But the concept of music as such, if it appears (for instance, in the poems "Smychok i struny" [Bow and strings] or "On i ia" [He and I]), is very often intentionally intermingled with other notions—that of happiness, poetry, foreboding of threatening events, and so on. Here Annensky moves along the same path as Blok and Bely, in whose poems and articles the term "music" very often carries a special mystical meaning that has very little to do with music as art (mixing various notions, which are still occasionally overused by some émigré critics who have no relationship at all to Symbolism). The best explanation of this Nietzschean term is given by Annensky himself in his article on Tolstoi's *Vlast' t'my* (Power of darkness), where he demonstrates Tolstoi's antimusical nature: "But here I understand music as something else: I consider music the most direct and most enchanting *assurance* for man of the possibility of a happiness that exceeds not only reality, but even the most daring fantasy." This is not, of course, what Blok meant by "the spirit of music," but still it is closer to Blok's symbol-metaphor than to any real musical art.

With Nietzsche showing the way, among the most recent composers Wagner seemed the most congenial to Russian poets of the beginning of the twentieth century. Blok felt it necessary to attend performances of the *Ring of the Nibelungs*, which he found boring. It is difficult nowadays to take seriously Kuzmin's "discussions" of *Tristan* in his novel *Kryl'ia* (Wings). An excellent description of a symphony concert in Andrei Bely's narrative poem *Pervoe svidanie* (The first rendezvous) clearly depicts a

---

[2] After this article was written, a book in English on Annensky was published: Vsevolod Setchkarev, *Studies in the Life and Works of Innokentij Annenskij* (The Hague: Mouton, 1963). The book has an interesting chapter on Annensky's colorism, with a detailed analysis of the colors and shades mentioned above and with an indication of their percentages.

performance of some score by Wagner. In one of his most characteristic poems ("O net, ne stan ..." [Oh no, it is not your form ...]), Annensky also refers to *Parsifal*, but at the same time intuits that the waltz ringing in the "banal and motley hall"—rather than the operatic music of Wagner, to which he appeals in his soul—is closer to his theme, to the expression of a "longing for beauty radiating somewhere far away."

The real music in Annensky's poetry, the presence of which gives this poetry a totally new and special sound, is much more interesting than Wagner and Nietzschean mystical music. His concrete sound, or rather noise instrumentation, is at times reminiscent of the experiments of Pierre Schaeffer and Pierre Henry with musique concrète in the 1950s, when recordings of rain, a train, or the beating of a heart were used as musical material. In Annensky's poems we encounter an impressive collection of all kinds of bells, large and small: "the ringing bells of a funeral," "wounded brass," "the brass language of funereal languor." The sighs of a train; the remarkably depicted and realized crackling of an alarm clock to which two poems are devoted; the clicking of billiard balls; the noise of rain, of trees, of a railroad station; the buzz of a mosquito; a barrel organ; the hiss of a pendulum—*The Cypress Chest* is filled with tangible, well-formed sounds depicted in relief, up to and including the completely stunning, totally unexpected military wind band that performs the poems of the poet:

> To you I send my verses, which once
> Soldiers played in the distance!
> Only your trumpets, without quatrains
> Sang them more mournfully and softly.

All these noises are extremely expressive, and, with their associations, open up as it were aural windows into the inner world of the poet.

The artistic application of these everyday sounds and noises in Annensky's poetry allows us to make a comparison which at first might appear rather unexpected: a comparison with the eleventh chapter of James Joyce's novel *Ulysses*. In his book on the novel, the commentator Stuart Gilbert gives the subtitle "The Sirens" to the eleventh chapter, pointing out that it corresponds to the episode of the sirens in *The Odyssey*, and that all its principal images and comparisons come from the area of musical art. Essentially, Gilbert is, of course, correct: in this eleventh chapter a good deal is relayed about concerts, about singers, about opera. However, the primary emotional content of the episode in the bar described in this chapter—the feelings and moods of the protagonist of the novel, Leopold Bloom—is conveyed not by conversations about music, not by a Donizetti aria performed in the bar, not by an excerpt from the operetta *Floradora* hummed by the barmaid Lydia Douce. The main emotional weight of this chapter is carried by the noises: the bell on the carriage of Bloom's rival, who is traveling to a rendezvous with Bloom's wife, Marion; the game of *sonnez la cloche*, in which the barmaids snap their garters to entertain the customers (both the name of the game and its erotic essence remind Bloom of his wife's behavior); and at the end of the chapter, the hopelessness and despair of the protagonist, which are well conveyed by the description of a persistent strumming of a piano tuner. The chapter overflows with music and conversations about it, but the decisive role in the chapter is given, just as in Annensky's poetry, not to musical harmony but to dissonant noises. In the final pages of the chapter, where the piano tuner appears, one is surprised by an almost literal coincidence with the second half of Annensky's poem "He and I":

> And for the beams of a different star
> I search in doubt and fear,
> Like a piano tuner, all the harmonies
> I finger cautiously.
>
> It grows dark … the room is empty,
> With difficulty I remember something,
> And pure and without an answer
> Note after note dies away.

Annensky's mature poetry from the time of *The Cypress Chest* is held together by a mutual interplay of concrete reality and dream. Here is the source, notwithstanding the frequent and carefully planned prosaic expressions, of the special dressed-up quality and animation of this book, which fits well in its bright and diversely plumaged era, which gave us *The Sea Gull* and *The Firebird*, *The Golden Cockerel* and *The Silver Dove*.

From the intertwining of life and dream arises the theme that is the sum of the two: literature. Two characteristic poems, which in our opinion touch upon the essence of Annensky's poetics, are devoted to it: "To the Other" and "Muchitel'nyi sonet" (An agonizing sonnet). It appears that Gumilyov and later commentators are right in interpreting "To the Other" as a reflection of Annensky's attitude toward other, more or less "official," Russian Symbolists. To the ecstatic and disconnected qualities of their poetics ("your insane thrust" [*bezumnyi tvoi poryv*]) Annensky opposes precision, clarity, and a "strict stylus" (*strogii karandash*). And in his total honesty Annensky is forced to introduce into the poem his "best dream"— his beloved ancient Greece, which, generally, appears rarely in his lyrics:

> My best-favored dream—Andromache at her weaving.
> Échafaudage atop her head,
> And it, coquettishly covered by a kerchief.

The image of Andromache—i.e., of Greece—weaving is immediately and, it would appear, intentionally deflated by everyday details ("échafaudage" on the head of a tragic heroine, covered, at that, by a "coquettish scarf"); and as if in excuse, this is followed by a "but then":

> But then, my strict stylus
> Never ceded its harmonies to ellipses.

This is why real-life exactness and palpability are needed, if only to make the dream and symbol more expressive. This is well put in "The Agonizing Sonnet":

> I need melting snow beneath the yellow of fire,
> Shining wearily through the perspiring glass,
> And that a strand of hair so close to me,
> So close to me, uncurled, would tremble.
>
> I need the smoky clouds from the darkening height,
> The circling of the smoky clouds, which have no past,
> Half-closed eyes and the music of a dream,
>
> And the music of a dream, which has no word yet …
> Oh, give me only a moment, but in life, not in a dream,
> So that I could become fire or be consumed in fire!

In this snatched moment the poet would be given insight, but for this to happen life has to be photographed, as with a flash of magnesium, with extreme clarity. This is the way the poet challenges not only rain, but life in general:

> Oh no! Enough of your transformations!
> Take on some permanent shape.

Precision and materiality are what Annensky bequeathed to the best Russian poets of the Postsymbolist generation—to Mandelstam, Khodasevich, Tsvetaeva, Pasternak, Mayakovsky, but above all, to Anna Akhmatova.

* * *

We have decided in this instance, as in a few cases below, to provide Russian titles (in transliteration) along with translations for the benefit of those interested in identifying the original texts. SK was particularly fond of the edgy subject matter, linguistic virtuosity, lexical innovativeness, and rhythmical verve of Annensky's poetry. He could be persuaded on occasion to perform dramatic recitations of poems like "Kek-uok na tsimbalakh" and "Kolokol'chiki," together with similar specimens from the poetry of Tsvetaeva, Khlebnikov and Mayakovsky. Such performances were in great demand at gatherings of the Berkeley Slavic department in the 1970s and 1980s.

Zinaida Gippius and Russian Poetry[1]

*P*age 14 of Temira Pachmuss's book shows a photograph of an exquisitely flower-like young girl in a frilly white frock; on page 5, there is a reproduction of a Léon Bakst watercolor that depicts a sneering young dandy in stylized male attire of the Napoleonic era. Both pictures are portraits of Zinaida Gippius (her German ancestors spelled the name Hippius before they emigrated to Russia in the sixteenth century), Russia's most profound religious poet, a guiding spirit of the Russian Symbolist movement, one of the main initiators of the religious revival among the liberal intelligentsia of the turn of the century, and a spectacular early practitioner of psychological unisex, who rejected the traditional male/female roles as early as the 1890s. Unpublishable and virtually unknown in the Soviet Union, she is the subject of two highly informative studies that have appeared recently in the West.

In 1889, at the age of twenty, Gippius was married to the rising novelist and critic Dmitry Merezhkovsky. They lived together for the rest of their lives in a fraternal, never-consummated marriage which was an intellectual partnership more than anything else. Although it was Merezhkovsky who eventually attained international fame with his book on Tolstoi and Dostoevsky and with his historical novels (one of them, *The Romance of Leonardo da Vinci*, has been shown to have served Sigmund Freud as a primary source for his psychoanalysis of Leonardo), all their friends agree that Gippius supplied Merezhkovsky with the stimuli and ideas for everything he wrote. And indeed, in retrospect, there can be no doubt that she was by far the more significant and influential writer of the two. The poems she published in 1893 and 1894 spelled the beginnings of

---

[1] Review of *Paradox in the Religious Poetry of Zinaida Gippius*, by Olga Matich (Munich: Wilhelm Fink, 1972), and *Zinaida Hippius: An Intellectual Profile*, by Temira Pachmuss (Carbondale: Southern Illinois University Press, 1971). Originally published as "The Dostoevsky of Russian Poetry" (not SK's choice of title) in *Nation*, 21 August 1972, 117–19.

modern Russian poetry. In them she expanded the boundaries of nineteenth-century meters and popularized the accentual verse and assonance rhymes that were later developed and perfected by Aleksandr Blok, Anna Akhmatova, and Osip Mandelstam. At a time when Russian criticism was dominated by utilitarian-minded Positivists who tolerated poetry only if it preached a simplistic moral or contained social criticism, Gippius was one of the first to take up the basic themes of Symbolism (which were to remain central to all her subsequent writings): man's need for religious faith, the problem of achieving freedom in a necessity-bound world, the ambiguities of sexual roles in any love relationship, and the inevitability of death as an ever-present factor in our lives. Andrew Field was not exaggerating when he wrote that the poetry of Gippius "can be nothing less than what Dostoevsky himself would have written had he been a poet."[2] In a very real sense, the position of Gippius in Russian poetry is indeed almost exactly analogous to that of Dostoevsky in the Russian novel. And of course, without her pioneering example neither Blok nor Mayakovsky would have been what they later became.

In most of her poems Gippius spoke of herself in the masculine gender (much more fully expressed in Russian grammar than in English). In her love lyrics, this masculine persona addresses now a female, now a male lover. This ambivalence was also present in her personal life. Her intellectual partnership with Merezhkovsky remained the most important of her relationships, but it left Gippius unsatisfied emotionally. A few incipient affairs with young poets and politicians in the late 1890s all ran aground on her inability and unwillingness to assume the traditional female role. She also had some close emotional involvements with other women and even addressed love lyrics to a few, but these attachments all seem to have been of secondary importance. Believing herself to be a woman physically but a man spiritually and emotionally, Gippius finally came to the conclusion that her ideal soul mate had to be a male homosexual who would be interested in neither a dominant masculine nor a submissive feminine stance. Her choice fell upon Dmitry Filosofov, the spectacularly handsome son of the Russian feminist leader Anna Filosofova. Filosofov was a literary critic, and, at the time, the lover of his cousin

---

[2] Andrew Field, *The Complection of Russian Literature: A Cento* (New York: Atheneum, 1971), 274.

Sergei Diaghilev, with whom he edited the pathbreaking journal *The World of Art*. With Merezhkovsky's willing assistance, Gippius resolutely set out to break up the relationship between Filosofov and Diaghilev, using as her main lever Filosofov's religious and mystical inclinations and interests, which Diaghilev was not able to share. The tug of war between Gippius and Diaghilev over the young critic's affections, which developed over a period of several years and which finally culminated in the victory of Gippius in 1905, had an effect on the entire future of Russian culture that is not generally realized and that had ramifications going far beyond this apparently private emotional tangle. In order to keep Filosofov more securely within their orbit, Gippius and Merezhkovsky initiated the famous encounters between Russian intellectuals and writers on the one hand and the Orthodox clergy on the other at the Religious-Philosophical Society. Russian intellectuals and Russian clergymen had been almost totally estranged since some time in the 1860s, and the resulting rapprochement led to the religious-cultural renascence that helped assert the reputations of such religious philosophers as Nikolai Berdyaev and Lev Shestov, supplied the essential religious strains in the poetry of the early Blok and the late Pasternak, and had an influence that can still be felt in such major works of Soviet literature as Bulgakov's *The Master and Margarita*, Pasternak's *Doctor Zhivago* and Solzhenitsyn's *August 1914*. For his part, Sergei Diaghilev was so crushed by the defection of his lover that he lost all interest in editing the remarkable journal the two of them had founded and decided to shift the center of his interest from painting and literature (with which he had been principally involved in the preceding ten years) to music and ballet. The impact of the ensuing series of concerts and ballet performances which Diaghilev took to Paris (he organized them partly in order to be away from St. Petersburg and to avoid seeing Gippius or Filosofov) on music, ballet, and the visual arts, both in Russia and throughout the world, is too well known to require documentation.

From 1905 until 1920, the group that was known in Russian literary circles as "the Merezhkovskys" consisted of the triumvirate of Gippius, Merezhkovsky, and Filosofov. Like many Russian intellectuals of the time, all three were strongly radicalized by the failure of the abortive Revolution of 1905. They collaborated on the antimonarchist tract *The Tsar and the Revolution*, which was banned in Russia but was published in France and Germany. They also jointly wrote a remarkable play, *Poppy Blossoms* (*Makov tsvet*; in her book, Temira Pachmuss translated this title as *The Red Poppy*, apparently confusing it with Glière's ballet of that name), a picture of the generational conflict occasioned by the 1905 Revolution and aggravated by the polarization of opinion over the desirability and ethics of the Russo-Japanese War. Reading *Poppy Blossoms* today, one experiences an almost hallucinatory sense of déjà vu: if Vietnam is substituted for Russia's ill-advised attack on Japan, the problems of Russian intellectuals in 1905 as depicted in the play become uncannily similar to those of today's Americans. Even more recognizably, Gippius's play *The Green Ring* (which is available in English and would make a worthwhile project for some university theater group) depicted the revolt of a group of articulate teenagers against the mercenary and hypocritical values of their parents and elders. In a brilliant production by Vsevolod Meyerhold, *The Green Ring* was the major event of the 1916 theatrical season; it remains to this day one of the finest genuinely revolutionary and genuinely poetic plays in the Russian language.

The objections of Zinaida Gippius to the tsarist autocracy were that it perpetuated the artificial division of people into social classes and, by supporting an official church and by persecuting religious dissenters and minorities, prevented the individual from seeking his or her own path to God. She saw the aim of the Russian revolutionary movement (which she came to revere) in the establishment of total universal freedom and equality in all aspects of social life; she also believed that the revolution would give people a freedom of choice in their pursuit of religious experience and sexual fulfillment. Lenin's version of the revolution, with its insistence on the primacy of class structure, restriction of sexuality to its most bourgeois forms, and, above all, its total ban on all spiritual life and religious growth, was for Gippius worse than oppression or betrayal of revolutionary ideals: it was sacrilege and deicide. No one among the Russian émigrés denounced the Soviet regime with greater fury and virulence than she, but the relentless bitterness and hatred of her anti-Bolshevik diatribes and poems poison her message and render her jeremiads unpalatable even for those who might sympathize with her reasons.

The loss of Filosofov, who in 1920 left the Merezhkovskys to join a group of revolutionary anarchists based in Poland, was as shattering a blow to Gippius as the October Revolution. In emigration, Gippius produced two volumes of literary memoirs, some critical articles, and a slim book of verse in her best metaphysical manner.³ Otherwise, the outside world knew her during those years as the wife of the noted writer Merezhkovsky. She outlived him by four years and died in 1945 in Paris, after completing her literary biography of him.⁴

Gippius became an Orwellian unperson in the Soviet Union after about 1925, and for several decades the position of literary historians there was that she had simply never existed. Her name began to reappear in Soviet encyclopedias and references after the 1960s, but she is mentioned only to be denounced as a decadent and a benighted reactionary who dared disagree with Lenin and Gorky.⁵ Because of her historical and artistic importance, it was inevitable that Gippius would be rediscovered by foreign scholars. The book by Olga Matich, originally a UCLA doctoral thesis, was published in Germany (but in the English language) by a Munich publishing house that specializes in important Russian writers and works which are banned in the Soviet Union for nonliterary reasons. Ostensibly a study of a particular aspect of Gippius's poetry, the book is actually a balanced and thoroughly objective outline of this poet's system of thought. The introductory chapter should lay to rest the many spurious legends and invidious myths that are still to be found about Zinaida Gippius in many non-Russian sources. The remainder of the book examines, under the suggestive chapter headings, "God," "Love," "Despair," "Devil," and "Death," the unique personal cosmogony and the powerful religious vision embodied in this astounding woman's poetry. Were it not for the fact that the poetry itself is quoted in the original Russian and without

---

3   Zinaida Gippius, *Zhivye litsa*, vols. 1 and 2 (Prague: Plamia, 1925). SK underestimates the sheer number of critical articles and the prose fiction that Gippius published in the 1920s and the 1930s. Three volumes comprising her "unknown prose" of the émigré period, totaling over 1,500 pages, have now been published in St. Petersburg by the publishing house Rostok: *Mechty i koshmar* (2002); *Chto ne bylo i chto bylo* (2002); and *Arifmetika liubvi* (2003). Her final collection of poetry appeared on the eve of World War II: Zinaida Gippius, *Siianiia* (Paris: Dom knigi, 1938).—Ed.
4   Z. Gippius-Merezhkovskaia, *Dmitrii Merezhkovskii* (Paris: YMCA-Press, 1951).
5   There has been an explosion of interest around Gippius in post-Soviet Russia. See especially Z. N. Gippius, *Stikhotvoreniia*; *Zhivye litsa*, ed. N. A. Bogomolov (Moscow: Khudozhestvennaia literatura, 1991); Z. N. Gippius, *Stikhotvoreniia*, ed. A. V. Lavrov (St. Petersburg: Novaia biblioteka poeta, 1999); and a nine-volume set of her collected works, *Sobranie sochinenii*, published in Moscow by Russkaia kniga, between 2001 and 2005 (a supplemental volume followed in 2006).—Ed.

translation, this book could be recommended as the most thorough and intelligent introduction to the thought and poetry of Zinaida Gippius ever written.

The "Intellectual Profile" by Temira Pachmuss is broader in scope and more ambitious than Professor Matich's study. Based on an enormous amount of research and drawing on a large body of unpublished manuscripts and documents, the volume builds up an impressive case for the importance of the entire Gippius phenomenon for the development of Russian poetry and culture as they exist today. All serious students of Russian literature, who are already indebted to Professor Pachmuss for her recent publications in France and Germany of the diaries of Zinaida Gippius, of her collected poetry, and of her memoirs (the latter two through the good offices of the same German publisher that brought out Olga Matich's book),[6] should be grateful for the thorough documentation and the great deal of new information on the life and writings of Gippius that the book contains. If the portrait of Zinaida Gippius that ultimately emerges is not entirely satisfactory, it is because the book is handicapped by the author's attitude of excessive adulation toward her subject, paradoxically combined with a lack of genuine affinity for Gippius's views and interests. The sexual ambivalence, so very important in both the poet's life and her poetry, is either lifted to a metaphysical level or coyly swept under the carpet (even the nature of Gippius's attachment to Filosofov, discussed in print by a number of previous commentators, is never made explicit in the book). The interpenetration of the sexual urge and the quest for God, so very basic to the thought of both Gippius and Merezhkovsky, is likewise treated with skittish prudery. The poet's plays, so significant and relevant for today's readers, are dismissed by Professor Pachmuss in a few curt paragraphs, and instead she concentrates her biggest guns on asserting the reputation of Zinaida Gippius as a literary critic.

---

[6] Z. N. Gippius, *Stikhotvoreniia i poemy*, vol. 1, *1899–1918*, and vol. 2, *1918–1945*, ed. Temira Pachmuss (Munich: Wilhelm Fink, 1972). See also Temira Pachmuss, *Intellect and Ideas in Action: Selected Correspondence of Z. N. Gippius* (Munich: Wilhelm Fink, 1972). Professor Pachmuss was also the editor responsible for diaries and memoirs of Gippius which appeared in various émigré periodicals; an abridged version of them in English is to be found in *Between Paris and St. Petersburg: Selected Diaries of Zinaida Gippius*, ed. Temira Pachmuss (Urbana: University of Illinois Press, 1975).—Ed.

Now, both before and after the revolution, Gippius indeed published a great deal of criticism under the pen name of Anton Krainy ("Anton the Extreme"). As a critic she was unbelievably narrow-minded and almost totally blind to literary quality as such. She expected her own kind of metaphysical subtlety from all other writers and was simply not interested in any writing that did not in one way or another descend from the Dostoevskian tradition. This *parti pris* led her to condemn as frivolous and insignificant prose writers of the caliber of Maksim Gorky, Anton Chekhov (who for Gippius was a provincial dullard able to describe only the animal side of human existence), and Vladimir Nabokov ("a writer who has absolutely nothing to say"), and to treat with contempt almost all the important Russian Postsymbolist poets, including such figures as Mayakovsky, Esenin, Pasternak, Anna Akhmatova, and Marina Tsvetaeva. Instead of trying to explain why the very qualities that made Gippius such an original thinker and poet also made her blind as a critic, Temira Pachmuss hastens to agree with all of her subject's foibles and prejudices, quoting with approval such patent absurdities as the assertion that Chekhov held all women in contempt (as supposedly proven by the character of Natasha in *Three Sisters*). "Hippius deserves recognition as an original and perceptive critic, whose judgment in literary matters has stood the test of time," Professor Pachmuss writes at the end of her detailed chapter on the poet's criticism, but everything she herself cites in the preceding eighty pages belies this sanguine evaluation.

"The religious thought which was typical of the Russian intelligentsia at the turn of the century has no validity today," writes Professor Pachmuss at the beginning of her book, leaving one wondering where she has been for the past ten years and why she bothered to write a book on Zinaida Gippius in the first place. For anyone who is at all aware of the recent trends in modern sensibility in the Western countries, Temira Pachmuss's own fact-filled book and Olga Matich's perceptive study should offer ample proof that the religious thought of Zinaida Gippius and of her contemporaries is remarkably valid and fascinating today and that this poet's tortuous search for freedom from sexual stereotypes can be understood far better now than it was in earlier decades. The English translations of Gippius's poems offered in Professor Pachmuss's book are regrettably pedestrian in quality and are frequently inexact. Should some talented translator come up with better renditions as a result of these two new books on Gippius, there would very likely be an eager and receptive audience in the West for the poems, plays, diaries, and memoirs of this unfairly and undeservedly forgotten writer who changed the course of poetry in her own country and who foreshadowed so many of our present-day insights and attitudes.

* * *

With this review, SK deeply offended Temira Pachmuss, who had long devoted much of her scholarly research to Zinaida Gippius and, as a result, had also inherited the papers of Gippius left to Vladimir Zlobin, the erstwhile factotum of the Merezhkovskys. She bided her time, but when SK published his edition of an English translation of Zlobin's memoirs, with a reiteration and expansion of his criticism of Pachmuss's views and allegations of censorship, she published an impassioned defense of her own work and a rebuttal of SK's trust in the veracity of Zlobin's memoirs.[7] To some readers, SK's tracing of cause and effect in the interpersonal relationships and careers of the Merezhkovskys, Filosofov, and Diaghilev may seem overblown.

This essay also provoked a standard denunciation of SK in the Soviet press. In a polemical article published in the official newspaper of the Union of Writers, he was taken to task for denigrating Dostoevsky's alleged "Socialist-Realist" credentials and, on the other hand, championing a vociferously anti-Bolshevik representative of the emigration.[8] The lengthy diatribe, with its several quotations from SK's writings, however, had the result of airing the selective and blinkered treatment of Dostoevsky in party-line literary criticism in the Soviet Union and of introducing Zinaida Gippius—together with her political and religious heterodoxy and her unconventional views of sexuality—to readers who never knew she existed. (Indeed, this may well have been the journalist's not-so-hidden agenda.)

---

[7] Temira Pachmuss, review of *A Difficult Soul: Zinaida Gippius*, by Vladimir Zlobin, ed., annotated, and with an introduction by Simon Karlinsky (Berkeley: University of California Press, 1980), in *Slavic Review* 40, no. 3 (Fall 1981): 505–6. SK's response and Professor Pachmuss's reply appeared in *Slavic Review* 41, no. 1 (Spring 1982): 195–96.

[8] A. Ponomarev, "Grimiruia pod velikikh: Neliteraturovedcheskie operatsii amerikanskogo literaturoveda," *Literaturnaia gazeta*, 5 November 1972.

Died and Survived[1]

"I am glad that you are studying Blok," Vladimir Nabokov wrote to Edmund Wilson in 1943. "But be careful: he is one of those poets that get into one's system—and everything (else) seems unblokish and flat." Most people who read poetry in Russian—whether their command of the language is native or learned—sooner or later succumb to Blok's magic. Of the dazzling galaxy of Symbolist and Postsymbolist Russian poets who wrote in the first two decades of this century, Aleksandr Blok (1880–1921) was the most spellbinding. Much of Russian poetry, from Pushkin to Mandelstam, is lucid and appeals to the intellect. But Blok's poems and plays are hypnotic, a blend of sorcery, banality and subtle verbal music. As the critic Kornei Chukovsky put it, "his [Blok's] poetry affected us as the moon affects lunatics."[2]

Blok retained his popularity throughout the postrevolutionary period. His writings remained in print even in Stalin's time, when Symbolism and other Modernist trends of the early twentieth century were treated as nonexistent. In the 1960s he was honored with an eight-volume annotated edition of his collected writings that included even earlier drafts, diaries, and a selection of letters.[3] With the exception of the two official patron

---

1 Review of *Selected Poems*, by Alexander Blok, trans. Alex Miller (Moscow: Progress Publishers, 1981); *Hamayun: The Life of Alexander Blok*, by Vladimir Orlov, trans. Olga Shartse (Moscow: Progress Publishers, 1980); *The Life of Aleksandr Blok*, vol. 1, *The Distant Thunder 1880–1908*, and vol. 2, *The Release of Harmony 1908–21*, by Avril Pyman (New York: Oxford University Press, 1979 and 1980, respectively). Originally published in *New York Times Book Review*, 9 May 1982, 8–9, 23–26.
2 "Его лирика … действовала на нас как луна на лунатиков." A literary critic, translator, memoirist, and famed writer for children, Kornei Chukovsky (1882–1969) was a friend and colleague of Blok's, particularly in the years immediately preceding his death in August 1921. Chukovsky published his reminiscences of Blok in 1922, and these "winged words" persisted through the frequent iterations of his accounts of Blok.—Ed.
3 Further evidence of Blok's remarkably enduring popularity is provided by the twenty-volume variorum edition of his complete collected writings that has been under way for several years: A. A. Blok, *Polnoe sobranie sochinenii i pisem v dvadtsati tomakh* (Moscow: Nauka, 1997–).—Ed.

saints of Soviet literature, Maksim Gorky and Vladimir Mayakovsky, such complete editions are normally reserved only for nineteenth-century classics.

In the 1970s, with the approach of the centenary of the poet's birth, there was a flood of Blok biographies, textual and documentary studies, and memoirs published in the Soviet Union, among them the three excellent Blok miscellanies brought out by the Tartu University in Estonia and the currently appearing four volumes in the prestigious Literary Heritage series.[4] As if that were not enough, Progress Publishers in Moscow has taken to exporting translations of books by and about Blok, as exemplified by the *Selected Poems* and an abridged version of Vladimir Orlov's biography, *Hamayun*, the latter published in Russian in 1978 and again in 1980. Also coinciding with the centenary is the appearance of the monumental two-volume biography of Blok by Avril Pyman, an English scholar and translator who spent twelve years in the Soviet Union, where she gained access to archival sources not usually available to researchers and interviewed a number of Blok's associates who were still alive in the 1960s.

The significance of the explosion of Blok scholarship and publication in the Soviet Union can be best understood by looking at the situation of other major figures of early twentieth-century Modernism. The poet and novelist Andrei Bely, who was linked to Blok through a complex mixture of amity and enmity, which was central to both of their lives, also had, in 1980, a centenary of his birth. But there were no new editions or critical studies to commemorate the date. Other important literary associates of Blok—Vyacheslav Ivanov, Zinaida Gippius, Mikhail Kuzmin—had complete collections of their poetry published in recent years by foreign scholars who live in the West, but in the USSR there was only one slim volume of Ivanov's poetry and nothing at all for Gippius or Kuzmin. There are no Soviet biographies of, or collections of critical articles about, Blok's great

---

[4] The valuable series of publications entitled *Blokovskii sbornik*, initially under the general editorship of Iu. M. Lotman, began appearing from the Tartu State University in 1964. It continued for many years and by 2010 had published eighteen volumes. The venerable *Literaturnoe nasledstvo* (Moscow: Nauka) issued five volumes under the title *Aleksandr Blok: Novye materialy i issledovaniia* between 1980 and 1993; the same institution had already published *Aleksandr Blok: Pis'ma k zhene* (Moscow: Nauka, 1978).—Ed.

younger contemporaries—Anna Akhmatova, Osip Mandelstam, and Marina Tsvetaeva.[5]

The reasons, as for everything else in Soviet cultural life, are ideological. Blok gave his allegiance to the Bolshevik regime at the time of the October Revolution, and he wrote a famous, if ambiguous, narrative poem about that Revolution, *The Twelve*, which Soviet authorities found objectionable in 1918 but which later exegetes proclaimed politically acceptable. And Blok died in 1921, thus escaping the denunciations and literary hounding that was the fate of all Modernist poets in the next three decades. In a cycle of poems about Blok, *The Wind*, which Boris Pasternak wrote shortly before his death in 1960, he lashed out at the "influential flunkeys" who alone decide which poets are "to be alive and lauded and which to be silenced and slandered" in the Soviet Union. Pasternak rejoiced that Blok was beloved "outside of programs and systems," and "has not been forced on us by anyone" or compelled to adopt Soviet writers retroactively as his offspring.

As the propagandistic blurbs in the English editions of Blok's *Selected Poems* and the Orlov biography show, subsequent developments proved Pasternak wrong. Ways were discovered to reduce Blok's complex biography and outlook to a catechistic instance of a wayward nobleman's conversion to the verities of Socialism. It is precisely as the progenitor of Soviet poetry, as a "citizen-poet," that this lifelong Symbolist and mystic is now being popularized at home and abroad and put to the task of indoctrinating later generations.

Aleksandr Blok was a scion of two notable academic families, and he married into a third one. Like many young intellectuals of his generation, he turned away from the positivistic values of the milieu into which he was born to espouse a more idealistic and mystical view of reality. In the philosophy and poetry of Vladimir Solovyov (1853–1900), a seminal figure for the whole of Russian Symbolism, Blok found the central image of his poetic vision: St. Sophia, the personification of Divine Wisdom in female form, the female hypostasis of Christ according to Byzantine mystics, and

---

[5] The literary landscape changed dramatically within ten years after this essay of SK's, with the fall of the Soviet Union. The several writers listed in this paragraph have been the subject of a good deal of attention over the past twenty-five years, and multiple works of criticism and editions of their writings have been published in post-Soviet Russia.—Ed.

the equivalent of *Das Ewig-Weibliche* of German nineteenth-century philosophers and poets. In his first collection of poems, *Verses about the Most Beautiful Lady* (1901–2), Blok announced her imminent advent, destined to transform the world. Blok perceived the incarnation of St. Sophia not only in future history and his own poetry, but also in the woman he married, the daughter of the famed scientist Dmitry Mendeleev, developer of the periodic table in chemistry.

An aspiring young actress, Lyuba Blok was cast by her husband and his circle of friends in the part of God's wisdom personified and, for good measure, the Blessed Virgin. Blok's almost medieval separation of love into sacred and profane spheres has been often blamed for their strange, almost sexless marriage. Avril Pyman, who had access to Lyuba's frank and rancorous memoirs (published only in fragments in the Soviet Union and in complete form by the Hebrew University of Jerusalem in 1977),[6] suggests a hitherto unperceived factor which is a key to much in Blok's poetry and plays: Blok's lifelong compulsive search for casual sex with prostitutes and pickups was the reason he left untouched the wife he loved and revered, eventually driving her into other men's arms. This was preferable to exposing her to the risk of venereal disease, for which he himself had to be periodically treated.

The revelation of this side of Blok in the Pyman biography and his wife's memoirs is not merely a piece of lurid literary gossip. It places into focus his cardinal theme of woman exalted vs. woman degraded. It can now be seen that the situation between the poet and his wife was the point of departure for his three dramatic masterpieces: the lyric comedy *The Puppet Booth*, the visionary drama *The Incognita* (both written in 1906; the latter also translated as *The Stranger*) and the historical tragedy *The Rose and the Cross* (1913). In the three plays, for all their disparities, the hero yearns for a woman who loves him and yet is totally unattainable. While these three plays belong at the summit of Russian poetic drama, Blok's other works for the stage, where this theme is absent, are all curiously lifeless and contrived.

---

[6] L. D. Blok, *Byli i nebylitsy*, ed. I. Paul'mann, foreword and commentary by L. S. Fleishman (Bremen: K-Presse, 1977). Another version of this text was published in the two-volume *Aleksandr Blok v vospominaniiakh sovremennikov* (Moscow: Khudozhestvennaia literatura, 1980), 1:134–87.—Ed.

The momentous events of the Russo-Japanese War and the first Revolution of 1905 did not bring about the coming of St. Sophia, as Blok had hoped. What they brought instead was the suppression of the revolutionary groundswell. Then came gradual reforms, followed, around 1910, by unprecedented economic prosperity. Like Gogol and Dostoevsky before him, Blok detested the civil liberties and the elective forms of government that existed in the West. Like Tolstoi, he mistrusted material well-being if it was not accompanied by improvements in the spiritual and moral spheres. His poetry of 1906–16, which contains his most haunting and melodious lyrics, is permeated with the poet's sense of an impending universal catastrophe, which he welcomed. *Retribution*, the title of both an important cycle of lyrics and a long narrative poem on which he worked during the last ten years of his life, was what Blok yearned to be visited upon the Russian government, the Orthodox Church, and all educated or prosperous Russians for delaying with their materialistic values the spiritual transfiguration of the world.

Many of his readers ignore this side of Blok. The brilliant émigré poet of the 1920s, Boris Poplavsky, who saw himself as Blok's disciple, wrote that Blok "is a poet of absolute pity, angry at nothing, condemning nothing."[7] In a memorable 1914 poem, Blok himself expressed the hope that posterity would forgive him his misanthropy and see him as "a child of goodness and light" and a "triumph of freedom." But freedom was the last thing that interested Blok. Soviet critics are quite right when they stress his negativism (though they interpret it simplistically as an indictment of the tsarist regime). Vladimir Nabokov had the same thing in mind when he wrote that Blok was "a superb poet with a muddled mind," in whom there was "something somber and fundamentally reactionary ... a murky vista with a bonfire of books at the end."[8] This is indeed an essential dimension of Blok, which the prophetic historical vision of his *On the Field of Kulikovo* poems, the iridescent textures of his

---

[7] "Блок православный поэт, поэт абсолютной жалости, не сердящийся ни на что, ни что не осуждающий." This statement is from one of Poplavsky's journals which are now part of the Simon Karlinsky Papers, BANC MSS 2010/177, The Bancroft Library, University of California, Berkeley. This and other excerpts from Poplavsky's journal for 1929 are cited in SK's "In Search of Poplavsky: A Collage," included in the present volume.—Ed.

[8] Vladimir Nabokov, "Cabbage Soup and Caviar," *New Republic*, 17 January 1944.

Italian Poems, or the festive love lyrics of the *Carmen* cycle should not make us overlook.

After the liberal-democratic Revolution of February 1917, Blok took a job (the first in his life) on a commission that investigated the abuses of the Romanov monarchy. But the Constitutional Democrats and moderate Socialists of the Provisional Government were too drab for his taste. In Lenin's and Trotsky's seizure of power Blok saw the same promise as in the advent of St. Sophia for which he had hoped prior to 1905: not a change of government in Russia, but a transubstantiation of reality (through the Nietzschean "spirit of music") into some higher form of existence. In a few days in January 1918, guided by what he believed to be an elemental roar emanating from other worlds, Aleksandr Blok affixed on paper his great poem of the Revolution, *The Twelve*.

In a montage of popular songs, political slogans, and biblical allusion (few Russian poets could write of the October Revolution without evoking the Bible), *The Twelve* depicts twelve Red Guards who march through a blizzard that is both meteorological and symbolic. As the poem makes amply clear, they are not ideologically conscious Marxists but members of the prerevolutionary criminal underworld who were swept into the Revolution and are now harassing and terrorizing the populace under the cover of idealistic and quasi-religious verbiage. The plot of the poem is not a story of class conflict but a deliberately trite love triangle between one of the Red Guards, a Red Guard deserter, and a prostitute whom they both love and whom one of them accidentally kills. Yet, through all the murdering and looting, the Twelve are gradually shown as the modern incarnation of the twelve apostles in the Gospels. Marching ahead of them with a red flag is their true leader, whom they do not recognize and try to shoot. He is revealed in the final section to be Jesus Christ.

The Twelve is a beautiful, multilayered poem whose colloquial pungency has defeated innumerable translators. Its meaning is complex enough to justify having an entire book devoted to its exegesis, Sergei Hackel's amazingly thorough *The Poet and the Revolution*.[9] It makes sense that the Bolshevik authorities tried to ban its public readings in 1918, and it makes sense that the Soviet literary authorities today call it the foun-

---

[9] Sergei Hackel, *The Poet and the Revolution: Aleksandr Blok's "The Twelve"* (Oxford: Oxford University Press, 1975).

tainhead of all Soviet poetry. While the importance of the poem is beyond dispute, the fate of its author in the three years he had left to live after its completion is a topic that will be debated, as Avril Pyman rightly assumes, as long as the Russian language exists.

The whole vast Soviet scholarship on Blok insists that writing *The Twelve* was the logical outcome of his earlier poetry and that it made him the bard of the Revolution. But his notebooks and some of the memoirs about him that were published abroad (and are not reprinted in the Soviet Union) show that after a year or so of initial enthusiasm he realized that the metamorphosis of the world had not occurred after all. The selfishness, vulgarity, and lack of spirituality he so hated in the old Russia had not disappeared after the Revolution but had survived in new, often uglier forms. At the age of forty-one, Blok died in acute mental depression, ceaselessly muttering "God forgive me." In a haunting memorial poem, Anna Akhmatova described him as "the Sun of Russia, extinguished in torment."[10]

Avril Pyman tells the story of Blok's life with authority and sympathy. Her demonstration of how his poetry sprang from his life and in turn determined its subsequent events is exhaustive, masterful, and wholly convincing. Her touching love for Blok prevents her from attaining the necessary critical distance and leads her to agree with his often unfair assessments of his contemporaries. As is the case with Richard Wagner and Ezra Pound, with both of whom Blok had similarities, taking him seriously as a civic thinker can only detract from the appreciation of his art.

The scope of her research and the total grasp of her topic make Avril Pyman's two volumes the most valuable biography of Blok to have so far appeared. Even as one disagrees with some of her interpretations of facts, one recognizes and respects the freedom with which she has reached them. This intellectual freedom is precisely what is missing in Vladimir Orlov's biography of Blok. An enormously erudite and productive scholar, Orlov has to his credit an impressive list of publications of Russian writers of the eighteenth, nineteenth, and twentieth centuries. He was the chief editor of the epoch-making eight-volume edition of Blok in 1960–63, and he is the most prominent of the Soviet scholars who have since the 1960s spearheaded the "rehabilitation" of the previously banned major poets of

---

10 Anna Akhmatova, "A Smolenskaia nynche imeninnitsa …" (August 1921).

the early twentieth century. In 1966 he got into hot water with the literary authorities for allowing a volume of Andrei Bely's poems to appear in a series he edited with an introduction that was deemed too sympathetic and too factually explicit.[11]

While Orlov's other writings have a more conventional scholarly format, *Hamayun* (the title refers to the prophetic bird of old Russian folklore) is a *biographie romancée*, written in a manner apparently inspired by Henri Troyat's books on Russian writers. The English version from Progress Publishers in Moscow contains about one half of the text of the Russian original. The seams occasionally show. Orlov writes with verve and probably knows more about Blok and his time than any other person now living. His book is also a good example of how Soviet censorship forces the biographer into the stance of a defense lawyer, minimizing or explaining away the politically incorrect views of his client and exaggerating whatever favorable evidence he can find. *Hamayun* is a lively, readable, and dishonest book—not because the distinguished scholar, Vladimir Orlov, wanted to be dishonest, but because that was the only way he was permitted to write about this particular poet and his life.

One of the pleasures of Avril Pyman's biography is her copious citing of Blok's poetry in her own resourceful and sensitive translations (she published a volume of them in 1972). In two of her footnotes, Avril Pyman refers admiringly to renditions of Blok by another English translator, Alex Miller. A volume of his translations now comes to us from Moscow. There are a few stanzas here and there and occasionally an entire poem in this collection that come close to conveying Blok's meaning with fidelity. But there are none that suggest Blok's evocative power. Blok's rhymes are always unexpected. Alex Miller, by settling for the most hackneyed rhymes in the English language, often reduces this great poetry to doggerel. How is the reader with no Russian to guess that the lines "The dancer at the Monarch's wish, / Serves him the Poet's head on a dish" are not comical but achingly beautiful in the original?[12]

---

[11] Andrei Belyi, *Stikhotvoreniia i poemy*, ed. T. Iu Khmel'nitskaia, N. B. Bank, and N. G. Zakharenko (Moscow and Leningrad: Sovetskii pisatel' [Biblioteka poeta, bol'shaia seriia], 1966). Khmelnitskaya's introduction was deemed unsatisfactory by Soviet hardliners.—Ed.

[12] From the second of the poems about Venice in Aleksandr Blok's cycle *Ital'ianskie stikhi* (1909).

Because it was published in the Soviet Union, Miller's collection features such Soviet specialties as historically distorted footnotes and tendentiously slanted mistranslations. Blok's last poem, "To Pushkin House," asks the spirit of Pushkin for help "in the silent struggle" against the new Soviet censorship. Alex Miller's version of this line, "Show us how to battle through!," makes it sound as if Blok were recruiting Pushkin for the revolutionary cause. The famous last line of *The Twelve*, the line to which Sergei Hackel devoted almost a hundred pages in his book, "Just ahead is Jesus Christ," is falsified into "In the distance—Jesus Christ." Readers curious about the quality of Blok's poetry would get a better notion of it by reading Avril Pyman's, Sergei Hackel's, and, for all its reticences and half-truths, Vladimir Orlov's books.

Symphonic Structure in Andrei Bely's *Pervoe svidanie*[1]

A student of Russian poetry would have to go back to Lomonosov to find another Russian poet whose poetry is comparable to Andrei Bely's in its scope and variety of erudition, spanning the most diverse fields. Certainly, no other twentieth-century poet has Bely's grasp of physical and mathematical sciences, of speculative philosophy, of aesthetics, of linguistics, and of musical theory and practice.[2]

Mikhail Kuzmin and Boris Pasternak, two poets who originally intended to become composers and who received extensive musical training, would reasonably be expected to write of musical matters with considerable assurance, yet neither of them does. Kuzmin can convey his own impressions of musical performances with great charm (e.g., his vivid evocation of a Wagnerian orchestra in the first section of *Forel' razbivaet led*), but he is sparing in the use of concrete musical terminology in his poetry. Boris Pasternak evokes scenes of piano playing in vivid, expressionistic imagery ("Roial' drozhashchii penu s gub oblizhet" or "Ia klavishei staiu kormil s ruki"); yet his one attempt to use technical musical terms, in his translation of Verlaine's "Art poétique," is startlingly inept, considering his earlier music studies.[3]

Andrei Bely, on the other hand, could write of musical theory and practice both in his prose (descriptions of concerts, recitals, and private

---

[1] Originally published in *California Slavic Studies* 6 (1971): 61–70. This volume was dedicated to Gleb Struve, one of the founders of the series. Its guest editors were Robert P. Hughes, Simon Karlinsky, and Vladimir Markov, all of whom had written their PhD dissertations under the direction of Professor Struve.—Ed.

[2] See also SK's concise survey of Bely's literary career in *Columbia Dictionary of Modern European Literature*, 2nd ed. (New York: Columbia University Press, 1980), 70–71.—Ed.

[3] E. Vinokurov and L. Ginzburg, eds., *Zarubezhnaia poeziia v russkikh perevodakh* (Moscow, 1968), 300–1. In the fourth stanza Pasternak seems to confuse the musical intervals of whole and half tone (*poltona*) with nuances of color (*poluton*). He also does not know the Russian word for bassoon (*fagot*) and uses for it a pointless French borrowing, *bason* (from *basson*).

musical performances in his *Second Symphony*, the chapter on Emily Metner (Emil Medtner) in *Nachalo veka*, and the numerous passages on music in the rest of the autobiographical trilogy) and in verse (especially in *Pervoe svidanie*[4]) with a consummate understanding of the subject and with fluent use of technical vocabulary. Derzhavin and Annensky have written impressively of individual musical instruments, but Bely is unique in Russian poetry in his detailed and knowledgeable evocations of individual orchestral timbres in *Pervoe svidanie*. For all the mystical and symbolic overtones of the scene at the concert, Bely finds remarkably apt and precise verbal means to convey the tone coloring of a quartet of horns set off antiphonally by bassoons,

> И в строгий разговор валторн
> Фаготы прорицают хором,[5] (429)

or the effect of a trombone crescendo on a single note,

> И стаю звуков гонит он,
> Как зайца гончая собака
> На возникающий тромбон. (431)

Only a person totally at home with various orchestral timbres could have imagined the nightmarish metaphors and the alliterative howl of *u*'s Bely uses to convey the auditory chaos of an orchestra tuning up before a performance:

> Возня, переговоры ... Скрежет:
> И трудный гуд, и нудный зуд—
> Так ноет зуб, так нудит блуд ...
> Кто это там пилит и режет? (427)

---

[4] There seems to be no satisfactory way to render the title of Bely's poetic masterpiece into English. *The First Meeting* and *The First Encounter* have both been tried and both miss the point; *The First Date*, although far from ideal, would be somewhat closer to what the Russian conveys, if it did not bring in undesirable Andy Hardy associations. Very reluctantly, one is forced to settle for the pretentious, but reasonably close *The First Rendezvous*.

[5] Andrei Belyi, *Pervoe svidanie*, in *Stikhotvoreniia i poemy* (Moscow and Leningrad, 1966). The numbers here and later refer to the page numbers of this edition.

This is immediately followed by an equally onomatopoetic depiction of a set of kettledrums being tuned up:

> Натянуто пустое дно,—
> Долдонит бебень барабана,
> Как пузо выпуклого жбана:
> И тупо, тупо бьет оно .... (428)

Equally apt are Bely's visualization of an orchestra conductor's typical gestures (429–31) and his felicitous epithet for the chord of the diminished seventh which is about to be resolved: *vozdukholetnyi septakkord*. Bely's paean to the versatility of the diatonic scale is remarkable for its subtle ambiguity, because the term *zvukoriad* (an old term for "mode") corresponds etymologically to the German *Tonreihe* and is used here in a context that may suggest the dodecaphonic composition systems of Schoenberg and Webern, already evolving, but not yet fully stated or practiced at the time *Pervoe svidanie* was written (1921):[6]

> Интерферируя наш взгляд
> И озонируя дыханье,
> Мне музыкальный звукоряд
> Отображает мирозданье—
> От безобра́зий городских
> До тайн безо́бразий Эреба
> До света образов людских
> Многообразиями неба. (426)

The fivefold paronomastic and prosodic permutation of the stem *obraz* in the above passage suggests a typical procedure of serial musical composition, and is in its way as disconcertingly and inexplicably prophetic as Bely's famous mention of the atomic bomb in the same *poema*.

Although familiar with music since infancy, Bely probably acquired his thorough knowledge of the symphonic form through Metner's de-

---

[6] Schoenberg's first systematic application of the *Tonreihe* dates from his Five Piano Pieces, op. 23, and Serenade, op. 24 (1923); Webern followed his example one year later in his *Drei Volkstexte*, op. 17.

tailed commentary on Schubert's C-Major Symphony during their joint visits to Arthur Nikisch's orchestral rehearsals in 1901.[7]

Four of Bely's early prose works bear the title "Symphony."[8] The use of the term was not figurative or metaphorical: it was Bely's intention to apply the principles of musical form to literary, verbal structures. Therefore, while these works can and have been studied by literary scholars,[9] they are unique in world literature in that methods of musical scholarship and analysis are equally applicable to them. For example, the *Second Symphony (The Dramatic)* has its themes arranged in the discernible structure of a four-movement classical symphonic cycle, as practiced by Haydn or Beethoven: the first part is a traditional sonata-allegro, the second part a dreamy adagio with religious themes, and also with sonata features. The third and fourth parts can be seen as the scherzo and the traditional rondo-finale.[10] The *Third Symphony (The Return)*, although divided into three parts, is in terms of its musical structure not a symphonic cycle but a vast one-movement sonata-allegro, with the exposition of the themes in the first part, their restatement and development in another tonality (in another universe, in this case) in the second part, and their recapitulation and synthesis in the original key in the last part.[11] These are only brief indications of the kind of musicological analysis that could and should be profitably applied to Bely's four symphonies in prose.

However, his most thorough and systematic application of the classical symphonic structure was made in a work written in verse and not containing the word "symphony" anywhere in its title. The autobiographical narrative poem *Pervoe svidanie*, written in 1921, at the time Bely was expecting to leave Soviet Russia to join his anthroposophic mentor Rudolf Steiner and the woman he loved (Anna Turgeneva) in Switzerland, is a

---

[7] Andrei Belyi, *Nachalo veka* (Moscow and Leningrad, 1933), 78–80.
[8] On all four of Bely's symphonies, see Gleb Struve, "Andrej Belyj's Experiments with Novel Technique," *Stil- und Formprobleme in der Literatur: Vorträge des VII Kongresses der Internationalen Vereinigung für moderne Sprachen und Literaturen in Heidelberg* (Heidelberg, 1959), 459–67.
[9] *Third Symphony* was analyzed by Oleg A. Maslenikov, "Andrej Belyj's Third 'Symphony,'" *American Slavic and East European Review* 7, no. 1 (1948): 78–92; on *Second Symphony*, see Elena Szilard, "O strukture *Vtoroi simfonii* A. Belogo," *Studia Slavica Hungarica* 13 (1967): 311–22.
[10] The authentically musical structure of the *Second Symphony* has been noted by Szilard.
[11] The sonata-allegro structure of the *Third Symphony* was pointed out several years ago in an unpublished paper on this work by my colleague, Professor Erica Brendel.

work permeated with the poet's lyrical joy. The narrative covers the period described by Bely later in his prose memoir *Nachalo veka*: his student days and his realization in May of 1900 that he would become a professional writer. Autobiographical elements that we know from the memoir (Bely's friendship with the family of Mikhail Solovyov, his infatuation with the wealthy merchant's wife Margarita Morozova, his pilgrimage to the tomb of Vladimir Solovyov) are interwoven in the poem with themes treated in Bely's *Second Symphony (The Dramatic)*—a mystical encounter at the symphony concert, the ghost of Vladimir Solovyov hovering over the city of Moscow, the satirical glimpses of Moscow's academic intelligentsia.

Another work of Bely's connected to *Pervoe svidanie* is his most baffling piece of writing, the long prose poem on language, *Glossolaliia: Poema o zvuke*, written at the time of the October Revolution. Ostensibly a linguistic treatise, the work is in fact a set of inchoate, instinctive, illogical meditations on language, to which, as Bely himself was the first to admit, scholarly linguistic criticism would not be applicable. The Bely who wrote *Pervoe svidanie*, even more than the author of *Glossolaliia*, is no longer the typically Symbolist poet he was when he wrote the symphonies and his first collection of verse. By 1921 Bely had read Khlebnikov (including *his* inchoate, instinctive theories of language), Mayakovsky, possibly even Boris Pasternak. He was assuredly familiar with the writings of Viktor Shklovsky, Roman Jakobson, and other Russian Formalists. The stylistic and lexical texture of *Pervoe svidanie* shows the unmistakable impact of Russian Futurism and Formalism.[12] Combined with this impact is some seepage from *Glossolaliia*, which leaves its precipitate in the forms of certain verbal devices and the mystical idea of salvation through language and linguistics, expressed in the Introduction to the poem.

Classical Russian literature provides two additional ingredients: deliberate stylistic reminiscences from Pushkin's *Evgeny Onegin* in the passages on the Solovyov family and the Gogolian demon of trivia (*bes poshlosti*) who appears prominently in chapters 3 and 4. All these heterogeneous themes and elements are brilliantly fused by Bely into a verse

---

[12] The author's insistence that *Pervoe svidanie* is a purely Symbolist work and his refusal to consider it within the context of the time of its writing weakens Oleg Ilinsky's article on this poem (Il'inskii, *Novyi zhurnal*, no. 90 [1968]: 98–111). Another defect is that Ilinsky repeatedly sees free verbal association in passages that in fact contain profound and multileveled meaning.

texture almost without equal in Russian poetry for its sustained inventiveness and carefully organized into a strict and regular four-movement symphonic cycle consisting of a sonata-allegro (with a separate introduction), an adagio in the form of a three-part Lied, a scherzo with a trio (in which a reprise of the end of the first movement serves as an introduction) and a rondo-finale with a coda.

The brief thirty-two-line Introduction is absolutely astounding in its concentration of numerous levels of meaning. The initial image of the miner-gnome who crushes crunching consonants to form tomes is a clever personification of the mechanical aspects of human language, dead sounds not yet brought to life by spirit and meaning. The gnome is metamorphosed into the "I" of the poem: at first a personified stylistic device and then a tired, aging poet, likened to a broken object and an extinguished bakery oven, baking indifferent verse to order.[13] The tired, extinguished poet starts to pray to God and the poet-oven immediately catches fire. The prayer to God becomes an invocation to language. Images of nature transcending its limitations (an inflated leaf on a dead stick, an ermine in the sky) powerfully convey the idea of spiritual resurrection, central to the entire Introduction. Animals symbolic of the Evangelists—the lion, the ox, and the eagle—which also figure in the Apocalypse, are evoked and the spiritual qualities assigned to them in Christian theology are compared to various capabilities of human language. This theological digression culminates in a complex explanation of the Christogram which combines the initial letters of "Jesus Christ" to form the symbol for Life,

"Ха" с "И" в "Же"—"Жизнь": Христос Иисус—
Знак начертательного смысла, (405)

followed by a paraphrased quotation of an appropriate verse from the Gospel according to John and the direct mention of the Evangelists, represented until now by their symbolic animals. In the last four lines of the Introduction, the pedantic gnomes of the inert language matter are left behind, the crunching (*khrust*) of consonants and of dying flames is re-

---

[13] Il'inskii, *Novyi zhurnal*, 103, seems to miss Bely's witty pun on the word *priem* (*приём*), which means a stylistic device in line 3 of the Introduction, but refers to the bakers' practice of renting their ovens to customers (*Peku priem: stikhi v nachinku*) in line 6.

placed by the crackling sounds of finely-honed sound instrumentation (*instrumentatsii grannyi tresk*), and the extinguished oven and the worn-out poet of the beginning are both ablaze with sacred fire. Language is the agent that accomplishes the progression from mineral to fire, from inert matter to vibrant life, and is thus assigned divine powers. As in *Glossolaliia*, but in a more convincing and successful manner, the Introduction fuses theology and linguistics: Bely's concentrated poetic art manages to combine into a harmonious whole such seemingly heterogeneous elements as paraphrases from the New Testament and literary terminology of Russian Formalists: *stilisticheskii priem* (stylistic device), *iazykovye idiomy* (idioms of language) and *instrumentatsiia* (sound instrumentation); the latter may refer not only to language phenomena treated in the Introduction but also to the orchestral instrumentation described at length in chapter 3 of the poem.

In Bely's prose symphonies distinctive verbal structures were used as equivalents of musical themes (this applies less to his *Third Symphony*, where thematic functions are more likely to be taken by characters or situations). In the sonata-allegro of the first chapter of *Pervoe svidanie*, the symphonic structure utilizes complexes of ideas as its basic structural element. The principal theme of this first movement (and in a way, of the entire poem) is the theme of reminiscences of Bely's experiences in 1900; subsumed within this theme are the ideas of creative imagination and of poetry. The principal theme is stated in the first twenty-two lines of chapter 1 and is then followed by three related subordinate themes that in turn take up Bely's activities and interests at that juncture of his life.

Subordinate theme I is his daily and social life as a student at Moscow University. It begins with the lines:

> Меня пленяет Гольбер Гент …
> И я—не гимназист: студент. (406)

Subordinate theme II has to do with young Bely's interest in mythology, mysticism, and the history of religions, an interest considered inappropriate and even shocking by his mathematician father. This theme is brought in with the ironic discussion of Hindu mystics and sacred texts (407) and is soon contrasted with subordinate theme III: the physical sciences that Bely was then studying:

> Мне Менделеев говорит
> Периодической системой. (407)

The exposition of themes is completed by two humorous restatements of subordinate theme II, which contrast the role of mythology in ancient times and in the modern world.

The development section, beginning with the lines

> Из зыбей зыблемой лазури,
> Когда отвеяна лазурь, (409)

combines and varies the principal and the three subordinate themes in various combinations. This section is particularly notable for its inventive use of Khlebnikov-like neologisms:

> Туда серебряные роги,
> Туда, о месяц, протопырь!
> Взирай оттуда, мертвый зорич,
> Взирай, повешенный, и стынь,—
> О, злая, бешеная горечь,
> О, оскорбленная ледынь. (409)

The recapitulation section takes up the subordinate themes II and III (in reverse order),

> И строгой физикой мой ум
> Переполнял: профессор Умов (410)

(this is the section which contains the celebrated prediction of the atomic bomb), then the principal theme,

> В душе, органом проиграв,
> Дни, как орнамент, полетели,
> Взвиваясь запахами трав,
> Взвиваясь запахом метели. (411)

and concludes with a developed restatement of subordinate theme I, which this time incorporates some new imagery and syntactic structures that turn out to foreshadow thematic and structural elements of chapter 3 of the poem. The interrupted evocation of the concert hall and of Beethoven at the end of chapter 1 is analogous to the musical effect of an interrupted cadence, the resolution of which has been postponed until chapter 3, where this theme is fully stated and developed. The reversal of thematic sequence in the recapitulation, although not usual in musical practice, is not unprecedented. I. V. Sposobin[14] calls this type of recapitulation *zerkal'naia repriza* ("mirror recapitulation") and cites instances of it in Wagner's overture to *Tannhäuser*, Liszt's *Les préludes*, and the first movement of Rachmaninoff's Fourth Piano Concerto.

Chapter 2 of *Pervoe svidanie* is, as previously stated, a simple three-part Lied in form. The apartment where Mikhail Solovyov, his wife, and their son Sergei opened the new world of poetry and imagination to the young Borya Bugaev, the future Andrei Bely, is described with wit, humor, and enormous affection. Mikhail Solovyov is assigned as constant background several objects (his "bistre"-colored armchair, his glittering pince-nez, his cigarette) which accompany every mention of his name like refrains. Two principal characters of the poem, Vladimir Solovyov and Nadezhda Zarina (fictitious poetic name for Margarita Morozova), who are later given prominent roles, make their first brief appearances in this first section of chapter 2. The contrasting second section of this chapter, describing Bely's and Sergei Solovyov's visit to Vladimir Solovyov's grave at the cemetery of the Novodevichy Monastery (similar to the analogous episode in the *Second Symphony*), is set off from the rest of the poem by its versification. It is written in couplets of iambic tetrameter, using only masculine rhymes, whereas the rest of the poem freely alternates masculine and feminine rhymes. The final section of the chapter takes the reader back to the Solovyov apartment, but this time Vladimir Solovyov is the center of attention. The philosopher and poet to whom Bely owed so much of his spiritual development is, as it were, conjured from his grave, and he appears, not as a ghost (as will be the case later on in chapter 4), but as a memory of Bely's actual brief encounters with him in his brother's apartment. Fragments of the concert passages from chapter 3 intrude even more insistently than they did at the end of chapter 1 into the portrait of the philosopher, a portrait that is a unique mixture of grotesquerie, satire,

---

[14] I. V. Sposobin, *Muzykal'naia forma* (Moscow and Leningrad, 1947), 198.

and affection. In the last evocation of Vladimir Solovyov in this chapter, however, grotesquerie and satire disappear for a moment and we are given a tremendously moving brief requiem,

> Он—канул в Вечность: без возврата;
> Прошел в восторг нездешних мест:
> В монастыре, в волнах заката,—
> Рукопростертый белый крест
> Стоит, как память дорогая, (424)

which the irrepressible humorist in Bely cannot resist from topping with a last lapse into the ridiculous a few lines later:

> Так всякий: поживет, и—помер,
> И принят под такой-то номер. (424)

I have attempted to demonstrate the thoroughness and logic with which Bely applied the procedures of musical form to the structural organization of his most important narrative poem. The scope of this paper does not allow for detailed examination of the scherzo form in chapter 3, the chapter that is the focal point of the poem, with its final realization of the musical themes presaged in the first two chapters, its dialectical development of the images associated with the Evangelists in the Introduction, and, most important of all, the poet's mystical encounter at the concert (the music serving as a catalyst) with Nadezhda Zarina, Bely's equivalent of Vladimir Solovyov's Sofiya and Blok's Prekrasnaia Dama. The trio in the scherzo is realized not only formally, but also symbolically, in the threefold contrast between the poet, Zarina, and the Gogolian demon of trivia brought into the concert hall by the philistine members of the Moscow society and academic world.

The recurrent rondo theme of chapter 4 is provided by the poet's wanderings through Moscow streets after the concert. Memories of other similar wanderings through snowy streets return throughout the chapter to serve as rondo refrains. The rondo episodes interspersed with these refrains form a retrospective synthesis of the thematic material of the first three chapters. The religious motifs of the Introduction and the theme of Vladimir Solovyov from chapter 2 dominate the end of the chapter.

The final appearance of Vladimir Solovyov as an invisible ghost in a snowstorm may have been suggested to Bely by the figure of Christ in Blok's *The Twelve*, but this Blokian image is ingeniously fused with the last echo of the concert hall imagery:

"Ты кто?"
—"Владимир Соловьев:
Воспоминанием и светом
Работаю на месте этом …"

И никого: лишь белый гейзер …
Так заливается свирель;
Так на рояли Гольденвейзер
Берет уверенную трель. (441)

The image of the Virgin in the last lines of chapter 4 and the final brief conclusion reaffirm the religious mood of the initial Introduction, not ecstatically and vibrantly as there, however, but on a note of peace and serenity.

Pervoe svidanie is an astoundingly successful piece of poetry, rewarding on many levels of perception. It is also a work that could and should be studied from the most diverse angles. Its debt to the Apocalypse and to the Gospel according to John; its relationship to *Glossolaliia*, to the *Second Symphony* and to Bely's autobiographical trilogy; its treatment of the person and the writings of Vladimir Solovyov; its debt to Russian Futurists (especially Khlebnikov) and Formalists—these are some of the problems this complex poem raises. A full-length study of the musical structural devices Bely used in this poem (which the present paper has only sketched out) could easily result in a book-length treatise.

Such future scholarly attention would be well deserved. Written during a decade when Russian narrative poetry scaled such astounding peaks as Mayakovsky's *Pro eto* (About this), Marina Tsvetaeva's *Krysolov* (The pied piper), Kuzmin's *Forel' razbivaet led* (The trout breaks through the ice) and Zabolotsky's *Torzhestvo zemledeliia* (Triumph of agriculture), Bely's autobiographical verbal symphony can make a valid claim to being one of the two or three most profound, most complex, and most verbally dazzling narrative poems in the entire history of the Russian *poema*.

The Death and Resurrection of Mikhail Kuzmin[1]

The last volume of poetry that Mikhail Kuzmin (1872–1936) was able to publish during his lifetime was *The Trout Breaks through the Ice*. A sequence of narrative and lyric poems, couched in the strikingly original surrealistic and visionary mode characteristic of this poet's later work, the book appeared in Leningrad in 1929. Where Kuzmin's first two major collections, *Nets* (*Seti*), published in 1908, and *Autumnal Lakes* (*Osennie ozera*), published in 1912, had been acclaimed and eulogized by many of the leading poets and critics of the time, *The Trout Breaks through the Ice*, except for two contemptuous brief notices, was passed over in silence by the Soviet press.

Still, the book had its admirers among the more discerning members of the Soviet literary community. Among them was Lidiya Chukovskaya, who confided to Anna Akhmatova in 1940 that she began to understand and to love Kuzmin only after *The Trout Breaks through the Ice*.[2] Akhmatova, whose own early poetry betrayed Kuzmin's strong influence and who, in 1912, had asked Kuzmin to write a foreword to her first collection of verse, *Evening* (*Vecher*), inscribing the copy she gave to him "To my wonderful teacher," had, it turned out, not yet read her erstwhile teacher's last book. Chukovskaya lent it to her and one month later recorded Akhmatova's judgment. Apart from a few individual poems which she liked, Akhmatova thought the entire book derived from German Expressionist cinema and therefore lacking in originality. She found what she called the book's "obscenity" (*nepristoinost'*) most depressing: "Kuzmin has always been homosexual in his poetry, but here he exceeds all boundaries. Before, one could not do this: Vyacheslav Ivanov might

---

1   Review of *Sobranie stikhov*, 3 vols., by Mikhail Kuzmin, ed. John E. Malmstad and Vladimir Markov (Munich: Wilhelm Fink Verlag, 1977–78). Originally published in *Slavic Review* 38 (1979): 92–96.
2   Lidiia Chukovskaia, *Zapiski ob Anne Akhmatovoi*, vol. 1 (Paris: YMCA-Press, 1976), 149.

wince. But in the twenties, there was no longer anyone to be wary of (*uzhe ne na kogo bylo ogliadyvat'sia*). Perhaps Villon was able to manage this sort of thing, but as for Mikhail Alekseevich—no. It is utterly disgusting."³

For a person familiar with Kuzmin's literary career and with the Russian cultural history of the twentieth century in general, the statement is astounding. Male homosexual love, it is true, has always been a major (but by no means the only) theme in Kuzmin's poetry. Before he made his name as a poet, he acquired considerable notoriety for his autobiographical *roman à thèse*, *Wings* (*Kryl'ia*). Initially published in 1906 in a special issue of *Vesy*, one of the most prestigious literary journals of the day, and later as a separate volume that became a best seller, *Wings* sought to demonstrate that for people who are homosexually inclined it is better to accept their orientation, making it a part of a productive and satisfying life, than to reject and fight it. This presupposition also underlies much of Kuzmin's poetry. In this sense, his last collection, which so shocked Akhmatova, did not "exceed" any boundaries that had not already been crossed in all his other writings, beginning with the earliest. Nor is the treatment of the homosexual theme in *The Trout Breaks through the Ice* and Kuzmin's other collections any more or less explicit than it is, for example, in the "Calamus" section of Walt Whitman's *Leaves of Grass* (a book which Akhmatova much admired in Kornei Chukovsky's translation) or in the cycles *Parallèlement* and *Hombres* of Paul Verlaine (surely it was Verlaine whom Akhmatova must have compared with Kuzmin, since Villon did not write on homosexual themes). Furthermore, graphic descriptions of male homosexuality are to be found in the poetry of Kuzmin's contemporary, Nikolai Klyuev, a poet who lost his freedom and eventually his life because of a poem he wrote in defense of Akhmatova (a line from which appears as an epigraph in her *Poem without a Hero*) and of whom she has written with warmth in her memoir of Osip Mandelstam.

Could Akhmatova have really forgotten the liberalized air of that last prerevolutionary decade, when all sorts of previously unmentionable themes—social, religious, political, and sexual—had become acceptable for literary treatment? The content of Kuzmin's love lyrics did not prevent poets as diverse as Annensky, Blok, Khlebnikov, and Tsvetaeva from

---

³ Ibid., 166.

regarding him as one of the greatest poets of their time. The only major poet of that period who chose to make an issue in print of Kuzmin's homosexuality was Gumilyov, who in 1912, in his review of *Autumnal Lakes* (written while he was still married to Akhmatova), complimented Kuzmin on being what in the parlance of the 1970s would have been called "a spokesman for Russia's gay community."[4]

As for Vyacheslav Ivanov—whose collection *Cor ardens*, published one year before Kuzmin's *Nets*, contained a whole section ("Eros") inspired by Ivanov's own homosexual experiences—he was surely the least likely person to have acted as Kuzmin's censor. Akhmatova may not have known Vyacheslav Ivanov's journal for 1906, where Kuzmin is described as a pioneer of the future age of sexual tolerance,[5] but she must have been aware that Kuzmin had shared a residence for a number of years with Ivanov and, until her untimely death, with Ivanov's wife Lidiya Zinovieva-Annibal, a fiction writer who specialized in the theme of lesbian love.

Akhmatova's statement on Kuzmin recorded by Chukovskaya, on which I have dwelt at such length, is important in two ways. It is a key to the genesis of Akhmatova's own much-admired but often misunderstood poetic masterpiece *Poem without a Hero* (*Poema bez geroia*), which is in essence her response to Kuzmin's *The Trout Breaks through the Ice* and possibly also to his earlier novel *Travelers by Sea and Land* (*Plavaiushchie-puteshestvuiushchie*, 1915).[6] It is also indicative, in general, of the extent to which Kuzmin's role in prerevolutionary cultural life and the reception of his work by his contemporaries have been forgotten and his writings unread in postrevolutionary times.

In his essay on Kuzmin's poetry included in the edition under review, Vladimir Markov makes abundantly clear that everything printed

---

4 "Kuzmin occupies one of the most important places among the contemporary Russian poets. Very few are able to achieve such astounding harmoniousness of the whole [combined] with such free variety of the component parts. Furthermore, being a spokesman for the views and emotions of a whole array of people, united by a common culture, who have quite justly risen to the crest of life's wave, Kuzmin is a poet with organic roots (*pochvennyi poet*)." N. Gumilev, *Sobranie sochinenii*, vol. 4 (Washington, D.C., 1968), 307; originally in *Apollon*, 1912, no. 8.

5 Viacheslav Ivanov, *Sobranie sochinenii*, vol. 2 (Brussels, 1974), 750. Kuzmin appears in this diary under the name of "Antinous."

6 See R. D. Timenchik, V. N. Toporov, and T. V. Tsiv'ian, "Akhmatova i Kuzmin," *Russian Literature*, July 1978, 213–305, for a detailed examination of the literary relationship between these two poets.

about Kuzmin in literary histories, encyclopedias, and textbooks, from the 1930s to this day, is misleading, wrong, or incomplete. Kuzmin is often listed as an Acmeist poet, which he never was. His best or most important works are usually said to be the verse cycles *Alexandrian Songs* and *Chimes of Love* (*Kuranty liubvi*) and the essay "On Beautiful Clarity," which, in terms of his overall achievement, is comparable to saying that Tolstoi's most important works are *Childhood* and *Sevastopol Stories*. A wide-ranging poet whose output encompasses important historical, metaphysical, and mystical themes, as well as erotic, humorous, and light verse, Kuzmin is invariably dismissed as a frivolous hedonist who was able to write only of trivia and trifles.[7] His three major collections of verse that were published in the 1920s constitute about one-half of his total poetic output by volume and represent some of his most serious and original work. Until now, however, they have remained unnoticed by literary scholars and historians.

Coming as it does after some four decades of critical and popular neglect of Kuzmin, the new edition of his complete poetry prepared by John E. Malmstad and Vladimir Markov produces the impression of a wide gate suddenly flung open onto a whole new country, partly forgotten and partly unexplored. A slow and careful reading of the seven major collections[8] leaves one astounded at the scope and variety of this supposedly "graceful minor poet" (Renato Poggioli's term for Kuzmin). The unprecedented precision and intimacy with which Kuzmin's poetry of 1906–8 reflected life, its insistence on the concrete beauty of our world and the joys of here and now, which so struck his contemporaries, began alternating already in the later sections of *Nets* with mystical insights derived from Kuzmin's study of Gnosticism as well as from his Old Believer heritage. This alternation continued in his later work, and its persistence makes mincemeat out of all critical attempts to fit Kuzmin into either the Acmeist or the Symbolist mold. Aleksandr Blok was neither whimsical nor paradoxical when he

---

[7] A typical example of this kind of uninformed treatment of Kuzmin is found in Renato Poggioli, *The Poets of Russia 1890–1930* (Cambridge, MA, 1960).

[8] Kuzmin's major collections are *Nets*, *Autumnal Lakes*, *Clay Doves* (*Glinianye golubki*, ca. 1915), *The Guide* (*Vozhatyi*, 1918), *Otherworldly Evenings* (*Nezdeshnie vechera*, 1923), *Parabolas* (*Paraboly*, 1923), and *The Trout Breaks through the Ice*. The edition under review also contains six lesser collections of verse published by Kuzmin, his verse play for puppets, *Tuesday at Mary's* (*Vtornik Meri*, 1921), and, in vol. 3, a large number of previously uncollected or unpublished poems.

saw the roots of Kuzmin's art in "the awakening of the Russian Schism, in the dark religious forebodings of fifteenth-century Russia, in the memory of the trans-Volga *startsy* (elders) who would come out of obscure marsh bogs into squat, smoke-filled peasant huts."[9]

An aspect of Kuzmin not found in other poets of his time is his habit of organizing his lyric poetry into cycles with easily discernible plots, which results in a hybrid genre that combines the features of the traditional lyric with those of a narrative *poema*. This is the form in which much of his autobiographical poetry is couched. It culminates in the remarkable novellas in verse of *The Trout Breaks through the Ice*, which belong among the finest examples of Russian twentieth-century narrative poetry. Kuzmin is a master of a variety of larger narrative verse structures, such as the remarkably beautiful *Cavalier* (*Vsadnik*) (included in *Autumnal Lakes*), which was surely the point of departure of Marina Tsvetaeva's epic poems *On a Red Steed* and *Tsar-Maiden*; the extended ode in free verse, "The Hostile Sea" ("Vrazhdebnoe more"), written in 1917 and dedicated to Vladimir Mayakovsky, which mingled Homeric themes with the mood of Russian revolution; or the visionary and surrealistic longer poems of the last two collections.

The Malmstad-Markov three-volume edition shows us the full stature of the poet Kuzmin, with all his stylistic and metrical virtuosity, verbal elegance, cultural range, and spiritual depth. But the two editors have done a great deal more than assemble the corpus of Kuzmin's poetry. John E. Malmstad's "Mikhail Kuzmin: A Chronicle of His Life and Times" occupies three hundred twelve pages in the third volume. It is not an introductory essay, but rather a substantial, full-scale, critical biography which also happens to be one of the very finest biographies of a twentieth-century Russian poet that we have. Kuzmin was a central figure in the literary life of his day as well as a friend or associate of many important writers and poets. He was also deeply involved in the worlds of music, art, and the theater. Among the dramatis personae of his biography were his school friend Georgy Chicherin (the future famous diplomat), Blok and Diaghilev, Meyerhold and Komissarzhevskaya, and the painters Sapunov and Sudeikin. It was an exciting and eventful life, and John E. Malmstad reconstructs it with sympathy and erudition. Its bilingual format (the nu-

---

9   Aleksandr Blok, *Sobranie sochinenii* (Moscow and Leningrad, 1960–63), 5:183.

merous citations of Russian texts are left untranslated) limits the number of potential readers of this excellent biography. It would be a shame if it were not eventually published as a separate book and thus made available to the general reading public.[10]

Every bit as impressive is Vladimir Markov's one-hundred-four-page critical appreciation of Kuzmin's poetry, "Poeziia Mikhaila Kuzmina" (also in the third volume). Markov has set himself the difficult and usually thankless task of demonstrating that a literary figure whom most critics have come to regard as peripheral or minor is actually an unfairly neglected major poet. His assertion and demonstration of the value of Kuzmin's poetry is a model of lucid and logical literary argument. The two editors provided the entire corpus with detailed annotations, which display an admirable command of the diverse cultural spheres reflected in Kuzmin's poetry.

At a ceremony in honor of Kuzmin's birthday in 1920, the speakers included, inter alios, Aleksandr Blok, Nikolai Gumilyov, Boris Eikhenbaum, and Viktor Shklovsky. In his speech, Blok expressed a wish that conditions be created in the future such that a literary artist as unique as Kuzmin would have the right "to remain himself."[11] We know that things did not turn out as Blok had wished, and that, after Soviet culture took the form it did, the mere fact of Kuzmin's sexual orientation contributed to reducing an admired poet to a pariah and a nonperson, so that even a poet of Akhmatova's stature and independence was able to turn against him with puritanical vindictiveness and depict him in *Poem without a Hero* as an evil demon responsible for bringing on cultural decline.[12] The new publication of his complete poetry, combined with the important critical contributions by John E. Malmstad and Vladimir Markov, should help restore Kuzmin to his rightful place among the foremost Russian poets of the twentieth century.

---

[10] Malmstad later collaborated with a Kuzmin specialist in Moscow on a revision of his original text: John E. Malmstad and Nikolay Bogomolov, *Mikhail Kuzmin: A Life in Art* (Cambridge, MA: Harvard University Press, 1999).—Ed.

[11] Blok, *Sobranie sochinenii*, 6:440.

[12] The authors of an otherwise fine and informative study, "Akhmatova i Kuzmin" (see note 6 above), jeopardize their scholarly probity by their occasional moralizing attempts to justify Akhmatova's later aversion to Kuzmin by referring to the latter's supposed misogyny and amorality. Their strictures, when placed next to John E. Malmstad's informed and sympathetic biography, make instructive reading.

***

In later years, SK wrote frequently about Kuzmin for the gay press. His review of Michael Green's English translation of selected prose writings (including *Wings*) and poetry by Kuzmin is of particular interest and is included in Simon Karlinsky, "Gay Life before the Soviets: Revisionism Revised," *Advocate*, 1 April 1982, 31–34. See also his entry on Kuzmin in *Gay Histories and Cultures: An Encyclopedia*, ed. George E. Haggerty (New York: Garland Publishing, 2000), 526–27.

Among SK's translations of Russian poetry is the following love lyric by Kuzmin:

> Nine delightful birthmarks
> I count with my kisses
> And as I count them, I read
> A mystery, sweeter than heavenly mysteries.
> On your cheeks, on your dear neck,
> On your chest, where your heart is beating—
> That which is darker than musk
> Will not be erased by kisses.
> Thus, over the heavenly staircase,
> As I tell the beads of caresses,
> I shall reach the gates of paradise
> Of your miraculous beauty.
> Now, that eighth birthmark
> Is the most precious one in the world,
> Sweeter than the shade in sultry summer
> And lovelier than the breeze in May.
> And when I reach the ninth one
> I no longer bother counting,
> I simply melt, I melt, I melt,
> Enveloped in a tender flame.
>
> —From *Clay Doves*, ca. 1915[13]

In the late 1970s and the 1980s SK took up the cause of a young contemporary poet who was strongly influenced by Russia's homosexual poets of the

---

13 Simon Karlinsky, trans., "Three Russian Poets," in *Gay Roots: Twenty Years of Gay Sunshine*, ed. Winston Leyland (San Francisco: Gay Sunshine Press, 1991), 652.

early twentieth century such as Mikhail Kuzmin and Nikolai Klyuev. Gennady Trifonov (1945–2011) was unabashedly gay and delineated his homosexual experiences in his lyric poetry. It is hardly surprising that he was not allowed to publish and, indeed, in 1976 was sentenced to four years of incarceration for homosexuality (*muzhelozhestvo*, article 121 of the Soviet criminal code), hooliganism, and dissident activities. SK's several articles about this young man and translations of his poetry were important in drawing attention in the West to Trifonov's plight. Among them were Simon Karlinsky, "The Case of Gennady Trifonov," *Christopher Street*, January 1979, 65–66; Simon Karlinsky, "The Case of Gennady Trifonov," *New York Review of Books*, 10 April 1986, 44; and Simon Karlinsky, "The Soviet Union vs. Gennady Trifonov," *Advocate*, 19 August 1986, 42–49. Upon release from prison in 1980, Trifonov was forced to eke out an existence for himself and his mother by manual labor and lived in fear of rearrest. By 1998, however, he was being published in a few journals in Leningrad and was soon allowed to travel abroad. His improved situation undoubtedly was at least partially caused by the pressure of international opinion, in which SK played no small role.

Nikolai Gumilyov and Théophile Gautier[1]

> И не одно сокровище, быть может,
> Минуя внуков, к правнукам уйдет,
> И снова скальд чужую песню сложит
> И как свою ее произнесет.[2]
>
> —Osip Mandelstam, 1914

Revival of poets condemned by the poetics of the preceding decades was a prominent feature of the Russian Silver Age. That was the time when Vladimir Solovyov rehabilitated Fet, that bête noire of the radical utilitarians (Lev Tolstoi and Chaikovsky may have loved Fet's poetry, but the entire dynasty of nineteenth-century *vlastiteli dum*,[3] from Belinsky to Mikhailovsky, never tired of mocking and reviling it). Sergei Andreevsky rescued Baratynsky from Belinsky's curse. Bryusov brought Karolina Pavlova back from near-total obscurity, and Aleksandr Blok, in his remarkable essay "Sud'ba Apollona Grigor'eva" (The fate of Apollon Grigoriev), saw the poet and critic Grigoriev as the "only bridge that unites us with Pushkin and Griboedov—a flimsy [bridge] suspended over the terrifying precipice of intellectual stagnation (*bezvremen'e*)."[4]

The one prominent exception among the senior Symbolists was Zinaida Gippius, whose abiding sympathy for Belinsky, Chernyshevsky, and Pisarev was motivated by her radical politics; her misguided contempt for Chekhov; her animosity (for intimate personal reasons) toward Diaghilev

---

[1] Originally published as "Nikolai Gumilev and Théophile Gautier" in *Cultural Mythologies of Russian Modernism: From the Golden Age to the Silver Age*, ed. Boris Gasparov, Robert P. Hughes, and Irina Paperno (Berkeley: University of California Press, 1992), 327–36.

[2] "And not just one treasure, perhaps, / Passing grandsons by, will go on to great-grandsons, / And anew a skald will arrange another's song / And deliver it as though it were his own."—Ed.

[3] So-called intellectual authorities.—Ed.

[4] Aleksandr Blok, *Sobranie sochinenii v vos'mi tomakh*, vol. 5 (Moscow and Leningrad, 1962), 513–14.

and the developments in the visual arts launched by *Mir iskusstva* (World of Art); and her aversion to the early productions of the Moscow Art Theater, which she saw as the theatrical equivalent of Diaghilev's aesthetics.[5] But many Postsymbolist poets sided with Diaghilev and Blok on the subject of nineteenth-century radical-utilitarian *vlastiteli dum*.

Examples extend all the way from Gumilyov's 1910 essay "Zhizn' stikha," where he lauded Russian Symbolism for "defending cultural values subjected to rough treatment [by writers] from Pisarev to Gorky" and for "instilling in the savages of the Russian press if not respect for great names and ideas, then at least a fear of them"[6]—to Vladislav Khodasevich's 1938 defense of Vladimir Nabokov's novel *Dar* (The gift). Khodasevich foresaw that the novel's jaundiced view of the Russian literary critics of the 1860s, shown in parodistic and grotesque terms in chapter 3 of *Dar*, "will undoubtedly cause the author many troubles. All the disciples and admirers of the progressive mental police that oversaw Russian literature since the forties of the last century are sure to become infuriated. Their hegemony is not yet quite over and they are sure now to soar over the author of *Dar* in a classical swarm of newspaper gadflies and mosquitoes."[7] Like his senior Symbolist contemporaries, Nikolai Gumilyov also undertook the rehabilitation of a poet rejected and reviled by the votaries of nineteenth-century utilitarianism, only in this case the poet whose champion Gumilyov became was not a Russian one, but the French Romantic Théophile Gautier (1811–72).

Romantic poetry appeared in France later than it did in Germany, England, or Russia. Poems with clear Romantic features were published by Lamartine and Hugo in the 1820s, but it was the turbulent opening night of Hugo's *Hernani* on 25 February 1830 that gained for the poets of the Romantic movement their general recognition. The nineteen-year-old Théophile Gautier, who had not yet published anything of note, was a prominent presence at that riotous opening night, with his long hair and wearing a vest of scarlet red velvet, the vest that became his trademark in the popular imagination, comparable to Vincent van Gogh's amputated ear or Mayakovsky's blouse of yellow necktie silk. As Gautier was to note

---

[5] Zinaida Gippius, *Zhivye litsa*, vol. 2 (Prague, 1925; repr. Munich, 1971), 158–59.

[6] N. Gumilev, *Sobranie sochinenii v chetyrekh tomakh* (Washington: V. Kamkin, 1962–68), 4:169–70.

[7] Vladislav Khodasevich, "*Sovremennye zapiski*, kn. 66-aia," *Vozrozhdenie* (Paris), 24 June 1938, 4–5.

at the end of his life: "That red vest! I wore it only once and yet I'm dressed in it all my life. Our poetry, our books, our essays, our travelogues will be forgotten, but our red vests will be remembered."[8]

Trying to pinpoint the nature of Gautier's Romanticism, Maurice Bouvier-Ajam found that the one common denominator which united Gautier with other French Romantics, Parnassians and even the early Symbolists (e.g., Baudelaire) was that they all rejected the literature and the poetics of the long reign of Louis XIV (1643–1715).[9] Recoil from neoclassical poetics of the seventeenth and eighteenth centuries was, of course, typical of the Romantic movements in various countries, but in Russia, for example, the poets of Pushkin's time could jettison Sumarokov and Kheraskov while continuing to admire Fonvizin, Knyazhnin, and Derzhavin. In France, things were more sweeping: there was the tremendous authority of Boileau, revered from the end of the seventeenth to the first third of the nineteenth century, to be overthrown. And there had been a swarm of splendid poets, from Villon and Charles d'Orléans in the early fifteenth century to Ronsard and Saint-Amant, to free, as Gumilyov put it, "from the curse laid on them by Boileau" and to restore to their earlier luster. This is precisely what Gautier, following the example of Charles Sainte-Beuve, did in his *Les grotesques* (1844).

The parallels between the revolt against the radical-utilitarian domination in which Acmeist poets followed the Symbolist example and the clearly similar revolution in aesthetics whereby the young Gautier and other French Romantics overthrew the neoclassical and rationalistic dogma codified by Boileau were sufficient reason for Gumilyov to regard Gautier as a kindred spirit. But there were other affinities that united these two poets across the eight decades that separated their respective formulations of their literary theories. Unlike his one-time classmate and close friend, Gérard de Nerval, Gautier had no interest in Romantic mysticism. He expressed this in his oft-cited motto, "I am one of those for whom the exterior world exists," a statement borne out by his poetry, if not by certain of his novels.

---

8   Cited by René Jasinski in *Europe* (Paris), no. 601 (May 1979), 4. This special issue devoted to Gautier contains, inter alios, René Jasinski, "Situation de Théophile Gautier"; Maurice Bouvier-Ajam, "Le romantisme de Théophile Gautier"; Jacques Gaucheron, "Ombres et lueur de l'art pour l'art"; Serge Fauchereau, "Où Pound et Eliot recontrent Goumilev, Mandelstam et Akhmatova"; and Russell S. King, "*Émaux et camées*: sculptures et objets-paysages."
9   Maurice Bouvier-Ajam in *Europe*, no. 601, 25ff.

Gautier also shunned all political involvement. In the 1833 preface to his narrative poem *Albertus* (the first two stanzas of which were brilliantly rendered into Russian by Gumilyov in his essay on Gautier) the French poet stated that "[the author of this book] has no political coloring; he is neither red, nor white, nor even tricolored; he is none of these and he takes notice of revolutions only when their bullets break his windows."[10] After the compulsory politicization of Russian criticism in the second half of the nineteenth century, this must have seemed like a fresh breeze in the second decade of the twentieth. Like Gumilyov, Gautier traveled to remote areas in search of romantically picturesque visual impressions. He, too, saw the task of any artist, including a poet, in wrestling with the inert matter of this world until it yields a new kind of beauty (compare his programmatic poem "L'art," which concludes *Émaux et camées*, with Paul Verlaine's vastly different "Art poétique"). But even apart from ideological or aesthetic considerations, it would be hard to think of another earlier figure who embodied the Acmeist ideal, as expressed in Gumilyov's theoretical writings, as closely as did Gautier.

During his lifetime and at the time of his death in 1872, the position of Gautier in the French literary pantheon seemed secure. His plays and ballets with his scenarios were performed, his novels and travelogues were read and admired, Hector Berlioz and other composers set his poetry to music, and his most comprehensive collection of verse, *Émaux et camées*, went through six editions between 1852 and 1872. In 1857, Charles Baudelaire dedicated his *Fleurs du mal* to Gautier, calling him "the impeccable poet," "the perfect magician of French literature" and "my very dear and very venerated teacher and friend." In the memorial volume *Le tombeau de Théophile Gautier*, brought out after the poet's death, we find contributions by several generations of French writers, ranging from Victor Hugo's homage, "À Théophile Gautier," which is virtually a history of the French Romantic movement and of Gautier's role in it, to Stéphane Mallarmé's much-anthologized "Toast funèbre."

But within a decade or two, Gautier's reputation suffered a precipitous decline in his native country. Turn-of-the-century French critics, such as Émile Faguet, Ferdinand Brunetière, and Gustave Lanson found Gautier

---

[10] Cited by Claudine Gothot-Mersch in Théophile Gautier, *Émaux et camées* (Paris: Gallimard, 1981), 9, and by Jacques Gaucheron in *Europe*, no. 601, 80.

minor, obsolete, "a poet who entered literature with absolutely nothing to say" (Faguet's formulation, which will be more than familiar to any student of Russian nineteenth- or twentieth-century literature). In the first decade of the twentieth century, Gautier was remembered in France chiefly as the author of *Capitaine Fracasse*, a novel considered suitable to be read by schoolchildren. As a poet, he was given credit for his ability "to copy, without thought or emotion, fragments of the surrounding world that he happened to experience"[11]—a description that repeats with hallucinatory precision the judgments published in the 1880s by Skabichevsky and Mikhailovsky about the writings of the man they called "Gospodin Chekhov."

In the 1930s, with a renewed interest in the Romantic age, Théophile Gautier's oeuvre began making the comeback that gradually restored it to the position it deserves. In 1979 the French literary monthly *Europe*, founded by Romain Rolland, which had earlier devoted special issues to such luminaries as Mozart, Mikhail Sholokhov, Voltaire, Shakespeare, Maksim Gorky and Nazim Hikmet, among others, brought out an excellent collection of Gautier studies, which included Serge Fauchereau's essay on Gautier's impact on the American Imagists and Russian Acmeists. For, decades before the French reclaimed Gautier, he was taken up almost simultaneously by the Anglo-American Imagists and in Russia by Mikhail Kuzmin, the presiding spirit of Acmeism, and Nikolai Gumilyov, its most vocal theoretician.

As Clarence Brown put it in his book on Osip Mandelstam, "the fact is that some four or five years earlier [than 1917, i.e., ca. 1912], and apparently independently of each other, Gumilyov and his associates on the one hand, and [Ezra] Pound and [T. E.] Hulme and their associates, on the other, had invented or reinvented more or less the same thing. The points of similarity between the goals of the Anglo-American Imagists and those of the Russian Acmeists are so striking that they tease the mind almost intolerably. They had rediscovered the viability in their own age of the kind of poetry advocated by Théophile Gautier—whom both Pound and Gumilyov, incidentally, explicitly hailed as their preceptor."[12] Gautier's impact on the poetry of Pound and, especially, T. S. Eliot has been

---

11 Dismissive turn-of-the-century views on Gautier cited by Jasinski, *Europe*, no. 601, 12–13.
12 Clarence Brown, *Mandelstam* (Cambridge: Cambridge University Press, 1973), 137.

exhaustively demonstrated by René Taupin.[13] Edmund Wilson[14] and Serge Fauchereau[15] have drawn on Taupin's findings.

The Russian rediscovery of Gautier seems to predate the Anglo-American one. Sergei Diaghilev, Aleksandr Benois and other members of the World of Art group were deeply involved with Gautier, as can be seen from the programs of the first Diaghilev ballet seasons in Paris. In 1909, the company made its debut with *Le pavillon d'Armide*, a ballet whose scenario Benois based on a *conte* by Gautier. In 1910, Diaghilev repatriated the ballet with Gautier's most famous scenario, *Giselle*, to France after its many years of exile in Russia. Next year came *Le spectre de la rose*, with a plot credited to Jean-Louis Vaudoyer, yet actually based on a poem by Gautier that had been earlier set to music by Hector Berlioz.[16] (Berlioz's *Les nuits d' été*, op. 7, no. 2, "Le spectre de la rose," is a setting of a poem from Gautier's *La comédie de la mort*.)

It was that same year, 1911, that Nikolai Gumilyov published his essay on Gautier, accompanied by his translations into Russian of four Gautier poems. They appeared in the prestigious art journal *Apollon* (no. 9). In the essay, Gumilyov praised not only Gautier's formal perfection, but also his "boundless Rabelaisian merriment" and his "wildly joyous thinking."[17] "The secret of Gautier is not that he is perfect, but that he is powerful—like Rabelais, like Nimrod, like a big and brave beast of the forest," Gumilyov wrote. Among the poems by Gautier which Gumilyov translated to accompany this essay were the programmatic "L'art," with its assertion that "L'art robuste / Seul a l'éternité"; and "L'hippopotame" (from Gautier's *Poésies diverses*) which asserts the poet's total independence from all current opinion, and which was later developed and expanded by T. S. Eliot into his anticlerical "The Hippopotamus."[18]

---

[13] René Taupin, *L'influence du symbolisme français sur la poésie américaine (de 1910 à 1920)* (Paris: H. Champion, 1929), in particular 134, 135, and 155–58 on Pound and 236–40 on Eliot.

[14] Edmund Wilson, *Axel's Castle: A Study in the Imaginative Literature of 1870–1930* (New York: C. Scribner's Sons, 1931), 98–99.

[15] Serge Fauchereau in *Europe*, no. 601.

[16] John Percival, *The World of Diaghilev* (New York: E. P. Dutton, 1971), 136–37; Boris Kochno, *Diaghilev and the Ballets Russes* (New York: Harper & Row, 1970), 24, 48, and 60.

[17] Gumilev, *Sobranie sochinenii*, 4:386–94.

[18] Ibid., 1:189–95; Taupin, *L'influence du symbolisme*, 238–40.

The apex of Gumilyov's involvement with Gautier came with the publication in 1914 of his translation of the complete text of Gautier's most comprehensive collection of verse, *Émaux et camées*. His later essay on translating verse postulated a number of basic requirements that must be met: reproduction of the meter and the rhyme scheme of the original, finding the appropriate vocabulary in the target language, keeping the same number of lines, etc.[19] He said nothing about preserving the imagery of the original, and this is the area where Gumilyov's translations make some very drastic departures from Gautier's originals.

The volume as a whole is a remarkable labor of love. Some of the poems, such as "Premier sourire du printemps," "Rondalla," "Bûchers et tombeaux," "Le souper des armures" and "Dernier vœu" have been rendered into Russian with astounding fidelity, preserving both the form and the tone of the originals. But some of Gumilyov's versions are flawed. The blemishes come in the following varieties: (1) incomprehension of French (there are very few of these, but they are spectacular); (2) introduction of new ideas or imagery not found in Gautier; (3) passages that emerge as comical in Russian but were dead serious in French; and (4) misinterpreting references to music or opera (Gautier worked for decades as a music critic; Gumilyov had no expertise in this area, though he must have consulted someone because some of the musical terminology was translated correctly).

Among the failures to understand the text, three may be cited. In the introductory sonnet that opens the collection, Gautier alludes to Goethe's *West-östlicher Divan*, where the song of the hoopoe is mentioned. Gautier cited from Goethe the Persian name of this bird, *Hudhud* (apparently related etymologically to the Russian *udod*). Gumilyov mistook this Persian bird for a woman's proper name and translated the line as "Pel o Gudut, zhivushchei siro" (Sang of Gudut and her lonely life).[20] In the poem "Impéria," about an Italian sixteenth-century courtesan, Gautier imagined as one of her pastimes wild outings on horseback with a group of bohemian friends:

> Courses folles dans les bohèmes
> Sur le dos des coursiers sans frein.

---

19 Gumilev, *Sobranie sochinenii*, 4:190–96.
20 Cf. Gautier, *Émaux*, 25, and Teofil' Got'e, *Emali i kamei*, trans. N. Gumilev (St. Petersburg: M. V. Popov, 1914), 5.

Gumilyov must have read *bohème* as *bohémien*, "Gypsy," because he translated these lines most poetically but incorrectly as:

> Езда на лошади цыганской,
> На дикой лошади равнин
>
> (Riding a Gypsy horse,
> The savage horse of the plains).[21]

Finally, the most amazing misreading is found in the poem "La mansarde," which ends with a portrait of an old woman with a gaunt profile who is scolding her kitten:

> Et l'on ne voit contre la vitre
> Qu'une vieille au maigre profil,
> Devant Minet, qu'elle chapitre.

Gumilyov somehow mistook the usual nickname for French kittens, Minet, for an Orthodox calendar of saints, and replaced Gautier's rather cozy picture with a very grim one indeed:

> И за окошком все страшнее
> Старуха тощая молчит,
> Погружена в Четьи–Минеи
>
> (And beyond the window, ever more terrifying,
> The gaunt old woman remains silent,
> Engrossed in her Calendar of Saints).[22]

Imagery not present in Gautier is strewn about liberally by Gumilyov, a procedure that Vladimir Nabokov once condemned as *otsebiatina* (roughly "adding one's own stuff"). Nabokov even coined a new English verb from this well-known Russian term, "to otsebiatinate." In the poem "Ce que disent les hirondelles," the Hajjis (i.e., Moslems who have made

---

[21] Gautier, *Émaux*, 33, and Got'e, *Emali*, 23.
[22] Gautier, *Émaux*, 134, and Got'e, *Emali*, 218.

a pilgrimage to Mecca) count their amber prayer beads in Gautier, but Gumilyov has them play a game of checkers instead:

> Хаджи играют в шашки мирно,
> С ногами сидя на софе.

In the second stanza of "La rose-thé," a butterfly alights on the rosebush. Gumilyov turns it into a nightingale, which then bursts into song, something a butterfly couldn't do. What's more, Gumilyov smuggles a line from Tyutchev into this stanza: the rose listens to the nightingale's love song, "Vnimaia povesti liubovnoi" (Tyutchev had "Vnimaet povesti liubimoi"; there are also instances of Pushkin lines slipped into Gautier in other poems).

Moments of unintended comedy occur when Gumilyov deprives of dignity the historical personages whom Gautier treated with reverence. In the prefatory sonnet, Goethe withdraws from the turmoil of the Napoleonic wars to seclude himself and write his *West-östlicher Divan*:

> Comme Goethe sur son divan
> À Weimer s'isolait des choses.

Gumilyov changes that divan into an actual piece of furniture, *takhta*, to which the aged German poet rushes (and on which he possibly even leaps) quite indecorously:

> Как Гете на свою тахту
> В Веймаре убегал от прозы.

And in the poem about the old veterans of Napoleon's campaigns, "Vieux de la vieille," where Gautier had the ghost of the emperor review the ghosts of his soldiers who perished at Austerlitz, Gumilyov undermines the image by dressing Napoleon in incongruous civilian garb:

> Где Император на параде
> Проходит в шляпе и пальто
>
> (Where the emperor at the parade
> Passes by in hat and coat).

Gumilyov got into difficulties about music and musical terminology in two specific instances. One was his rendition of the poem "Contralto," Gautier's homage to the voice of his common-law wife, the singer Ernesta Grisi.[23] Gumilyov's one real failure in the collection is the sequence of four poems, called jointly "Variations sur le Carnaval de Venise." Almost all the poems in *Émaux et camées* are written in French octosyllabic verse with cross rhymes that alternate feminine and masculine endings, which Gumilyov quite appropriately conveyed with the familiar Russian iambic tetrameter. But the lines of the "Carnaval de Venise" poems, especially the second one, "Sur les lagunes," also suggest the popular barrel organ melody which serves as the theme for the cycle, the song known in most Western languages as "The Carnival of Venice," except in German, where it is called "Mein Hut der hat drei Ecken." The tune is hummable to a French octosyllabic line with a feminine ending, but there is no way to fit into it lines of Russian iambic tetrameter, which is what Gumilyov offers. To fit this tune to a Russian meter would require an amphibrachic trimeter with a truncated first foot:

$$\smile - \circ \;/\; \smile - \smile \;/\; \smile - \smile$$

Nor did Gumilyov manage to preserve the imagery of the second poem of the cycle, particularly of the two passages that Oscar Wilde cited in *The Picture of Dorian Gray* as the quintessential verbal reflections of the visual impression produced by Venice. In the first of these citations, the all-important musical image, "Sur une gamme chromatique," is replaced by Gumilyov with a literary one, "V volnen'i legkogo razmera," while in the second fragment cited by Wilde,

> Devant une façade rose,
> Sur le marbre d'un escalier,

---

[23] See the detailed analysis of this particular poem and its handling by Gumilyov in S. Karlinsky, "Contralto: Rossini, Gautier and Gumilev," in *Language, Literature, Linguistics: In Honor of Francis J. Whitfield on His Seventieth Birthday, March 25, 1986*, ed. Michael S. Flier and Simon Karlinsky (Berkeley, 1987). [Reprinted in the present volume.]

the equally central image of marble was omitted by Gumilyov:

> Пред розовеющим фасадом
> Я прохожу ступеней ряд.²⁴

But all these shortcomings should not obscure the fact that Gumilyov's *Emali i kamei* is an astounding achievement. In the arts, if not in biology, one is free to select one's parents or ancestors. Whether it was a case of Goethean elective affinity or a Bakhtinian literary dialogue, Gumilyov constructed a monument to his love for and closeness to a French poet who died a decade and a half before Gumilyov was born and who was disdained in France throughout Gumilyov's life. This monument deserves to be read and studied more than it has been until now.

*　*　*

Among SK's first published reviews were those of the path-breaking edition in four volumes of the writings of Nikolai Gumilyov prepared in the 1960s by Gleb Struve and Boris Filippov. (Translations were not included.) His acute formulations of the stature of Gumilyov (who was executed by the new Bolshevik regime in August 1921) deserve to be cited:

> Although no work of his was reprinted in the Soviet Union since 1923, and although his name has been unmentionable in the Soviet press until very recently, Gumilyov has steadily continued to exercise an influence on the Russian poetry of the present century, both Soviet and émigré. Even those who are not attracted to the military and exotic themes of some of his poetry (Gumilyov's occasional showy heroics are similar to Kipling's bouts of manliness that irked Max Beerbohm and to the compulsive manly stance of Hemingway that Gertrude Stein saw fit to ridicule) have to recognize Gumilyov's work not only as the major phenomenon of Russian poetry that it is but also as an important fact of modern Russian sensibility.²⁵

---

24   Gautier, *Émaux*, 38, and Got'e, *Emali*, 36.
25   Simon Karlinsky, review of *Sobranie sochinenii v chetyrekh tomakh*, vol. 1, by Nikolai Gumilev, ed. G. P. Struve and B. A. Filippov (Washington: Kamkin, 1962), *Books Abroad* 37 (Autumn 1963): 471–72.

SK refined his opinions upon reading Gumilyov's more mature poetry:

> As Professor Struve points out in his lucid survey of Gumilyov's literary evolution, and as is amply illustrated by the poetry gathered in this second volume, there are several tenacious clichés about the nature of Gumilyov's work which in the light of his later and more mature poems no longer make sense. Gumilyov's own tragic and violent death generated a legend, nourished by the earlier poetry of adventure and exploration, Gumilyov as a purveyor of dashing heroic, and somewhat juvenile, poetry that was supposedly redeemed only by the poet's deliberate and precise craftsmanship.
>
> With all his lyric poetry gathered and perusable in its entirety, we see that the Gumilyov of the popular cliché represents only one aspect of this poet. Gumilyov the maître of the Acmeist school, with his championing of simple and direct poetic communication and his admiration for Théophile Gautier, also turns out to be a particular aspect or mask of this protean poet—although in this case the Acmeist image has been fostered by literary historians rather than by the popular legend. The startling new image that emerges after one reads the second volume of his collected works is that of Gumilyov the visionary neo-Symbolist mystic who tends to couch his visions in authentically surrealistic imagery. We have been aware of this side of Gumilyov because of one of his most famous and frequently anthologized poems, "The Lost Streetcar"; we can see now that this poem was not exceptional in his work, but that it represents a definite and major strain in the poetry Gumilyov wrote in the last five years of his life. Nor is this the only unexpected side of Gumilyov revealed by the second volume: there is an equally surprising orthodox religiosity; a gentle humor we do not usually associate with this poet; fine and subtle treatments of contemporary themes, as in the delightful brief novella in verse "When I Was in Love ..." (pp. 193–95). We owe a debt of gratitude to the editors of this volume for making us realize that Gumilyov was not only a brilliant poet, but a deep and many-sided one as well.[26]

---

[26] Simon Karlinsky, review of *Sobranie sochinenii*, vol. 2, by Nikolai Gumilev, ed. G. P. Struve and B. A. Filippov (Washington: Kamkin, 1964), *Books Abroad* 40 (Winter 1964): 106–7. SK went on to publish reviews of vols. 3 and 4 of this 4-volume edition of Gumilyov's collected writings: *Books Abroad* 41 (Autumn 1967): 480; and *Books Abroad* 43 (Spring 1969): 278–79.

An Emerging Reputation Comparable to Pushkin's[1]

For almost a quarter century after his death in a remote Siberian labor camp in 1938, Osip Mandelstam's name was consigned to oblivion in his own country. In the West he was vaguely remembered by a few scholars as one of the Acmeist poets who had rebelled against the mysticism of the Symbolists around 1910, a poet secondary in interest to such leading Acmeists as Anna Akhmatova and Nikolai Gumilyov and not to be compared in any meaningful way to such giants of twentieth-century Russian poetry as Aleksandr Blok or Vladimir Mayakovsky. Yet today Mandelstam is a tremendous cult figure in Soviet underground publications (*samizdat*), and the State Publishing House has just released a collection of his poems that has been repeatedly announced since 1959.[2] Articles about him are appearing in the West with increasing frequency, at least two major American universities are offering graduate seminars on his work, and the first full-scale biographical and critical study of him in English has just been published. Almost simultaneously, there has now appeared the second volume of the memoirs of Mandelstam's widow—whose passionate *Hope against Hope* was enthusiastically received here four years ago—and two comprehensive collections of his poetry in English translation.

---

1 Review of *Hope Abandoned*, by Nadezhda Mandelstam, trans. Max Hayward (New York: Atheneum, 1974); *Selected Poems*, by Osip Mandelstam, trans. Clarence Brown and W. S. Merwin (New York: Atheneum, 1974); *Complete Poetry of Osip Emilievich Mandelstam*, trans. Burton Raffel and Alla Burago (Albany: State University of New York Press, 1973); and *Mandelstam*, by Clarence Brown (New York: Cambridge University Press, 1973). Originally published in *New York Times Book Review*, 20 January 1974, 1, 10, 12.

2 O. Mandel'shtam, *Stikhotvoreniia*, ed. N. I. Khardzhiev, intro. by A. L. Dymshits (Leningrad: Sovetskii pisatel', 1973 [Biblioteka poeta, bol'shaia seriia]). Needless to say, there was a flood of editions and publications of Mandelstam's poetry and prose in late- and post-Soviet Russia. The editions prepared by Gleb Struve and Boris Filippov and published in the US (and mentioned by SK below) are widely acknowledged as pioneering efforts.—Ed.

It is all part of a momentous rediscovery and reevaluation, currently winning for this poet a reputation of towering proportions and generating among students and lovers of Russian poetry an excitement comparable to that of astronomers who are in the process of discovering that a minor outer planet is actually a solar system's second sun. Russian poetry's central sun—Aleksandr Pushkin—has been considered a figure without peer for a century and a half. Recently, a few brave voices have been raised here and there to suggest that in Mandelstam Russian poetry at last has a poet of a stature comparable to Pushkin's—a claim that even the most fanatical admirers of Blok, Mayakovsky, or Pasternak would not dream of making.

The phenomenon we now call Osip Mandelstam has been put together before our very eyes during the past eighteen years. The first post-Stalinist collection of Mandelstam's poetry and prose was brought out in 1955 (in New York, and in Russian) by Gleb Struve and Boris Filippov. It contained only what the poet had been able to publish during his lifetime—less than half of his output, as we now know. The early 1960s saw first a trickle, then a minor flood of unpublished Mandelstam manuscripts brought back by visiting Western scholars from the Soviet Union, manuscripts that had been carefully hidden and preserved by the poet's widow and a few loyal friends during the bleak years when the government was bent on obliterating all evidence that Osip Mandelstam had ever existed. By 1964, Struve and Filippov had enough material for an updated two-volume Mandelstam, which was in turn superseded by their three-volume edition, published between 1967 and 1971.

It is these hitherto unknown later works of Mandelstam—poetry written between 1930 (when he returned to writing verse after a five-year silence) and 1937, including the poems he wrote in his Voronezh exile just before being shipped off to a labor camp, the poems in which he reaches the probable peak of his lyric and visionary powers—that make him the awesome figure he is. They also enable us to see his early poetry in a revealing new light.

Osip Mandelstam grew up in St. Petersburg, in a cultivated Russian-Jewish family. The years that followed the unsuccessful Revolution of 1905 (when Mandelstam was fourteen) were an exciting time to be young. Poetry was scaling new heights; Russian literature, the visual arts, and political and philosophic thought were as free of governmental pressure and ideological harassment as they would ever be. The young Mandelstam studied philosophy, art history, and classical literature, and all these interests were reflected in his early poetry. His poems began appearing in the best literary journals of the time from 1910 on; his first collection of verse, *Stone* (1913), brought him instant recognition as one of Russia's finest young poets.

Accomplished and elegant technically, full of fresh perceptions, Mandelstam's early poetry was concerned with various aspects of human culture from the architecture of the Hagia Sophia to the cathedral of Notre Dame, from the music of Bach and Beethoven to silent movies and the choreography of a tennis game. Such references to history, literature, and the arts remained a frequent trait of Mandelstam's later poetry as well, and this preoccupation has led certain critics, both Russian and foreign, to see Mandelstam as a poet divorced from actual life. This was a charge brought against him by his Soviet detractors of the 1920s (who were wont to contrast him with the politically committed Mayakovsky), and we can discern an echo of those old denunciations in a recent American reference book, *Atlantic Brief Lives* (1971), where we read of Mandelstam's poetry that it "reflect[s] life in art and literature, rather than direct experience. Chiefly concerned with form and technique, it is impersonal and erudite."

Such a view of Mandelstam as some kind of Russian Parnassian is misguided. Like W. B. Yeats and Rainer Maria Rilke—two poets whom he equals in pure power and whose counterpart in Russian poetry he may well be—Mandelstam uses references to cultures of the past not to escape but to grasp and express his own sense of present reality. This is true of such an early masterpiece as the haunting "Solominka" (1916), in which the ghosts of Poe's and Balzac's heroines (Lenore, Ligeia, and Séraphita) float through the huge bedroom of a beautiful woman while "the twelve months are singing of the hour of death" and the room itself is gradually invaded by the black river Neva, the whole conveying the poet's sense of the doom and decay that pervaded the final years of the Russian empire.

In one of the very last poems Mandelstam ever wrote (no. 382 in the Struve-Filippov edition), ancient Egypt, "adorning itself in choice bitchery" and concerned primarily with the welfare of its corpses, whose "trifling pyramids still jut out," is strikingly contrasted with the sinful, imperfect, but infinitely more livable age in which that "insolent scholar and thieving angel," François Villon, could despise illusory "spidery civil rights" and create great humanistic poetry. This ostensible excursus into ancient and medieval history was written in March of 1937, during the building of the White Sea canal by Soviet slave labor and on the eve of the worst of Stalin's purges.

As early as 1916, Mandelstam had begun to expand his thematic and emotional range, and his poetry grew in depth and stature in the 1920s and 1930s. Though it has none of the outward trappings of novelty or innovation, Mandelstam's mature poetry is nevertheless totally unprecedented in both form and content. Its full originality and the acutely twentieth-century sensibility that underlies it reveal themselves fully only after repeated readings. Turns of phrase, epithets, images, or ideas that may at first appear familiar and clear turn out to be laden with fresh and rich meaning. One keeps returning to these poems month after month, year after year, always discovering new depths, new perspectives, new ambiguities that arise from some intangible substratum on which Mandelstam's poetry is built.

The postrevolutionary Mandelstam developed into a genuinely vatic poet, an observer and a barometer of his time, able to respond to the changes of his epoch with a kind of visceral totality and to predict future developments accurately in one unbearably beautiful poem after another—such as "Twilight of Freedom" (1918), "The Age" (1923), "Leningrad" (1930), "To the German Language" (1932), and the shattering "You're Still Alive" (1937). The work of Mandelstam's final years, when he was no longer allowed to publish anything and lived under constant threat of arrest, combines a tragic vision with a warmly expressed love of his country and his people and mingles a defiant defense of Western cultural traditions (his poems on Ariosto and Villon and his great, book-length poetic essay on Dante) with bursts of grateful joy at being alive and experiencing to the very last this world's beauty and radiance.

These final poems of Mandelstam are as good as anything in twentieth-century poetry, Russian or foreign. His stylistic range reaches from Pushkinian simplicity to visionary Surrealism and metalogical mutterings that bring to mind both García Lorca and William Blake; his thematic variety encompasses love lyrics, reflections on sharply observed contemporary Soviet reality, poems about the horror and despair of his own situation, historical and philosophical meditations, and vivid records of a multitude of visual experiences; and his verbal texture has a grandeur, richness, and density never before attained in Russian poetry, forcing one to turn for comparisons to Villon, Baudelaire and—well, all right—Shakespeare.

The cresting of the new wave of interest in Mandelstam's poetry among Western scholars coincided with the publication in 1970 of his wife's first volume of memoirs, *Hope against Hope*, which brought Mandelstam to the attention of many people, including some who are not usually concerned with poetry, Russian or otherwise. One of the most eloquent records of life under Stalin, *Hope against Hope* told the full story of how the outwardly gentle poet of iron inner integrity was hounded, ostracized, exiled, and finally destroyed. It is a book of great passion and immediacy which ought to be read not only by anyone interested in Mandelstam but by those who want to know what the first half of the twentieth century was really all about.

Nadezhda Mandelstam's new book, *Hope Abandoned*, is not, strictly speaking, a sequel to her first one. It is, rather, a retelling of the same events from a different point of view. The emphasis is now not on Mandelstam and on his wife's heroic and successful struggle to save his manuscripts from destruction, but rather on the author herself, her views and her opinions. The narrative sequence is again deliberately scrambled, and the writing manner is as flamboyantly virtuosic as in the first book. (Max Hayward's English translations of the two books, while conscientious and adequate, have unfortunately toned down the brilliance and verbal exuberance of Mandelstam's Russian style and eliminated her occasional flights of colorful vulgarity.)

But there is a new element: "In my old age, there awoke in me a woman convinced of her own infallibility," Nadezhda Mandelstam confesses at one point. It is this infallible woman who now sits in judgment not only over Mandelstam's enemies and persecutors, but over the whole of Russian twentieth-century culture both before and after the Revolution. The condemnation is sweeping and the verdict grim indeed. With an almost Tolstoyan recklessness, she lashes out at the good along with the bad: Symbolist and Futurist poets (including some about whom Mandelstam himself had written with great admiration), all of Russian Modernist painting, almost all of Soviet literature, the stage productions of Meyerhold, the films of Eisenstein, and the literary theories of Tynyanov. Even the poet Anna Akhmatova, the most loyal friend Mandelstam had, who in *Hope against Hope* emerged as a magnificently heroic figure, now comes in for her share of knocks, while every friend or associate Akhmatova ever had is invariably portrayed as either a predator or a silly puppet.

It is all too understandable humanly and, after what she's been through, Nadezhda Mandelstam is as entitled as anyone to her rages and aversions. Still and all, *Hope against Hope* was a marvelously gallant and generous book, and it is a pity this cannot be said of *Hope Abandoned*. Nadezhda Mandelstam nevertheless remains one of the finest and most informed commentators on Mandelstam's and Akhmatova's poetry. *Hope Abandoned* explains some of her husband's more difficult poems with an insight and authority no one else could match. (Mandelstam's memoir is available in Russian from Association Press in New York. Her long essay "Mozart and Salieri," published in English as a separate book in a sympathetic translation by Robert A. McLean,[3] is a meditation on Mandelstam and the nature of poetic creativity which clearly belongs with the literary commentary sections of *Hope Abandoned*, but was for some reason not included in the body of the book.)

Can Mandelstam's poetry be translated into another language? His verbal splendors, his deliberate ambiguities, the multiple levels of perception which his Russian conveys would seem to make the task of translating him almost superhuman. Yet Paul Celan has managed to transpose Mandelstam into German almost intact and there exist some astoundingly resourceful and faithful renditions of his poetry into Polish. Until now, Mandelstam has been far less fortunate in English.

Clarence Brown and W. S. Merwin's attractively turned-out volume *Selected Poems* comes closer to conveying the flavor of this poetry than any of its predecessors or competitors. Brown and Merwin have an affinity for Mandelstam, and they have matched his verbal elegance with an elegance of their own. Those able to read Mandelstam in Russian will miss the rich rainbow hues and the magnificent Wagnerian sonorities in these frequently austere and monochromatic renditions. At times there are problems of comprehension, but Mandelstam's limpid precision and his sharpness of focus are often very much there: "My animal, my age, who will ever be able / to look into your eyes? / Who will ever glue back together the vertebrae / of two centuries with his blood?"

The more ambitious *Complete Poetry* translated by Burton Raffel and Alla Burago is, regrettably, not likely to enhance anyone's understanding or appreciation of Mandelstam. At best, these translations manage to con-

---

[3] Nadezhda Mandelstam, *Mozart and Salieri* (Ann Arbor, MI: Ardis, 1973).

vey the basic meaning of the poems in plodding, unimaginative prose arranged on the page to look like verse and occasionally varied by pointless repetitions of words ("We drank mead there," turned into "We've drunk honey-wine there, we have, we have," is one such instance out of many). Again and again, however, Mandelstam's text has been read carelessly. For example, could this fastidious poet have written, in a poem that evokes romantic Scotland: "And hear, or seem to hear, crows and harps / Shouting back and forth, in ominous silence"? *Shouting* harps, doing their shouting *in silence*? In Russian these lines read: "And I seem to hear a raven and a harp / Calling to each other amidst an ominous stillness." What does the *persona* in the poem about Lamarck mean by "I'll wear a horny robe"? In Russian he was about to wrap himself in the corneous mantle of mollusks.

Non sequiturs, misread idioms, and garbled historical and literary references are all generously scattered throughout the volume. There are also a number of poems where Raffel and Burago clearly don't have the foggiest notion of what Mandelstam is saying from beginning to end (the poem about ancient Egypt and Villon, cited above, is one of these).

A reader who knows no Russian and is curious about Mandelstam's poetry and personality would be far better served by Clarence Brown's excellent critical and biographical study. The author of numerous essays and articles on Mandelstam and a translator of his prose and poetry, Clarence Brown (now professor of comparative literature at Princeton) first became involved with Mandelstam as a graduate student in the mid-1950s. He knows the poet's widow and his surviving friends. He knows as much about Mandelstam as anyone in the Western world and he has done more than anyone, with the possible exception of Gleb Struve and Boris Filippov, to spearhead appreciation in the West of the man he unequivocally calls the greatest modern Russian poet.

An intensely personal book, Brown's *Mandelstam* outlines all the known facts about the poet's life, drawing on and quoting numerous sources—memoirs, historical documents, letters—which until now were not available in English and mostly unknown even to specialists. Mandelstam's life and literary development are solidly placed in their historical framework and shown against the background of the brilliant period of poetic flowering which nurtured him and to which he so richly contributed. The significance of the city of St. Petersburg in Mandelstam's work, the theories of the Acmeist group, of which Mandelstam was one of the charter members, the poet's involvement with architecture and with the Greek and Latin classics—all these and numerous other pertinent topics are treated by Brown authoritatively and in depth.

Even more impressive is Brown's reading of the poetry itself. Drawing on his own background in modern English and American literature, Brown quite early in the book puts Mandelstam in the company of Yeats, Joyce, Wallace Stevens, Eliot, and Pound. The real proof of this claim lies in Brown's extensive examination of Mandelstam's works, period by period and sometimes poem by poem, and this adds up to a knowledgeable and wholly convincing demonstration of Mandelstam's international significance and stature.

Brown's analyses of individual poems—which include the Russian text, a verbatim English translation, and a detailed commentary and explication—contain some of the book's most valuable insights, but these sections are also, unfortunately, its one vulnerable aspect. For all his persuasive authority and grasp of the subtlest nuances of Mandelstam's verbal art, Brown now and then misreads some perfectly simple Russian word or grammatical construction (this is also the case with his and Merwin's translations of the poems), thus undermining his and our understanding of the text.

For example, one of Mandelstam's best early poems, "Silentium" (his answer to a famous nineteenth-century poem of the same name by Tyutchev), sets up a dichotomy between silence (refusal to speak) and muteness (inability to speak). But Brown reads "silence" as "stillness" and "muteness" as "quietness" and therefore fails to notice this contrast, basic to the conception of the poem. Two of Mandelstam's most important poems, "1 January 1924" and the untitled one that begins "No, I was no one's contemporary," feature the image of a personified despotic age who makes his son ill and prematurely old, but who will eventually come to kiss this son's hand in repentance and contrition. Again Brown misses the point, reading *k ruke pripadet*, "will fling himself down to kiss the hand," as if it were *upadet na ruku*, "will fall on the arm." In the same two poems, the phrase "two sleepy apples" actually means "two sleepy eyeballs," since the word *iabloko* can mean either "apple" or "eyeball" in Russian.

There are a few other similarly annoying misreadings in the book—but for each of them there are pages and pages of perceptive and imaginative commentary, sympathetic, scholarly, and right on target. Brown's reading of the poem about the star over St. Petersburg (poem no. 101) is a sheer delight, correcting earlier misinterpretations and telling us for the first time what this most widely anthologized of Mandelstam's poems really says. The book examines Mandelstam's poetry only up to 1925, which suggests that it may be the first part of a projected two-volume work. But even as it stands, despite its linguistic lapses, Clarence Brown's *Mandelstam* is an excellent and most welcome introduction to the poet and a fine, knowing guide to his work.

* * *

SK pays tribute to the depth of Mandelstam's historical understanding in another review a few years later, of *Osip Mandel'štam and his Age: A Commentary on the Themes of War and Revolution in the Poetry 1913–1921*, by Steven Broyde. Initially compelled, as was his custom, to point out misreadings and mistranslations, he ultimately gave the book a thumbs-up and concluded with the following:

> [The author's] approach to the poems is twofold. First there is the method of establishing the poem's context within the rest of the poet's work. Here Broyde follows his teacher Kiril Taranovsky, who was the director of the original dissertation and whose recent essays on Mandelstam are remarkable for their insight and acumen. However, Taranovsky's analysis of context and subtext (not dissimilar in method to Harold Bloom's much acclaimed recent studies of English poets), with its ultimate implication that a poem exists primarily as a sum of the echoes of its author's other poems and of the poets he has read, stands in curious contradiction to the basic thesis of Broyde's book. The contradiction is resolved, however, when Broyde applies his second approach and, thus, very ably demonstrates that much of Mandelstam's poetic response to war and revolution was parallel to the response of his contemporaries, especially Mayakovsky, Esenin, and the proletarian poets. While these *engagé* poets responded to events simplistically, Mandelstam recognized the full complexity of historical developments.[4]

---

[4] Review of *Osip Mandel'štam and his Age: A Commentary on the Themes of War and Revolution in the Poetry 1913–1921*, by Steven Broyde (Cambridge: Harvard University Press, 1975), *Slavic Review* 79 (1974): 386–87.

Tsvetaeva in English: A Review Article[1]

*I*n June 1923 Marina Tsvetaeva, then living in the village of Mokropsy outside of Prague, wrote to the young literary critic Aleksandr Bakhrakh, contributor to Russian émigré publications in Berlin. The correspondence between the poet and the critic, who at that time had not yet met in person, soon took on a tone of strong emotional involvement. By August Tsvetaeva realized that she had misinterpreted the tenor of Bakhrakh's letters and that the excessive intimacy of their correspondence was making him uncomfortable. Her later letters to him are accordingly far less personal or intense in tone. The temporary emotional crisis into which Tsvetaeva's correspondence with Bakhrakh plunged her is also reflected in eight remarkable poems which she appended in her letters to him.[2] Seven of these poems were eventually included in Tsvetaeva's finest and most mature collection, *Posle Rossii* (After Russia). The seventh poem of the sequence addressed to Bakhrakh, untitled when sent to him, was given the title "Pis'mo" (Letter) in the collection.[3] Written on 11 August 1923, the poem depicts the poet's agony of waiting for Bakhrakh's reply to the several letters she had sent him, asking him to define their relationship and the future of their correspondence.

This poem has a rather curious history of publication. After what apparently was its first appearance in print in *Posle Rossii*, it was included (as a new and unpublished poem) in 1946 in the collection *Russkii sbornik*, which also contained Bakhrakh's obituary of Tsvetaeva.[4] In 1961, Bakh-

---

[1] Originally published as "Cvetaeva in English: A Review Article" in *Slavic and East European Journal* 10, no. 2 (1966): 191–96.
[2] Marina Tsvetaeva's letters to Aleksandr Bakhrakh appeared in *Mosty*, no. 5 (1960): 299–318, and no. 6 (1961): 319–41. The poem "Pis'mo," in the form originally mailed to Bakhrakh, is reproduced in no. 6, 345–46.
[3] M. Tsvetaeva, *Posle Rossii* (Paris, 1928), 108–9.
[4] *Russkii sbornik* (Paris, 1946), 136. In this edition, line 5 of the poem is erroneously placed at the beginning. There are minor textual differences between the version sent to Bakhrakh (the one in *Mosty* and in *Russkii sbornik*) and Tsvetaeva's final version, which appears in *Posle Rossii* and in *Tarusskie stranitsy*.

rakh included "Pis'mo" in his publication of Tsvetaeva's letters and poems addressed to him. In the same year the poem was finally published in the Soviet Union, along with a number of other poems from *Posle Rossii*, in the celebrated, much-criticized by the orthodox, collection *Tarusskie stranitsy*.[5] Although the magnificent poetry of *Posle Rossii* has been available in Western libraries for decades, it is typical and significant that it was only after the furor occasioned by *Tarusskie stranitsy* and its hostile reception by some Soviet critics that some of the poems from *Posle Rossii* were finally translated into English. This happened when *Pages from Tarusa*, an English translation of large portions of the controversial Soviet collection, appeared in 1964.[6]

The translation of "Pis'mo" is to be credited to a fine contemporary English-American poet, Denise Levertov. When *Pages from Tarusa* was reviewed in the American press, critics, including those of the special journals devoted to Slavic studies, were unanimous in their praise of the high quality of Denise Levertov's translations. "A Letter" was apparently the most admired of her translations, for it has been reprinted in a special edition of *TriQuarterly* devoted to "Creativity in the Soviet Union"[7] (although a poem written by the exiled Tsvetaeva in Czechoslovakia in 1923 would hardly seem pertinent to that general topic). It had evidently not occurred to any of the enthusiastic critics to compare the translation

---

5   *Tarusskie stranitsy* (Kaluga, 1961). Tsvetaeva's prose and poetry, mainly selections from *Posle Rossii*, is on 252–61 (including "Pis'mo," with one misprint, 257–58).

6   Andrew Field, ed., *Pages from Tarusa* (Boston, 1964). The five poems by Tsvetaeva were translated by Denise Levertov (four) and Andrew Field (one). The ordering of the poems, based on that of the Soviet original of the book, places a juvenile poem written by Tsvetaeva at the age of 17 ("Osen' v Taruse," first printed in *Volshebnyi fonar'* [Moscow, 1912], 43) in the midst of the sophisticated, mature poems from *Posle Rossii*. No dates are provided, and the style of Denise Levertov's English translation leaves no doubt that she was unaware of the tremendous stylistic difference between the early poem and the later ones. The volume also contains Tsvetaeva's prose memoir "Khlystovki" (Women of the flagellant sect), ably translated by Collyer Bowen as "The Kirillovnas." When this memoir, originally published in Paris as part of a series of Tsvetaeva's family memoirs (*Vstrechi*, no. 6 [1934], 243–48), was reprinted in *Tarusskie stranitsy*, the title was changed to "Kirillovny," possibly to avoid undesirable religious implications. The American translator (or his editor), apparently unaware of the original title, retained the Soviet substitution.

7   Marina Tsvetaeva, "A Letter," trans. Denise Levertov, *TriQuarterly*, [no. 3] (Spring 1965): 64. The issue also contains Andrew Field, "A Poetic Epitaph: Marina Tsvetaeva's Poems to Blok," and three poems translated by Lydia Pasternak Slater (57–63).

of "A Letter" with its Russian original, yet such a comparison is highly instructive and points out most vividly both the dangers of translating complex poetry without sufficient qualification and the ease with which experts will accept and praise what is in fact a catastrophic bungle.

Письмо

Так писем не ждут,
Так ждут—письма.
Тряпичный лоскут,
Вокруг тесьма
Из клея. Внутри—словцо.
И счастье. И это—всё.

Так счастья не ждут,
Так ждут—конца:
Солдатский салют
И в грудь—свинца
Три дольки. В глазах красно.
И только. И это—всё.

Не счастья—стара!
Цвет—ветер сдул!
Квадрата двора
И черных дул.

(Квадрата письма;
Чернил и чар!)
Для смертного сна
Никто не стар!

Квадрата письма.

The poem is carefully structured. The two six-line stanzas (lines 1–12) develop two contrasting images, the contrast being reinforced by the fact that the second stanza recapitulates the syntactic and the semantic structure of the first one. The two four-line stanzas alternate the content of the first twelve lines in compressed form, while line 21 sums up the message of the entire poem.

Lines 1–6 state the poet's yearning for a letter. The meaning of the first two lines is: This is not how you (they, one, people) wait for letters (*pisem*); this is how you wait for a letter (a particular expected letter, *the* letter: genitive singular *pis'má*). Tsvetaeva, with her phenomenal feeling for the nuances of spoken Russian, based the structure of the entire poem on an elementary fact of Russian grammar: the government of the verb *zhdat'*, "to wait." The genitive plural in line 1 (the case of the direct object of a negated verb *and/or* the case required by the given verb) is combined and contrasted with a slightly different kind of genitive in the second line (a clear case of verb government). This sort of grammar-school parsing probably never occurred to Tsvetaeva or to her Russian readers—they would take the grammatical aspects of the poem for granted. But a translator has to be aware of it, for the government of the verb *zhdat'* is what determines the meaning and the structure of the remainder of the poem. Here is Denise Levertov's equivalent of Tsvetaeva's first stanza:[8]

> So they don't expect
> letters. So they wait for—
> letters.
>
> A ragged scrap
> circled by
> sticky tape. Inside—
>
> a scribble,
> and happiness.
> And that's all.

It is easy to see what has happened. The last word of line 2 has been read with an incorrect stress and mistaken for the accusative plural form. Yet at least three things point overwhelmingly to the fact that Tsvetaeva meant *pis'má* and not *pís'ma* in line 2: the government of the verb *zhdat'*, the stress required by the meter, and, if that were not enough, the rhyming of this word with *tes'má*, which certainly admits no other stress. And so in the English version the contrast between letters in general and a particular expected letter—the whole point of the beginning of the poem—has

---

[8] Denise Levertov's translation is cited here from Field, *Pages from Tarusa*, 288–89.

been lost (the English definite article could have done the job so well). Instead, we get three lines with a vaguely Brooklynese-Yiddish intonation and almost no meaning at all. Tsvetaeva's *Vokrug tes'ma / Iz kleia* ("A braid of glue around the edges") is a mildly metonymic description of an ordinary envelope; Denise Levertov's "circled by / sticky tape" suggests some exotic and messy-sounding postal customs and difficulties with the vocabulary of the original. "A scribble" is a poor substitute for the warm and casual *slovtso* that Tsvetaeva uses to describe the contents of the desired missive.

The second stanza of the original is an example of the kind of parallel construction that is so typical of the later Tsvetaeva. The letter that was so joyously expected in the first stanza may also bring her unhappiness. It may indicate that the friendship she values so highly is ended. So the second stanza recapitulates the structure of the first one, but this time the arrival of the letter is visualized in terms of an execution by a firing squad. This the translator apparently understands, but since she missed the point of the first stanza she is unable to do justice to the nuances of the second one:

> So they don't expect
> happiness. So they expect—
> the end.
>
> A soldierly
> salute, and
> three slugs of lead in the breast.
>
> Their eyes are red,
> and just that.
> That's all.

Things become quite catastrophic again at the equivalent of Tsvetaeva's lines 11 and 12. In Russian, everything goes red before the eyes of the condemned and shot person or persons, who, as the very expressive *I tol'ko* suggests, experience an utter sense of finality. "Their eyes are red, / and just that," which Miss Levertov offers us at this point, only testifies that the text of the original has not been understood. The very subtle ambiguity of the repeated last phrase of the two stanzas (*I eto—vse*), conveying plenitude in the first stanza ("And this is everything," i.e., everything one needs), but futility and finality in the second one ("And that is all there is," i.e., all there will ever be) is not felt within the context of the English version.

After line 12, the remainder of Tsvetaeva's poem becomes elliptic and consists predominantly of verbless clauses, with most of the nouns in the genitive case. Extreme syntactic ellipsis is one of Tsvetaeva's favorite and most typical devices. The comprehension of her elliptic speech in the second half of the poem hinges on two simple things: the realization that the poet is referring to herself in all the impersonal "you" or "they" constructions and that the basic grammatical fact of the entire poem is the requirement that the masculine or neuter direct object of the verb *zhdat'* be in the genitive case. The verb itself, firmly and memorably established in the first two stanzas, need no longer appear: the case that it governs will unfailingly suggest it to the native Russian ear. In Tsvetaeva's mature poetry, the reader is often required to supply the omitted verbs that are represented only by their objects in the oblique cases; a translator of this particular poem is hopelessly lost if he fails to account for all those genitives in elliptical clauses.

A possible English literal version of lines 13–21, with the ellipses filled out in brackets, would read as follows:

> [I] no [longer expect] happiness—[I am] too old [for that]!
> [My] bloom—the wind blew it away!
> [I am waiting for] the square of a courtyard
> And for black muzzles of rifles.
>
> ([I am waiting for] the square of a letter:
> For ink and magic!)
> No one is too old
> For the sleep of death.
>
> [I am waiting for] the square of a letter.

There may be other ways of conveying in English the implications of Tsvetaeva's ellipses; a different English version is needed, if the poetic quality of the original is to be perceived. But, basically, this is what these lines mean in the Russian. Denise Levertov's version of this part of the poem is:

>It's not happiness, old girl!
>The wildflower color—
>the wind blew it away.
>
>A square courtyard
>and black thoughts.
>Of a square letter,
>ink, sorcery.
>When it comes to
>death, the
>
>last dream, no one's
>old.
>A square letter.

Syntactic ellipses were not even noticed. Simple idioms, e.g., *stará*, were misunderstood. Because of a misprint in *Tarusskie stranitsy*, the genitive plural *dul* "rifle muzzles" was misread as *dum* "thoughts," an error which could have been avoided by a simple check of the original in *Posle Rossii*, available in most major libraries. The contrast between being too old for happiness and not being too old for death, which dominates the final portion of the poem, was simply overlooked.

It is dismaying to have to write all of this about a translation by Denise Levertov, a poet for whom I have great admiration. What, in the long run, is wrong with this translation (and with numerous others like it) is not any given mistake or set of mistakes, but the sheer idea of translating a poem which the translator understands neither structurally nor semantically. The able poet and the editor of the volume in which her translation first appeared (Andrew Field, who has elsewhere shown himself to be a capable propagandizer of Russian literature and an alert observer of the Soviet literary scene), in their desire to acquaint the American public with the work of a Russian poet they obviously admire, have overlooked considerations so basic and so self-evident that one would think they need not be mentioned at all.

Marina Tsvetaeva is a difficult poet to translate. Of the few examples of her work available in English, the rhymed translations of Boris Pasternak's sister, Lydia Pasternak Slater, are by far the finest, both in their fidelity to the original and in their literary sophistication. Translations of Tsvetaeva's poetry by Olga Andreyev Carlisle[9] and by Dimitri Obolensky[10] are evidently not intended as poetic versions: they aim only at conveying the basic meaning of the Russian original. The English version of "A Letter" is intended to be an English poetic equivalent of the Russian original. It is based on a procedure that is becoming more and more widely practiced as the interest in Russian twentieth-century poetry spreads among American intellectuals. Denise Levertov has had the collaboration of unnamed persons who are presumably specialists in Russian language and Russian poetry. Here is how this translating procedure is described by the editor of *Pages from Tarusa*: "The poetry translations have been done from literal versions and metrical schemes supplied to the poets, in addition, of course, to oral readings. While there is a close proximity to the originals in all instances, the poets have taken certain liberties. The poems stand first as English poems in their own right, the only valid standard, it seems to me, by which to judge poetry translations."[11]

There can be no reasonable objection against this method of translating poetry. On occasion it has proven to be spectacularly successful, as for example in W. H. Auden's version of Bella Akhmadulina's poem "Volcanoes," which is not only faithfully rendered, but vastly superior as poetry to the rather undistinguished Russian original.[12] But, as the above comparison of Tsvetaeva's poem with its English translation demonstrates, this method has a built-in danger that is very real indeed. The poet-translator who cannot read the original is completely at the mercy of an informant whose competence he cannot evaluate. Given a garbled version of the original poem as a point of departure, the most resourceful or

---

9   Olga Andreyev Carlisle, *Voices in the Snow* (New York, 1962), passim. [SK reviewed this (and another) anthology elsewhere at length, criticizing the selection and lamenting—"but carp we must," he writes—the quality of the trots provided the major American poets who were contributing to the volume (Simon Karlinsky, "Hosting Russian Poetry," *Nation*, 7 July 1969, 28–30).—Ed.]
10 Dimitri Obolensky, *The Penguin Book of Russian Verse* (Baltimore, 1962), 363–68.
11 Field, *Pages from Tarusa*, xiii.
12 Bella Akhmadulina, "Volcanoes," trans. W. H. Auden, *Encounter* 20, no. 4 (April 1963): 53.

inspired translator becomes helpless. Whole vast areas of twentieth-century Russian poetry await translators, but if their translations are to be of any value at all these translators have, as a minimal requirement, to be able to understand the basic meaning, the structure, and the implication of the text they are translating. Some recent translations of Tsvetaeva, Pasternak, and Mandelstam, and especially the selection of Anton Chekhov's letters edited by Lillian Hellman and now available in paperback, full of the most unbelievable mistranslations and howlers on its every page,[13] show that this minimal condition is not as absurdly obvious as it might appear to some. The problem of faulty, shoddy translations of Russian literature into English is as much with us today as it was in the days of Marian Fell and Constance Garnett. Denise Levertov's translation, spotlighted in this paper at length and perhaps a little unfairly, serves as a handy illustration of what happens when the minimum-comprehension criterion is not met. As Marina Tsvetaeva herself has remarked about a critical article by Ivan Bunin: "Luchshe nikak, chem tak!"[14]

* * *

This skillful *explication de texte* demonstrates SK's extraordinary expertise in dealing with problems of translation from Russian to English, particularly of works as complex semantically, lexically, and rhythmically as Tsvetaeva's poetry. Nearly every review of English-language works on Russian literature he wrote exhibits a similar concern. Elaine Feinstein, another translator—and later biographer—of Tsvetaeva, emerged relatively unscathed from under his scrutiny:

> Many of the things that make Tsvetaeva the poet she is are missing from [Elaine] Feinstein's translations. There are no poetic fireworks, no virtuosity, none of the verbal music of the originals. The parallel syntactic constructions, the repetitions of some key words around which a poem is often built are likewise not to be found in the English. But also, by and large, there are almost no comprehension problems. Mrs. Feinstein has translated Tsvetaeva with fidelity and at times with

---

[13] *The Selected Letters of Anton Chekhov*, ed. Lillian Hellman (New York, 1965).
[14] "Better not at all than like this!" Marina Tsvetaeva, "Poet o kritike," *Blagonamerennyi* (Brussels, 1926), 2:118.

remarkable resourcefulness. It is a measure of the shoddiness of recent translations of modern Russian poetry that the honesty and integrity of Elaine Feinstein's translation should seem to us such an unprecedented luxury.[15]

SK once designated the devices common to the poetry of Tsvetaeva and Boris Pasternak (and the difficulty of rendering of it into English), in a devastating review of two translations from Pasternak: "sudden shifts and compressions of meaning, emphasis on the phonetic and the lexical aspects of the poetic craft ... syntactic ellipses frequently found in Russian colloquial speech."[16] (For SK's discussion of a specific link between the two poets, see below his essay "Pasternak, Pushkin and the Ocean in Marina Tsvetaeva's *From the Sea*.") In what is perhaps his final public statement, over a quarter of a century on, about Tsvetaeva—and after numerous publications of his own on the poet, including two book-length monographs—SK reviewed positively a study of intertextuality in Tsvetaeva's longer works by Michael Makin.[17] He did, however, yet again find it necessary to take an author to task for lapses in translation, "frequently out of focus or simply sloppy," errors that might often be avoided by "looking things up or checking with native speakers."

Pasternak's early prose, like Tsvetaeva's, makes many of the same demands as his poetry, and may be nearly as difficult to translate. See the following excerpts from SK's highly positive review—in which he also praises the translator's "brilliant introduction"—of Angela Livingstone's excellent annotated English edition of Pasternak's essays, his autobiography *A Safe Conduct*, and his speeches and essays:

> In all things I would like to reach
> Their very essence.

---

[15] Review of *Selected Poems*, by Marina Tsvetaeva, trans. Elaine Feinstein, foreword by Max Hayward (New York: Oxford University Press, 1971), *Russian Review* 32 (January 1973): 101–2.

[16] "The Crime Against Pasternak," review of *The Poems of Doctor Zhivago*, by Boris Pasternak, trans. Eugene M. Kayden (Kansas City, MO: Hallmark Editions, ca. 1971), and *Sister My Life*, by Boris Pasternak, trans. Philip S. Flayderman (New York: Washington Square Press, 1967), *Nation*, 22 January 1968.

[17] Review of *Marina Tsvetaeva: Poetics of Appropriation*, by Michael Makin (Oxford: Clarendon Press, 1994), *Times Literary Supplement*, 30 December 1994.

These two lines open the first poem in Boris Pasternak's last collection of verse, *When the Weather Clears Up*, begun in 1956 and completed in 1959, one year before his death. Essences, in life and in art, are what much of Pasternak's poetry and prose were about. He strove to uncover, as he wrote in the poem just cited, "the crux of bygone days, their cause, the foundations, the roots, the very core." And yet, as the poet Marina Tsvetaeva, his passionate admirer and correspondent, warned in an essay (1933), readers' response to Pasternak often reminded her of dialogues in *Alice in Wonderland*. Reality, as perceived by Pasternak, resembles the ordinary, pragmatic reality, but he viewed and described it from an angle all his own, an angle whose eccentricity was less apparent to him than to some of his readers. This accounts for his honest surprise at the storm and fury unleashed in the Soviet Union by the publication abroad of his novel *Doctor Zhivago* and the awarding to him of the Nobel Prize....

His understanding of the terms "realism" and "realistic" was so idiosyncratic that it enabled him to consider the music of Chopin, the poetry of Verlaine and the plays of Heinrich von Kleist as representative works of realist art. For Pasternak, art was realistic "in that it did not invent metaphor, but found it in nature and faithfully reproduced it."

Similarly, the terms "romantic" and "romanticism" were appropriated by the poet "for quite a narrow and negative meaning. 'Romantic' means whatever is made up, ungenuine, and not experienced in real life." Other literary and philosophical terms, such as "identity" or "originality," underwent semantic mutations, while "subjectivity" and "objectivity" became, in Livingstone's words, "quite unmoored and float about until we are dizzy." This is not willfulness or caprice. Pasternak saw everything "in the light of its ability to change, to shift and to reveal itself as extraordinary." Critics have often pointed out Pasternak's power to see the world anew, to discover in humdrum everyday trifles aspects that had never been observed before. This also applies to his theoretical writings about art.[18]

In point of fact, SK's admiration for the poetry of Pasternak preceded his intense involvement with the equally singular lyric voice of Tsvetaeva. We in-

---

[18] Simon Karlinsky, "Realistically Speaking," *Times Literary Supplement*, 22 November 1985.

clude here an except from one of his earliest published writings, an introduction to German translations of Pasternak's poetry, dating from 1950:

> For Boris Pasternak poetry was never a form of magic or ritual, but always a strict exercise in art, an exercise that was both conscientious and universal. Pasternak did not indulge in formal experiments; his poetry is new and unusual all the same. He uses conventional poetic forms for expressionistically subjective content, for a system of crisscrossing allusions, and for a brilliance that was unheard of in Russian poetry.
>
> Boris Pasternak was born in 1890, the son of Leonid Pasternak, a well-known portrait painter. He studied in Germany at the University of Marburg. It was perhaps there that he began greatly to admire Goethe and Lenau. Other literary models are, in particular, Shakespeare, Pushkin, and Lermontov.
>
> Pasternak's first poems were published in 1912. In them we can already discern the fundamental tone, the leitmotif of his future poetic creation: *the constant amazement over the miracle of being alive.*
>
> Ilya Erenburg, who in the 1920s wrote about Pasternak's poetry, praised him for having again confirmed the right to existence of "chamber poetry"— a poetry in the vein of chamber music, written in small format, for a more sophisticated and therefore smaller public. In the years following, it became clear that Pasternak's reading public was larger than Erenburg had believed.
>
> The first two volumes of Pasternak's poetry appeared before the Revolution. They were called *A Twin in the Clouds* and *Above the Barriers*. In these volumes Pasternak's specific style is clearly marked. His meters are strictly classical, but the rhymes are unconventional; sometimes he uses near rhymes, just as Aleksandr Blok did. The whole structure of Pasternak's poetry is characterized by the presence of a lively spirit that is hungry, perhaps too hungry, for life, almost uncanny in its scintillating vitality, built on the basis of a staccato rhythm. A concentration of these traits can be found in Pasternak's third volume of poetry, *My Sister Life*. This volume was written in 1917 and published in Berlin in 1923. A remarkable book, it was apparently created at the time when Pasternak left the literary group LEF. Mayakovsky, who was then the recognized and authoritative leader of this group, propagated the idea that the only task of poetry was its usefulness for the revolutionary cause. This conception was, of course, entirely alien to the passionate and individualistic poetry of Pasternak, and he had the courage to admit this

by breaking with LEF. In *My Sister Life*, the poem "Definition of Poetry" develops Pasternak's unique conception of literary counterpoint—two completely different themes are simultaneously developed to a parallel effect, while safeguarding the unity of the poetic whole. The poet lives through and transforms his life experience so intensely that his occasional literary signals can be understood only by readers who have sufficient imagination to understand his comprehensive metaphors and allusions. In his collection of poems *Themes and Variations*, Pasternak raises his purely poetic virtuosity to heights that had never been reached in Western literature. These short poems are the literary equivalent of the etude as a musical genre. They stimulate and astonish us, but it cannot be denied that their charm is mainly of an intellectual nature. The main group of poems in this volume consists of variations on the topic of Pushkin in the Crimea; they comprise a poetic description of a well-known portrait that shows Pushkin on the Crimean sea coast. Among the six subsequent variations, the first is written in Pasternak's most extreme fashion, and it deals with the conflict of Pushkin's Russian environment, on one hand, and his alleged African origins, on the other; the second variation is written in Pushkin's own style and provides an impressive maritime picture, with Pushkin gazing into "the misty twilight of shipwrecks."

After this third volume of poems Pasternak wrote two long narrative poems, *Lieutenant Schmidt* and *1905*, a short novel, *Lyuvers's Childhood*, and an autobiography. In the 1930s it became increasingly difficult for him to publish his works (his most important writings of the 1920s were all published abroad), and—unwilling to make any compromise, either in his style or in his choice of topic—he turned to the art of literary translation.[19]

---

[19] Translated by Joachim Klein, from S. Karlinsky, "Drei russische Dichter," *Das Lot* 4 (October 1950): 48–50.

A New Edition of the Poems of Marina Tsvetaeva[1]

The literary fate of Marina Tsvetaeva, who in my view is one of the most remarkable Russian poets of the twentieth century, took its ultimate shape sadly and instructively. The highest point of Tsvetaeva's popularity and reputation during her lifetime came approximately between 1922 and 1926, i.e., during her first years in emigration. Having left Russia, Tsvetaeva found the opportunity to print a whole series of collections of poetry, narrative poems, poetic dramas, and fairy tales that she had written between 1916 and 1921: *Mileposts 1* (*Versty 1*), *Craft* (*Remeslo*), *Psyche* (*Psikheia*), *Separation* (*Razluka*), *Tsar-Maiden* (*Tsar'-Devitsa*), *The End of Casanova* (*Konets Kazanovy*), and others. These books came out in Moscow and in Berlin, and individual poems by Tsvetaeva were published in both Soviet and émigré publications. As a mature poet Tsvetaeva appeared before both Soviet and émigré readership instantly at her full stature; her juvenile collections *Evening Album* (*Vechernii al'bom*) and *The Magic Lantern* (*Volshebnyi fonar'*) were by that time forgotten. Her success with readers and critics alike was huge and genuine. If one peruses émigré journals and newspapers from the beginning of the 1920s, one is easily convinced of the popularity of Marina Tsvetaeva's poetry at that period. Her writings appeared in the Russian journals of both Prague and Paris; her arrival in Paris and appearance in February 1925 before an overflowing audience for a reading of her works was a literary event. Soviet critics similarly published serious and sympathetic reviews.

But later, the situation began to change. By that time, *Contemporary Annals* (*Sovremennye zapiski*) and Prague's *Will of Russia* (*Volia Rossii*) had published Tsvetaeva's recollections of the days of the October Revolution and the Civil War: "Free Passage" ("Vol'nyi proezd"), "My Jobs" ("Moi sluzhby"), and "October Revolution in a Railroad Car" ("Oktiabr' v vagone"). These sketches, which gave a vivid and merciless picture of the

---

[1] Translated by Joan Grossman. Originally published as "Novoe izdanie stikhov Mariny Tsvetaevoi" in *Novyi zhurnal*, no. 84 (1966): 295–300.

epoch, aroused the wrath of orthodox Soviet criticism. With their publication began the Soviet press's hostile attitude toward Tsvetaeva's work, which in the 1930s changed to total silence. A negative attitude toward Tsvetaeva among émigré critics began at about the same time, though it was provoked by entirely different reasons.

By the time they appeared, those works that particularly pleased the émigré critics—*Verses to Blok* (*Stikhi k Bloku*), the play *Fortuna*—belonged for the poet herself to a phase already past. After her emigration, Tsvetaeva's talent underwent a profound and rapid evolution. By the middle of the 1920s she had reached her mature writing manner, having assimilated the best achievements of styles attempted earlier: the highly excited Romanticism of her early poetry collections and "Romantic" plays; stylization in the manner of folk laments, underworld jingles similar to limericks, sentimental "cruel" ballads, and other folklore genres in the collection *Mileposts 1* and, in part, in *Craft* (and of course in her folktales); and finally, high-style Church-Slavic lexicon and Tsvetaeva's extremely individual version of the Russian Baroque. In her new manner Tsvetaeva wrote some highly original and profound pieces: *Poem of the End* (*Poema Kontsa*), *The Stairs* (*Lestnitsa*), *The Pied Piper* (*Krysolov*), tragedies based on stories from Greek mythology, and the collection *After Russia* (*Posle Rossii*). These appear to us now, well after the poet's death, to be the summit of Tsvetaeva's creative work, her most precious contribution to the development of Russian poetry in the twentieth century.

Tsvetaeva's contemporaries thought otherwise. With all the variety of aesthetic positions of writers of the older generation of that time, the unanimity with which Maksim Gorky (in letters to Pasternak), Ivan Bunin, and Zinaida Gippius, all failing to understand Tsvetaeva's mature writings, paid them scant attention or wrote of them with obvious disdain, is striking. In Tsvetaeva's complex style of the 1920s, many émigré critics saw empty wordplay, unmotivated virtuosity, ostentatious "originality," and hysteria, where now we who approach her work with good will and attention see brilliant and genuine verbal power, superb mastery of verse form, spiritual depth, and expressive transmission of delicate psychological nuances.

In the 1930s Tsvetaeva's reputation began to wane. In the Soviet Union only rarely was she mentioned, and then with contempt and unvarying references to her "White counterrevolutionary sympathies" and "reactionary" position. For the older émigré writers Tsvetaeva was linked with constant attention to the verbal side of poetry and artistic prose, which was unacceptable to them. (In a way they were right—Tsvetaeva's mastery oversteps the boundaries of schools and trends and, as one of the outstanding instances of Russian "verbalism" of the twentieth century, she is the literary ally of Bely, Remizov, Mayakovsky, and Pasternak.) For the younger Paris poets and critics of the 1930s, Tsvetaeva as poet was, it might be said, rather too brilliant, vivid, and life-loving. The Paris school was attracted rather to despair, weariness, murmurs, little peculiarities of speech—that same murmuring that Tsvetaeva earlier, already in 1921, had rejected:

> Not for these flattering garments, deceitful cassocks—
> Vociferous was I born to this world!
>
> My dreams are not nocturnal—[they're] in broad daylight!
> Unlike you, I don't live by hissing, whispering!
>
> (Не для льстивых этих риз, лживых ряс—
> Голосистою на свет родилась!
>
> Не ночные мои сны—наяву!
> Шипом-шопотом, как вы, не живу!).

Of course, there were critics in the emigration who wrote of Tsvetaeva warmly and with understanding: Marc Slonim, Yury Ivask, Alfred Bem, and, by the thirties, Vladislav Khodasevich (who earlier had written of her with reserve or negatively). In the émigré press two articles appeared about Tsvetaeva by Prince Dmitry Svyatopolk-Mirsky (on *The Swain* [*Mólodets*] and on *The Pied Piper*)—until now in general the best criticism written about Tsvetaeva. But in the 1930s the tone in émigré criticism was dominated by the Paris school—and the great poet Marina Tsvetaeva in the last years of her life abroad remained, in her own words, "without readers and without criticism."

The Second World War and the end of the 1940s were a time when Tsvetaeva was almost forgotten. After her suicide in Elabuga, unmentioned by the Soviet press, her name totally disappeared from Soviet books, newspapers, and even encyclopedias. In the emigration only Georgy Fedotov in 1942 proclaimed Tsvetaeva "the number one Russian poet of our era."[2]

---

2 Fedotov's statement is from his "On Parisian Poetry" (first published in *Kovcheg: Sbornik russkoi zarubezhnoi literatury* [The ark: A collection of Russian literature abroad], compiled by V. F. Mansvetov [New York, 1942]).

He was an exception. Much more typical in the 1940s were the constant attacks and slurs on Tsvetaeva by Georgy Adamovich and Nikolai Otsup. It was typical that even Tsvetaeva's correspondent Aleksandr Bakhrakh, in his obituary (which appeared in the Paris-based *Russian Miscellany* [*Russkii sbornik*] and was the sole public notice of her death), felt it necessary to underline her "mannered style," her "failures and blunders." He also proclaimed *Psyche* and *Craft* to be her finest collections, leaving unmentioned her greatest works, written and published after 1921.

But Tsvetaeva's oblivion lasted a relatively short time. The Thaw set in, and Tsvetaeva was remembered in her homeland and almost simultaneously (what caused this constant and surprising parallel?) in the emigration. In the 1950s, Tsvetaeva emerged before a new generation of readers who had not heard of her—in the memoirs of Ilya Erenburg, in the "Autobiographical Sketch" of Boris Pasternak (so far unpublished in the Soviet Union, but translated into many languages), and in her own works, which in the Soviet Union have been gradually reprinted and republished since 1956.

At the same time there appeared abroad a collection of her prose, her volume of verse about the civil war called *The Demesne of the Swans* (*Lebedinyi stan*), and letters to Bakhrakh, Ivask, Roman Goul, Fedotov, and Anatoly Steiger. All this revealed to the reader some completely new, unknown features of Tsvetaeva's literary and personal image. From around 1960 one encounters more and more rarely in the émigré press complaints about Tsvetaeva's "spoiled" talent, her "incomprehensibility" and "hysteria"—which were so common in the 1930s and 1940s. Certain critics (for example, Vladimir Weidlé) who at one time wrote rarely and negatively of Tsvetaeva now treat her work with attention and respect.

In 1961 the one-volume collection of selected lyrics that had been promised in 1956 appeared in the Soviet Union. Despite a certain tendentious selection of material that narrowed and limited the general image of Tsvetaeva's poetry, that volume, which sold out in Moscow in two days, actually revealed to the Soviet reader the range and variety of that poetry.[3] Now, in much-expanded form, this volume has been republished in the series "Poet's Library" (Moscow/Leningrad, 1965), edited by Tsvetaeva's

---

[3] Marina Tsvetaeva, *Izbrannoe*, ed. V. Orlov (Moscow: Gos. izd-vo khudozhestvennoi literatury, 1961).

daughter Ariadna Efron and Anna Saakyants, with an introductory article by Vladimir Orlov (an expanded, augmented and corrected version of his introduction to the 1961 volume).[4] The book contains not only lyrics, but also narrative poems and dramatic works by Tsvetaeva.

Along with *Poem of the End* and *Poem of the Hill* (*Poema Gory*), which became known to Soviet readers in the 1961 volume, it includes the fairy tale narrative in verse *Tsar-Maiden*, the lyrical satire *The Pied Piper*, *Poem of the Staircase* (originally printed in *Freedom of Russia* under the title "The Staircase"), the tragedy *Ariadna*, and other major pieces by Tsvetaeva that were almost unknown to readers abroad and were completely new to Soviet readers. Immense labor was expended in collecting poems of Tsvetaeva that had appeared in rare émigré publications. Fifty-five poems, unpublished but preserved in the archive of Tsvetaeva's daughter, are printed here for the first time. All the same, despite the wealth of material represented in the volume, one is struck by the omission of many significant poems and cycles. This is not a matter of differing tastes or disagreement among the compilers about the significance of one or another of Tsvetaeva's pieces. The rehabilitated Tsvetaeva, previously accused of "White" sympathies and reactionary leanings, now was subject to an effort at refashioning her image in official Soviet style and transforming her, after the fact, into a stereotype of Soviet respectability. It was difficult, of course, to expect that a volume published in the Soviet Union would contain verses from *The Demesne of the Swans*, which praised the White movement, or the splendid counterrevolutionary poems "Riotous Carnival!" ("Maslenitsa shiroka!") and "Like Migrants to Some New York?" ("Pereselentsami— / V kakoi N'iu-Iork?") from *Craft*. But also excluded were Tsvetaeva's relatively few, but significant, religious lyrics (for example, the profound and original "God" ("Bog") from *After Russia*). Deliberately omitted from her most important collection, *After Russia*, were poems expressing Tsvetaeva's peculiar Platonic idealism, her striving for "other worlds"—such poems as "The Blindly Flowing Sobbing of Lethe" ("Lety slepotekushchii vskhlip") or "Sybilla to the Infant" ("Sivilla—mladentsu"). (True, the selection does include the splendid "The Train" ("Poezd"), where these "Platonic" motives are interwoven with domestic-social criticism.) Finally, also omitted

---

[4] Marina Tsvetaeva, *Izbrannye proizvedeniia*, introd. by V. Orlov, ed. A. Efron and A. Saakiants (Moscow/Leningrad, 1965).

from the volume was the high point of Tsvetaeva's patriotic lyric, her stunning cycle on the death of Mayakovsky (with the superb description of the meeting of the two suicides Mayakovsky and Esenin in the Kingdom of Heaven). In Orlov's foreword this cycle is referred to as a "contradictory piece," in which "some false notes are heard." Moreover, the cycle is represented by a tendentious choice of excerpts. In this manner, Tsvetaeva as poet is presented to the Soviet reader incompletely.

Along with the tendentious selection of works, it must be noted that two major pieces included in the volume suffered cuts by the censor. In the first instance this refers to *The Pied Piper*. In form the largest of Tsvetaeva's works, this poem at the time of its appearance called forth the ecstatic responses of Pasternak and Fedotov and the extremely interesting article by Svyatopolk-Mirsky. However, the work passed unnoticed by the majority of émigré critics (though Mikhail Osorgin, in a well-meaning piece about the "romantic" Tsvetaeva, called *The Pied Piper* a "very musical piece of nonsense").

The Pied Piper is a work exceptional for its genre: satire, as indicated in the subtitle, actually is interwoven with lyric and even philosophy in an original, fantastic blend. In the poem, keen satire is directed against bourgeois stupidity and malice in all its guises—including the Soviet variety. This is underlined by the fact that the rats from which the hero frees the town of Hamelin speak in quasi-Communist jargon (they have not only *glavkhvost* and *glavshish* [common disrespectful nicknames for superiors], but also their own rat version of NEP [New Economic Policy]). In an effort to restrict the poem's meaning to a satirical portrayal of German bourgeoisie, the editors actually maimed *The Pied Piper*. In the notes it is said that this poem is printed "with insignificant omissions." In fact, from the third chapter 134 lines are eliminated. The fourth chapter is treated almost as ruthlessly, since the passages cut are essential for understanding Tsvetaeva's idea, and their absence leads to a distorted understanding of the entire poem. From *Poem of the Staircase* (*Poema Lestnitsy*) a quatrain containing an ironic parallel of Marx and the devil is omitted.

Yet despite the cuts and misquotes in the book's commentaries (for example, in the notes to the poem "The Naiad" ("Naiada"), p. 755, there is attributed to Tsvetaeva—who, at the end of the 1920s was writing about the White defenders of Perekop—the glorification of their Red opponents), and despite the necessity of reducing Tsvetaeva's complex and inimitable worldview, in the foreword and notes, to the usual Soviet formulae, the publication of *Selected Works* of Marina Tsvetaeva is a great and joyous event for those who value Russian poetry. In the Soviet Union at the present time, Tsvetaeva is one of the most loved and most sympathetic poets, especially among the young literary generation. In her originality, her freedom from any dogma, her profound contemporariness, and her genuine ethical purity, young Russians see not only poetry, but also, as many foreign visitors report, a valuable lesson about life. This recognition and reevaluation, of which Pasternak wrote, are already, to a degree, occurring. But to print Tsvetaeva's creative work in full, in all its variety and independence, is at present impossible in the Soviet Union. It would be good if émigré publishers would fill this gap and reprint Tsvetaeva's "forbidden" works: first of all, the complete *Pied Piper*, then *Perekop*, *The Red Bull-Calf* (*Krasnyi bychok*), the cycles on the death of Voloshin (*Ici-Haut*) and the death of Mayakovsky, the drama on the French Revolution, *Fortuna*, and the interesting cycle of reminiscences of the epoch of the Civil War.

* * *

SK was perfectly placed to evaluate the two Soviet editions (1961 and 1965) of the works of Marina Tsvetaeva, once he had completed the revision of his PhD dissertation, which was published within a few short months of this review (Simon Karlinsky, *Marina Cvetaeva: Her Life and Art* [Berkeley: University of California Press, 1966]). This pioneering work made him, as it were, the godfather of a burgeoning field of study and the instigator of intense interest in the oeuvre of Tsvetaeva. He eventually determined that the vast amount of new information which had come to light in the intervening twenty years necessitated a new look at his subject, and wrote *Marina Tsvetaeva: The Woman, Her World, and Her Poetry* (Cambridge: Cambridge University Press, 1986). In the meanwhile, he had published a number of reviews and essays in Russian on her life and work, and for this volume we have translated four of them, since the material they contain is treated cursorily if at all in his two English-language, book-length studies of the poet.

The review translated here also comprises a remarkably succinct but comprehensive introduction to Tsvetaeva. Again, we have chosen here and below to supply transliterated Russian titles of the poet's writings for the use of readers who can consult the original texts.

New Information about the Émigré Period of Marina Tsvetaeva

(Based on Material from Her Correspondence with Anna Tesková)[1]

With the increasing popularity of Marina Tsvetaeva, both in the USSR and abroad, the literature about her life and work also continues to grow. Her early unknown works and translations are being published, along with remembrances by contemporaries. A person well versed in her literary and epistolary legacy is forced to respond warily to some of the works of a memoiristic nature that have appeared in the last few years. Rather frequently, friends of Tsvetaeva's provide mutually contradictory information or cite her using verbatim quotes from her own articles, once published in émigré newspapers and journals that are now difficult to get hold of. In one memoir which appeared a few years after my 1966 biography of Tsvetaeva came out,[2] I chanced to read not only a series of paraphrases of my book, but also some inaccuracies and errors that I'd made, all of which the author placed in Marina Tsvetaeva's own mouth and transposed to the mid-1920s.

Therefore, despite all the value of the testimony of memoirists, the letters of Tsvetaeva herself—even granted her well-known subjectivity, sometimes amounting to bias—represent the most reliable and interesting source for understanding her literary and personal biography. To the already familiar letters of Yury Ivask, Roman Goul, Georgy Fedotov, Anatoly Steiger, and Aleksandr Bakhrakh, and the more recently published letters to Vladislav Khodasevich and Zinaida Shakhovskaya, as well as the

---

[1] Translated by Kevin O'Brien. Originally published as "Novoe ob emigrantskom periode Mariny Tsvetaevoi (po materialam ee perepiski s A. A. Teskovoi)" in *Russkaia literatura v emigratsii: Sbornik statei* [Russian émigré literature: A collection of essays], ed. Nikolai P. Poltoratskii (Pittsburgh: University of Pittsburgh Dept. of Slavic Languages and Literatures, 1972), 209–14.

[2] Simon Karlinsky, *Marina Cvetaeva: Her Life and Art* (Berkeley: University of California Press, 1966).

fragments from letters to various people which appeared in the journal *Novyi mir* (New world) and the still unpublished, fascinating correspondence with Salomeya Halpern, we may now add a separate little volume of letters to Anna Tesková, published in Prague in 1969 by the Czechoslovakian Academy of Sciences.[3]

Anna Tesková, a Czech journalist and writer (1872–1954), was one of the organizers of the Prague Czech-Russian Society (Édnota), which was dedicated to helping Russian refugees. Tsvetaeva became friends with her at the very end of her stay in Czechoslovakia, though it appears that they had been acquainted earlier. One hundred thirty-five letters from Tsvetaeva to Tesková have been preserved, beginning with a formal ("Dear Madame") response to an invitation to take part in a literary soirée (November 1922) and ending with a despairing letter, written when she was already on the train taking her away to the USSR (12 June 1939). The book contains roughly two-thirds of these letters. However, several thousand lines have been cut from the texts that are included. According to the volume's editor, Vadim Morkovin, the missing passages "refer to people still living" and "many relate to the poetess's personal or family matters" or contain "less interesting or frequently repeated domestic details." Evidently, in the letters from the 1930s, descriptions reflecting the strained relations between Tsvetaeva and her daughter, Ariadna Efron, who is still alive, have been left out. When one considers that the publication of the book was conceived during the liberal Dubček government, but published only after the Soviet seizure of Prague, it seems likely that the editors had to leave out some pronouncements by Tsvetaeva about Soviet power, as well as her hesitations and doubts about returning to the USSR. Nevertheless, in an improvement over Soviet journals, snipping away without a twinge of conscience in their reprints of Tsvetaeva's work, as well as over émigré editors who subjected her while she was still living to the "despair of abridgements" (rarely has a writer been subjected to censorship from such a variety of positions, and on such diverse grounds, as Tsvetaeva), the conscientious Czech editors at least indicate exactly how many lines they have omitted.

---

[3] Marina Tsvetaeva, *Pis'ma k A. Teskovoi* (Prague: Academia, 1969). [A full edition of these letters was published only some forty years later: M. I. Tsvetaeva, *Pis'ma k Anne Teskovoi*, ed. L. A. Mnukhin (Bolshevo: Memorial'nyi Dom-muzei Mariny Tsvetaevoi v Bolsheve, 2008).—Ed.]

Despite the sad fact of abridgements (and the equally sad circumstance that in a book published by the Czechoslovakian Academy of Sciences, the Russian translations of the French and German texts, including poems by Rilke, are rendered with unbelievable clumsiness, in hopeless translations done by people who clearly know neither French nor German), the collection of letters to Tesková provides a great deal of new material for deepening our understanding of both the literary and the personal biography of Tsvetaeva. Tsvetaeva's letters frequently provide an essential key for reading her more difficult works. For example, in light of the correspondence with Tesková, we can read afresh her essay-memoir of Valery Bryusov: "The task was difficult—in spite of the repulsion which he inspired in me (and not in me alone)—to give an idea of his unique greatness. To judge, without having convicted him, although the sentence seemed already prepared. I wrote, alas, without sources, using quotes cited from memory." Just as instructive are Tsvetaeva's pronouncements: about her article in response to the death of Rilke ("Your Death"); about the dramatic trilogy about Theseus created during the years of the correspondence (the first two parts, *Ariadne* and *Phaedra*, were completed and published, while a planned third part, *Helen*, was abandoned after the mockingly hostile reviews of *Phaedra* in the émigré press);[4] about the creation and fate of the long poem *Perekop* ("No one will take it. Its form is too radical for the right wing and its content is too rightist for the left") and other works by Tsvetaeva. The writer of these lines must reject his earlier reading of the poem *The Red Bull-Calf* (*Krasnyi bychok*).[5] A letter to Tesková dated 11 March 1928 (no. 41 in the collection) shows that the poem was based on the death (from tuberculosis) and funeral of a young Russian, a former volunteer, and his conversation with his mother before his death. Despite annoying cuts, the connection between this letter and the poem is unquestionable, and the letter reveals the subject of *The Red Bull-Calf* from a completely new perspective.

---

[4] For a more extended discussion of Tsvetaeva's dramatic output, consisting of six "Romantic" verse plays written in 1918–19 (a time when she was associated with the actors of the Third Studio of the Moscow Art Theater) and two neoclassical verse tragedies, *Ariadne* and *Phaedra* (written in the 1920s), see Simon Karlinsky, "Kuzmin, Gumilev and Tsvetayeva as Neo-Romantic Playwrights," *Russian Theatre in the Age of Modernism*, ed. Robert Russell and Andrew Barratt (New York: St. Martin's Press, 1990), 106–22.—Ed

[5] Karlinsky, *Marina Cvetaeva*, 203–4.

The extensive information about émigré publishing houses, journals, and political groups will interest historians of Russian émigré literature. The correspondence provides many confirmations of the hostile attitude (already well established in the literature) of many literary figures abroad toward Tsvetaeva's innovations and the antipathy to her artistic evolution by editors and critics who had valued her earlier works, which were more traditional in form (she writes in 1928 that in the newspaper *Poslednie novosti* [The latest news] "they very much like the old me, i.e., the young me").

Letter no. 82 (24 November 1933) is of exceptional literary-historical interest: in it Tsvetaeva shares with Tesková her thoughts regarding Ivan Bunin's Nobel prize.

> On the 26th I am to sit on a platform and to congratulate Bunin. To try to avoid it would be to protest. I make no protest, I simply disagree.

Tsvetaeva felt that both Gorky and Merezhkovsky deserved the prize much more than Bunin,

> for if Gorky is an era, and Bunin is the end of an era, then Merezhkovsky is the era of the *end* of an era, and his influence both in Russia and abroad is incommensurable with that of Bunin, who has had absolutely *no* influence either there or here.

One should point out that Tsvetaeva grew up in a family in which the name of Gorky was held in high esteem; that Katya, Gorky's daughter from his first marriage, who died young, was an early childhood friend to whom Tsvetaeva dedicated a poem in her first published collection, *Evening Album* (*Vechernii al'bom*); that Gorky, who was as little attracted to the mature poetry of Tsvetaeva as Bunin was, nevertheless managed in 1924 to get the poems of Tsvetaeva (who had already emigrated) into the Leningrad journal *Russkii sovremennik* (Russian contemporary), edited by himself and Evgeny Zamyatin; and that in 1927 Gorky arranged a trip to Sorrento and Paris for Tsvetaeva's sister Anastasiya (who published under the name A. Mein), which gave the sisters the chance to see one another after five years apart. As for Bunin, despite the warm and friendly relations between Tsvetaeva and his wife, Vera Muromtseva-Bunina, he invariably gave Tsvetaeva's work scornfully contemptuous reviews (and in his *Memoirs* didn't refrain from kicking her viciously when recalling her tragic death). We must assume that here the personal aspect somewhat showed through in Tsvetaeva's literary judgments.

In the same letter we find a description of the reaction of the Merezhkovsky couple to the awarding of the Nobel to Bunin.

> Merezhkovsky and Gippius are furious. Perhaps this is the only simple, natural feeling felt by that complex pair in their entire life.... Everyone fears them right now because both, especially she, are evil. As in evil spirits.

The letters to Tesková provide many new details that clarify her relationships with Rainer Maria Rilke and Boris Pasternak, and with the young émigré poets Nikolai Gronsky and Anatoly Steiger. The motives which led to her return to the USSR also become clearer. The letters reflect the ideological divide, which extended over many years, between Tsvetaeva and her husband Sergei Yakovlevich Efron, who by the 1930s had switched to a pro-Soviet position:

> Sergei is entirely immersed in Soviet Russia, he sees nothing except it and in it he sees only what he wants to see. (16 October 1932)

Gradually, the father converted both children to his new faith.

> Mur [Tsvetaeva's son, Georgy] lives torn between my humanism and the near-fanaticism of his father ... (here four lines are left out of the text; 28 December 1935).

Finally, in a letter dated 15 February 1936, the question of returning is out in the open:

> In short—Sergei and Alya and Mur are eager. All around: the threat of war and revolution—in general, catastrophic events. There's nothing for me to live on—alone—here. The émigré community *doesn't like* me.... Finally—Mur has no prospects here. I see these young people in their twenties—they're at a loss.

But it's clear from the same letter that Tsvetaeva harbored no particular illusions about her future in the USSR:

> I, with my *Furchtlosigkeit* [fearlessness], I who *cannot* refrain from responding, I who cannot sign a salutary address to the great Stalin, for it was *not* I who called him great, and even if he is great it is not my kind of greatness, and perhaps the most important thing—I hate every triumphant, bureaucratized church.

The penultimate letter to Tesková, written five days before her final departure from Paris, testifies to the depth of Tsvetaeva's despair, offering herself as a sacrifice for the sake of her son and her husband ("you can't abandon a person in trouble, I grew up with that"):

> God, what anguish! Right now, in the heat of the moment, with everything in a fever—my hands and my head and the weather—I still have not sensed it fully. But I know myself, I know what awaits me! I'll break my neck looking back: at you, at your world, at our world. (7 June 1939)

Lately in the West people have been saying and writing a good deal—sometimes with considerable exaggeration—about a question that has seemingly been long decided—that of the woman without rights within her family. The life of Tsvetaeva would seem to offer an incontrovertible argument for the latter-day (female) champions of women's equality. Tsvetaeva the poet paid a terrible price for the right to be a wife and mother, and there's plenty behind the assertion that escaped her in one of her letters:

> Marriage and love are destructive to one's personality, they are a trial. This was what both Goethe and Tolstoi thought. And an early marriage, such as mine, is a total catastrophe, a blow from which you can't recover for the rest of your life. (26 May 1934)

Many remarkable Russian poets of this century have had to live in poverty. At the same time, for Osip Mandelstam in the "Lethean cold" of Voronezh there was the loving and caring Nadezhda Yakovlevna; for

Georgy Ivanov in that almshouse in the south of France where his talent ripened so astonishingly at the end of his life, there was no need to wash the floors or linen; as for Boris Poplavsky—frequently hungry and—to the indignation of many—refusing to work, he could loaf around Montparnasse at will. All of these male poets, living in poverty, had the elementary physical possibility to write. Tsvetaeva did not.

Her husband, mild, polite Sergei Yakovlevich, was often ill, often gone from home, busy with his shady political ventures. Her daughter Alya, a twenty-something young lady, studied, sometimes worked, and then was the first of the family to depart for the Soviet Union. Her son, Mur, was a wild boy, a hooligan without any spiritual interests. Tsvetaeva supported all of them with her Czech pension, with her rare literary earnings, with handouts from well-wishers and friends. She feeds, serves, and makes clothes for all of them. All of her time and all of her energy went to that housework, while there remained at most an hour or an hour and a half a day for her main work—writing—and neither Sergei Yakovlevich nor Alya, even while knowing the worth of Tsvetaeva's creative work, knowing that she is an extraordinarily rare poet, helped in any way to lighten her domestic hard labor. (The story by Olga Chernova-Kolbasina in the journal *Mosty* (Bridges), no. 15, about how Tsvetaeva, in Czechoslovakia, forced the young Alya to do the housework while she herself wrote, hardly tallies with what we know from all other accounts.)

Complaints about the lack of time for writing form a constant leitmotif in the letters to Tesková. Having escaped to a seaside resort during the summer of 1926, Tsvetaeva immediately wrote three long poems, one after another. In a letter from London she announced that in a week she wrote an article which at home would have taken a month and a half to write, while she managed to write the essay on Andrei Bely, "A Captive Spirit" ("Plennyi dukh"), one of the high points of her prose, "only because Mur and Alya had the measles, and I had *time*" (26 May 1934).

It would be the easiest thing in the world to pass sentence on Tsvetaeva's household ("my people at home, interested in everything but me, for at home I'm [just] dishes, broom, cutlets—and I understand why") for preventing her from writing, and in the end, leading to her death, offering her no option but to leave for the Soviet Union. But they're not responsible for the terrible conditions in which the family found itself both abroad and on their return to their homeland. They're not responsible for the "biological necessity" and a whole series of habits and practices of everyday familial life which demanded from Tsvetaeva the poet absolutely unique sacrifices, with which no other poet had to contend.

We can learn a great many other things from the letters to Tesková: about the joint appearance of Tsvetaeva and Vladislav Khodasevich, 2 February 1935, at an evening devoted to the memory of Blok, where she read her reminiscences of encounters with Blok (where is the text of these reminiscences now?); about how Aleksei Remizov was the godfather of Mur; about Tsvetaeva's emotional reaction to Hitler's invasion of Czechoslovakia (the pension from the Czechoslovakian government was one of the chief sources of Tsvetaeva's livelihood in Paris, as becomes clear from the correspondence); about how she cherished the works of the Scandinavian women novelists Selma Lagerlöf and Sigrid Undset for their descriptions of the heavy lot of woman as wife and mother. Still, it seems that the chief value of the publication of these letters is that for those who value the verse and prose of Tsvetaeva's last decade, they reveal under what conditions and at the price of what effort that deeply spiritual verbal art arose.

Pasternak, Pushkin, and the Ocean in Marina Tsvetaeva's *From the Sea*[1]

I

Children who grow up in cultured or somewhat-cultured Russian families are introduced to the poetry of Aleksandr Pushkin at an early age. In the last decades of the nineteenth century this introduction usually occurred through the primer *Native Word* (*Rodnoe slovo*), which was compiled by the pedagogue Konstantin Ushinsky and went through more than fifty editions in the first two decades after its appearance in 1864. This mode of using primers to introduce children to poetry was part of the national cult of Pushkin, a cult Marina Tsvetaeva summed up in part six of her essay "The Poet about the Critic" ("Poet o kritike") in the phrase "primers, bad grades, exams, busts, masks," and so forth.[2] In fact, exams and bad grades were not always the extent of it. In more cultured families, a child might be callously humiliated for insufficient or overly individualistic understanding of one of Pushkin's texts. Examples can be found in Tsvetaeva's "My Pushkin" ("Moi Pushkin"). In less cultured families, if one is to believe Anton Chekhov's story "Out of Sorts" ("Ne v dukhe"), published in 1884, it could reach the point of beatings because of Pushkin.

As a little girl, Marina Tsvetaeva came upon the same excerpt from *Evgeny Onegin* (the second stanza of the fifth chapter) that poor Vanya

---

[1] Translated by Liza Knapp. Originally published as "Pasternak, Pushkin i okean v poeme Mariny Tsvetaevoi 'S moria'" in *Boris Pasternak and His Times: Selected Papers from the Second International Symposium on Pasternak*, ed. Lazar Fleishman (Berkeley: Berkeley Slavic Specialties, 1989), 46–57.

[2] SK's source in this essay for Tsvetaeva's texts was the exemplary edition of her prose and poetry published in New York between 1979 and 1990, masterminded by Aleksandr Sumerkin: Marina Tsvetaeva, *Izbrannaia proza v dvukh tomakh* (New York: Russica, 1979); Marina Tsvetaeva, *Stikhotvoreniia i poemy v piati tomakh* (New York: Russica, 1980–90). However, in lieu of multiple references to these seven volumes, we have chosen to provide the titles of her writings in both English translation and the original Russian (in transliteration) for the benefit of readers who have access to other or later editions of Tsvetaeva's writings.—Ed.

Prachkin is learning from Ushinsky's reader in Chekhov's story. True, for little Marina, in the line "Winter, the peasant triumphing ..." Pushkin appeared "not stolen, but given, not mysterious, but revealed." Before that had come a secret and forbidden reading of *The Gypsies* at the age of five or six in the room of Valeriya, her half-sister. Valeriya's room was a forbidden realm in the mythology of Tsvetaeva's childhood. It was enemy territory, attractive for this very reason. It was a place of liberation from maternal prohibitions and the place of encounters with the imagined and beloved devil, described in the sketch "The Devil" ("Chort"). In Tsvetaeva's reminiscences of childhood the image of the devil personifies revolt (first of all, against her mother), eroticism, and, at the same time, Russian literature with Pushkin at its head—literature that little Marina, raised on German literature, became acquainted with behind her mother's back and in an atmosphere of prohibition and danger.

One should not, I am well aware, mix life with literature and fictional characters with real, live people (although Tsvetaeva herself, as we shall see, loved to do this). Nevertheless, there is a remarkable parallel in the theme of parental punishment for the reading of Pushkin in Chekhov's tiny story and in the memoiristic sketch by Tsvetaeva. At the end of Chekhov's story the father beats the boy, not just on account of Pushkin but also out of annoyance with himself over a loss at cards. The highly cultured Mariya Aleksandrovna Tsvetaeva, née Mein, certainly did not beat Marina. But she did recognize in Pushkin some form of incendiary power, since the girl was punished for Pushkin: for her interest—premature, according to her mother—in Onegin and Tatyana, for her ignorance of who Bonaparte, referred to by Pushkin, was, and for her inappropriate use of new words read in Pushkin.

And yet little Marina held on to her love of Pushkin despite prohibitions and ridicule during childhood, and Pushkin remained for her the heart of Russian literature her whole life long. None of the Russian poets and prose writers of the nineteenth century was as dear to her. Tsvetaeva would hold forth in admiration of individual poems by Baratynsky, Lermontov, or Fet; she had an affinity for Leskov's *Cathedral Folk* and Aksakov's *Family Chronicle*; but she did not know the full scope of their oeuvre as she did the oeuvre of Pushkin and her beloved German poets, Goethe, Heine, and Rilke. Only among her older contemporaries and her peers did Russian poets emerge whom she studied and placed on the same level as Pushkin: Blok, Bely, Kuzmin, Akhmatova, and, above all, Boris Pasternak.

The young Tsvetaeva's study of Pushkin went through three early stages: the quasi-infantile forbidden reading of *The Gypsies* and *The Captain's Daughter*, with a very approximate understanding of the meaning but with complete faith in the poetic enchantment; next, an authorized reading in the primer of excerpts from *Onegin* and *Poltava*, minor poems like "The Drowned Man" ("Utoplennik"), as well as her mother's reading aloud of Pushkin's fairy tales; and, finally, at the age of ten, her fascination with a poem that might appear to be inaccessible to the understanding of a child, "To the Sea" ("K moriu"). The whole final part of the sketch "My Pushkin" is devoted to the description of the young Marina's murky but not distorted perception of Pushkin's epistle to the sea. It is significant that this little girl, who didn't understand many of the words or the realia of the text, interpreted the content of the poem as a love story—the separation of two lovers, the poet and the sea.

This situation is probably the most unusual in the polymorphous-androgynous love stories in the poetic world of Tsvetaeva, where the limitations of sex, age, or the feasibility of a meeting are often not taken into account.[3] One may point to relevant examples such as the "love plot" between Grinyov and Pugachov, spotted by Tsvetaeva in *The Captain's Daughter*,[4] or, in the memoiristic sketch "My Jobs" ("Moi sluzhby"), the hypothesis about the desirability of Pushkin's marrying not Nataliya Goncharova, but instead Natasha Rostova from *War and Peace*. Her reproaches to Natasha Rostova for having married Pierre instead of waiting for Pushkin overlook not only Rostova's and Pushkin's existence in two incommensurate worlds, but also something even more substantive from the point of view of the epoch: the inappropriate age of the proposed bride. Natasha Rostova, thirteen in 1805, at the time of her first appearance in *War and Peace*, would have been nearly forty at the time of the marriage of the thirty-year-old Pushkin to the sixteen-year-old Goncharova. The romantic encounter between Psyche-Natasha and the inspired blackamoor imagined in "My Jobs" is undermined by the overripe age of Tolstoi's heroine. However, in the poetic world of Marina Tsvetaeva such practical obstacles are not taken into account.

---

[3] "My God! How a human being is diminished by taking on sex." Marina Tsvetaeva, "Moi Pushkin." See also Tsvetaeva's "Natal'ia Goncharova."

[4] See Tsvetaeva's "Pushkin i Pugachev."

Fate offered the ten-year-old Marina the opportunity of seeing whether the grand picture which so captivated her measured up to reality: the poet's parting from the ocean which was in love with him, against the background of Napoleon expiring on a cliff and a genius by the name of Byron racing across the sky, "with his head made up of rays of light and his body of clouds."[5] Because of her mother's illness, the whole family went to Italy "to the sea" in the fall of 1902, at the height of her infatuation with the poem "To the Sea." But the sea turned out to be the bay of Genoa, a cove or tourist beach in Nervi, which in no way compared to the powerful and loving ocean in Pushkin's poem. Tsvetaeva, in "My Pushkin," and, following that text, her sister Anastasiya in her memoirs, describe Marina's disappointment when the sea turned out not to be as it was for Pushkin:

> At first sight, I did not fall in love with the sea; gradually, as everyone does, I learned to make use of it and play in it: collecting pebbles and dancing in it—just like a youth, dreaming of a great love, gradually learns to take advantage when opportunity presents itself.[6]

This ambivalent attitude toward the sea—dislike of the actual sea and a certain recognition of the value of the sea as a traditional literary theme—runs through Tsveateva's whole poetic and epistolary legacy. To renounce the sea once and for all was impossible for her, if only because of her name, whose marine etymology she understood and valued.[7] From this etymology, marine-Marina, are constructed two poems from Tsvetaeva's early collection *Magic Lantern* (*Volshebnyi fonar'*): "Prayer to the Sea" ("Molitva moriu") and "Soul and Name" ("Dusha i imia"). In the latter, the poet asserts that not only her name but also her dreams and her soul are marine, though it seems more a matter of paronomasia than true conviction. References to her connection to the sea are to be found also in lyrics of the mature Tsvetaeva, such as, for example, "Some are created from stone" ("Kto sozdan iz kamnia"), 1920, and "Naiad" ("Naiada"), 1928. In a somewhat salonesque poem of 1913 (not completely successful,

---

[5] Marina Tsvetaeva, "Moi Pushkin."
[6] See also Anastasiia Tsvetaeva, *Vospominaniia* (Moscow, 1983), 95–96.
[7] See her dialogue with Asya Turgeneva in the memoiristic sketch "A Captive Spirit" ("Plennyi dukh").

in my view),⁸ Tsvetaeva envisioned an imaginary encounter with Pushkin on the seashore in Gurzuf, using the setting Pasternak would later use in *Theme with Variations* (*Tema s variatsiiami*).

However, to shift from Tsvetaeva's poetry, we find in her letters the recurrent leitmotif of dislike of the sea. It appears especially often during Tsvetaeva's émigré period, when more than once for the sake of her children she took pains to gather the means for summer trips to the sea, only then to curse it in letters to friends. Of numerous examples, we can cite the letter to Anna Tesková:

> The Ocean. I recognize its grandeur, but I don't like it (I never liked the sea, only once, the first time, in childhood, under the sign of Pushkin's "Farewell, free element!"). It is free, whereas I am "constrained";⁹

or the letter to Raisa Lomonosova, who was setting off for America:

> At the sea—the simplest, almost familial ...—I languish, don't know what to do with myself.... How many times have I tried to fall in love with it!¹⁰

Tsvetaeva made the most significant of these attempts to love the sea not only in the poetic but in the existential sense at the end of May 1926 when her goal was to intensify her contact with her most beloved contemporary poet, Boris Pasternak. This attempt flowed into the writing of the *poema* dedicated to Pasternak, *From the Sea* (*S moria*).

II

The foundation for studying the interrelations of Marina Tsvetaeva and Boris Pasternak was laid in an article by Olga Raevsky-Hughes, published in 1971.¹¹ From then on these relations were explored in a series of studies,

---

8 SK is referring to "A Meeting with Pushkin" ("Vstrecha s Pushkinym").—Trans.
9 Marina Tsvetaeva to Anna Tesková, 8 June 1926, *Pis'ma k A. Teskovoi* (Prague, 1969), 39.
10 Tsvetaeva to Raisa Lomonosova, 1 February 1930, from the Archive of Leeds University, courtesy of Richard Davis. [This letter is now available in Marina Tsvetaeva, *Sobranie sochinenii v semi tomakh*, vol. 7 (Moscow: Ellis Lak, 1995), 316–19, after a first publication by Richard Davis in *Minuvshee*, no. 8 (1989).—Ed.]
11 Ol'ga Raevskaia-Kh'iuz, "Boris Pasternak i Marina Tsvetaeva: K istorii druzhby," *Vestnik Russkogo studencheskogo khristianskogo dvizheniia* (Paris), no. 100 (1971).

most extensively in Lazar Fleishman's book *Boris Pasternak in the Twenties*[12] and in the introductory essay to the collection of letters by Rilke, Tsvetaeva, and Pasternak, compiled by Konstantin Azadovsky and Elena and Evgeny Pasternak.[13] For our purposes here, we need only note that, prior to the beginning of the two poets' correspondence and her essay about Pasternak, "A Cloudburst of Light" ("Svetovoi liven'"), published in 1922, Tsvetaeva was only familiar with his book *My Sister Life* (*Sestra moia zhizn'*), also published in 1922, which she thought was the only one he had published. In early 1923, she became familiar with the collection *Themes and Variations* (*Temy i variatsii*), about which she wrote Pasternak in a letter of 11 February 1923.[14] The cycle *Theme with Variations*, found within this collection, shares some common ground (as mentioned above) with Tsvetaeva's poem "A Meeting with Pushkin." As is well known, the theme on which Pasternak wrote variations in the cycle was the painting by Aivazovsky and Repin depicting Pushkin on Crimean cliffs above the breakers. The poem depicts Tsvetaeva herself with Pushkin in this very landscape. However, if *Theme with Variations* in all fairness may be considered to be one of the loftiest of Pasternak's poetic flights, Tsvetaeva's "Meeting with Pushkin," with its speech addressed to Pushkin by a young poetess (specifically, a poetess, and not yet a poet), written in the style of Edmond Rostand, beloved by Tsvetaeva at the time, does not poeticize Pushkin, but, to be blunt, vulgarizes him.

---

[12] Lazar' Fleishman, *Boris Pasternak v dvadtsatye gody* (Munich: Wilhelm Fink, 1980). A revised edition of this indispensable study was published in St. Petersburg by Akademicheskii proekt in 2003.—Ed.

[13] In abridged form, *Voprosy literatury*, 1978, no. 4. In unabridged form, the collection was published in German, French, and Italian. The Russian text is cited in the present essay from an unpublished typescript, kindly provided to the author by Serena Vitale and Angela Livingstone. [SK presented this paper in 1984, a year before the collection appeared in English: *Letters, Summer 1926: Boris Pasternak, Marina Tsvetayeva, Rainer Maria Rilke*, ed. Yevgeny Pasternak, Yelena Pasternak and Konstantin M. Azadovsky (San Diego: Harcourt Brace Jovanovich, 1985); 2nd ed. (New York: New York Review Books, 2001). In 1990 the same editors' Russian version was published in Moscow. See also: *Nebesnaia arka: Marina Tsvetaeva i Rainer Mariia Ril'ke*, ed. Konstantin Azadovskii (St. Petersburg: Akropolis, 1992); Marina Tsvetaeva and Boris Pasternak, *Dushi nachinaiut videt': Pis'ma 1922-1936 godov*, ed. E. B. Korkina and I. D. Shevelenko (Moscow: Vagrius, 2004).—Ed.]

[14] Marina Tsvetaeva, *Neizdannye pis'ma*, ed. G. Struve and N. Struve (Paris: YMCA-Press, 1972), 279, where several poems from the collection *Themes and Variations* are enumerated.

It is hard to say whether Tsvetaeva, on reading the collection *Themes and Variations*, noticed this contrast, so unflattering to her, in the treatment of the theme of Pushkin in the Crimea. In her letter to Pasternak about this collection she did not mention his Pushkin cycle. However, she subsequently cited it at least three times: (1) in the first poem of her cycle *Verses to Pushkin* (*Stikhi k Pushkinu*), 1931, which contains the words "Brows more blue than olives" ("Лбы голубей олив") from the fourth poem of Pasternak's cycle; (2) in the essay "My Pushkin," into which Tsvetaeva inserted his lines

Стихия свободной стихии
С свободной стихией стиха

(An element of a free element [the sea]
with the free element of a line of verse);

and (3) in *From the Sea*, where the lines

Лучше волны гложу,
Осатанев на пустынном спуске

(Better than a wave am I gnawing away,
Possessed, atop a steep deserted slope)

appear as an amalgam of the Pasternak line "В осатаненьи льющееся пиво" (Beer aswirl as if possessed) and the Pushkin line cited later by Pasternak "На берегу пустынных волн" (On the shore of deserted waves). These three lines make it safe to assume that at the time of composition of *From the Sea*, not just Pushkin but also Pasternak was associated with the thematics of the sea.

This triple association—Pushkin, Pasternak, and the sea—reached its height of intensity for Tsvetaeva in May of 1926, when she was staying on the shore of the Atlantic Ocean in the fishing village of Saint-Gilles-sur-Vie. This was the period of furious attacks on Tsvetaeva in the émigré press for her article "The Poet on the Critic," attacks that augured the possibility of a break between her and part of the expatriate literary community.[15] At this

---

[15] On this, see Irma Kudrova, "Polgoda v Parizhe," in *Marina Cvetaeva: Studien und Materialien, Wiener slawistischer Almanach* 3 (1981).

same time, in May of 1926, the three-way correspondence between Tsvetaeva, Pasternak, and Rilke reached its culmination. Over the course of four days, from Sunday to Wednesday, 23 to 26 May, Tsvetaeva wrote Pasternak an extended letter, which, as the compilers of the volume of correspondence of Rilke, Tsvetaeva, and Pasternak point out, contains invaluable commentary on *From the Sea*. In particular, on the 26th Tsvetaeva writes:

> Boris, I don't live backwards, I don't try to foist on anyone either my six-year-old self or my sixteen-year-old self,—why, then, am I so drawn to *your* childhood, why am I so drawn to drawing you into mine? ... With you now, in the Vendée, in May of 1926, I have been playing nonstop some kind of game, so that in the game—in the games!—I am collecting seashells with you.

Further on, Tsvetaeva sets forth in detail and poetically the causes of her dislike of the sea, after which she cites the first lines of the chapter "Marine Mutiny" ("Morskoi miatezh") from Pasternak's *The Year 1905* (*Deviat'sot piatyi god*). The chapter had been published in *New World* (*Novyi mir*) three months prior to this letter. The opening of "Marine Mutiny" in its own way treats some of the basic motifs of Pushkin's "To the Sea," especially the theme of the contrast between the quiet and the stormy sea. Tsvetaeva writes that she went to the Atlantic Ocean in the hopes of finally seeing the sea with the eyes of Pushkin and Pasternak and that she again—for the nth time—failed:

> That, with which and for which I went: *your verse*, that is, transfiguration of the thing. I'm an idiot to have hoped to see *your* sea *with my own eyes*—beyond sight, above sight, out of sight. "Farewell, free element" (I was ten years old) and "I am getting fed up with everything" (my thirty years)—there you have my sea.

This juxtaposition of the first lines of "To the Sea" and of "Marine Mutiny,"

> Everything can become bland.
> It's only you who are never the same
>
> (Приедается все.
> Лишь тебе не дано примелькаться),

confirms yet again that *From the Sea* was envisioned as the antithesis of the marine landscapes of Pushkin and Pasternak. This point is indicated by the very title *From the Sea*, which opposes Pushkin's "To the Sea." Two days later, on the 25th, Tsvetaeva describes a fresh attempt to come to love the sea and writes that the sea attempted to reciprocate her feelings: "as I was walking just now on the beach, the waves were clearly trying to kiss my feet."

The passages cited contain some of the basic themes of *From the Sea*: (1) visiting one another by means of an extratemporal journey into childhood; (2) games on the seashore with seashells and various other objects washed up by the sea; and (3) a meeting at the edge of the seashore, but not a quiet, stormy, or furious one, like those in Pushkin and in Pasternak's *Themes and Variations* and "Marine Mutiny," but a welcoming one that "tries to kiss your feet." It is surprising that for the poetic meeting with Pasternak, Tsvetaeva, deprived of entry into the Pushkinian-Napoleonic-Byronic ocean of "Marine Mutiny," turned to the seashore not of her own childhood but of that of her younger sister Anastasiya. "Asya, other than pebbles and seashells, had no marine dreams in reserve. Sometimes I would hit her because of those seashells," according to "My Pushkin." And there on this beach of her childhood was conjured up the spirit of Boris Pasternak.

The mode of conjuring his spirit—the opening theme of the *poema*—was for Tsvetaeva a beloved means of transport into forbidden and inaccessible realms: a mutually agreed-on meeting in a dream. Her first collection, *Evening Album* (*Vechernii al'bom*), published in 1910, included a poem "Link through Dreams" ("Sviaz' cherez sny") dedicated to Vladimir Nilender, with whom Tsvetaeva was in love at the time. The poem describes the continuation of meetings, forbidden in waking life, by means of mutual dreams. At the very start of the correspondence with Pasternak, Tsvetaeva wrote to him:

> My favorite means of communication is otherworldly: the dream: to see in a dream. And my second is correspondence. A letter, like some form of otherworldly communication, not as perfect as a dream, but its laws are the same.[16]

---

[16] Tsvetaeva to Pasternak, 19 November 1922, Tsvetaeva, *Neizdannye pis'ma*, 271.

Tsvetaeva bases *Attempt at a Room* (*Popytka komnaty*), dedicated to Rilke and written immediately after *From the Sea*, on this same idea. Tsvetaeva wrote about the same thing many years later to Anatoly Steiger:

> With you I want only this, only that which can't be named, not: dream while awake, dream—while asleep, to enter together with you into sleep and live there.[17]

From the Sea draws together these themes and thoughts. For the sake of a meeting with Pasternak, Tsvetaeva penetrates into a zone forbidden to her, Soviet Moscow, just as during her childhood she would enter another forbidden zone, her sister Valeriya's room (and the realm of the devil) for the sake of a meeting with Pushkin. From its very beginning *From the Sea* establishes the impossible and the unthinkable as reality and norm:

> With the North-Southerly
> I know: impossible!
> Possible—when needed!
>
> (С Северо-Южным
> Знаю: неможным!
> Можным—коль нужным!).

The north-southerly wind, which doesn't exist in nature, carries the sleeping Tsvetaeva from the west to the east, from the Atlantic coast of France to Moscow, from her own dream into the dream of Boris Pasternak and simultaneously into his and her childhoods. According to the logic of the dream, the action occurs simultaneously in the bedroom of Pasternak in Moscow and on the seashore in France. According to this same dream logic, the interlocutors are children playing on the beach as well as adult poets discussing literature and politics. The beach playthings, called to the attention of the child hypostasis of Pasternak—seashells, pebbles, pumice—carry at the same time an utterly adult poetic load, serving as allegorical representations of longing, love, conscience, poetry, glory, jealousy, and envy.

---

[17] *Opyty* [Experiments] (New York), 1955, no. 5, 59–60.

Pasternak then recollected these objects washed ashore by the sea from Tsvetaeva's *poema* in the meditations of Yury Zhivago on how to depict Lara in his poetry in the chapter "In Varykino, Again" in the novel *Doctor Zhivago*: "In a broken, winding line the sea throws down pumice, cork, seashells, seaweed, whatever was lightest and most weightless that could be lifted up from the bottom. Stretching out endlessly in the distance, this was the border marked on the shore by the high point reached by the surf. Thus, you, my pride and joy, were washed up to me by the storm of life. Thus, will I depict you."[18] The lyrical tone of the *poema* becomes satirical when one remembers Soviet censorship and the "*napostovtsy*," the contributors to the journal *On Guard* (*Na postu*), who in the fall of 1923 rebuked the State Publishing House for publishing the counterrevolutionary Tsvetaeva and in May 1924 characterized the poetry of Pasternak as "the monstrous caprices of a young loafer, who has found the opportunity to publish his notebook of trivialities and disseminate it for general use" (from Pertsov's article "Invented Figure").[19]

The last of those marine playthings found on the shore, a starfish, undergoes a series of semantic metamorphoses: from a marine object, the star becomes the star of Bethlehem, and then a red star, the symbol of the government of the USSR. At this point Tsvetaeva for perhaps the only time reminds Pasternak of the possible difference in their political stands, a difference about which she wrote more openly to Rainer Maria Rilke ("and Boris calls himself a Socialist! Can you believe it?").[20] The Atlantic starfish is presented, as she writes, "to a republican—from the hand of a Chouan." Tsvetaeva wrote *From the Sea* in the Vendée, a locale associated with the counterrevolutionary, royalist revolt of the peasant-Chouans at the time of the French Revolution in the eighteenth century. For Tsvetaeva, from the very start of the October Revolution, the Vendée became synonymous with resistance. It is recalled in this same context in poems of the collection *The Demesne of the Swans* (*Lebedinyi stan*) and the drama *Fortuna*.

---

[18] Boris Pasternak, *Doktor Zhivago* (Ann Arbor, 1959), 464.

[19] See S. Rodov, the section "Greshnitsa na ispovedi u Gosizdata" in the article "Original'naia poeziia Gosizdata," *Na postu*, nos. 2/3 (1923): 148–50; and V. Pertsov, "Vymyshlennaia figura," *Na postu*, no. 5 (1924): 221.

[20] Rainer Maria Rilke, Marina Zwetajewa, and Boris Pasternak: *Briefwechsel* (Frankfurt am Main: Insel, 1983), 120. [This was subsequently published in English; see n. 13.—Ed.]

But for Tsvetaeva politics was always capable of dissolving in poetry: recall her unconditional admiration for Mayakovsky, which completely overlooked his political views and activities. After an ironic request to Pasternak to "inform the authorities":

> That on the stern of the ship Russia
> The total shipwreck:
> An object with five ends

> (Что на корме корабля Россия
> Весь корабельный крах:
> Вещь о пяти концах)

(that is, a red star). Then the finale of the *poema* begins, tranquil and lucid. The essences of the two poets, as it were, interpenetrate—spiritually and even erotically, but in the complete absence of physical contact: one of Tsvetaeva's "exits from visibility." For the sake of this maximal proximity with her beloved poet-contemporary, Tsvetaeva freighted the *poema* with an element alien to her but close to Pasternak—the sea. But at the same time she transferred this sea (just as Pushkin transferred the sea "into the forests, into silent wildernesses") into her Tsvetaevan zones of dream and childhood.[21]

---

[21] An interesting and detailed analysis of *From the Sea* was done by Ieva Vitins in her dissertation, "Escape from Earth: A Study of the Four Elements and Their Associations in Marina Tsvetaeva's Work" (University of California, Berkeley, 1974), and also in her presentation at the Tsvetaeva conference in Lausanne in the summer of 1982. [See Ieva Vitins, "Marina Cvetaeva's Poèma 'S Morja'" in *Marina Tsvetaeva: Trudy 1-go mezhdunarodnogo simpoziuma* [Lausanne, 30 June–3 July 1982], ed. Robin Kemball, E. G. Etkind, and Leonid Heller (Bern, Switzerland: Peter Lang, 1991), 250–61.—Ed.]

"Traveling to Geneva ...":
On a Less-than-Successful Trip by Marina Tsvetaeva[1]

"The whole point of it is that he didn't love her, and it is only for that reason that she loved him *so*, choosing *him* because she secretly *knew* that he would not be able to love her back.... People with this fatal gift for unhappy and unrequited love simply have a genius for hitting upon unsuitable objects of affection."[2] In these words about Pushkin's Tatyana, written by Tsvetaeva just after the end of her epistolary romance with Anatoly Steiger, we see her penchant for combining literature with autobiographical confession. Throughout her creative career, short-lived intimacies with one person or another tended to be immortalized in a literary work just before (or after) they broke up: a cycle of verse, a long poem, or a short memoir written as a sketch.

All sorts of relationships might serve as the impetus for this kind of creative incarnation. Examples include her friendship of many years with Prince Sergei Volkonsky, her delight at the literary talent of Osip Mandelstam, and her tribute to the recently deceased Aleksei Stakhovich, with whom she had been only slightly acquainted. However, the most significant things written by Tsvetaeva on the basis of temporary intimacy with another person were those born of a feeling of love.

> Love! Love! Both in convulsions and in the grave,
> I am wary—am tempted—am shy—rush forward.

---

[1] Translated by Eric Naiman. Originally published as "'Puteshestvuia v Zhenevu ...': — ob odnoi neudavsheisia poezdke M. I. Tsvetaevoi" in *Marina Tsvetaeva: Trudy 1-go mezhdunarodnogo simpoziuma* [Lausanne, 30 June–3 July 1982], ed. Robin Kemball, E. G. Etkind, and Leonid Heller (Bern, Switzerland: Peter Lang, 1991), 72–80.

[2] Marina Tsvetaeva, "Moi Pushkin," in *Izbrannaia proza v dvukh tomakh 1917–1937* (New York: Russica, 1979), 2:262.

In Tsvetaeva's literary biography "love" is quite a capacious concept, encompassing an extensive spectrum of shades and gradations. Love for her husband and daughter; her literary infatuation (obviously erotically tinged) with Boris Pasternak and Rainer Maria Rilke; her tempestuous love affairs with the hero of *The Poem of the End* (*Poema Kontsa*), Konstantin Rodzevich, and with the heroine of the cycle *Woman Friend* (*Podruga*), Sofiya Parnok—all these different types of love lie at the foundation of Tsvetaeva's works. For the biographer or the commentator there is no getting around them.

So far, all the work I've mentioned flowed from real and mutual relationships. But Tsvetaeva has cycles of poems which arose from unfulfilled love, love that never came to be or, as she herself wrote, "one-sided" love. In the collection *After Russia* (*Posle Rossii*), these are the poems written to Abram Vishnyak, whom she would soon reject, and to Aleksandr Bakhrakh, whom she did not know at the time. Such is the cycle *Verses to an Orphan* (*Stikhi sirote*), dedicated to Anatoly Steiger, who she knew was not susceptible to a woman's love or motherly tenderness. The cases of Bakhrakh and Steiger are the most obvious examples of Tsvetaeva's "fatal talent" for choosing "inappropriate objects of affection." She would mythologize the chosen one, ascribe to him nonexistent qualities and desires, place demands on him that were impossible to fulfill, invest him with hopes that could not possibly come true.

Whether purposefully or not, such "one-sided" love, built on illusions, caused the poet to suffer, but at the same time it was the soil from which poetry grew. Tsvetaeva yielded to the illusion of mutuality with such fearlessness for the sake of poetic leavening. In her creative work, as she explained in her remarkable letter to Vladislav Khodasevich, "the only full and true" conception of a man (or of a city) is an internal one, "with eyes closed, no peeking."[3] Her meeting in person with Khodasevich—and in a café, at that—could end in disenchantment, just as London, when she saw it for herself, "crumbled before my eyes," turning out to be not the London described in the lines in the poem "The ancient fogs of love …."

While she was corresponding with Anatoly Steiger and writing *Verses to an Orphan*, two different Steigers existed for Tsvetaeva—a real, living

---

[3] Tsevtaeva to V. F. Khodasevich, 15 April 1935, in "Pis'ma Mariny Tsvetaevoi," *Novyi mir*, 1969, no. 5, 206.

one and an imaginary one—along with two Switzerlands: the country next door, which her neighbors from Château d'Arcine often visited, and another Switzerland, in which her internal Steiger dwelt. Initially, she wasn't drawn to the real Switzerland:

> People often go to Geneva from here, i.e., to Switzerland, and that is a bit irritating, but I am not envious and know that in the final analysis all good things have been fairly distributed: I have been given a talent for dreaming so powerful that it outstrips any automobile. (Letter of 14 August 1936[4])

The next day Tsvetaeva was "invited from the morning on to Geneva—for a whole day," but she declined.[5] This would have been the real Switzerland, but she would have liked to meet with Steiger in an oneiric castle or room, "in a dream, to enter with you into a dream—and to live there."[6] This room, the imagined place of their imaginary meeting, had already been described in Tsvetaeva's poems *Attempt at a Room* (*Popytka komnaty*) and *Poem of the Air* (*Poema Vozdukha*), and Tsvetaeva would envision it vividly in a diary entry in the form of a letter which she sent to Steiger by letter on 18 August.[7]

In a letter written the next day, Tsvetaeva returned to that prospect of a one-day trip to Geneva. It wasn't Geneva that attracted her, but the possibility of making her way from there to the sanatorium in Berne where Steiger was being treated. She rejected this idea as impractical, but in subsequent letters continued to play with the notion that Geneva might serve as the gateway for a face-to-face meeting, whether through Steiger's arrival in St. Pierre de Rumilly or Tsvetaeva's at the sanatorium of Heilige Schwendi. And when on 2 September Tsvetaeva was again asked to take part in a group trip to Geneva, she agreed. There were two reasons for the journey: to show Geneva to her son Mur, and to profit from the domestic Swiss mail to send Steiger a package. Steiger was recovering from an operation in a decent sanatorium, his parents were there, and he did not

---

[4] *Opyty* (New York), 1955, no. 5, 59.
[5] Ibid., 56.
[6] Ibid., 59–60.
[7] Ibid., 61.

seem to need anything. Nevertheless, Tsvetaeva bought him a jacket out of her meager means.

On 4 September 1936, in a letter entitled "My Geneva," which never found its way into the collection published by K. Vilchkovsky, Tsvetaeva ironically described the day which she had not ended up spending in that city.[8] Calling upon Pasternak's "all-powerful god of details," she recreates for Steiger the events (or anti-events) of 3 September. The departure had been set for ten in the morning. Tsvetaeva hurriedly wrapped up her parcels and dressed herself and Mur "so that we looked more or less like the Swiss." Ten o'clock came, eleven o'clock, twelve—and there still was no car. The landlord's son informed Tsvetaeva that all the other traveling companions—the owner of the castle (formerly a Russian colonel), his Swiss-Russian wife, and one other woman—had thought better of it and would not be going.

> I go to the landlady and try just a bit to persuade her (one thing is for sure—I absolutely have to send off those things!). In a vague manner she both refuses and agrees to go. And it is already one o'clock, lunchtime (endless), now it's already two, and there is still no car.

At four the car ordered for ten a.m. arrived, and at half past four the whole group departed for Geneva. The ride was marvelous, three potential pitfalls were successfully navigated—there was enough gasoline, the French and the Swiss borders were crossed. Tsvetaeva was shown the English Garden and Lake Geneva. But she had one concern:

> I haven't been to Switzerland since 1903—and then I didn't send any packages—will I manage to send them off from a foreign post office? And will I find the courage to stop a car full of people in front of the post office.... But this, too, was dealt with.

She folded a note inside the package for Steiger: "I myself would like to be this jacket: to warm [you] and to know when and for whom I am

---

8 Unpublished letter, M. I. Tsvetaeva to A. S. Steiger, kindly provided to me by Steiger's sister, A. S. Golovina. The passages describing the trip to Geneva on 3 September are cited in accordance with this letter. [The complete corpus of Tsvetaeva's letters to Steiger is now available in Marina Tsvetaeva, *Sobranie sochinenii v semi tomakh* (Moscow: Ellis Lak, 1995), 7:565–635.—Ed.]

needed. M. Ts."⁹ "Now"—Tsvetaeva writes—"I can ride back." However, Mur and the other passengers had other goals and other plans.

> But here they come—the Uniprix, the arcades, in a word that household and female version of hell. Immediately Mur wants a fountain pen and a whole bunch of other things, I keep making him multiply by five, the landlady (Russian-Swiss—very sweet) picks out collars for her daughters in Russia (she sends them in letters), the colonel, her husband, wants beer. Mur *can't* multiply by five—in a word, a good hour of standing around over things, of immersion—face first—in the sorts of detail which I hate. As a reaction to all the chocolate, I don't buy any. (After your operation you probably are not supposed to have any, and my landlady bought some for Mur)—we sit in a café, the heat is insane, I write you a postcard, and Mur takes advantage of this by ordering himself an unbelievably large mug of beer (Gargantua!)—and again Uniprix and again the demand for a pen (Mur now has two).

A postcard with a view of the store "Au Grand Passage" has survived; on it Tsvetaeva, sitting with Mur in the hot café, wrote to Steiger: "Perhaps only in the times of Herzen and Ogaryov and their Natashas have greetings been sent with such bitterness from Switzerland to Switzerland. M.Ts."¹⁰ Leaving the café with Mur, she found that her companions had vanished: "For a long time nobody comes back. Absolutely nobody." Later it turned out that her landlady had suffered heart palpitations in the Uniprix and been taken to a doctor.

Tsvetaeva spent the following hours waiting, sitting alone in the burning heat of the car. (All the while Mur and the driver kept going off to drink beer.) She yielded to only one of Geneva's many temptations: she bought herself a cigarette lighter that cost one Swiss frank. "But since I already have my own with me and I have to take it across the border, I stuff it down my bosom—rather deeply." And as the fatal inevitability of Tsvetaeva's destiny would have it, the punishment was about to begin for this miniscule whim.

---

[9] Cited from a text transcribed by K. S. Vilchkovsky. The publication of Tsvetaeva's letters to Steiger in the journal *Opyty* was made on the basis of this text. A copy of the unpublished part of Vilchkovsky's transcript was in turn furnished to me by the editor of *Opyty*, Yury Ivask, during the preparation of my monograph about Tsvetaeva.

[10] The text of the postcard was kindly provided to me by A. S. Golovina.

> 7 o'clock. 7:30.... All the stores have closed. And—pay attention—I begin to feel it burn. That is, it has been burning me for a long time, from the first minute. In the little pit between the parting of my ribs. And—it really burns. *It*. The lighter. And as luck would have it, it is full of fuel.

With gallows humor Tsvetaeva tells Steiger that she was wearing a tight dress which buttoned at the back, so that she could not extract the scorching lighter, without undressing right there, on the square in front of the store. From the heat, the scorching metal seemed to have fused into her skin. There follow humorous observations about whether the fuel in the lighter might explode from the hot weather and the temperature of her body.

> And what if it suddenly bursts into flame—on the border? That's the sort of thing that happens with me. (And the dress will burn, and the automobile will burn, and the *border* will burn!) From time to time (and it is already well past 8), I check, running my hand over my dress—could it be smoldering—and I sniff, does it smell burnt? No! But it smells of fuel. As though I had been bathed in it. And my companions are still not back, and Mur keeps drinking beer with the driver, they come back again, and then go away again.

Finally at nine the colonel turned up, they set off to get his ill wife, and the trip back began. Tsvetaeva joked with the driver and watched the moon rise. ("For me the moon is loneliness itself. All the inhumanity of loneliness. I don't have a poet's feelings for the moon, but rather a wolf's.") But this description of the trip back to Château d'Arcine recalls a different animal from the canine order: the fox cub mentioned several times in Tsvetaeva's poetry, hidden by a young Spartan under his clothes and gnawing away at his stomach. Despite the continuous pain, Tsvetaeva did not tell anyone about the lighter. Only after they have returned to the castle:

> I run upstairs and—I can only see the surface of the lighter—it has *become a part* of me. I tear it away with difficulty: *raw flesh*. A terrific burn—and two lighters (at one point I had moved it). Now I can say on the basis of experience (my raw flesh): a lighter, full of fuel and thrust down the bosom, (1) does not light (2) but burns through.

It is hard to imagine a more fitting symbol for the catastrophic consequences of all Tsvetaeva's encounters with real-world phenomena—in daily life, in politics, or in love—than this ill-fated lighter. But she would not have been Tsvetaeva, had she not tried to extract some sort of metaphysical lyrical profit from this unmerited burn:

> I haven't told you about my thoughts on the road (accompanying the quiet burning of the lighter)—about how I would have agreed to spend the rest of my life being burned (I'd get used to it)—if you could be sitting next to me instead of the driver.

Through a further string of associative ideas, it occurs to Tsvetaeva that on this imaginary automobile ride Steiger would be cold and that she might not know how to warm him ("except with the lighter within"). Then comes a vision of a polar expedition, during which Tsvetaeva, as the senior participant, warms a young explorer—Steiger—with her body and thus saves his life. And Tsvetaeva imagines that the French driver sitting next to her as she engaged in this fantasy was probably thinking *Drôles de gens, les Russes, mais bien gentils* (Funny people, these Russians, but nice all the same). She closes the letter with the words "What is left to us, *Russes* or not *Russes*, than to be *bien gentils* with one another—[than baying] at the solitude of the lunar planet?"

The principle of contrast had transposed Steiger, connected with the idea of the lighter burn, to the North Pole as a participant in the Chelyuskin expedition, about which Tsvetaeva had written two years earlier with such enthusiasm in the poem "Cheliuskintsy." On the following day, this contrast between the polar ice on one hand, and, on the other, the unbearable heat in the café, the sweltering car, and the hellishly burning, potentially exploding lighter provided the impetus for the most frenzied poem of the cycle *Verses to an Orphan* (*Stikhi sirote*):

> On the iceberg—
> Beloved,
> On a landmine—
> Beloved,
> On an iceberg, in Guyana, in Gehenna—beloved.

And with its final chord of triumphant pity:

> And there is no pit, there is no abyss—
> Beloved! Desired! Pitied! Poor Darling!

Finally, a few words should be said about the opening of "My Geneva," which I have intentionally kept for the end. The letter begins as follows:

> Yesterday, after the trip to Geneva, I became utterly convinced of the impossibility of our ever meeting face-to-face. And suddenly I recalled those words, so strange in their cruelty, spoken by the extremely young Tsar—to zemstvo deputies, it seems:—"Don't dare to dream." (And—they dared.) And so, after yesterday's trip I understood that I don't dare even to dream.

Tsvetaeva had in mind the controversial declaration made on 17 January 1895 by Nicholas II shortly after his accession to the throne, when he told the deputies of the nobility, zemstvos, and urban officials not to get carried away by "senseless dreams about the participation of members of the zemstvos in the affairs of internal administration." The young monarch's discouraging words about democratization had a devastating effect on society. Lev Tolstoi responded in an angry article, "Senseless Dreaming,"[11] and Anton Chekhov made veiled references to it in two of his letters.[12]

It would seem that Marina Tsvetaeva had achieved the two goals of her trip—she had shown Geneva to her son and had sent the packages. But the general failure of the whole day and the physical pain from the burn fed into her habitual train of thought about the impossibility of ever fulfilling her desires. This theme found only approximate expression in the tactless words of the last Russian autocrat. It was expressed more succinctly in a couplet from a narrative poem by Victor von Scheffel (1826–86), *The Trumpeter of Säckingen*, which for Tsvetaeva had come

---

[11] Cf. L. N. Tolstoi, *Sobranie sochinenii v dvadtsati tomakh*, vol. 16 (Moscow, 1964), 605–14, and the commentary on 664. Nicholas II's words are cited on p. 606.
[12] Letters, Chekhov to A. S. Suvorin, 19 January and 23 March 1895, in A. P. Chekhov, *Polnoe sobranie sochinenii i pisem*, letters, vol. 6 (Moscow, 1978), 14–15, 40–41.

to represent the way her social relationships always turned out wrong. By the start of the twentieth century Scheffel's poem, which had gone through over one hundred editions in the nineteenth century and been distributed in millions of copies, was already being placed in the category of *Trivialliteratur*. As a historian of German literature, Richard Meyer, has written, "the popularity of this book brought into disrepute the very idea of popularity."[13] However, Tsvetaeva, an admirer of Lidiya Charskaya and Edmond Rostand, would not give up a beloved quotation simply because its source had been compromised.

In the thirteenth chapter of *The Trumpeter of Säckingen*, the hero of the poem, the musician Werner, pays court to Margareta, a nobleman's daughter, and receives a humiliating rejection in the form of a long, mocking monologue by Margareta's father about the inappropriateness of marriage between a poor musician and a girl from a good family.[14] Both the development of the episode and the name of the bride point to the connection between this chapter and the fifth chapter ("In the Rathaus") of Tsvetaeva's *Pied Piper* (*Krysolov*). And the next chapter of Scheffel's poem, the fourteenth, consists of a collection of songs composed by Werner, one of which, beginning with the words "Das ist im Leben hässlich eingerichtet,"[15] expresses yearning for a lost love. It had a huge success—first as a poem and then as an aria from an opera written in 1884 by another Victor, the composer Victor E. Nessler, on the subject of Scheffel's *Trumpeter*.[16] In 1888 alone Nessler's opera had 900 performances in the cities of northern Germany, everywhere evoking delight with an aria,

---

[13] Richard M. Meyer, *Die deutsche Literatur des 19. Jahrhunderts* (Berlin, 1912), 307. "*Der Trompeter von Säkkingen* gehört zu den Büchern, die die Popularität bei uns unpopulär gemacht haben."

[14] Joseph Victor von Scheffel, *Der Trompeter von Säkkingen*, "Dreizehntes Stück: Die Werbung," in *Werke in zwei Bänden* (Zurich, 1969), 2:140–48.

[15] Scheffel, *Werke*, 2:155–56.

[16] *Der Trompeter von Säkkingen: Oper in 3 Akten, nebst einem Vorspiel; Mit autorisierter theilweiser Benutzung der Idee und einiger Originallieder aus J. Victor von Scheffels Dichtung von Rudolf Bunge; Musik von Victor E. Nessler* (Leipzig, 1884). The young Werner's "Farewell" ("Abschied," Lied für Baryton), "Behüt dich Gott!," is on p. 263. In Nessler's opera the heroine is named Maria rather than Margareta; in Rudolf Bunge's libretto the theme of social inequality between the musician and the nobleman's daughter is absent. All this shows that this text was known to Tsvetaeva from its literary source and not from its operatic version, despite the wide popularity of the latter.

"Das ist im Leben," which became a kind of national song. Each stanza of the aria ended with a couplet:

> Behüt dich Gott! Es wär zu schön gewesen,
> Behüt dich Gott, es hat nicht sollen sein!
>
> (Farewell! It would have been so beautiful,
> Farewell, it wasn't meant to be!).

With this couplet that she had known from childhood little Marina had shocked her tutor in the Black Forest pension, when the owner of the hotel Angel did not come, as he had promised, for her and Asya ("The Ivy-Clad Tower" ["Bashnia v pliushche"]).[17] With these words Tsvetaeva had summed up her own friendship with Sonechka Holliday, which ended after three months ("The Tale of Sonechka" ["Povest' o Sonechke"]).[18] And it was with this couplet that her correspondence with Steiger concluded.

Es hat nicht sollen sein—it wasn't meant to be. If Marina and Asya had been called for as arranged, they would not have ended up in the castle of Princess von Thurn und Taxis, and the sketch "The Ivy-Clad Tower" would never have been written. If the grown-up Tsvetaeva had been better at sorting through trains and schedules, she would have made her way to Anatoly Steiger in the middle of August 1936, and the idea for *Verses to an Orphan* would never have arisen. The impossibility of a face-to-face meeting, submersion in the everyday hell of Geneva's stores, and her imaginative tale of the lighter burn were necessary for the idea's incarnation in verse.

As is becoming increasingly apparent with each publication, Tsvetaeva's epistolary legacy provides a subtle and essential key to the history of her works' creation and to the interpretation of their content. As I have tried to show, the letter "My Geneva," concealed by Vilchkovsky when he published her letters to Steiger in the journal *Opyty*,[19] illuminates both the theme and the system of images of the poem "On the Iceberg." Other

---

17   Tsvetaeva, *Izbrannaia proza*, 2:193, with the attribution of the quotation to Scheffel.
18   "Povest' o Sonechke," in Marina Tsvetaeva, *Neizdannoe: Stikhi, teatr, proza* (Paris: YMCA-Press, 1976), 350.
19   In the copy by Vilchkovsky (see n. 9), the letter "My Geneva" is listed as number XVII. Its text is replaced by one dotted line.

unpublished letters to Steiger—or letters hitherto published only with cuts—can provide further analogous material. One can only hope that the collections of letters from Tsvetaeva to Anatoly Steiger and Yury Ivask which have been announced for publication by Russica will reproduce these letters in their entirety and without vexing cuts.[20] Cuts might have seemed desirable upon first publication of these letters in 1955 and 1956. Now, however, when scholars of Tsvetaeva have received full access to the cycle *Woman Friend* and to *Letter to an Amazon* (*Lettre à l'Amazone*), such Victorian squeamishness is neither necessary nor appropriate. As Tsvetaeva quite justifiably wrote to Ivask about Steiger, "I don't give away his secret, it is evident in every one of his published lines."[21] About this very secret Steiger himself said:

> It is not my duty, but an honor, a special honor
> To mention it, without lowering my eyes.[22]

It would be unfortunate if publishers and commentators prove more bashful than the poets themselves and, lowering their eyes, bar the way to a more complete understanding of Marina Tsvetaeva's poetry.

---

[20] These were eventually published in Russia. See n. 8.—Ed.
[21] Letters, Tsvetaeva to Iu. P. Ivask, in *Russkii literaturnyi arkhiv*, ed. M. Karpovich and D. Chizhevskii (New York, 1956), 229.
[22] Anatolii Shteiger, *2 x 2 = 4* (New York, 1982), 59.

Isadora Had a Taste for "Russian Love"[1]

When Isadora Duncan returned to the United States in October 1922 after her triumphant appearances in Moscow, she brought back a boundless enthusiasm for the Soviet system and a Russian husband almost two decades her junior. Her return was widely covered in the press because she and Sergei Esenin, her new husband, were briefly detained by the immigration authorities at Ellis Island under suspicion of being "Bolshevik agents." The *Herald* described Esenin as "super-blond," "of a slim, athletic build, broad-shouldered and slim-waisted" and "the most cheerful Bolshevist that ever crossed the Atlantic." The *New York World* added that Esenin spoke French and was "a boyish chap, who looks as though he might make an excellent halfback for any football team."

Actually, Esenin did not speak French—or any other language except Russian. Throughout their brief marriage he and Duncan communicated through interpreters. It was an oversimplification to call him a "Bolshevist," and he was far from cheerful at the time of his arrival in America. He was probably the most popular poet in Russia, with a following that resembled that of a matinee idol or an operatic tenor more than that of a literary figure. It was a rude shock to Esenin to learn that in Western Europe and America he was merely the boyish husband of a celebrated dancer and that his poetry was unknown outside Russia. His resentment led to heavy drinking, wild furniture-smashing brawls in hotels from Paris to Chicago, and to repeated, well-publicized beatings of his aging, overweight, and adoring wife (their romance began when the drunken Esenin slugged Duncan at a party after one of her Moscow recitals, awakening an unsuspected masochistic streak in her and arousing her appetite for what she called "Russian love," all too often expressed in black eyes that she had to cover with makeup and veils).

---

1   Review of *Esenin: A Life*, by Gordon McVay (Ann Arbor, MI: Ardis, 1976). Originally published in *New York Times Book Review*, 9 May 1976, 3, 38.

Nine months after their marriage, Esenin walked out on Duncan, declaring in an interview: "I married [her] for her money and for a chance to travel." The length of the marriage was about par for Esenin's involvements with women. Besides Duncan, he had been married to a well-known Russian actress and to the granddaughter of Lev Tolstoi, and he had a number of children by various mistresses, but he left all of them in a year or less. After his break with Duncan, Esenin returned to Russia and embarked on a self-destructive course that led to his suicide two years later at the age of thirty.

An archetypal instance of the violent, alcoholic, doomed poet, Esenin was driven by a series of irreconcilable love-hate conflicts that pervaded all areas of his life and consciousness: his confused feelings about the Revolution, which he had hailed and whose results he came to loathe; his ambiguous sexuality; his mixed attraction to and detestation of the Jews; and his sense of having betrayed his peasant heritage in his later, sophisticated and decadent poetry.

The poet's inner contradictions have now been ably documented in Gordon McVay's thoroughly researched, lavishly illustrated new biography, the most detailed and knowledgeable account of Esenin's life to have appeared so far. Crammed with new facts that McVay discovered during twelve years of research, much of it in secret Soviet archives, the book avoids the romanticized approach of some of the earlier writings on Esenin and punctures numerous holes in the image of Esenin as saintly peasant sage and revolutionary that has become de rigueur in the Soviet Union in the last two decades.

In 1915, when he was twenty, Sergei Esenin (the name has also been transcribed as Yesenin and Essenine) made a tremendous hit in St. Petersburg literary circles with his fresh and lyrical early poems, which sang of his native Ryazan countryside and voiced a touching compassion for wild and domestic animals mistreated and tormented by humans. His personal beauty and charm and his peasant origins all contributed to his success and popularity. The fashion for literary *paysannerie* had been launched somewhat earlier by Nikolai Klyuev (1887–1937), a brilliant, powerful poet whose work combined the folklore of the Old Believer sects of northern Russia with the literary culture of the Symbolist movement, and who was seen by many as the authentic spokesman for the whole of the

Russian peasantry.[2] Klyuev was openly homosexual, something that was widely accepted in literary circles of the time. Esenin became his disciple and eventually his lover.

In response to the fad for peasant culture, Esenin and Klyuev affected fantastic folk costumes straight out of opera and filled their poems and personal speech with incomprehensible words from remote dialects. The masquerade was so successful that it brought them to the attention of the imperial court (the last Romanovs were notoriously blind to the cultural renaissance that marked their reign, noticing only those artists who, like Esenin and the basso Chaliapin, publicized their peasant roots). In 1916 Esenin was a protégé of Empress Alexandra, reading his poetry at her court and planning to dedicate his next book to her.

Less than two years later, Esenin lent his support to the October Revolution. Like the other peasant poets around Klyuev, Esenin saw in Lenin a new peasant tsar who would restore the patriarchal ways and religious piety of the Russian countryside and protect the village culture from the threat of modernization and Westernization. Esenin welcomed the October Revolution with a series of baroque, visionary poems couched in biblical diction, in which he equated Russia giving birth to world revolution with nature yielding a harvest, a cow producing a calf, and the Virgin Mary giving birth to Christ. Equally offensive to Marxists and to Orthodox Christians, these poems, culminating in the utopian narrative poem *Inoniia*, remain a unique poetic statement that mingles the remnants of an ancient fertility cult with a vision of cosmic revolutionary change.

It took Esenin several years to realize that his view of the Revolution as a peasant utopia was misguided. When he did, he changed his peasant garb to elegant Western attire and joined the Imaginists, a postrevolutionary, modernistic, urban literary group. His marriage to Isadora Duncan gave him a chance to escape from Soviet realities, but Germany, France,

---

2 SK's high opinion of Klyuev's poetry was reflected in a series of publications in the gay American press. See, for example, Simon Karlinsky, "Kliuev, Nikolai (1887–1937)," in *Gay Histories and Cultures: An Encyclopedia*, ed. George E. Haggerty (New York: Garland Publishing, 2000), 520–21. He and Esenin also figure in Simon Karlinsky, "Introduction: Russia's Gay Literature and History," in *Out of the Blue: Russia's Hidden Gay Literature; An Anthology*, ed. Kevin Moss, intro. by Simon Karlinsky (San Francisco: Gay Sunshine Press, 1997), 15–25. This same volume (151–52) contains SK's translation of two poems by Klyuev.—Ed.

Holland, and America all seemed equally alien, incomprehensible, and devoid of all appreciation of literature (which for Esenin meant Russian literature only). Esenin's poetry written after his return mourns the disappearance of traditional rural ways and customs ("The Receding Russia"), laments the imminent passing of his own youth and beauty, and expresses his solidarity with the alcoholics and derelicts of Moscow's skid row, who like Esenin could find no place for themselves in postrevolutionary society ("Moscow of the Taverns").

To his credit, Gordon McVay's book takes up an important theme until now avoided by Esenin's biographers: his sexual ambivalence. McVay examines Esenin's relationship with Klyuev and concludes that Esenin "may have succumbed to the pressure of the milieu and discovered in himself a latent bisexuality." This points in the right direction, but it does not begin to cover the subject. There is nothing "latent" about the seventeen-year-old Esenin confessing to Mariya Balzamova, a young woman infatuated with him, that the great love of his life might turn out to be either a man or a woman; nor is there anything "latent" about the love letters and poems Esenin and Klyuev exchanged. "Pressure of the milieu" cannot account for Esenin's recurrent close relationships with men who were either homosexual or had bisexual episodes in their lives (Gorodetsky, Ryurik Ivnev and Leonid Kannegiser, to name a few), or for his widely attested-to habit of sharing his bed with his male friends. Esenin's alternating attraction to homosexuality and his revulsion against it (strikingly illustrated in Nicolas Nabokov's memoir *Bagázh*[3]) may well have contributed to his alcoholism and his suicide. His battered and abandoned wives and mistresses seem to have been the principal victims of this poet's inability to come to terms with his bisexuality.

McVay fails to notice that this entire complex is a key to understanding a number of Esenin's more significant poems, such as "The Day Departed" (1916), where the poet sends his shadow to make love to other men in his stead; "Farewell to Marienhof" (1922) with its homoerotic imagery; the opening section of "Prayers for the Dead" ("Sorokoust"), where the poet's self-disgust bursts forth in the deliberately shocking images of oral and anal sex with animals and objects; and, finally, Esenin's famous

---

[3] A few months later SK published a review of *Bagázh: Memoirs of a Russian Cosmopolitan*, by Nicolas Nabokov, *Russian Review* 36 (1977): 116–17.

suicide poem, which is also a love letter to the young man who had spent the night with him a few days earlier (McVay's discussion of this poem is handicapped by his failure to convey the grammatical gender of the addressee, unequivocally stated in the second line of the Russian original; in general, one could wish for more fluent and idiomatic renditions of verse quotations throughout McVay's book).

Esenin was at the height of his celebrity when he killed himself. Had he survived until the collectivization of the 1930s, he would undoubtedly have been branded a "kulak" and have perished in the labor camps, as did Klyuev and other poets of the peasant group. Esenin's attitude and his popularity were repeatedly denounced as reactionary and harmful in the Soviet press in the 1920s; from the 1930s on, much of his work was banned and it became dangerous to own a volume of his verse. Under Khrushchev, the official view was reversed. This native son and superpatriot, who had welcomed the October Revolution and repeatedly expressed his dislike of Western countries and Western culture, now suddenly seemed a more suitable candidate for the title of great modern Russian poet than the cosmopolitan Jews Pasternak and Mandelstam or the émigrée Marina Tsvetaeva. Today there is an officially fostered Esenin cult in the Soviet Union and publications about him have become an industry.

In human profundity and poetic mastery, Esenin is no match for Blok or Mayakovsky, Mandelstam or Tsvetaeva. But he has something that these other, greater poets lack—a popular touch which makes his poetry equally accessible and moving, as the poet Georgy Ivanov suggested, to a literary scholar, to a teenaged Soviet girl who is a member of the Communist Youth, and to an aged White Army general living in retirement in Paris.[4] Gordon McVay's biography has little to say about the quality of Esenin's poetry, but it contains enough new material on the poet's life and personality to enable future commentators to read this poetry with more understanding and in greater depth than before. Sergei Esenin with all his complexities and contradictions restored is a far more interesting poet than the standardized patriotic icon now promoted in the Soviet Union. He deserves to be known here.

---

[4] SK paraphrases freely from memoirs of Esenin in Georgii Ivanov, *Peterburgskie zimy*, 2nd ed. (New York: Izd-vo imeni Chekhova, 1952).—Ed.

II. Modernism, Its Past, Its Legacy

* * *

The foregrounding of Esenin's "sexual ambivalence" in this essay provoked a storm of controversy in the New York Russian émigré newspaper *Novoe russkoe slovo* after Valery Pereleshin, a gay poet living in Brazil and frequent contributor to the paper, published a paraphrase and partial translation of it in the issue of 9 July 1976 under the title "Pobol'she by takikh statei!" (Let's have more articles like this!). The first response ("Napraslina na Esenina"), alleging slander, came from a certain Vladimir Rudinsky (29 August), to whom SK replied at length on 30 September. Subsequent interventions came in the form of letters; SK's only further reply was published on 1 December, and he silently called a halt to the discussion, undoubtedly owing to a lack of any mutual understanding of the subject, by the end of the year. This minor "scandal" also generated a flood of private correspondence, part of which is preserved in the Simon Karlinsky Papers at the Bancroft Library, University of California, Berkeley. A lively and prolonged exchange of letters between SK and McVay, who was by that time writing a second book, *Isadora and Esenin*,[5] is of particular interest.

One of SK's translations of Klyuev's vivid and exotic poetry is the following:

> That fellow with the green eyes
> Smells of ginger and mint.
> What Pripyat and what Euphrates
> Might be flowing in the blood in his veins?
> Isn't there a desert sunset in his earlobes,
> Leopards at their water hole?
> In the tart buds of aspen trees
> There's the biblical vinegar of sultry Chaldea.
> The shouts of a Russian carpenters' guild
> Are an echo of an Arab encampment.
> In a Lapland snowstorm you discern
> An African's coral-hued dance.
> Corals and Russia leather—
> Such things cause poetry's spring floods.
> In an Orthodox chapel, an arabesque-clad mufti
> Is in tears over an ancient liturgy book.

---

[5] Gordon McVay, *Isadora and Esenin* (Ann Arbor: Ardis, 1980).

This is an encounter, amidst our native furrows,
Of grain and earthy nipples.
In the fellow's eye sockets, star-like,
Is a green nocturnal flame,
As if amidst bamboo thickets
Tiger cubs slink in their mother's wake,
As if on pussy willows, biliously,
Ginger and Chilean mint have sprouted.

(1924)[6]

---

[6] Simon Karlinsky, trans., "Three Russian Poets," in *Gay Roots: Twenty Years of Gay Sunshine*, ed. Winston Leyland (San Francisco: Gay Sunshine Press, 1991), 650.

Surrealism in Twentieth-Century Russian Poetry: Churilin, Zabolotsky, Poplavsky[1]

All her life Zinaida Gippius remembered how startled she was when as a young girl she was told that the Russian word *predmet* was devised and introduced into the language by Karamzin at the very end of the eighteenth century.[2] The discovery left her wondering how the Russians who lived before that time could discuss all sorts of basic things without a word denoting "object" in the language. We may well be startled in a similar way when we stop to realize that the handy adjective "surrealistic" was coined only in the late 1920s. Furthermore, the word did not initially mean what it came to mean later. When Vladimir Mayakovsky encountered the French Surrealists during his trip to Paris in 1927, he was not sure just what their movement was about but from their behavior concluded that they must be the French equivalent of his own LEF group.[3] The Paris-centered movement in poetry, painting, and cinema, which was to have a considerable impact on the arts of this century and which contributed the word "surrealistic" to many languages, was, it is rarely realized today, primarily dedicated to synthesizing the insights of Sigmund Freud with those of Karl Marx.

Although the participants of the original Surrealist movement styled themselves revolutionary and Marxist, the Soviet cultural establishment refused to recognize them as any such thing, and the refusal, we can now plainly see, was motivated not only by the adherence of André Breton and Paul Éluard to Freud but also, and overwhelmingly, by the insistence of the Surrealist poets and painters on their right to use revolutionary twentieth-century techniques and images. At the time when the Soviet cultural policy was about to set up "Socialist Realism"

---

[1] Originally published in *Slavic Review* 26 (1967): 605–17.
[2] Z. N. Gippius, *Zhivye litsa*, vol. 2 (Prague, 1925), 126.
[3] Maiakovskii, "Ezdil ia tak," in *Polnoe sobranie sochinenii*, vol. 8 (Moscow, 1958), 334.

as the only acceptable artistic method, surrealistic techniques and imagery, viewed from the Soviet Union, could not but appear bourgeois and decadent. To the Surrealists themselves the rejection by Moscow seemed a tragic mistake. The English Surrealist David Gascoyne described the various developments in this protracted mutual misunderstanding and the genuine pain the Surrealists felt at being told that they had to adhere to techniques and styles *they* felt were antiquated and bourgeois.[4] The Russian artists in the Soviet Union faced by similar demands at the time had no choice. The French and Spanish poets, painters, and film-makers of the Surrealist movement did have a choice, and the result was that by the mid-1930s the original Surrealist movement had to all intents and purposes fallen apart. Various representative participants went each his own way. Breton tried to cleave to the earlier Surrealist purity for the next few decades, Aragon became an orthodox Stalinist in politics if not in his art, Salvador Dalí steadily drifted toward wealth and Catholicism, while Luis Buñuel somehow manages to amalgamate the original Freudian-Marxist orientation of the Surrealists in his later non-Surrealist films.

By the time the movement fell apart, the adjective "surrealistic" became commonly used and universally understood in broader connotations. A suburban matron understands perfectly when she reads in the society column of her Sunday paper that one of her neighbors went on a surrealistic shopping spree (how did one express such things before the 1920s?). In recent literary criticism the term "surrealistic" is commonly used (without reference to the original Surrealist movement) to denote the kind of fantasy that arises not from the unfamiliar and the traditionally fantastic but rather the kind of fantasy that results from the unexpected juxtaposition of images that are already familiar and preferably even prosaic. The classic illustration of this type of fantasy is provided by Lautréamont's celebrated description (so admired by the Surrealists) of the encounter between a sewing machine and an umbrella upon a dissecting table. Three objects not at all fantastic in themselves produce an unmistakably fantastic effect merely by the unexplained fact of their conjunction. Similarly, when Nikolai Zabolotsky (to jump the gun a bit) describes a Leningrad crowd in which one man carries a boot on a platter

---

[4] Gascoyne, *A Short Survey of Surrealism* (London, 1936).

and another one sings a poodle-dog,[5] the reader is at once shifted into a surrealistic context by such ordinary things in such unexpected context. To the same order of surrealistic devices in the arts belong the reversal of expected size relationships (huge combs or apples that fill an entire room in René Magritte's paintings); unmotivated reversal in expected sequences of events; separate, independent existence of parts of familiar objects or of parts of human anatomy (Lautréamont probably did not know Gogol's "The Nose" when he wrote his prose poem about the man who encounters one of his own hairs as a fellow customer in a brothel).

Interest in surrealistic types of imagery usually goes hand in hand with interest in the subconscious, in delirium, in free association, in automatic writing, and, of course, in dreams. The logic of most of our dreams is likely to be surrealistic, as Lev Tolstoi well realized. Aleksei Remizov's unvarnished transcriptions of his own dreams in his book *Martyn Zadeka* are almost inevitably surrealistic. But not all dreams in literature have to be surrealistic. Gogol's work offers us pertinent examples in this respect: the dream of the Mayor in *The Inspector General*—the one about the two rats which sniffed at him and then went away (contributing a popular saying to the Russian language as they left)—is certainly a perfectly prosaic and realistic dream. Levko's dream in "May Night," on the other hand, is pure Romanticism, with its water nymphs, evil witch, and the crumbling house becoming new again. But Gogol also provides us with an authentically surrealistic literary dream in his "Ivan Fyodorovich Shponka and His Aunt." Here the hero dreams that his future wife *is* a bolt of textile, and later in the dream his wife is located simultaneously in his hat and in his pocket. An equally fantastic scene of this dream, in which Shponka

---

[5] "Odin—sapog neset na bliude / Drugoi—poet sobachku-pudel'." Zabolotskii, "Obvodnyi kanal," in *Stikhotvoreniia* (Washington, 1965), 48. The English translation of these lines in *The Penguin Book of Russian Verse*, ed. Dimitri Obolensky (Baltimore, 1962), 419, which reads "One [character] is carrying a boot on a dish, another is chanting the praises of a poodle [he is selling]," deprives the passage of its surrealistic quality by substituting a rather forced prosaic explanation, not really warranted by the deliberately ungrammatical Russian original. The new Soviet edition, Zabolotskii, *Stikhotvoreniia i poemy* (Moscow and Leningrad, 1965), 212, prints the version of the poem "Obvodnyi kanal" amended by the poet during the Stalinist period, when he consciously tried to edit all surrealistic imagery out of his earlier work. In this amended version the second quoted line reads: "Drugoi poet khvalu Iude" [The other chants praises of Judas], thus replacing a bit of surrealistic whimsy with a not-very-appropriate romantic-demonic note.

dreams that he is a bell being hoisted atop a belfry which is really his aunt, becomes doubly surrealistic when a precisely identified colonel of a certain regiment, who happens to be passing by, assures the terrified Shponka that he is in fact a church bell. A twentieth-century descendant of this colonel is to be found in Velimir Khlebnikov's *poema* called *Gibel' Atlantidy* (The end of Atlantis), in the person of the passer-by (*putnik*) who strolls past the cataclysmic scene at the end of the poem, when a continent is collapsing and sinking into the ocean. If the bizarre and the unusual placed in believable or prosaic surroundings make a romantically fantastic impression, the effect of the prosaic and the believable placed within a bizarre or incongruous context is, as Gogol's colonel and Khlebnikov's passer-by demonstrate, likely to be surrealistic.[6] And, of course, a genuinely surrealistic type of fantasy resists any kind of paraphrasable explication and excludes any possibility of allegorical interpretation.

Once the specific type of imagination entailed in surrealistic imagery becomes clear, one can take a fresh look at a number of Russian writers

---

6   In his review of *Russian Futurism*, by Vladimir Markov (Berkeley: University of California Press, 1968), *Nation*, 10 February 1969, 182, SK had remarked on Khlebnikov's "verbal flair, surrealistic imagery and anarchic inner freedom." Along with Pasternak and Poplavsky, Khlebnikov had featured in SK's introduction to a German translation of several poems as early as 1950:

> "Khlebnikov was the Columbus of new poetic continents, which are at the moment populated and spiritually explored by only a few of us," wrote the most significant poet of revolutionary Russia, Vladimir Mayakovsky.
>
> There are very few poetic inventions or devices that were not analyzed in Khlebnikov's poetic laboratory. More than any other personality of the twentieth century, with the possible exception of the American prose poet Gertrude Stein, Khlebnikov awakened the hidden potentials of vowels and word roots. That his influence did not extend to other countries can be explained by the fact that Khlebnikov's extraordinary research was done in the Russian language and syntax, which is why his most surprising inventions cannot be translated....
>
> Already in his first poems, Khlebnikov is surprisingly powerful and original. The Russian language is very flexible, as word classes can be modified by the use of corresponding suffixes, prefixes and other forms (for example, verbs can be changed into nouns, nouns into adjectives, etc.). Moreover, there is a complex system of diminutives and derivatives of a different type, which can be used with astonishing ease for similar transformations. All these elements of language had never before been used to poetic ends. It was Khlebnikov's achievement to demonstrate their magical power and to show how they could be mastered. (Translated by Joachim Klein, from S. Karlinsky, "Drei russische Dichter," *Das Lot* 4 [October 1950]: 46–48.)—Ed.

and works. Gogol and Khlebnikov emerge as major Russian Surrealists, though not full-time ones. Tatyana's dream in Pushkin's *Evgeny Onegin* acquires a new look, as do the dreams of Anna Karenina, the deathbed delirium of Andrei in *War and Peace,* and the dream of Andrei's young son at the end of that novel. Some of the best-known poems of Konstantin Sluchevsky, Nikolai Gumilyov (especially "The Wayward Tram" ["Zabludivshiisia tramvai"]), and Georgy Ivanov are authentically surrealistic. And although the Surrealist movement had no discernible impact on Russian literature—there was no Russian Surrealism in the sense that there was Czech or Serbo-Croatian Surrealism—the broadened definition of the term as outlined above enables us to consider three extremely interesting Russian twentieth-century poets as Surrealists. These three are not the only possible candidates for such a designation within Russian poetry (a thorough search for surrealistic imagery will certainly reveal it in a number of prerevolutionary, Soviet, and émigré Russian poets), but they are the most likely, the most obvious, the most thoroughly surrealistic ones.

The surrealistic poetry of Tikhon Churilin (1885–1946) was mostly written during the second decade of the present century and thus belongs chronologically with the Acmeist and Futurist generation of prerevolutionary Russian poetry. Nikolai Zabolotsky (1903–58), it is becoming more and more clear, is the most important and interesting poet to develop in the Soviet period and environment. His contemporary Boris Poplavsky (1903–35) is probably the most outstanding poet produced by the Russian emigration. Because of the frequently reactionary orientation of Russian literary criticism, both in the Soviet Union and at times in the diaspora, these three poets have been by and large overlooked and neglected for decades. The poetry of Zabolotsky is going through a major revival at the present time, both in the Soviet Union and abroad. In 1965 there appeared almost simultaneously two large collections of this poet's work, one in the Soviet Union and one abroad,[7] which made available for the

---

[7] See n. 5. The Soviet edition, edited by A. M. Turkov, offers a more comprehensive selection of Zabolotsky's poetry, but the almost simultaneous Washington volume, edited by Gleb Struve and Boris Filippov, is indispensable in that it offers the text of the collection *Stolbtsy* and of a few later poems as originally published by Zabolotsky. In the new Soviet edition, *Stikhotvoreniia i poemy,* the poems of this collection have been quite systematically tampered with (apparently by the poet himself in the 1940s)

first time in almost three decades Zabolotsky's startlingly original early work, his first collection *Stolbtsy* (Columns) and the long-banned *poema* on collectivization *Torzhestvo zemledeliia* (Triumph of agriculture). Also in 1965, attracting considerably less attention, there was privately printed in Paris a small edition of Boris Poplavsky's slim posthumous book of verse, *Dirizhabl' neizvestnogo napravleniia* (Dirigible of unknown destination). The volume contained some of his most remarkable and successful poems, which clearly place Poplavsky among the major Russian poets of the twentieth century. But if Zabolotsky is finally given the recognition he so richly deserves, and if Poplavsky has a certain minority following among Russian speakers abroad,[8] Tikhon Churilin's person and poetry might possibly be the single most thoroughly forgotten phenomenon in the whole history of Russian letters. Certainly, even the secondary poets of the Karamzinian epoch receive more attention in Soviet publication and criticism.

Yet, if one looks through the literary journals published in the heyday of Russian Futurism, one easily finds his poetry represented there alongside Khlebnikov, Mayakovsky, Kamensky, and the various Burlyuks. A poet of peasant origin, Churilin became insane shortly after beginning his literary career around 1910. After several years of treatment at mental institutions he was cured and shortly thereafter published his first volume of verse, *Vesna posle smerti* (Springtime after death; Moscow, 1915). The volume met with considerable critical acclaim, and several of the poems from it were widely anthologized at the time. Nikolai Gumilyov wrote about *Vesna posle smerti*:

> The poems of Tikhon Churilin are on the borderline between poetry and something extremely significant and exciting. It has long become customary for prophets to use verse to express their revelations, moralists their laws, and philosophers their deductions. Every valid or even simply peculiar worldview tends to be formulated in verse.

---

with the clear aim of eliminating all surrealistic imagery and of making the syntax, the grammar, the spelling, and the punctuation of the original poems more customary, more prosaic, and less startling.

[8] "I did not meet Poplavski, who died young, a far violin among near balalaikas.... His plangent tonalities I shall never forget, nor shall I ever forgive myself the ill-tempered review in which I attacked him for trivial faults in his unfledged verse." Vladimir Nabokov, *Speak, Memory* (New York, 1966), 287.

It would take us too long to establish the causes for this in this brief notice. But, of course, this tendency in the majority of cases has nothing in common with poetry.

Tikhon Churilin is a fortunate exception [to this rule]. From the literary point of view, he is connected with Andrei Bely and more remotely with the Cubo-Futurists.[9] He frequently succeeds in twisting his verse in such a manner that usual, even trite words assume the quality of some kind of pristine savagery and novelty. His theme is a human being on the very verge of insanity, at times actually insane. But while real madmen incoherently describe birdies and little flowers, his poems retain insanity's severe logic and the imagery of genuine ravings:

> Побрили Кикапу—в последний раз.
> Помыли Кикапу—в последний раз.
>   С кровавою водою таз
>   И волосы, его.
>   Куда-с?
> Ведь Вы сестра?
> Побудьте с ним хоть до утра[10]

(They've shaven Kickapoo—for the last time.
They've washed Kickapoo—for the last time.
  A pail with bloody water
  And his hair:
        What should be done with it?
  Aren't you the sister?
  Stay with him at least until morning).

Vesna posle smerti also made a very strong and lasting impression on Marina Tsvetaeva, who became friendly with Churilin at the time of the

---

[9] Gumilyov's parallels are certainly valid, but one can't help suspecting that the term "surrealistic," nonexistent at the time, conveys what he was trying to express with greater precision.

[10] Quoted from N. Gumilev, *Pis'ma o russkoi poezii* (Petrograd, 1923), 205. The article originally appeared in *Apollon*, 1915, no. 10 (December). It may be worthwhile to point out that the name Kickapoo was known to the Russians of 1915 as a currently popular dance (see also Maiakovskii, *Oblako v shtanakh* [A cloud in trousers]) and conveyed no associations with either minstrel shows or Li'l Abner.

publication of his book.¹¹ In 1929, while writing her monograph on the painter Nataliya Goncharova (who did the illustrations for Churilin's first book), Tsvetaeva remembered Churilin and his book in several passages. Here are two representative quotations: "I first heard about this Nataliya Goncharova from Tikhon Churilin, a poet. A poet of genius. To him and by him were given the best poems about the war, not sufficiently circulated or appreciated at the time. Nor are they known now."¹² And

> I can see it, this huge book, published, it seems, in only two hundred copies. The book, written after the departure from the insane asylum where Churilin spent two years. Springtime after death. There was a verse in it that said more about immortality than volumes and volumes:
>
> > Быть может—умру
> > *Наверно* воскресну!
> >
> > (I shall possibly die
> > I shall be resurrected *for certain!*).
>
> The entire book unfolded (*shla*) under the sign of resurrection and of recent death.¹³

Only recently did we learn from a memoir of Lilya Brik that Churilin's "The End of Kickapoo" (the same poem that Gumilyov quoted in his review) was one of Vladimir Mayakovsky's favorite poems, and that Mayakovsky frequently recited it in such a manner as to bring out the tragic theme of the poem.¹⁴

Few things illustrate the paradoxes and vicissitudes to which the evaluation of twentieth-century Russian poetry is subject as does this case of

---

11 In 1916 Churilin dedicated to Tsvetaeva a fragment from an autobiographical prose poem "Iz detstva dalechaishego" [Out of remotest childhood], which appeared in the collection *Giulistan 2* (Moscow, 1916). On his friendship with Tsvetaeva, see my book *Marina Cvetaeva: Her Life and Art* (Berkeley: University of California Press, 1966), 40.

12 Tsvetaeva, "Natal'ia Goncharova," *Volia Rossii* (Prague), nos. 5/6 (1929), 47.

13 Ibid., 49.

14 L. Brik, "Chuzhie stikhi," in *V. Maiakovskii v vospominaniiakh sovremennikov* (Moscow, 1963), 344. The extent to which Churilin has been forgotten in the Soviet Union can be gauged by the fact that the committee of distinguished Soviet scholars that edited this volume was unable to state his correct dates in the index.

a poet so highly regarded and taken so seriously by Gumilyov, Tsvetaeva, and Mayakovsky (with all their differences in aesthetic approach) and so totally neglected by Soviet and émigré criticism.

Churilin's surrealism in his first book is, to be sure, a very special case. Much of the special imagery is due to the poet's desire to convey the mental states of paranoia and delirium. Already in *Vesna posle smerti* there is a strong tendency toward what the Surrealists later were to call automatic writing. In Churilin's second book of verse, *L'vu—Bars* (To lion—[from] leopard), first published in Moscow in 1918,[15] the tendency toward free association based on phonetic pattern gets almost out of hand at times. But in this volume as well Churilin remains a Surrealist *en avance* in his deliberate agglomerations of unrelated and disturbing images. The following poem from *Vesna posle smerti* might perhaps be used to illustrate this poet's art. Within twelve lines, with no story to tell, relying only on the use of imagery and of sound associations and patterns, Churilin takes the reader from comfortable placidity to the verge of nameless terror and back. The final suicidal mood is also a feature of several other of his poems.

Полночь на святках

Пламя лампы ласковой потухает: полночь.
В каске, в маске, с плясками подступает полночь.
Тихо-тихо-тихонько шла бы полночь, полночь.
Прямо пряно-пьяною приступаешь, полночь.

Вьюгой—ффьюю ты—вьюгою попеваешь, полночь.
Среброструнной домрою донимаешь, полночь.
Балалайкой, лайкою, лаешь, лаешь полночь.
—И ушла на кладбище—с пляской, в каске, полночь.

Утро. Струны добрые домры—где ты, полночь?
Солнце светит, вечное,—где ты, где ты, полночь?
Мёты взмёт, метельные,—засыпают полночь.
О, могила милая,—где ты? где ты, полночь.[16]

---

[15] I wish to thank Professor Vladimir Markov for providing me with a copy of this otherwise utterly unobtainable volume.
[16] Tikhon Churilin, *Vesna posle smerti* (Moscow, 1915), 57.

Midnight at Christmastime

The flame of the gentle lamp is dying: midnight.
In helmet, in mask, with dances, she approaches—midnight.
Quiet, quiet, so quietly, won't you go away, midnight?
Direct, heady, drunken, you attack, midnight.

Like a blizzard (just look at it!), in blizzard gusts you sing, midnight.
With silver-stringed *domra* you taunt, midnight.
Balalaika-like, sled-dog-like, you bark and bark, midnight.
—And [then] she went off to the cemetery—the dancing,
                                        helmeted midnight.

Morning. Kindly *domra* strings—where are you, midnight?
The eternal sun is shining—where are you, where are you, midnight?
Whirling blizzard swirls [gradually] cover midnight.
O, sweet grave, where are you? Where are you, midnight?

After the October Revolution Churilin underwent a political conversion and devoted himself to the "theory of Communist culture." He wrote no verse after 1920, having come to consider lyric poetry "not a valid aesthetic aim in itself."[17] As late as 1925 he was considered sufficiently well known and important to have a sizable section devoted to his poetry in the popular anthology of twentieth-century Russian poetry compiled by I. S. Ezhov and E. I. Shamurin.[18] Because his poetry was available in this widely read collection, it is reasonable to assume that his use of surrealistic imagery was familiar to his two younger contemporaries, Zabolotsky and Poplavsky, during their formative years.

These two poets present a fascinating contrast in terms of environment, personality, and literary orientation, but there is also a set of equally fascinating, at times uncanny, parallels in their individually developed styles, their systems of imagery, even the chronology of their literary careers. Both are metaphysical poets. Both were born in 1903, Zabolotsky on 24 April, Poplavsky exactly one month later on 24 May. Both came from

---

17 Churilin's own statement as quoted in the biobibliographical note on him (which for all its brevity is apparently the most detailed factual source on this poet) in I. S. Ezhov and E. I. Shamurin, *Russkaia poeziia XX veka* (Moscow, 1925), 588–89.
18 Ibid., 314–16. Twelve poems by Churilin are included.

families of liberal-minded Russian intelligentsia. Zabolotsky's parents were of peasant origin, and Poplavsky's came from the nobility; but the intellectual and educational level of the two families appears to have been about the same. Poplavsky spent a part of his childhood abroad; after 1919 his family emigrated, first to Constantinople, then to Paris. Poplavsky's literary associations in the Russian Paris of the 1920s, his contacts with Merezhkovsky and Gippius, with Khodasevich and Otsup, with the French literary world could not have been in the least similar to Nikolai Zabolotsky's simultaneous experiences in the Red Army, his literary apprenticeship in children's journals under the tutelage of Samuil Marshak, and his association with the young Evgeny Shvarts and with Konstantin Vaginov in the literary group *Oberiu (Ob"edinenie Real'nogo Iskusstva)*.[19]

The literary influences and parentage of these two poets could not be more diverse. The only possible influence they could have shared is that of Mandelstam. Otherwise, the undoubted literary progenitor of Zabolotsky, the poet who influenced him more than anyone, is of course Velimir Khlebnikov. The impact of Khlebnikov would be obvious even if the name of this poet did not recur in Zabolotsky's poems. The profundity of Zabolotsky's love and gratitude to his literary master is demonstrated in the oddly touching homage that the forest animals pay to Khlebnikov's grave in *Triumph of Agriculture*. Poplavsky's literary genealogy, on the other hand, leads us straight to Aleksandr Blok, the Blok of the mystical and lyrical prose essays most of all. In his own literary criticism Poplavsky venerated Lermontov, Dostoevsky, and Rozanov. He thought Pushkin devoid of deeper insight, mysticism, and human compassion. However, Poplavsky's Russian literary background constitutes less than one half of his literary roots, far more important being the impact of French poetry, Baudelaire above all but also Rimbaud, Lautréamont, and Apollinaire. At times, especially in his essays and prose fiction, he almost appears to be a Frenchman who has somehow learned to write idiomatically but not always correctly in Russian.

Continuing their odd parallel chronology, both poets made their literary debuts in periodicals in 1927. Zabolotsky's first and most surrealistic book, *Stolbtsy*, appeared in 1929 in Soviet Leningrad. Poplavsky's first and most surrealistic book, *Flagi* (Flags), was printed in Estonia and published

---

[19] Note *real'nogo*, not *realisticheskogo*; Association of Real Art.

in Russian émigré Paris in 1931. It is hardly likely that Zabolotsky and Poplavsky ever knew of each other's existence, even though Zabolotsky's *Stolbtsy* was briefly reviewed in the émigré press by Khodasevich, who failed to grasp its originality and thought the whole thing a possible hoax,[20] and Poplavsky was mentioned adversely and briefly quoted in an article by the Soviet critic Zelinsky in the 1930s.[21] Quite independently, each of them devised a system of imagery that we now can call surrealistic, and they devised it simultaneously with each other and also simultaneously with the international group of official Surrealists. In their early poetry both Zabolotsky and Poplavsky describe a big city seen as a phantasmagoria—at times because of the fantastic juxtaposition of realia but mostly because of the genuinely dreamlike absence of logical motivation for what is described. At its most extreme, this illogical city is a nightmare. Thus in Zabolotsky:

> Покойник из царского дома бежал!
> Покойник по улицам гордо идёт
> Его постояльцы ведут под уздцы
>
> . . . .
>
> Он—в медных очках, перепончатых рамах,
> Переполнен до горла подземной водой[22]

(The corpse has escaped from the royal house!
The corpse walks proudly through the streets,
Tenants lead him by his bridle;

. . . .

He is wearing copper spectacles, webbed frames,
Chock-full with subterranean water up to his throat);

---

20 Quoted in the commentary to the Struve-Filippov edition of Zabolotskii, *Stikhotvoreniia*, 312–13. Khodasevich also advanced the supposition that Zabolotsky might be a genuine madman or cretin. Vladimir Nabokov shows a better perception of the literary technique involved in his statement that "Zabolotskii found ... a method of writing, as if the 'I' of the poem were a perfect imbecile, crooning in a dream, distorting words, playing with words as a half-insane person would." "An Interview with Vladimir Nabokov," conducted by Alfred Appel, Jr., *Wisconsin Studies in Contemporary Literature* 8, no. 2 (Spring 1967): 148.
21 Kornelii Zelinskii, *Kriticheskie pis'ma*, book 2 (Moscow, 1934), 144.
22 Nikolai Zabolotskii, "Ofort," in *Stikhotvoreniia*, 29. The first line surrealistically paraphrases the beginning of A. K. Tolstoi's poem "Vasilii Shibanov."

and in Poplavsky:

> Но вот грохнул подъезд и залаял звонок.
> Весна поднималась по лестнице молча.
> И каждый вдруг вспомнил, что он одинок.
> Кричал, одинок! задыхаясь от желчи.
> И в пении ночи, и в рёве утра,
> В глухом клокотании вечера в парке,
> Вставали умершие годы с одра
> И одр несли как почтовые марки[23]

> (But now the entrance door slammed
>   and the bell started barking.
> Springtime was silently mounting the stairs.
> And each one suddenly remembered he was lonely.
> Shouted, I'm lonely! choking with bile.
> And in night's singing, in morning's roar,
> In evening's dampened boiling in the park,
> Dead years would arise from their deathbed
> And carry the deathbed like postage stamps).

But at other times, life in this city is bearable, for it can be merely astounding and fantastic, rather than tragic. But even when the two poets describe something realistic or prosaic, the undertone of a visionary surrealism is unmistakable. Here are some beer-hall barmaids in Leningrad during the NEP period, as seen in Zabolotsky's "Krasnaia Bavariia" (Red Bavaria):

> И в том бутылочном раю
> Сирены дрогли на краю
> Кривой эстрады. На поруки
> Им были отданы глаза.
> Они простерли к небесам
> Эмалированные руки
> И ели бутерброд от скуки[24]

---

[23] Boris Poplavskii, "Vesna v adu," in *Flagi: stikhi* (Paris: Chisla, 1931), 20. The image of "dead years" probably comes from Baudelaire's "défuntes Années" in the first tercet of his sonnet "Recueillement."

[24] Zabolotskii, *Stikhotvoreniia*, 23.

> (And in that paradise of bottles
> Sirens [felt] chilled on the edge
> Of a crooked stage. Under security
> They were issued eyes.
> They stretched heavenward
> [their] enameled arms
> And ate a sandwich in their boredom).

And Poplavsky's circus parade passing a beer hall in the south of France in "Poslednii parad" (The last parade):

> А сквозь город под эскортом детским,
> Под бравурный рёв помятых труб,
> Проходила в позах молодецких
> Лучшая из мюзик–хольных трупп.
>
> . . . .
>
> Солнце грело вытертые плюши,
> А в тени пивных смотрели рожи.
> Их большие розовые души
> Улыбались музыке прохожей[25]

> (While through the town, escorted by children,
> To the jaunty roar of bashed-in trumpets,
> There marched in rakish poses
> The best of music-hall companies.
>
> . . . .
>
> The sun warmed the threadbare velvet [upholstery],
> While in the shade of beer halls mugs were staring.
> Their large pink souls
> Smiled at the passer-by music).

In Zabolotsky's surrealistic Leningrad and Poplavsky's equally surrealistic Paris (or, in his case, also the French Riviera or some megalopolis of the future) people constantly levitate, die, and kill each other casually without anyone being really hurt; seasons, times of day, or planets are personified in accordance with their respective genders in Russian: night,

---

[25] Poplavskii, *Flagi*, 34.

springtime, and the moon casually walk around among the populace. All these personifications are Baudelairian—that is, they are not explained in terms of any paraphrasable allegory. Even Zabolotsky's powerful personification of the night in the form of a winged witch in *Triumph of Agriculture* is not easily reducible to a symbol of evil and misfortune. Poplavsky is more specifically poetic, for there is more of a French elegance in his surrealistic visions. Zabolotsky's surrealism in *Stolbtsy* often draws on a Zoshchenko-like world of communal kitchens, an abundant supply of questionable food, and the flea markets of the NEP period.

An extremely surrealistic device widely used by Zabolotsky is a simple reversal of components. In mathematics the sum will not be affected if the sequence of the components is altered. In art, that can make all the difference. Hence the sense of unreality achieved by Zabolotsky by the very primitive means of turning things upside down:

> И этих девок упокой
> На перекрестке вверх ногами![26]
>
> (And rest those wenches in peace
> Upended at the crossroads!);

or

> Спи, форвард, задом наперед![27]
>
> (Sleep, O forward, in reverse!);

or

> И жизнь трещала как корыто,
> Летая книзу головой[28]
>
> (And life chattered like a trough
> Flying about head downwards).

---

[26] Zabolotskii, "Ivanovy," in *Stikhotvoreniia*, 40.
[27] Zabolotskii, "Futbol," in *Stikhotvoreniia*, 27.
[28] Zabolotskii, "Tsirk," in *Stikhotvoreniia*, 67.

Even fish, in Zabolotsky's poem "Rybnaia lavka" (The fish store), manage to use their gills in reverse:

И жабры дышат наоборот!²⁹

(And the gills breathe backwards!).

Occurring in the final lines of each of the quoted poems, these inexplicable reversals end the poems on a note of utter unreality.

Another of Zabolotsky's amazingly direct ways of achieving surrealistic *ostranenie* (making-it-strange) is his constant use in his early poetry of burlesquely distorted quotations or reminiscences from Pushkin—bits of *Onegin* or *Ruslan i Lyudmila* or the strange collage of themes and phrases from *Skazka o tsare Saltane* (Tale of Tsar Saltan) in his magnificent early poem "Iskushenie" (Temptation), published for the first time in the recent Soviet volume. We find a similar use of literature for *ostranenie* in Poplavsky's "Podrazhanie Zhukovskomu" (Imitation of Zhukovsky), in which the whole point of the title seems to be the total absence of even the remotest connection between the poem and Zhukovsky.

As their gifts matured, the respective ideologies of Zabolotsky and Poplavsky began to play a more overt role in their poetry. Here, despite the similarity of some of their imagery and poetic devices, they are quite different from each other. Zabolotsky's ideology, or rather his philosophy of life, is a kind of animism, a pantheism, similar to Victor Hugo's but more directly inspired by the philosophy of Nikolai Fyodorov, by the Soviet utopian biologist Tsiolkovsky, and by the image of the union of humanity with gods and animals as outlined in Khlebnikov's utopia *Ladomir*. Poplavsky, on the other hand, was a chaotic Christian mystic fascinated by the *bogoiskatel'stvo* (God-searching) of Dostoevsky and by the mystical trances of St. Teresa of Avila.

Both poets chose to give up their surrealistic imagery in the early 1930s—Poplavsky out of deference to the Parisian school of fashionable existential *angoisse* that became dominant in the émigré literature at that time. His two later collections, *Snezhnyi chas* (Snowy hour; 1936) and *V venke iz voska* (In a wreath of wax; Paris, 1938), attest to his genuine

---

29 Poplavskii, *Flagi*.

mystical experience and were praised for that reason by his literary associates. As poetry these books are often amorphous and at times simply dull. The publication of *Dirizhabl'* revealed a synthesis between Poplavsky's mysticism and his earlier surrealism and visual inventiveness. The result is some of his most personal and important poetry. Poplavsky died in Paris in utter indigence, a victim of a bizarre experiment with drugs in 1935 at the age of thirty-two. Zabolotsky, subjected to a savage campaign of vilification in the party press led by the notorious Ermilov, tried to achieve a more traditional style of poetry. His *Triumph of Agriculture* was totally misunderstood by the party critics: a poem about the collectivization that used surrealistic imagery was assumed ipso facto to be hostile and dangerous. Around 1934 we see both Zabolotsky and Poplavsky almost willingly trying to give up the most distinctive and personal features of their poetic personalities (trying unsuccessfully—but the similarity of ideological pressures so similarly exercised in such diverse environments is noteworthy). Two years after Poplavsky's senseless and tragic death, Zabolotsky's ordeal by labor camps began. He returned in 1946 a broken man, tubercular and possibly alcoholic. In the last twelve years of his life he wrote a number of conventional poems in the eclectic nineteenth-century manner approved by the authorities. He remained a tremendously gifted poet to the end, and in some of the quasi-realistic poems of his last period he managed to scale the heights of poetry, which is all the more amazing because he was clearly working in an alien medium. Poplavsky once wrote that a second-rate poem by a great poet is preferable to a good one by a mediocre poet. He could have been speaking of Zabolotsky's last period.

The vivid and unique early work of these two poets offers testimony to something else as well: the division of Russian literature into Soviet and émigré is at times a mere convention. The division of poetry into good and mediocre, however, remains eternally valid. Both Poplavsky and Zabolotsky are good poets and deserve to be known as such. Together with their predecessor Churilin, they can now be seen to form an extremely interesting minor strain within twentieth-century Russian poetry. A further study of the work of these three poets and a comparison of their work with the achievements of the French, Czech, and Yugoslav Surrealists would deepen our understanding of the origin and uses of their surrealistic techniques and enhance our admiration for the matchless scope and variety of Russian poetry in the first three decades of the twentieth century.

Evtushenko and the Underground Poets[1]

The more one studies the Symbolist-Acmeist-Futurist creative explosion in Russian poetry of the first three decades of our century, the more staggered one is by its total scope and accomplishment. By the early 1930s, that great age was forcibly brought to an end by what in retrospect amounts to a governmental ban on all creativity and imagination. While Mayakovsky was being acclaimed *the* great Soviet poet and his work nationalized, while Pasternak was being decried by the Soviet press for his uniqueness and individuality, no younger poet was any longer allowed to try to equal the stylistic daring and modernity of either of these two. Victorian-age poetic techniques, themes, and styles were brought back, proclaimed the latest word, and institutionalized as the only possible way for Socialist-Realist poetry, whereupon all Russian poetry worthy of the name ceased until after Stalin's death. As Boris Slutsky, a poet who survived the Stalinist period, described the plight of Russian poetry during those years:

> Only yesterday she was on the run,
> Wringing her hands in terror.
> Only yesterday she was on the executioner's block
> For perhaps the tenth time.

---

[1] Review of *Antiworlds: Poetry by Andrei Voznesensky*, ed. Patricia Blake and Max Hayward (New York: Basic Books, 1966); *The New Russian Poets, 1953–1966: An Anthology*, ed. and trans. George Reavey (New York: October House, 1966); *Yevtushenko Poems*, trans. Herbert Marshall (New York: E. P. Dutton, 1966); *Voznesensky: Selected Poems*, trans. Herbert Marshall (New York: Hill and Wang, 1966); *Selected Poems of Andrei Voznesensky*, trans. Anselm Hollo (New York: Grove Press, 1964); *Selections from "The Bratsk Hydroelectric Station" and Other Poems*, by Yevgeny Yevtushenko, trans. Bernard L. Koten (New York: New World Review, 1965); *Stikhotvoreniia i poemy* [Selected poetry], by Iosif Brodskii (Washington, D.C.: Inter-Language Literary Associates, 1965); poems by Nikolai Morshen, in *Novyi zhurnal*, nos. 82 and 83 (1966); *Bulat Okudzhava Sings His Songs*, 12-inch record, recorded and pressed for ARFA by RCA Victor Custom Records Division; and "Lots of Luck, Kid!," by Bulat Okudzhava, trans. Robert Szulkin, in *Pages from Tarusa*, ed. Andrew Field (Boston: Little, Brown, 1964). Originally published in *Nation*, 21 November 1966, 549–53.

Since 1956, however, there has been a definite poetic revival in the Soviet Union.[2] Within the country, the most striking development of the past decade is the grudging recognition now granted to the great Russian poets of the early twentieth century and, most important, the partial availability of their work. The recognition and availability are limited and subject to certain carefully observed ideological rules, but with all that, the really momentous phenomenon in Russian poetry of the past ten years is that the poems of Anna Akhmatova, Boris Pasternak, Marina Tsvetaeva, Velimir Khlebnikov, Nikolai Zabolotsky and, most recently, Andrei Bely can actually be read, after decades of suppression, vilification, and officially imposed oblivion. But at least a dozen other major poets who were exiled, condemned to silence, or physically destroyed by the Soviet regime (Kuzmin, Gumilyov, Mandelstam, Zinaida Gippius, Vyacheslav Ivanov, and Khodasevich, to name a few) have not yet been republished and are still treated very gingerly in the Soviet press and scholarship.

Outside the Soviet Union, the younger post-Stalinist poets have been making the biggest news. The international attention now attracted by Evtushenko and Voznesensky is nothing short of phenomenal. Their poetry is read in translation and acclaimed by thousands of young Europeans and Americans for whom Akhmatova and Pasternak were merely names, and who have probably never heard of Mandelstam or Tsvetaeva or Zabolotsky. This situation is paradoxical: the reverse would be if a generation of Russian readers who had never heard of Yeats or T. S. Eliot or Auden or Marianne Moore were suddenly to acclaim Allen Ginsberg as the first significant English-language poet since Whitman and Wilde. But this situation is also a sign of the times. The fact is that Evtushenko and Voznesensky represent two of the possible options that a Russian poet has today. Examining the respective situations and accomplishments of these poets and contrasting them to the alternative options, exemplified by such poets as Bulat Okudzhava, Joseph Brodsky, and Nikolai Morshen, may perhaps throw light on the actual state of Russian poetry.

Evgeny Evtushenko is undoubtedly the biggest name in Soviet poetry today. There has not been such a matinee idol in Russian poetry since

---

[2] Once again the reader is reminded that SK is addressing a particular moment in time (here the 1960s in the history of Russian poetry) and will encounter a high number of time-specific references.—Ed.

the days when Igor Severyanin used to recite his Ego-Futuristic poems to audiences on the eve of World War I. Despite Evtushenko's vehement denials, there is an unmistakable kinship: he shares Severyanin's penchant for a pseudoelegant foreign vocabulary and has on occasion the same surefire sentimentality and the same facile and bouncy optimism. He also possesses Severyanin's theatrical flair. To hear Evtushenko recite his versified editorials is a spellbinding experience, but deprived of the author's delivery and reduced to a printed page, his poems inevitably disappoint.

Evtushenko's main strength is in being topical. Such poems as *Babi Yar*, "The Ballad on Poaching," the still-unpublished "Letter to Esenin" and the recent, dreadfully maudlin "Italian Tears" can state the thoughts and attitudes of the younger Soviet generation in ways that could not be safely printed in the Soviet Union unless dressed up as verse. There is an obvious analogy in this with the tsarist Russia of the 1860s: Nekrasov's verse and Chernyshevsky's literary criticism also had ways of bringing up certain "burning issues" otherwise too hot to be aired publicly. Considering the role his poetry plays within present-day Soviet society, Evtushehko's success and fame at home are both understakable and well deserved. But when his foreign admirers accept his mixture of grandstand histrionics and mawkish sentiment as a major poetic utterance of our age, there is evidence of a total misunderstanding of what poetry is all about.[3]

---

[3] One of SK's first published reviews—of *Vzmakh ruki* (Moscow: Molodaia gvardiia, 1962), by Evtushenko, in *Books Abroad* 37 (Summer 1962): 355—contains a succinct summary of the popular young poet's impact.—Ed.:

> Evtushenko is predominantly a civic poet. As such, he voices, in versified editorials and within certain prescribed limits, the aspirations of the Soviet younger generation.
>
> Abroad, his poems are often read as a sort of political barometer. Both at home and abroad his popularity seems to be due to extraliterary reasons. His more orthodox pieces, such as the protestations of fealty to the Revolution or the odes in honor of Fidel Castro, are not very different from the sort of thing Soviet poets wrote under Stalin, except possibly for the "Evtushenko rhyme." (The method of rhyming in which the first rather than the last syllable of the final word in a line is rhymed, with an assonance in the stressed syllable where the rhymed syllable is unstressed, was introduced in Russian poetry at the turn of the century, evidently by Zinaida Gippius, and was later used by Gumilyov in "Zavodi." It is at present very popular with the younger poets and Evtushenko is usually credited with having invented it.) …
>
> For all that, the sheer fact of Evtushenko's popularity may yet lead to new and salutary developments in Russian poetry. Despite the orthodox tone of

Evtushenko can be admired for his editorial daring. The daring of Andrei Voznesensky is largely stylistic and thematic. His poetry tries to be frankly original and unabashedly imaginative—two qualities that are of course essential for any true poetry, but which were considered grave sins in Stalin's era. Voznesensky, more than any other young Soviet poet, also brings back the emphasis on the verbal aspects of the poet's craft. His strident assonances, out-of-control alliteration, and overly insistent play on verbal stems are all borrowed from his great predecessors Khlebnikov, Pasternak, and Marina Tsvetaeva; however, they used such devices both with more restraint and with greater expressive effect. But these poets are dead, while Andrei Voznesensky is alive and celebrated and, besides, Soviet poetry can certainly use a transfusion of technical originality, whatever the source. A far more talented and accomplished poet than Evtushenko, Voznesensky shares with him a certain provincial limitation of outlook and the habit of interspersing his more daring efforts with more conventional or even conformist utterances on the standard themes of official Soviet poetry: the greatness of the Russian people, the tenderness and affection inspired in the poet by Lenin's name, and the horrors of American militarism, Western decadence, and the FBI. When Mayakovsky treated similar themes back in the 1920s, there was no doubt that they represented his actual convictions; in Evtushenko and Voznesensky, whatever their feelings may be, the reader gets the inevitable clichés which all Soviet writers (and especially those allowed to travel abroad) have been required to reiterate ad nauseam for the past thirty years.

For the third most popular Russian poet now writing, Bulat Okudzhava, freedom from the compulsory cliché has become *the* crucial freedom within the context of Soviet literature. Although he has published several slim volumes of verse, Okudzhava is primarily a *chansonnier* in the French tradition. The effect of his poems depends equally on the melodies he composes for them and on his own subdued and intimate delivery. The

---

much of what he has to say, he does make a conscious effort to bring Russian verse back into the twentieth century from the limbo of the Soviet neo-Victorianism to which it was relegated under Stalin. Above all, there is in his work an open concern for problems of technique and versification. In the work of Evtushenko's more talented contemporaries (Voznesensky, Akhmadulina, Novella Matveeva), his example has already led to some fresh and promising poetic departures.

most original and popular of his songs were not included in his published collections, nor are they commercially available on Soviet-made records, but privately made tapes of Okudzhava's songs enjoy an enormous circulation in the Soviet Union, and no party in Moscow or Leningrad has been complete without them for the past five years. The recording recently released in this country contains some of his best-known pieces. A good half of the songs included represent underground poetry.

The concept of literature, including poetry, as a lesson or a sermon has always been central to Soviet culture. In his minor and modest way, Okudzhava now revives the opposite, nondidactic concept of art, stemming in the Russian tradition from Pushkin and Chekhov. His songs simply show or describe things as he sees them, and his attitude to his subject matter is contained within his manner. He can also be quite refreshingly irreverent. His "Paper Soldier" treats the whole notion of military heroics, Soviet or otherwise, as absurd (the same kind of scoffing in Okudzhava's amusing novella *Lots of Luck, Kid!* was literally horrifying to the orthodox Soviet critics).

Another Okudzhava song tells of waterfront prostitutes and of some Soviet sailors who are frightened to go out to sea. Prostitution is not indicted, the sailors' cowardice is neither defended nor condemned—there is an implied presupposition of an adult audience that has outgrown Sunday school. Okudzhava's "The Midnight Trolley" has particularly irked those who uphold the orthodox Soviet mentality. The hero of this song tells of his remedy against loneliness and acute depression: take the midnight trolley in Moscow and sit in it next to others who have also experienced shipwreck in the night. Neither Lenin nor the great Russian people are evoked. Instead:

> Who would have thought that there is so much kindness
> In silence. In silence.

Quietly, unobtrusively, Okudzhava brings back the things that are most inimical to the Soviet brand of Socialist-Realist aesthetics, a detached irony, freedom to be either optimistic or pessimistic, depending on the subject at hand, and at times a genuine sense of human tragedy. His refusal to take out insurance in the form of occasional repetition of official clichés is apparently what makes some of his most popular work unpublishable in the Soviet Union to this day. Other younger Soviet poets who have come into prominence in the past decade—Bella Akhmadulina, Evgeny Vinokurov, Viktor Bokov, Novella Matveeva—do take out such insurance. The remaining alternatives for a Russian poet today are to publish clandestinely in the Soviet Union (and perhaps to send work to be published abroad at great personal risk) or to be an émigré poet.

Shortly before her death, Anna Akhmatova stated in several interviews that today's important and lasting Russian poetry does not appear in the official press and is unknown abroad.[4] The underground poetry Akhmatova had in mind has a minuscule circulation in the Soviet Union in mimeographed publications, the very names of which constitute a challenge to what is officially acceptable: *Syntax* (an open invitation to a charge of Formalism), *Sphynxes* (an assertion of the mystery of poetic creation) and *Phoenix* (a rebirth of poetry from the ashes). In these privately circulated publications (some of which have been reprinted in toto in a West German émigré journal), young and unknown poets can achieve a full measure of freedom from ideological fetters and can write in any style about anything they please. Their stylistic inspiration comes for the most part from Khlebnikov's experiments with language of some fifty years ago; Marina Tsvetaeva (who committed suicide in 1941 after her voluntary return from exile) and Nikolai Gumilyov (shot for counterrevolutionary activities in 1921) are here objects of a cult. The poetry in these little journals is by no means great, and it is rarely even good, but it *is* fresh and free in a way Evtushenko's is not.

The most notable poet to have so far emerged from these clandestine publications is Joseph Brodsky, who became famous after the Soviet authorities put him on trial for being a "parasite" and a "sponger." The transcript of his trial, published in the West, left no doubt that what was really indicted in Brodsky's person was the whole notion of writing socially useless poetry. After being sentenced to five years at hard labor, and spending almost two years carting manure in a remote northern area, Brodsky was quietly released this year. A piece of poetry he has written since his release has just reached the West; it is a cycle of poems dedicated to the memory of T. S. Eliot. A selection of Brodsky's poems,

---

[4] See Alexander Werth, "Akhmatova: Tragic Queen Anna," *Nation*, 22 August 1966, 157–60.

most of which appeared in Soviet underground journals, was published in 1965 by the Inter-Language Literary Associates of Washington, D.C. Brodsky's poetry is uneven, and often murky and verbose, but at its best it has a seriousness and a profundity no other Soviet poet can match. He uses surrealistic imagery freely; his acknowledged foreign influences—John Donne and Eliot—are not on any Soviet-approved list; and if Okudzhava's jaunty songs admit only a possibility of a tragic view of life, Brodsky's brooding elegies are at times permeated with an oppressive sense of doom which only the eternal values of art and nature are allowed to overcome.

The best present-day Russian poetry is not produced by any of the four by-now internationally famous poets discussed so far. Since the death of Anna Akhmatova, the finest living Russian poet is a man whose poetry is known to perhaps a few hundred people at most. His name is Nikolai Morshen. In originality of content, profundity, literary culture, and craftsmanship, neither Voznesensky nor Brodsky can even touch his work. Morshen has been publishing for over a decade, yet his name remains virtually unknown in the Soviet Union. It is all a question of the peculiar role of geography in modern Russian literature. Saint-John Perse or Thomas Mann could reside in America and maintain their positions in their respective literatures, but a modern Russian writer who leaves his country inevitably loses not only his Russian audience but any claim to international attention.

Nikolai Morshen, the most important of several interesting Russian émigré poets now active in the West, left Russia as a very young man during World War II and lives at present in Monterey, California. His one small book of verse was published in West Germany in 1959. Entitled *The Seal*, the book uses this pinniped mammal, with its breathing hole in the Arctic ice, as the central metaphor for the collection, whose theme is the situation of a restless and inquisitive intellectual in an environment of totalitarian orthodoxy. Since the publication of *The Seal*, Morshen's poetry has been steadily growing in scope and stature. This year he has published in the New York–based Russian literary journal *Novyi zhurnal* two sets of poems which clearly place him in the front rank of twentieth-century Russian poets. Influenced initially by Mandelstam, Pasternak, and Zabolotsky, and later by Teilhard de Chardin, Morshen has more recently matured into a wholly original poet, unlike any other in Russian literature. His latest poetry draws on completely new areas of human thought (cybernetics and paleontology, for example); the elegance of his verbal texture, which is light years away from the strident pyrotechnics of a Voznesensky, is comparable to the best of Pasternak. A recent poem in which the grasses and weeds of the North American wilderness are made to recite a tiny anthology of classical Russian poetry is a tour de force of truly dazzling proportions. There is no doubt that a large and enthusiastic audience awaits Morshen's poetry in the Soviet Union, should it be made available there (at which time, presumably, translators into other languages will also deign to notice it).[5]

In the meantime, there is a veritable flood of English translations of Evtushenko and Voznesensky. Anselm Hollo's versions of Voznesensky, inexplicably endorsed by the poet himself and now available in paperback, are a particularly blatant example of that all-too-frequent recent phenomenon of translation of Russian literature by guesswork. Knowing the language only sketchily and apparently not wishing to use a dictionary, Hollo translates "hunting hound" as "rodent"; "Ah, those home-grown Iagos!" as "O they are hothouse flowers"; and "Poetesses hasten to become market-women" (*Poetessy begut v lotoshnitsy*) as "And the poet-girls, running, running ... / Toward the trembling black grove." Whenever the text gets too idiomatic for comfort, Hollo simply drops the passage and develops an earlier or later phrase. He throws in Anglo-Saxon obscenities or French words, apparently just for the hell of it, when there is not the slightest pretext for them in Voznesensky's Russian original. At times he totally misses the point of an entire poem.

Compared to Hollo's "translations," even Herbert Marshall's versions of Evtushenko and Voznesensky look good. But the improvement is only relative. Marshall understands many more Russian words, and he tries to convey something of Voznesensky's style and verbal structure. But as an English stylist, Marshall is naive, to say the least, and he, too, has considerable difficulties with the Russian idiom. Voznesensky's introduction to his "Triangular Pear" begins, "I am writing a work of major proportions, with a plot. It is about 'the discovery of America.'" Marshall's rendition of this is "I am working on a big thematic subject 'About the Discovery

---

[5] Morshen's development as a poet remained of particular interest to SK. See the two later essays on Morshen (published in 1982 and 1993) in the present volume.—Ed.

of America.'" (Hollo's version of the passage is "I am working on a great theme: the discovery of America.")

Marshall's own wildly ungrammatical Russian sentences, quoted by him in his largely irrelevant introduction to the Voznesensky volume, leave no doubt how ill-equipped he is to translate anything at all from that language. Copious footnotes have been supplied by Marshall for both the Evtushenko and the Voznesensky volumes, and the only word for some of them is "unbelievable." Natasha Rostova, in a footnote appended to a spectacularly garbled and misunderstood Evtushenko passage, is described as a character from Tolstoi's "great novel *Anna Karenina*,"[6] while the Queen of Sheba and Bathsheba, mentioned in Voznesensky's "Ballad of Work," are left in their Russian transcriptions and helpfully identified by Marshall as "a Tsarina of Russia, patron of the arts, of whom many portraits were painted," and "a lake in Estonia," respectively.[7]

Fragments from Evtushenko's long epic *The Bratsk Hydroelectric Station* have been translated by Bernard L. Koten. (How odd that this sprawling, verbose opus should become available in some three English translations, while such authentic masterpieces of Russian twentieth-century narrative poetry as Bely's *The First Rendezvous*, Tsvetaeva's *Poem of the End*, and Zabolotsky's *Triumph of Agriculture*, to name a few, still remain untranslated.) Koten worked with greater care than Marshall, in whose volume this poem is also partly represented. At least Koten conveys the meaning of the title, while Marshall's equivalent, "Bratsky GES," makes no sense in English and throws the gender agreement of Evtushenko's Russian title out of kilter. But Koten, alas, also has his vocabulary trouble (Evtushenko speaks of Lermontov's "bilious gaze," which Koten renders as "bitter vision"), and as poetry, even on Evtushenko's level of the term, Koten's translation is often plodding and uninspired.

The same has to be said, unfortunately, of the translations in George Reavey's anthology, though they are on a far superior level than the grotesqueries of Hollo or Marshall. In addition to the inevitable Evtushenko, Reavey's book offers a sampling of Voznesensky, Brodsky, Okudzhava, the underground poet Galanskov, the witty and whimsical Novella Matveeva

---

6   *Yevtushenko Poems*, 149.
7   *Voznesensky: Selected Poems*, 115. SK was to subject the translator to further scathing scrutiny a year later in his review of *Mayakovsky*, trans. and ed. Herbert Marshall (New York: Hill and Wang, 1965), in *Russian Review* 26, no. 4 (October 1967): 413–15.—Ed.

(her least typical work, it seems), and a few others, but all of them somehow emerge flat and unrewarding in English, with Okudzhava, stripped of his direct and laconic manner and relentlessly explicated to the full, faring about the worst. Whatever one can say about the new post-Stalinist Soviet poets, one thing is certain: they deserve better from their English translators.

Voznesensky, for one, does get better (and then some) in the unusual volume *Antiworlds*, edited by Patricia Blake and Max Hayward. The contrast between this volume and the others mentioned is dazzling. Not only have Voznesensky's poems been translated by those who have understood all his Russian words and who have no problems with Russian idiom or syntax (an elementary requirement, of course, though it is rarely met these days), but most of the poems in this volume stand up remarkably well as English poetry. In fact, the paradoxical fault of *Antiworlds*, if regarded as a set of translations, is that the results are too spectacularly good. Put into English by the likes of W. H. Auden, Robert Lowell (who on this occasion, for once, was given reliable trots), and Richard Wilbur, Voznesensky loses the naive and provincial tone he often has in Russian, sheds his often crude and overemphatic alliteration, and indeed becomes the kind of poet he undoubtedly could be had he the literary culture and sophistication of his translators. But this is probably mere carping. Everybody who contributed to *Antiworlds* is to be congratulated (Voznesensky on his good fortune). Is it too much to hope that a similar venture may be organized by the editors to furnish an equally successful English volume of Mandelstam or Tsvetaeva or Khodasevich or Zabolotsky?

* * *

As SK remarks in the essay above, Joseph Brodsky was surely the most considerable figure in Russian poetry to emerge in the post-Stalin era. Regrettably, SK never wrote at length on Brodsky, and his only other recorded statement about him—so far as is known to the present editors—is contained in an answer (apparently never published) to a questionnaire about the poet solicited from SK in early February 1980. He chose to reply only to the second of five questions: "What features of Brodsky's poetry are particularly valuable for you?" His response follows.

Evtushenko and the Underground Poets

My first contact with the poetry of Joseph Brodsky was through a tape recording made by Clarence Brown in Leningrad of a reading by Brodsky of his poems dedicated to the memory of T. S. Eliot. The originality of Brodsky's poems was striking, and striking, too, was the manner of reading, which went against their metrics: a mixture of the Comédie-Française and a Jewish cantor.

For me the most memorable reading aloud of Brodsky's verse was in the kitchen of a friend of mine in San Francisco: against a background of a pile of dirty dishes and wine glasses, Mikhail Baryshnikov was fervently declaiming:

> И если что-нибудь взлетало в воздух,
> то был не мост, то Павлова была

> (And if anything took flight into air,
> it was no bridge, it was Pavlova).

No personal encounter ever actually took place. There was once a reception at my home in his honor. The house was full of noisy people, most of them unknown to me. Brodsky was besieged by Berkeley students wanting to know why he left the progressive Soviet Union for the citadel of imperialism. He had a toothache, and had little patience with them. Right there beside him were Russians, recently arrived in America, who were instructing other Russians (who had lived in America for decades) how one was to behave here and generally just what's what. Some sort of scandal out of Dostoevsky's *Possessed* was brewing, though it never actually erupted. Someone burned the table with a cigarette. Someone, attempting to leave, couldn't manage the front door and broke the lock (a locksmith had to be called). And left behind, a woman's knitted jacket of gigantic proportions was hanging long afterward in the entryway. It was eventually donated to a charitable organization with other rubbish.

Any real encounter with Brodsky occurs in the poems he began writing a couple of years after that evening. They appeared first in the *Messenger of the Russian Christian Movement* (*Vestnik Russkogo khristianskogo dvizheniia*) and later in the elegant gray volumes published by Ardis, *The End of a Beautiful Epoch* (*Konets prekrasnoi epokhi*) and *A Part of Speech* (*Chast' rechi*). Brodsky as poet had matured to the point of being unrecognizable in them. *Twenty Sonnets to Maria*

Stuart (*Dvadtsat' sonetov k Marii Stiuart*), "Mexican Divertimento" ("Meksikanskii divertisment"), "Classical Ballet" ("Klassicheskii balet") sum up the epoch of Akhmatova and Mandelstam, the way the young Pushkin subsumed everything that had been done in Russian poetry before him and then advanced beyond.

Voices that were heard even earlier in Joseph Brodsky's poetry—those of the Englishmen John Donne, William Blake, and T. S. Eliot—are still heard in it. Above all, his own can be heard in it, inimitable and absorbing.

Comparing poets who are contemporaries with each other *odiosa sunt*. But one can hardly doubt that, of all the Russian poets who have appeared in the second half of the present century, Brodsky is the most outstanding. And, as Mirsky once wrote about Tsvetaeva, it is pleasant to sense that you live at the same time as Brodsky.[8]

---

[8] Translated from the Russian from the original document in carton no. 7, Simon Karlinsky Papers, BANC MSS 2010/177, The Bancroft Library, University of California, Berkeley. Correspondence between SK and Gregory Poliak, editor-publisher of Silver Age Publishing, indicates that a section of a volume to be published to mark the 40th birthday of Joseph Brodsky was to be devoted to responses to a questionnaire also to be sent to Mikhail Baryshnikov, John Updike, Mstislav Rostropovich, Andrei Sinyavsky, Nina Berberova, Susan Sontag, and others. In the event, they were not published in the volume, *Chast' rechi: Al'manakh literatury i iskusstva*, no. 1 (New York: Serebrianyi vek, 1980).

POETRY ABROAD

In Search of Poplavsky: A Collage[1]

An Introductory Digression

I first ran into Boris Poplavsky's name in 1940 or 1941, and it was a case of mistaken identity. I was in Beverly Hills, California, at the home of a remarkable woman named Anna Semyonovna Meller, who in the days of my childhood was Madame Antoinette, the best known and most elegant couturiere in Harbin. My mother's dressmaking establishment, Levitina-Karlinskaya, was not even a close second, but theirs was a friendly rivalry. Anna Semyonovna's adopted son Alex, six years my senior, was the idol and the despair of my Manchurian childhood: a champion ice skater, a concertizing pianist at the age of twelve, and a stoic who, during a hike in Chalantung, went on talking with a smile after a sharp rock had opened a bleeding gash on his knee. (I was half his age at the time and I remember screaming my head off at the mere sight.) Now, in California, he was a Surrealist painter, had been awarded a Guggenheim grant, and had spent a summer in New York, where he had met Pavel Tchelitchew (Chelishchev) and the son of Max Ernst and a number of other persons of equally supernatural stature. Staying as a boarder at Anna Semyonovna's was Alex's friend Eddie, a young man of similar origins and background (his parents owned a dress shop on the Bubbling Well Road in Shanghai, and my mother had worked for them in her early youth), a former Berkeley architecture major who was now studying costume design at an art school somewhere near Westlake Park. Eddie's sketches usually took first prize at school competitions, with the second prize going to his principal rival and fellow student, a melancholy-looking German refugee boy named Rudi Gernreich.

---

[1] Previously published in *The Bitter Air of Exile: Russian Writers in the West 1922–1972*, ed. Simon Karlinsky and Alfred Appel, Jr. (Berkeley: University of California Press, 1977), 311–33; an earlier version appeared in *TriQuarterly*, no. 27 (Spring 1973): 342–64.

Waves of pure happiness would wash over me every time I waited for the Wilshire bus to take me for a day or a weekend to the Meller home in Beverly Hills, away from everything that made my life in Los Angeles glum and barely endurable: the incomprehensible courses in civics and physics (even their names seemed interchangeable) at Belmont High; the hopelessly boring afternoon job at the grocery store; and the pointless weekly exchange of mutual insults between Jack Benny and Rochester on the living room radio. ("It is all probably very funny and subtle, if we could only truly understand it," my father would assure me after denying me permission to turn the dial to some concert music. But I *did* understand it all and it was *not* funny.) At the Mellers', things were altogether different. To begin with, it was perfectly all right to speak Russian and to have been born in China without having everyone exclaim, as they did at school, "How did you ever manage *that*?" or "Were your parents missionaries?" Instead of Jack Benny on the radio, there were real live stars to be encountered in Beverly Hills. Once I had to jump back when a long black car swung into a driveway with George Raft at the wheel and Rita Hayworth next to him. Another time, Eddie and I were walking past the John Frederics millinery shop on Beverly Drive and were stopped dead in our tracks by the sight of the most unbelievably beautiful woman either of us had ever seen. She was selecting a hat inside. We stood there staring, exchanging whispered conjectures as to who this magical creature might be; then a saleslady came out, not to ask us to move, but to announce, "Miss del Rio would like to know which of the two models you gentlemen consider more becoming." None of the Dolores del Rio films I saw later even began to do justice to the unforgettable radiance of her beauty.

Many years later, I felt a shudder of recognition as I watched that same scene reenacted (transposed into a comical key) in Billy Wilder's film *Witness for the Prosecution*. Could Eddie have recounted it to someone during his brief career at the film studios? He was designing costumes for Gene Tierney and Maria Montez at Universal—or was it United Artists?—when he was run over and killed by a drunken driver. It happened as he was crossing Beverly Drive one evening in 1945, about half a block from where he and I had once stood admiring Dolores del Rio. Eddie also had connections in the world of burlesque. Rose La Rose wanted a new kind of stage costume and he came up with one that featured a quivering pink lobster over the G-string. One night he sneaked me backstage at the burlesque house on Main Street (I was too young to purchase a ticket), and I watched from the wings a performance of a tassel-twirler named Ermaine Parker. Afterward we went out for coffee with her and her tall, handsome husband, the straight man for the foul-mouthed, baggy-pants comedian in the show. The talk was mostly about the couple's infant son, who had developed a liking for classical music before he learned to speak.

There were art exhibits of new painters, to which Alex or Eddie would take me: Salvador Dalí at the Ambassador Hotel, Eugene Berman and Christian Bérard at little galleries on Sunset Strip. But above all, books and poems were a part of daily life at the Mellers'. It was there that I was introduced to, or urged to read, *Look Homeward, Angel*; *To the Lighthouse* (which I couldn't get through on the first try); *Portrait of the Artist as a Young Dog* (the book that provided the model for the title came later); a volume of short stories by Noel Coward (which I still think quite good); and collections of poems by Wallace Stevens, Dylan Thomas, and (whatever happened to him?) George Barker. While everyone at home and at school kept urging me to forget about those useless Russian books I was forever dragging about, Alex and Eddie, older and wiser, never considered giving up their cultural heritage. Alex had his cult of the "three fellow-Alexanders"—Pushkin, Blok, and Scriabin; he had given up playing the piano when he decided that, compared to the later period of Scriabin, all music was primitive and dull. The three of us used to get high reciting Blok to each other, mostly from *The Mask of Snow* and *The Nightingale Garden* cycles. But here I could contribute as well as receive. One day, after leafing through *A Synthetic History of the Arts*, by a Soviet scholar named Ioffe, at the Los Angeles public library, I learned of the existence of Boris Pasternak and Velimir Khlebnikov. There was no Khlebnikov at the library, but I immediately copied out his poem about the grasshopper, which Ioffe had cited to illustrate some principle of modern painting or other. They did have *My Sister Life* and *Themes and Variations*. I took these over to the Mellers' the next weekend, and while the older generation (Alex's parents and his aunt Madame Olga) pronounced Pasternak incomprehensible, Alex and Eddie both agreed that here was a major discovery.

I also introduced them to my favorite modern Russian novelist, a man I knew only as V. Sirin, with whose work I had become involved several years earlier. When I brought over my copy of *Invitation to a Beheading*, Eddie tried reading it out loud, but his long sojourns in Shanghai and

Berkeley had done something to his Russian stress. (This was not noticeable when he spoke, only when he read aloud.) I took the book away from him and began to read slowly, getting all the stresses right, but after three pages I had to stop: Eddie was on the floor, his legs kicking in the air, a beatific smile on his face. "Stop it, I can't stand it, it's too beautiful," he was moaning. Alex's reaction was a little more reserved. He kept the book for several days and when he returned it, he remarked, "If I were a writer, this is how I would want to write." And a little later: "I had the damnedest feeling I wrote some of it myself." Sirin then joined Pushkin, Blok, Pasternak, Thomas Wolfe, and Dylan Thomas in our literary pantheon.

It was on one such enchanted Sunday afternoon, leafing through the New York Russian newspaper *Novoe russkoe slovo* [published until 2010], to which Anna Semyonovna subscribed, that I came upon Poplavsky's name—and this is where the mistaken identity part comes in. A memoirist (Yury Terapiano? Vladimir Varshavsky?) was reminiscing about the Russian Montparnasse of the 1920s. He could vividly remember the poet Boris Poplavsky drunkenly declaiming:

> And the nightingale in the Sanskrit tongue
> Shouts "More wine! More wine!" over the yellow rose.

The name was unfamiliar, but there was something about those two lines that made me resolve to look up their author. As a matter of plain fact, however, the lines were not by Poplavsky. I could never find them in any of his books, and after years of fruitless searching I finally, through sheer accident, discovered the awkward truth. The lines are a quotation from the *Rubaiyat* translated into Russian by Ivan Tkhorzhevsky. In connection with that translation Vladislav Khodasevich, when asked one morning why he looked so poorly, quipped: "I had a terrible nightmare. I dreamed that I was a Persian poet and that Tkhorzhevsky was translating me." But never mind. These two lines of Tkhorzhevsky's pseudo-Omar did direct me to Poplavsky.[2]

---

[2] The passage corresponds to stanza 6 of Edward Fitzgerald's version, where the nightingale speaks in Pahlavi and the rose is *sallow*. The notes to my (New York, 1888) edition explain that the rose was yellow in the first edition of Fitzgerald's translation and identify Pahlavi as the "old, heroic Sanskrit of Persia." This seems to suggest that Tkhorzhevsky was translating Fitzgerald into Russian, rather than the original Omar.

III. Poetry Abroad

The Discovery

The strange Aztec-Mayan pyramid that houses the main public library in downtown Los Angeles will always remain for me one of the endearing spots in Southern California. Its dark tile walls that kept the air comfortably cool on the muggiest days; the long, Alhambra-like vistas that opened from one room to another; the purling fountains in the inner yards (if I'm making it sound garish and eclectic, it no doubt was) I still find unforgettable. There was a Russian lady in the Foreign Books Room, whose name I never learned, who made it a point to purchase everything worthwhile in contemporary Soviet and Russian émigré literature. The library's collection of volumes on Russian painters and painting and on the Soviet theater of the 1920s was nothing short of opulent.

Yes, of course they had Poplavsky at that library. There were two slim volumes: a selection from his journals and a volume of verse called *Flags*. I got *Flags*, opened it in the middle, and immediately felt as though I were falling through a hole in the ice. Nikolai Tatishchev described his first impression of reading *Flags* thus: "A pure and piercing sound. Hardly anything can be made out. Now and then something breaks through and stings you. 'O Morella, come back, it will all be different one day.' Alarm, apprehension. The barometer needle quiveringly indicates a storm. A degree of agitation that can be expressed only in deliberately approximate terms."[3] This was how a mature person, a close friend of the poet and the publisher of his posthumous books, reacted to *Flags*. My own impression (and it remains one of the most vivid of my entire life) was somewhat different. I was struck first of all by the bright colors, the swirling images, the authenticity of the dreamlike states the poems conveyed:[4]

> In the emerald waters of the night
> Sleep lovely faces of virgins
> And in the shadow of blue pillars
> A stone Apollo slumbers.
>
> Orchards blossom forth in the fire,
> White castles rise like smoke
> And beyond the dark blue grove
> Vividly dark sand is ablaze.

---

[3] N. Tatishchev, "O Poplavskom" [On Poplavsky], *Krug* [The circle], vol. 3 (Paris, 1938).
[4] The translations of the Poplavsky poems are mine.—Author.

> Flowers in the garden hum,
> Statues of souls come to life
> And like butterflies from the fire
> Words reach me:
>
> Believe me, angel, the moon is high,
> Musical clouds
> Surround her, fires
> Are sonorous there and days are radiant.

My English cannot reproduce the pulsating music that emanates from these lines in Russian, nor does it convey the artful and often startling rhymes. There are pages and pages in this little book that project this blend of color and music, but there are also other things:

> We shelter our caressing leisure
> And unquestioningly hide from hope.
> Naked trees sing in the forest
> And the city is like a huge hunting horn.
>
> How sweet it is to jest before the end
> This is understood by the first and the last—
> Why, a man vanishes, leaving fewer traces
> Than a tragedian with a divine countenance.

There was an attitude in those poems, a vision, a sensibility quite new to me, but one that I instantly recognized and accepted:

> But now the main entrance thundered
>   and the bell started barking—
> Springtime was ascending the stairs in silence.
> And suddenly each one remembered that he was all alone
> And screamed "I'm all alone!" choking with bile.
> And in the singing of night, in the roar of morning,
> In the indistinct seething of evening in the park
> Dead years would arise from their deathbeds
> And carry the beds like postage stamps.

I did not know enough about poetry at the time to recognize Poplavsky's sources, to discern his French influences: Baudelaire (who had a greater impact on him than anyone except Blok), Nerval, Rimbaud, Laforgue, Apollinaire, Breton. I did not know then, as I know now, that Boris Poplavsky was in a sense a very fine French poet who belongs to Russian literature mainly because he wrote in Russian. But much of his sensibility was also a verbal equivalent of the visual imagery I knew and loved in the work of the exiled Russian neo-Romantic painters Pavel Tchelitchew and Eugene Berman.[5]

An uncritical acceptance? I knew at once that much of what Poplavsky was doing was highly artificial. But I knew even then that artifice was a natural component of some of the finest art and had no objections. Despite its artificiality (and partly because of it), the book hit me with a wave of lyrical power I would not have believed possible, a wave that swept me off my feet and held me prisoner for many weeks. This was not like getting intoxicated on Blok's verbal magic, nor was it like the intense intellectual pleasure afforded by Pasternak's formal perfection and his freshness of perception. Poplavsky came to me more like a fever or a demonic possession. I went around reciting Poplavsky's lines by heart. I tried composing melodies to them. I discovered that stanzas 3 and 4 of his poem "To Arthur Rimbaud" could be conveniently sung to the tune of the clarinet solo from Chaikovsky's *Francesca da Rimini*, and I did sing them, obsessively. The next thing I knew, my mother, normally infuriatingly indifferent to poetry, was muttering Poplavsky to Chaikovsky's music in an undertone while fixing dinner.

It was a heavy burden to keep to oneself at sixteen. I was fortunate indeed to have two older friends with whom I could share it. Alex and Eddie were almost as enthusiastic about Poplavsky as I. The three of us

---

[5] "But Poplavsky's surrealistic world is created illegitimately, using means borrowed from another art, namely painting (some of the critics have pointed out that Poplavsky is actually a visual rather than a musical poet; his poetry has been compared to Chagall's paintings …)." Gleb Struve, *Russkaia literatura v izgnanii* [Russian literature in exile] (New York, 1956), 339. The observation is absolutely correct, but why is cross-fertilization between the arts illegitimate? Russian poetry of the twentieth century in particular has a deep-going and highly legitimate symbiotic involvement with both painting (Voloshin, Mayakovsky, Khlebnikov) and music (Bely, Blok, Kuzmin, Pasternak).

leafed through the fragments of his journals. We did not find his religious quest congenial, but the seriousness and depth of his spiritual experience got through to us, and his ways of formulating it we also found impressive. Seeing that Russian poetry could be this closely allied with Surrealism in painting, Alex was moved to write a few Russian poems, which were meant as literary parallels to his paintings. He submitted them to *Novoe russkoe slovo* and one of them was printed, not in that newspaper's Sunday poetry section as he had hoped, but as an illustration to an editorial which discussed the poor quality of Russian émigré poetry and asserted that Surrealism as a whole was an unimportant trend, by now entirely passé and forgotten. Then Alex was drafted into the army. He wrote me asking for the library copy of *Flags*. I sent it to him, he returned it, then he wanted it again, and it was lost in the mail. I ruefully paid the charges for the lost book ($2.50, I think). A few months later it turned up at Alex's training camp. When I tried to return it, I was told that there was no need, because the library had replaced it. I now had my own copy of a book by Poplavsky....

But just who, exactly, was Boris Poplavsky?

Some Biographical Materials

Exhibit A: His Father

[The vice president of the Moscow Association of Manufacturers] was Yulian Ignatievich Poplavsky, an extremely original and colorful personality even for the Moscow of those days.

Poplavsky was a musician. He graduated (with very high grades) from the Moscow Conservatory where he majored in piano and was one of the favorite pupils of Pyotr Chaikovsky, with whom he was on intimate terms, as can be seen from his memoirs. I do not remember what it was that moved him to give up his musical career and take up industrial relations.... Poplavsky was a talented person; one seldom encounters such facility with word and pen. He could discuss any topic and could treat the most serious subject in a frivolous vein. His speech mannerisms, which corresponded to his manner of dress, irritated many and Poplavsky was widely disliked. It was said that he was "barred from the stock exchange." This seems to be factually correct: invitations were not extended to him and this would cause clashes between the

Manufacturers' Association and the Stock Exchange Committee. He was also active in St. Petersburg where he was the representative of his organization, together with Jules Goujon [the president of the Manufacturers' Association] at the Convention Council. When a petition had to be drafted or a summary of a discussion prepared, he was irreplaceable and was able to draft them with the utmost ease and elegance. Gradually, people became accustomed to his manners, and he began receiving invitations to Stock Exchange Committee sessions, especially when labor problems were involved, inasmuch as the antiquated organization of the Stock Exchange Committee was falling behind the times in collecting current statistical data and the documentation pertaining to labor problems. Poplavsky's office on Miasnitskaia Street was excellently organized and the Association (it was in existence for only twelve years) was able to accumulate much valuable material.

> —A portrait of Boris Poplavsky's father, from Paul Bouryschkine, *The Merchants' Moscow*.[6]

Exhibit B: His Sister

1. I can still see one [of these poetesses]—tall, feverish, everything about her dancing: the tip of her shoe, her fingers, her rings, the tails of her sables, her pearls, her teeth, the cocaine in the pupils of her eyes. She was hideous and enchanting with that tenth-rate enchantment which cannot but attract, to which people are ashamed to be attracted, to which I am openly and shamelessly attracted....

2. I can say in general that I was met with kindness in this alien world of female practitioners of drug-addicted poetry. Women are in general kinder. Men do not forgive felt boots or having starving children. But this very same P——skaya, I am convinced, would have removed the sables from her shoulders had I told her that I had a starving child at home....

---

[6] P. A. Buryshkin, *Moskva kupecheskaia* (New York, 1954), 256–57. This little-known volume is an astoundingly thorough and convincing record of the contribution made by the traditionally maligned and despised Russian merchant class to the development of Russian culture, literature, and the arts during the century preceding the Revolution.

3. I did not get to hear the feverish, fur-clad beauty recite her poetry, but I doubt that cocaine could have disposed her to write of love....

> —Three glimpses of Boris Poplavsky's sister Natasha, gleaned from Marina Tsvetaeva's memoir *A Hero of Labor* (1925).[7] Tsvetaeva and Natasha Poplavskaya both appeared at a reading of women poets in the cold and starving Moscow of 1920.

Exhibit C: His Biography

Boris Poplavsky was born in Moscow on 24 May 1903. His father was a free artist—a musician, a journalist, and a well-known social figure; his mother, née Kokhmanskaya, came from an old, cultivated, aristocratic family, had a Western European education, and was a violinist with conservatory experience. As a child, Boris Poplavsky was first looked after by his nanny, Iraida, and then by a German nurse and a French governess. Later, as an adolescent, he had Swiss and English tutors, and when he reached school age, he was taught by Russian university students, hired to give him lessons. He also studied music, but showed no enthusiasm; lessons in drawing, however, were always his favorites.

In 1906, his mother had to take the children abroad because of the severe illness of her daughter. They lived alternately in Switzerland and Italy, while his father remained in Moscow. While abroad, Boris forgot his native tongue to such an extent that, when he returned to Moscow, his family had to enroll him and his brother at the French lycée of Saint Philippe Néri, where he remained until the Revolution.

Boris took to reading early ... and it was hard to tear him away from a book. When his elder sister Natasha, a dazzlingly educated and talented girl, published a collection of verse in Moscow, where she was considered an avant-garde poetess, Boris, either through competitiveness or imitation, also began to practice writing verses in his school notebooks, accompanying them with fanciful illustrations.

---

[7] Marina Tsvetaeva, *Proza* (New York, 1953), 239, 240, 247.

III. Poetry Abroad

When the Revolution broke out in February 1917, Boris was fourteen years old. In 1918 his father was forced to travel to the south of Russia, and he took his son along. Thus, while still quite young, Boris had to part from his family and experience all the horrors of the civil war. In the winter of 1919, when he lived in Yalta, he gave his first reading as a poet at the Chekhov Literary Circle. And in March of the same year he and his father emigrated to Constantinople.

This period of his life can be summed up in two words: he meditated and prayed. All the money his father gave him, his own belongings, even his food, Boris gave to the poor; at times several homeless people would spend the night in his room: students, officers, monks, sailors, and others, all of whom were literally refugees. In Constantinople, Boris attended a makeshift equivalent of high school, did a great deal of sketching, read a lot, occasionally took incidental jobs, and spent much time with the cub scouts at the Russian Hearth, which was organized by the YMCA.

At the same time, Boris saw life through a veil of profound mysticism, as if sensing the breath of Byzantium which gave birth to the Orthodox faith, to which he yielded himself unconditionally. In June 1921, his father was invited to Paris to attend a conference on Russian trade and industry. For ten years Boris lived in the Latin Quarter, during the last four on the rue Barrault near the place d'Italie. There he died in the little annex at number 76-bis, located on the roof of the immense Citroën garage.

The exciting and intriguing city of Paris absorbed Boris so much that he left it only once, in 1922, to spend a few months in Berlin. There he moved in the avant-garde literary circles, often appeared at literary gatherings and artistic soirées, and made a number of literary acquaintances. The Poplavsky family gradually all assembled in Paris and Boris's life seemed to enter upon a normal course. He regularly attended the Art Academy at La Grande Chaumière and was later enrolled at the Sorbonne, majoring in history and philology. He immersed himself in philosophy and theology and spent long hours in the rare manuscript room of the Bibliothèque Sainte-Geneviève. He was a passionate book collector; he had two thousand volumes at his death. He regularly visited museums, where he would stay for days on end. He studied assiduously, practiced sports, and wrote. As in earlier days, he was interested in poetry, literature, economics, philosophy, sociology, history, aviation, music, and everything else. He was always in a hurry to live and work, and he sometimes dreamed of becoming a professor of philosophy in Russia ... not merely when collective farmers got to wear top hats and drive around in Fords, as he put it, but when the persecution of faith would end and a free life of the spirit would begin.

    His novel *Homeward from Heaven*, which is partly autobiographical, gives an idea of how Boris lived and worked in Paris. He frequently appeared at literary gatherings, debates, and conferences as the principal speaker or as a discussant; he was well known in literary and artistic circles. His close friends valued him as a religious mystic, a God seeker, and a perceptive philosopher and thinker. The last years of his life were profoundly enigmatic. Many found in him not only a friend, but a source of support for attaining an ideological turning point in their lives. He was destitute at the time, but he would still share his last penny with the poor.

    A tragically absurd incident brought his life to an end. On 8 October 1935, Boris met a half-mad drug addict, who under the pressure of his own adversity decided to commit suicide and wrote a suicide note, addressed to the woman he loved. He persuaded Boris, "on a dare," to try out a "powder of illusions," but instead, excited by the maniacal idea of taking a fellow traveler along on his journey to the beyond, gave him a fatal dose of poison, taking one himself at the same time.

    Boris left behind two parts of a trilogy in the form of two large novels, *Apollon Bezobrazov* and *Homeward from Heaven*, and sketches for the third part, *The Apocalypse of Therese*. Then there are three volumes of verse ready for publication, a philosophical treatise on logic and metaphysics, the essay "Solitude," a multi-volume diary, notations, drawings, letters, his favorite books which contain many jottings on the margins, and a great deal of other material, which so far has not been sorted out.

Paris, October 1935

                        —Yulian Poplavsky's biography of his son, slightly abridged.[8]

---

[8] Iu. I. Poplavskii, "Boris Poplavskii," *Nov'* (Tallinn), no. 8 (1936): 144–47.

Exhibit D: A Friend

I began writing verse quite early, and in 1920 Boris Poplavsky and I organized a Poets' Guild in Constantinople.

—Vladimir Dukelsky, alias Vernon Duke.[9]

Exhibit E: Self-Portraits

1. "Poverty is a sin, retribution, impotence, while luxury is like a kingdom in which everything reflects, extends, incarnates the slightest flutter of God's eyelashes. And nevertheless, stoically, heroically, Oleg managed to bring his life to a realization, extricated it out of its wraps, despite poverty, inertia, and the obscurity of his underground destiny. Having received no education, he wrenched one for himself from the stained, poorly illuminated library books, read while his behind grew numb on the uncomfortable benches. Anemic and emaciated, by abstinence and daily wrestling with heavy iron weights, he forced life to yield him cupola-like shoulder muscles and an iron handgrip. Not handsome, unsure of himself, he used his hellish solitude, know-it-all-ism, valor, asceticism to master that fierce eye mechanism which was able to subjugate, at times to his own amazement, female heads radiant with youth. For Oleg, like all ascetics, was extraordinarily attractive, and his ugliness, rudeness, and self-assurance only enhanced his charm. Life refused him everything and he created everything for himself, reigning and enjoying himself now amidst the invisible labors of his fifteen-year effort. Thus, in a conversation he would calmly and slyly radiate the universality of his knowledge, which astounded his listeners as much as did the ease with which he could, while sitting on a sofa, lift and toss about a thirty-kilogram weight or a chair, held horizontally by its back in his hand, as he laughed at the gloomy, lifeless, unascetic, sentimental, disbelieving Christianity of the Paris émigré poets."

2. "You thought, Oleg, that you could at last do without God, rest from His insatiable demands; and see, now He is doing without you.... Look, nature is about to enter upon her sad, brief summer

---

[9] Autobiographical note in the anthology *Sodruzhestvo* (Washington, 1966), 521. Although both wrote poetry at the time, it was the future composer of *Cabin in the Sky* and *Le bal de blanchisseuses* who considered himself a poet then, while Poplavsky saw himself as a future painter.

triumph and you were asleep, your heavy head full of the hot waters of sleep, and you dreamed of earthly, full-blooded, bearded life. Once again you were insolent to God, Oleg, and tried living without Him, and your face hit the ground, heavily, stupidly, clownishly. You finally awoke from the pain, took a look around, and see, the trees are already in bloom and have hung out their vivid, abundant new leaves. It is summer in the city and again you are face to face with God, whether you want to be or not, like a child that conceived the wish to hide from the Eiffel Tower behind a flowering shrub in the Trocadero garden and after walking around it was instantly overtaken by the iron dancer-monster that takes up the entire sky. You try not to notice it, but it hurts you to look at the white sky and a heavy, sweaty stuffiness is pressing on your heart. You are again in the open sea, in the open desert, under an open sky covered up by white clouds, in the intolerable, ceaseless, manifest presence of God and sin. And there is no strength not to believe, to doubt, to despair happily in a cloud of tobacco smoke, to calm yourself at a daytime movie. The entire horizon is blindingly occupied by God; in every sweaty creature He is right there again. Eyesight grows dim and there is no shade anywhere, for there is no home of my own, but only history, eternity, apocalypse. There is no soul, no personality, no I, nothing is mine; from heaven to earth there is only the fiery waterfall of universal existence, inception, disappearance."

—Two of Boris Poplavsky's self-portraits as Oleg in his novel *Homeward from Heaven*.[10]

Exhibit F: The Critical Response

1. ...[R]ecently *Will of Russia* (*Volia Rossii*) discovered the amazingly gifted B. Poplavsky. Of all his delightful poems it printed, not a single one could have possibly appeared in *Contemporary Annals* (*Sovremennye zapiski*)—they are far too good and uniquely original for it.

—Georgy Ivanov in *Latest News* (*Poslednie novosti*), Paris, 31 May 1928.

---

10 Fragments from *Homeward from Heaven*, in *Krug*, vol. 3.

2. Among the Parisians, Boris Poplavsky is particularly outstanding. Some of his poems (especially the one with the epigraph from Rimbaud that appeared in volume 2 of *Poetry* and the "Manuscript Found in a Bottle" in *Will of Russia*, number 7) force one to stop and listen in astonishment to the voice of a genuine and entirely new poet. What is interesting about Poplavsky is that he has severed all ties with Russian subject matter. He is the first émigré writer who lives not on memories of Russia, but in a foreign reality. This evolution is inevitable for the whole of the emigration.

—D. S. Mirsky (Prince Dmitry Svyatopolk-Mirsky), in *Eurasia* (*Evraziia*), Paris, 5 January 1929.

3. ...Poplavsky's pseudonaiveté and sleek imitation of the correctly grasped literary fashions. There is no point in mentioning Poplavsky's name next to the names of Blok and Rimbaud (and yet this has been done by Weidlé and Adamovich and Mochulsky).

The scribblings (*pisaniia*) of Mr. Poplavsky, whose critical articles are as deliberately insolent as his verse, would not even deserve mention were it not for the fact that these puerile and shrill scribblings found an echo in Georgy Adamovich.

—Gleb Struve in *Russia and Slavdom* (*Rossiia i slavianstvo*), 11 May 1929; 11 October 1930.[11]

---

[11] Gleb Struve attacked Poplavsky's work vehemently when it first appeared in print, and he remained Poplavsky's most consistent critical opponent. The only other adverse response to Poplavsky's literary beginnings in émigré criticism, Vladimir Nabokov's review of *Flags* in *Rul'* [The rudder]—which Nabokov subsequently repudiated (see n. 20, below)—is far milder in both its tone and its conclusions. Although Nabokov took Poplavsky to task for his violations of meter, ungrammatical usages, and abuses of inappropriate colloquialisms, he ended the review with the admission that some of the poems in the collection "soared with genuine music."

In his later history of Russian émigré literature (see n. 5), Professor Struve cites the highly favorable opinions of various important émigré writers and critics about Poplavsky's poetry with exemplary scholarly objectivity; he even seems to see some promise in Poplavsky's novels. But his ultimate judgment on Poplavsky can be summed up in this quote: "He was a gifted man and an interesting phenomenon, but he never became any kind of writer, no matter what his numerous admirers may say" (Struve, *Russkaia literatura v izgnanii*, 313).

Exhibit G

THE TRAGIC DEATH OF THE POET B. POPLAVSKY

The lower depths of Montparnasse have claimed the lives of two more young Russians. Under circumstances that are still being investigated, the poet Boris Poplavsky and nineteen-year-old Sergei Yarko, well known in certain shady cafés of boulevard du Montparnasse, died of narcotics poisoning.

ACCIDENT OR SUICIDE? The police commissioner of the Maison Blanche quarter immediately initiated an investigation. At first, the possibility of a double suicide was not ruled out. But upon examination of the evidence, it became clear that the young men were the victims of a drug overdose. It is also possible that the drug, purchased on Montparnasse from nameless dealers, contained an admixture of some kind of poison.

Boris Poplavsky never thought of suicide. Sunday evening he visited Dmitry Merezhkovsky and discussed literature and politics with him. On Monday he was seen on Montparnasse. His parents, with whom he had a conversation several hours before his death, categorically reject the possibility of suicide. Their son was a victim of "white powder" vendors.

Apparently Poplavsky and Yarko had been addicts for a long time. In the poet's wallet, his own photograph was found, bearing a revealing inscription: "If you are interested, I found a source of cocaine, etc. Reasonably priced: heroin 25 fr. a gram, cocaine—40 fr." This was written in Poplavsky's hand—apparently in some café, where he was not able to announce the news out loud to his friend.

NO FUNDS FOR BURIAL. At 4 p.m. yesterday, Poplavsky's and Yarko's bodies were taken to the Institute of Forensic Medicine for autopsy. The funeral is planned within the next few days. But there are absolutely no funds available for Boris Poplavsky's burial. His family is destitute. There is not a sou in the house. Boris Poplavsky's parents are appealing to all his friends and to all generous people to help them pay for a coffin and a burial plot for the poet whose life ended so tragically. Donations may be sent to *Latest News*.

> —Selected passages from the lengthy news story in *Latest News* (*Poslednie novosti*), Paris, 11 October 1935

III. Poetry Abroad

Excerpts from "The Book of Blessings,"
Poplavsky's Unpublished Journal for 1929

109. I need only those writers whom I can apply practically in my life, from whom I can learn a particular form of pride or pity and, of course, whom I can develop and alter in my own way. Chekhov teaches me to endure in a special way, not to surrender, to hope, for in Chekhov there is much that is Roman, there is much of "no matter what happens," of *quand même*. With Dostoevsky one can be ill and die, separate and perish, but it is impossible to live with him. As for Tolstoi, with his ancient Hebraic family idylls, I find him repulsive. But Chekhov I hope to put to use, after first rendering him harmless. How? By expanding and developing his admiration for the perishing, beautiful failures, by cleansing him of his disgusting squeamishness and his dignified contempt, contempt for what has failed, what has perished, i.e., extending him in a Christian or, more correctly, specifically Orthodox direction.

110. Chekhov is the most [Russian] Orthodox of Russian writers or, more correctly, the only Orthodox Russian writer. For what is Russian Orthodoxy if not absolute forgiveness, the absolute refusal to condemn which we hear in the voice of Sonya and of the Little Priest of the Swamps?[12]

111. Blok is also an Orthodox poet, the poet of absolute pity, angry at nothing, condemning nothing....

115. It seems to me that the closest work we have to the spirit of the Prometheus of Aeschylus is Chekhov's *Ivanov*. Let us note, *en passant*, that the Prometheus of Aeschylus is one of the most pretentious heroes in world literature. But then, is there anything more beautiful than heroic pretentiousness, for is not the perishing hero higher than the smugly successful hero? And is not the point of a perishing hero in his pretense at being a hero?

116. All my poetry is only the voice of Sonya, or at least I would like for all my poetry to be the voice of Sonya, consoling Uncle Vanya abandoned by everyone in the midst of the demolished estate....

123. Oh, how the lower strata of the émigrés are irritated and outraged by the sight of an impoverished and merry friend of books and stars, with his tattered pants and a monocle in his eye! It is their enormous, base yearning for power that is outraged within them.

---

12 I.e., Sonya from Chekhov's play *Uncle Vanya*, and the elfin creature from Blok's poem of that name, who prays with equal fervor "for the injured leg of a frog and for the Pope in Rome."

What! He dares to be joyous, that owner of worn-out shoes? Isn't he in the same position as we? He has no money, no power, and he dares to be joyous. Where does he get his joy? Surely not from that bookish, intellectual stuff—the very thing that ruined Russia? From Culture and Social Conscience? Thus the poor people. And a huge disgust hangs suspended in perplexity from their curled lip, while the friend of the stars goes his own way in his worn-out shoes, waving his handsome athletic arms in the air as he recites poetry to his neighbor.

124. The attitude of the wealthy émigrés toward the friend of the stars is even more base. What! We've done our best, we've achieved, we've recovered our own, and this one dares to be joyous while the seat of his pants is in patches? What was the point of our struggle?

125. But the attitude of foreigners is delightful. It can be seen from their glances in the street, for in them there still survive the ancient, beautiful ideals, merry and profound, of ancient stoical poverty. There was once this delightful philosopher—Anaximenes of Dorcrete seems to have been his name—a fine athletic old man. Diodorus tells us that he was once invited to some ritzy party, by some tyrant or other. Coming to the table, he bared himself and beshat the company and the table, and with this excellent deed he indubitably deserved his immortality. His other works were forgotten, but compared to this they could not have been important.

Poplavsky Yesterday and Today

When I first read *Flags*, I had no idea of Poplavsky's position in the Russian literary hierarchy. I had simply assumed that he was a poet as famous as Blok and Pasternak. I knew little about Russian poetry as a whole at the time, and there were many important modern poets I was yet to discover and read. It took me a few years to realize that apart from a small cult centered in Paris, almost no one had ever heard of his name. In the late 1940s my colleagues at the Control Council for Germany, Alain Bosquet and Edouard Roditi, were publishing a literary journal in Berlin. They asked me to write something about Russian poetry for it, "about somebody modern and famous, like Selvinsky or Bagritsky," as Roditi put it. I had no idea who Selvinsky and Bagritsky were, but I offered to write about the three poets who had been my favorites during my school years in Los Angeles. They let me, and I wrote three brief pieces on Khlebnikov,

Pasternak, and Poplavsky; these were translated into German and published in *Das Lot* in 1950, with a selection of translated poems by each of these poets.[13] The overindulgent accompanying note identified me as the author of "numerous articles published in American newspapers and magazines," but apart from a few pieces in the college newspaper, this was actually my debut in print. I'm glad it had to do with Poplavsky and that I already then called him the most interesting poet produced by the Russian emigration between the two world wars.

By then I had already read his two posthumous collections of verse (they contain some astounding poems, but I found them on the whole a bit of a letdown after *Flags*); the published portions of his novels (*Homeward from Heaven* contains some of his finest lyrics, inserted between passages of prose and printed to look like prose); his paradoxical critical essays; the highly original short story "The Ball"; his pieces on painting and boxing. When in 1965 Nikolai Tatishchev privately published a new volume of Poplavsky's previously uncollected poems, *Dirigible of Unknown Destination*, my torch for the poet flared up again. The volume contained some of his most typical and most perfectly realized poems ("On the Frontier," for instance, with its striking central metaphor of a poet as a customs official trying to stop the two-way smugglers' traffic between the Land of Good and the Land of Evil; or "The Biography of a Clerk," with its transposition of the humiliated clerk of Gogol's "The Overcoat" and Dostoevsky's *Poor Folk* into a Kafkaesque and surrealistic tonality). I read a paper on Poplavsky's surrealistic techniques at a scholarly gathering in Washington, D.C., and published it as an article in *Slavic Review*.[14] A few graduate students purchased copies of the *Dirigible* as a result, but I knew that, with one or two exceptions, I had failed to convince my fellow Slavicists of the value of Poplavsky's work. Just how badly I had failed was made clear to me by one of my most respected and discerning colleagues, who referred to him as a Parisian Vertinsky (a popular émigré nightclub singer) for the elect few.

Doing literary research in Europe in the fall of 1969, I made a point of seeking out and talking about Poplavsky with those who knew him or were his friends in an effort to reconstruct the reality of the man behind the po-

---

[13] S. Karlinsky, "Drei russische Dichter," *Das Lot* 4 (October 1950): 46–51. [See postscript to present article.—Ed.]

[14] See SK's essay "Surrealism in Twentieth-Century Russian Poetry: Churilin, Zabolotsky, Poplavsky" in the present volume.—Ed.

etry and the prose: the poets Alla Golovina and Sofiya Pregel; the painters Ida Karskaya (a marvelously warm and compassionate woman and a far more important painter than I had previously realized) and Constantine Terechkovitch; the critic Georgy Adamovich; the literary scholar Sophie Laffitte (née Glickman, later Sophie Stalinsky and Sophie Bonneau); and of course Poplavsky's closest friend and the curator of his archive, Nikolai Tatishchev. All of them had observed Poplavsky at close range at one or another time in his life, all but the first two had poems dedicated to them in *Flags*, and all were willing to talk about him candidly and openly. Some day I hope to transcribe these interviews in full, but for the moment I can say that their sum total has helped me to formulate the two sets of polarities that I feel primarily motivated and shaped Poplavsky's literary art. The never-resolved dichotomy between poetry and painting is what accounts for the intensely visual nature of his imagery and much of his subject matter. According to Terechkovitch, Poplavsky thought of himself during his first few years of exile not as a poet but as a painter. In 1922, Terechkovitch and Poplavsky traveled together to Berlin to study art. In Berlin, Poplavsky met the leading Soviet abstractionists as well as Chagall, Tchelitchew, and Chaim Soutine. But everyone, and particularly his teachers and colleagues, kept assuring him that he had no talent for painting. At first he tried to ignore their verdict. When he realized that they were right, the result was a total nervous breakdown that kept him bedridden for several weeks. Not only his highly personal articles on art exhibitions and painters, which appeared later in the journal *Numbers* (*Chisla*), but much of his prose and poetry testify to his never-ending yearning for mastery of the visual arts. His literary development reflects not so much the development of Russian émigré poetry as the evolution of the Paris schools of painting in the late 1920s and early 1930s—especially those of the Surrealists and the neo-Romantics.

The other central polarity has to do with his insatiable hunger for mystical experience (any kind of mysticism) and drug experience (any kind of drugs). It was his sister Natasha, that "dazzlingly educated and talented girl" his father wrote about, who introduced Boris to drugs by the time he was twelve. Her search for the ultimate high eventually took her to Madagascar, to Africa, to India, and finally to Shanghai, where she died in the late 1920s—of pneumonia, according to her father's biography of Boris, but of a hopeless opium addiction according to everyone else.

Drugs remained a constant presence in Poplavsky's life, both in Berlin and in Paris, and they (rather than imitation of his idol Rimbaud) account for the psychedelic swirling of images and the vivid, violent colors so typical of his verse. There are vast riches of authentic psychedelia to be mined in twentieth-century Russian poetry—Balmont and Khlebnikov are the names that come to mind most easily—but no one in the Russian tradition exploited the openings to other realities that drugs afford as systematically as did Poplavsky in the service of his poetry. There was, unfortunately, no LSD or mescaline to be had in those days, and he had to do it the hard way. (A tremendous stimulus for writing much of *Flags* came when his friend, the minor poet Boris Zakovich, the "Pusya" of Poplavsky's journals, inherited a large supply of pain-killers and mind expanders from his dentist-father.) Those who are capable of appreciating the unique kind of beauty Poplavsky was thus able to glimpse and convey are the beneficiaries.

Poplavsky's religious quest was as intense as it was eclectic. A devout and loyal member of the Russian Orthodox Church (as his journals leave no doubt), he was powerfully drawn to Roman Catholic rite and lore, to Hindu mystics, to freemasonry, and to various forms of spiritualism. One of the most intense experiences of his life, according to Tatishchev, occurred in 1918, when he met Jiddu Krishnamurti, the philosophical and spiritual teacher, who took his hand and addressed a few words in English to him. Poplavsky understood no English, but he was moved to tears. In Berlin he had several discussions about anthroposophy with Andrei Bely. (His mother and aunt were close to Moscow anthroposophic circles.)

Boris Poplavsky was loved by a number of exceptional and brilliant women in his day, but the central relationship of his life, its keynote, was what he himself called his love affair with God (*roman s Bogom*). This affair is the subject of many poems in *Snowy Hour*; it is basic to his novels, and it is vividly reflected in the portions of his diaries which his friends Dina Shraibman and Nikolai Tatishchev published after his death. It was also discussed in print by no less a thinker than Nikolai Berdyaev in his puzzled, perplexed, and not entirely sympathetic review of Poplavsky's journals.[15] I'll venture to say, with all due respect, that the celebrated philosopher simply failed to grasp the point of Poplavsky's mysticism. Like art, like drugs, mysticism was for Poplavsky both a way of expanding

---

[15] In *Sovremennye zapiski* [Contemporary annals] (Paris), no. 68 (1939).

his personal vision and a means of transforming unbearable social reality. Poplavsky's lecture on Marcel Proust and James Joyce (he is the only Russian writer I can think of besides Vladimir Nabokov who responded creatively to *Ulysses*), of which I have the outline, concludes with a surprising prediction of impending social revolution in Western Europe, which would combine social, sexual, and personal-mystical elements. For Poplavsky, the reason the Soviet experiment turned Russia into a "vast, barbarous, snow-clad field" was that in its attempt to build a better society it suppressed the human spirit and its most precious manifestations. This was well understood by Poplavsky's friends Zinaida Gippius and Dmitry Merezhkovsky; yet one can easily imagine the shock that this conclusion of the Proust-Joyce lecture occasioned among the émigré audience when Poplavsky delivered it at the Kochevie Club on 22 October 1931.

Poplavsky's career in the world of émigré letters was brief and meteoric. Only six years separate his literary debut from his death. During that time he impressed some of the most important older writers-in-exile (Merezhkovsky, Khodasevich, Georgy Ivanov) and was acclaimed by the finest émigré critics (Mirsky, Mochulsky, Adamovich, Weidlé). He must have made an enormous impression on the émigré writers of his own age group, for he looms as a momentous presence in the subsequently written autobiographies and memoirs of Nina Berberova,[16] Yury Terapiano,[17] Vladimir Varshavsky,[18] and V. S. Yanovsky.[19] Vladimir Nabokov on two occasions singled out Poplavsky as the only poet of importance among the younger émigrés.[20] At Poplavsky's funeral, homage was paid to him by such diverse figures as Mark Aldanov, Aleksei Remizov, and Vladislav Khodasevich, whose eloquent obituary of Poplavsky was later reprinted

---

16 Nina Berberova, *The Italics Are Mine* (New York, 1969). Original Russian version, *Kursiv moi* (Munich, 1972).
17 Iurii Terapiano, *Vstrechi* [Encounters] (New York, 1953).
18 Vladimir Varshavskii, *Nezamechennoe pokolenie* [The unnoticed generation] (New York, 1956).
19 Vasilii Ianovskii, "Eliseiskie polia" [Les Champs-Élysées], an excerpt from his memoirs, in *Vozdushnye puti: Al'manakh* [Aerial ways: An anthology], vol. 5 (New York, 1967), 175–200.
20 "I did not meet Poplavsky who died young, a far violin among near balalaikas. His plangent tonalities I shall never forget, nor shall I ever forgive myself the ill-tempered review in which I attacked him for trivial flaws in his unfledged verse." V. Nabokov, *Speak, Memory* (1951), 216. This is repeated, with the addition of a quoted line from Poplavsky's poem "Morella," in the expanded version of *Speak, Memory* (1966), 287.

in a collection of his critical essays.[21] And yet, if we were to take a count, there would probably be fewer people in the world today who are aware of Poplavsky's existence than there were in 1935.

I am convinced that Boris Poplavsky has his readers somewhere. But where? Russians, either abroad or in the Soviet Union, don't seem to want to read him. When Olga Carlisle included Denise Levertov's fine translation of his poem, "Manuscript Found in a Bottle," in her book *Poets on Streetcorners*, the Moscow *Literary Gazette* took her to task for including this "tramp of whom no one has heard" among the other fine Russian poets in her anthology. Publication of a few excerpts from *The Apocalypse of Therese* in George [Yury] Ivask's Russian literary journal *Experiments* (*Opyty*) in the late 1950s was met with similar scorn by Russian newspapers in Paris and New York. I tried submitting several of his unpublished poems and a highly interesting essay on Russian painting (which I obtained from Nikolai Tatishchev and which Jean-Claude Marcadé carefully annotated) to the New York Russian literary journal *Novyi zhurnal*. Two of the poems were published, with distorting "corrections" by the editor, while the remainder of them and the article were rejected after a two-year wait.[22] In a personal letter to me, the editor of *Novyi zhurnal*, Roman Goul, wrote that Poplavsky was "an utter madman" and proudly recalled how he and a group of friends once threw Poplavsky out of a Berlin beer hall.

And yet, as Vladimir Nabokov put it when I informed him of my interest in Poplavsky: "Yes, write something about him. He was, after all, the first hippy, the original flower child." This might simplify things a bit, but it is not wrong.[23] During the past few years young Slavic scholars in

---

[21] V. Khodasevich, "O smerti Poplavskogo" [On Poplavsky's death], in *Literaturnye stat'i i vospominaniia* [Literary essays and memoirs] (New York, 1954).

[22] An English translation (by Peter Lawless) of Poplavsky's article about the Berlin Exhibition of 1922 was eventually published: "The Notes of Boris Poplavsky," intro. by Simon Karlinsky, annotations by Jean-Claude Marcadé, *Art International* 18 (1974): 62–65.—Ed.

[23] His involvements with drugs and Hindu mystics are two of the more striking ways in which Poplavsky seems to foreshadow the hip culture, but that is by no means all. He dressed unconventionally, was never without a pair of dark glasses, thought bathing unnecessary, and would wear the same shirt for weeks on end. His favorite music was by Bach, Scriabin, and Stravinsky. A beard and long hair are the only ingredients that were missing, but that tonsorial style was inextricably connected with the priestly caste in Russian culture. There clearly would have been no point in Poplavsky's trying to pass for an Orthodox priest.

the West, those in their early twenties, have been repeatedly taking to Poplavsky like the proverbial duck to water. I've read with pleasure the intelligent papers Olga Bazanoff and Mike Hathaway wrote about him for Vsevolod Setchkarev's seminar on émigré literature at Harvard, and Hélène Paschutinsky's first-rate MA thesis on Poplavsky's imagery,[24] written under Sophie Laffitte's direction at the Sorbonne. I am excited about Anthony Olcott's Stanford thesis.

Perhaps Poplavsky was an émigré in more senses than one. Caught between cultures, he was also trapped in the wrong historical period. Many young non-Russians today should have no trouble identifying with him and seeing him as one of themselves. As Emmett Jarrett and Dick Lourie wrote,[25] when I sent them some trots of his poetry for translation: "He's dynamite ..."

How to detonate him?

* * *

It is of interest to read SK's early publication—dating from 1950—which was written as an introduction to a German translation of three of Poplavsky's lyrics (see note 13 above):

> Boris Poplavsky's name is completely unknown in his own country. Poplavsky was perhaps the most gifted representative of a generation

---

[24] Particularly impressive is Mlle Paschutinsky's demonstration of the central function of the states of flying, floating, and levitation in Poplavsky's poetry, and of his systematic use of objects and beings capable of these states: fish, ships, dirigibles, balloons, submarines, interplanetary rockets, clouds, comets, and angels, as well as the role of Poplavsky's ubiquitous bridges, balconies, and towers, functioning as stepping-stones to flight and levitation. The resultant antithesis of lightness and heaviness is then used by Mlle Paschutinsky to construct a highly convincing and logical system that provides us with a key not only to Poplavsky's imagery, but also to the whole of his complex metaphysics. Should Poplavsky's poetry ever gain the wide readership it so very much deserves, Hélène Paschutinsky's study will certainly be a fundamental source on this poet. [In subsequent years Paschutinsky, under the name of Elena Menegaldo, published widely on Poplavsky. See, for example, her important edition of Boris Poplavskii, *Neizdannoe: dnevniki, stat'i, stikhi, pis'ma*, ed. A. Bogoslovskii and E. Menegal'do (Moscow: Khristianskoe izd-vo, 1996), and subsequent editions of Poplavsky's collected works. See also Dmitrii Tokarev, *"Mezhdu Indiei i Gegelem"* (Moscow: Novoe literaturnoe obozrenie, 2011).—Ed.]

[25] Emmett Jarrett and Richard Lourie translated three poems by Poplavsky for the same collection from which the present memoiristic essay by SK is taken. This same volume contains a chapter from *Homeward from Heaven*, translated by Charty Bassett.—Ed.

of Russian émigré poets who were born in Russia but whose literary activity between the two wars took place everywhere: from Warsaw to Addis Ababa. Poplavsky spent his short life (1903–35) mostly in Paris. His literary reputation was based on a small volume of poems with the title *Flags*. This book was published in Paris and Tallinn in 1931. After his death, a collection of poems with the title *In a Wreath of Wax*, a short novel (*Homeward from Heaven*), and *Diaries* were found among his papers. A selection of these works was published by Poplavsky's friends. In *Diaries*, Poplavsky gives a detailed description of his poetic method. In this context, Poplavsky quotes an old Hindu poem in which an unknown poet is not satisfied with the sentence "The tree of my life yearns on a hill"; a few lines later the same poet gives a modified version of the same sentence: "The blue tree of my life yearns on a hill." As Poplavsky noted, the color blue is added to express the intangible.

Nowadays Poplavsky's poetic method seems to be similar to French Surrealism, and *Diaries* shows that he had studied and admired the writings of André Breton. When reading Poplavsky's poems one is reminded of surrealistic paintings.[26]

Some years later, SK prepared a three-volume edition of Poplavsky's collected poetic oeuvre: Boris Poplavskii, *Sobranie sochinenii* (Berkeley: Berkeley Slavic Specialties, 1980–81). The first of these volumes contains a brief essay by the editor, "An Alien Comet," which is a distillation of his earlier publications about the poet, as well as a brief biography of Poplavsky by Anthony Olcott.

---

[26] Translated by Joachim Klein, from S. Karlinsky, "Drei russische Dichter," *Das Lot* 4 (October 1950): 50.

Morshen,
or a Canoe to Eternity[1]

Some poets are astonishingly precocious: Arthur Rimbaud, for example, wrote everything he had to write by the time he was nineteen. Nikolai Morshen's development as a poet offers an opposite example. Gradually maturing in a leisurely and deliberate manner over almost four decades, this poet's work, when viewed in its totality, is a study in ever deepening philosophical thought and ever more finely honed verbal mastery. The stages of Morshen's development and their chronology are obvious enough: the verse of 1936 to 1946 (written prior to Morshen's first published collection and, for the most part, not included in it); the three published books of verse, *Tiulen'* (The seal, 1959), *Dvoetochie* (Punctuation: Colon, 1967), and *Ekho i zerkalo* (The echo and the mirror, 1979); and a few poems that have appeared in émigré journals from his fourth, unpublished collection, "Umolkshii zhavoronok" (The now-silent lark).[2] To read this poetry in the order in which it was written is to realize that the concept of Darwinian evolution—a major theme in Morshen's poetry—applies not only to the examples of related animal species or related language groups, but also to the model of one man's slowly maturing poetic vision.

Nikolai Nikolaevich Marchenko, who took the German word for "little Blackamoor" as his pen name, was born in Kiev on 8 November 1917, exactly one day after the October Revolution. His mother, Elizaveta Petrovna Toropova, came from a St. Petersburg family of government officials. His father, Nikolai Vladimirovich Marchenko (1887–1969), was

---

[1] Originally published in *Slavic Review* 41, no. 1 (Spring 1982): 1–18.
[2] See Nikolai Morshen, *Tiulen'* (Frankfurt am Main: Posev, 1959); Morshen, *Dvoetochie* (Washington, D.C.: Victor Kamkin, 1967); and Morshen, *Ekho i zerkalo* (Berkeley: Berkeley Slavic Specialties, 1979). The poems intended for "Umolkshii zhavoronok" appeared in *Russkii al'manakh* (Paris, 1981), 103–6; and in *Perekrestki* [Crossroads] 2 (1978): 10–13, 3 (1979): 17–18, and 4 (1980): 27. [*Umolkshii zhavoronok* was first published in its entirety in 1996; see n. 3 of the following article.—Ed.]

born in Kazan but grew up and spent most of his life in Kiev, where he studied at the Polytechnic Institute. Strongly drawn to the theater, the senior Marchenko managed to combine teaching mathematics with a career as a stage actor. He fought with General Denikin's forces in the Civil War, was captured by the Bolsheviks, escaped, and managed to return to his double vocation of mathematics and acting. His theatrical activities had to be given up at the beginning of the First Five-Year Plan, when the government banned all private theaters and introduced strict control of the repertoire and acting and directing methods of remaining theaters. After World War II, in emigration, Nikolai Vladimirovich Marchenko found a new calling which brought him considerable recognition in the sixth and seventh decades of his life. He became the novelist and essayist Nikolai Narokov, the author of the novels *Mnimye velichiny* (translated into English as *Chains of Fear*) and *Mogu* (I can) and of short stories and literary essays that appeared in almost all the important émigré journals. *Chains of Fear*, an in-depth psychological study of life among Stalin's secret police, enjoyed international success and was translated into German and French as well as English.[3]

Some of Morshen's earliest recollections are those of backstage life: rehearsals and performances of plays by Beaumarchais and Ostrovsky and prerevolutionary operettas. The poet remembers reading Pushkin as a child—a traditional, complete Russian edition, of course, which included even the letters—sitting on a sofa piled high with mimeographed play scripts. But he was not personally drawn to the theater, as he was later not drawn to the prose genres, possibly because they were his father's sphere.

At the beginning of the 1930s Morshen witnessed the famine in the Ukraine that was brought about by forced collectivization. Living next to a railroad station, the fifteen-year-old boy could observe nightly the passing freight trains crammed full of peasants being taken to Siberian labor camps. His father was temporarily arrested the same year. To that time the poet dates his realization of the basic inhumanity of the Soviet system, a realization that was later to be reflected in some of his most powerful poems in *The Seal*.

---

[3] Nikolai Narokov, *Mnimye velichiny* (New York, 1952). The book is available in English as *Chains of Fear*, trans. Christopher Bird (Chicago, 1958), in French as *Grandeurs imaginaires* (Paris, 1959), and in German as *Wenn das Salz schal wird*, trans. Siegfried von Vegesack (Graz, [1956]). *Mogu* was published in Buenos Aires in 1965.

Like most Russian adolescents, Morshen was familiar with the classics of his native poetry, and Derzhavin, Pushkin, and Baratynsky became lifelong favorites. His personal involvement with poetry, however, was the result of a fortuitous accident. Leafing one day through a traditional anthology of popular texts suitable for public recitation, Morshen came upon a poem by Gumilyov. It turned out that a collection of Silver Age poets had been bound together with the anthology, possibly for safety's sake. Gumilyov's "muse of distant journeys," irresistible to the adventure-starved, adolescent mind, infected the young Morshen with poetry. His early love for this secret prince of Soviet poets was later reflected in the Gumilyov citations and reminiscences in *The Seal*. Eventually Morshen found a group of like-minded coevals interested in reading and, in some cases, writing poetry. In the Soviet Union of 1935 the Silver Age Russian poets (with the exception of Bryusov and Blok, spared because of their political stands at the end of their lives) were banned and generally forgotten. The discovery of Gumilyov led Morshen and his friends to other poets of their parents' generation, resulting in some important rediscoveries.

The earliest verse that has been preserved in the poet's archive is dated 1936. Morshen himself considered his poetry of the years 1936–38 derivative and imitative, "now of Bryusov, now of Balmont, but mostly of Gumilyov."[4] It is significant that during the period subsequently named after the dreaded secret police chief Ezhov, when the country was terrorized by some of Stalin's worst purges, many young people turned for comfort to Gumilyov's proscribed neo-Romanticism, with its glorification of swashbuckling sea captains and Kiplingesque explorers in Africa. Yet, for all the derivative quality of Morshen's prewar verse, a few poems from that period found their way, in revised form, into *The Seal*, including some remnants from an extensive cycle of 1938 and 1939 about an unhappy love affair.[5]

Morshen graduated from secondary school in Odessa, where his family had moved in 1933. In 1935 he began his studies at Odessa University, majoring in physics. When his family moved to Kiev, a regulation prohib-

---

[4] Personal communication. A study should one day be written about the phenomenon of the persistent and parallel cults of the three officially disapproved poets in the pre-1960s USSR—the romantic and escapist cult of Gumilyov, the sentimental cult of Esenin, and the intellectual cult of Khlebnikov.
[5] See, for example, "Zakaty" [Sunsets], in Morshen, *Tiulen'*, 27–28. See also the untitled poem, ibid., 16.

iting transfers of students from one city to another delayed his acceptance at the university there for one year. Consequently, he was still a student at the outbreak of the war and was therefore not drafted into the army. In September 1941 Kiev was occupied by the German army. In February 1942 Morshen married Nataliya Vasilievna Zozulya. The entire family left Kiev at the time of the German retreat, moving first to Königsberg, then to Berlin. The end of the war found them in Hamburg.

Despite the constant threat of forced repatriation (under the terms of the Yalta Agreement, the three Western allies rounded up thousands of natives of Russia all over Germany and handed them over to the Soviet authorities), there quickly arose in the displaced persons camps of West Germany what later came to be called the literature of the Second Emigration. The prospect of writing and publishing without any ideological or stylistic controls must have been intoxicating indeed. In this intellectually stimulating atmosphere Morshen again took up writing poetry, which he had all but abandoned during the war years. In 1946 he made his debut in print, publishing the poem "Iskhod" (Exodus; subsequently included in *The Seal*) in one of the new émigré journals[6] under the pen name he continued to use. The poem is couched in his somewhat eclectic early manner, but the line "V potok nesushcheisia vselennoi" (Into the stream of the rushing universe—the poet suggests to his companion that they immerse their legs up to the knees in this stream) offers a foretaste of the themes and manner of his second collection, *Punctuation: Colon*. During the rest of Morshen's stay in Germany, his poetry regularly appeared in émigré periodicals, primarily in the journal *Grani* (Facets; published in Frankfurt am Main). He supported himself during that period as a laborer in shipyards and in construction work.

In 1950 Morshen and his family left for the United States, an experience he described in the moving poem "Slovno lastochkin khvost, za kormoiu" (Like a swallow's tail, behind the stern).[7] After brief employment at an automobile plant in Syracuse, New York, Morshen obtained a position as a teacher of Russian in Monterey, California, which he occupied until his retirement in 1977, and settled permanently on the West Coast.

---

[6] This was in a mimeographed edition, of which no copy has been preserved. See "Iskhod," ibid., 41.
[7] Ibid., 49–50.

After the grim years of Stalinist terror, after the turmoil of the war and the uncertainties of postwar existence as a displaced person, with its threat of forced repatriation, came a secure and comfortable life by the Pacific Ocean on the Monterey peninsula. Acquiring a home for his entire family (which later also comprised his parents and his aunt), raising his four children, teaching Russian to young Americans, exploring California's mountains, forests, and rivers on long hiking and boating trips with his wife, Morshen must have felt the urge to sum up in poetic form what he had witnessed and experienced in the first thirty years of his life. The result was *The Seal*, the book of verse in which Morshen found his own poetic voice and attained his full stature as a poet. The collection includes poems written in Kiev, Germany (where the basic theme of the collection had already taken shape), and California. But the book as a whole is focused on the Soviet experience before, during, and after World War II.

The pinniped mammal after which the collection is named (its title has a clumsy sound in Russian and is ambiguous when translated into English) serves as the book's central symbol and provides its keynote. The significance of the seal is explained in the second poem of the book, also entitled "The Seal."[8] The poem tells of a student at an unnamed Soviet university who attends a compulsory meeting where the entire student body is required to approve the death penalty for whomever the government has designated as "enemies of the people" at the latest show trial (the poem is couched in quatrains of traditional Russian rhymed iambic pentameter, but a prose fragment of hackneyed political oratory is brutally wedged into the middle of the first stanza). His eyes lowered, the protagonist of the poem obediently raises his hand with everyone else, "trying to think of nothing." Later that night he wanders in a public park, still trying to keep that afternoon's experience out of his consciousness and forcing himself instead to think of a seal he had read about in his childhood. To survive, the seal has to break a secret breathing hole in a layer of permanently frozen ice.

Ever since Zamyatin wrote his story "The Cave" a few years after the Revolution, Russian writers have repeatedly likened postrevolutionary spiritual and intellectual life to the coming of a new ice age. Morshen

---

8 Ibid., 10–11.

narrows this widely used image to the situation of a particular individual in a totalitarian state. He explains that the political poems in *The Seal* or, more precisely, the poems that deal with the situation of the individual enslaved by the all-powerful machinery of the state, reflect only what the poet himself had felt, seen, or experienced. In this sense much of *The Seal* is a poetic response to the urge to testify about the nature of the time in which one lives—just as André Chénier's *Iambes* and Anna Akhmatova's *Requiem* were testimonies inspired by the same urge. Only very rarely did Morshen permit himself to alter, for artistic reasons, the exact facts of the experience described. Thus, in the poem in which his lyric hero overhears someone whispering a few lines by Gumilyov and realizes that this person must be a kindred soul, Morshen substituted the contextually appropriate lines from Gumilyov's "Fra Beato Angelico" ("There is God, there is the world. They live forever / While human life is instantaneous and wretched") for the Gumilyov poem he actually overheard.[9]

    The Seal contains a number of purely lyrical evocations of Kiev and of nature in the Ukraine. The most memorable poems of the collection, however, and the most accomplished technically, are clearly the political ones. In addition to the poem that gave the collection its title, they are "V chas, kogda solov'iami" (In the hour, when like nightingales), about the suicide of a Ukrainian collective farmer; "Groza proshla" (The storm is over), in which a vividly captured sketch of the Ukrainian landscape serves as the background for a brief glimpse of an aged peasant trudging on foot to the city to see the public prosecutor about someone who has been—apparently unjustly—arrested; and the quite remarkable "Na Pervomaiskoi zhdu tramvaia" (I wait for the streetcar on the Street of the First of May), where the initially realistic sketch of an employee unable to get to work on time because the right streetcar does not come is gradually blown up into a suffocating nightmare about a society in which everyone is at all times presumed guilty by the state (this poem is based on a concrete historical phenomenon, the draconian Soviet law of 1940 that made not only

---

[9] The cited lines from Gumilyov's "Fra Beato Angelico" appear as an epigraph to the untitled poem, ibid., 18, and fragments from these same lines are scattered in the fourth stanza of this poem. Morshen remembers that the Gumilyov lines he actually overheard in the situation described in the poem were from that poet's "Indiuk" [The tom-turkey].

absenteeism but also being late for work a state crime).[10] The powerful psychological impact of "Na Pervomaiskoi zhdu tramvaia" is achieved by relatively simple means: the hypnotic reiteration of the refrain "A streetcar comes, but it's not mine" and the gradual transformation of workaday reality into a Kafkaesque dream from which the narrator is allowed to awaken in the very last line.

Similar poems employ structures of considerable complexity. In "Vecherom 7-go noiabria" (On the evening of the 7th of November"), the loneliness and alienation of the protagonist, unable to participate in the "carefully rationed merriment" that celebrates the October Revolution anniversary, is contrasted with the dance rhythms of "two orchestras playing from three balconies ... for the toiling millions."[11] The three alternating dance rhythms (a waltz, a polka, and a krakowiak) produce a deliberately discordant effect, oddly reminiscent of the three simultaneous orchestras in the first-act finale of Mozart's *Don Giovanni*. A further internal contrast is provided by unexpectedly appropriate, ironic quotations from Pushkin's *The Bronze Horseman*, A. K. Tolstoi, Pasternak, and popular songs. The deliberate clash between a merry dance tune and the tragic theme it expresses is also found in the brief poem "Po tropinke po lesnoi" (Along a forest path), a lament for two soldiers killed in the war which is couched in the rhythm of a boisterous polka.[12] The hackneyed text of a popular polka with which the poem ends serves as an apt reminder of life's and nature's indifference to individual tragedy and loss.

The most densely textured poem in *The Seal* and one that ushers in the verbal imagination and lexical virtuosity of Morshen's later poetry is "Kak krugi na vode" (Like ripples on water).[13] Stylistically a bridge between *The Seal* and *Punctuation: Colon*, the poem derives its entire imagery from the multiple meanings of a single Russian word, *krug*. Meaning basically circle, *krug* can in certain contexts also mean ripples on water, cycle, sphere, circuit, and even nautical life preserver, and Morshen exploits all these meanings. He opens the poem with a picture of pervasive fear, spreading out like ripples on water, filling every nook and cranny, lurking in all dark corners, and even seeping in through the pores of one's

---

10 Ibid., 15, 23, and 17, respectively.
11 Ibid., 12.
12 Ibid., 40.
13 Ibid., 19.

skin. The loner hero, typical of many poems in *The Seal*, tries to hide from the omnipresent terror within his own four walls:

> Дверь на крюк! Но тебе не заклясть свой испуг
> Конурою, как норы понурой:
> Он порочен твой круг, твой магический круг
> Нереальный своей квадратурой.[14]

Other images of enclosing circles follow: a citation of Ecclesiastes 1:6 ("The wind returneth again according to his circuits," which in its biblical formulation is a Russian proverb); the horizon that girdles the city and congeals into an impermeable wall; a life preserver that is so drenched with bitter water that it sinks. The final stanza points out both the cause and the effect of the fear that blankets the country:

> А вдали, где полгода (иль более) мрак,
> Где слова, как медведи, косматы:
> Воркута, Магадан, Колыма, Ухтпечлаг …
> Как терновый венец или Каина знак—
> Круг полярный, последний, девятый.[15]

The "words as shaggy as bears" are the names of concentration camps in the arctic regions, whose existence was denied by the Soviet government for decades, but which had been known to most Russians since the 1930s. The rest of the world became aware of them (to the extent that it ever did) with the publication of Aleksandr Solzhenitsyn's *Gulag Archipelago*. Morshen was spared the central experience of Solzhenitsyn's life, but the poem just described shows that he realized the cardinal importance of the concentration camp experience for the mentality of *homo sovieticus*. *The Seal* was published a few years before Solzhenitsyn's first novel made its sensational appearance. For all the obvious differences in the two writers' personalities and their respective literary genres, Morshen's first book

---

[14] "Latch your door! But you won't exorcise your fright / With this cubbyhole as depressing as a burrow: / Your magic circle is a vicious circle / Because its squaring is unreal." Ibid.

[15] "And far away, where the darkness lasts half the year or longer / There are words as shaggy as bears: / Vorkuta, Magadan, Kolyma, Ukhtpechlag … / Like the crown of thorns or the mark of Cain— / The polar circle, the ultimate, the ninth one." Ibid.

often explores in the lyrical mode experiences remarkably similar to those Solzhenitsyn's novels probe. The parallels extend from the obvious ones, such as the evocation of Dante's circles of hell when writing of the labor camps and Nerzhin's determined effort to keep his prohibited volume of Esenin (just as Morshen's lyric hero hangs on to his Gumilyov quotations), to more complex ones, such as the kinship between the lyrical voice in *The Seal* and Solzhenitsyn's loner heroes, the Nerzhins and the Kostoglotovs, or the subtle correspondences between the poem "Andreevskaia tserkov'" (St. Andrew's Church) and chapter 23, "The Church of St. John the Baptist," in Solzhenitsyn's *The First Circle*.[16] These parallels, which would make a fitting subject for a separate study, are neither accidental nor the result of any possible mutual influence. Morshen simply has the same remarkable ability to bring into focus the essential core of Soviet experience that Solzhenitsyn had so admirably manifested in another literary medium.

In his introductory essay to *The Seal*, Vladimir Markov justly wrote that this was "poetry of high quality, unfeigned modesty, unostentatiously independent in its themes and its choice of artistic means," containing "keen thinking, internal logic, and, at times, exciting play of semantic contrasts and viewpoints."[17] The publication of *The Seal* placed Morshen's name in the forefront of Russian émigré poetry, and it must have also initiated his present high reputation among underground poetry lovers in the Soviet Union. Like any poet who had found his true voice and discovered his particular subject matter, Morshen might have gone on exploring this successfully inaugurated manner. Instead, he turned to entirely new themes and evolved a fresh poetic manner for dealing with them in the poems that comprise his second published collection, *Punctuation: Colon*.[18]

In the late 1950s there occurred an important shift of perspective in Morshen's poetry. Until then his poetry had been concerned with the experiences of a particular person in a particular country during a clearly delimited period in history. Now the poet's vantage point soared upward. His horizon expanded vertiginously. His vision encompassed both minute close-ups and cosmic vistas. Even his literary and intellectual genealogy

---

16 Ibid., 26 and Aleksandr Solzhenitsyn, *V kruge pervom* (New York, 1968), 112–18.
17 Morshen, *Tiulen'*, 3–4.
18 *Dvoetochie* was reviewed by SK in *Novyi zhurnal*, no. 88 (1967): 297–99. The present essay is an elaboration and extension of his readings of Morshen's poetry in the review.—Ed.

underwent a metamorphosis, so that a quarter of a century after he began writing verse, Morshen suddenly acquired a new set of literary predecessors and—impossible as it may sound in biological terms—changed his intellectual ancestry.

The beginning of this inner transformation coincided roughly with the publication of Pasternak's *Doctor Zhivago* and the ensuing controversy of *l'affaire Pasternak*. During approximately the same period, Morshen, like a number of others in the West who were concerned with modern Russian poetry, rediscovered Osip Mandelstam and became newly aware of the significance of Nikolai Zabolotsky. As Morshen recalls it, he was familiar with the work of Pasternak, Mandelstam, and Zabolotsky while he was still in the Soviet Union, but it was at this particular juncture in his life that all three began exercising a powerful influence on his own work. The congenial elements that Morshen found in Pasternak's joyous precision, Mandelstam's transfigured lucidity, and the later Zabolotsky's life-affirming pantheism brought to his own writing a new and, on the whole, more optimistic conception of the tasks and functions of poetry.

His continuing interest in new developments in the physical and biological sciences led Morshen to discover the philosophy of Pierre Teilhard de Chardin. In the writings of the author of *The Phenomenon of Man*, Morshen found a convincingly argued verification of some of his own poetic intuitions. He was attracted not so much by Teilhard's ingenious synthesis of Christian theology and Darwinian evolution as by his powerful arguments for the teleological aim of this evolution, for the inevitable spiritualization of the cosmos through the agency of humanity. To a mind that has experienced firsthand the totalitarian dehumanization of society, the Teilhardian noosphere is understandably more attractive as the next stage in our development than the soulless anthill or termites' nest to which Marx, Lenin, and Mao have so resolutely condemned us. In Teilhard's long-range view, the horrors and cruelties of our century take their logical place in the long line of atrocities that humanity has been periodically inflicting upon itself in the course of its tortured but irreversible progress.

The cross-fertilization of Morshen's poetry by the philosophy of Teilhard is comparable to nineteenth-century symbiotic relationships between Schelling and Tyutchev and between Schopenhauer and Fet. Just as Schelling's thought revealed to Tyutchev his "heavenly vault ablaze with stellar glory" ("nebesnyi svod, goriashchii slavoi zvezdnoi"), Teilhard and, before him, the new discoveries of twentieth-century physical and biological sciences opened up for Morshen new perspectives both for humanity's future and for poetry. The tradition of finding poetic inspiration in the realm of the exact sciences goes back to Lomonosov in Russian poetry, but it fell into disrepute in the nineteenth century—one can mention the total contempt in which such figures as Gogol and Lev Tolstoi held scientific disciplines based on precise observation and direct study of nature. In more recent times, however, Chekhov, Nabokov, and Solzhenitsyn were led by their involvement with the exact sciences to new avenues of literary expression. In poetry, Osip Mandelstam, with his genuine interest in Linnaeus and Lamarck,[19] and Nikolai Zabolotsky, whose poetry moved from benign Khlebnikovian pantheism to a troubled examination of man's relationship to the rest of the universe, offer clear precedents for some of Morshen's concerns in his second collection.

The harsh, restricted, and congealed universe of *The Seal* opens up in *Punctuation: Colon* into the cosmos and nature, of which humanity is but a component part. The hopeless loner who was the lyrical voice of the first book is now the proud descendant of magnificent evolutionary processes and the ancestor of godlike beings of the future in whose minds time and space will be transformed in ways we cannot imagine.[20] The poet has not forgotten that police states and concentration camps are still a part of our reality; but it is equally a part of his—and our—reality that "Amidst the universal silence / Sharing its suffering with no one / The Earth flies, whirls, sings / Enveloped in the haze of the Word."[21]

---

[19] Mandelstam's interest in Linnaeus, Lamarck, Buffon, and other eighteenth-century predecessors of Darwin's ideas on evolution runs like a constant thread through his *Journey to Armenia* and also finds expression in his poems "Lamarck" and "A nebo budushchim beremenno ..." [And the sky is pregnant with the future ...]. See Osip Mandel'shtam, *Sobranie sochinenii*, 3 vols. (Washington, D.C., 1967–71), 2:137–76, 1:177–78, and 1:145–47.

[20] "Klubilis' nochi u reki," in Morshen, *Dvoetochie*, 18–19. The poem has been translated into English with miraculous precision by Richard Wilbur as "Nights rolled upon the river's face," *TriQuarterly*, no. 28 (Fall 1973): 426–27; reprinted in *The Bitter Air of Exile*, ed. Simon Karlinsky and Alfred Appel, Jr. (Berkeley: University of California Press, 1977), 334–35.

[21] Среди молчанья мирового,
Ни с кем страданья не деля,
Летит, кружит, поет Земля,
Окутанная дымкой Слова. (Morshen, *Dvoetochie*, 10)

III. Poetry Abroad

The frightened, hunted animal that served as the central image in *The Seal* is replaced in *Punctuation: Colon* by the image of a plant that confidently germinates and grows amidst adverse conditions. The plant imagery of *Punctuation: Colon* operates on various symbolic levels: the wisdom and harmony of recurrent natural processes, as contrasted to the shoddiness and clumsiness of human politics and history, or the triumph of the forces of life over inert matter.[22] Above all, the growing plant is Morshen's symbol for the inexorable striving of art and the human spirit for freedom:

> В мире тусклых надежд и бездомных собак
> По утрам расцветают цветы.
> И встает Будапешт. И ведет Пастернак
> Разговоры с бессмертьем на ты.
>
> Возникают живые как ртуть полыньи.
> Собираются в строчки слова.
> Загораются солнца. Гремят соловьи.
> И асфальт разрывает трава.[23]

In a letter of 3 November 1888 to his friend Aleksei Suvorin, Anton Chekhov pointed out the similarity of the basic laws that govern natural processes and artistic creation: "We know that nature has a, b, c, d, do, re, mi, fa, sol, and curves, straight lines, circles, squares, green, red, blue. We know that all this in a given combination will yield a melody or a poem or a picture, just as simple chemical elements in a given combination yield a tree or a stone or the sea, but all we know is that they are combined; yet the principle according to which they are combined is concealed from us. Anyone who is at home with the scientific method senses intuitively that a piece of music and a tree have something in common and that both one and the other are created in accordance with identically regular and simple laws. Hence the question of what these laws are."[24] But Chekhov

---

[22] See "Urok botaniki" [Botany lesson], ibid., 61–62; "Tsvetok" [The flower], ibid., 63–64; and "Bylinka" [A blade of grass], ibid., 58.

[23] "In the world of dim hopes and homeless dogs / Flowers blossom every morning. / And Budapest rises. And Pasternak conducts / Informal conversations with immortality. // Unfrozen water, alive as quicksilver, bursts through ice. / Words gather into lines. / Suns blaze forth. Nightingales thunder. / And grass tears up asphalt." Ibid., 43.

[24] A. P. Chekhov, *Sobranie sochinenii*, 12 vols. (Moscow-Leningrad, 1960–64), 11:281.

was critical of attempts by his contemporaries Boborykin and Merezhkovsky to devise a quasi-scientific "physiology of creativity," feeling that such a project was beyond human capabilities, given the current state of scientific knowledge. He did, however, see a possible approach to the problem by means of intuitive speculation: "the philosophy of creativity."

One of Morshen's central insights in *Punctuation: Colon* (and in some poems in *The Echo and the Mirror*) is that creative imagination is just as much a part of nature as organic life and inorganic matter:

> Ударят трижды в берег воды,
> И трижды крикнут петухи,
> Что нужно ждать к зиме приплода,
> Что люди, звери и стихи—
> Все братья, все одной породы,
> Не прихоть—но закон природы,
> Ее успехи, не грехи.²⁵

The idea of nature becomes basic to Morshen's poetry, beginning in *Punctuation: Colon*. His nature is not merely lyrical, but is also humanized, endowed with morality and sentiments, and at times frankly allegorical. Contemplation of a sunset on the seashore in "Na zakate" (At sunset) becomes a meditation on the enslavement of Russian literature by opportunistic windbags, with the moon cast in the unexpected role of a fat-faced liar and the phosphorescence of the sea serving as the faithful memory of the past.²⁶ Other seascapes in the book provide the poet with intimations of spirituality, with images of cosmic slaughter and of his own unity with the universe.²⁷ Seasons, rivers, mountains, and plants are all equally spiritualized and given human significance. The poet of *Punctuation: Colon* is very much aware of the tragic aspects of existence—he is anything but a Pollyanna—and in at least one poem of the collection he admits that

---

25 "Thrice will the waters strike the shore, / And thrice will the cocks crow, / That new offspring is to be expected by winter, / That beasts, people and poems / Are all brothers, all of the same race, / Not nature's whim, but her law. / Her successes, not her sins." "U slovarei" [At the dictionaries], in Morshen, *Dvoetochie*, 30.
26 Ibid., 43–44.
27 "Noch' na vzmor'e" [Night at the seaside], ibid., 52; "More, kholodnyi perpetuum mobile" [The sea, a cold perpetuum mobile], ibid., 48; and "Segodnia tikho na more" [The sea is quiet today], ibid., 54.

mankind just might turn out to be too self-destructive to survive.[28] But he also knows that limitations can again and again be overcome against impossible odds, whether by flying fish escaping their native element, a Mesozoic saurian becoming the ancestor of a present-day mammal named Nikolai Morshen, a blade of grass growing through the asphalt, or the poetry of Osip Mandelstam surviving government-decreed destruction and winning a huge new audience.

Hand in hand with the poet's confidence in the higher cosmic order goes his confidence in the power of the human imagination and the ability of language to express what the mind and spirit perceive. This is the message of Morshen's witty poem "Otvet na notu" (Reply to the note),[29] a deliberate challenge to one school of Russian émigré poetry with its obligatory existential despair, mistrust of verbal virtuosity, and negation of the ability of language or literature to communicate anything at all, as expressed in the famous maxim "Esli nado ob"iasniat', to ne nado ob"iasniat'" (If you need to explain it, it's not worth explaining). In Morshen's view, this so-called Paris Note is "poetry's capitulation in the face of what is obvious (for shame!), / in the face of what is known in advance."[30] Morshen, on the contrary, is a poet who believes in what he has to say and sees nothing wrong in saying it with verve, brilliance, and maximal use of all the resources of the Russian language and poetic tradition. His deep roots in his native language and culture are evident not only in those poems of *Punctuation: Colon* that meditate on linguistic and poetic topics, but in the elaborate system of references, reminiscences, and direct quotations of Russian proverbs and poets sprinkled throughout the book. The high point of such "collage poetry" (a device Morshen shares with one of the leading Paris Note poets, Georgy Ivanov, with whom he otherwise has little in common) is the finale of the poem "Ia svoboden kak brodiaga" (I'm as free as a tramp).[31] In this handsome tribute to the landscape and nature of his adopted country, Morshen has the weeds and grasses of the North American wilderness sing a ten-line rhymed song made up entirely of cited lines of Pushkin, Khomyakov, A. K. Tolstoi, Fet, Blok, and other Russian poets.

---

[28] "Balerine" [To a ballerina], ibid., 47.
[29] Ibid., 31–32.
[30] Ibid., 32.
[31] Ibid., 65–66.

One seemingly paradoxical aspect of Morshen's poetry is its combination of extremely modern themes and thought with traditionalist external form. His poetry up to and including *Punctuation: Colon* is all couched in traditional Russian syllabotonic meters and exact, nineteenth-century-type rhymes. In this respect, Morshen is comparable to two modern American poets, Robert Frost and Richard Wilbur (his inner correspondences with and similarities to the latter extend beyond matters of poetic technique, and it is only fitting that Morshen and Wilbur translated each other's poetry). However, if we remember that the contemporaries of Johann Sebastian Bach considered him an outmoded composer who had fallen behind the times technically, we can see that it is dangerous to make pronouncements on an artist's modernity on the basis of his technique alone. Besides, as Vladimir Weidlé has perceptively pointed out, Morshen's meters sound far from standard when applied to his themes and outlook: "There is a particular metrical vigor (*stikhotvornaia bodrost'*) in this and his other poems, which the poets of recent decades either avoided or simply lacked. It is hard to define it; it is as if they failed to add lemon peel to certain bitter drinks. Morshen's poems have it. It can be smelled in his iambic tetrameters and therefore he need not be embarrassed of them."[32]

After the publication of *Punctuation: Colon*, there came a new turn in Morshen's poetry, the nature of which was not at first apparent even to his more attentive readers. He had always been concerned with verbal textures and sonorities, but his poems that appeared in *Novyi zhurnal* from about 1970 on and that were eventually incorporated in *The Echo and the Mirror* acquired such textural density that individual lines at times sounded like several lines of verse collapsed or telescoped into one. Where the poems of *Punctuation: Colon* found new perspectives and new solutions to the eternal problems of nature, art, and man, the poems of the next book seem actually to fuse these three categories into one unity. The agency of this fusion is Morshen's exploration of lexical devices not usually associated in recent times with serious (let alone philosophical) poetry: onomatopoeia, paronomasia, anagrams, and puns. This entire area of language had, of course, been explored with great thoroughness earlier in the twentieth century by Russian Futurist poets, especially Khlebnikov, Mayakovsky,

---

[32] Vladimir Veidle, "Zhretsy edinykh muz: 7. Dvoe drugikh," *Novoe russkoe slovo*, 28 October 1973.

and Kruchyonykh, and, in her own somewhat different manner, by Marina Tsvetaeva. Of the many words used to describe the phenomenon, Aleksei Remizov's term "verbalism" is perhaps the most suitable.

Yet, Morshen's new verbalism is different in kind from Khlebnikov's or Tsvetaeva's. Their usage of it was Dionysian and intuitive, his is Apollonian and filtered through a mind versed in mathematics, cybernetics, and modern probability theory. It would be wrong to apply the term "experimental" to Morshen's later poetry, because, as Leonid Rzhevsky has pointed out, "his discoveries in this area are so unique and significant in their richness and their striving to fuse the sound and the sense" that they are "no longer a game but a fulfillment." Rzhevsky goes on to say that Morshen's new fusion of sonority and meaning is "structurally perfect and harmonious" and that it derives "from euphony and from philosophic meditations and from Pasternak and from Khlebnikov, but most of all from the exceptional talent of the poet himself."[33]

By adapting the Kruchyonykh-Khlebnikov term for metalogical or trans-sense language, *zaum'*, to his own usage (in one poem he makes it an anagram for *muza*, muse, and in another draws a witty parallel between *zaum'*, Kruchyonykh's famous *dyr bul shchyl*, and the Einsteinian formula $E = mc^2$), Morshen acknowledges his debt to his predecessors in Russian verbalism. On the one hand, he is more conservative than these predecessors, because he keeps his verbalist explorations within the confines of traditional meters and rhymes (his poems and passages in free verse are few and exceptional). On the other hand, he often goes beyond his predecessors by making his meaning depend on anagrams and palindromes (as in "Pereverten'" [Changeling, or Palindrome], his ironical epitaph for Ilya Erenburg),[34] by introducing mathematical formulas into his text, and by resorting to a kind of cloning, whereby a poem is split into two or three connected poems while retaining its overall identity as a poetic unit. Morshen has coined the terms *dvustikh* (double poem) and *tristikh* (triple poem) to describe such multiple poems. Some of them are connected by having the rhyming last word or words of one section also serve as the title of the next section. A more complex form of cloning occurs in "Raz-

---

[33] Leonid Rzhevskii, "Strofy i 'zvony' v sovremennoi russkoi poezii," *Novyi zhurnal*, no. 115 (1974): 137.
[34] Morshen, *Ekho i zerkalo*, 16.

dvoiniki" (Split twins),[35] in which the narrator's separation from his other self and his search for it are graphically represented on the page by the poem's splitting about halfway through into two parallel columns which become two separate poems. The possibility of the ultimate reunion of the two selves is indicated by the final long line printed across the page, which can serve as the last two lines for either one of the two poems that have split off from the poem's beginning.

Morshen, though not ordinarily given to theoretical pronouncements about his work, coined a term to describe his later verbalist and structural procedures: *deepodrazhanie*. Constructed by analogy with *deeprichastie* (adverbial participle) and *zvukopodrazhanie* (onomatopoeia, literally imitation of sound), *deepodrazhanie* can be approximately translated as imitation of action or imitation of deed. Morshen saw the procedure as an intuitive search for meaning based not on verbal stems (as had been the case with both Khlebnikov and Tsvetaeva), but on chance and intuition. The object of the search is to have the words both speak the poem's meaning and perform this meaning for the reader. Morshen's continuing involvement with Teilhard de Chardin and with modern physics and cybernetics convinced him that a teleological approach to existence is possible and that profound insights can be arrived at through seemingly absurd and aimless paths. If such things as the mechanism of the subconscious, intuitive insight, and even the laws of evolution are operative in the progress of the exact sciences (as illustrated for Morshen by Arthur Koestler's account in his *Sleepwalkers* of the fumbling and devious methods by which Copernicus, Kepler, and Galileo gradually unraveled the mysteries of the solar system),[36] they should all the more be the province of the poet and of poetry.

This entire complex of ideas informs Morshen's poetry with its overall confidence in life and in the ultimate aims of mankind, a confidence that is highly unusual in émigré poetry and one which Weidlé described in a slightly different connection as the presence of lemon peel in Morshen's poems. On the personal plane, this confidence is further justified by the symbiotic relationship between Morshen's poetic evolution and his continued residence in Monterey. He has always loved boating and hiking in

---

[35] Ibid., 35.
[36] Arthur Koestler, *The Sleepwalkers: A History of Man's Changing Visions of the Universe* (New York, 1959).

the woods and has always connected these activities with poetry. Fishing from a boat in the Pacific Ocean, canoeing on California's rivers, and exploring its forests and mountains, he feels, provide him with the themes of his poems and determine their forms.[37]

The third collection of Morshen's poems, *The Echo and the Mirror*, comprises his output between about 1967 and 1974. In a sense, the collection is something of a synthesis between *The Seal* and *Punctuation: Colon*. The poems couched in the new *deepodrazhanie* manner develop brilliantly (and in a hopelessly untranslatable way) Morshen's major theme of the basic unity between language, nature, and art. In a poem that compares a formal garden and a wild forest, Morshen shows the inner logic of the growth of a forest through a graphic device. A jumble of letters yields, on closer examination, first a sentence of prose and then a quatrain of rhymed verse, with the rhymes placed where no one could expect them:

Однаковнимательныйвзорвнемувидитпрелестьумаистрогостьлюбви

Однако внимательный взор в нем увидит прелесть ума и строгость любви.

> Однако внима-
> тельный взор в нем уви-
> дит прелесть ума
> и строгость любви.[38]

In the dense poem "Primety" (Omens),[39] dealing with the providential aspects of Pushkin's death, the names of a large number of animals, hidden within or between the words of the poem, create the additional image of a forest full of lurking creatures.

---

[37] The reader is reminded that SK was writing during Morshen's lifetime (1917–2001). We have chosen not to bring the texts of the four essays about SK's contemporaries, Nikolai Morshen and Valery Pereleshin, into the present.—Ed.

[38] "howevertheattentiveglancewilldiscerninitthecharmofintelligenceandtheseverityoflove
However, the attentive glance will discern in it the charm of intelligence and the severity of love.

> However, the atten-
> tive glance will dis-
> cern in it the charm of intelligence
> and the severity of love." ("Sad i les," in Morshen, *Ekho i zerkalo*, 23)

[39] Ibid., 69–70.

The practice of *deepodrazhanie* accommodates Morshen's serious themes, but because it involves puns, it has led, not surprisingly, to some humorous poems—something new in Morshen's poetic practice. Thus, in "Na vystavke" (At the art exhibit), the poet plays with unexpected meanings he gets from dismembering the names of masters of modern painting, while at the same time evoking the lilting tune of the old cakewalk "La petite Tonkinoise" (known in Russian as "Kitaianochka").[40] In "Norma braka" (meaning either The norm of marriage or The norm of rejecting defective goods), the heroine, who is at first equated with the maiden in the peasant song from *Evgeny Onegin*, Bogdanovich's Dushenka (that is, Psyche), and Blok's girl from the church choir, quickly mutates, in fewer than two lines, via Blok's Beautiful Lady into the Queen of Spades, Chekhov's Lady with the Little Dog, and, most ominous of all, into Gogol's "lady pleasant in all respects."[41]

But the new manner can also be used for the grim political themes previously treated in *The Seal*, which were mostly relegated to the background in *Punctuation: Colon*. In "Volch'ia vernost'" (Wolves' fidelity),[42] the accumulation of standard epithets and sayings associated with wolves in Russian culture turns the protest against the senseless extermination of these "free stepchildren of the enslaved earth" (the ostensible theme of the poem) into an allegory of a lone-wolf poet, whom the Soviet state also exterminates because it can neither tame him nor teach him to perform tricks. "Ukho i ekho" (The ear and the echo), by simple altering of word boundaries in some standard slogans, reveals the situation the official propaganda hides:

"На родине—счастье!"
—Народ … и … несчастье!

"На родине воля!"
—Народ … и … неволя!

"Коммуну же надо! Ставьте!"
—Кому … нужен … ад … Оставьте![43]

---

40   Ibid., 12.
41   Ibid., 24.
42   Ibid., 65.
43   "'In our country there's happiness!' / —The people … and … misfortune! // 'In our country there's freedom!' / —The people … and … captivity! // 'But we need the commune! Build it!' / —Who needs … [this] … hell? Let it be!" Ibid., 14.

The poet of the third volume has the advantage of a greater distance from and a more balanced perspective on Soviet realities than did the poet of *The Seal*, who wrote from immediate experience. His new perspective is conveyed with tragic honesty and considerable verbal elegance in "V miniatiure" (In miniature), a poem built entirely on the exploration of Russian diminutives. The poet imagines himself leaving the earth, having abandoned his earlier illusions:

> И за кормою астрокорабля
> Сужается российская земля,
> Сжимается в земельку и в землицу,
> На ней мелькают личики, не лица,
> В журнальчиках хвалебные стишки,
> Психушки, вытрезвилки, матючки—
> Язык, и тот стремится измельчиться.[44]

At that distance, all the patriotic and military glories in which the Soviet state takes such inordinate pride look small and insignificant. Even the Russian spirit (*russkii dukh*) becomes its diminutive and thus comes to mean a bad smell (*dushok*). All this hardly makes the poet happy:

> Ликую? Нет: скорее трепещу.
> Мельчаю? Да: я съежиться хочу
> И вот уже не с верой в постоянство—
> Лишь с родинкой на памятке лечу
> В чужбинищу свободного пространства.[45]

Even more daringly challenging to accepted Russian traditions, both prerevolutionary and Soviet, is the poem "Poslanie k A. S." (Epistle to A. S.).[46] Morshen addresses the epistle to Aleksandr Sergeevich Pushkin,

---

[44] "And behind the stern of the spaceship / The land of Russia narrows down / Compresses itself into a landlet, a land-drop, / On it there flicker facelets, not faces, / Laudatory verselets in teensy journals, / Teensy psychoclinics, tiny sobering-up stations, diminutive obscenities— / Even the language itself strives to be petty." Ibid., 79–80.

[45] "Do I rejoice? No, rather I tremble. / Am I becoming petty? Yes, I want to shrivel / And now, no longer with faith in constancy / But only with a birthmark on a memento [instead of Motherland in memory] I fly / Into the immense alien realm of free space." Ibid.

[46] Ibid., 75–78.

casting the poem, with sovereign, unselfconscious mastery, in a close approximation of Pushkin's own poetic tone and voice. The subject is Pushkin's contempt for political rights and such issues as freedom from unfair taxation and censorship and for other "vaunted rights," as stated in one of the last poems he wrote, "Iz Pindemonti" (From Pindemonte). On behalf of his own generation of "seals and deer" (*tiuleni i oleni*; the image of the "deer" refers to the hero of Solzhenitsyn's play *Olen' i shalashovka*, known in English as *The Love Girl and the Innocent*), Morshen asks Russia's "national genius" whether such an attitude, given Pushkin's oft-expressed enthusiasm for military glory and nationalistic conquest, might not add up to a "logically consequent [national] vice / Which is of use only to tyrants." The extended middle section of the poem describes a baby deer (a real one this time) encountered in the California woods, which preserves its freedom by risking its life in a perilous escape. Pushkin's concept of "secret freedom," to which Blok appealed in his desperate last poem, is thus brought into contrast with the concrete and genuine freedom won by the American fawn.

At the end of "Epistle to A. S.," Morshen stands on its head the long Russian tradition of civic poetry by mentioning two poets who are not in the same league as Pushkin in terms of their poetic genius, but whose commitment was to actual freedom, not to an illusory "secret" one. These are Ryleev, who lost his life in the Decembrist rebellion, and Ralph Waldo Emerson, whose lines about "the shot heard round the world" from "Concord Hymn" (in Morshen's own rhymed translation) serve as a kind of concluding epigraph to the poem, in juxtaposition with the beginning of "From Pindemonte."

Morshen's ability to challenge the giants of the past and get away with it is further borne out by the remarkable double poem "Al'piiskaia vesna" (Springtime in the Alps),[47] where a mountain brook is heard by the poet to recite a Russian translation of Goethe's "Über allen Gipfeln," driving home once again Morshen's cardinal theme of the unity of nature and man-made art. Goethe's poem had been previously rendered into Russian by Lermontov (whose version is one of the best-known brief lyrics in the language) and by Annensky. Undaunted, Morshen incorporates into his lovely poem a new version that need not fear comparison with its illustrious predecessors.

---

[47] Ibid., 19–20.

Like *The Seal* and *Punctuation: Colon*, *The Echo and the Mirror* also has a living being as its presiding keynote image. This time it is *Mimus polyglottos*, the American mockingbird. The collection opens and closes with poems about the mockingbird, and a veritable aviary of other birds is scattered throughout the rest of the book. The birds of the third collection do not merely survive, like the seal, or triumph over history and inert matter, like the blade of grass in *Punctuation: Colon*. "Posledniaia lastochka" (The last swallow)[48] opens for the poet a window into eternity, as other swallows did for Derzhavin, Fet, and Mandelstam. The poet's muse in the poem "Muza" appears to him in a variety of avian guises, including a dove, an eagless, and the firebird and swan princess of Russian folk tales. The poet yearns to possess this bird-woman, by violence if necessary, "So that from her clenched lips / Complaints of verse lines would burst forth / In nightingale whistlings / On dry-storm [literally, sparrow] nights."[49]

It is the mockingbird, however, that emerges as the supreme embodiment of the three highest values in Morshen's poetry: nature, art, and freedom. All art is a form of mimicry; the abilities of the *Mimus polyglottos* are, like the mirror reflection and the echo, art's counterpart in nature. In the concluding poem of the third collection, "Mnogogolosyi peresmeshnik 2" (Mockingbird 2),[50] the poet's own path and progress through life are traced in six stanzas, in which the mockingbird impersonates six other birds. Only the nightingale in the second stanza is named outright, its identity further driven home by references to nightingales in Pushkin, Delvig, and the *Igor Tale*. The rooster in the first stanza, the lark in the third, the siskin in the fourth, and the swallow in the fifth are not named or mentioned. They are recognizable to a person versed in Russian tradition by the quoted phrases associated with them in Russian poetry, folklore, or popular songs. Morshen's new American roots, strongly expressed in the "Epistle to A. S.," are here personified by the bird which the mockingbird imitates in the sixth and final stanza. Its Russian manifestation, *grai voronii*, belongs to the dawn of the poet's life, a dawn which has

---

[48] Ibid., 38–39.
[49] Чтоб из губ ее стиснутых
Рвались жалобы строчек
Соловьиными свистами
В воробьиные ночи. (Ibid., 27)
[50] Ibid., 89.

fled over the seas (*uporkhnula za moria*). The impossibility of retrieving one's youth is expressed through the single English word that concludes the poem and identifies the bird, "Nevermore."

It is too early to discuss as a coherent whole the poems Morshen has written since the completion of *The Echo and the Mirror*. They comprise what he calls a "half-collection" that bears the title "The Now-Silent Lark." The poems continue the manner of *The Echo and the Mirror*, though in a more subdued mode. The most memorable of these new poems add to Morshen's formula of "poetry equals nature equals poetry" a cozy familiarity with mythology (Greek and biblical) and with classical antiquity. In two hauntingly beautiful poems, "Stikhi i stikhii" (Verses and elements) and an untitled one that begins "V nezhnom plene sladkoi slepoty" (In the tender captivity of sweet blindness), images from Homer, Ovid, and the Book of Genesis serve to attenuate the poet's sense of unity between eternal nature and the imaginative processes of the human mind that produce art. A striking stanza in "Stikhi i stikhii" works the titles of comedies by Aristophanes into a description of the creation of the world:

> Гудели ритмы в смутном океане,
> Текла и пела первая река,
> Летели, плыли по-аристофаньи
> Лягушки, птицы, осы, облака.[51]

These new, mature poems may represent a summary of Morshen's earlier poetry, or they may indicate a turning point in his poetic development. In either case, it is hard to imagine how his future work could surpass the profundity and mastery he has already attained.

Over the years, Morshen has done a considerable amount of literary translation. His numerous translations into Russian of American poets (Emily Dickinson, Robert Frost, Randall Jarrell, Phyllis McGinley) and prose writers (Shirley Ann Grau, Bernard Malamud, John Updike, Eudora Welty, Joyce Carol Oates, Isaac Asimov) appeared in the magazine *Amerika* published by the United States Information Agency for distribution in the Soviet Union. For the same magazine he also translated William

---

51 "Rhythms hummed in a murky ocean, / The first river flowed and sang, / There flew [or] floated, in an Aristophanian manner / Frogs, birds, wasps, clouds." (Morshen, "The Now-Silent Lark")

Faulkner's Nobel Prize acceptance speech, portions of Louis Armstrong's autobiography, and a variety of essays on such diverse subjects as science, architecture, film, and rock music. Unknown to anyone in the United States (where *Amerika* did not circulate), these translations deserve to be studied by those interested in problems of literary translation. Morshen brings to them the same verbal imagination and lexical resourcefulness we know and admire in his poetry. Two tiny examples will have to serve as evidence of his ability to solve seemingly insoluble translation problems. The title of Pauline Kael's book of film criticism *Kiss Kiss Bang Bang* was rendered by Morshen as *Chmok-chmok, pif-paf*. Even more astoundingly, considering the lack of both definite and indefinite articles in Russian, the name of the rock group The Who found its Russian equivalent in *Te, kto* (The Ones Who).

Not too many years ago, Evgeny Evtushenko came to give a reading on the Berkeley campus. The overflow crowds had to be accommodated by a closed-circuit television hastily installed in an additional auditorium. Nikolai Morshen and his wife sat quietly in the back listening to Evtushenko. Only the faculty of the Slavic department and a few students knew who they were. Watching the ovations for Evtushenko, I tried to think of historical precedents: Faddei Bulgarin's *Ivan Vyzhigin*, regarded by English and Polish critics of the 1830s, unaware of the prose Pushkin and Gogol were then writing, as the finest Russian novel of the age; American journalists of around 1900 mentioning Anton Chekhov as the man to whom Gorky himself had dedicated a novel; or Osip Mandelstam outside a St. Petersburg movie theater about 1915, lost in the midst of a crowd that hysterically acclaimed Igor Severyanin as *the* great modern poet. Before too many years pass, Morshen's presence at Evtushenko's recital will take its place within this series of events.

Morshen
after *Ekho i zerkalo*[1]

*E*ver since the publication of his first collection of verse, *Tiulen'*, in 1959 (with a preface by Vladimir Markov), the poet Nikolai Morshen has produced a new volume of poetry at the end of each succeeding decade. *Dvoetochie* came out in 1967 and *Ekho i zerkalo* in 1979.[2] In the early 1980s poems intended for Morshen's next collection, whose title was known to be *Umolkshii zhavoronok*, began appearing in Russian publications in the West, among them *Russkii al'manakh* and *Perekrestki*.

Umolkshii zhavoronok is now complete, though as yet unpublished (the poet was kind enough to lend me a copy for this article).[3] Unlike its three predecessors, each of which possesses an organic unity, the new collection, subtitled *Dva polusbornika*, consists of two sections, the first bearing the same title as the whole volume (it contains nineteen poems) and the second one called "Eretik" (eighteen poems). This last "half-collection" contains poems on topics from the Old and New Testament and Russian cultural traditions which may indeed strike some as heretical. The first half addresses itself to matters that some critics have singled out in Morshen's earlier collections as his central themes. What are some of them?

---

[1] Originally published in *Readings in Russian Modernism: To Honor Vladimir Fedorovich Markov*, ed. Ronald Vroon and John E. Malmstad (Moscow: Nauka [Oriental Literature], 1993), 165–72. This essay can best be read in conjunction with the preceding one, which includes translations of titles, explains terminology, and elucidates context.—Ed.

[2] Nikolai Morshen (Nikolai Nikolaevich Marchenko), *Tiulen'* (Frankfurt am Main: Posev, 1959); *Dvoetochie* (Washington, D.C.: Victor Kamkin, 1967); *Ekho i zerkalo* (Berkeley: Berkeley Slavic Specialties, 1979). For publication data, thematic description of Morshen's first three collections, and the poet's biography, see Simon Karlinsky, "Morshen, or a Canoe to Eternity," *Slavic Review* 41, no. 1 (Spring 1982): 1–18 [reprinted in the present volume].

[3] *Umolkshii zhavoronok* was first published in its entirety in Nikolai Morshen, *Sobranie stikhov*, ed. O. Raevsky-Hughes (Oakland: Berkeley Slavic Specialties, 1996). See also Nikolai Morshen, *Pushche nevoli: Stikhi*, ed. V. V. Agenosov (Moscow: Sovetskii sport, 2000).—Ed.

Vsevolod Setchkarev defined Morshen's "three great themes" as (1) "poetry and its materials: the word, verse [and] speech"; (2) "nature, but not in the usual sense of 'nature poetry'"; and (3) "science *about* nature (evolution, primarily)." He continues, "It is the interconnection, the fusion, the interweaving of these three thematic strands that give Morshen's poetry its unique quality."[4] G. S. Smith had the same phenomenon in mind when he wrote of "ex-Kievan Nikolai Morshen, who is preoccupied with paronomastic *Naturphilosophie*."[5] One could add to this Morshen's frequent insistence that the arts and sciences are ultimately children of nature in exactly the same sense as living beings are (including the germinating plants that are the dominant image of *Dvoetochie* and the talented birds whose song keynoted *Ekho i zerkalo*). So is the organic matter that forms the earth and its atmosphere.

This view is freshly reiterated in the untitled fourth poem of *Umolkshii zhavoronok*, which begins with the words "Ledniki i moreny ..." (Icebergs and moraines ...). Unlike the majority of this poet's work, the poem is couched in free verse. Metrical organization is rudimentary. There are a few rhymes or assonances, strategically placed where they would illustrate the point of the poem, which is that glaciers and moraines carved palpable forms long before the first sculptor, winds whistled intelligible melodies before the first musician, and sunrises and sunsets painted vivid canvases on the sky before there were painters. Only verse had to be born together with humans, "blindly / at an unknown place." The poem ends with a clearly iambic and self-rhyming line that drives home the message of the preceding stanza: "Primer—Gomer" (An example is Homer).

This poem is an example of Morshen's structural procedure of *deepodrazhanie*, which he launched in *Ekho i zerkalo*.[6] The intermittent meters and the few carefully placed rhymes in the first three stanzas show the transitory quality of the art produced by inanimate matter. Meter and rhyme vanish in the fourth stanza, where human beings first appear, only to blaze forth triumphantly in the iambic and rhyming last line that signals the advent of Homer, one of the earliest human poets.

---

[4] Vsevolod Setschkareff, "Naturwissenschaft und Poesie (Bemerkungen zur Dichtung Nikolai Moršens)," *Die Welt der Slaven* 27, no. 2 (1982): 235–36.

[5] G. S. Smith, "Another Time, Another Place," *Times Literary Supplement*, 26 June 1987, 692.

[6] Karlinsky, "Morshen, or a Canoe to Eternity," 12.

In *Umolkshii zhavoronok*, as in *Ekho i zerkalo*, *deepodrazhanie* enables the reader not only to understand and hear the text, but also to visualize what is being described. This can be seen in the following brief poem:

> Стихи предлагают любому
> Свою подъяремную грудь—
> Возможность, как по чернозему,
> По лексике плуг потянуть.
>
> Стихи обнажают не сразу
> Свою подколодную стать—
> Наклонность узорчатой фразой,
> Чешуйчатой рифмой блистать.
>
> Стихи открывают не многим
> Свою поднебесную суть—
> Способность ожить за порогом,
> Из рук у тебя упорхнуть.

The central images of each of the three stanzas—the ox, the snake and the bird, respectively—are neither mentioned nor identified in the poem. Yet the standard epithets and activities associated with each of these animals cause them to materialize in the reader's mind.

This instance of *deepodrazhanie* is akin to other poetic procedures favored by Morshen, such as literary metamorphosis (ox turning into snake turning into bird in the cited poem); intertextual collage; paronomasia and other forms of sound organization; and, of course, the creation of neologisms, which range from simple ones (the adverb *arkhimetko* in the poem, "Stikhi na sluchai," where Archimedes appears in the final line) to complex ones that verge on *zaum'*. In "Flora i favn"—the title itself is a pun on the Russian version of "flora and fauna"—the poet takes the plant called cow wheat in English and *ivan-da-mar'ia* in Russian as his basic verbal model to tell an unhappy rustic love story where the traditional names of field plants are used in their nonbotanical connotations to provide the vocabulary for this narrative poem's plot.

In "Charodeika" Morshen follows the precedent of Vladimir Soloukhin's book on mushroom gathering, *Tret'ia okhota*, in undertaking the rehabilitation of the aspen tree.⁷ The aspen has been slandered in Russian folklore (its quivering leaves are said to remember Judas, who hanged himself from an aspen—which does not grow in Palestine as per Soloukhin—and werewolves can be defeated only if aspen stakes are driven through their hearts) and in literature (such as Turgenev's story "Svidanie" in *Zapiski okhotnika*, where the pure heroine is symbolized by a birch, while the aspen is associated with the false and pretentious butler who betrayed the girl). Unlike Soloukhin, Morshen does not deny the magical and even diabolical qualities traditionally associated with the aspen. Instead he metamorphoses the feminine-gender tree, *osina*, into a seductive enchantress, a doomed beauty who is then further metamorphosed into three bewitching beings from three Ukrainian tales by Gogol: *rusalka* (river nymph, in "Maiskaia noch'"), *pannochka* (young lady, in both "Taras Bul'ba" and "Vii") and *ved'ma* (witch, the true nature of the *pannochka* in "Vii"). The line containing the Gogolian reference dissolves whatever little resistance the poet offered to this tree-turned-into-woman. He will allow her to enter his "enchanted gaze" and thus be transformed into a poem he will compose about her.

In his essay about the poet Georgy Ivanov, Vladimir Markov defined Ivanov's style as "a mélange of colloquialism, 'music,' and quotations," adding in a footnote that "perhaps there is a law: the last man in any series resorts to quotation."⁸ Different as Morshen's poetry is from Ivanov's, Markov's stylistic definition fits, oddly enough, both poets. As for the law about the last man in a series resorting to quotation, Morshen is as given to it as Ivanov, possibly even more so. Some of his poems are so saturated with quotations and/or deliberate references to other poets that their texture deserves to be called an intertextual collage. The most striking of these collages is the ten-line rhyming song at the end of the poem, "Ia svoboden, kak brodiaga …" in *Dvoetochie*, in which every line is a quotation from a different Russian poet, beginning with Aleksei Khomyakov and A. K. Tolstoi and ending with two lines of Pushkin, one from "Prorok" and the other from "Besy."⁹

---

7   Vladimir Soloukhin, *Tret'ia okhota* (Moscow: Sovetskaia Rossiia, 1968), 51–55.
8   Vladimir Markov, "Georgy Ivanov: Nihilist as Light-Bearer," in *The Bitter Air of Exile: Russian Writers in the West 1922–1972*, ed. Simon Karlinsky and Alfred Appel, Jr. (Berkeley: University of California Press, 1977), 146 and 150; originally published in *TriQuarterly*, no. 27 [Spring 1973]).
9   Morshen, *Dvoetochie*, 65–66.

The following poem from *Umolkshii zhavoronok* is a case in which intertextuality does not attain the density of a collage, but is quite evident and striking nonetheless.

> В нежном плене сладкой слепоты,
> В плоском свете одноглазой кривды
> Не пройдут бескормчие плоты
> Мимо Сциллы и Харибды.
>
> Нужен киль да руль и нужен глаз да глаз,
> Чтобы розоперстей стали зори
> И ладья не в Лету пронеслась—
> В Ионическое море.
>
> Где вода, как правда, солона,
> И, как ложь, недолговечна пена,
> И бесхитростная глубина
> Отрезвляет постепенно.
>
> Где волна с волною не спеша
> Коротает вечность в разговоре.
> Вспоминай же море, о душа,
> Вспоминай (memento) море!

The first eight lines tell of the perilous passage of Odysseus and his crew between Scylla and Charybdis, once two beautiful women, who had been turned into voracious sea monsters by the vengeful gods, as recounted in the twelfth canto of the *Odyssey*. While hewing closely to the situation in Homer, Morshen introduced his own theme: the need for intelligence and skill to make the passage and for appropriate nautical technology to escape the two monsters. The "rafts devoid of steersmen" in line 3 cannot overcome the danger, even though the appealing adjectives *nezhnom* and *sladkoi*, and the unobtrusive but elegant alliterations of *plene*, *ploskom* and *ploty* (with their suggestion of waves lapping the shore) and of *sladkoi slepoty* might lull the reader into thinking that the danger can be escaped.

Only a craft equipped with a keel and a rudder and guided by a watchful steersman will assure that the travelers not rush into death (the river Lethe), but emerge into the Ionian Sea. In this Homeric ambience, the standard, even hackneyed epithet for the goddess of dawn, Eos, "the rosy-fingered," coexists without the least friction with a line from Griboedov's *Gore ot uma*, "nuzhen glaz da glaz" (from the maid Liza's opening monologue in act one of the play). The Griboedov quotation obviously generated the Homeric-sounding phrase, "Nuzhen kil' da rul'," that precedes it.

But as the second line of the poem serves notice, the theme is not only the nautical skill of Odysseus, but also the ability to steer one's way between truth and falsehood. The "affectionate captivity in sweet blindness" in line 1 suggests the earlier imprisonment of Odysseus by the amorous demigoddesses Calypso and Circe, which, though it was affectionate and sweet, was also debilitating. This would cause the hero to see things in the "trite light of one-eyed falsehood" of line 2, a condition likened to sailing on pilotless rafts incapable of conveying Odysseus to the Ionian Sea, revealed in the third stanza of the poem as the realm of truth.

The imagery and the vocabulary of this contest between truth and falsehood suggest certain intertextual echoes, perhaps unconscious ones, from two later poems by Osip Mandelstam. The late poetry of Mandelstam, with its deep concern with officially imposed falsehood, is highly valued by Morshen.[10] We can compare Mandelstam's *shestipalaia nepravda* with Morshen's *odnoglazaia krivda* (in both cases falsehood personified by a female entity marred by physical deformity); or, in a poem of 1937 which also begins with the imagery of sailing the seas, Mandelstam's "gor'ka morei trava / Lozhnovolosaia—i pakhnet dolgoi lozh'iu" with Morshen's lines 9 and 10:[11]

> Где вода, как правда, солона,
> И, как ложь, недолговечна пена.

The "guileless depth that gradually sobers one up" in lines 11 and 12 marks the hero's final attainment of safety and also evokes the earlier departure of Odysseus from the island of the Sirens. After the escape from blindness and peril and the acquisition of life-supporting skills and truth

---

10 Karlinsky, "Morshen, or a Canoe to Eternity," 7.
11 Osip Mandel'shtam, *Sobranie sochinenii v trekh tomakh*, ed. G. P. Struve and B. A. Filippov, vol. 1 (Munich: Inter-Language Literary Associates, 1967), 164 and 250.

in the first three stanzas of the poem, peace and security are reached in the fourth stanza, with its evocations of Pushkin's *govor voln* and Batyushkov's and Mandelstam's cozy, everyday eternity (*vechnost'*). But the poet does not want the hero to forget the perils and escapes that he has endured and therefore concludes the poem with the clever pun on the Russian word for sea, *more*, and the familiar Latin maxim *memento mori*.

Umolkshii zhavoronok differs from Morshen's earlier collections in the profusion of its biblical and classical allusions. They are particularly dense in the second *polusbornik* of the volume, "Eretik." Like Lev Tolstoi, Morshen has difficulty accepting the validity of certain New Testament miracles. The opening poem of this section, also bearing the title "Eretik," expresses doubt about the assertion in Matthew 17:20 that a mustard seed's worth of faith is sufficient to move a mountain. Such thinking, the poem implies, easily leads to burning live people for a supposed lack of faith:

> Потому что, как ни скверно,
> Еретик и сам постиг:
> Кто сжигает—правоверный,
> Кто горит, тот еретик.

Likewise, "Predpaskhal'noe" points out the injustice committed by Christ (as told in Matthew 21:19 and Mark 11:13–14) in cursing a fig tree and causing it to wither for not bearing any fruit. The time, the poet points out, was Easter and the tree could not have produced fruit before having blossomed.

Even more attractively heretical is the poem "Stikhi i stikhii," where not only is a poet (*stikhotvorets*) casually equated with the Creator (*Tvorets stikhii*), but the Book of Genesis is contaminated with Greek and Roman classics. The creation of the mountains is equated with the creation of "Exegi monumentum" by Horace (in its Pushkin redaction and with the added alliterative bonus of *gory* and *Goratsii*). The creation of amphibians, birds, insects, and clouds is likened to Aristophanes's choice of titles for his comedies:

> Летели, плыли по-аристофаньи
> Лягушки, птицы, осы, облака.

Finally, the Serpent in the Garden of Eden is said to be an earlier incarnation of Ovid, the author of *Ars amandi*:

> Где, в ироническом являясь виде,
> Пел языком стихов (или стихий?)
> Любви искусство райский пра-Овидий,
> Накликавший изгнанье змий.

Let us now return to Vladimir Markov's remark about the last man in a series (the one who quotes). As early as 1974, Leonid Rzhevsky pointed out that Morshen's poetic language was moving in the direction of the verbally-conscious art of Russian Futurists of the early twentieth century. Rzhevsky saw this new fusion of sonority and meaning in Morshen's later poetry as something derived "from euphony and from philosophic meditations and from Pasternak and from Khlebnikov, but most of all from the exceptional talent of the poet himself."[12] When Lazar Fleishman spoke of the same aspect of Morshen's poetry at a conference on the literature of the Russian emigration,[13] the older scholar Nikolai Andreev insisted that Morshen's poetic evolution "did not happen in a vacuum" and that its cause was that "there lives in America Morshen's friend, the remarkable literary scholar, Professor Vladimir Markov, who wrote, as you well know, a splendid book on the Futurists and published many things in the journals."[14]

Morshen may well be the last poet to continue the traditions of Russian "Verbalism" (Aleksei Remizov's expression), because none of today's younger poets, not even the ultramodern Meta-metaphorists, such as Ivan Zhdanov, Aleksei Parshchikov and the gifted Nina Iskrenko, explore the possibilities of *slovotvorchestvo* in such depth as Morshen. There are many poems one could cite from *Umolkshii zhavoronok* to illustrate his varied uses of *korneslovie* and quasi-*zaum'*. In the humorous "Kva-s," the Russian version of the frogs' croaking, *kva*, the national soft drink *kvas*, the

---

[12] Leonid Rzhevskii, "Strofy i 'zvony' v sovremennoi russkoi poezii," *Novyi zhurnal*, no. 115 (1974): 137.

[13] G. Nivat, ed., *Odna ili dve russkikh literatury? Mezhdunarodnyi simpozium, sozvannyi Fakul'tetom slovesnosti Zhenevskogo universiteta i Shveitsarskoi akademiei Zheneva, 13–14–15 aprelia 1978* (Lausanne: l'Age d'Homme, 1981), 63–76.

[14] Ibid., 81–82.

expression *kvasnoi patriotizm* (jingoism), and the national favorite source of quotations (Griboedov again) are all combined to suggest that life during what is now called "the period of stagnation" was as monotonous and parochial as the croaking of frogs in a swamp. The interrelated poems "Azbuka kommunizma" and "Azbuka demokratii" use the modern Russian and Old Russian alphabets to bring out in an unexpected way the contrast between freedom and oppression, a theme present in all Morshen's collections, beginning with *Tiulen'*.

"Chelovek-nevidimka," couched in the rare meter of anapestic pentameter (with a few lapses into *dol'nik*), states the seldom-noticed fact that history remembers those who engaged in violence or were victimized by it, but forgets those who changed the world with their decency and good deeds. Thus, everyone knows about the Decembrists who were hanged, but the names of the Decembrists who had granted freedom to their serfs are forgotten:

> Ни строки, ни доски, никоторого нет им признанья!
> Но усмешкою циник отторгнет мое восклицанье.

Here, as in the rest of this poem, the all-but-invisible internal rhyme is formed when the words *nikotorogo net* are echoed across the word boundary in the last syllable of *tsinik* and the first two syllables of *ottorgnet*, illustrating the historical invisibility of the people in question.

Morshen's poetry is so rich and varied that one is tempted to describe and analyze every poem of *Umolkshii zhavoronok*. To resist this temptation, I would like to conclude by quoting the densely neologistic poem "Raiskoe utro" in its entirety. The poem takes place in the Garden of Eden before Adam was given the power to name things. At this stage nothing has a name yet and the poet is obliged to describe everything with neologism suggestive of function or typical form of motion. The profusion of affectionate diminutives conveys Adam's (and the poet's) delight at discovering all these unfamiliar entities. To facilitate comprehension, it can be stated that lines 1–4 describe a stream; lines 5–6, a fluffy tree branch; lines 7–8, a songbird; lines 9–10, dew on leaf stems; lines 11–12, bees and flowers; line 13, huge coniferous trees; line 14, a clear sky. Lines 15–16 are self-explanatory. A particularly rich neologism is *zelenitochka* in line 9. Combining the words for green and thread, it well conveys the

III. Poetry Abroad

image of leaf stems. But also, because *selenit* is the word used in Russian science fiction in the meaning of moon dweller, *zelenitochka* also suggests a little lunar girl:

> Райское утро
>
> Течет себе зеркалинка,
> Струилка, омывалочка,
> По-омутам-молчалинка,
> По-отмелям-журчалочка.
>
> Пушистой машет кисточкой
> Приветка-свежелисточка,
> Щебечет свиристаловка,
> Порх-порх-перелеталовка.
>
> На каждой зелениточке
> Сверкалки, водослиточки,
> Для каждой прижужжальницы
> Открылись расцветальницы.
>
> Иглогиганты храмовы.
> Высокосинь блистательна.
> И утро так адамово
> Так первоназывательно.

Morshen's fourth collection of poems (or two half-collections, as he prefers) is further testimony to this astonishing poet's ever-growing profundity and skill. In conversation he stated repeatedly that *Umolkshii zhavoronok* was his last book and that he did not intend to write any more verse. This would disappoint the huge new audience he has gained through recent publications of his work in Russia. But even as his oeuvre now stands, the four volumes that comprise it are clearly one of the treasures of twentieth-century Russian poetry.

A Hidden Masterpiece:
Valery Pereleshin's *Ariel*[1]

In the nineteenth century, an expatriate Russian writer, such as Turgenev, was not subjected to any special treatment because of his residence abroad. His writings could be published both in Russia and in foreign countries, and no one ever assumed that the quality or interest of his work was affected by his exile. The Revolution changed all that. After the mid-1920s, Russian writers who lived abroad automatically lost their Russian audience, since their books could no longer be imported. During the first two postrevolutionary decades, the tremendous enthusiasm for the new Soviet society in the West brought about a flood of translations of Soviet fiction, drama, and poetry. Not many people knew or cared that the finest Russian writing of those decades was being done by exiled writers—Bunin, Remizov, Marina Tsvetaeva and the young Vladimir Nabokov—whom no one in the West wanted to publish or read. Western hostility to non-Soviet Russian writing reached a zenith during World War II, when a large number of prominent American intellectuals signed a protest against the selection by the Book-of-the-Month Club of a novel they had not read by an author of whom they had not heard (*The Fifth Seal* by Mark Aldanov), merely because he was a Russian exile and therefore presumably an enemy of freedom and democracy.

The zigzags in Western-Soviet relations since that time—the Cold War and its thaw, Solzhenitsyn's revelations in *The GULAG Archipelago*, the recent popularity of Nabokov's Russian novels in translation—have not substantially changed the picture. Today, a satire on the Soviet bureaucracy such as Vladimir Voinovich's *The Ivankiad*, an amusing enough book, gets translated and widely reviewed as a matter of course, while Alla Ktorova's brilliantly perceptive studies of interpersonal relationships between Soviet women, in her novel *The Face of the Firebird* and her stories, remain untranslated. The only possible explanation is that Voinovich

---

[1] Originally published in *Christopher Street* 2, no. 6 (December 1977): 37–42.

lives and writes in Moscow, while Ktorova has moved to Washington, D.C. Similarly, a superficial media creation like Evgeny Evtushenko has his poetry translated into English by some of America's foremost poets, while a Russian poet of true depth and magnitude, such as Nikolai Morshen, who happens to live in California, remains untranslated except for the two fine adaptations of his poems that were included in Richard Wilbur's last collection.

All this needs to be said so that the reader may understand the literary fate of the poet and the book about to be discussed. Valery Pereleshin is the pen name of Valery Salatko-Petrishche. He was born in Siberia and grew up in China, where he lived until his mid-fifties, before moving to Brazil, where he now lives. [Pereleshin died in Brazil in 1992.—Ed.] His first collection of poetry, *En Route*, was published in Harbin in 1937. *Ariel*, brought out in 1976, is his most recent book. It is his ninth volume of verse. In addition to his original work, Pereleshin has also translated into Russian a large body of poetry by Chinese, Brazilian and Portuguese poets as well as a number of English ("The Rime of the Ancient Mariner" by Coleridge among them) and Spanish poems. His first four collections, published in China, created for Pereleshin a reputation as one of the most gifted young poets among the Far East émigrés. But his work was only known to the Russians who lived in China and to a very small number of connoisseurs of émigré poetry in Paris, New York, and a few other Western capitals. His more recent collections, beginning with *Southern Home* (1968),[2] are read by an equally small number of people: the few poetry lovers among the Russians who live in the West, a few academics in American, Canadian, Australian, and West German universities, and a miniscule number of underground admirers in the Soviet Union, who manage to get hold of his books through clandestine channels. And yet people who evaluate modern Russian poetry on the basis of quality, rather than the poet's place of residence, are gradually becoming convinced that Pereleshin belongs in the front rank of Russian poets of the second half of the twentieth century. One of the first to state this in print was Alexis Rannit (the curator of Russian and East European Studies at Yale University

---

[2] This book—Valerii Pereleshin, *Iuzhnyi dom: Piataia kniga stikhotvorenii* (Munich: Pereleshin, 1968)—was reviewed by SK upon publication: Semen Karlinskii, "*Iuzhnyi dom* Valeriia Pereleshina," *Novoe russkoe slovo*, 9 February 1969.—Ed.

and by general consent the finest living Estonian poet), in his detailed study of Pereleshin's poetic techniques in *Russian Language Journal*.[3]

Ariel should lay to rest whatever doubts might have remained about the significance of Pereleshin's poetry. The book is not a simple collection of poems, but rather four superimposed works, belonging to four totally different genres. It is a narrative sequence of 168 sonnets, which is also the poet's personal diary for a three-year period, a story of one man's love for another told in a sort of epistolary novel in verse and, finally, a survey of celebrated instances of older men loving younger ones in the Western literary tradition. Because of its autobiographical background, the circumstances of the book's genesis form an essential part of its plot.

The tradition of Russian poetry on homosexual themes that had flourished in the first two decades of the twentieth century was interrupted by the Revolution. The tradition had, however, a somewhat unobtrusive continuation in Russian émigré poetry, especially in the work of Anatoly Steiger (1907–44). Pereleshin's poetry prior to *Ariel* spoke of his love life only in cryptic and ambiguous terms. A few of his poems of the early 1970s were the beginning of his self-revelation. *Ariel* and the still unpublished long autobiographical poem called *Poem without an Object* (on which he worked for many years and which he completed after the publication of *Ariel*) constitute a full-fledged literary coming out.[4] In *Poem without an Object*, the poet tells of the Chinese and Russian male lovers he had during his youth in the Far East. Some of his recent poems are addressed to Brazilian male friends or lovers. His most important involvement prior to the romance which is the subject of *Ariel* was apparently with a young Chinese bookseller in Shanghai.

An absorbing episode in *Poem without an Object* describes the poet's efforts to secure the release of his Chinese lover from jail, where he was imprisoned by the Kuomintang authorities for Maoist political sympa-

---

[3] Aleksis Rannit, "O poezii i poetike Valeriia Pereleshina: Shest' pervykh sbornikov poeta (1937–1971), *Russian Language Journal* (East Lansing) 30 (Spring 1976): 79–104.

[4] Chapters of *Poem without an Object* were serialized in *Sovremennik* (Toronto); see n. 16 of the following article. The *poema*—finished in Rio de Janeiro in March 1976— was eventually published in its entirety over a decade later: Valerii Pereleshin, *Poema bez predmeta*, ed. Simon Karlinsky (Holyoke: New England Publishing, 1989). The lengthy introduction by SK (pp. 7–31) is a detailed analysis of the eight cantos of this narrative in verse (comprised of linked *Onegin* stanzas), the poem's literary heritage, and its historical and personal context.—Ed.

thies and for possessing Communist tracts. Ironically, the affair came to an end (described in several telling poems in *Southern Home*) when the Chinese lover responded to the pressures of the traditional Confucianist pro-family philosophy, combined with Maoist puritanical teachings, and decided it was his duty to his people to marry and raise a family. This episode seems to be the starting point for Pereleshin's theory of Spiritual Left-Handedness, which divides men into those who are guided by the imperatives of the species and by racial and family traditions, and those who have liberated themselves from such imperatives and have thereby become spiritually and metaphysically "left-handed."

Pereleshin's earlier love affairs were with people who, no matter how attractive, could not share his literary interests or understand the scope of his poetic achievement. Then, on 17 February 1971, a letter from the Soviet Union arrived. A literary translator and lover of poetry named Evgeny ("Zhenya") Vitkovsky, who had become aware of Pereleshin's poetry, was writing to express his interest and admiration. Thus began what Pereleshin has subsequently called his "romance with a ghost." A cultivated, sensitive young man, thirty years his junior, was ostensibly offering himself as a son, lover, and disciple all in one. He was thus providing a direct, personal link to the culture which Pereleshin had left as a child but to whose service he had devoted himself as a poet all his life, even though today he calls himself a Brazilian poet who happens to write in Russian. The poet's intoxication with the correspondence that ensued and his subsequent sobering up are captured in the sonnets of *Ariel* and constitute the book's central subject.

Like most gay men in the Soviet Union, Vitkovsky was married (see George Schuvaloff, "Gay Life in Russia," *Christopher Street*, September 1976, for an explanation of this frequent survival tactic). His family, consisting of himself, his mother, his wife, and his small son, is typical—from what one knows from other sources—of the living arrangements of gay men in the Soviet Union. As the correspondence brings into sharper focus Vitkovsky's home life and his daily routine, we can perceive the poet's resentment and envy of those who were in daily contact with the object of his love. The poet realizes that this particular young man is attracted to what is most valuable in him—his poetic gift. He responds in ways that are unprecedented in his earlier poetry. His poetic power, his expressivity, his verbal mastery grow and expand, seemingly before the reader's eyes. This expansion parallels the gradual intensification of the two men's mutual fascination and need.

Since the exchange is carried out entirely by mail, there is always the danger of the Soviet selective censorship of private letters, poignantly mentioned in several of the sonnets. The younger man consciously braves this danger for the sake of being immortalized in a major poetic creation (one must remember that the prestige of poetry in Russian and Soviet culture is beyond anything we know in the West). The poet understands his correspondent's need, and he caters to it by his frequent and extended parallels with historical and literary predecessors: Socrates and Alcibiades, Shakespeare and the apocryphal Willie Hughes, Verlaine and Rimbaud, Stefan George and Maximin, Oscar Wilde and Bosie. The most astounding thing is that Pereleshin's brilliance, eloquence, and verbal pyrotechnics save these comparisons from appearing presumptuous or far-fetched within the context of the cycle.

On one level, then, *Ariel* is an account of the day-to-day lives of two Russian men of two different generations, one of whom lives in Moscow and the other in Rio de Janeiro, and who have only their mutual need and a shared literary culture in common. But on another level it is a rich and absorbing philosophical treatise on the nature of love, a study of the ways in which love can develop and thrive without the lovers ever experiencing each other's physical presence.

Recognizing his distant friend's obligations to his family, the poet nevertheless cannot help dreaming of an eventual personal encounter. The beauty of Brazil and the pleasures of Rio de Janeiro are vividly conveyed in several sonnets by way of enticing Vitkovsky to sever his family ties and to undertake the enormously difficult feat of getting an exit visa. Then a letter from Moscow brings a devastating blow. The distant lover and disciple has left his mother, wife, and child not in order to join the poet, but to move in with another woman, right there in Moscow. Several sonnets give vent to the sense of having been used and betrayed.

But bitterness is ultimately sublimated in the astonishing crown of sonnets that concludes *Ariel* and sums up the experience that inspired it. In this sequence of fourteen sonnets, the last line of each sonnet also serves as the first line of the next one, and the first lines of all fourteen are arranged at the end to form a separate sonnet, which is also an acrostic that spells out "Zhenya Vitkovsky."

An epilogue to the entire affair is found in one of the last stanzas of canto eight of *Poem without an Object*, written a year after the last sonnets of *Ariel*: "Perhaps mere hollow mischief / Guided his ingratiating pen / But for those three golden years / I will still speak of him kindly / And bless him with valedictory light."

It is a fact of literary history that misdirected and unconsummated love affairs can give rise to some of the greatest poetic insights about the nature and ways of love. The two parallels to Pereleshin's "romance with a ghost" in twentieth-century Russian poetry are Vyacheslav Ivanov's collection *Eros* (1908), inspired by his brief affair with the primarily straight younger poet Gorodetsky, and Marina Tsvetaeva's seven-poem cycle *Verses to an Orphan* (1936), which reflected her misguided infatuation with the gay poet Anatoly Steiger. Pereleshin's *Ariel* is larger in scope than these two illustrious predecessors and it reflects the poet's emotional experience in broader and also more concrete and coherent terms.

Already in his earliest published poetry, Pereleshin had shown himself a virtuoso of traditional Russian poetic techniques (a number of the finest Russian poets of this century have preferred to restrict themselves to traditional nineteenth-century verse, among them such undoubtedly modern figures as Anna Akhmatova and Vladislav Khodasevich). In *Ariel*, Pereleshin's neoclassically conservative form is a vehicle for an acutely modern sensibility. On the more obvious level this can be seen in the contrast between the masterfully wrought Petrarchan sonnets in which most of *Ariel* is couched (there are also a few Spenserian sonnets, which Pereleshin calls "English") and the present-day urban landscapes of Moscow and Rio de Janeiro, with their governmental agencies and formalities, cafés and cruising areas which the sonnets describe. Citations from the Bible, the lives of the saints, and the theory of sexuality ascribed to Aristophanes in Plato's *Symposium* coexist in *Ariel* side by side with Soviet labor camps, the commercial billboards of Rio, and an unexpectedly funny reference to the American TV actor Dennis Weaver.

Translated into its Anglo-American equivalents, *Ariel* could be described as a book that uses the outer form we would associate with Elizabeth Barrett Browning and Dante Gabriel Rossetti to express a sensibility halfway between Marianne Moore and James Merrill (with a few side excursions into the respective territories of Brother Antoninus and John Rechy). This description might give an idea of what an English translation of this unclassifiable book would sound like; such a description is as close as those who cannot read Russian are ever likely to get to the tone and style of *Ariel*. Its stylistic and verbal richness and the precision of its language are likely to defeat the best efforts of translators for some time to come.

This richness and the unprecedented candor of the book make regrettable its inaccessibility to the readers of other cultures, to say nothing of readers in the Soviet Union, where its publication would have caused the biggest sensation in decades. The book is a major event in contemporary Russian poetry and a breakthrough that is significant for the whole of Western culture. It is also unarguably its author's finest achievement, crowning a remarkable oeuvre that spans four decades. But present-day Russian exiles, many of whom were raised in the Soviet Union under Stalin, are far more homophobic than cultivated Russians were at the beginning of this century or than the Paris émigrés of the 1930s who saw nothing wrong with honoring and appreciating Anatoly Steiger. Today's émigrés may regard such earlier figures as Konstantin Leontiev or Mikhail Kuzmin (both mentioned at crucial points in *Ariel*) with respect, carefully overlooking their homosexuality, but Pereleshin's total frankness is something that cannot be conveniently ignored.

The publication of *Ariel* might well cost Valery Pereleshin the loss of a considerable segment of the small following he has so laboriously acquired. Despite an enthusiastic introductory essay by George [Yury] Ivask, a noted American scholar and an important émigré poet in his own right, *Ariel* has not so far been reviewed by any of the émigré journals. Russian language bookstores in major American cities and the agents who had distributed Pereleshin's earlier books have refused to handle *Ariel*. The book is at the present time available only directly from the publishing house in West Germany that brought it out or from the poet himself.[5]

But it is a book that anyone who cares for either Russian poetry or gay literature should know about. If poetry on gay themes is read and studied a century from now, it is a safe bet that *Ariel* is one of the books by which the decade of the 1970s will be remembered.

---

[5] Valerii Pereleshin, *Ariel'*, with an introductory essay by Yury Ivask (Frankfurt am Main: Possev-Verlag, 1976).

III. Poetry Abroad

* * *

The original article concluded with the following three sonnets from *Ariel* translated by SK. They were republished in *Out of the Blue: Russia's Hidden Gay Literature: An Anthology*, edited by Kevin Moss, introduced by Simon Karlinsky (San Francisco: Gay Sunshine Press, 1977), pp. 187–88, and were accompanied by three other poems by Pereleshin in SK's translation: "To One Who Confessed," "Straight from the Shoulder," and "Admiration" (pp. 184–86). SK also published a comprehensive survey of Pereleshin's life and career, with bibliography, in *Gay and Lesbian Literature*, vol. 2, edited by Tom Pendergast and Sara Pendergast (Detroit: St. James Press, 1998), pp. 285–87.

Without a Mask[6]

You willed it so—and you've become my fate.
About the twilight of the waning world,
About the flame of Plato and of Shakespeare,
About myself I now converse with you.

My friends (they—almost every one of them—
Are caustic scoffers, cavilers, fault-finders,
Their trump cards mockery and biting satire)
Are dying to know everything about you.

So I betray you in smoke-filled cafés
Amidst the talk of sports and Leonard Bernstein,
But even at such times we are alone.

Only at night, without a screen or mask,
I blend with care the colors for these sonnets
And am tormented that you are not here.

(14 November 1972)

---

[6] Translator's Note: Unrhymed versions from the Russian by Simon Karlinsky. In the original, all the sonnets in *Ariel* are written in lines of precisely rhymed iambic pentameter. The rhyme scheme for "Without a Mask" and "A Declaration of Love" is abba abba ccd eed. The virtuosic "Not for Publication" has only two sets of rhymes throughout, rhyming abba abba bba bab.

Not for Publication

I am resigned (though inwardly I scream).
You, too, must now endure the hurt of failure.
Try to snatch but a half an hour from your jailer.
Don't be ashamed of self-abasing gestures,

Or else, he will snuff out on the spot
All of our dreams and hopes for an encounter,
And, victim of a modern immolation,
They'll dump you at the foot of Lenin's tomb.

A living dog's more blessed than dead lions.
You'd better lie. Humiliate yourself.
For cover, use some shreds of a red banner.

God doesn't ask you for insane bravado.
He knows that when you trample on the icons
You still have not betrayed your inner self.

(10 September 1973)

A Declaration of Love

That's quite a sweet confession that I got:
You write you love me for my verbal powers
Though I am not renowned among the poets
And other masters have a greater fame.

Well, why turn down the lesser good that comes our way?
I, too, love Sergio because on Sundays
He gives me rides in his three-seat sedan.
I love Antonio as a splendid house painter.

Among the barbers, I love the black barber Nilo.
Among the soaps, it's cocoa-butter soap.
No salt but Morton's will for pickles do.

There's Dennis Weaver—I just love him as an actor.
Bald-domed Anselmo—him I love as tram conductor.
And you—I only love the translator in you.

(6 November 1974)

Russian Culture in Manchuria and the Memoirs of Valery Pereleshin[1]

When Anton Chekhov sailed eastward by riverboat on the Amur during his trip to Sakhalin (Amur then marked, as it still does, the border between China and Siberia), he was struck by the abundant wildlife and sparse population. In his letter to Aleksei Suvorin, 27 June 1890, he wrote: "Cliffs, crags, forests, thousands of ducks, herons and all sorts of long-beaked rascals, and utter wilderness. The Russian bank is on the left, the Chinese on the right. If I feel like it, I can look at Russia, and if I feel like it, I can look at China. China is as barren and savage as Russia: villages and sentinel huts are few and far between."[2] Even though China had been ruled for centuries by Manchu emperors, the homeland of that dynasty, Manchuria, was a vast nature preserve with far fewer towns and villages than the area could accommodate.

In 1896 the Russian government obtained permission from the Chinese to construct, through Manchuria, a continuation of the Trans-Siberian Railroad to Vladivostok. This was the Chinese Eastern Railway. A bit later, a southern branch was constructed toward the Russian towns of Dalny (Дальний; Dairen after the Russo-Japanese War, now Dalian in China) and Port Arthur, on the Liaotung peninsula by the Yellow Sea. Because of all this vast railroad construction, thousands of people of various nationalities who inhabited the Russian Empire moved to Manchuria. In 1898 a settlement was founded at the point of intersection of the eastern railroad branch and the wide river Sungari, a tributary of the Amur.[3]

---

[1] Review of *Russian Poetry and Literary Life in Harbin and Shanghai, 1830–1850: The Memoirs of Valerij Perelešin*, ed. Jan Paul Hinrichs (Amsterdam: Rodopi, 1987). Originally published as "Memoirs of Harbin" in *Slavic Review* 48, no. 2 (Summer 1989): 284–90.

[2] *Anton Chekhov's Life and Thought: Selected Letters and Commentary*, trans. Michael Henry Heim, ed. Simon Karlinsky (Berkeley: University of California Press, 1973), 167.

[3] A detailed account of Russian railroad construction in Manchuria during the 1890s and of the foundation of Harbin is contained in E. Kh. (Evgenii Khrisanfovich) Nilus, *Istoricheskii obzor kitaiskoi vostochnoi zheleznoi dorogi, 1896–1923 gg.* (Harbin, 1923), vol. 1. Nilus was married to the poet Aleksandra Parkau.

Initially named the Sungari Settlement, the new town soon became Harbin, a distorted name of a Chinese fishing hamlet later absorbed by the town. Arseny Nesmelov, the foremost Harbin poet of the 1920s and 1930s, depicted the founders and planners of Harbin in one of his poems: "Inzhener. Rasstegnut vorot. / Fliaga. Karabin. / —Zdes' postroim russkii gorod, / Nazovem—Harbin."[4] Nesmelov wondered whether the whole project might be a belated manifestation of the ferment inherited from Peter the Great. Indeed, Harbin was a boomtown, comparable in the speed of its growth to St. Petersburg (but without the attendant cruelty) or to San Francisco during the Gold Rush. Within five years there were Russian hotels, schools, churches, and theaters. The Russo-Japanese War, which Russia lost, enriched Harbin. It became the rest and recuperation place for Russian officers and soldiers. Many of these men were so impressed by the opportunities for jobs, the inexpensive way of life, and the seeming absence of national or racial animosities that they resolved to move to Harbin after demobilization. Both sets of the present reviewer's grandparents moved to Manchuria at the urging of their sons who had served there as soldiers during the war of 1904–6.

Several misunderstandings about the Russian presence in Harbin ought to be cleared up before addressing the volume under review. It was not primarily a city of refugees, as the back cover of the book implies. It is true that the Russian-speaking population, which included large contingents of Ukrainians, Jews, Poles, Georgians, and Tatars, rose to some 127,000 after the October Revolution. This figure includes only those who stayed. Uncounted thousands made brief stops in Harbin on their way to other cities in China or to other countries. Unlike the Russian émigrés who went to Paris or Prague or even to Shanghai, the new residents of Harbin were not a minority surrounded by a foreign population. They found themselves instead in an almost totally Russian city, populated mainly by people with roots in the south of European Russia. Speakers of Russian who grew up in Harbin and later moved to the Soviet Union or the United States were often surprised to learn that they spoke the dialects of Kharkov or Odessa.

---

4 "An engineer. Collar open / A canteen. A carbine. / —Here we'll build a Russian city. / We'll call it—Harbin."—Ed.

III. Poetry Abroad

On this one point Jan Paul Hinrichs is mistaken in his otherwise excellent introduction to the memoirs of the Harbin poet Valery Pereleshin: Harbin did not look like "any provincial Siberian city," because many of its buildings, boulevards, and parks were planned—well before the October Revolution—by distinguished Russian architects and also by Swiss and Italian town planners (I found the models for Harbin's Municipal Garden in Switzerland and the north of Germany, rather than anywhere in the Soviet Union). Nor was Harbin "a lifelike reconstruction of prerevolutionary Russia on Chinese soil"—it had been a Russian city all along, one that had escaped the Revolution, the civil war, and Stalin's collectivization and had managed to keep well into the 1940s the high standard of living that typified Russia during the decade that preceded World War I.[5]

---

[5] The economic prosperity of Russian Harbin in the second, third, and fourth decades of the twentieth century was interconnected with the economic boom in the rest of Manchuria, occasioned by the mass influx of Chinese farmers, fur trappers, and tradesmen. This led to a great demand for American-made agricultural machines and implements, which were distributed by several firms based in Harbin. Manchurian soybean products, animal skins, lumber, and other commodities were also exported to Germany and other European countries. See Frederick Simpich, "Manchuria, Promised Land of Asia: Invaded by Millions of Settlers, This Vast Region Now Recalls Early Boom Days of the American West," *National Geographic Magazine*, October 1929, 379–428; and Owen Lattimore, "Byroads and Backwoods of Manchuria: Where Violent Contrasts of Modernism and Unaltered Ancient Tradition Clash," ibid., January 1932, 101–30. There *were*, as other commentators have pointed out, Russian beggars, prostitutes, and drug addicts in Harbin, but these were very small minorities.

Transient foreign visitors, who often assumed that the entire Russian-speaking population of Harbin had recently escaped from the Soviet Union, were hard put to explain the prosperous appearance of the street crowds. Jan Paul Hinrichs cites a long excerpt from Harry A. Franck's book *Wandering in Northern China* (New York, 1923). Franck wrote that the "ladies as well gowned as at the Paris races [who] strolled with men faultlessly garbed by European standards" all had "not a crust left at home" and sold their "necessary things" to achieve this deceptive appearance.

Lilian Grosvenor Coville ("Here in Manchuria. Many Thousand Lives Were Lost and More Than Half the Crops Destroyed by the Floods of 1932." *National Geographic Magazine*, February 1933, 233–56) visited Harbin in the fateful year that brought a major flood, the Japanese invasion, and an epidemic of cholera. She, too, was puzzled by the well-dressed look of Harbin Russians. She accepted the explanation that Harbin women were divided into two classes: the attractive ones, who were all cabaret hostesses, and the unattractive ones, who were all dentists. As to the men, they were either supported by their dentist wives or somehow managed to "exist and enjoy themselves on nothing at all." Coville also believed that Harbin's "excellent ballet dancers" and other performers were "trained in Moscow and smuggled out of Russia to Harbin" (all quotes from p. 235).

The only difference was the presence of numerous Chinese shopkeepers, itinerant vendors, artisans and servants. But it was *they* who had to learn to speak Russian or, rather, the amusing Russo-Chinese pidgin called "Moya-tvoya," originated by Chinese peddlers in Siberia in the nineteenth century, which became the lingua franca for Russo-Chinese transactions in Harbin.[6]

Hinrichs does a fine job of demolishing the other misapprehension about Harbin: that it was culturally provincial. He cites statements to that effect by compilers of anthologies of Russian émigré poetry and a regrettably dismissive passage from the late Gleb Struve's indispensable *Russkaia literatura v izgnanii* (1956). Harbin was an important cultural center from the first decade of its existence. The celebrated tenor Nikolai Figner and his Italian-born wife Medea sang there. When Leonid Andreev's first drama, *K zvezdam*, was banned in St. Petersburg and Moscow, it premiered in Harbin in 1907.[7] The fabled Vera Komissarzhevskaya brought

---

[6] The exact proportion of Harbin's Russian-speaking population in comparison with the Chinese is hard to pinpoint. The section called Fudiedzian, inhabited only by the Chinese, where street names and shop signs were in their language, occupied approximately one-sixth of the city's area. But it was far more densely populated than any of the Russian sections.

For description and analysis of "Moya-tvoya," see the two articles on it by Johanna Nichols: "Pidginization and Foreigner Talk: Chinese Pidgin Russian," in *Papers from the Fourth International Conference on Historical Linguistics*, ed. Elizabeth Closs Traugott et al. (Amsterdam, 1980), 397–407; and "The Bottom Line: Chinese Russian," in *Evidentiality: The Linguistic Coding of Epistemology*, ed. Wallace Chafe and Johanna Nichols (Norwood, New Jersey, 1986), 239–57. Both articles cite earlier descriptions of "Moya-tvoya" and its occurrences in literary sources, especially in the writings of the ethnographer Vladimir Arseniev (1872–1930), whose book, V. Arsen'ev, *Dersu Uzala*, was turned by Akira Kurosawa into the film of the same name, made in the Soviet Union.

Since in Arseniev's books the Russo-Chinese pidgin is used by speakers of Tungusic languages (the central character in *Dersu Uzala* is a Nanai tribesman), Professor Nichols postulates a substratum in "Moya-tvoya" that comes from neither Russian nor Chinese but from Nanai. This would explain the reduplication of Russian words in such locutions as *malo-malo* (used instead of *nemnogo* or *slegka*), said to be a feature borrowed from Nanai. In the second of her cited articles, Professor Nichols proposes that "Moya-tvoya" "arose when the Russians and the Chinese began regular trading in 1768 in Kyakhta, located on the present Russian-Mongolian border south of Lake Baikal" (p. 240). [Included here is SK's corrected and expanded footnote for this article, to be found in carton 7 among his papers in the Bancroft Library, University of California, Berkeley, which remained unpublished.—Ed.]

[7] See James B. Woodward, *Leonid Andreyev: A Study* (Oxford: Clarendon, 1969), 135.

her company in 1909. During World War I, another major actress, Ekaterina Roshchina-Insarova, performed with an itinerant company of her own. Fyodor Chaliapin came in the 1930s to give several recitals and was lionized and feted at numerous banquets. Chaliapin did not sing with the Harbin Opera Company, as Hinrichs has it, but two singers of the Harbin opera were of a caliber to go on to international careers. The tenor Sergei Lemeshev went to the Soviet Union where he enjoyed great popularity. He made several Soviet films in the 1930s and was a guest star in the opera houses of Berlin and Prague in the late 1940s. The mezzo-soprano Irina Petina, noted in Harbin for her Carmen, eventually sang the same part at New York's Metropolitan Opera, appeared in Hollywood films (as "Irra Petina"), and had special parts composed for her by Leonard Bernstein (in *Candide*) and Heitor Villa-Lobos (in *Magdalena*).

Even apart from opera and theater, Harbin was a cultural city. The large number of Russian schools (most of which emphasized the study of Russian literature), periodicals, theaters (including such specialized ones as the highly popular theater of Ukrainian musical comedy and a company that performed only in Tatar), and libraries—all testify to the outstanding intellectual level of the multinational Harbin community.[8] It was inevita-

---

[8] An enormous amount of information about economic, cultural, medical, culinary, and numerous other aspects of life in Russian Harbin is found in *Politekhnik*, no. 10, a special tenth anniversary issue, 1969–79, Sydney, Australia. (I would like to thank my Berkeley colleagues and former fellow Harbiners, Boris Bressler and Gregory Grossman, for bringing this fascinating publication to my attention.) Ordinarily published as a newsletter by the graduates of the Harbin Polytechnic Institute who live in Australia, the anniversary issue of 1979 is a volume of 300 pages with some sixty articles and essays.

Among the highlights is an illustrated account of Harbin churches and temples. Besides the numerous Orthodox churches there were two large Jewish synagogues, a handsome mosque on the Artillereiskaia ulitsa, and Catholic, Protestant, and Old Believer churches. This article is followed by an eyewitness account of the demolition and burning during China's Cultural Revolution of the most beautiful and famous of Harbin churches, the St. Nicholas Cathedral, built in 1899 in the traditional Vologda style of wooden architecture. On 23 August 1966, Red Guards, for the most part hysterical teenagers, destroyed the cathedral and burned its priceless icons while beating drums and shouting Maoist slogans (*Politekhnik*, no. 10, 134–44).

Hinrichs cites in his annotations (132n14) two minor newsletters published in the West by former Harbin residents. He apparently did not have access to the two most substantial of such publications, *Politekhnik* in Sydney and the magazine-format *Biulleten'* of the "Igud Iotsei Sin," printed in Russian (with a brief supplement in English) in Tel Aviv. *Biulleten'* is now in its thirty-fifth year of publication. The latest edition availble that a literature in Russian would arise in this atmosphere.[9] There was no one of a stature comparable to that of Bunin or Tsvetaeva or Nabokov in Harbin. Novels and collections of stories were published in the 1920s and 1930s, but the only prose writers worthy of note were Nikolai Baikov, author of highly readable accounts of Manchuria, its nature and folklore, who also wrote works of fiction about the interaction of Russians with Manchuria's indigenous population (his first book on Manchuria was published in St. Petersburg in 1914; he died in Australia in 1958); and Boris Yulsky (Юльский), whose stories appeared in the illustrated weekly *Rubezh* and who died too young to have fulfilled his promise.[10]

Harbin's literary life manifested itself most intensely and memorably in poetry. An account of this poetry has now been written by the last still active Harbin poet, Valery Pereleshin (pen name of Valery Frantsevich Salatko-Petrishche, born in 1913 in Irkutsk), and edited with loving care by Jan Paul Hinrichs, a noted translator of exiled Russian poets into Dutch, who is also responsible for publishing the work of various other Russian writers in Holland.[11] Hinrichs teaches at the University of Leiden and is the Slavic librarian of that university.

---

able at this writing (no. 298, June 1988) commemorates the fortieth anniversary of the arrival of some 6,000 Jewish residents of Manchuria and the rest of China in Israel. The issue features several memoirs about that event, including one by the magazine's editor, Boris Mirkin. There is also an installment of the posthumously published chronicle of the earliest period of Jewish presence in Harbin by A. I. Kaufman (see n. 13 below).

9   On the beginnings of Harbin's literary life, see Iu. (Iustina) Kruzenshtern-Peterets, "Churaevskii pitomnik: O dal'nevostochnykh poetakh," *Vozrozhdenie* (Paris), no. 204 (1968): 45–70. This article provides information on the period 1917–30, which antedates the time described in Pereleshin's memoirs. See also Mikhail Volin, "Russkie poety v Kitae," *Kontinent* (Paris), no. 34 (1982): 337–57.

10 For a biographical sketch of Baikov, see the special issue of *Politekhnik* cited in n. 8 above (181n6). It was depressing to learn from Pereleshin's memoirs that the talented Yulsky was a cocaine addict and a regular contributor to the Fascist newspaper *Nash put'*. Founded by the führer of the Russian Fascist movement Konstantin Rodzaevsky in 1932 and financed by the Japanese, this newspaper was the lowest example of gutter journalism that Harbin had ever seen. On *Nash put'* and the Russian Fascist movement in the Far East, see John J. Stephan, *The Russian Fascists: Tragedy and Farce in Exile, 1925–1945* (New York, 1978).

11 See *Europese Nacht: Vladislav Chodasevitsj, Georgij Ivanov, Boris Poplavskij, Gedichten*, ed. and trans. Jan Paul Hinrichs (Maastricht, 1984); and Valerij Perelešin, *Gedichten*, ed. and trans. Jan Paul Hinrichs (Leiden, 1983). The latter has appeared in two more printings since its first publication, 1984 and 1985. Hinrichs is responsible for Dutch editions of, among others, Anna Akhmatova, Nikolai Gumilyov, and Vasily Rozanov.

Pereleshin is a remarkable instance of a "twice-born" poet. He began publishing poetry at the very end of the 1920s in various Harbin periodicals. By the mid-1930s he was one of the best-known and most admired of Harbin poets. His first collection of verse appeared in 1937. Soon thereafter, he took monastic vows and departed first for Beijing, then for Shanghai. Three more collections of Pereleshin's poetry were published in Harbin between 1939 and 1944 by his mother, a well-known journalist.[12]

By leaving Harbin, Pereleshin escaped the fate of Russian poets who had remained there, such as Arseny Nesmelov (Несмелов; real surname: Mitropolsky [Митропольский]) and Aleksei Achair (Ачаир; real surname: Gryzov [Грызов]), who were deported to the gulags when Soviet troops occupied Harbin in August 1945.[13] In 1950 Pereleshin tried to join his younger brother in California, but upon arriving in San Francisco he was imprisoned. An anonymous accuser had denounced him as a Soviet agent because, before giving up his monkhood, he had worked as a translator for the Soviet news agency TASS. Pereleshin was a rare example of a Russian writer in the Far East who took the trouble to study Chinese language and literature. His duties at TASS entailed nothing more than translating clippings from Chinese periodicals into Russian. But those were McCarthyite times and Pereleshin was deported back to China. From 1953 on, Pereleshin has lived in Rio de Janeiro. He is now a Brazilian citizen and considers himself a Brazilian poet who happens to write in Russian (though in 1983 he brought out a volume of his verse written in Portuguese).

Pereleshin's "second birth," to borrow Boris Pasternak's well-known phrase, took place when the last vestiges of Russian presence and culture

---

[12] For a good thematic and technical analysis of Pereleshin's early collections of poetry, see Aleksis Rannit, "O poezii i poetike Valeriia Pereleshina: Shest' pervykh sbornikov poeta (1937–1971)," *Russian Language Journal* (East Lansing) 30 (Spring 1976): 79–104.

[13] On the fate of Achair (the name has three syllables) and other poets after the Soviet invasion of Manchuria, see Valerii Pereleshin, "Konets Alekseia Achaira," *Novoe russkoe slovo*, 10 December 1972, 5. A shattering account of how various prominent members of the Harbin community, who had welcomed the Red Army as liberators from the Japanese, were invited by the Soviet command to receptions at which they were arrested and then deported, can be found in A. I. (Abram Iosifovich) Kaufman, *Lagernyi vrach* (Tel Aviv, 1973). Kaufman (1885–1971), a well-known Harbin physician, scholar, and Jewish civic leader, spent sixteen years in Soviet camps before he was allowed to join his family in Israel in 1961.

had vanished in Manchuria and when Manchuria itself had ceased to exist as a separate entity—it now constitutes the four northeastern provinces of the People's Republic of China. From 1967 on, Pereleshin's poems and essays began to appear in *Novoe russkoe slovo* (New York), *Novyi zhurnal* (New York), *Vozrozhdenie* (Paris), and *Grani* (West Germany), thus breaking a quarter of a century of literary silence.

Since then, Pereleshin has published eight more collections of his verse including *Iuzhnyi dom*, a volume of poetry about the cultures of ancient and modern China and his involvement with them both; *Kachel'*, a book of highly original metaphysical and religious poetry, which includes the long poem *Poema o mirozdanii* and the wreath of sonnets *Krestnyi put'*; and *Ariel'*, astounding in its profundity, virtuosity, and thematic unconventionality.[14] With these books, Pereleshin has outgrown in magnitude his Harbin contemporaries of the period 1930–50. He has by now become one of the four or five most important Russian poets of the second half of the twentieth century. He is also a diligent and resourceful translator of poetry. After his very moving rendition into Russian of *Li Sao*, a long "politico-erotic elegy" written by the Chinese poet Ch'u Yuan ca. 300 BC, came his anthologies of Chinese and Brazilian poets in Russian and a Portuguese translation of Mikhail Kuzmin's *Aleksandriiskie pesni*.[15]

Yet, through it all, Pereleshin's literary beginnings in Harbin's congenial cultural environment have remained the center of his interest. During the decade of the 1970s he produced two major autobiographical texts: the memoirs under review, whose full title is *Dva polustanka: Vospominaniia svidetelia i uchastnika literaturnoi zhizni Kharbina i Shankhaia* (Two waystations: Memoirs of a witness to and participant in the literary life of

---

14 Valerii Pereleshin, *Iuzhnyi dom* (Munich, 1968); *Kachel'* (Frankfurt am Main, 1971); *Ariel'*, with an introductory essay by Yury Ivask (Frankfurt am Main, 1976). On the metaphysical dimension in *Kachel'* and other poetry by Pereleshin, see Valentin Evdokimov (Moscow), "'Chertovy kacheli' i sed'moe nebo" (the first half of the title refers to a well-known poem by Fyodor Sologub), *Vestnik Russkogo khristianskogo dvizheniia* (Paris), no. 139 (1983), 173–91. On *Ariel'*, see Simon Karlinsky, "A Hidden Masterpiece: Valery Pereleshin's *Ariel'*," *Christopher Street* 2, no. 6 (December 1977): 37–42 [included in the present volume].

15 Ch'u Yuan, *Li Sao: Poema*, trans. Valerii Pereleshin from the Chinese original (Frankfurt am Main, 1975); *Stikhi na veere: Antologiia kitaiskoi klassicheskoi poezii* (Frankfurt am Main, 1970); *Iuzhnyi krest: Antologiia brazil'skoi poezii* (Frankfurt am Main, 1978); M. Kuzmin, cotrans., *Canticos de Alexandria* (Rio de Janeiro, 1986).

Harbin and Shanghai), and the long autobiographical poem, written in Onegin stanzas, *Poema bez predmeta*, six of whose eight cantos have been serialized in the literary journal *Sovremennik*.[16]

As the reader learns from both the memoirs and the narrative poem, Pereleshin matured as a poet through joining Churaevka, an association of younger Harbin writers founded by the older poet Aleksei Achair. What impresses one today about the young people who belonged to Churaevka is the breadth of their culture and the sureness of their literary choices. They knew the classics of Russian literature (any graduate of a Harbin high school did). They also knew the literature of early twentieth-century Modernism, which was at that time suppressed and withdrawn from circulation in the USSR. They were aware of what was going on in both the Soviet and the émigré literatures (individual issues of such émigré journals as *Sovremennye zapiski* or *Chisla* were regularly reviewed in the Harbin press). While the arbiters of taste in Russian Paris argued over whether Tsvetaeva had entered a period of decline or whether Sirin (Vladimir Nabokov) was a genuinely Russian writer or whether Boris Pasternak should be discarded for selling out to the Soviets, the young Harbin poets knew these writers' importance and applauded their achievements.

Harbin had no particular poetic school. Nesmelov's antecedents came from Russian Futurism and from Marina Tsvetaeva. Most of the Churaevka poets chose the Acmeist mold. Pereleshin's masters were Gumilyov and the Parisian heir of the Acmeists, Georgy Ivanov. Lidiya Khaindrova's model was Akhmatova, and Nikolai Shchyogolev's was Mandelstam. Harry (really Grigory) Satovsky-Rzhevsky, Jr., adored the poetry of Boris Poplavsky. Yet, these and other Harbin poets had poetic voices of their own. Pereleshin's memoirs resurrect names familiar to those interested in literature during the 1930s in Harbin: Marianna Kolosova, a poet of great vehemence, whose thematic monotony (she wrote of nothing but the horrors of Stalin's regime) makes some of her verse seem bathetic today; Larisa Andersen, equally gifted as poet, actress, and character dancer (who could ever forget her dance "Tabu," performed

---

[16] The first six cantos of Pereleshin's *Poema bez predmeta* were serialized in the following issues of *Sovremennik* (Toronto): no. 35–36 (1977), 127–53; no. 37–38 (1978), 70–95; no. 39–40 (1978), 132–59; no. 41 (1979), 29–58; no. 42 (1979), 52–80; no. 45–46 (1980), 35–64. See n. 4 of the preceding essay.

in a leopard skin to the music of Ernesto Lecuona at a *kino-kontsert?*),[17] whose admirable poetry has stood the test of time quite well; and Nataliya Reznikova, whose once acclaimed novels, stories, and poems seem somewhat faded now.

Pereleshin is by no means an impartial chronicler. He draws a nasty caricature of Viktoriya Yankovskaya, whom I have always considered a rather interesting poet. His account of the visit to Harbin by the famed painter and stage designer Nikolai Roerich (1874–1947) is patently wrong. Roerich could not have been "almost one hundred years old" in the mid-1930s and he could not have published "a book of his memoirs at the end of the last century," since he graduated from the St. Petersburg Art Academy in 1897. It was disappointing to find nothing about the well-wrought light verse of Aleksandra Parkau, even if we do get an anecdote about her unconventional domestic arrangements.

The book will put those who are familiar with Harbin literature in a nostalgic mood, as the readers of this review must have gathered by now. Those who know nothing of Harbin will be introduced to a fascinating and mostly unfamiliar chapter in the history of Russian culture. The second part of the memoirs traces the fate of several Harbin writers who moved to Shanghai at the end of the 1930s because the Japanese occupation of Manchuria made things uncomfortable and a Soviet invasion seemed imminent. There, in the international settlement and the French concession, they tried to continue the literary life they had known in Harbin. Volumes of poetry were published; Russian literary journals were started. But cosmopolitan Shanghai did not possess the Russian readership that had existed in Harbin. The triumph of Mao's revolution in 1949 spelled the end of all Russian culture in China.

---

17 *Kino-kontserty* were afternoon performances, usually on Saturdays, where before seeing the latest Marlene Dietrich or Shirley Temple film (a Shirley Temple fan club existed in Harbin in the 1930s) or one of the Ginger Rogers–Fred Astaire musical comedies, one could watch a live variety show. The latter could include performances by singers (Sofiya Redzhi, a Harbin precursor of Edith Piaf, with her *pesni ulitsy* or the more sedate Mariya Sadovskaya); the beloved comedian Fyodor Khmarin; one of the popular dance duos, such as the ballerina Olga Manzhelei and her husband Boris Serov; modest corps-de-ballet numbers; and, especially, exotic dancers, such as Larisa Andersen, Nina Antares, or Mara Vasilevskaya (one of whose dances, "Satanella," depicted a she-devil and was performed in a black satin evening gown of extremely complex cut with a pair of silver horns on her head).

The publication of Pereleshin's memoirs in the Netherlands is one more signal of the current renewal of interest in Harbin both in the West and in the Soviet Union. The erstwhile Harbin and Shanghai resident Nataliya Ilina, now a Soviet writer, achieved considerable success with her semiautobiographical two-volume novel *Vozvrashchenie*. Pereleshin is quite right to point out that the novel slanders Harbin's Russian community. Ilina's more recent collection of autobiographical essays is still fairly slanderous but less so, while its currently serialized sequel is almost objective and contains an admiring section on Larisa Andersen.[18] Ilina's great popularity indicates that Soviet readers are interested in learning about Harbin, now so distant both geographically and historically. In the West, the unexpected recent publication of Nesmelov's selected prose fiction[19] and Pereleshin's ceaseless efforts, expressed in numerous articles and essays and crowned by the appearance of his memoirs, suggest that there might be a comparable interest outside the Soviet Union. The following lines from Arseny Nesmelov's poem about the founding of Harbin, which was cited at the beginning of this review, may well turn out to be prophetic:

> Milyi gorod, gord i stroen,
> Budet den' takoi,
> Chto ne vspomniat chto postroen
> Russkoi ty rukoi.
>
> Pust' udel podobnyi gorek,—
> Ne opustim glaz:
> Vspomiani, starik-istorik,
> Vspomiani o nas.[20]

---

[18] Compare Nataliia Il'ina, *Dorogi i sud'by* (Moscow, 1985), and the section "Larisa" in her "Vstrechi," *Oktiabr'*, 1987, no. 5, 83–92.

[19] Arsenii Nesmelov, *Izbrannaia proza*, ed. Emmanuil Shtein (Orange, CT, 1987).

[20] "Dear city, proud and graceful, / There will come a day / When it won't be remembered / That you were built by a Russian hand // Though such a destiny be bitter,— / We will not lower our eyes: / Remember, aged historian, / Remember us."—Ed.

IV

ON CHAIKOVSKY

A Review of *Tchaikovsky: A Self-Portrait* by Alexandra Orlova[1]

*P*yotr Chaikovsky repeatedly expressed in his letters a dread that, because of the popularity of his music, people would one day examine his personal life and write biographies. What he could not have foreseen was that books would appear claiming to speak in his name, with the implication that they are his *autobiographies*. After *Tchaikovsky: A Self-Portrait* by V. Volkoff (1974) and *Piotr Ilyich Tchaikovsky: Letters to His Family; An Autobiography* by Galina von Meck (1981), we now get another "self-portrait," this time by the Soviet music historian Aleksandra Orlova. This is a reworked version of a book that was first published in Leningrad in 1976 under a more suitable title, *P. I. Chaikovskii o muzyke, o zhizni, o sebe: Literaturnaia kompozitsiia A. A. Orlovoi* (P. I. Chaikovsky on music, on his life, on himself: A literary compilation by Aleksandra Orlova).

As Aleksandra Orlova tells us in the preface to the English edition, she established an affinity with this composer when she worked for two years (1938–39) at the Chaikovsky Museum in Klin, housed in what was once his home. She felt so close to him, she writes, that she had the feeling she could at any moment hear his voice or see him enter the room. This privileged affinity apparently gives her the right to regard her collage of excerpts from Chaikovsky's letters, diaries, and articles as the equivalent of his "autobiography" and even as his "confessions," comparable to those of Jean-Jacques Rousseau.

As Chaikovsky's English biographer John Warrack had occasion to observe in his review of this book, published in the *Times Literary Supple-*

---

[1] Review of *Tchaikovsky: A Self-Portrait*, by Alexandra Orlova, trans. R. M. Davison with a forward by David Brown (Oxford: Oxford University Press, 1990). Originally published in *Slavonic and East European Review* 70 (July 1992): 541–44.

ment under the suggestive title "Poisonous Rumours," Orlova's way of handling Chaikovsky's texts leaves a great deal to be desired.[2] In a freewheeling paste-and-scissors method, she glues together snippets from the composer's frank and open letters to his younger brothers Anatoly and Modest, from more guarded ones to his friends and colleagues, and from formal letters to various musicians (to say nothing of his published essays on musical topics) and shapes it all into a continuous narrative, supposedly written by Chaikovsky. Another feature of the book is the constant tampering with chronology, with tenses of verbs, and with other aspects of the original texts. The words may be for the most part Chaikovsky's own, but they are shuffled around so that they say what Aleksandra Orlova wants them to say. All this is most unfortunately reminiscent of the rearrangement of quotations developed by Soviet cultural historians in Stalinist and post-Stalinist times to distort the political views of various writers and artists, even though, in this particular case, the agenda is obviously not political.

Aleksandra Orlova is right to chide Soviet censorship for removing all evidence of the composer's homosexuality from his writings published from the 1930s onwards. But it somehow never occurred to her to try to learn more about this subject, and about how it affected Chaikovsky and his contemporaries. In an article she published in the New York Russian-language newspaper *Novoe russkoe slovo* in 1987, Orlova pointed out that she had repeatedly "described how [Chaikovsky] was tormented by this anomaly throughout his life, the anomaly that was a calamity, a curse laid on him by fate." And further in the same article she states that "being a highly decent and honorable man, he regarded his anomaly as a disgrace that could never be effaced."

Now, anyone who has read Chaikovsky's diaries, published by his brother Ippolit,[3] or his letters to his younger brothers, will know that this does not reflect the composer's feelings. He always maintained that he was not guilty for the way nature made him. If anything tormented him, it was the possibility of invidious gossip that could make his father or sister ashamed of him. This fear led to his ill-advised marriage, followed by a

---

2 *Times Literary Supplement,* 9 November 1990.
3 Petr Chaikovskii, *Dnevniki* [Diaries], *1873–1891* (Moscow and Petrograd: Glavlit, 1923).

nervous breakdown, after which he made a comfortable adjustment to his sexual orientation. Because Orlova is unable to perceive evidence of homosexuality in Chaikovsky's writings and in memoirs about him, her "self-portrait" says nothing about the formative influence of his classmate, the poet Aleksei Apukhtin, or the happiness he experienced in his homosexual liaisons with his valet-lover Aleksei Sofronov, with Ivan Klimenko (referred to in the composer's letters as "Climena") and with the violinist Iosif Kotek, among others.

A similar lack of information underlies Orlova's view that, in the 1890s, the attitude to homosexuality in Russia was similar to that in the USSR under Stalin and in England in the reign of Queen Victoria. But if one looks at the Russian press at the time of Oscar Wilde's trial in 1895, when the periodicals of the English-speaking world wrote of him with revulsion and fury, one will see that Russian journalists, even such conservative ones as Vasily Rozanov, took the side of Wilde and saw him as a brilliant artist, unfairly persecuted by hypocritical authorities. The most visible homosexual in Russia at the time of Chaikovsky's death was the Grand Duke Sergei Aleksandrovich, brother of Alexander III and uncle of Nicholas II. His love affairs with men were known to everyone in Russia and written about in the press of Western countries. The explorer Nikolai Przhevalsky, Chaikovsky's friend Aleksei Apukhtin and most of the World of Art circle, headed by Sergei Diaghilev, were all quite openly homosexual.

Unaware of any of this, Aleksandra Orlova set about spreading her hypothesis of Chaikovsky's enforced suicide and of a conspiracy to hide it. Shortly after her departure from the Soviet Union in 1979, her articles on this subject began appearing in the West in Russian and in English. Two prominent musicologists, Joel Spiegelman in America and David Brown in England, became Orlova's disciples.[4] The latter wrote in his entry on Chaikovsky in the authoritative *New Grove Dictionary of Music and Musi-*

---

[4] Joel Spiegelman (b. 1933) is actually a pianist, harpsichordist, conductor, and composer who divides his time between the United States and Russia. Spiegelman's article for *High Fidelity* magazine ("The Trial, Condemnation and Death of Tchaikovsky," February 1981, 49–51), in which he uncritically retailed Orlova's contentions as established facts, was more or less the sum total of his musicological output.—Ed.

cians, reprinted in *The New Grove Russian Masters 1*, "That [Chaikovsky] committed suicide can hardly be doubted ... That he died of cholera ... cannot be credited."[5]

The gist of Aleksandra Orlova's revised version of the composer's death, accepted by David Brown and numerous others, is that shortly before the first performance of his Sixth Symphony, the composer became erotically involved with the nephew of a Count Stenbock-Fermor, who threatened to complain to Tsar Alexander III about this.[6] A group of Chaikovsky's fellow alumni from the School of Jurisprudence in St. Petersburg heard about this and convoked a "court of honor," which condemned the composer to death for sullying the uniform of their alma mater. He obediently took poison (arsenic according to the *New Grove*). Then, a monstrous conspiracy that involved the composer's family, some of the best-known physicians in Russia, and the imperial court covered up the suicide and palmed it off as a cholera infection. How does Aleksandra Orlova know all this? She was told by a man named Aleksandr Voitov in 1966 that he had heard about it as a teenage boy in 1913 from the widow of one of the members of the "court of honor" who heard about it from her husband, who died in 1902.

Actually, Chaikovsky's death is one of the best documented on record. Almost every hour of the last five days of his life is accounted for.

---

[5] David Brown, "Tchaikovsky," in *The New Grove Dictionary of Music and Musicians*, ed. Stanley Sadie, vol. 18 (London: Macmillan, 1980), 606–36; Brown, "Piotr Il'yich Tchaikovsky," in *The New Grove Russian Masters 1: Glinka, Borodin, Balakirev, Musorgsky, Tchaikovsky* (London: Macmillan, 1986), 145–250. Citations are from *Russian Masters*, 223–24.

[6] Actually (and quite ironically), it was Aleksandr Poznansky, the author of the book SK recommends at the end of this review, who introduced this now famous nephew into the story in his first, and very effective, rebuttal of Orlova's account. In recounting the version of the rumor that she had heard, Orlova had only stated that it was a certain Count Stenbock-Fermor who had brought the charges against Chaikovsky. Poznansky, diligently researching the possibilities thus raised, determined, on the basis of the *Genealogisches Handbuch der baltischen Ritterschaften* (Golitz, 1930), that "the only young man who might answer Orlova's description would have been Aleksandr Stenbock-Fermor, the son of Count Vladimir Stenbock-Fermor" (see Poznansky's "Tchaikovsky's Suicide: Myth and Reality," *19th-Century Music* 11, no. 3 [Spring 1988]: 203). As soon as Poznansky came up with his name, this Aleksandr was ensconced as the official victim in Orlova's subsequent retellings and those of her followers, to Poznansky's considerable amusement.—Ed.

There is no known poison that can mimic cholera symptoms and cause a person to die slowly over a period of four days. Why did those fellow students of long ago pick on Chaikovsky, who kept his sex life private, and why did they not condemn to death other School of Jurisprudence alumni, such as Apukhtin or Prince Vladimir Meshchersky, who flaunted their sexual orientation, were involved in major homosexual scandals, and yet escaped with impunity? Shortly after Orlova's revelations, Ivan Stenbock-Fermor of Palo Alto, California, informed me that he had the family tree of the various branches of his family and that both the Count Stenbock-Fermor, who was a friend of Alexander III and went hunting with him, and the count's wife were their parents' only children, so that there could not have been a nephew to be involved with Chaikovsky.

The claims of Aleksandra Orlova and her followers were eagerly accepted in the West. As the music critic of the New York Times Donal Henahan wrote,[7] he wanted to believe it because it reminded him of a nineteenth-century Russian novel. (What novel could he possibly have had in mind? Or did he confuse Russian novels with Italian opera?) But from 1981 on, Orlova's version was repeatedly challenged in print by critics and historians. Alan M. Kriegsman, the dance critic of the Washington Post, described her evidence as "a tissue of inferences from one unsupported conjecture to another" and wrote that "by the same logic we could also decree that Tchaikovsky ... was the real author of Wagner's Ring of the Nibelung."[8] The hypothesis was thoroughly debunked by the historian Aleksandr Poznansky in his essay "Tchaikovsky's Suicide: Myth and Reality" in 19th-Century Music,[9] a part of his subsequently published book.

To Aleksandra Orlova's collection of third-hand rumors, never traceable to anyone who knew Chaikovsky, Poznansky opposed a large number of statements, letters, diaries, and memoirs by the composer's relatives, friends, and doctors who were with him at the time of his death. He also offered a profusion of new information about such matters as the cholera

---

[7] Donal Henahan, "Did Tchaikovsky Really Commit Suicide?," New York Times, 26 July 1981.
[8] Alan M. Kriegsman, "The Great Suicide Debate," Washington Post, 28 March 1982.
[9] Poznansky, "Tchaikovsky's Suicide," 199–220.

control regulations that were in force at the time, the unfortunate series of circumstances that delayed the diagnosis of Chaikovsky's illness, and the attitudes to homosexuality in the 1890s at the School of Jurisprudence and the court of Alexander III. Orlova is clearly aware that her critics have proven her wrong on almost every count, because the depiction of the composer's death that we find in *Tchaikovsky: A Self-Portrait* differs in most particulars from the versions offered in her earlier articles on this topic. But she still insists on rejecting all factual evidence surviving from the period and cites some new "testimony," consisting, as usual, of unverifiable rumors.

Aleksandra Orlova's book does contain many interesting statements by Chaikovsky on his life, music, and friends, as well as other composers, not otherwise available in English. But because this material is often chronologically skewed and because Orlova does not know the actual nature of Chaikovsky's relationships with his various friends and lovers, the book would be most profitably read after Aleksandr Poznansky's factually informed and genuinely new and revealing recent book, *Tchaikovsky: The Quest for the Inner Man*.[10]

* * *

Prior to writing this piece and its companions in this volume, and long before Aleksandr Poznansky embarked on his ultimately dispositive refutation of the suicide rumor, SK had participated, along with Malcolm Hamrick Brown and Nina Berberova, in the first detailed public challenge to it. This took the form of a letter to the editor of *High Fidelity* magazine,[11] which had published Joel Spiegelman's sensationalistic Orlova paraphrase.[12] The letter shows that Poznansky's efforts, impressive and valuable as they were, were after all unnecessary to undermine the veracity of the hardy fable. The trio of reputable Slavists pointed out that no one who actually knew Chaikovsky (including

---

10 Alexander Poznansky, *Tchaikovsky: The Quest for the Inner Man* (New York: Schirmer, 1991).
11 Nina Berberova, Malcolm Brown, and Simon Karlinsky, "Tchaikovsky's 'Suicide' Reconsidered: A Rebuttal," letter to the editor, *High Fidelity*, August 1981, 49 and 85.
12 See n. 4.

the composers Glazunov and Rachmaninoff, Chaikovsky's brother Anatoly, or the art connoisseur Vladimir Argutinsky-Dolgorukov, who was actually on the scene when Chaikovsky was taken ill at his brother Modest's apartment in St. Petersburg—all of whom Berberova had interviewed in the course of researching her novelized biography, *Chaikovskii: Istoriia odinokoi zhizni*, published in 1936) had ever doubted that he died of complications from cholera, whereas proponents of the suicide rumor were invariably people without direct access to him. They assessed the role of contemporary attitudes toward homosexuality as an incubator of scandalous rumors during the composer's lifetime. They showed that public health standards in Russia (revised and widely published the year before Chaikovsky's death) were consistent with the way in which the composer's body was treated at his funeral. They used contemporary documents, including Tolstoi's last novel, *Resurrection*, to show that public attitudes toward homosexuality had become more tolerant by the 1890s, rendering the possibility of a mortal threat of exposure implausible. They had a bit of fun detailing the escapades of homosexuals prominent in Russian public affairs in the late nineteenth century, including members of Tsar Alexander III's court (and even the tsar's own brother). They showed that Russian journalists, unlike those in the English-speaking countries or in Germany, treated Oscar Wilde sympathetically at the time of his trial for "gross indecency," which took place two years after Chaikovsky's death. "So," they concluded,

> even though Tchaikovsky indeed feared the exposure of his homosexuality for much of his life, he had less cause to fear the consequences in the early 1890s than before. Furthermore, at the end of his life, he associated with Sergei Diaghilev and other younger homosexuals who later were to form the World of Art group. Unlike the generation to which Tchaikovsky belonged, these younger men felt no qualms about their homosexuality. Had any of them been aware of his being forced into suicide due to the sexual orientation they all shared, surely someone in the World of Art group would have taken advantage of the relaxation of censorship after the 1905 revolution to draw public attention to such an outrage inflicted on the composer they all venerated.

Alas, to no avail. The racy rumor continued to spread on the strength of its sheer value as titillation, and the chief music critic for the *New York*

Times, Donal Henahan, did his best to abet it, deriding the *High Fidelity* letter as "scattershot and undocumented[!]," and declaring himself ready (indeed, "yearning") to believe Orlova's version because it "reeks so heavily of the conspiratorial atmosphere of old Russian novels."[13] "We have no idea what novels he means," wrote Berberova, Brown, and SK in weary rejoinder, "but we do know that a music critic should not confuse history with fiction."[14]

---

[13] Henahan, "Did Tchaikovsky Really Commit Suicide?"
[14] Nina Berberova, Malcolm H. Brown, and Simon Karlinsky, "Doubts about Tchaikovsky," letter to the editor, *New York Times*, 9 August 1981.

Should We Retire Chaikovsky?[1]

Much as I enjoyed reading Lawrence Mass's interview with my Berkeley colleague and almost-neighbor Philip Brett,[2] there is a statement toward the end of the interview with which I couldn't disagree more. That was when Philip said: "It's time for poor old Tchaikovsky to retire. For so long, he and his 'homosexual tragedy' symphony were all there was to our music; and that is worth a book in itself." Such a book is currently being written by the historian Aleksandr Poznansky.[3] Pending its appearance, anyone interested in Chaikovsky or in gay history should read Poznansky's essay "Tchaikovsky's Suicide: Myth and Reality."[4]

With great erudition and a profusion of factual information, Poznansky demonstrates the utter absurdity of the story about the composer being forced to poison himself by a "court of honor" constituted by his fellow alumni from the School of Jurisprudence. These classmates of yore supposedly feared that the disclosure of Chaikovsky's homosexuality (widely

---

[1] Originally published as "Should We Retire Tchaikovsky?" in *Christopher Street*, no. 123 (May 1988), 16–21.

[2] "Homosexuality and Music: A Conversation with Philip Brett," *Christopher Street*, no. 115 (October 1987), 12–26; reprinted in Lawrence D. Mass, *Dialogues of the Sexual Revolution*, vol. 2, *Homosexuality as Behavior and Identity* (New York: Harrington Park, 1990), 36–54. Philip Brett (1937–2002), a member of the music faculty at the University of California, Berkeley from 1966 to 1991, was the pivotal figure in the emergence of LGBT studies in musicology. He began as a student of English Renaissance music, concentrating on William Byrd, but his interests shifted to Benjamin Britten when he sensed that the times were right for an honest treatment of Britten's sexuality in relation to his creative work. His article "Britten and Grimes," *Musical Times* 118 (December 1977): 995–1000, was a turning point not only in Brett's career, but in the wider world of music scholarship, and led to his selection as an interview subject by Lawrence Mass. Brett's plea to retire Chaikovsky was sooner a plea to include others (by now, many others indeed) in the narrative than a call for surcease.—Ed.

[3] Subsequently published as Alexander Poznansky, *Tchaikovsky: The Quest for the Inner Man* (New York: Schirmer, 1991).

[4] Alexander Poznansky, "Tchaikovsky's Suicide: Myth and Reality," *19th-Century Music* 11, no. 3 (Spring 1988): 199–220.

known about for decades, as the letters and diaries Poznansky cites show) might besmirch the honor of their alma mater.

The suicide hypothesis, launched by the Soviet musicologist Aleksandra Orlova in a series of articles she published from 1980 on, after moving here from the Soviet Union, was debunked by critics, historians, and scholars familiar with Russian social and musical history, myself included. Alan M. Kriegsman, in his article "The Great Suicide Debate," described Orlova's "proof" as "a tissue of inferences from one unsupported conjecture to another" and wrote that "by the same logic we could also decree that Tchaikovsky consorted with grizzly bears and was the real author of Wagner's *Ring of the Nibelung*."[5]

But Orlova's version was enthusiastically embraced by such luminaries of music and dance criticism as Donal Henahan of the *New York Times*, whose wildly uninformed account was reprinted by newspapers all over the English-speaking world; Arlene Croce of the *New Yorker*; and David Brown, the British author of the projected four-volume biography of Chaikovsky, of which three volumes have already appeared.[6] Brown is also responsible for getting the suicide version into the pages of the authoritative *New Grove Dictionary of Music and Musicians*, and into three music dictionaries published by Oxford University Press between 1983 and 1986.[7]

Poznansky's essay comes as a breath of fresh air, because unlike the proponents of the forced suicide theory he really knows and can demonstrate the key issues involved: the amply documented circumstances of the composer's actual death; the attitudes toward homosexuality in Russia during the 1890s, with particular reference to the court of Alexander III and the School of Jurisprudence; the health precautions taken against the cholera epidemic during which the composer died; the unfortunate series

---

[5] Alan M. Kriegsman, "The Great Suicide Debate," *Washington Post*, 28 March 1982.

[6] David Brown, *Tchaikovsky: A Biographical and Critical Study*, 4 vols. (New York: W. W. Norton, 1978–92). Vol. 4 was published four years after this article.—Ed.

[7] The three Oxford University Press dictionaries: *The New Oxford Companion to Music*, ed. Denis Arnold (1983); *The Oxford Dictionary of Music*, ed. Michael Kennedy (1985); and *The Concise Oxford Dictionary of Opera*, 2nd ed., ed. Harold Rosenthal and John Warrack (1980). Brown's article on Chaikovsky in *The New Grove Dictionary of Music and Musicians* (London: Macmillan, 1980) was replaced in the second edition (2001) with one by Roland John Wiley that reverted to an equivocal stance about the circumstances of the composer's death.—Ed.

of circumstances that delayed the diagnosis of the disease, which was curable then if caught in time; and even the actions of various known poisons on the human organism in comparison with the symptoms experienced by Chaikovsky. Where Orlova and those who believe her offer conjecture, legend, and rumor, Poznansky has amassed a profusion of solid, verifiable evidence which slowly but surely dissolves the bogus construct of Aleksandra Orlova and David Brown right before the reader's eyes. Those who read French might also want to look at Nina Berberova's new preface to the 1987 edition of her biography of the composer, *Tchaïkovski*, where she describes the various gay coteries that existed in Moscow and St. Petersburg in the 1890s and the relative tolerance with which individual homosexuals were treated in the army, the arts, and at the imperial court during the time when "poor old" Chaikovsky was allegedly forced to kill himself for being gay.[8]

No, this is not the time to retire him and his "homosexual tragedy" symphony (his Sixth Symphony in B Minor), if only because during the past two decades the study of Chaikovsky's life has been left to people with little sympathy for—and even less understanding of—what it means to be a homosexual. I lost all interest in David Brown's highly acclaimed multivolume biography-in-progress when I read in the first volume about the "growths of psychological abnormality which insidiously bound themselves round him" and which, according to Brown, "unbalance[ed] his emotional life" so that it could not "channel itself into the closest of personal relationships."[9] Reviewing that first volume, the knowledgeable American musicologist Malcolm Hamrick Brown wrote that if Chaikovsky were as psychotic as David Brown portrayed him he "would have ended in a mental institution, not in the halls of Cambridge University to receive a Doctor of Music degree, *honoris causa*."[10]

---

[8] See "Préface à l'édition de 1987," in Nina Berberova, *Tchaïkovski: Biographie* (Paris: Actes Sud, 1987 [paperback repr., 2004]). The book was originally published in Russian (*Chaikovskii: Istoriia odinokoi zhizni* [Berlin: Petropolis, 1936]) and was at that time the only serious treatment by a Western writer of Chaikovsky's sexuality. The new preface, translated by Vincent Giroud as "Looking Back at Tchaikovsky," was published in *Yale Review* 80, no. 3 (July 1992): 60–73.—Ed.

[9] Brown, *Tchaikovsky*, 1:50.

[10] *Journal of the American Musicological Society* 33 (1980): 405. To appreciate the wittiness of the good Brown's retort to the bad, one needs the original context. David Brown had justified his crude description of Chaikovsky's "psychological abnorma-

Even more offensive is the biography *Tchaikovsky* by Edward Garden.[11] Quite early in his book, Garden equates homosexuality with the inability "to feel sexually aroused" or "to establish a firm, constant, and loving relationship with any other human being."[12] Later in the book we read that "the frustrations of his endemic homosexuality" marred the music of Chaikovsky's Fourth Symphony and that the composer's sex life was either autoerotic or confined to homosexual fantasies. No wonder that Garden found reading Chaikovsky's diaries (published by his brother Ippolit in 1923) "quite frankly rather dull."[13] The diaries contain several instances of Chaikovsky's loving and, if read carefully, sexual relationships with various men, but Garden's obvious homophobia prevented him from taking into consideration the evidence of these diaries.

As for Aleksandra Orlova, whose authority in Chaikovsky studies has been taken for granted by so many American critics and journalists, here are some excerpts from her article "Tchaikovsky's Tragedy and Gorbachev's *Glasnost*," which appeared in the New York Russian newspaper *Novoe russkoe slovo* on 25 January 1987. The tone is typical of Orlova's other writings on the subject. "It's no secret that the composer suffered from the congenital anomaly of being a homosexual. In my other publications I have described how he was tormented by this anomaly throughout his life, the anomaly that was a calamity, a curse laid on him by fate," Orlova says. And a few lines later: "Being a highly decent and honorable man, he regarded his anomaly as a disgrace that could never be effaced." This, despite Chaikovsky's descriptions in his letters and diaries of the happiness that his relationships with other men had brought him! Elsewhere, Orlova denied the possibility that the composer and his former classmate, the poet Aleksei Apukhtin, were lovers at one time, as suggested in certain memoirs. That was impossible, Orlova claimed, because both Chaikovsky and Apukhtin were "active homosexuals" and as such,

---

lity" by citing "the extremity of his case." Malcolm Brown: "An 'extreme case' would have ended in a mental institution, not in the halls of Cambridge," etc. Chaikovsky's career was evidence of "a highly adaptive, even successful adjustment to his psychological condition."—Ed.

11 Edward Garden, *Tchaikovsky* (London: J. M. Dent, 1973); reissued in paperback in 1976 and still available in most music stores.
12 Ibid., 16–17.
13 Ibid., 45.

they could relate sexually only to "passive homosexuals." No, let's not "retire" Chaikovsky just when his biography has become the province of ignorance and homophobia.

As for his Sixth Symphony, the degree to which it was and is misunderstood is shown by the fact that it still can be called an expression of "homosexual tragedy." The subtitle of this symphony is usually rendered with the French word *pathétique*. This is quite misleading because the prime meaning of this French adjective is the same as that of the English "pathetic," that is, "arousing pity." The Russian *pateticheskii*, according to *The Oxford Russian-English Dictionary*, has the following meanings: (1) enthusiastic; passionate; (2) emotional; (3) bombastic.[14] I am reasonably sure that the meaning Chaikovsky had in mind was "passionate," a meaning vastly different from the English "pathetic" or its French cognate.

We know that his two earlier symphonies, the Fourth and the Fifth, were program music. The program of the Fourth, described in detail in the oft-cited letter from Chaikovsky to his grandmotherly patroness Nadezhda von Meck, had to do with an individual's difficulties in integrating himself into the larger society. The Fifth described the conflict between a human being's desires and plans and the implacable fate that could thwart them.[15] Chaikovsky found it hard to begin his Sixth Symphony until, as he confided to his gay younger brother Modest, he decided to embody in it a private, secret program that would not be revealed to the public. Modest pointed out that the proposed subtitle, *Programmnaia* (Programmatic), would expose its author to endless questions as to the nature of that program. Modest then suggested *Tragicheskaia* (Tragic) and, when that was rejected, came up with *Pateticheskaia* (Passionate).

---

[14] *The Oxford Russian-English Dictionary* (London: Clarendon Press, 1972).

[15] For the letter about the Fourth Symphony, see P. I. Chaikovskii, *Polnoe sobranie sochinenii: Literaturnye proizvedeniia i perepiska*, vol. 7 (Moscow: Gos. muzykal'noe izd-vo, 1962), 124–27; trans. in full in *Music in the Western World: A History in Documents*, selected and annotated by Piero Weiss and Richard Taruskin, 2nd ed. (Belmont, CA: Thomson/Schirmer, 2008), 339–42. The very sketchy program of the Fifth was found after Chaikovsky's death among his papers: "Intr[oduction]. Complete submission before Fate, or, which is the same, before the inscrut[able] predestination of Providence. Allegro. (1) Murmur of doubt, complaints, reproaches to XXX. (2) To leap into the embrace of *Faith*??? A wonderful program if only it can be carried out…. *Consolation*. A ray of light…. No, no hope!" (as translated in Poznansky, *Tchaikovsky*, 490).—Ed.

Almost all books on Chaikovsky mention that the Sixth Symphony had a secret program. I heard something about that program when I was about seventeen or eighteen and too young and careless to sit down and write what I had heard. I realize that what I am about to offer is poorly remembered hearsay, and that by doing so I descend to the level of Aleksandra Orlova, whom I have twice criticized in print for relying on unverifiable statements of people long since dead. But I do not maintain that what I say is true, only that it was told to me.

Some time in 1941, a friend of my youth named Alex came back to Los Angeles from New York, where he had spent several months associating with the Russian-born painter Pavel Tchelitchew (more correctly, Chelishchev; those who want to know more about Alex may look up my memoir, "In Search of Poplavsky: A Collage").[16] Alex was gifted as both a pianist and a painter. From Tchelitchew, who had in the 1920s designed scenery and costumes for Sergei Diaghilev, in his turn a close friend in his youth of Modest Chaikovsky's, Alex had heard about the composer's private life and the secret program of his Sixth Symphony.

"Did you know that Chaikovsky enjoyed being screwed by his servant Alyosha?" Alex asked me casually one day. (I now know that Alyosha was Aleksei Sofronov, Chaikovsky's long-time loyal valet and his frequent bed partner.) "And that the climax of the Sixth Symphony depicts that enjoyment?" Then, as we listened to a 78 r.p.m. recording of the symphony, I was told the following outline of its first movement.

The murky bassoon and viola music at the opening of the first movement (inspired by the beginning of Wagner's *Das Rheingold*) shows early, half-conscious stirrings of the attraction to other men. The fast Allegro non troppo section that follows is a feverish search within oneself and in the external world for ways to express this attraction. The expressive melody in D major, marked Andante (the second theme of the movement), portrays the feeling of loving and being loved by the man of one's choice. This theme comprises all the notes of the D-major scale except for the leading tone (C-sharp), so that although this is authentic love music,

---

16 In *The Bitter Air of Exile: Russian Writers in the West 1922–1972*, ed. Simon Karlinsky and Alfred Appel, Jr. (Berkeley: University of California Press, 1973), 311–33 [reprinted in the present volume].

it is incapable of the usual resolution (into, say, a marriage) as the more conventional forms of love can be.

The love music is given a powerful build-up. Then it subsides in a drooping clarinet solo. Next it is furiously pounced upon by the brutal rhythms of the Allegro vivo. The theme of the feverish search scurries frantically trying to escape or to hide from this incomprehension and hostility. Everything seems lost. During a brief lull in this raging orchestral storm, the low brass intones a portion of the Russian Orthodox funeral canticle "May He/She Rest with the Saints." But the "search theme" does not give up and with the arrival of a prolonged pedal tone (the low F-sharp in the basses and timpani that lasts for thirty-six bars), it finds a safe haven. In the powerful new section that begins at the eleventh bar of this pedal, the two male lovers have found a safe environment in which they can finally achieve the physical union they crave.

In the middle range, the brief, stabbing phrases of the trombones and the tuba represent the actual penetration of the composer by his sexy servant (or, possibly, the other way around), while in the ethereal heights above, the slowly descending D-major scale, the key of the preceding love music, is the happiness and gratitude the two lovers feel as they obtain what they so desperately need. This time, the scale does have the C-sharp, but because it is descending, there is still no conventional resolution.

The climax of this sexual act is not shown. (In the twentieth century, Richard Strauss would use horn glissandos to depict an ejaculation in the prelude to *Der Rosenkavalier*, while still later Shostakovich was to portray through suggestive trombone slides the actual copulation of his heterosexual lovers and the man's subsequent detumescence in *Lady Macbeth of the Mtsensk District*.) Instead of a climax, Chaikovsky transfigures the love music of the second theme by transposing it into the key of B major and placing it in a new harmonic and instrumental environment, which suggests that love survives into the postcoital stage. A gentle, sighing coda concludes this encounter between two male lovers who succeeded in escaping from the disapproval and anger of the outside world.

I remember the program of the first movement because I told it to someone or other every few years since I first heard it. There were more explanations about the program of the rest of the symphony, but I am sorry to say that I forgot them. I cannot recollect what the stumbling waltz in five-quarter time of the second movement represented, nor the mischievous march, built on the ceaseless interval of leaping fourths. I do recall that the finale of the symphony was meant as a requiem for a friend and former lover who died.

This could have been a number of men: Edouard, whose death the composer mourns in one of his diaries; Ivan Verinovsky, an army officer with whom he had an affair in the Caucasus, during a visit to his brother Anatoly and his wife (Verinovsky, to Chaikovsky's horror, shot himself after the composer refused to make their relationship permanent); or Aleksei Apukhtin, who died at about the time the symphony was composed.

The Sixth Symphony was dedicated to the composer's gay nephew Vladimir ("Bob") Davydov, with whom Chaikovsky was in love since Bob was a teenager and who was by 1893 old enough to respond, perhaps, to his uncle's love. The program of the symphony could thus be Chaikovsky's confession of his past loves to Bob (who was the first to learn that the new symphony was to have a private, intimate program).

Yes, I know, this is speculation based on hearsay. But after about a month of reading Chaikovsky's diaries and letters and then turning to Aleksandra Orlova's and Edward Garden's writings on one of my favorite composers, I can't help feeling that I prefer what I heard in 1941—at least until some biographies appear that understand his times and his love life as well as do Nina Berberova and Aleksandr Poznansky, whom I cited at the beginning of this *cri de cœur* on Chaikovsky's behalf. An ad for a book on Chaikovsky which I tore out of a magazine a few years ago proclaims in large blue letters: A SCARED, PSYCHOTIC GENIUS. See what I mean?

* * *

Opinions differ as to the seriousness with which SK advanced his sexual hermeneutics in this now-celebrated article. As always, context is key. His writings on Chaikovsky can be read as an index to his increasingly open, engaged, and uninhibited participation in gay journalism. Read in sequence, they track his mounting enjoyment of his new role. His tone modulates from severe reproof to endearing *méchanterie*, the implied facial expression from furrowed brow to winking grin. There are many winks in "Should We Retire Chaikovsky?" to serve as signals that he was, in a spirit of parody, committing an Orlovian or Brownian sin of his own, producing a reading, based on an oral tradition, that was calculated to shock or titillate the Orlovas and Gardens and Browns. The most obvious winks are the pseudoapologies that serve as preface ("I realize that what I am about to offer is poorly remembered hearsay, and that by doing so I descend to the level of Aleksandra Orlova") and epilogue ("Yes, I know, this is speculation based on hearsay [, b]ut ... I prefer what I heard in 1941") to his *explication de texte*—which, by the way, offers, in its musical details, far more evidence than Orlova or David Brown have ever offered for their confident diagnoses.[17] Best of all is the deadpan announcement that "I do not maintain that what I say is true, only that it was told to me." That effectively demolishes the suicide theory, which had been advanced by naive scholars incapable of making that crucial distinction.

Withal, SK implies, hearing the Sixth Symphony as a description of gay lovemaking is a perfectly legitimate enhancement of one's pleasure in the work, so long as one makes no specious claims as to the composer's intentions. Here he writes in solidarity with so-called opera queens who freely substitute their own imagined plot twists, either ironic or subversive, for those of the score and libretto, both for the sake of private enjoyment and as political armor.[18]

---

[17] The editors of *Christopher Street* tried to help out with a few score pages for illustration, but chose some from the wrong movement of the symphony, much to SK's annoyance: "If there was to be any musical citing, surely the 'homosexual tragedy' passages in the finale were the least suitable for the points I tried to make!" SK to Frank Conway, 27 June 1988, carton no. 7, Simon Karlinsky Papers, BANC MSS 2010/177, The Bancroft Library, University of California, Berkeley.

[18] See Mitchell Morris, "Reading as an Opera Queen," in *Musicology and Difference: Gender and Sexuality in Musical Scholarship*, ed. Ruth A. Solie (Berkeley: University of California Press, 1993), 184–200; and Wayne Koestenbaum, *The Queen's Throat: Opera, Homosexuality, and the Mystery of Desire* (New York: Poseidon, 1993). Both are roughly contemporary with the present essay.

Man or Myth?
The Retrieval of the True Chaikovsky[1]

A look at any CD catalogue or at the yearly plan of any symphony orchestra around the world will confirm the secure place of Chaikovsky's music in the repertoire. Conductors, instrumentalists, and singers, from his day to ours, have loved to perform his music. But the enthusiasm of the public and the performers has not yet been matched by a corresponding appreciation or even acceptance by his biographers, music critics, and other commentators. In what used to be the Soviet Union, compulsory nationalistic idolatry of Chaikovsky went hand in hand with a ban on all information about his personal life or his conservative political views. In the West, interest and enthusiasm have always been accompanied by critical incomprehension and hostility.

A comment by the venerable Eduard Hanslick at the time of the 1881 Vienna world premiere of Chaikovsky's Violin Concerto to the effect that this was music one "could hear emit a stench" is attributable to Western prejudice against Eastern Europe; people then could not quite believe that a Russian could produce a world-class masterpiece. But the contemptuous dismissal of Chaikovsky's music by such heavyweights of twentieth-century musicology and criticism as Donald Francis Tovey, Paul Henry Lang and Edward Lockspeiser was due, as Richard Taruskin pointed out in a recent article, not to the quality of the music itself but to the critics' perception of the composer and his character.[2]

---

[1] Review of *Tchaikovsky: A Biographical and Critical Study*, vol. 4, *The Final Years, 1885-1893*, by David Brown (New York: W. W. Norton, 1992); and *Tchaikovsky: The Quest for the Inner Man*, by Alexander Poznansky (New York: Schirmer, 1991). Originally published as "Man or Myth?: The Retrieval of the True Tchaikovksy [sic]" in *Times Literary Supplement*, 17 January 1992, 20–21.

[2] The article referenced here is "Tchaikovsky, Fallen from Grace," *New York Times*, 30 June 1991; for a more comprehensive treatment of the same material, see R. Taruskin, "Pathetic Symphonist: Chaikovsky, Russia, Sexuality, and the Study of Music," *New Republic*, 6 February 1995; repr. with an update in Taruskin, *On Russian Music* (Berkeley: University of California Press, 2009), 76–104.—Ed.

IV. On Chaikovsky

As someone who considers Chaikovsky one of the great composers of all time and tries to read everything published about him, I was tremendously heartened by the appearance a few years ago of two studies of his music written by younger scholars: *Tchaikovsky's Ballets* by Roland J. Wiley and *Tchaikovsky's Musical Style* by Henry Zajaczkowski.[3] Both authors demonstrated the freshness and originality of Chaikovsky's musical procedures, and Zajaczkowski, in particular, stressed the organic nature of Chaikovsky's handling of form, harmony, tonality, and orchestration. In neither book was there a trace of the squeamish distaste so usual in serious critical writing on this composer in English.

These two specialized studies stand in curious contrast to the three critical biographies produced in England over the past two decades.[4] Of the latter, John Warrack's lavishly illustrated *Tchaikovsky* is an attractive, straightforward guide to the man and his music, treating both with fairness, but breaking no new ground and offering no new research. Edward Garden's *Tchaikovsky* reverts to the earlier pattern of incomprehension and hostility. Quite early in the book, the reader is informed that Chaikovsky's homosexuality meant that he was "unable to feel sexually aroused" and could not "establish a firm, constant and loving relationship with any other human being," and therefore suffered from "loneliness which was the lot in those days of the homosexual." Later in the book we read that "the frustrations of his endemic homosexuality" marred the music of Chaikovsky's Fourth Symphony and that his love life was either autoerotic or confined to homosexual fantasies. Chaikovsky's rich and rewarding love life and his sexual adventures are recorded in his published correspondence and in the diaries brought out by his brother Ippolit.[5] But, like many others, Edward Garden was not interested in finding out about the real Pyotr Chaikovsky who lived from 1840 to 1893. He chose to depict, instead, the widespread popular myth of the lonely,

---

[3] Roland John Wiley, *Tchaikovsky's Ballets: Swan Lake, Sleeping Beauty, Nutcracker* (Oxford: Oxford University Press, 1985); Henry Zajaczkowski, *Tchaikovsky's Musical Style* (Ann Arbor, MI: UMI Research, 1987).

[4] John Warrack, *Tchaikovsky* (New York: Scribner's Sons, 1973); Edward Garden, *Tchaikovsky* (London: J. M. Dent, 1973); David Brown, *Tchaikovsky: A Biographical and Critical Study*, 4 vols. (New York: W. W. Norton, 1978–92).

[5] Petr Chaikovskii, *Dnevniki* [Diaries], *1873–1891* (Moscow and Petrograd: Glavlit, 1923), published in English as *The Diaries of Tchaikovsky*, trans. Wladimir Lakond (New York: W. W. Norton, 1945).

guilty, frustrated homosexual living out his life on the verge of a nervous breakdown or even insanity.

David Brown's four-volume *Tchaikovsky: A Biographical and Critical Study* began to appear in 1978 and is complete with the publication of its fourth volume. With its vast bulk, it is surely the most ambitious work on the subject ever undertaken. As a biographer, Brown amassed more information on Chaikovsky than any predecessor, and as a musicologist, he examined the composer's entire corpus. Because of the scope of the whole, each succeeding volume was hailed in the press of English-speaking countries as part of one of the greatest biographies of a cultural figure written in any language. Yet, now that all four volumes are available, I feel painfully disappointed. The understanding of Russian culture is often shaky, there is a poor grasp of the historical period, and Chaikovsky's individual qualities are barely perceptible.

Reviewing Brown's first volume in 1980, Malcolm Hamrick Brown expressed regret over the narrow range of biographical sources to which David Brown restricted himself. In this and in some other respects, David Brown shows himself to be a disciple of the Soviet music historian Aleksandra Orlova, whose help he acknowledges in the prefaces to each one of his volumes. In her writings on Chaikovsky published since her departure for the West in 1979 and especially in her sensationalist claims about the circumstances of the composer's death, Orlova limited her purview and manipulated the available evidence to foster her singular conception of the man and his music. In her view, Chaikovsky suffered all his life from being unable to overcome his homosexuality, a condition he regarded as "a curse laid on him by fate" and "a disgrace that could never be effaced." Much of his music is interpreted by Orlova as a sort of howl of despair caused by this ceaseless suffering.

Little of this is borne out by the composer's diaries or the memoirs about him, but David Brown must have found Orlova's interpretations congenial. In his first volume, he disqualified himself from "any deep elucidation of [Chaikovsky's] personality" on the grounds that he is "not a medical psychologist." But no medical qualifications were needed by the people who wrote successful biographies of Lytton Strachey, E. M. Forster, Somerset Maugham and other notable homosexuals—only a minimal understanding of what homosexuality is and how homosexuals fared in a particular culture during a given historical period. Instead of examining

IV. On Chaikovsky

Chaikovsky's individual situation against the background of his society, Brown follows the examples of Edward Garden and Aleksandra Orlova and sets up the familiar anguished, suicidal homosexual figure of the popular myth. We read about the "growths of psychological abnormality which insidiously bound themselves round him, constricting, distorting and unbalancing his emotional life," thus making the composer unable to form "the closest of personal relationships." In his four volumes, Brown writes of a number of men with whom Chaikovsky formed relationships of precisely this kind. But the author's obvious distaste for the entire subject prevents him from recognizing them for what they were.

The epithets that most frequently occur in Brown's discussions of Chaikovsky's music are "flawed" and "second-rate." His enthusiasm is reserved for the composer's most acclaimed works: the Violin Concerto, the Sixth Symphony, the ballets, and the two most familiar operas, *Evgeny Onegin* and *The Queen of Spades*. Otherwise, some of Chaikovsky's most beautifully wrought scores receive either curt dismissals or ill-tempered scoldings. His lovely last opera, *Iolanta*, with its unique subject—a musical portrayal of blindness and of the trauma experienced upon gaining sight as an adult—is judged a failure, a "slender, pretty, but also insipid piece." The wonderful string sextet, "Souvenir de Florence," is proclaimed second-rate. The symphonic fantasy *Francesca da Rimini* is "flawed" because it is an expression of Chaikovsky's own "feelings of sexual guilt." (Ten pages earlier, Brown cited the composer's letter to his brother Modest where he maintained that he had never felt guilty for the way nature made him.) The Third Symphony, the finale of the Fourth, and the Second Piano Concerto ("irredeemably handicapped") are described in a tone of condescension shading off into contempt.

Of course, no composition by Chaikovsky is contemptible, not even the Piano Sonata, which receives a veritable tongue-lashing in Brown's book. Nor is it usual for biographers of composers who enjoy a worldwide fame to take such a jaundiced view of their subject and his oeuvre. The ultimate impression is that David Brown loves some of Chaikovsky's music, but detests his way of life to the point where his idea that the man is "flawed" spills over into the evaluation of his work. This would account for the continuous efforts to discredit the composer's less well-known works and to cast doubt on Chaikovsky's universally admired melodic inventiveness by either suggesting that the melodies are derivative (unconvincingly illustrated by musical citations from Berlioz, Beethoven, Glinka, etc., which Chaikovsky supposedly copied), or by finding in these melodies codes and ciphers that purportedly spell out names of people and places. Hugh Macdonald, a critic who seems to despise Chaikovsky ("a prancing pouf"), nevertheless published in 1983 a searching review of David Brown's second volume where he showed how arbitrary and unreliable this decoding of Chaikovsky's melodies is.[6]

After all the recent biographies that lack a minimal understanding of Chaikovsky's sexual orientation and reduce his life to stereotypes, the publication of Aleksandr Poznansky's *Tchaikovsky: The Quest for the Inner Man* comes like a fresh breeze through a stuffy room.[7] For the first time since the appearance of Nina Berberova's *biographie romancée* in 1936 (it was reissued in French in 1987), Chaikovsky's story is told by someone who knows his period and his milieu intimately and has taken the trouble to understand his emotional experiences. Poznansky is not a musicologist but a social and cultural historian. The complaints by a few of the earlier reviewers of his book about the lack of musical analysis miss the whole point. No figure of comparable importance has had his biography and personality so utterly distorted by musicologists. It is the personal story of Chaikovsky, placed within the context of his time, that was desperately needed in English, and this is exactly what Poznansky provides. His is the first factually reliable literary portrait of this composer ever written and certainly a welcome one.

Poznansky draws on a larger body of source material than any other biographer—not only the censored and uncensored publications that appeared in Soviet times, but also a considerable body of prerevolutionary publications, such as the memoirs of Chaikovsky's wife, which Aleksandra Orlova (and, following her example, David Brown) did not bother to consult. We learn that certain character traits considered by some to be typically Russian, and by others as peculiarly Chaikovskian—sentimentality, melancholy, a penchant for weeping—were the result of his upbringing in the family headed by his father Ilya, a man who belonged

---

[6] "Tchaikovsky: Crises and Contortions," review of *Tchaikovsky*, vol. 2, *The Crisis Years, 1874–1878*, by David Brown, *Musical Times* 124 (October 1983): 609, 611–12.

[7] More recently Poznansky published a 2-volume biography of Chaikovsky in Russian: Aleksandr Poznanskii, *Petr Chaikovskii: Biografiia* (St. Petersburg: Vita nova, 2009).—Ed.

in a sentimentalist novel of the end of the eighteenth century rather than in the second half of the nineteenth. Without any prejudice, Poznansky examines the various levels of the homosexual subculture that existed in Chaikovsky's time. As anyone who has studied that period in depth will know, there was an amazing degree of tolerance for homosexuality during the reigns of the last two tsars, something that can be verified by examining the lives of such contemporaries of Chaikovsky as the explorer Nikolai Przhevalsky, the poet Aleksei Apukhtin and the publisher Prince Vladimir Meshchersky. Many names that float barely identified through the other biographies—Nikolai Bochechkarov, Aleksei Sofronov, Iosif Kotek—acquire concrete reality as the composer's lovers or gay friends.

Poznansky's book easily disproves Aleksandra Orlova's story that the composer committed suicide by taking poison on the orders of a "court of honor" convoked by his one-time fellow students at the School of Jurisprudence. Where Orlova based her version exclusively on unverifiable, third-hand rumors and the testimony of people who never knew Chaikovsky, Poznansky, facts and historical evidence in hand, shows that this composer's death from cholera was one of the best-documented deaths on record and that because of a whole series of historical circumstances, the events described by Orlova could not possibly have happened.

The Chaikovsky portrayed in this biography is tremendously likeable: kindly, generous, cultivated and, quite often, happy. The book joins the musicological works of Wiley and Zajaczkowski as an instance of the new type of Chaikovsky studies: informed, imaginative, and treating both the man and his music with sympathy and respect.

**

Of course SK's review enraged David Brown and incited a blustery letter of protest to the editor of the *TLS*, which appeared in the issue of 7 February 1992. "I am honoured to find myself aligned beside 'such heavyweights' of musical criticism as Donald Francis Tovey and Paul Henry Lang," he began, as if oblivious to the invidious context in which those names had been invoked. He defended himself, together with Edward Garden, against the imputation of prudish hostility toward Chaikovsky with a well-aimed boomerang: "I think the trouble may be that we examine the evidence, then attempt to establish the truth, rather than make up our minds what we want the truth to be, and then try to square the evidence with this." He attempted to laugh off Poznansky's book by quoting from a scurrilous review that matched his own prejudices.[8] "But what I simply cannot stomach," he finally confessed, "is to be found wanting beside a *biographie romancée* of Nina Berberova. How, sir, do you think H. C. Robbins Landon or Julian Budden would have felt if, say, Barbara Cartland had written a romantic biography of Haydn or Verdi, and their views of these composers had then been judged less perceptive than hers?"

Terrible, no doubt; but the analogy was shaky. Robbins Landon and Budden were, like Brown, authors of multivolume monographs.[9] But placing himself on the level of these distinguished nonacademic writers was as big a blunder as was placing Nina Berberova, a major scholar as well as a *romancière* (and a writer with whom Dr. Brown was evidently unfamiliar), on a level with Barbara Cartland. SK was no Postmodernist à la Hayden White,[10] but he did recognize (and, in this review, forcefully affirmed) the principle that knowledge of facts without precise knowledge of social context is as fatal to historiography as imagination without knowledge of social realities is to the writing of fiction.

---

8   Paul Griffiths, "Outing Peter Ilyich," *New York Times Book Review*, 5 January 1992.
9   H. C. Robbins Landon, *Haydn: Chronicle and Works*, 5 vols. (London: Thames and Hudson, 1976–80); Julian Budden, *The Operas of Verdi*, 3 vols. (London: Cassell, 1973–81).
10 In, say, *The Content of the Form: Narrative Discourse and Historical Representation* (Baltimore: Johns Hopkins University Press, 1987), a study of figurative language in historical writing, which is often accused of attempting to erase the line between history and fiction.

Chaikovsky
and the Pantomime of Derision[1]

After thirty years of teaching and writing about Russian literature and culture, I've discovered a principle that is something halfway between a paradox and a parlor game. It amounts to the question: what do prerevolutionary Russia and homosexuality have in common? Answer: both are regarded by many people in this country as rather distasteful topics about which they'd rather not hear. And both are discussed with great vehemence and self-assurance by people who know little or nothing about them. I can think of no other subjects to which this situation would apply. We cannot imagine anyone writing or lecturing about, say, Shakespeare or nuclear physics or even home gardening without first gaining some firsthand knowledge about these things. Yet, for much of my life, I've been hearing and reading people holding forth on either homosexuality or Russia's pre–October Revolution past from positions of either partial or total ignorance.

Thus, when Boris Yeltsin was elected president of the Russian Republic (before the disintegration of the Soviet Union), then-president George H. W. Bush took to calling him the first man ever elected to office in Russian history. As far back as the fourteenth and fifteenth centuries, however, the city of Novgorod in the north of Russia was an independent mercantile republic which chose its aldermen and other officials by popular elections. Just before its subjugation by Moscow in the 1470s, Novgorod even had a woman mayor, Marfa Boretskaya. During Russia's parliamentary period, 1905–17, hundreds of representatives were elected all over the country and sent to the State Duma. Between the Revolutions of February and October 1917, there were democratically elected mayors in both Moscow and St. Petersburg. Hundreds of deputies, from

---

[1] Originally published as "Chaikovskii and the Pantomime of Derision" in *O Rus!: Studia Litteraria Slavica in Honorem Hugh McLean*, ed. Simon Karlinsky, James L. Rice, and Barry P. Sherr (Oakland: Berkeley Slavic Specialties, 1995), 47–56.

all over the country, came to the Constituent Assembly at which they were to choose the form of postrevolutionary government in Russia. All this makes Boris Yeltsin not the first Russian elected to office, as President Bush would have had it, but perhaps the seven-thousandth.

As for instances of discussing homosexuality by people who know nothing at all about it, one could quote quite a selection, from Maksim Gorky's "Destroy homosexuality and fascism will disappear from this world" to Anita Bryant's memorable "They cannot reproduce, so they have to recruit."[2] One area where the lack of information on prerevolutionary Russia and the lack of understanding about homosexuality converge into a focus is the study of the life and music of the great composer Pyotr Ilich Chaikovsky, who lived from 1840 to 1893. His music was appreciated and loved in his lifetime, both in his country and abroad. It was performed by the finest orchestras, soloists, and opera companies of his time (as it still is). Chaikovsky was invited to Cambridge University in England to receive an honorary doctorate, and travelled to New York to conduct his music for the opening of Carnegie Hall.

Chaikovsky was also a life-long homosexual, something that was generally known through the grapevine when he was alive. The situation of Russian homosexuals in the last decades of the nineteenth century was more similar to the one in France (the country where many gay Englishmen, threatened with disclosure or scandal, would flee throughout the nineteenth century) than the one in Germany, England, or the United States. For example, during the trial of Oscar Wilde in 1895, two years after Chaikovsky's death, the press of the English-speaking countries unanimously wrote of Wilde with revulsion and contempt. But the Russian press, like the press in France, took Oscar Wilde's side, seeing his case as persecution of a talented artist by the hypocritical and puritanical British authorities.

If you study the period, you find many prominent homosexuals, quite a few of them lesbians, in society, in the arts, and at the imperial court.[3]

---

2   Maksim Gor'kii, "Proletarskii gumanizm," in *Sobranie sochinenii v 30 tomakh* [Collected writings in 30 volumes], vol. 27 (Moscow: Gosizdat, 1953), 238. This essay originally appeared in both *Pravda* and *Izvestiia* on 23 May 1934.
3   Simon Karlinsky, "Russia's Gay Literature and Culture: The Impact of the October Revolution," in *Hidden from History: Reclaiming the Gay and Lesbian Past*, ed. Martin Bauml Duberman, Martha Vicinus, and George Chauncey, Jr. (New York: New American Library, 1989), 347–64 and 552–59.

IV. On Chaikovsky

At the apex of the gay pyramid stood the Grand Duke Sergei Aleksandrovich, the brother of Tsar Alexander III and the uncle of Nicholas II. The Grand Duke Sergei was quite open about his orientation, bringing his current lover to court functions, parades, balls, and the theater and opera. One of the Paris newspapers, announcing his visit to that city, wrote that the grand duke was accompanied by his mistress, Mr. So-and-so.[4] The reactionary editor and newspaper publisher Prince Vladimir Meshchersky, whom Chaikovsky knew from school, was openly gay and a valued advisor of the last two tsars. When Meshchersky got into major trouble after seducing a bugle boy from the imperial marching band, Alexander III had the case quashed and the witnesses silenced.[5] All this needs to be pointed out because so many biographies of Chaikovsky stress his constant fear of exposure and his resulting depressed state during much of his life.

This is a widespread view, to which I myself used to subscribe before I learned how wrong it was. In a survey of Russian gay history published eighteen years ago, I wrote that "Chaikovsky's oft-described life was a continual round of pain, fear of exposure and desperate sporadic efforts to change his inner nature."[6] Eventually I came to understand that this popular image was not factual. It was definitively demolished with the publication of Aleksandr Poznansky's thoroughly researched biography *Tchaikovsky: The Quest for the Inner Man* (see note 5). This book was especially important, coming as it did after two decades, the 1970s and the 1980s, when the field of Chaikovsky studies in English came to be dominated by people ignorant of both Russian history and the phenomenon of homosexuality.

Chaikovsky's first biographer was his younger brother Modest. It was in Modest's St. Petersburg apartment that Chaikovsky died of complications from cholera on Sunday, 25 October 1893. Late in the evening of

---

[4] Alexander Poznansky, "Tchaikovsky's Suicide: Myth and Reality," *19th-Century Music* 11, no. 3 (Spring 1988): 203.

[5] Alexander Poznansky, *Tchaikovsky: The Quest for the Inner Man* (New York: Schirmer, 1991), 235ff. and 482ff.

[6] Simon Karlinsky, "Russia's Gay Literature and History (11th–20th Centuries)," *Gay Sunshine*, nos. 29/30 (Summer/Fall 1976): 1–7. [See *Gay Sunshine*, no. 31 (Winter 1977) for polemics about this piece and correction of errors. A revised version is in *Gay Roots: Twenty Years of Gay Sunshine* (San Francisco: Gay Sunshine Press, 1991), 81–104.—Ed.]

the 20th, the composer had supper at Leiner's restaurant, where, as it was shown later, he was served a glass of unboiled water. The symptoms of the illness first appeared the next morning, but the composer and his brother both assumed it was a case of upset stomach, something from which Chaikovsky often suffered. There was a cholera epidemic in the city and the water supply of St. Petersburg was known to have been contaminated with cholera bacilli.

Many biographers of Chaikovsky believed that his death could be blamed on the negligence of Modest Chaikovsky, who was supposedly preoccupied with the rehearsals of his new comedy and did not get medical aid for his brother until it was too late. But as the recent reconstruction of the composer's illness and death by Valery Sokolov (based in part on the unpublished book on the same subject by the microbiologist Nikolai Blinov) shows, Modest brought in two of the most distinguished physicians in St. Petersburg, the brothers Vasily and Lev Bertenson, on the very day that the cholera symptoms appeared. According to Sokolov, cholera was cured by 23 October, but it had weakened Chaikovsky's heart and, especially, kidneys, leading to uremia, of which he actually died.[7]

As Poznansky's book shows, rumors of foul play began almost at the time of Chaikovsky's funeral. Journalists accused his doctors of lack of competence. Cholera was considered the illness of the poor who lived in unsanitary conditions. The only known path of infection was ingesting food or water contaminated by human excrement. How could the affluent and universally admired composer, who was sure to have used only cooked food and boiled water, have gotten cholera? Rumors were concocted that the composer had deliberately played Russian roulette with his life by drinking a glass of unboiled water (an idea to which George Balanchine subscribed).[8] Actually, the composer was in fine shape when the illness struck—making hotel reservations in towns where he was to conduct in the next few weeks and writing friends whom he hoped to visit.

A powerful stimulus for the rumor mill was provided by the composer's last work, Symphony No. 6, the "Pathétique," whose first perfor-

---

[7] Valerii Sokolov, "Do i posle tragedii: Smert' P. I. Chaikovskogo v dokumentakh," *Znamia*, November 1993, 148–49.
[8] Solomon Volkov, *Balanchine's Tchaikovsky* (New York: Simon and Schuster, 1985), 219.

mance he had conducted about ten days before his death. Received with incomprehension and indifference when it was premiered by Chaikovsky, the Sixth Symphony was played at a memorial concert two weeks after his death, and it was now read as Chaikovsky's farewell to life, a kind of musical suicide note and, later, as a depiction of a lifetime of wretchedness entailed by living a homosexual life. By the end of the 1890s, the sexologist Havelock Ellis in England had dubbed the "Pathétique" "the homosexual tragedy symphony."[9]

Brother Modest's biography appeared in three volumes at the turn of the century. Modest's once-popular plays are now firmly forgotten, but his biography still remains an attractive piece of writing and an indispensable source about Chaikovsky's life.[10] But as Poznansky rightly warns in his book, it is a slanted source. Being a man of his time, Modest Chaikovsky resolutely concealed his own and his brother's homosexuality from the readers. By doing so, he also omitted some of the happiest periods and relationships in his brother's life: his rewarding liaisons with his one-time classmate Sergei Kireev and with the violinist Iosif Kotek, his durable affair with his valet Alyosha (Aleksei Sofronov) and so on.

To learn about such things, we have to turn to Chaikovsky's personal diaries, published in 1923 by his other brother, Ippolit, or to the remarkably frank and well-annotated volume of correspondence with his younger brothers and other relatives that somehow slipped past the Soviet censorship as late as 1940 (the editors were punished and the volume withdrawn, but not before copies found their way to libraries in the West).[11] Modest's biography appeared in 1906 in English in an abridged translation by Rosa Newmarch. This remained the standard source in English, a biography full of holes, with many episodes, such as the composer's brief, disastrous marriage, making no sense at all in Modest's and Rosa Newmarch's telling.

However, Chaikovsky's sexual orientation was generally known to scholars in the West. This awareness must surely have contributed to the

---

[9] Herbert Weinstock, *Tchaikovsky* (New York: Alfred A. Knopf, 1943), 365.
[10] Modest Chaikovskii, *Zhizn' Petra Il'icha Chaikovskogo* (Moscow and Leipzig: Jurgenson, 1900–3).
[11] Petr Chaikovskii, *Dnevniki* [Diaries], *1873–1891* (Moscow and Petrograd: Glavlit, 1923); idem, *Pis'ma k rodnym* [Letters to relatives] (Moscow: Gos. muzykal'noe izd-vo, 1940).

judgment of his music by some heavyweights of mid-twentieth-century musicology: Donald Francis Tovey (who considered him "a composer of light music" who cannot handle a symphonic movement); or Paul Henry Lang: "The development of his themes often becomes hysterical."[12] This whole critical attitude has been described by the scholar Henry Zajaczkowski as "the musicological pantomime of derision that has passed as serious critical assessment of [Chaikovsky's] music for so many years."[13]

The low point of this mid-century pantomime was reached in the collection of essays edited by Gerald Abraham published in 1946, reissued in 1974, and available at most libraries. In the introductory biographical essay by the then well-known critic Edward Lockspeiser, we read of a life of fear, despondency, and self-pity and of "neurotic character" that "drove him into homosexuality with all its attendant complications of furtiveness, deception and guilt." And then: "It is the music to gorge on, shameless in its sensuousness and splendor. And it was no accident that such music was conceived by a warped neurotic, shy and tortured."[14] (Except for homosexuality, not a single trait mentioned by Lockspeiser is confirmed by any memoir about Chaikovsky or by his own diaries and letters.) Some of the other contributors to Abraham's volume played variations on the theme of how inept a composer Chaikovsky was due to his neurosis: he had no sense of form, could not put a concerto together properly, did not know how to orchestrate, and so forth.[15]

There were other midcentury biographies of Chaikovsky that did not see his private life as a handicap to his talent or to his technical abi-

---

12 Richard Taruskin, "Tchaikovsky, Fallen from Grace," *New York Times*, 30 June 1991.
13 Henry Zajaczkowski, *Tchaikovsky's Musical Style* (Ann Arbor: UMI Research, 1987), vii.
14 Gerald Abraham, ed., *The Music of Tchaikovsky* (New York: W. W. Norton, 1946), 9–23.
15 In addition to the cited biographical sketch by Lockspeiser, Abraham's collection also contains Eric Blom's chapter "Works for Solo Instruments and Orchestra," where the author seeks to vindicate Nikolai Rubinstein's initial judgment of the First Piano Concerto (known from Chaikovsky's oft-cited letter to Nadezhda von Meck) as "bad as a whole," "worthless and repellently trivial"; "Miscellaneous Orchestral Works" by Ralph W. Wood, with frequent references to the composer's supposed ineptitude and vulgarity and the pronouncement that *Francesca da Rimini* is "really a very low-grade piece of music"; and a section "The Ballets" by Edwin Evans, which is so uninformed and error-ridden as to be practically worthless.

lity. Such were, for example, the books in English by Herbert Weinstock (1943), and by John Gee and Elliott Selby (1960), authors who did not see Chaikovsky's homosexuality as something that gave them the right to despise him.[16] But they did follow the general trend of perceiving the composer's story as a lifetime of unrelieved pain and suffering in his closet. A rare instance of a book written with understanding of Russian society during the period when Chaikovsky lived was the *biographie romancée* written by the exiled Russian poet and novelist Nina Berberova.[17]

By the 1930s, there were rumors that Chaikovsky did not die of cholera, but was forced to commit suicide because of his homosexuality. These rumors came in many versions. The composer, supposedly, got involved sexually with a son or a nephew of the tsar, or of some noble family, or of the yard-keeper of the building where he lived. He was then given a choice—usually by the tsar, but sometimes by the father or the uncle of the young man: "suicide or Siberia!" The purveyors of these rumors did not know that Alexander III, whose brother and closest adviser were openly gay, was not likely to have taken such an attitude. With the postrevolutionary clampdown on the topic of homosexuality, people forgot the conditions that had existed in the 1890s. Berberova's research revealed that people who knew Chaikovsky and were near him when he died remembered his death from cholera. The suicide version was always asserted by people who did not know the composer, but had heard the story from someone they thought reliable.

But things were to get still worse later in the century. With the publication of *Tchaikovsky* by the Englishman Edward Garden in 1973, the real dark ages of Chaikovsky studies began. At a time when a great deal of information about variant forms of sexuality was becoming known even to the general public, what Garden offered was not only what today is called homophobia, but a sort of militant ignorance of the entire subject. Since Chaikovsky was a homosexual, wrote Garden, "he was unable to feel sexually aroused," and was thus continuously frustrated. He also could not "establish a firm, constant and loving relationship

---

[16] Weinstock, *Tchaikovsky*; John Gee and Elliott Selby, *The Triumph of Tchaikovsky: A Biography* (New York: Vanguard, 1960).
[17] Nina Berberova, *Chaikovskii: Istoriia odinokoi zhizni* (Berlin: Petropolis, 1936).

with any other human being." The result was "a propensity for nervous breakdowns unparalleled by any other great composer," which repeatedly brought him to the verge of insanity. Much of Chaikovsky's music is marred for Garden by his "morbid inversion" or "by the frustrations of his endemic homosexuality."[18]

In 1978, Garden's associate, another senior English musicologist, David Brown, published the first volume of his four-volume critical and biographical study, completed with the appearance of its fourth volume in 1991. Brown established his point of view in his first volume, where he wrote in a simplistic Freudian vein that the death of the composer's mother when he was a teenager led to the "growths of psychological abnormality which insidiously bound themselves round him, constricting, distorting and unbalancing his emotional life," thus preventing him forever from forming any close personal relationships.[19] Of course, there were relationships with various men documented in Chaikovsky's diaries and letters, but Garden's and Brown's detestation of the entire topic led them to ignore this. Like Garden before him, Brown tried to establish causal relationships between what he saw as flaws in Chaikovsky's music (he judged about two-thirds of his output artistic failures) and the pathology of his orientation.

The third recent obfuscator to muddy the understanding of Chaikovsky's life and music is the Soviet music historian Aleksandra Orlova. She departed for the West in 1979 and within two years became internationally famous through her sensationalist articles about Chaikovsky's death. He did not die of cholera, she claimed, but was forced to take poison by a so-called court of honor convoked by his fellow alumni from the School of Jurisprudence, a kind of junior college he had attended in his youth. These men, whom he had not seen for decades, found out about Chaikovsky's homosexuality and condemned him to death for besmirching the uniform of their school. Then, *teste* Orlova, a monstrous conspiracy, involving the composer's family, three distinguished doctors, the police, and the tsar's court covered up the suicide and palmed it off as a cholera infection. And how does Aleksandra Orlova know all this? Why,

---

18 Edward Garden, *Tchaikovsky* (London: J. M. Dent, 1973)
19 David Brown, *Tchaikovsky: A Biographical and Critical Study*, vol. 1, *The Early Years, 1840–1874* (London: Gollancz, 1978), 50.

she was told in 1966 by a man named Aleksandr Voitov, who had heard it as a teenaged boy in 1913 from the widow of one of the members of the "court of honor," whose husband had died in 1902.[20]

It was all, of course, one of those "death or Siberia" rumors that Nina Berberova had investigated back in the 1930s, rumors that cannot ever be traced to anyone who was anywhere near Chaikovsky at the time of his death, rumors whose acceptance depends on total ignorance of the situation of Chaikovsky or of the homosexuals of his time. But in the conspiracy-hungry West, Orlova's claims were eagerly accepted. David Brown became her ally and placed her version of the events in the authoritative *New Grove Dictionary of Music and Musicians* and into two other music dictionaries, published between 1983 and 1986.[21]

Clearly, Orlova's version satisfied people like David Brown and Edward Garden, who believe that all homosexuals lead lives of ceaseless misery, from which suicide offers a welcome escape. Orlova herself belongs to this group: as she has written, Chaikovsky was "tormented by his anomaly throughout his life, the anomaly that was a calamity, a curse laid upon him by fate." And a little further: "Being a highly decent and honorable man, he regarded his anomaly as a disgrace that could never be effaced."[22] (Once again, there is no support for this in any document that stems from Chaikovsky or his contemporaries.) Orlova believes that the suffering heroines of Chaikovsky's operas, especially the suicidal Liza in *Pikovaia dama*, are musical portrayals of the composer's ceaseless pain and despair. Curious, isn't it, that no one ever says this of the suffering women in the operas by Verdi and Puccini?

As Aleksandr Poznansky showed in his 1988 essay, all the hypothesizing about Chaikovsky's endless misery and ultimate suicide was based not on the facts of his biography or the content of his music but rather on the widespread myth about how homosexuals were supposed to have fared in the nineteenth century. The suicide version, in particular, was ably refuted by two authors in Russia, who were aware of Poznansky's 1988 essay

---

[20] Alexandra Orlova, "Tchaikovsky: The Last Chapter," trans. David Brown, *Music & Letters* 62 (1981): 125–45; idem, *Tchaikovsky: A Self-Portrait* (Oxford: Oxford University Press, 1990).
[21] Poznansky, "Tchaikovsky's Suicide," 214n3.
[22] Aleksandra Orlova, "Tragediia Chaikovskogo i gorbachevskaia glasnost'," *Novoe russkoe slovo*, 25 January 1987.

and who fully supported his conclusions.[23] It is indicative of Aleksandra Orlova's and David Brown's scholarly probity that neither she in her 1990 book nor he in the last volume of his Chaikovsky biography made any mention of the considerable number of publications that disagreed with their "misery-cum-suicide" interpretation of the composer's life.[24]

Since the tragic mood of the Sixth Symphony and the seemingly hopeless atmosphere of its last movement have been repeatedly adduced as evidence that in his last work Chaikovsky bid his farewell to life, it might be appropriate to point out that the sketches for this last movement go back at least two years before the symphony's premiere.[25] Moreover, while working on the Sixth, he made preliminary drafts for his unrealized Seventh Symphony. These drafts eventually ended up as his one-movement, posthumous Third Piano Concerto, an energetic piece of music that does not contain a single despondent passage. If we take the (always dubious) path of reconstructing the man and his character through his music, we have to point out that he left behind not only "Sérénade mélancholique," "Autumn Song," and such possibly uncheerful operas as *Evgeny Onegin* and *Mazepa*, but also the radiant First Piano Concerto, the lively comic opera *Cherevichki*, and his final work for the operatic stage, *Iolanta*, with its jubilant finale celebrating the heroine's deliverance from blindness. The last major composition before the Sixth Symphony was the coruscating ballet *Shchelkunchik* (*The Nutcracker*)—surely a piece of music that the hopeless psychotic described by Lockspeiser, Garden, David Brown, and Orlova could not possibly have composed.

* * *

In a somewhat later piece that covered much the same ground as this one, but which appeared in a publication that served a readership with a specific interest in LGBT concerns, SK balanced his account of Chaikovsky's alleged suicide—as a myth created by, and appealing to, homophobia—with a complementary report of its reception in the homosexual community, where it

---

23 B. S. Nikitin, *Chaikovskii: Staroe i novoe* (Moscow: Znanie, 1990); Gennadii Shokhman, "Vzgliad s drugikh beregov," *Sovetskaia muzyka* 6 (1990): 134–41.
24 Orlova, *Tchaikovsky: A Self-Portrait*; David Brown, *Tchaikovsky: A Biographical and Critical Study*, vol. 4, *The Final Years, 1885–1893* (New York: W. W. Norton, 1991).
25 Nikitin, *Chaikovskii*, 188.

was not always greeted with skepticism, but where, in a fashion that was on the face of it surprising (but on reflection less so), was often eagerly appropriated by journalists and activists. He called out for rueful censure the especially erroneous version of the American composer Ned Rorem, who "in the pages of *Opera News* (1 February 1986) mentioned a 'state-enforced suicide' because of the composer's 'liaison with his nephew.'" As SK perhaps somewhat hyperbolically remarked, the "gay community in America took to the suicide story *en masse*, as it furnished a famous gay martyr from the past." He pointed with dismay to "an unholy alliance ... between the benighted homophobes in England and gay liberationists and historians in America"—a phenomenon that furnished this essay (largely a review of yet another homophobic British biography) with its title.[26] With the exception of a dictionary entry published in 2000,[27] this was SK's final contribution to Chaikovsky studies and his last article on music.

---

[26] "Tchaikovsky and the Unholy Alliance," review of *Tchaikovsky: A Biography*, by Anthony Holden (New York: Random House, 1996), *Harvard Gay and Lesbian Review* 3, no. 4 (Fall 1996): 31–33.

[27] "Tchaikovsky, Pyotr Ilich (1840–1893)," in *Gay Histories and Cultures: An Encyclopedia*, ed. George Haggerty (New York: Garland, 2000), 865–66.

V

ON STRAVINSKY

The Composer's Workshop[1]

Maturing slowly as a composer, Igor Stravinsky caught up with the musical present of his age when he composed *The Firebird* at twenty-eight. One year later, with *Petrushka* (1911), he overtook that age and remained in the lead ever since, mapping out the future course of the art of music, both predicting its trends in his work and bringing them about by the force of his example. Several generations of music critics, puzzled by his continuous evolution, have ridiculed and deplored what they saw as the composer's unpredictable scurrying from style to style in heedless, pointless search of novelty. Their books and articles remain as historical curios, and Stravinsky's evolution can now be seen for what it always was: the rich, purposeful, astoundingly fruitful search for a synthesis between the musical culture of the past and the gradually emerging musical forms, both serious and popular, of the twentieth century. The vantage point of Stravinsky's art has remained youthful: open, fresh, inquisitive. He never composed a bar of what may be termed "old man's music." If his recent *Requiem Canticles* do not seem the trail blazer that *Petrushka* and *The Rite of Spring* were sixty years ago, it is because by now we are used to Stravinsky. The same *Requiem Canticles*, coming from some young unknown, would have been hailed as an amazing new departure and the probable threshold of a major musical career.[2]

---

[1] Review of *Retrospectives and Conclusions*, by Igor Stravinsky and Robert Craft (New York: Alfred A. Knopf, 1969); *"The Rite of Spring": Sketches 1911–1913; Facsimile Reproductions from the Autographs*, by Igor Stravinsky (London: Boosey & Hawkes, 1969); and *Rannie balety Stravinskogo: "Zhar-ptitsa," "Petrushka," "Vesna sviashchennaia"* [Stravinsky's early ballets: *The Firebird, Petrushka, The Rite of Spring*], by Irina Iakovlevna Vershinina (Moscow: Nauka, 1967). Originally published in *Nation*, 15 June 1970, 730–33.

[2] As noted earlier, we have chosen not to bring all of the text of these articles, which were written over many years, into the present. This will be especially noticeable to the reader in essays about individuals alive when SK was writing and about matters involving the former Soviet Union.—Ed.

Stravinsky has been increasingly active as a writer in recent decades. The sixth volume of his and Robert Craft's miscellanea (interviews, diaries, and assorted commentary) has just been published, the *New York Review of Books* frequently features his opinions, and at this writing he has apparently become a regular columnist for *Harper's Magazine*. One recognizable impulse behind all this writing activity (there are many others) is the desire to document his own past, to point out the roots of his art in the great Russian artistic renaissance of the early twentieth century, the brilliant period whose significance is so widely misunderstood or underestimated in the West. This documentary aspect of the Stravinsky-Craft volumes has been a great boon to musical historians and Western Stravinsky biographers, and, indeed, the books contain vast riches of musical and historical information gleaned from an almost unprecedented six-decade span of intense artistic creativity.

Not everything Stravinsky remembers should be taken as gospel, however. Lawrence Morton has demonstrated the master's lapse of memory in enumerating his Chaikovsky sources for *The Fairy's Kiss*.[3] In *Expositions and Developments* we are told about *Renard*: "The original title of my barnyard fable was *Skaska o petuhyeh, Leesyeh, kotyeh y baranyeh*, 'Tale about the Cock, the Fox, the Cat, and the Ram.'"[4] This was reverently cited in Eric Walter White's biography of Stravinsky and on the jacket of the Columbia recording of *Renard*. But that is *not* the original Russian title of *Renard*, as a glance at any printed edition of that work will establish. What Stravinsky is quoting, through the haze of that absurd, three-headed transliteration system, is the original Russian title of *Histoire du soldat*, but with the four beasts of *Renard* replacing the soldier and the devil of the other work. The Russian title of *Renard* began with the word *baika*, the regional and colloquial word for "story," and continued quite differently.[5]

---

[3] Lawrence Morton, "Stravinsky and Tchaikovsky: *Le baiser de la fée*," *Musical Quarterly* 48, no. 3, Special Issue for Igor Stravinsky on His 80th Anniversary (July 1962): 313–26; repr. in *Stravinsky: A New Appraisal of His Work*, ed. Paul Henry Lang (New York: W. W. Norton, 1963), 47–60.

[4] Robert Craft and Igor Stravinsky, *Expositions and Developments* (Garden City, New York: Doubleday, 1962; repr. Berkeley: University of California Press, 1981), p. 119 in the 1981 edition.

[5] To wit: *Baika pro lisu, petukha, kota da barana: Veseloe predstavlenie s peniem i muzykoi* [The story of the fox, the cock, the tomcat and the ram: A merry performance with singing and (instrumental) music].—Ed.

A few lines later, Stravinsky recollects how the music of *Renard* was inspired by the *guzla* which, as he explains, is "a kind of fine metal-stringed balalaika ... strapped over the player's head like the tray of a cigarette girl in a night club." This is a very precise description of the instrument called *gusli* in Russian and psaltery in English, which is the instrument Stravinsky means. The *guzla* is a Balkan bowed string instrument used to accompany the recitations of south Slavic folk epics and not related to *Renard* in any way (Stravinsky must have been thinking of Mérimée's collection of faked folk poems, *La guzla*, translated into Russian by Pushkin).[6] Such memory lapses are probably unavoidable, given Stravinsky's huge storehouse of remembered experience. Western musicologists will continue quoting them in good faith until eventually their Russian colleagues will set them right.

That there is a substantial Soviet contribution to be made to our understanding of Stravinsky is startlingly evident with the publication of Irina Vershinina's masterful study of Stravinsky's first three ballets. Everything of significance written elsewhere about *The Firebird*, *Petrushka* and *The Rite of Spring* is right there in her book; but the author's insight into the Russian cultural history of the period and into Russian folk song and folklore (what Western musicologist could realize that the flute and cello themes at the very beginning of *Petrushka* are adapted from the street vendors' cries used to sell coal, herring, and marinated apples?) enables her to locate these ballets in a historical and cultural context with a knowledge and precision that are beyond the reach of most non-Russian commentators.

A trained, competent musicologist, she draws on ethnography, anthropology, the history of Western and Russian painting, and the social and political currents of the time to achieve a coherent and meaningful total picture. She is addressing a new generation of Russian readers who grew up during those three decades when the music of the greatest composer Russia ever produced could not be played in the USSR, and when he himself was persistently denounced as a traitor and a Wall Street lackey. The book is the first significant Soviet contribution to Stravinsky studies

---

6   Actually, the error originated with Charles-Ferdinand Ramuz, the Swiss novelist, who translated the text of *Renard* for its first publication (Geneva: A. Henn, 1917). Ramuz, of course, might well have been thinking of Mérimée.—Ed.

(discounting the pedestrian 1964 biography by Boris Yarustovsky) since Igor Glebov's brilliant *A Book about Stravinsky* was published in 1929, only to be banned soon after and relegated to library shelves, classified "limited circulation."

It is instructive to compare Irina Vershinina's account of the genesis and reception of *The Rite of Spring* to Robert Craft's similar effort in his introduction to the elegant, if overpriced, Boosey & Hawkes facsimile edition of Stravinsky's working sketches. Craft draws on the memories of the composer, on some of his letters, on the statements of his French colleagues, and on the record in the Western press. Vershinina uses unpublished Stravinsky letters from Soviet archives, the reactions of the Russian press to the work's premiere, and fragments from the private correspondence of various Russian critics and composers (e.g., Myaskovsky and Prokofiev). Craft's is the story of the creation of *The Rite of Spring* as it is remembered *now*; Vershinina's is the account of that creation as seen from Russia and within the context of Russian culture. Craft's most glaring omission is Stravinsky's essay (liberally quoted by Vershinina), "What I Wanted to Express in *The Rite of Spring*," written by the composer immediately after finishing the score and published in the journal *Muzyka* in 1913.

In the Russian text of that essay, there is a curious stylistic spillover from the ballet: Stravinsky uses the same archaic, shamanistic, bogyman style he devised for the titles of various sections of the music. The composer and Robert Craft wrestle with the problem of translating these titles into English, both in the notes to the sketchbook and in *Retrospectives and Conclusions*, and they often lose. "Igra umykaniia," the Russian title of the section usually called "Jeu du rapt," means "Mock Abduction of the Bride," *umykanie* being the kind of bridal abduction practiced by exogamous societies to avoid intermarriage within the tribe. Stravinsky's new translation, "Game of Seizing the Girl," doesn't begin to cover the topic.

Nor is "Leading-Moving" a satisfactory rendition of the wonderfully evocative "Idut-vedut" (transcribed as "Eedoot-veedoot" by Craft); literally, "they are coming–they are bringing them," where the rhyming pair of impersonal third-person plural verb forms conveys both the idea of a massive round dance and the spooky implication that some unknown entities are coming and bringing someone else, possibly against that someone's will. "The Evocation of the Human Ancestors," which Craft finds "unhelpfully ... specific," is actually "Evocation of the Forefathers of Humans." Appropriately for the totemistic, prehistorical world of *The Rite of Spring*, the wording leaves open the question of whether these forefathers are gods, beasts, or humans ("Forefathers of Humans," by the way, is the name of a 1911 painting by Roerich, the original set designer of the ballet, which indeed shows a group of prehistoric shamans in quasi-animal garb). Finally, Craft solemnly offers us a nonexistent Russian word, telling us that he is correcting an earlier misprint in the score. Couldn't Irina Vershinina or *somebody* have been consulted?

But even with all the shortcomings of the translation and commentary, the sketchbook itself is a delight. Anyone who knows and loves the work and who disregards all those music critics who every ten years or so announce that *The Rite* has had its day and is no longer relevant can now go to the local library and follow, with awe and fascination, the gradual taking-shape in its creator's mind of the still-startling score which Robert Craft imaginatively compares to a prize bull that has inseminated the whole modern movement. The nature of the imaginative and creative mental processes is probably ultimately not susceptible to paraphrased explanation, but study of the sketchbook does provide us with a number of interesting insights into Stravinsky's laboratory.

This same invitation to enter the composer's creative workshop was often the subject of the first five Stravinsky-Craft volumes, and in this respect *Retrospectives and Conclusions* is different from its predecessors. The book is mainly about illness, death, and other men's music. Stravinsky remains a fascinating music critic, as his passages on Gesualdo, Monteverdi and Beethoven's last quartets show. The gem of the book is a brief, two-page meditation on *The Magic Flute*—exploring the presence of death in its music and the predictions of many future musical styles that hindsight can now discover in it. Henceforth, no collection of critical opinions on Mozart will be complete without these pages. However, to the list of works and composers (Beethoven, Wagner, Verdi, Ravel) that Stravinsky says are anticipated in *The Magic Flute*, we could add the last bars of his own Larghetto concertante from *Symphony in C*, recalling as it does the ending of Mozart's first-act quintet.

Stravinsky's literary judgments, especially those on Tolstoi and Gorky, are trenchant and knowledgeable. Robert Craft narrates in his usual witty and readable manner Stravinsky's encounters with the English and American literary figures who are or were his friends: Eliot, Auden, Evelyn Waugh, Graham Greene. Craft's account of the opinions of Stravinsky's erstwhile mentor and friend, the cofounder of the Eurasian movement, Pyotr Suvchinsky, demonstrates the peculiarly Russian form of confrontation between the creative genius and the sterile theoretician. Suvchinsky's reactions are exactly those of a typical nineteenth-century Russian literary critic faced with a masterpiece by Pushkin or Tolstoi. Recognizing the achievement, such critics would inevitably complain of the artist's philosophical shallowness, political turpitude, and Russian provincialism. Certainly, Suvchinsky's political slurs should be seen as a part of the Byzantine web of Parisian émigré rivalries rather than as any factual revelations.

The most memorable pages in *Retrospectives and Conclusions* move away from the format of diaries and commentaries of the earlier volumes and enter the realm of literary confessions. The wealth of medical information, the precise accounts of Stravinsky's various illnesses and close brushes with death, his realization of its imminence, Robert Craft's agonies of apprehension (the two are clearly closer than most fathers and sons)—all this would make depressing reading were it not for Stravinsky's overriding intellectual curiosity about these new experiences and his steadfast determination to survive and to write more new music. Intensely concerned with the present, and more aware of and sympathetic to its problems than many a man half his age, Igor Stravinsky at eighty-eight remains a young and active musician with, we hope, more books like this one and more musical masterpieces like *Requiem Canticles* to offer to an amazed and grateful world.

* * *

Exceptional interest attaches to SK's writings on Stravinsky, because, appearing when they did, they document the confluence of two streams, or rather the abutment of two eras: the era in which Stravinsky himself was the dominant—or rather dominating—source of information about his life and work, and the subsequent era of proper documentary and archival research. SK was the only Western scholar then writing who possessed both intimate knowledge of Stravinsky and his work, on the one hand, and vast erudition within the world of Russian culture, on the other. He was acutely aware of the disjunction between Stravinsky, an émigré since 1910, in whom there was massive interest among musicians in the West (and, increasingly, within the Soviet domain), and the deficient cultural purview from which he was approached by, for the most part, subscholarly investigators. His writings on Stravinsky amounted to the first sustained effort to bridge that gap.

In his earliest piece on the composer, a review essay titled "Igor Stravinskii—East and West," SK took note of the problem:

> The roots of Stravinsky's art are deeply Russian. The point of departure, the selection of subject matter, the entire aesthetic approach of his earlier successful works can be best understood within the framework of the marvelous Russian cultural renaissance of the early twentieth century. *The Firebird, Petrushka,* and *The Nightingale* are musical parallels and counterparts of the poetry of Balmont and Kuzmin, the early prose of Bely and Remizov, and the painting of Roerich and Goncharova. An understanding of the Russian cultural context is indispensable in order to have a thorough grasp of almost all of Stravinsky's work up to and including *The Fairy's Kiss* (1928). Since much of his later output is either a reaction against his Russian musical origins or an occasional sentimental return to them (*Danses concertantes,* 1942; *Scherzo à la russe,* 1944), a critic or musical historian writing of Stravinsky's later work should also be able to understand just what Stravinsky is abandoning or returning to. Under normal conditions there would be a large body of informed scholarship and criticism written in Russian about this Russian, whose work has been the central phenomenon of Western music for the past six decades. But the conditions governing Russian musical scholarship and criticism during the greater part of Stravinsky's career have, of course, been anything but normal.[7]

In that early piece, SK recognized only one worthy Russian contribution to Stravinsky scholarship or criticism: *Kniga o Stravinskom* (A book about Stravinsky) by Boris Asafiev, writing under his pen name of Igor Glebov, also men-

---

[7] "Igor Stravinskii—East and West," review of *Themes and Episodes,* by Igor Stravinsky and Robert Craft, *Stravinsky: The Composer and His Works,* by Eric Walter White, and *Stravinsky,* by Roman Vlad, *Slavic Review* 27 (1968): 453.

tioned in the article to which this note is appended. For the rest, there was only incomprehension and hostility, leading to an informational vacuum that Western scholarship, still linguistically ill-equipped and burdened with its own ideological prejudices, was incapable of repairing. Indignation modulates into sorrow when SK confronts, and is forced to dismiss, the first monograph on Stravinsky to appear in Russia since Asafiev's after a hiatus of thirty-five years.[8] This book, and also a heavily bowdlerized, "rather lame" translation of Stravinsky's 1936 autobiography that appeared in 1963 on the heels of Stravinsky's official visit to the Soviet Union the year before, indicate that "Soviet literature on Stravinsky has been somewhat schizophrenic in recent years: interest in his work and pride in his achievement as a Russian constantly clash with the continual need to reassert the conservatism of Socialist Realism in music (a concept obviously incompatible with everything Stravinsky stands for) and the need to apologize for, or attack, his expressed views on musical aesthetics and his status as an émigré."[9] The article proceeds to a melancholy conclusion, enumerating the inadequacies of two Western monographs and welcoming the latest volume of memoirs and diaries jointly authored by Stravinsky and his assistant Robert Craft, which, although "every bit as rewarding and significant as the other books in the series,"[10] pertains entirely to the "Western" sector of Stravinsky's bifurcated life.

The above essay is much more hopeful, thanks to the appearance, in 1967, of the first really solid piece of late-Soviet Stravinsky scholarship: Irina Vershinina's monograph on the three early ballets. That encouraging phenomenon, with its implied promise of more to come, gave SK the nerve, as it were, to suggest at last (and it was high time) that the Stravinsky-Craft volumes were not the impeccable sources they appeared to be. For the first time their errors and insufficiencies were exposed alongside those of the other books under review—and that provoked (surely to the great delight of the *Nation*'s editors) a huffy reply from "Igor Stravinsky."[11]

The name must go between scare quotes, because by 1970, and for at least two years before that, all writing signed "Stravinsky" was the single-handed work of Robert Craft (as were the final volume of memoirs, the *New*

---

8   Boris Iarustovskii, *Igor' Stravinskii: Kratkii ocherk zhizni i tvorchestva* (Moscow: Muzyka, 1964).
9   "Stravinskii—East and West," 454.
10 Ibid., 457.
11 *Nation*, letter to the editor, 3 August 1970, 66, 83.

York Review interviews, and the *Harper's* reviews mentioned at the beginning of the present article).[12] "Prof. Simon Karlinsky's review," the letter begins, "of some recent books concerning my music ... is so generous to me that I feel ungrateful taking issue, as I shall, with some points both of fact and of emphasis." The first issue discussed is the quality of Glebov's/Asafiev's *Book about Stravinsky*, which Stravinsky did not like (as Craft had evidently discovered by looking at "the rubrics with which I [sic] decorated it at the time," and as will surprise no one who has read the book). The first substantial issue concerns the authorship of "What I Wanted to Express in *The Rite of Spring*," the article whose absence from Craft's account of the ballet in the facsimile sketchbook SK had complained about. Not for the first time (or the tenth), "Stravinsky" here disavows authorship of this essay, claiming on this occasion that "it was concocted by a French journalist, and the Russian version is a translation." The journalist in question was Ricciotto Canudo, the Italian-born editor of an arts magazine called *Montjoie!* The article, titled "Ce que j'ai voulu exprimer dans *Le sacre du printemps*," appeared in the magazine on the day of the fabled premiere performance, 29 May 1913. Like almost all Stravinsky's public writings, then, this one was the work of a ghostwriter. But, like all those other writings, it enjoyed Stravinsky's input and approval. Stravinsky himself sent the piece to the Moscow journal *Muzyka* as his own work, and when it appeared, tried to get the editor, Vladimir Derzhanovsky, to republish it with his own corrections to the translation. It is as much his work as were his *Chroniques de ma vie* (ghostwritten by Walter Nouvel), or his *Poétique musicale* (ghostwritten by Pyotr Suvchinsky and Alexis Roland-Manuel), and rather more than his letter to the *Nation*.

---

[12] Craft has acknowledged this, though inconspicuously and somewhat deviously. In an obviously ghost-written "Author's Foreword" in *Themes and Conclusions* (London: Faber and Faber, 1972; repr. Berkeley: University of California Press, 1982), a conflated British reissue credited to Stravinsky alone and consisting more or less of the nondiary portions of the last two Stravinsky-Craft volumes (*Themes and Episodes* and *Retrospectives and Conclusions*), we read that "I can now confess to the partly mercenary motive behind some of my prefaces, reviews, interviews. Bluntly, then—or is it an open secret?—the balance between my income and my needs has, for a decade or more, rested on the 'deductibility' of the latter; and my deductibility 'status' has depended, in turn, on the production, if not of music, then, *faute de mieux*, of words. For to write, in America, is to 'write-off'" (p. 15). There is, as well, a note not expressly attributed to "Stravinsky," added for the UC Press reprint edition, stating that "Mr. Robert Craft ... conducted the interviews on behalf of the journals and institutions represented" as themselves throughout the volume (p. 8).

One rather trivial issue raised by "Stravinsky" gives certain proof that he was not the author of the letter. It concerns the "'nonexistent Russian word' which Karlinsky objects to, but which, perhaps only because I coined it, I still like." There is a word among the titles of the dances in *The Rite of Spring* that Stravinsky is well known to have coined: *vypliasyvanie*, the first noun in the title of the concluding dance from part 1, "Vypliasyvanie zemli," known in French as "Danse de la terre" and in English as "The Dance of the Earth." The word is derived from the Russian verb *pliasat'*, which means to do a (folk) dance. (Ballroom or theatrical dancing has a different verb in Russian.) Since it is Stravinsky's ad hoc coinage, it cannot be translated with any certainty; but its prefix, often rendered "out" in English, suggests something violent, an attempted breakthrough (and the scenario and music certainly support that suggestion): hence, perhaps, as Craft himself suggested, "The Dancing Out of the Earth," or "The Dance Overcoming the Earth."[13]

But that was not the word about which SK was complaining when he noted in exasperation that "Craft solemnly offers us a nonexistent Russian word, telling us that he is correcting an earlier misprint in the score." An early edition of the score, now the most widely available one thanks to its being pirated (owing to the lack of copyright on Russian works before the 1970s) by the American publisher Edwin F. Kalmus and later by Belwin Mills, has an obvious misprint in the Russian title of the "Jeux des cités rivales" (or "The Ritual of the Two Rival Tribes," to give its inaccurate but standard English version): "Игра двухъ горо довъ" ("Igra dvukh" goro dov"") in prerevolutionary orthography. It is an error of registration: an extra space has been interpolated into городовъ (gorodov", *cities* or *tribes*). Craft remembered this, probably because Stravinsky had pointed it out to him one day, but forgot to which word it applied. His solemn footnote reads: "A misprint in the Russian has been carried over to the 1965 edition: *dvukhgoro* is one word, not two." Alas, among those who might have been consulted in 1969, Igor Stravinsky, suffering in the last years of his life from progressive dementia, was not available.

SK had the courtesy, of course, to avoid peremptory correction of this or any other of "Stravinsky's" vagaries. It was surely as obvious to him as it is to us in retrospect that the chief purpose of the letter to the *Nation* was to uphold one of the lies that he had exposed, the one about Canudo and *Montjoie!* At that time it was just the word of the reviewer against the word

---

13 Stravinsky, *"The Rite of Spring": Sketches*, xxi.

of the composer's ventriloquist, and in responding, SK did not insist, but his correctives have since been vindicated many times over.[14] On one point, however, his judgment needs revision in the light of subsequent research, and that is the matter of Suvchinsky's "slurs," as reported by Craft in *Retrospectives and Conclusions*. It must have been painful at the time to read, "If Stravinsky had not gone to America in 1939 … he might have compromised himself politically," followed by a random harvest of details about Stravinsky's interwar flirtation with Fascism.[15] It was reasonable to suppose that this waspish narrative, delivered (if Craft's translation of Suvchinsky's French is to be trusted) with crude and venomous aplomb, "should be seen as a part of the Byzantine web of Parisian émigré rivalries," about which SK was far better informed than was Craft (or anybody else writing at the time about Stravinsky), "rather than as any factual revelations." But the evidence has been mounting since Stravinsky's death and the opening of his archives, both in Russia and in the West, and there can be no gainsaying that this distasteful material is not just the revenge of the sterile theoretician on the creative genius but a part of the factual record of Stravinsky's life—ripe (like the record of Chaikovsky's sexual proclivities) for sensationalist abuse, to be sure, but also for legitimate scholarly use.

---

[14] On the matter of *Montjoie!*, see Philippe Rodriguez, *L'affaire Montjoie!: Canudo et Stravinsky* (Fasano: Schena; Paris: Didier Érudition, 2000).
[15] *Retrospectives and Conclusions*, 195ff.

The Repatriation of Igor Stravinsky[1]

*I*n July 1970, when the composer had less than a year left to live, his niece Kseniya Stravinsky (the daughter of his elder brother Yury) traveled from Leningrad to Évian-les-Bains on an official mission. The aim of that mission was interpreted by the composer's intimates as: bring him home, "dead or alive." To quote from Robert Craft's *Chronicle of a Friendship*, "If it is the latter [i.e., alive], he will receive the world's best medical care, as well as a house, car, chauffeur, and every comfort and even luxury. If it is the former [i.e., a voluntary posthumous return], he may be assured of the highest state honors as well as a niche next to Pushkin or Tolstoi."[2] It was clearly to be one of those symbol-laden repatriations which the Soviet government holds so dear, works so hard to achieve, and which it invariably represents to the world (as it had in such divergent cases as those of Aleksandr Kuprin, Sergei Prokofiev, and Marina Tsvetaeva) as the returning artist's total and unreserved endorsement of the entire Soviet system.

Stravinsky chose to remain in the West and to be buried in Venice. Nevertheless, the officially permitted repatriation of his music, memoirs, and critical writings, initiated at the time of his state visit to the USSR in 1962, has been gathering momentum since the time of his death. Articles and books by Soviet authors about him have been appearing every year or so; pictures of Stravinsky can now be seen in the phonograph record sec-

---

[1] Review of *I. F. Stravinskii: Stat'i i materialy* [I. F. Stravinsky: Essays and materials], compiled by L. S. D'iachkova, ed. B. M. Iarustovskii (Moscow: Sovetskii kompozitor, 1973). Originally published in *Slavic Review* 33 (1974): 528–32.

[2] Robert Craft, *Stravinsky: Chronicle of a Friendship 1948–1971* (New York: Alfred A. Knopf, 1974), 388. Kseniya Yuryevna published a small book of her own on her 1970 visit, and also about her first meeting with her uncle in Leningrad in 1962: Kseniia Iur'evna Stravinskaia, *O I. F. Stravinskom i ego blizkikh* [On I. F. Stravinsky and members of his family] (Leningrad: Muzyka, 1978). The chief value of the book lies in its inclusion of letters home from Kseniya's late elder sister Tatyana, who had spent some months with the composer and his family in Nice in 1925.—Ed.

tions of the Beriozka hard-currency stores in Moscow and Leningrad, next to those of other great Russian composers; and in 1971, *Dialogi*, a carefully selected (and heavily censored) volume of excerpts from the first four volumes of the Stravinsky–Robert Craft discussions and reminiscences,[3] was brought out. Now Stravinsky has been given the ultimate official Soviet accolade, one of those *Stat'i i issledovaniia* (Essays and research articles) or *Stat'i i materialy* volumes which are the musician's or painter's equivalent of a writer's having an issue of *Literaturnoe nasledstvo* devoted to his life and work. An imperial-sounding edict by the minister of culture, Ekaterina Furtseva, with its capitalized PRIKAZYVAIU (I HEREBY COMMAND), printed on the reverse of the title page, makes any future hostility to Stravinsky in the Soviet press a potential *lèse-majesté* and sets the tone for the new official approach to his person by referring to him as the "outstanding Russian composer."

And thus the musician reviled for decades as a traitor to his people, a capitalist lackey of Wall Street, and a reactionary mystic has now been returned to the fold. One has to marvel at the adaptability of the Soviet cultural establishment, when one considers the obstacles and inner contradictions it had to overcome in order to grant full recognition to Stravinsky. It was not simply the mere fact of his emigration. Glazunov and Rachmaninoff had also emigrated, yet their music had always remained a part of Soviet musical culture (the Glazunov equivalent of *Stat'i i materialy* was published in two volumes in 1959; at least four analogous collections devoted to Rachmaninoff have appeared between 1945 and 1957). But Stravinsky, unlike the conventional Glazunov and the musically conservative Rachmaninoff, was one of the creators and presiding genii of the musical sensibility of our century, the very embodiment of that Modernist spirit which the aesthetics of Socialist Realism, with its total commitment to the nineteenth-century views of Chernyshevsky and Stasov, is duty-bound to abhor and to execrate. Yet the Soviet musicologists are now being COMMANDED by their government to study and to appreciate Stravinsky. It is hard not to be reminded of Stalin's similar order on the subject of Mayakovsky, issued in 1935. The result of Stalin's command was the appearance of a whole school of Mayakovsky criticism

---

[3] Igor' Stravinskii, *Dialogi: Vospominaniia, razmyshleniia, komentarii* (Leningrad: Muzyka, 1971).

dedicated to proving that Mayakovsky, the founder and leader of the Russian Futurist movement, was all along an enemy of Modernist art. Are we now in for studies of Stravinsky as an enemy of modern music?

For the moment, at least, the emphasis is not on Modernism, but on patriotism. The first of four sections of *Stat'i i materialy* consists of eulogies and testimonials by prominent Soviet musicians. They devote most of the space allocated to them to assertions of Stravinsky's Russian authenticity—as meaningful a pursuit, one would think, as a search for military themes in *War and Peace* (Stravinsky's equally self-evident internationalist outlook, however, is hardly mentioned, lest anyone take him for a cosmopolitan). Dmitry Shostakovich, who in the 1950s had called Stravinsky a traitor to his country on the pages of *Sovetskaia muzyka*, now admits that he has always loved and studied Stravinsky's music. "The spirit of Russia is inextinguishable in the heart of this genuine, truly major talent, brought forth by Russian soil and united to it by blood," writes Shostakovich, probably not realizing how closely he echoes the *Blut und Boden* phraseology of certain German critics who wrote in a similar vein about Beethoven during the National Socialist period.[4] Aram Khachaturian admits he does not care for Stravinsky's later work and cautions the Soviet readers against taking seriously any of Stravinsky's criticism of "great Russian musicians" or his "anticivic" statements, since these sacrileges must actually have been committed by some unnamed "businessmen" who supposedly surrounded Stravinsky and kept speaking on his behalf.[5] Just to be on the safe side, Khachaturian concludes by evoking Lenin and asserting his own fealty to Leninist principles in music. Tikhon Khrennikov sanctimoniously bemoans Stravinsky's long absence from his homeland, which cheated him of the opportunity to compose patriotic epics, such as Prokofiev's *Semyon Kotko* and *Aleksandr Nevsky*. Refreshingly free from the cant and hypocrisy that characterize the rest of the testimonial section are violinist David Oistrakh's candid admission that he forced himself to

---

[4] There is no reason, of course, to assume that these words, printed under Shostakovich's byline, were actually written by him, any more than were the many official speeches he was given to read (where his earlier negative commentary on Stravinsky had appeared), or the public documents (such as the denunciation of Sakharov that was published in *Pravda* over his signature) that he was given to sign (and which he sometimes did not actually sign); see Irina Shostakovich, "An Answer to Those Who Still Abuse Shostakovich," *New York Times*, 20 August 2000.—Ed.

[5] And herein SK slyly raises that very possibility with respect to Khachaturian.—Ed.

lose interest in Stravinsky's music when "certain attitudes" to it became mandatory "during a particular period"; and composer Rodion Shchedrin's (with whose recent ballet *Anna Karenina* Soviet music seems to take its first tentative step into the second half of the twentieth century) recollection of the explosive impact of Stravinsky on the Soviet music students of the late 1950s, when his previously forbidden music suddenly became available and performable.

The second section of the book offers the Soviet reader selected portions of Stravinsky's *Poetics of Music* (without so much as a mention of its fifth section, "The Avatars of Russian Music," a trenchant analysis of Russian aesthetics and Soviet musical policies)[6] and some fragments from *Themes and Episodes* and *Retrospectives and Conclusions*, the last two of the Stravinsky-Craft literary collaborations. The translations from the English (*Poetics of Music* was translated, quite decently on the whole, from the French original) are occasionally inexact, but more often they are downright sloppy. In the brief commentary on *Orpheus*, an example from the Concerto for Strings is identified as coming from the Violin Concerto; the violist for whom the Elegy for Viola Solo was composed is identified as a "violinist"; and the phrase "the tantara which almost spells 'Taps'" (i.e., the military bugle signal called *otboi* in Russian) is rendered as "the fanfares which almost replace 'light tapping'" (*postukivaniia*). One page later Stravinsky's description of the pitch series on which his *Variations* is based, "a succession of notes that came to my mind as a melody," is translated as "a succession of notes that arose in my consciousness as a ready model." Since the work of Soviet translators is usually highly competent, the wretched quality of the translations in this collection and of the Stravinsky texts in the 1971 *Dialogi*—where the title of the *Symphony in Three Movements* was rendered throughout as "Symphony in Three Motions" (*Simfoniia v trekh dvizheniiakh*, instead of *v trekh chastiakh*)—seems hard to account for.

---

[6] Now known conclusively (owing to the discovery of his original manuscript in Russian) to have been ghostwritten by Pyotr Suvchinsky and subsequently translated into French (by Stravinsky's son Sviatoslav, known as Soulima, with a final edit by Alexis Roland-Manuel); see Svetlana Savenko, "P. P. Suvchinskii i *Muzykal'naia poetika* I. F. Stravinskogo" [P. P. Suvchinsky and I. F. Stravinsky's *Poetics of Music*], in *Petr Suvchinskii i ego vremia* [Pyotr Suvchinsky and his time], ed. Alla Bretanitskaia (Moscow: Kompozitor, 1999), 273–83.—Ed.

In terms of censors' cuts (indicated by series of dots in brackets or at times not indicated at all), the texts in the present volume were gone over with greater stringency than those in the 1971 *Dialogi*. A casual spot check reveals that among the passages from which Soviet readers had to be protected are Stravinsky's mild praise for wealthy patrons of the arts in the West, his statement that many people preferred the music of Wagner to that of Verdi merely because they thought of Wagner as a revolutionary, and the information that Stravinsky's one-time son-in-law (Yury Mandelstam, who is, however, identified in the notes to Stravinsky's letters in a later section as an "émigré poet") was a contributor to the émigré journal *Sovremennye zapiski*. In Stravinsky's letter to Diaghilev about the significance of Chaikovsky's ballets, which is translated from the English text found in Eric Walter White's *Stravinsky*,[7] the statement that the city of St. Petersburg was connected for Stravinsky with the recollection of Tsar Alexander III, whom the composer once saw in his childhood, is replaced by a few dots.

The third section of the collection is taken up with studies of Stravinsky's music by Soviet musicians and musicologists. It is, by and large, on the disappointing side. The conductor Gennady Rozhdestvensky compares the orchestration of the original score of *Petrushka* with the composer's 1947 revision of it, without saying anything that is not obvious to anyone who has taken the trouble to look at the two scores. The composer Edison Denisov tabulates the percussion instruments found in various Stravinsky scores but does not seem to have anything to say about them. G. Alfeevskaya's essay on the *Symphony of Psalms* documents the unexpected similarities between the last movement of that work and Sergei Rachmaninoff's *Vespers* (*Vsenoshchnoe bdenie*, 1915), including Stravinsky's use of two melodies found in the Rachmaninoff work, which may, however, have been drawn by both of them from some common source in the Russian ecclesiastical musical tradition.

The two genuinely valuable contributions to Stravinsky scholarship that this section contains are the fragments from the journals of the choral conductor and authority on Russian folk music Aleksandr Kastalsky (1856–1926) and the essay "Paradoxality as a Feature of Stravinsky's

---

[7] Eric Walter White, *Stravinsky: The Composer and His Works*, 2nd ed. (Berkeley: University of California Press, 1979), 573–74.

Musical Logic" by the composer Alfred Schnittke. Kastalsky heartily disliked both *The Rite of Spring* and *Les noces*, but his command of the Russian folk song idiom enabled him to perceive with clarity and insight the exact manner of Stravinsky's use of this folk idiom in these two works. Schnittke, writing in a jaunty, irreverent manner which is utterly untypical of Soviet criticism when dealing with an admired figure, but which is so much more suitable to discussing Stravinsky than the customary hushed tones and mechanical genuflections, very ably discerns and documents a hitherto unperceived principle in Stravinsky's musical thinking.

The real showpiece of the book is its fourth section, which contains sixty-two letters by Stravinsky from various Soviet archives.[8] As the composer's close associate, Robert Craft, pointed out in his *New York Review of Books* piece on *Stat'i i materialy*, these letters are documents of major biographical and cultural significance. Stravinsky's letters to his teacher Nikolai Rimsky-Korsakov of 1907 testify to the fledgling composer's closeness to and respect for the older musician in a manner that one would not expect from Stravinsky's later recollections of that period. The same warmth and intimacy permeates the young Stravinsky's correspondence with Rimsky-Korsakov's widow and two sons, who were for a time Stravinsky's closest friends. The letters to Andrei Rimsky-Korsakov contain marvelously detailed accounts of Stravinsky's search for the new musical language he discovered in *Petrushka* and in *The Rite of Spring*, which was called *The Great Sacrifice* (*Velikaia zhertva*) in the initial stages of composition. Following a visit to St. Petersburg in December 1910, Stravinsky announced that he had found the right ambience for the final scene of *Petrushka*: "The final act is shaping up in an interesting way: continuous rapid tempi, major keys that reek of some kind of Russian vittles (*sned'*)—cabbage soup, perhaps—of sweat, of high glistening boots, of concertinas. Intoxication! Gambling fever! What's Monte Carlo in comparison?" But Andrei Rimsky-Korsakov failed to respond to this winning enthusiasm. After the international success of *Petrushka*, the entire

---

[8] These were assembled by Igor Ivanovich Blazhkov (b. 1936), a Kiev-born conductor resident in Leningrad, who had been avidly promoting Stravinsky's music from the podium since 1958, and who had been in vigorous correspondence with Stravinsky since that remarkably early date.—Ed.

Rimsky-Korsakov clan turned against Stravinsky, as did the majority of prominent Russian music critics of the time, causing the young composer chagrin and pain with their barrage of *"gustaia gazetnaia rugan'"* (heavy-handed abuse in the press). Andrei actually preferred the music of his brother-in-law Maksimilian Steinberg to that of Stravinsky, as can be seen from his monograph on Steinberg published in 1928.

Pending the publication of *Selected Letters of Igor Stravinsky* that has been announced by the "Sovetskii kompozitor" publishing house, the selection of letters in *Stat'i i materialy* is a major new source of information for any student of the composer's work or of Russian culture during the last decade before the Revolution.[9]

---

[9] That task was eventually undertaken—after "Sovetskii kompozitor" had become, simply, "Kompozitor"—by Victor Pavlovich Varunts (1945–2003), an indefatigable researcher who by the time of his death had issued three volumes in a series called *I. F. Stravinskii: Perepiska s russkimi korrespondentami; Materialy k biografii* [I. F. Stravinsky: Russian-language correspondence; Materials toward a biography] (Moscow: Kompozitor, 1997–2003), which took the project as far as 1939.—Ed.

Igor Stravinsky and Russian Preliterate Theater[1]

At the beginning of *Petrushka*, a tune is heard first in the bass at rehearsal number 2 and then in the full orchestra at 5, with the stage direction: "There passes, dancing, a small crowd of drunken carousers." Western sources, such as Eric Walter White's *Stravinsky: The Composer and His Works*, identify this tune as "an Easter Song known as the 'Song of the Volochebniki' from the province of Smolensk."[2] This

---

[1] Originally published in *19th-Century Music* 6 (Spring 1983): 232–40, and in *Confronting Stravinsky: Man, Musician, and Modernist*, ed. Jann Pasler (Berkeley: University of California Press, 1986), 3–15.

[2] Eric Walter White, *Stravinsky: The Composer and His Works* (Berkeley: University of California Press, 1966), 162. White cites Stravinsky's sources from Frederick W. Sternfeld, "Some Russian Folk Songs in Stravinsky's *Petrouchka*," which initially appeared in *Notes* (Music Library Association) 2nd ser., vol. 2, no. 2 (March 1945): 95–107 and was reprinted in the Norton Critical Scores edition of *Petrushka* (New York: W. W. Norton, 1967), 203–15. The same identifications are also cited in Vera Stravinsky and Robert Craft, *Stravinsky in Pictures and Documents* (New York: Simon and Schuster, 1978). All these authors repeat Sternfeld's out-of-focus translations of Russian song titles ("Song of the Volochebniki" instead of "Easter Carol" and "Down in the Petersky" instead of "Along the St. Petersburg Road") and cite his nonexistent geographical locations ("Totemsk" and "Tombosk" instead of the correct Tot'ma and Tambov; the spurious forms are attributable to the inability to distinguish Russian nouns from their adjectival derivations). [Actually, Sternfeld was aware of the more idiomatic translation in the first example, as he had written "*Down the Petersky* or *Petersburg Road*" (*Notes*, p. 100), while White and Craft, evidently relying on him, chose to reproduce only the more literal, less idiomatic variant.—Ed.] Sternfeld and those who rely on his identifications fail to distinguish between rural folk songs of anonymous origin and the urban popular ditties whose authorship can be established and that Stravinsky also quotes in his score. Thus, the organ-grinder's melody, first stated in a disjoined form by clarinets in octaves two measures after 10 and at 12 and then fully at 15, is the sentimental romance, "Toward Evening, in Rainy Autumn," whose text was written by Aleksandr Pushkin (at the age of fifteen). The music was composed by Nikolai Titov. [The situation is actually a bit more complicated: the young Pushkin's poem, published in 1827, was set by two composers of sentimental

information is correct, though confusingly expressed. The *volochebniki*, also known as the *lalyn'shchiki*, were people who went around Belorussian villages on the Monday after Easter Sunday singing *volochebnye pesni*, that is, Easter carols. The cited identification is thus tautological because it says "an Easter song known as the 'Song of the Singers of Easter Carols.'"

In Russian, the carol is known as "Dalalyn'." A look at its lyrics as cited by Irina Vershinina reveals the humorous implications of Stravinsky's placement of the tune in *Petrushka*.[3] The passing carousers have to be out-of-towners because the custom of Easter caroling existed only in Belorussia, in areas bordering on Poland, and was unknown in St. Petersburg, where the action of *Petrushka* takes place. In their drunken state they are disoriented both geographically, thinking they are in their native Belorussian village, and chronologically, confusing the pre-Lenten Carnival with the Monday after Easter Sunday, still six weeks away, on which their announcement that Christ has arisen and request for Easter eggs would be customary and appropriate.

This very small example illustrates how familiarity with Russian cultural background can enhance our understanding of Stravinsky's music. I had occasion to realize the truth of this during the twelve years it took me to write a survey of Russian drama from its prehistoric beginnings to the age of Pushkin. In studying indigenous forms of Russian drama,

---

romances, Titov and Nikolai De Witte (both in 1829). The melody in *Petrushka*, however, was neither Titov's nor De Witte's, but one that circulated in Russia from mouth to mouth in many guises, best known as a song of the post-Decembrist period with words by Fyodor Glinka, "No City Noise is Heard" (*Ne slyshno shumu gorodskogo*). See R. Taruskin, *Stravinsky and the Russian Traditions* (Berkeley: University of California Press, 1996), 701–4.—Ed.]

3   Irina Iakovlevna Vershinina, *Rannie balety Stravinskogo* [Stravinsky's early ballets] (Moscow: Nauka, 1967), 73. Stravinsky found this song in Nikolai Rimsky-Korsakov's collection of arrangements *Sto russkikh narodnykh pesen dlia golosa s fortepiano, soch. 24* [One hundred Russian folk songs for voice and piano, op. 24], where it appears as no. 47. The translation of the cited portion of the text, with ellipses filled out in brackets, is: "Easter carol, Easter carol! [Give us] each an Easter egg! Christ is risen." In the remainder of the text the singers threaten to harm the livestock of those who fail to offer them gifts of holiday foods. See N. A. Rimskii-Korsakov, *Sto russkikh narodnykh pesen* (St. Petersburg: V. Bessel, 1877, repr. Moscow and Leningrad: Muzgiz, 1951), 90–91.

I kept stumbling on phenomena that were familiar from Stravinsky's oeuvre between 1910 and 1918. Conversely, examining his output from that period, I saw that his stage works from *Petrushka* to *Histoire du soldat* (*The Soldier's Tale*) add up to a compendium of the native theatrical genres of old Russia.

Prior to the introduction of literary drama, in the form of amateur theatricals in Orthodox religious seminaries (school drama) and at the court of Tsar Alexis (German-derived court drama) during the last quarter of the seventeenth century, dramatized rituals and folk entertainments that can be collectively described as Russian preliterary theater had existed in postbaptismal Russia. With some allowance for mutual contamination between categories, this theater existed in the following forms: (1) enactments of surviving pagan rituals that dated back to pre-Christian times, initially had agrarian significance, were timed to the change of seasons, and were usually (though not always) disguised as Christian holidays or ceremonies; (2) highly dramatized village customs of betrothal, wedding, and postwedding celebration, which also combined pre-Christian and postbaptismal elements; and (3) performances by itinerant folk entertainers, the *skomorokhi*, Russian minstrels who also doubled as buffoons, musicians, and animal impersonators.

In addition to these three forms of folk theater that go back to Kievan Russia and earlier, there existed in post-Petrine Russia the institution of (4) pre-Lenten Carnival (*maslenitsa, maslenichnoe gulianie*), with its bearded carnival barkers, puppet shows, masked mummers, and trained bears; and (5) the performances of orally transmitted folk plays about peasants, devils, and foreign royalty that were put on by illiterate soldiers and by convicts in Siberian penal settlements. If we consider Stravinsky's major works for the period 1910–18, we can see that *The Rite of Spring* (*Vesna sviashchennaia, Le sacre du printemps*) is a musical dramatization of the first of these categories—a pagan seasonal agrarian rite; *Svadebka* (*The Wedding*) sets to music the second of our categories; *Renard* (*Baika pro lisu*) is, as most Soviet commentators have realized, a modern revival of the spirit of the *skomorokhi*; *Petrushka*, apart from its protagonist's drama, is a catalogue of *maslenitsa* customs; and *Histoire du soldat*, despite its Swiss disguises, shares features with the soldier and convict folk drama.

Why this musical innovator chose to compose some of his most revolutionary works on subjects taken from archaic and, in his day, mostly defunct preliterary dramatized folklore is a fascinating problem in creative psychology. The years 1907 to 1917 were the time of a great wave of new interest in native Russian art, stripped of the hybridization with Western themes and forms that had predominated in the nineteenth century. Pushkin could write his Russian fairy tales *The Tale of the Fisherman and the Fish* and *The Golden Cockerel* on subjects borrowed from the Brothers Grimm and Washington Irving, respectively. His *Ruslan and Lyudmila*, ostensibly a folktale about Kievan Russia, combines Russian folklore elements with themes drawn from Western chapbook romances and with stylistic mannerisms borrowed from Voltaire and Évariste de Parny, just as the opera that Glinka based on this poem weds Russian and Tatar folk songs to musical textures borrowed from Rossini and Weber. A not-dissimilar procedure was followed, mutatis mutandis, in the pseudo–folk operas, such as *Sadko* or *The Snow Maiden*, by Stravinsky's teacher, Rimsky-Korsakov. All this is said not to disparage the artistic quality of Pushkin or Glinka or even Rimsky-Korsakov, but to pinpoint the difference between their view of folklore and the one embodied in the work of Stravinsky and his contemporaries, the Symbolist and Postsymbolist poets and Russian Modernist painters of the first two decades of the twentieth century.

Considered from this angle, Stravinsky's first ballet, *The Firebird* (*Zhar-ptitsa, L'oiseau de feu*), is a product of the nineteenth-century aesthetic. The libretto mingles themes from Russian folklore with elements drawn from Chaikovsky's *Swan Lake* and Fyodor Sologub's play *Nocturnal Dances*, for which Mikhail Fokine did the choreography one year before he staged *The Firebird* and which had a plot based on a Brothers Grimm tale. The folk songs in *The Firebird* come from a reputable folk song collection and are cited verbatim.[4] They have been selected for their exotic beauty and are couched in the most advanced and elegant musical idiom of the time, French Impressionism, just as Glinka and Rimsky-Korsakov used to set tastefully selected folk melodies in internationally approved musical styles of their day.

---

[4] Vershinina, *Rannie balety*, 50–52, 58–59.

The use of musical folklore in *Petrushka* could not be more different. As Irina Vershinina has pointed out, Stravinsky's Russian contemporaries were actually shocked by what they saw as his lack of selectivity.[5] Trained musicologists were needed to identify the folk melodies in *The Firebird* (and later in *The Rite*), but any Russian child could recognize the tunes that accompany the street dancers, the coachmen, or the nursemaids in *Petrushka*, because they were as familiar as "Home on the Range," "Three Blind Mice," or "When Irish Eyes Are Smiling." Combined with street vendors' cries, barrel organ ditties, the humorous use of an old Easter carol, and hackneyed waltzes by Lanner, this struck the early Russian listeners of *Petrushka* as a gaudy, tasteless mixture, leading the young Prokofiev to qualify the musical materials of *Petrushka* as "rotten trash" (*trukha*).[6]

In *Petrushka* Stravinsky had turned his back on both the ethnographic approach and the Western-style sugarcoating of folklore that were implicit in the Russian nineteenth-century musical aesthetic. This process was deepened in *The Rite*, where, in line with the archaist conception, the musical folklore utilized was largely Lithuanian—that is, not only non-Russian, but non-Slavic (the Balts and the Slavs supposedly had common origins in ancient times). But Stravinsky deformed both the Lithuanian and the Slavic materials with a sovereign freedom in a manner that may be termed cubistic. Lawrence Morton's and Richard Taruskin's best detective efforts were required to discern them at all.[7]

By the time he came to compose *Svadebka*, *Renard*, and the remarkable sets of peasant songs and choruses of 1914–19, Stravinsky no longer needed either to cite or to deform folk tunes or popular melodies because he had internalized the structural, modal, and melodic properties of Russian folk music. Pianist Aleksei Lyubimov declared that, in these works, "archaism of melodies and dynamism of rhythms create

---

[5] Ibid., 81–82.

[6] Prokofiev's letter to Nikolai Myaskovsky in S. Prokof'ev, *Materialy, dokumenty, vospominaniia* [Materials, documents, memoirs] (Moscow: Sovetskii kompozitor, 1961), 645. Cited in Vershinina, *Rannie balety*, 74.

[7] Lawrence Morton, "Footnotes to Stravinsky Studies: Le sacre du printemps," *Tempo*, March 1979, 9–16; Richard Taruskin, "Russian Folk Melodies in *The Rite of Spring*," *Journal of the American Musicological Society* 33 (Fall 1980): 501–43.

an extraordinary impression of a natural grasp of the spirit and style of ancient peasant folklore."[8] All that Stravinsky needed from the folk tradition at this point was the words (usually substandard or in phonetically transcribed dialect) and the subject matter in order to create dazzlingly original Russian music that was free of both ethnography and stylization.

Stravinsky's gradual internalization of Russian musical folklore, traceable from *The Firebird* to *Svadebka*, had a linear progression. The resultant manner had clear parallels in internalization of folklore observable in the work of other Russian artists of the period—the paintings of Nataliya Goncharova and Marc Chagall, for example, or the narrative poetry of Velimir Khlebnikov and Marina Tsvetaeva.[9] Stravinsky's utilization of folk theater forms during the same period does not follow a linear or chronological pattern, and it may therefore be more convenient to examine each individual case, beginning with the most ancient of these forms and going up to the more modern.

The Rite of Spring and Agrarian Vernal Rites

When the Grand Prince Vladimir decreed the imposition of Christianity as the state religion of Kievan Russia in AD 988, he lacked the power and the communications network to compel all his subjects to abandon their earlier Slavic religion. Christianization was followed by many centuries of *dvoeverie*, literally, "dual religion," and pagan survivals lingered on in the countryside well into modern times. With the nineteenth-century introduction of anthropology and ethnography, a wide array of seasonal folk customs and games was easily identified as directly descending from ancient rituals for welcoming the springtime and expelling the winter, such as had been common since prehistory among various Indo-European tribes. The cults of sun gods Yarilo and Kostroma (who may have been of Slavic, Finnic or Scandinavian origin) and of the mischievous river

---

[8] On the jacket of Lidiya Davydova's recording of Stravinsky's songs, Melodiia 33 C 10-08133-4 (stereo), 33⅓ rpm.
[9] See Richard Taruskin, "Stravinsky and the Painters" in Pasler, *Confronting Stravinsky*, 16–38.

nymphs (*rusalki*) and ceremonies of welcoming or expelling them at the onset of spring were practiced in more or less disguised form well into the nineteenth century.

As Vladimir Propp points out, the surviving vernal rites (*rusalia*) for either welcoming the solar gods or expelling the river nymphs followed a similar format.[10] The purpose of the expulsion was either to make the local bodies of water safe for a summer of swimming or else to move the *rusalki*, who represented water, from rivers and lakes to the fields and thus assure an ample harvest. There would be ceremonial songs and processions followed by *velichanie*, the honoring of a central figure, which corresponds to the episode "Velichanie izbrannoi" in the second part of *The Rite*, usually translated as "Glorification of the Chosen One." The sun god or the river nymph could be impersonated by people or represented by effigies. Whether the honored entity was welcomed or expelled, the effigy was put to ritual death, either by burning or by tearing to shreds. Propp compares this to ancient cults of dying and resurrected divinities, such as Osiris in Egypt and Adonis and Persephone in ancient Greece, cults that symbolized the return of springtime. To read the descriptions of the Yarilo, Kostroma, and *rusalia* ceremonies in V. Vsevolodsky-Gerngross's *History of Russian Theater* (1929), in *The Russian Folk Theater* by Elizabeth A. Warner (1977), or in Propp's cited book is to understand the long-range origins of the theme and the action of *The Rite*.[11]

Its immediate, short-range sources are to be sought in the great interest in prehistory and early Slavic religion in Russian arts in the years that immediately preceded the composition of that ballet. The Soviet Stravinsky specialist Valery Smirnov in his 1970 book and Lawrence Morton, apparently independently, in 1979 pointed out Sergei Gorodetsky's cycle

---

[10] V. Ia. Propp, *Russkie agrarnye prazdniki* [Russian agrarian holidays] (Leningrad: Izd-vo Leningradskogo gosudarstvennogo universiteta, 1963).

[11] Vsevolod Vsevolodskii-Gerngross, *Istoriia russkogo teatra* [A history of Russian theater] (Moscow and Leningrad: Tea-Kino-Pechat', 1929), vol. 1, chap. 2, 99–191, contains a detailed account of dramatically enacted pagan rituals that existed in Russian culture well into modern times. Elizabeth A. Warner, *The Russian Folk Theater* (The Hague: Mouton De Gruyter, 1977), contains accounts of Kostroma, Yarilo, and *rusalia* ceremonies and their later survivals and transformations. Its bilingual format (Russian texts are copiously cited without translation) makes its use by nonspecialists in Slavic studies difficult.

of poems about Yarilo, written in 1905-7, as a source of the idea and imagery of this ballet.¹² This is certainly plausible, but there are several other claimants: Aleksei Remizov's 1907 book about seasonal changes and ancient games connected with them, *Posolon'* (Follow the sun), for example, or the leading Futurist poet Velimir Khlebnikov's series of visionary narrative poems about Stone Age Russia, published in 1911 and 1912, especially *I and E*, in which a Stone Age maiden is caught in a competition between two rival tribes and condemned to be sacrificed to pagan gods. Another source that would bear more detailed investigation is the essays and paintings of the set designer for *The Rite*, Nikolai Roerich. He was involved in the project since its inception, and some of his earlier paintings bear titles or depict scenes that are reminiscent of certain episodes in the ballet.

Svadebka and Russian Village Weddings

The earliest native historical source, the *Primary Chronicle*, reports the existence of "pagan play acting" and dancing at the weddings of ancient East Slavic tribes. A sixteenth-century text, the *Stoglav* (Book of hundred chapters), complains of the enduring contamination of Christian weddings by pagan survivals. In the 1850s and 1960s, six volumes of *Ethnographic Studies* containing numerous transcribed wedding ceremonies from various regions were published by the Imperial Geographic Society. "The obviously theatrical character, as we understand it, of, for example, the wedding ceremony has enabled many ethnographers to record it in the form of theatrical play … the entire ceremony abounded in magic spells, incantations and, in general, obvious traces of paganism."¹³

With a few individual adjustments, the betrothal ceremony, the *devichnik* (a kind of bridal shower, with unbinding of the tresses and the bride's lament for the loss of her freedom), the blessing of the groom by his parents, and the wedding feast were not spontaneous transactions but

---

12 V. V. Smirnov, *Tvorcheskoe formirovanie I. F. Stravinskogo* [Igor Stravinsky's artistic development] (Leningrad: Muzyka, 1970), 87; Morton, "Footnotes," 9–16.
13 Vsevolodskii-Gerngross, *Istoriia russkago teatra*, 81–82.

enactments of a prearranged, prerehearsed script that had been traditional in that particular village for centuries. As Tatyana's nurse puts it in Pushkin's *Evgeny Onegin*: "They unbound my tresses with weeping / And led me to the church with songs." The actual marriage ceremony, which was a prescribed Christian rite, was the only part of the entire wedding not covered by the local ritual. The ritual's potential for theatrical adaptation has been realized since the eighteenth century, when two of the more successful Russian comic operas incorporated scenes of unbinding the bride's tresses, with texts similar to the one used in Stravinsky's ballet-cantata.[14] In 1875, a company of noted Russian actors and actresses brought to Paris an opulent staging of a transcript of a village wedding. In 1923, the State Experimental Theater presented in various cities of the Soviet Union a production called *The Russian Folk Wedding Ceremony*, an entire evening performance that reproduced the same ritual. That was, of course, the year when Stravinsky completed the instrumentation of his *Svadebka* (for some reason still known in this country under its French title of *Les noces*).

What Stravinsky got from Pyotr Kireevsky's collection of folk texts was not a group of songs to be set to music, but a complete script of a ritual that was actually a folk play. He then trimmed and rearranged it to suit his purposes. The version he chose was less riddled with pagan survivals than some other recorded versions (for example, there is no part for the Guard or the Polite One, euphemisms for a shaman who took over the priestly functions once the church ceremony was completed).[15] Still, when the Virgin Mary is commanded to bless the wedding and help comb the bridegroom's hair (at 44) and then is given a direct order by the divided bassos ("Pod' na svad'bu," which is roughly "Off to the wedding

---

[14] *The Miller Who Was a Wizard, a Cheat and a Matchmaker* (1779), with text by Aleksandr Ablesimov and with a pastiche of popular folk tunes arranged by Mikhail Sokolovsky, and *The St. Petersburg Bazaar* (1782), text by Mikhail Matinsky and best-known musical version by Vasily Pashkevich. The wedding customs depicted in these eighteenth-century works and subsequently reflected in Stravinsky's masterpiece continued in certain areas in postrevolutionary times. A number of such traditional songs and ceremonies were collected by Soviet folklorists between 1920 and 1960 and published in *Lirika russkoi svad'by* [Russian wedding lyrics], ed. N. P. Kolpakova (Leningrad: Nauka, 1973).

[15] Vsevolodskii-Gerngross, *Istoriia russkogo teatra*, 81–82.

with you!"), we realize that the mother of the Savior is here replacing some ancient fertility goddess. In monotheistic religions, divinities do not get ordered about, but in *The Iliad*, a warrior could order Aphrodite off the battlefield.

Renard and the Skomorokhi

In the early sketches for *Svadebka*, there was to be a role for a *skomorokh*, the minstrel-buffoon. *Skomorokhi* used to provide the entertainment at both royal and peasant weddings and are often mentioned in wedding songs. In the final score, at rehearsal number 16 of the first scene, there is mention of a "dashing little *skomorokh*, running in from another village" to distract the bride from her lamentations. In the C.-F. Ramuz translation, a singing bird replaces the clown. Ramuz's French translations of the three works of Stravinsky that are most closely connected with the lore and spirit of the *skomorokhi*, namely *Pribaoutki*, *Svadebka*, and especially *Renard*, systematically deprive them of that connection.

Renard is perhaps Stravinsky's least understood work among Western commentators. One gets to read in program notes that this is an Aesopian fable about barnyard animals, and Stravinsky gets praised for his clever imitation of these beasts. Soviet critics, from Boris Asafiev (Igor Glebov) in the early 1920s to Mikhail Druskin in the 1970s, invariably call *Renard* a *skomorosh'e deistvo*, a minstrel show or buffoon comedy. At its basic level, *Renard* depicts four *skomorokhi* in a pre-Petrine village who put on animal masks to perform a satirical, anticlerical skit about the victimization of a wealthy peasant (the Cock) by a con woman disguised as an itinerant nun (the Fox is a Vixen in the Russian text). The Cock's two fellow peasants, the Tomcat and the Ram, rescue him twice. Then the peasants kill the predator and blame the murder on the hounds of the local noblemen, whereupon the performers remove their masks and demand a payment of a crock of butter for their performance.

The *skomorokhi* are mentioned in chronicles and sermons since the beginning of recorded Russian history. Despite clerical denunciations, they enjoyed a great popularity as purveyors of humor and satire in old Russia. They ceased to exist as a social class as a result of Tsar Alexis's edicts, which outlawed them in 1648 and, in even harsher terms, in 1657. But they were remembered for centuries in folk songs, folk poetry, wedding rituals, drama, and opera. Their history has been studied by a number of scholars, most authoritatively by the musicologist Nikolai Findeizen, Stravinsky's occasional correspondent.[16] His work has been supplemented recently by two very good books on the *skomorokhi* by Anatoly Belkin and Russell Zguta.[17]

The instruments associated with the *skomorokhi* were the *gudok* (a vertically held fiddle), *volynka* (bagpipes), and *gusli* (the Russian psaltery). Stravinsky was fascinated with the sound of *gusli*. In early sketches for *Svadebka*, he intended to impersonate it with harpsichords and cimbaloms. Cimbalom as *gusli* is of course central to the conception of *Renard* (where this instrument is also prominently featured in the Russian text, but not in translations). Stravinsky's most realistic orchestral representation of *gusli* is in the piano and harp duet in the first trio of *Scherzo à la russe* (1944; this combination follows the example of Glinka's *Ruslan and Lyudmila*). He was to return to the *gusli* sound once more in the 1954 instrumentation of Four Songs (taken from two earlier sets of songs), where the flute, harp, and guitar suggest a *skomorokhi*-like bagpipe and *gusli* accompaniment.

---

[16] See his *Ocherki po istorii muzyki v Rossii* [Studies in the history of music in Russia] (Moscow and Leningrad: Muzgiz, 1928), vol. 1, 145–70. Cf. Nikolai Findeizen, *History of Music in Russia from Antiquity to 1800*, trans. S. W. Pring, ed. and annotated by Miloš Velimirović and Claudia R. Jensen (Bloomington: Indiana University Press 2008), vol. 1, 113-35 ("The Activities of the *Skomorokhi* in Russia").

In addition to being the founder of *Russkaia muzykal'naia gazeta* [Russian music gazette] (published 1894–1918), Findeizen was an important music historian who published monographs on Glinka, Dargomyzhsky, Grieg, and Anton Rubinstein, and books on early Russian music. Perhaps his most important work is the posthumous two-volume history of Russian music from antiquity to the eighteenth century cited above.

The Russian text of Stravinsky's letter to him, written in 1912, about the plan of *The Rite of Spring* (apart from a deleted postscript) appears in *I. F. Stravinskii: Stat'i i materialy* [I. F. Stravinsky: Essays and materials], compiled by L. S. D'iachkova, ed. B. M. Iarustovskii (Moscow: Sovietskii kompozitor, 1973). Portions of the letter appeared in translation in Igor Stravinsky, "*The Rite of Spring*": Sketches 1911–1913 (London: Boosey & Hawkes, 1969). Various excerpts cited by Craft, Vershinina, and Yarustovsky are all from the same letter. Yarustovsky seems to imply that there might be other correspondence between Stravinsky and Findeizen at the Saltykov-Shchedrin Library in St. Petersburg.

[17] A. A. Belkin, *Russkie skomorokhi* [Russian minstrels] (Moscow: Nauka, 1975) and Russell Zguta, *Russian Minstrels: A History of the Skomorokhi* (Philadelphia: University of Pennsylvania Press, 1978).

Folk Theater in *Petrushka*

The folk-theater components in *Petrushka* are not as ancient in origin as the ones so far discussed. They mostly date to no earlier than the eighteenth century, and they are also far more accessible to Western audiences. There are two points in this regard that I have not seen discussed. One is the importance of the figure of the long-bearded carnival barker, *balagannyi ded*, rather lamely translated as *le compère de la foire*, who appears in the first tableau. These barkers, whose job it was to entertain the crowd and to lure them into the *balagany* (the makeshift barracks where the various performances took place), spoke in lines of rhymed prose of unequal length, known as *raeshnik* [pronounced raYOSHnik]. The syncopated, limping rhythms of the *raeshnik* (rather similar in form to the poetry of Ogden Nash, with its wildly varying line lengths) are conveyed in the flute and oboe figure when the curtain goes up (at 4) in the first tableau of *Petrushka*. *Raeshnik* is also the rhythm of the subsequent passages, marked stringendo at 7, 17, and 22. They usually alternate with the cries of the coal vendor ("uglei! uglei!") that open that tableau.[18]

Raeshnik was also the standard verse of the oral folk theater of soldiers and convicts. Ramuz closely imitated its form in his text for *Histoire du soldat*, which makes for an interesting connection between that work and *Petrushka*. The other point concerns the episode of the maskers in the fourth tableau—men disguised as a devil, a pig, a goat, and (added in Fokine's choreography, though not indicated in the score) a woman. These masks, as both Propp's and Zguta's research suggests, go further back in history than the other customs depicted in *Petrushka*.[19] These

---

18   The identification of the motive of fourths as "uglei! uglei!" ("there's some charcoal!") was made in Vershinina, *Rannie balety*. The author cites Aleksandr Kastalsky's notations of street vendors' cries, selling coal, herring, and marinated apples, all either jumping up a fourth or filling a downward fourth with lesser intervals. Vershinina demonstrates the derivation from these vendors' cries of the rhythm and the intervals at the opening flute motive and also of the theme of the four cellos at 1 and the oboe solo at bar six of 2. As to the return of the initial motive in the "Dance of the Nursemaids," someone seems to be selling coal and pickled apples while the nannies are dancing.

19   See Propp, *Russkie agrarnye*, 111 (on the significance of animal disguises) and 116ff. (on cross-dressing of the sexes during winter holidays); and Russell Zguta, "Origins of the Russian Puppet Theater: An Alternative Hypothesis," *Slavic Review* 33 (December 1974): 712 (on the antiquity of these forms of disguise).

particular masks indicate connections with both old pagan rites and the usages of the *skomorokhi*.

The Soldier's Tale and Oral Folk Theater

The connection of the works so far mentioned with preliterate theater is self-evident. Stravinsky had during the gestation of these works friends and associates who encouraged this interest and could provide him with necessary expertise. The respective roles of Aleksandr Benois and Nikolai Roerich in the creation of *Petrushka* and *The Rite* were, as we now know, far more fundamental than Stravinsky remembered when he reminisced about those collaborations in *Conversations with Igor Stravinsky*.[20] The possible connection of Findeizen with the subject matter of *Svadebka* and *Renard* is a topic that will bear investigation.

Things may seem more dubious in the case of *Histoire du soldat*. After all, the only folkloric component here is the tale from Aleksandr Afanasiev's collection, which Stravinsky and Ramuz turned into a musical play and reset in Switzerland. Ramuz, who in his memoirs could not even recall Afanasiev's name and who had no knowledge of any Russian traditions, could not have been familiar with the institution of the oral folk theater of soldiers and convicts, which arose in Russia in the eighteenth century in imitation of literate, professional theater and which still existed in the early twentieth century.[21]

---

[20] In Igor Stravinsky and Robert Craft, *Conversations with Igor Stravinsky* (Garden City, NY: Doubleday, 1959; repr. Berkeley: University of California Press, 1980), the sections on Roerich, 94–95, and on Benois, 97–98, create the impression that Stravinsky selected these artists to design his ballets after his conception of the two works was formed and his music was almost completed. But, as Stravinsky's letters to Roerich dating from 1910–12 and Valery Smirnov's essay on the role of Benois in the genesis of *Petrushka* conclusively demonstrate, the two artists participated in creating the ballets they designed from the very inception. Each contributed important ideas for the stage action and musical realization of *The Rite* or *Petrushka*, respectively. See Igor Stravinsky's letters to Nikolai Roerich, introduced and annotated by Irina Vershinina, in *Sovetskaia muzyka*, no. 8 (August 1966): 57–63 and V. V. Smirnov, "A. N. Benua—librettist *Petrushki*" [A. N. Benois, the librettist of *Petrushka*], in D'iachkova and Iarustovskii, *I. F. Stravinskii*, 155–62.

[21] C.-F. Ramuz, *Souvenirs sur Igor Strawinsky* (Paris: Gallimard, 1929), 79. Pierre Meylan in his book on the collaboration between Ramuz and Stravinsky, *Une amitié célèbre* (Lausanne: Éditions du Cervin, 1962), denies that *Histoire du soldat* owes anything to Russian folklore (p. 65). Unaware of its Russian ties, Meylan attempts to

Yet the similarities of *Histoire du soldat* to plays of this genre cannot be overlooked. In chapter 11 of part 1 of his semiautobiographical novel *Notes from the House of the Dead*, Fyodor Dostoevsky described a performance by convicts in a Siberian penal colony of a folk play based on plays and operas about Don Juan, a performance he had actually witnessed in the late 1840s. The play was accompanied by a raucous little orchestra of squeaky violins and balalaikas, and it featured a virtuoso contribution by a tambourine player. Other plays of this type were collected and described in the early twentieth century. Aleksei Remizov, the influential writer, who may have had a hand in the libretto of *The Firebird* and whom Stravinsky helped out financially in Paris in the 1930s,[22] based his very successful *Comedy of the Devils* (1907) on such plays. He later adapted the most famous play of this genre, *Tsar Maximilian*, popular for almost two centuries in peasant amateur theatricals. Other twentieth-century playwrights, such as Zamyatin and Sologub, also drew on this type of play, whose logic, as Remizov remarked, is the logic of dreams.

Typical of this theater are deformations of foreign legends (*Histoire du soldat* is a deformation of the Faust legend, just as the play Dostoevsky saw was a deformation of Don Juan); interactions of common Russian folk (soldiers or peasants) with foreign, non-Russian royalty; the juxtaposition of everyday mundane reality of military barracks or peasant life with the supernatural, usually represented by the devil; and an anachronistic mixture of a fairy-tale world with ultramodern realia, such as the stock exchange, the telephone, tango, and ragtime in *Histoire du soldat*. Combined with the French versification that seems to imitate the *raeshnik* of Russian folk dramas, these features indicate that the Russian oral folk theater connections of *Histoire du soldat* deserve to be investigated in greater depth.

Conclusions

In a telling footnote to *Stravinsky in Pictures and Documents*, Robert Craft expressed regret that "Stravinsky never explained the anthropological

---

derive its dramatic conception from French medieval *fabliaux*. His book repeatedly implies that Ramuz was the author rather than the translator of the texts of *Svadebka* and *Renard*, though Meylan is clearly aware of the true facts.

[22] Stravinsky and Craft, *Pictures and Documents*, 642n10.

background of [*Svadebka*] ... the rituals and cultural traditions of which Western audiences are largely unaware."²³ The regret is of course also applicable to the rest of Stravinsky's oeuvre of the 1910s. When he was creating these epochal scores, he was addressing a Russian audience, for which such explanations would have been redundant. Foreign audiences, with whom these works were not yet established, might have been put off by too much ethnography or anthropology in program notes. In later years, Stravinsky was reluctant to discuss the folklore sources of his earlier compositions, not on account of snobbery or reactionary politics, as has sometimes been suggested, but because his artistic tastes had undergone a complex evolution that caused him to lose interest in that whole sphere and also because he had forgotten a great deal. Just how much he forgot can be seen in his discussion in *Expositions and Developments* of his *Podbliudnye* (Dish-divination songs). Stravinsky not only mistranslates the title as *Saucers* but gets the method of divination all wrong, the method that is described quite precisely in Pushkin's *Evgeny Onegin*, chapter 5, stanza 8, where the text of the first of these songs is also quoted.²⁴ Speak-

---

²³ Ibid., 619n236.

²⁴ As outlined by Propp, *Russkie agrarnye*, p. 108, dish-divination songs were sung during Yuletide by young women in rural areas as an accompaniment to a special fortune-telling game. The game consisted of placing on the table a large dish filled with water in which each participant would put her ring, comb, or some other small trinket, after which the dish was covered with a towel. Next came the singing of the *podbliudnye* (literally, "in the presence of the dish") songs, whose texts dealt with allegorical descriptions of agricultural activities, gigantic symbolic animals, and possession of gold, jewels, and other treasures. Most of these songs featured the obligatory refrain of "slava!" or "slavna!" ("glory!" or "glorious!"). During the singing, the trinkets were extracted one by one from under the towel over the dish, and as each trinket was withdrawn, its owner's fortune was predicted in accordance with the imagery of the line being sung.

In addition to studies by folklorists, such as Propp, this divination game was described in two of the best-known Russian literary works of the early nineteenth century: Pushkin's *Evgeny Onegin* and Vasily Zhukovsky's much-anthologized romantic ballad *Svetlana* (1812). Stravinsky himself, after completing his four dish-divination choruses (composed between 1914 and 1917), returned to this genre once more in 1919 in the third of his Four Russian Songs for voice and piano, which bears the title *Podbliudnaia* and has the typical refrain of "slavna!" Yet, discussing these choruses with Robert Craft in *Expositions and Developments* (Garden City, NY: Doubleday, 1962; repr. Berkeley: University of California Press, 1981), pp. 118–19 in the 1981 edition, Stravinsky stated: "Choruses of this sort were sung by the peasants while fortune-tellers read their fingerprints on the smoke-blackened bottoms of saucers."

ing of *Renard* in the same book, Stravinsky cannot remember the Russian title of this work and confuses the "Russian" *gusli* with the Yugoslav bowed instrument, the *guzla*.²⁵

This is either an aberration of memory or an ad hoc invention. No such method of fortune-telling is associated with *podbliudnye* songs by any Russian poet or student of folklore (nor does it seem likely that reading fingerprints was known to Russian peasants in the eighteenth and nineteenth centuries). The saucers, whose mention by Stravinsky has saddled these choruses with their unsuitable English title, may have come from his confusing the Russian word for *dish* (*bliudo*) with the one for *saucer* (*bliudtse*). Or Stravinsky may have been thinking that the English *saucer* had the same meaning as the French *saucière*. Be that as it may, the statement in *Expositions and Developments* had added further cultural barriers to appreciation in the West of this lovely choral work, made even more attractive by Stravinsky's 1954 rearrangement of it for voices and four horns.

Even a person as close to Stravinsky as Robert Craft is quite at sea about what the titles of the individual choruses should be. He calls the first of them "Saints' Day in Chigisakh" or "Christ in Chigisakh" or "Chigisakh across Yauza" in *Stravinsky in Pictures and Documents*, 604. In all three versions the name of the village Chigisy [*recte*: Chigasy] appears in the locative case, which suggests that Craft's informants did not know Russian grammar. [Chigisy, the erroneous form of the town's name, was Stravinsky's (not SK's) error, maintained in all autographs and editions.—Ed.] This is the song cited in *Evgeny Onegin*. In his commentary to his translation of this novel, Vladimir Nabokov (vol. 2, 497) includes the correct translation of the title, which is "In Our Savior's Parish in Chigasy beyond the Yauza," and of the entire text. There is no way of knowing from the existing English translations that the song opens with a description of a brick church built in 1485 and ends with a portent of death, information which Nabokov supplies.

The 1932 J. & W. Chester edition of *Podbliudnye* accompanies the title of the second chorus, "Ovsen'," with a note that this is "a beneficent solar deity honoured in Russian mythology." Eric Walter White repeats this information in *Stravinsky*, 211, though no study of pre-Christian Russian mythology mentions any such being. Robert Craft, *Pictures and Documents*, calls this chorus "Autumn," apparently because his informants have confused "Ovsen'" with *osen'*, which indeed means autumn. This is a particularly absurd mistake because a check with Vladimir Dal's standard *Dictionary of the Great Russian Language* (4 vols.; first published 1863–66) shows that *ovsen'*, known in some areas as *avsen'* or *tausen'*, was the name of the first day of spring in the pre-Christian Russian calendar, according to which the new year began on the first day of March. Although the meaning was lost in later centuries, the word remained in some peasant songs as an exclamation that conveyed the hope for a good harvest (see Propp, *Russkie agrarnye*, 38–39).

25 The Russian title of *Renard*, printed in recent editions of the score, is *Baika* (a regional word for *story* or *fairy tale*). The first edition had a more extended title that means "The Story of the Vixen, the Cock, the Tomcat, and the Ram." In Stravinsky and Craft, *Expositions and Developments*, p. 119 in the 1981 edition, Stravinsky, claiming to cite the original Russian title of this work, begins with a different word for *fairy tale*, *skazka* (which is the first word in the Russian title of *Histoire du soldat*),

V. On Stravinsky

During the years when Stravinsky was sharing his reminiscences with Robert Craft, his energies were still occupied with creating more new music. If the choice were between total recall of his Russian period and the composition of *Agon*, *The Flood* and *Requiem Canticles*, we would all surely choose music over documentation and memories. But now that Igor Fyodorovich is gone, those of us who know something about Russian culture must try to supply the missing pieces.

* * *

This dazzling piece displays with equal zest and magnificence both SK's erudition and his capacity for exciting speculation; and one of us (RT) must sacrifice decorum and revert to the first person in this commentary. It gave me an unforgettable thrill when I heard it in its original form, as a contribution to a roundtable on Stravinsky's Russian backgrounds at a Stravinsky centennial conference at the University of California, San Diego in September 1982. It was my first glimpse of SK in person, and no first meeting with a fellow scholar has ever been for me more *rokovoi*—to use that resonant Russian word not in its frequent meaning of "leading to disaster," but in the one that relies more on the literal meaning of the root noun, which means "fate." I knew that SK was someone with whom I would be fated to interact repeatedly and profoundly, for he had in this brief piece mapped out the territory I was to inhabit for the dozen-plus years that it took me (eerily mirroring the "twelve years it took me to write a survey of Russian drama" that SK invoked at the outset) to complete and see through to print the huge monograph, *Stravinsky and the Russian Traditions*, on which I had then just embarked. Every one of SK's examples has its chapter counterpart in that book, and, with the one exception duly to be noted, I found his spadework to be a trusty guide (to typology in the first place), without which my work would have been far more arduous and far less coherently concluded. The whole central section of my book, devoted to what is sometimes called Stravinsky's "Swiss period,"

---

and follows it with the wrong preposition, which puts the four animals (with the Cock preceding the Fox) in a different grammatical case from the one they were in in the first edition. The South Slavic *guzla* (possibly suggested to Stravinsky by Prosper Mérimée's volume of faked Yugoslav poetry, *La guzla*, which Pushkin translated into Russian) has nothing to do with the Russian psaltery, *gusli*, which inspired the sonority of *Renard*.

is in effect a gloss on SK's conference paper of 1982, and on its slightly more elaborate published version.

The Swiss period, for Stravinsky, encompassed the years 1910 to 1920, the years during which he was living in the Vaud, the French-speaking southwestern canton of Switzerland abutting Lake Geneva (or Leman, as it is locally known), where he repaired originally for the sake of the excellent maternity facilities its hospitals offered his pregnant wife (his son Soulima having been *in utero* at the time of the *Firebird* premiere and the removal of the whole family to Paris to witness it), where he then decided to make his base in the period of his wild early successes via Diaghilev's Russian Ballet, and where, finally, he chose to sit out the upheavals of World War I. In one of the few passages from his *Chroniques de ma vie* that can be quoted with confidence, Stravinsky's ghostwriter wrote, "My profound emotion on reading the news of war, which roused patriotic feelings and a sense of sadness at being so distant from my country, found some alleviation in the delight with which I steeped myself in Russian folk poems."[26] Brought on by homesickness, it was the most intensely nationalistic phase of Stravinsky's career, but, as SK very acutely points out toward the beginning of his essay, the nationalism that informs Stravinsky's Swiss-period music is of a very different sort from the familiar nationalism of nineteenth-century Russian art, as embodied musically in the work of the group that included his teacher, Rimsky-Korsakov. That difference was summed up in a single inspired sentence by Stravinsky's exact contemporary, Yakov Aleksandrovich Tugendhold (1882–1928), a Russian art critic living in Paris, who sent a review of *Firebird* back home to the Symbolist journal *Apollon*. "The folk," he wrote, "formerly the object of the artist's pity, are becoming increasingly the source of artistic style."[27]

Art historians have long had a name for this phenomenon, which showed up first and most distinctly (and was most widely practiced) in the visual and, particularly, the applied arts; and it is no accident that Tugendhold was commenting as an art historian on the visual aspects of the Russian ballet (in the case of *Firebird*, the sets and costumes of Konstantin Korovin and Aleksandr Golovin). The word art historians have coined is *neonationalism*. It was not a term anyone had ever applied to music, because hardly any musicians had been affected by the tendency. Until Stravinsky, that is, who learned of the

---

26 Igor Stravinsky, *An Autobiography* (New York: Simon and Schuster, 1936), 83.
27 Ia. A. Tugendhold [*sic*], "Russkii sezon v Parizhe," *Apollon*, 1910, no. 10, p. 21.

tendency from the painters with whom he was now willy-nilly collaborating, and who took it further than any other artist in any other medium, making it, in the process, more determinative of his own personal style during his Swiss years than anyone had done before or since.

I was in San Diego that fateful morning to give a paper in which I proposed that the term neonationalism be applied to Stravinsky at last—and, through him, employed as a lens for viewing and comparing the work of other composers. Imagine my combined delight and resentment to hear SK, who went immediately before me on the panel, steal my thunder, very accurately invoking neonationalism (in all—thankfully—but name) in detailing the crucial difference between the music of *Firebird* and that of *Petrushka*.

It is because the music of this most intense nationalistic phase of Stravinsky's career was composed with a Russian audience in mind but was for many decades published only abroad and performed only before foreigners that the anomaly arose of which SK complains when he notes that *Svadebka* is "for some reason still known in this country under its French title of *Les noces*." Believe me, he knew the reason. But he refused to accept the strange convention (which applies as well, of course, to *Pétrouchka* and *Le sacre du printemps* and even, often, to *L'oiseau de feu*, not to mention the "Swiss" songs (*Pribaoutki*, *Berceuses du chat*, and all the rest), maintaining a stubborn stance that bedeviled the lives of many editors in his time, and led to the shelving of at least one important piece of work.[28] I was younger and less exigent, but warmly sympathized with SK's crusade.

---

[28] SK addressed the subject in correspondence with his editor as he prepared an article about Diaghilev. "Now we come to a point about which I have very strong feelings. That is the outmoded custom of regarding works of Russian art, music, ballet, etc., as somehow more authentic if their names are cited in French. This was a snobbish British custom until ca. the 1920s, but I hoped that it had faded away. It makes no sense in the world to cite ballets by Russian composers, which have familiar and well-established names in English, in any form but the English. To put them into French or to add French diacritics not needed in English strikes me as a form of antiquated snobbery (as if English were not as cultured a language as French).... I would feel like a fool if an article I've signed follows that meaningless custom.... I couldn't live with myself if we Gallicize *The Firebird*, *Petrushka*, *The Rite of Spring*, *The Prodigal Son*, *Cleopatra* and *Scheherazade*. This would make me guilty of the kind of pretentious snobbery that I've been battling for years.... As to Fokine, I bow to the customary French *e muet* at the end of his last name (redundant in English), but his first name must be Mikhail (as in Baryshnikov) and that of Benois should be Alexander. Please accept my assurance that Russian names do not become less authentic when put into

The one point on which SK's brilliant typology of preliterate theatrical genres requires correction is in the matter of *Renard* (or as he would prefer, *Baika pro lisu, petukha, kota da barana*), about which he confidently asserted that it was, "as most Soviet commentators have realized, a modern revival of the spirit of the *skomorokhi*," the medieval Russian *jongleurs* or *Spielmänner*. Agreeing with the Soviets must have given SK a peculiar sensation, and perhaps it should have tipped him off: Asafiev's idea was a speculative hypothesis, and it has not been borne out by subsequent research.[29] Which is not to say that one must not think of the word *skomorokh* when watching or listening to *Renard*, only that there is no demonstrable connection between the *skomorokhi* and the preliterate Russian theater. They are not known to have engaged in dramatized performances, and so when SK writes that

> at its basic level, *Renard* depicts four *skomorokhi* in a pre-Petrine village who put on animal masks to perform a satirical, anticlerical skit about the victimization of a wealthy peasant (the Cock) by a con woman disguised as an itinerant nun (the Fox is a Vixen in the Russian text). The Cock's two fellow peasants, the Tomcat and the Ram, rescue him twice. Then the peasants kill the predator and blame the murder on the hounds of the local noblemen, whereupon the performers remove their masks and demand a payment of a crock of butter for their performance,

he is describing something that never happened in a pre-Petrine village, but only in a community of Stravinsky's (or Asafiev's) imagination. And so we should bear in mind that SK spoke not of the *skomorokhi* but of their "spirit," as Asafiev (and perhaps Stravinsky, too) imagined it. Nor is there any historical reason to suppose that the skit enacted in *Renard* was supposed to be allegorical, as SK asserts. He claimed a bit less, interestingly enough, when reading the paper aloud in San Diego. On that occasion he told his audience (according to Robert Craft's chance citation from the unpublished typescript) only that "*Renard* is a work that portrays a group of itinerant *skomorokhi*

English rather than French." SK to Karen Kevorkian/Ann Karlstrom, 22 August 1988, carton no. 7, Simon Karlinsky Papers, BANC MSS 2010/177, The Bancroft Library, University of California, Berkeley. (The reader will have realized that for the present republication of SK's articles, we have generally used the [transliterated] Russian form of names.)

29 For a thorough review of the evidence, see Taruskin, *Stravinsky*, 1237–46.

who don animal masks, perform a satirical, anticlerical skit for a rural audience in pre-Petrine Russia and demand a payment in barter at the end of the performance."[30] Even without the wealthy peasant and the con woman, this probably goes beyond what Stravinsky actually intended to portray—not a satire, just a *veseloe predstavlenie*, a "merry performance," as the work's subtitle would have it—and yet SK's version winningly displays his playful, speculative side, and I am glad it is in print. Similar strictures might be offered by strict-constructing historians to some of SK's other interpretive sallies, like the connection he draws (plausible from the Slavist side, less so from that of Stravinsky's biography) between *Histoire du soldat* and convict drama; and at times he reads the fruits of his own erudition a bit literalistically. (Did Stravinsky know or care that "Dalalyn', dalalyn'" was Belorussian? Did he expect his listeners to know?) But the speculations of a well-stocked imagination, verifiable or not, offer nonmatriculated listeners or spectators an enriched experience.[31]

---

[30] Quoted by Craft in *Stravinsky: Selected Correspondence*, vol. 1 (New York: Alfred A. Knopf, 1984), 421n.

[31] One last footnote may be the place to record the fact that (*pace* SK) Mikhail Semyonovich Druskin (1905–91), the musicological doyen of the Leningrad Conservatory who preserved an island of St. Petersburg there for the benefit (and to the gratitude) of his pupils, and who as a young Soviet pianist performed Stravinsky's Concerto for Piano and Winds in the composer's presence (Berlin, 1926), actually resisted Asafiev's interpretation of *Renard*, even though Asafiev had been his mentor. Nowhere in Druskin's monograph *Igor' Stravinskii: Lichnost', tvorchestvo, vzgliady* (Leningrad: Sovetskii kompozitor, 1974) did he mention *skomorokhi* in connection with Stravinsky's "merry performance," which deprived him of an easy way of characterizing the piece. In one place he calls it a "circus acrobatic performance" (p. 74), in another a "vulgar fairground spectacle" ("ploshchadnoe iarmarochnoe zrelishche," p. 92).

VI

ON SHOSTAKOVICH

"Our Destinies Are Bad"[1]

Few musicians have been as highly honored by the Soviet government as Dmitry Shostakovich. He was, it is true, the object of two savage campaigns of denunciation and vilification in the Soviet press, in 1936 and 1948, but in the intervening years he was quite regularly awarded Stalin and Lenin prizes; served on Soviet delegations to various peace congresses; and was appointed a People's Artist of the Soviet Union in 1954, one year after Stalin's death. He joined the Communist Party in 1960. He was elected a deputy to the Supreme Soviet of the USSR. He frequently issued statements in support of his government's policies. Then, at the end of his life, Shostakovich decided to speak his mind. In a series of conversations with the young musicologist Solomon Volkov, the composer expressed his uncensored views on musical, personal, and political matters. What emerges is a life dominated by fear for personal survival and by loathing for the system that honored the composer and which he had no choice but to serve.

The music of Shostakovich meant a great deal to me for a few years during the second decade of my life. I first heard it as a ballet, Léonide Massine's lovely *Rouge et noir*, choreographed to Shostakovich's First Symphony. That gripping, youthful work, together with certain portions of the Fourteenth and Fifteenth Symphonies, is the only music of Shostakovich that is still attractive to me today. In 1942 I was present at the Los Angeles premiere of Shostakovich's Seventh Symphony. Leopold Stokowski conducted, Nelson Eddy sang "The United Nations Song" by Shostakovich, and a Soviet woman sniper, famous because she had personally shot seventeen Germans, made an impassioned plea for the opening of the second front. Leningrad was under siege. There was a portrait of Shostakovich in his air-raid-warden gear on the cover of *Time*. Our press

---

[1] Review of *Testimony: The Memoirs of Dmitri Shostakovich; As Related to and Edited by Solomon Volkov*, trans. Antonina W. Bouis (New York: Harper & Row, 1979). Originally published in *Nation*, 24 November 1979, 533–36.

and Hollywood films kept assuring us that our valiant allies, the Soviet people, were united in their love for their all-wise and benevolent leader, Joseph Stalin. To doubt the artistic worth of Shostakovich's Seventh was tantamount to supporting Hitler. An elderly man who was heard muttering in the lobby that it was a trashy piece was almost lynched.

Listening to the Seventh on the radio recently, I marveled at the wishful illusions that accompanied its initial reception. That marching episode in the first movement—a phrase from *The Merry Widow* arranged and orchestrated in the manner of Ravel's *Boléro*—how fresh it sounded, how eagerly it was accepted as the new word in music. I recognized those same illusions in the whitewashing of the American cult of Stalin in the film *The Way We Were* a few years ago. The Barbra Streisand character had a picture of Lenin on her wall and she was shown as nobly striving to save women and children from being killed in Spain. In real life in those days, the portrait would have been that of Stalin, and her energies would have been devoted to discrediting Trotsky and to accusing anyone who dared mention the postcollectivization famine in the Soviet Union or Stalin's concentration camps of fascism. That was the way we of that generation, the film heroine's and mine, *really* were.

There is no escaping the fact that the wild success of Shostakovich's music in the West in the 1940s, especially among many people not otherwise noted for their interest in serious music, was due to the wartime alliance and the concomitant uncritical enthusiasm for everything Soviet, including Stalin. In light of the revelations of *Testimony: The Memoirs of Dmitri Shostakovich*, this is ironic. The figure of Stalin looms as the single biggest presence in the book, a murderous deity at once insane and infantile, poisoning the air people breathe by his existence, reducing everyone to quivering jelly, constantly demanding homage and human sacrifices.

Shostakovich came face to face with the full power of Stalin's displeasure during the purges of the 1930s. Nationally prominent figures close to him, such as Marshal Mikhail Tukhachevsky and the legendary stage director Vsevolod Meyerhold, were framed for nonexistent crimes and destroyed with no protest from any quarter. Millions of others perished for no reason at all. Shostakovich himself narrowly escaped with his life after Stalin ordered a press campaign against his hugely successful opera *Lady Macbeth of the Mtsensk District*. He survived by abasing himself, pleading guilty, and composing his Fifth Symphony in the officially approved "realistic" manner (which in practice amounted to imitating the clichés of nineteenth-century Romanticism).

Twelve years later, the internationally famous composer of the Seventh Symphony seemed to be headed for the executioner's block once again when he, Sergei Prokofiev, and several other Soviet composers were accused of "cosmopolitanism" (i.e., of not being chauvinistically patriotic in their music). This time round he escaped annihilation through Stalin's fortuitous whim of sending him as the Soviet delegate to the Conference for World Peace held at the Waldorf Astoria Hotel in New York City in 1949. There is a photograph in the book of Shostakovich flanked at that conference by the youthful Norman Mailer and Arthur Miller, the very image of the hands-across-the-sea amity of the artists of two peace-loving, democratic peoples. It is only now that we learn of Shostakovich's shame and disgust at the hypocritical charade he was forced to enact.

His two major ordeals left Shostakovich demoralized and frightened for the rest of his life. He was willing to sign any statement, make any speech the authorities prepared for him, tailor his music to any specifications. It is one of the great achievements of the volume of memoirs to show how an artist of this stature can be brought to such a pass. The keynote of the book is the composer's impotent rage. The Soviet rulers are "sick people" who feel that "they were called to set mankind," or at least their country, "on the right path." But the internal opponents of the Soviet regime are also treated with scorn, Aleksandr Solzhenitsyn for his messianism and supposed religious fanaticism and Andrei Sakharov for his contribution to the construction of the hydrogen bomb, which, in Shostakovich's judgment, deprives him of any right to speak out on moral matters.

Here is how Shostakovich sees life under Communism: "It's a huge ant hill in which we all crawl. In the majority of cases, our destinies are bad. We are treated harshly and cruelly. And as soon as someone crawls a little higher, he's ready to torture and humiliate others." His strongest contempt is reserved, understandably enough, for foreign "humanitarians" (mistranslated as "humanists" in the book) such as George Bernard Shaw, Romain Rolland, and Paul Robeson, who visited the Soviet Union during Stalin's rule and then wrote glowing accounts of the free and prosperous life they observed. "Once I was tormented by the question: Why?" says Shostakovich. "Why? Why were these people lying to the entire world? Why don't these famous humanitarians give a damn about us, our lives, honor, and dignity?"

The answer for him is that "their cozy life as famous humanitarians is what they hold most dear." Digging up the true facts of Soviet life is an ungrateful business: "You have to get involved, you have to write letters. And if you write a protest you won't get invited the next time and they'll ruin your good name. The radio and papers will smear you with dirt, they'll call you a reactionary." Shostakovich was well aware that Stalin's one-time Western supporters (and their biographers) had tended in recent years to exercise selective forgetfulness about their earlier fellow-traveling.

Shostakovich's embittered view of his life and his country left him with a residue of hatred which is at times directed at some unexpected targets. Arturo Toscanini, who did so much to win Shostakovich his popularity abroad, is denounced as a terrible conductor and a musical dictator comparable to Stalin. Prokofiev "had the soul of a goose, he always had a chip on his shoulder," and he is said to have hired others to orchestrate his work. Vladimir Mayakovsky, whose poetry Shostakovich admired and for whose comedy, *The Bedbug*, he composed the incidental music, is described as a boor, a snob, and a toady. The tone in which Shostakovich speaks of these artists and also of the Soviet political establishment is a mixture of revulsion, sarcasm, and forced humor, a mixture reminiscent of the musical style of his opera *The Nose*. This is a book that one cannot read without wincing.

Aside from Meyerhold, Tukhachevsky, and the satirist Mikhail Zoshchenko (who was persecuted by the Soviet authorities far more grimly than Shostakovich ever was), the person of whom the composer speaks with the greatest admiration and affection is his teacher, Aleksandr Glazunov. Regarded by most people as a secondary figure in the history of Russian music, Glazunov is for Shostakovich a "great musician." The impression left by the several sections devoted to Glazunov in the book is that Shostakovich not only loved the alcoholic and syphilitic old composer but envied him for having lived and worked before the Revolution. "He composed when he really wanted to, for his own pleasure, without giving a thought to 'ideological content [of his music].'" Glazunov enjoyed the patronage of wealthy publishers and merchant millionaires, who, says Shostakovich, "are always more generous than the state." When things got uncomfortable for him in Soviet times, Glazunov managed to defect during a visit to Vienna. He died peacefully in Paris in 1936, safe from ideological harassment.

In view of the extreme interest of the memoirs and the many startling and debatable revelations they contain, it is a pity that the book comes to us with so many unresolved questions in matters of authorship and veracity. Because of Solomon Volkov's musicological expertise and well-documented closeness to Shostakovich, there is no reason to doubt that he actually wrote down what Shostakovich told him. One is perplexed, nonetheless, to read two pages on Igor Stravinsky which are a verbatim reproduction of a statement by Shostakovich published in the Soviet Union in 1973 in a collection of essays on Stravinsky edited by Boris Yarutovsky. Beginning identically, the texts in *Testimony* and in the collection of essays then diverge and go their separate ways. Similarly, the section on Mayakovsky is almost identical with Shostakovich's brief memoir of him published in *Mayakovsky as Remembered by His Contemporaries* (Moscow, 1963), except that the passages depicting the cordial contacts between the poet and the composer have been replaced in *Testimony* by memories of hostility and rudeness.

It would have been far more comfortable for everyone involved if Volkov had been listed as the author of the book instead of its editor, and had chosen the format of "conversations with …" in the manner of J. P. Eckermann's classic *Conversations with Goethe at the End of His Life* or Aleksandr Gladkov's recent volume of conversations with Boris Pasternak.[2] Another major problem is that Volkov fails to annotate for the benefit of Western readers those passages where Shostakovich makes statements that are contrary to known facts. Thus, he blames Stalin's persecution of the writer Zoshchenko on Stalin's supposed envy of Zoshchenko's fame and popularity abroad. But Zoshchenko's work is practically untranslatable and, outside the Soviet Union, he never had any reputation to speak

---

[2] Alexander Konstantinovich Gladkov, *Meetings with Pasternak: A Memoir*, ed. Max Hayward (New York: Harcourt Brace Jovanovich, 1977). This book remained unpublished in the original Russian until 2002. (Volkov's *Testimony* has never appeared in Russian.)—Ed.

of. The actual causes and circumstances of his persecution are on record in several Western histories of Soviet literature.

If Stravinsky treated the Soviet musicologist Yarustovsky with contempt and refused to shake his hand, as Shostakovich says, how can we account for Stravinsky's inviting Yarustovsky to his home in Hollywood and quoting his insights with approval in print? Worst of all is Shostakovich's detailed account of the suicide in 1921 of the literary critic Anastasiya Chebotarevskaya, the wife of the major Symbolist poet and novelist Fyodor Sologub. As we know from numerous memoirs, she killed herself because of the inhuman cat-and-mouse game that Lenin's government was playing with her and her husband by first granting them an exit visa and then withdrawing it. Shostakovich attributes her suicide to a trivial spat with her husband and describes Sologub's despair in the wake of his loss in an insensitive, jeering tone that reduces a tragedy to ridiculous farce. The reader deserves at least a footnote stating the actual facts.

An additional handicap with which the book is saddled is the English translation. It can only be described as crude and occasionally semiliterate. On the one hand there is a profusion of anachronistic American slang which cannot possibly correspond to anything in Shostakovich's Russian: "beat the hell out of it," "those bums," "I don't want to be full of hot air." On the other hand, there is wholesale literal transposition of Russian idioms into English with no regard to what this does to the reader's comprehension. The Russian word for "power" (*vlast'*) can also be used to mean "government" or "system." The Russian words for "creativity" and "creative" more usually designate "art" and "artistic." Although these correspondences do not exist in English, the translator assumes they do and so we get "progressive realistic creativity" where "progressive realistic art" is meant, or "It's not enough to love Soviet power. It has to love you" where "Soviet power" stands for "Soviet Government." (Prospective readers are hereby advised to change "creativity" to "art" and "power" to "government" or "system" throughout the book, if they want to get at the meaning of the passages where these words occur.)

Western commentators have often been puzzled when Soviet persecution of artists is brought up, and they still seldom realize just what is involved. Reporting on the campaign against Soviet composers in his column in the *New York Herald Tribune* in 1948, Virgil Thomson found the whole business distasteful, but logical and reasonable, because the composers themselves "have determined their own ideal and accepted … the principles" under which they were being censured.[3] Another American music critic whom I admire, Peter Yates, describing Soviet composers' difficulties with their government in his book *Twentieth Century Music* (1967), pointed out that they are also given great privileges by the authorities and compared this to the plight of American composers, left to the mercies of commercialism. "So long as the officially endorsed attitude that music is a commercial product sold for entertainment persists in America," Yates concluded, "we have no better cause than the Russians to boast of 'freedom of the arts.'"[4]

I find such obligatory "comparison of oppressions," which is more popular today than ever, sadly uninformed. Shostakovich's pretending that his Fifth Symphony was a glorification of Socialist labor, when he in fact composed it as a memorial to the victims of Stalin's terror, or that the march in the Seventh represented advancing German troops, while he actually thought of his own Soviet leaders during its composition, is living a lie of such magnitude that few in the West can imagine it, let alone experience it. *Testimony* is one continuous illustration of Boris Pasternak's observation in *Doctor Zhivago* that people cannot be required to falsify their feelings day after day, to extol what they dislike and to feign joy about things that bring them misfortune, without sustaining serious physical and mental damage. A lifetime of pretense and hypocrisy on this scale cannot be understood by those who have not observed the Soviet system from within. The book should be required reading for those of us who think that Soviet dancers defect to the West only to get better roles and salaries.

* * *

In terms of sheer impact, this review of Solomon Volkov's notorious bestseller of 1979 was unquestionably SK's musical chef d'oeuvre, and this despite the fact that among his writings none stands in greater need today of contextualization and reconsideration. In the official memorial resolution commissioned

---

[3] Virgil Thomson, "Composers in Trouble," *New York Herald Tribune*, 22 February 1948; repr. in Virgil Thomson, *Music Reviewed 1940–1954* (New York: Vintage Books, 1967), 243.

[4] Peter Yates, *Twentieth Century Music: Its Evolution from the End of the Harmonic Era into the Present Era of Sound* (New York: Pantheon Books, 1967), 127.

by the University of California following SK's death in 2009, we called this remarkable piece "the butterfly's wing-beat that set off a thunderstorm in the form of the 'Shostakovich wars' that raged for decades."[5] The amazing thing about it is that, like many of us at the time, SK basically accepted the authenticity and veracity of the book on first impression, which (and this is something that the book's inveterate, and now victorious, debunkers often forget) was truly powerful. As SK wrote, no one could read this book without wincing. He paraphrased some of its wince-making—and news-making—contents, and closed with a peroration that more eloquently than any other conveys why the book was at first received so willingly and seemed so important.

But SK's review also contained a pair of paragraphs that effectively sealed *Testimony*'s fate. He noted two places where the new book reproduced passages he remembered from others that he'd read (one of them being the volume of *Stat'i i materialy* about Stravinsky that he had previously reviewed for *Slavic Review* in an essay, "The Repatriation of Igor Stravinsky," which is also included in the present book), and he remarked, in a passage that has echoed endlessly in the literature about Shostakovich, that Volkov should have cast himself, rather than Shostakovich, as the book's author. SK was the first to enunciate this now elementary stricture.

As most readers of these lines must know, *Testimony* has been conclusively exposed as a fabrication. The one who gets most of the credit for proving this, and rightly so, is Laurel Fay, who has been subjected by the book's defenders to a campaign of vilification that begins to rival the ones that took place decades ago in Stalin's Russia, or the ones SK describes in this very piece with respect to Western miscreants who learned, to their cost, that (as he says), digging up the true facts of Soviet life is—or was—an ungrateful business.

In an interview with a Canadian journalist that was first published in 2000 in *Lingua Franca*, the old academic gossip rag, Fay recalled that she first approached Volkov's book "with great excitement and enthusiasm, and with no idea that it might not be authentic." But, as her interlocutor reports:

> Shortly after she began reading *Testimony*, her attitude changed. "Something just didn't feel right," she says. "It was all just a little too convenient, both in terms of the explanation of the genesis and the background and then in the actual text itself." The tone also puzzled

---

[5] http://universityofcalifornia.edu/senate/inmemoriam/simonkarlinsky.html.

her. *Testimony* is filled with biting sarcasm, bitter recrimination, and gossipy asides. Apart from a warm tribute to his mentor, Alexander Glazunov, Shostakovich says nothing about his life's happy moments and expresses little gratitude. And why would Shostakovich, a devoted father and husband, recklessly endanger his family by agreeing to publish such a frontal attack on the Soviet system?

But there was something even more troubling. "I began to realize that I'd read some of this material before," Fay says, although at first she could not identify where. The breakthrough came in November 1979, when Simon Karlinsky published a review of *Testimony* in the *Nation*. Karlinsky noted that two substantial passages in *Testimony*—a book said to derive entirely from interviews with the composer—had already appeared in print under Shostakovich's name in Soviet publications. "Then it all began to click for me," Fay says, "and it didn't take me very long then to find another five passages."[6]

Since then, Fay has identified one more passage reproduced from the Soviet press, so that the beginnings of every one of the eight chapters in the book—the very pages Shostakovich signed as evidence of their authenticity—have all been exposed as recyclings.[7] It is obvious to all except Volkov's "useful idiots" (as Lenin would have said) that the whole process of authentication had been a sham, and that the first and most important victim of Volkov's chicanery was Shostakovich himself.

The point to emphasize with regard to SK's contribution to its exposure is that his commitment to advance the cause of truth took precedence over his commitment to uphold the actual contents of the book, even though he had found the book persuasive and inspiring, and wished to promote it. He was the single reader erudite enough to spot Volkov's recyclings without prompting or special research; and then he was the first reader to raise what proved to be fatal doubts about the book's provenance. Without him, Laurel Fay would not have been able to get started on what proved to be a grandly successful debunking. SK's review, in conjunction with Fay's interview, should be, as he says, required reading for all who think that disinterested commit-

---

[6] Paul Mitchinson, "The Shostakovich Variations (2000)," *Lingua franca* 10, no. 4 (May/June 2000): 46–54; repr. in Malcolm H. Brown, ed., *A Shostakovich Casebook* (Bloomington: Indiana University Press, 2004), 303–24; citation on p. 307.
[7] See Laurel Fay, "Volkov's *Testimony* Reconsidered," in Brown, *Shostakovich Casebook*, 22–67.

ment to scholarly standards is a chimera. Although, as we've seen, SK could be as playful as any Postmodernist, when it mattered no one was ever a sturdier pillar of rectitude.

His review of *Testimony* did not go without challenge from readers of the *Nation*, which is not surprising in view of that magazine's history as a former Stalinist redoubt. A reader named Leonard Boyer wrote in (9 February 1980) to counter the claims of Volkov's book by upholding the veracity of the older view of Shostakovich, which he supported by quoting from official Soviet documents, and from Western news accounts from the time of the War. His other tactic was to impugn the objectivity of émigrés from Soviet Russia, like Solomon Volkov. The letter ends with an exhortation to SK to "remove his cold-war goggles; they're frosted over." Here is the relevant portion of SK's answer, printed in the same issue of the *Nation*:

> Leonard Boyer believes that the statements attributed to Dmitry Shostakovich in press releases and concert programs dating from the 1940s represented the composer's true feelings. Back in the 1940s I might have agreed with him. Since that time I have met too many people who experienced Soviet life under Stalin and I have read too many eyewitness accounts of that period's repression to accept at face value such homilies, usually extracted under duress. As my review made clear, I do have problems with the total veracity of Solomon Volkov's book. But not because of the fact that the author has left the Soviet Union. Beginning with the earliest refugees from the October Revolution and all the way to today's Vietnamese boat people, the testimony of those who experienced the inhumanity of and enslavement by the so-called Socialist regimes and then fled has been discounted as "not objective" by people like Boyer—no matter how many millions have risked their lives and suffered privations to escape Socialism. If this persistent disregard of human suffering isn't a form of wearing goggles, I don't know what is.

Taking Notes for Testimony[1]

In Lidiya Chukovskaya's diaries, which chronicle the labors and days of the poet Anna Akhmatova, a telling episode is recorded. In 1946 Akhmatova was denounced in a resolution by the Central Committee of the Communist Party of the Soviet Union as a harmful writer, alien to the Soviet people. Andrei Zhdanov, the orchestrator of Stalin's post–Second World War persecutions of artists and other intellectuals, in a famous speech qualified Russia's great and beloved poet as "half nun, half harlot, mingling prayer with fornication."[2] There followed a massive press campaign urging the country to hate Akhmatova. She was berated at innumerable public meetings and ostracized from Soviet culture for a long time.

Several years later, a visiting delegation of students from England asked to meet Akhmatova. The encounter took place in the presence of officials of the party and of the then all-powerful Writers' Union. One of the students wanted to know Akhmatova's reaction to the party resolution and to Zhdanov's speech. She had no choice but to stand up and say: "I consider both documents, the speech of Comrade Zhdanov and the resolution of the Central Committee, to be entirely correct." The students made it clear that they found Akhmatova's response "not pleasing."

Setting down Akhmatova's story of this incident in her diary, Chukovskaya gave vent to her own sense of outrage. "What were those Englishmen, idiots or scoundrels? ... Someone was humiliated, beaten half to death and here they come asking: 'Did you enjoy the beating? Show us your broken bones!' And our own people—why did they allow this encounter? It's sadistic."[3] But, of course, the students meant no harm.

---

[1] Review of *The New Shostakovich*, by Ian MacDonald (Boston: Northeastern University Press, 1990). Originally published in *Times Literary Supplement*, 7 September 1990, 949.

[2] "Doklad t. Zhdanova o zhurnalakh 'Zvezda' i 'Leningrad,'" *Novyi mir*, 1946, no. 9, xi.

[3] Lidiia Chukovskaia, *Zapiski ob Anne Akhmatovoi*, vol. 2, *1952–1962* (Paris: YMCA-Press, 1980), entry for 8 May 1954.

They were typical of Western intellectuals who for most of Stalin's reign assumed that conditions in Communist countries were identical to those in Western democracies and that people there spoke what they thought. There was no way for them to imagine what the novelist Josef Škvorecký has called "the scientific methods of making terrified mice out of men and women."[4]

One of the most valuable aspects of Ian MacDonald's new biography of the composer Dmitry Shostakovich is his massive documentation of the terrorized state of Soviet society, including its artists, from the end of the 1920s on. Such fearless truth-seekers as Aleksandr Solzhenitsyn and Andrei Sakharov could appear and take on the system only after Stalin's death—in his time they would have been physically destroyed before they could make their mark.

Shostakovich is a good example of a major artist deprived both of the right to express his ideas and of his dignity by political pressure and intimidation. An honored figure in Soviet culture for most of his career, the recipient of numerous Stalin and Lenin prizes, Shostakovich was also the object, in 1936 and again in 1948, of two savage vilification campaigns by the Soviet regime and media. At those times, he lived in constant expectation of exile to the gulags or summary execution, sleeping in the lift so that the arresting officials would not disturb his children. But he weathered those periods of danger by making penitent statements and tailoring his music to the requirements of the state-imposed aesthetic of Socialist Realism.

In the 1960s Shostakovich became bolder, writing music that indicted the conformism and anti-Semitism of the Brezhnev era: the vocal cycle *From Jewish Folk Poetry* and the Thirteenth Symphony, with its settings of satirical poems by Evgeny Evtushenko.[5] But he was careful to intersperse his more daring works with safely conventional ones, such as his Twelfth Symphony, a paean to Lenin and the October Revolution, and the cantata *The Execution of Stepan Razin* (also to a Evtushenko text), which turns the seventeenth-century brigand-rebel into a politically correct proto-Bolshevik and preaches a Leninist message of class hatred. Still, for the

---

[4] Josef Škvorecký, *The Engineer of Human Souls*, trans. Paul Robert Wilson (Toronto: Lester & Orpen, 1977), 462.
[5] *From Jewish Folk Poetry* was actually written in 1948 and kept "in the drawer" until 1955, in the period of the so-called Thaw.—Ed.

outside world the composer remained a faithful son of the Communist Party (which he joined in 1960) and a loyal Soviet citizen.

This is the image that MacDonald seeks to overthrow. *The New Shostakovich* is constructed by the author with considerable ingenuity and eloquence even if its main foundation, as he admits at the outset, is shaky. This foundation is the odd book *Testimony: The Memoirs of Dmitri Shostakovich*, brought out in 1979 by the Soviet musicologist Solomon Volkov after he emigrated to America. Volkov claimed that the entire text was dictated to him by Shostakovich. Unfortunately, Western scholars soon discovered that the opening pages of each chapter of *Testimony* were taken verbatim from memoirs by Shostakovich published earlier in Soviet books and periodicals. Since the composer could not have memorized his old texts, the discovery cast doubts on the validity of the whole book. The refusal of Volkov's publishers to make the original Russian text available for scholarly examination made things look even more dubious.

Had Volkov styled himself as the author of *Testimony*, rather than as its stenographer and editor, had he refrained from "the editorial sleight of hand" (MacDonald's phrase), his revisionist view of Shostakovich's politics and outlook might have had a better chance of acceptance in the West. Shostakovich's hatred of the Soviet system, the false and misleading character of the programs of his Fifth and Seventh Symphonies, his life of fear and demoralization—all this has been confirmed since Volkov's book in the memoirs of people who knew the composer well, among them Galina Vishnevskaya and the violinist Rostislav Dubinsky, and in a television interview of the composer's son Maksim, cited by MacDonald.

The New Shostakovich accepts (with occasional hand-wringing by the author) the reliability of Volkov's *Testimony*, but it ups the stakes of the earlier book. In a detailed survey of Shostakovich's entire oeuvre, MacDonald seeks to demonstrate that, beginning with 1931, virtually all of his music embodied a repudiation of Communism and was a portrayal of the sufferings of the oppressed Soviet people. Under the present Gorbachev regime, when all accounts of Stalinist (and even Leninist) brutality are highly valued and encouraged, this could have been accomplished by interviewing the composer's surviving intimates and perhaps studying his archive in the Soviet Union. MacDonald chose a different path. He tries to show the composer's liberalism, humanitarianism, and political subversiveness by either describing a passage of his music and then juxtaposing it with quotations from literary works that do take an adverse view of Communist realities, such as Nadezhda Mandelstam's two volumes of memoirs or *The Captive Mind* by Czesław Miłosz; or else by identifying certain recurring musical formulae and cross-references which MacDonald then labels as codes for "Stalin," "tyranny," or "satire of Socialist Realism."

This search for programmatic codes is at times done with subtlety, as when a phrase from the last act of *Lady Macbeth of the Mtsensk District* is shown to represent the idea of betrayal, and then the fortunes of this phrase in Shostakovich's later symphonic and chamber works are traced. But all too often such analysis is simplistic and unconvincing. Two-note figures, usually involving the dominant and the tonic (the timpani at the opening of the last movement of the Fifth Symphony and the solo trombone squawks in the first movement of the Ninth) are invariably said to spell "Stalin." The reasons for this assumption are explained in a footnote that simply fails to persuade.

Because so much of MacDonald's book consists of musicological and historical commentary intended to demonstrate the image of Shostakovich that the author favors, one example will have to suffice to show how and why MacDonald's stratagems do not always work. He interprets the opera *Lady Macbeth of the Mtsensk District* as counterrevolutionary in spirit, "a deliberate, if necessarily disguised, expression of antagonism to Communism" and "strong evidence of Shostakovich's disenchantment with the Soviet regime." It's a pity he didn't see the musical and political study of the same opera by Richard Taruskin, which first appeared in the program booklet of its 1988 production at the San Francisco Opera and was then expanded in the *New Republic* (20 March 1989).[6] Taruskin compared the libretto of the opera to its literary source, a novella by Nikolai Leskov which is the story of a passionate murderess who exterminates anyone who stands in the way of her plans or desires.

Shostakovich decided to idealize this murderess, insisting that she was an "intelligent, talented and interesting woman." To this end, he eliminated from the opera the third of her murders, that of a little boy who

---

6 This much-traveled piece found its final resting place (as "*Entr'acte*: The Lessons of Lady M.") in R. Taruskin, *Defining Russia Musically* (Princeton: Princeton University Press, 1996), 498–510.—Ed.

stands to inherit the fortune of the husband she has assassinated (because, as Shostakovich put it at the time, "The murder of a child, no matter how it is explained, always makes a bad impression"). But the other murders—that of the heroine's father-in-law, then of her husband—are justified in the opera because she alone is given lyric and poetic music, while the men are portrayed in grotesque, subhuman musical terms.

The opera was composed, argued Taruskin, at the time of the expropriation of the kulaks, when any moderately successful farmer was declared an enemy of the people and sentenced to extermination together with his family. By turning the husband and the father-in-law into class enemies, whom it is all right to eliminate (and reducing other authority figures, the priest and the policemen, to vicious caricatures), the music of Shostakovich supported Stalin's genocidal policies, rather than disagreed with them, as MacDonald has it. The dictator and his henchmen later turned against this opera and denounced it only because their ears were too primitive to understand what its music was saying.

There are some attractive things in MacDonald's book—his love for the music of Shostakovich and his able demonstration of the self-referential nature of many of Shostakovich's compositions make one want to hear more of this music. He is aware of his hero's penchant for writing trashy, low-comedy music suitable for accompanying the antics of circus clowns and then placing it in some of his more serious symphonic and chamber works. MacDonald always calls such passages "satiric," but even he is hard put to decide just whom or what they are meant to satirize. Hardest of all to swallow is the book's claim for Shostakovich as the twentieth century's greatest composer on the grounds that he was the only one to portray the time's political and moral realities, while other composers addressed themselves mostly to musical form. There is even an invidious comparison of Shostakovich's Fifth Symphony, which in MacDonald's decoding speaks "for the hundreds of millions ... in the twentieth century who have suffered under political oppression," to Chaikovsky's Sixth, which "speaks primarily for Tchaikovsky."

In preglasnost times, there existed in the Soviet Union a vast critical industry that specialized in discovering revolutionary and anti-tsarist messages in the work of politically conservative artists of earlier times, such as Gogol and Chaikovsky. Many pages of *The New Shostakovich* make one think of the products of that unlamented industry—not because one disagrees with what Ian MacDonald has to say, but because wishful thinking so often takes the place of what should have been critical and historical rigor.

* * *

Once again SK took note of methodological or tactical failings in a book of which he basically approved, as if offering a colleague a friendly, eminently constructive critique. And once again his upright stance was attacked by those who insisted on bias. This time the attack came not from the unregenerate Stalinist party but from zealous revisionists who were ostensibly on the other side; and to the discomfiture of one of the present volume's editors (RT), who must again slip into the first person, it was I who inadvertently attracted their wrath to him. SK's citation of my essay on *Lady Macbeth* was to Ian MacDonald like waving a red rag at a bull, and he came charging, in a letter to the *Times Literary Supplement* that (as SK described it to me) revealed the writer's true colors to his formerly friendly critic.[7] Like MacDonald's musical exegeses, which reminded SK of the methods and objectives of Soviet criticism, but much more bluntly, the letter bore the earmarks of a McCarthyite campaign (or, which amounted to the same thing, a KGB campaign), targeting not only me, at whom derisive adjectives (eccentric, contorted, cross-eyed, etc.) were hurled by the handful, but also, and incredibly, poor Shostakovich. "Like Solomon Volkov and Galina Vishnevskaya," he wrote, "I see *Lady Macbeth* as the artistic foundation of Shostakovich's moral individualism."[8] The only evidence offered in support of this interpretation consisted of a record of the composer's personal relationships:

> As a professor of literature, Karlinsky will know that non-Party satirists like [Mikhail] Bulgakov, Zamyatin, Olesha and Zoshchenko were, long before 1930, convinced that Marxist collectivism was a disaster. Shostakovich knew these writers personally, collaborating with one

---

7 Ian MacDonald, letter to the editor, *Times Literary Supplement*, 28 September 1990, 1031.
8 The reference to Vishnevskaya, the famous Soviet soprano, is to her memoir, *Galina: A Russian Story*, trans. Guy Daniels (San Diego: Harcourt Brace Jovanovich, 1984). The discussion of *Lady Macbeth* is on p. 207ff. It places the opera, composed in 1930–32 and first performed in January 1934, in the historical context of the so-called Great Terror, which was unleashed in 1936.

(Zamyatin: on the opera *The Nose*) and exploring a major project with another (Bulgakov: an opera on his play about Pushkin, *Last Days*). There is nothing to suggest that the composer—like, say, Mayakovsky—opposed the non-Party writers; on the contrary, the evidence is that he sympathized with them—which is presumably why he read their books, watched their plays and socialized with them.

He knew them personally. He read their books. There is nothing to suggest that he opposed them. State Procurator Vyshinsky could not have built a better case for guilt by association. MacDonald may have thought of it as exoneration, not guilt, but attempting to proving anything on the basis of association, and placing the burden of (negative) proof on the accused, brought chilling reverberations to the mind of one familiar with the tactics of Soviet show trials. It was a horrifying display, and when it came my turn to review *The New Shostakovich* I was far less generous to the author than SK had been.[9] I owed to SK's prior experience the same debt that Laurel Fay had owed to his early critique of Volkov's *Testimony*.

---

[9] *Slavic Review* 52, no. 2 (Summer 1993): 396–97.

VII

SONG AND DANCE

The Uses of Chaliapin[1]

One of the earliest memories of the celebrated Russian basso, Fyodor Chaliapin, as recorded in the first of his two autobiographies (*Pages of My Life*), was the folk legend he heard from his mother about the fall of Satan from grace and the elevation of Michael to the rank of archangel. In the version that Avdotya Chaliapina told her five-year-old son, the Lord, angered by the rebellion of the archangel Satanael, decided to replace him with a strange, hairy, but meek supernatural creature named Misha, who just happened to be around in Heaven. "Well then, having driven away Satanael, God called Misha unto Him and said: 'Although thou art not intelligent, it would still be better if I make thee the commander of Heavenly Hosts, an archangel. Thou wouldst not cause trouble in Heaven. And henceforth, thou shalt be not Misha, but Mikhail, while Satanael shall be simply Satan!'"[2]

This the-last-shall-be-the-first story, so very relevant to Chaliapin's own subsequent myth, made an indelible impression on the little boy. In the current English version of this biography (an earlier American edition appeared in 1926 as *Pages from My Life*), the passage just quoted appears thus: "God sent for him and said: 'Although you are not clever, I will take you as head of the Heavenly forces and as arch-strategist. You will start no trouble here, and henceforth you will be called, not Mikh, but Satan.'"

Such inability on the part of the editors and translators of this beautifully produced and illustrated volume to tell the difference between Satan and Michael, between archangel (*arkhistratig*) and arch-strategist, or to discern the significance of the little legend for the rest of the autobiog-

---

[1] Review of *Chaliapin: An Autobiography As Told to Maxim Gorky*, translated, compiled, and edited by Nina Froud and James Hanley (New York: Stein and Day, 1967). Originally published in *Nation*, 27 May 1968, 704–6.
[2] Cf. Fedor Shaliapin, *Povesti o zhizni: Stranitsy iz moei zhizni, maska i dusha* (Perm: Permskoe knizhnoe izd-vo, 1969), 5–6. The story works better in Russian, in which language the name of the fallen angel is Satana (accent on the last syllable), thus yielding a cleaner parallel: Mikha+il/Satana+il.—Ed.

raphy, goes a long way toward explaining the vast amount of distortion, misinformation, and just plain absurdity about Chaliapin and his life that is found in the book.

The attribution of authorship to Gorky, to begin with, can only be qualified as opportunistic. *Pages of My Life* was dictated by Chaliapin to Gorky's stenographer and had the benefit of Gorky's editorial assistance. None of the earlier foreign or Russian editions (including the version in the two-volume collection of Chaliapin materials published in the Soviet Union by the Soviet musicologist E. A. Grosheva, from which the present English version is purportedly translated) lists Gorky as the author or even ghostwriter. The closest Gorky himself came to claiming any share in the book was in the letter he wrote at the behest of the Soviet Government, to be presented as evidence in the French court where Chaliapin, by then a rabidly anti-Soviet émigré, was suing for damages for an unauthorized republication of the biography in the Soviet Union. The lawsuit ended the decades-long friendship between the writer and the singer, but even in a document intended to discredit Chaliapin in every way, all Gorky lays claim to is editorial assistance and transcribing the stenographer's notes. None of the complete editions of Gorky's works in the USSR includes this book, although it has been announced for the forthcoming centenary edition as a work Gorky helped edit.

All the pertinent letters from Gorky on the origin of the book are reproduced in the current English edition of the autobiography, causing the "as told to" and the raves on the dust jacket about Gorky's "brilliant handling" of his subject to ring a bit hollow. And since the English text is a free rearrangement of the Russian original rather than a literal translation, a more accurate designation of the volume would have been: "Chaliapin's Autobiography As Edited by Gorky and Retold by Nina Froud and James Hanley."

In addition to the autobiography, the book contains a selection of Gorky-Chaliapin correspondence, portraits, and other Chaliapiniana. The acknowledgments section and introductions tell of twelve years spent in preparing the volume, of trips to the Soviet Union, and of digging up rare materials in Soviet archives. Just why all this traveling and research were necessary is utterly puzzling because, with the exception of a few letters published elsewhere and an article culled from a popular Soviet magazine, *all* the material in the book, including the annotations, is taken from the two-volume Grosheva collection. So resolutely did the editors restrict themselves to this one source that even the most important single Chaliapin publication, his second and far more detailed autobiography, *Maska i dusha* (Mask and soul), published in 1932 in France and in America (under the title *Man and Mask*), was read by them, as they admit, only in the bowdlerized selections included in the same Grosheva collection.[3] The sections of *Maska i dusha* censored for Soviet publication (approximately one-third of the original text) are indispensable for understanding the biography, the attitudes, and the politics of the singer. But these omitted passages and chapters would be too much at variance with the sentimentalized image of Chaliapin as the great democratic, nationalistic, and realistic artist of the Russian people, whose officially encouraged cult has been a prominent feature of the post-Stalinist period in Soviet cultural life. And while an American volume dedicated to fostering this patently false and slanted image is at least ludicrous, viewed within its Soviet context the Chaliapin revival (of which the Grosheva collection and its American Gorky-credited avatar are symptoms) is of considerable interest, and provides us with valid insights into recent Soviet cultural policies.

The partial amnesty being offered to the more daring and innovative twentieth-century Russian art prohibited under Stalin is still proceeding cautiously and hesitantly. Much of the earlier work of Sergei Prokofiev is still under virtual ban. While the poetry of Andrei Bely has been republished, his great experimental novels, *Petersburg* and *Kotik Letaev*, are still unavailable and unmentionable. Meyerhold has been posthumously rehabilitated politically, but none of his magnificent productions has been revived, and his practices and theories are relegated to the past and are not permitted to have any impact on the current Soviet theater. While these three innovators, who died as loyal Soviet citizens and members of Soviet artists' unions, are allowed what may be called a partial recognition, three sworn enemies of the Soviet regime whose works were previously taboo—Chaliapin, the writer Ivan Bunin, and the composer Sergei Rach-

---

[3] "Maska i dusha," in *Fedor Ivanovich Shaliapin*, ed. Elena Andreevna Grosheva, 2 vols. (Moscow: Iskusstvo, 1957–58), 1:239–351; Fyodor Ivanovich Chaliapin, *Man and Mask: Forty Years in the Life of a Singer* (Garden City: Garden City Publishing, 1932); Fédor Chaliapine, *Ma vie*, traduit du russe par André Pierre (Paris: Albin Michel, 1932). [The cuts remain in Grosheva's 3-vol. revision (1976–79), 1:213–303.—Ed.]

maninoff—are now enthusiastically accepted and propagandized by the Soviet cultural establishment. Such paradoxically selective rehabilitation makes sense only if seen as a triumph of the aesthetics of Socialist Realism over politics or historical justice. Neither Bunin nor Chaliapin nor Rachmaninoff was considered in any way progressive or revolutionary or even democratic when they made their respective artistic reputations in prerevolutionary Russia. But they were all close friends of Maksim Gorky's (until they broke with him over political issues after they emigrated to the West), which is practically a *cachet de noblesse* for purposes of rehabilitation.

Unlike Gorky, these three had no tolerance or understanding for any of the twentieth-century developments in the arts, remaining aristocratically aloof from the main trends in the Russian artistic revival of the first decades of the century. Chaliapin, in particular, was actively hostile to all methods of staging opera that deviated from the melodramatic Russian stagings of the 1890s, and he was opposed to all important twentieth-century music (with the exception of Rachmaninoff's). In his heyday, he was powerful enough to sabotage some of the newer music, preventing Russian productions of Richard Strauss and blocking Diaghilev's project of a joint instrumentation of Musorgsky's *Khovanshchina* by Ravel and Stravinsky. As Stravinsky tells it, "Unfortunately, however, Diaghilev cared less about establishing a good instrumentation of the opera and rescuing it from Rimsky-Korsakov than about our version as a new vehicle for Chaliapin. That idiot from every nonvocal point of view, and from some of these, could not realize the value of such instrumentation. He declined to sing, and the project was abandoned, though we had already done considerable work."[4]

---

[4] Igor Stravinsky and Robert Craft, *Conversations with Igor Stravinsky* (Garden City: Doubleday, 1959), 66–67. In this notably cryptic comment, "and from some of these" seems to mean "and from some vocal points of view." Chaliapin did not in fact impede the *Khovanshchina* production, which went on as scheduled in June 1913, and which was never intended wholly to replace the Rimsky-Korsakov orchestration. What Stravinsky here recalls with resentment is Chaliapin's refusal to relearn the part of Dosifei, or to sing Shaklovity's act 3 aria as Dosifei. This meant that Stravinsky's reorchestration of the latter item could not be included in the production, but his substitute finale (along with Ravel's orchestration of some numbers omitted from the Rimsky-Korsakov version) was indeed performed, and Chaliapin was finally persuaded to sing in the finale. See R. Taruskin, *Stravinsky and the Russian Traditions* (Berkeley: University of California Press 1996), 1038–39, 1045–46.—Ed.

In current Soviet aesthetics, traditional and nationalistic late-nineteenth-century art is still mechanically equated with such concepts as "progressive" and "realistic." It is their parochialism and their traditionalism that make the émigrés Bunin, Rachmaninoff, and Chaliapin so eminently acceptable to the post-Stalinist Soviet cultural authorities, rather than their artistic achievements, which are undeniable in the cases of the first two.

During his long musical career, Chaliapin was many things to many men. For Maksim Gorky, he was the very embodiment of the Russian nation. "Such men appear to remind us all how strong, handsome and talented the Russian people are," wrote Gorky. Nicholas II agreed (one of the few imaginable subjects on which the monarch and the writer could conceivably see eye to eye). He gave Chaliapin a gold watch and the title of His Majesty's Soloist (later Chaliapin demanded that the watch be exchanged for a showier one that would be more suitable for demonstrating the largess of the Russian tsar on trips abroad). Both Gorky and Nicholas II (as the whole Rasputin business well demonstrated) were susceptible to the peculiarly Russian mystique of the Divinely Inspired Peasant, as the Representative of the Masses.

This particular appeal was something on which Chaliapin, like his contemporary Rasputin, never failed to capitalize. He was not merely a singer to be judged on his vocal or dramatic abilities but always the Archangel Mikhail, who had to be loved and admired because he had once been the lowly and hairy Misha. His foreign audiences saw him primarily as an exotic and barbarous Russian, whose overwhelming voice and presence made them overlook his hammy acting and his monumental lack of the most elementary musical taste and culture. A singer with a narrowly provincial repertory, he made an international name for himself almost solely in the operas by the Russian Five. Back in Russia, despite an occasional Don Basilio or Mefistofele his favorite roles were in such god-awful third-rate works as Anton Rubinstein's *Demon* and Serov's *Judith*. If we are told that the interpretations of *Boris Godunov* by Pinza, London, or Christoff owe a lot to Chaliapin, it is only in the sense that Jeanne Moreau may owe some of her acting techniques to Theda Bara.[5]

---

[5] Here SK went a little overboard. George London quite proudly declared his debt to Chaliapin, which amounted to a claim of authority; early in his career, he wrote, he sought out as coach "a Russian bass-baritone by the name of George Dubrovsky," who was "a younger colleague of Chaliapin" and "a product of a school of acting which

It is of course understandable that a charismatic crowd-pleaser like Chaliapin should find his admirers both at home and abroad. His weepy, breast-beating Boris, his moaning and cooing renditions of Massenet's *Élégie* or Rubinstein's *Persian Love Song* are bound to be appreciated by the type of listener who is left cold by the far superior musicianship and vocal artistry of a Fischer-Dieskau, a Ghiaurov, or a Donald Gramm.

During his emigration, Chaliapin lived in Paris, where he became the rallying point for the most hidebound of the émigrés who now saw in him the embodiment of the vanished glories of Imperial Russia. For Vladimir Mayakovsky, who denounced him in a long poem and never tired of needling him in articles and topical poetry, Chaliapin stood for the worst and the most antiquated of Russian theater and music, and was a foreign imperialist flunky to boot.[6] To encounter him now in an American-published book as a pro-Soviet pal of Gorky and Lenin is paradoxical, but on the whole harmless. The official Soviet cult of Chaliapin, on the other hand, which can produce two 800-page volumes of materials dedicated to the proposition that Chaliapin's art was realistic and progressive, and that it represents the finest in early twentieth-century music (while dismissing Igor Stravinsky in a contemptuous footnote as a "militant apologist for Formalism in music"), can only be seen as ominous and profoundly reactionary in every conceivable meaning of that term.[7]

---

was typical of the Russian lyric theater and also of the Moscow Art Theater," from whom "I was able to learn an entire style of operatic acting, gestures and attitudes such as only one of his background could show me" (quoted in Nora London, *George London: Of Gods and Demons* [Fort Worth: Baskerville, 2005], 122). It is quite evident that the other singers named here all studied Chaliapin's recordings and assimilated his authoritative renditions, even if they ultimately departed from them in various ways.—Ed.

6 This poem, "Gospodin 'narodnyi artist'" [Sir People's Artist], was published in *Komsomol'skaia pravda* on 2 June 1927. What occasioned it was a report in the Paris émigré newspaper *Poslednie novosti* that Chaliapin had donated 5,000 francs for the relief of unemployment among Russians living in exile, to be dispensed through the Russian Orthodox Church in Paris. It accuses Chaliapin not of antiquated artistry but of class perfidy (Chaliapin having been one of the first to be named a "People's Artist" by the fledgling Soviet government in 1918). Its appearance in the newspaper made it an official declaration of Soviet hostility, showing that the Soviet cult of Chaliapin, like this earlier condemnation, was the product of a political calculation.—Ed.

7 The churlish characterization of Stravinsky was not a footnote, actually, but a capsule identification for Soviet readers in the index of Grosheva, *Shaliapin*, 2:712 (and was dropped, incidentally, for the late 1970s revision).—Ed.

VII. Song and Dance

* * *

This minority report or contrarian view of the usually idolized Chaliapin, SK's earliest publication on a musical subject, already sets the tone—or, more properly, the subtext—for most of the musical pieces reprinted in this volume, namely the vagaries of cold-war reception. Questions involving the fluctuating reputations of cultural figures and artifacts in light of political events and attitudes especially attracted SK, and that is what led him to participate so conspicuously in some of the most heavily fraught scholarly debates ever to engage musicians. These were the very debates—involving Chaikovsky and his alleged suicide, Shostakovich and his alleged memoirs, and the dramatic reevaluation of Stravinsky's heritage and legacy both in Russia and in the American academy—that brought Russian music out of its comfortable if low-status Romantic-nationalist ghetto and into the unruly mainstream of modern musicology. SK's position as a peerlessly well-informed disciplinary outsider gave his voice a special cachet within those debates. At the same time, like all subtexts, that of Cold-War reception casts light reciprocally on the objects discussed and on the discussants.

SK's musical essays are full of fascinating idiosyncrasies and fissures that are well worth the sort of analysis that is broached at times, though never aggressively and far from exhaustively, in the commentaries offered here. In the case of Chaliapin, it may be more obvious now than it was at the time of the article's original publication that the perhaps surprisingly insistent negativity of SK's critique betrays the discomfort many liberals felt when contemplating both the Communist and the anti-Communist sides of the cold war debate. For SK, Chaliapin was in a double bind, at once an icon of Stalinist *poshlost'* (aesthetic insipidity) and a spokesman for "rabid" and "hidebound" anti-Soviet factionalism. He had become in SK's eyes a political football, and SK, who opposed both teams, wanted no part of him.

Russian Comic Opera in the Age of Catherine the Great[1]

Comic opera was introduced in Russia in the early 1770s. It remained one of the country's favorite dramatic forms until the end of that century. The term "comic opera" may perhaps be misleading in this case. We are not talking of *La serva padrona* or *Le nozze di Figaro* or of any other eighteenth-century comic opera that requires opera singers to perform. Russian comic opera of the age of Catherine was essentially a literary rather than a musical-dramatic genre. It was a brief (one- or two-act) play that included songs, vocal ensembles, and occasionally choruses. The performers were actors with some singing ability rather than trained singers. The music for these productions was at times composed by Russian or resident foreign composers, but equally often there would be no original musical score, the performers being instructed to sing their vocal numbers to the tune of this or that popular air of the day.

In its native France, this form of music drama had a more appropriate name: *comédie mêlée d'ariettes*. Its main practitioner was Charles-Simon Favart (1710–92). During his four decades of writing musical comedies, Favart bridged the transition from the *comédie en vaudevilles*, associated with the theatricals at the two annual Paris fairs (*théâtre de foire*, in which Favart did his playwriting apprenticeship in the 1730s), to the true French *opéra-comique* at the end of the century. Favart's comedies treated a variety of themes and social situations, but some of his most lasting successes depicted peasant life in the countryside. The plot invariably showed two young peasant lovers overcoming obstacles to their union, be it parental opposition or interference by a villainous bailiff. A favorite plot device was to involve a naive, inexperienced peasant girl with a man above her on the social scale and in a position to hold her in his power. This was the situa-

---

[1] Originally published in *19th-Century Music* 7 (April 1984): 318–25, and subsequently as part of ch. 5 of *Russian Drama from Its Beginnings to the Age of Pushkin*, by Simon Karlinsky (Berkeley: University of California Press, 1985).

tion in Favart's *Le caprice amoureux, ou Ninette à la cour* (1755), *Annette et Lubin* (1762) and *Les moissonneurs* (The reapers, 1768), the last being a musical comedy version of the Book of Ruth in the Bible.

Favart's manner of presenting peasant life on the stage has been compared to the idealized and bucolic canvases of Boucher and Watteau. Because of his enormous popularity, these plays were soon exported to other countries and adapted to local tastes and conditions.[2] Thus *Ninette à la cour* reappeared in Germany as *Lottchen am Hofe*, in England as *Phoebe at Court*, in Italy as *La contadina in corte*, and in Sweden as *Lantflickan på hovet*. In 1783, it was incarnated as *La villanella rapita*, a comic opera with libretto by Giovanni Bertati and music by Francesco Bianchi, with two additional scenes composed by Mozart (K. 479 and 480) for the 1785 production in Vienna. Similar transformations occurred with other successes of Favart, leading to a great vogue for rustic settings and for peasant girl–peasant boy–nobleman (or bailiff) triangles in comedy and comic opera throughout the Western world.

By the time Lorenzo Da Ponte used this theme in his libretti for Mozart's *Le nozze di Figaro* (the Susanna, Figaro and the Count imbroglio) and *Don Giovanni* (Zerlina, Masetto and the Don), in 1786 and 1787, respectively, he was offering his own version of possibly the most widespread comedic plot situation of the century. The famous Don Giovanni–Zerlina duet "Là ci darem la mano" is a rare living survivor of the hundreds upon hundreds of duets of similar content and tone that resounded for half a century in every theater in Europe.

Another work whose international success helped enhance the fashion for *paysannerie* in musical comedies was Jean-Jacques Rousseau's *Le devin du village*, premiered in Paris in 1752. Considered the first genuine French comic opera (in that, unlike the earlier *comédies d'ariettes*, it was provided with a musical score of its own), Rousseau's brief idyll about a peasant couple brought together by a kindly quack consolidated the custom of letting the musical theater voice a preference for the wholesome rustic life over the supposedly corrupt life of the cities. *Le devin du village* became the object of innumerable imitations, one of the most

---

[2] On the impact of Favart on the whole of Europe (with the exception of the Slavic countries), see Alfred Iacuzzi, *The European Vogue of Favart* (New York: Institute of French Studies, 1932).

popular of which was Favart's parody of Rousseau, *Les amours de Bastien et Bastienne* (1753), also widely copied and imitated. Its progeny included the brief opera *Bastien und Bastienne*, composed by the twelve-year-old Mozart for a performance at the home of Dr. Anton Mesmer, the originator of the notion of animal magnetism.

A third French name essential for tracing the origins of the comic opera in Russia is Michel-Jean Sedaine (1719–97), author of comic-opera libretti for such popular composers of the second half of the eighteenth century as Philidor, Pierre Monsigny, Egidio Duni, and André Grétry. A follower and personal disciple of Denis Diderot, Sedaine obeyed in the libretti of his earlier period Diderot's behest that theater deal with all occupations and social classes. Thus the protagonists of Sedaine's *Blaise le savetier* (1759, music by Philidor) are a poor village cobbler and his wife; in *Le jardinier et son seigneur* (1761, also with Philidor), a kitchen gardener is humiliated and his wife and daughter are insulted during a visit from an inconsiderate noble and his entourage; and in *Le roi et le fermier* (1762, music by Monsigny), King Henri IV of France finds refuge in the hut of a peasant whose fiancée has been abducted by neighboring nobles.

Sedaine's most popular comic opera, *Le déserteur* (1769, also with Monsigny), deals with the adventures of a simple army private who gets into trouble because of a practical joke played on him by his future father-in-law. Through their great currency, these early libretti of Sedaine (his later ones, including the one for Grétry's *Richard Cœur de Lion*, 1784, dealt mostly with royalty) greatly expanded the social purview of comic opera.[3] Between them, Favart, Rousseau, Sedaine, and a host of their contemporaries and imitators made the poorer and humbler classes the expected and accepted protagonists in comic opera. Servants, peasants, artisans, or gardeners who could appear in subsidiary or episodic roles in neoclassical comedy and sentimental drama were now shown to have love lives of their own and interesting and at times paradoxical emotions. Although the surviving conventions of the dramatic pastorale could upon occasion force the rustic protagonists of the new genre into the poses and attitudes of Arcadian shepherds and shepherdesses, the extended social

---

[3] On the significance of Sedaine, see Louise Parkinson Arnoldson, *Sedaine et les musiciens de son temps* (Paris: Entente Linotypiste, 1934).

purview of the *opéra comique* did represent a step in the direction of a more democratic theater.

Russians became acquainted with this new genre during the guest appearances of a French touring company in St. Petersburg in the years 1764-68.[4] Because of the continuing orientation toward Parisian tastes and the widespread practice of "adaptation to our customs," it was inevitable that Russian comic opera would materialize. The earliest chronologically was *Anyuta*, a one-act comedy with music, which was performed for Catherine by the members of her church choir at Tsarskoe Selo on 26 August 1772. *Anyuta* is generally considered the ancestress of all Russian operetta and musical comedy. The text was written by Mikhail Popov (1742–ca. 1790), otherwise known as one of the actors of the Imperial Theaters and as a journalist and folklore collector. The music for

---

[4] R.-Aloys Mooser, *L'opéra-comique français en Russie au XVIIIe siècle* (Geneva: R. Kister, 1954), 45ff. The same author's *Opéras, intermezzos, ballets, cantates, oratorios joués en Russie durant le XVIIIe siècle* (Geneva: R. Kister, 1955) is a useful tabulation of foreign and Russian works for musical theater during the period in question.

The utilitarian-minded Russian scholars of the nineteenth and early twentieth centuries had little interest in studying the arts and the culture of the eighteenth century. Modern understanding of the nature of eighteenth-century comic opera begins with Nikolai Findeizen's *Ocherki po istorii muzyki v Rossii*, 2 vols. (Moscow and Leningrad: Gos. izd-vo Muzsektor, 1928), published posthumously but written, to a large extent, before the Revolution. This work has served as the basis of literary and musicological studies of comic opera that have appeared since its publication. From the 1930s and especially the 1940s on, understanding of Russian eighteenth-century music and literature has been handicapped by the ultranationalistic stance assumed by Soviet culture, which requires that Western sources of Russian art be minimized or altogether ignored.

Recent Soviet studies of Russian comic opera as a literary genre either have ignored its dependence on its French models or have gone to the extent of denying this dependence altogether. Thus, P. N. Berkov, in his often excellent *Istoriia russkoi komedii XVIII v.* (Leningrad: Nauka, 1977), 180ff., disregards the development of the genre in the West and the productions of representative French comic operas in St. Petersburg throughout the 1760s (of all of which he is aware, since he cites Mooser's studies) and seeks, quite unconvincingly, to derive Russian comic operas from native folklore traditions, such oral folk plays as *Tsar Maximilian*, and comedies by Russian neoclassical playwrights.

Soviet musicologists offer a somewhat more factual and historically balanced account of the genesis of the genre in Russia; see, for instance, Iu. V. Keldysh, *Russkaia muzyka XVIII veka* (Moscow: Nauka, 1965), ch. 6. But even they have not ventured a full-dress comparison of the Russian texts with Favart and Sedaine, which is the crux of the matter.

this piece is lost. It is not clear whether there was an original score composed for it or whether, as was often the practice with Favart, the musical numbers were simply sung to the melodies of currently popular songs (known as *timbres* in France).

Popov's play follows closely the mode of representing peasant life developed by Favart and Rousseau. The heroine, the adopted daughter of a poor peasant, is being forced into a distasteful marriage with a hired hand. A handsome young nobleman named Viktor falls in love with her and, upon investigating her origins, discovers that Anyuta is a noblewoman by birth, the daughter of a colonel, and thus a suitable match for himself. The disappointed foster father and the hired hand are easily placated by small sums of money. The concluding ensemble chants the praises of the stratified social system: "Do not try to possess things you were not meant to own.... / He who is pleased with his lot / Is the most fortunate man in the world!" While their extreme poverty and very hard life are made explicit in the play, Anyuta and the two peasant men are shown as crude, grasping, foul-mouthed creatures. Only the noble Viktor is endowed by the author with some semblance of dignity and humanity.

For all its lack of dramatic polish and human insight, Popov's *Anyuta* did set the pattern for the numerous comic operas that were written and produced in Russia during the following three decades. Popov's incorporation of native folk song texts into his play led his followers to feature such songs, either authentic or imitation, in their plays. The name Anyuta (probably inspired by Favart's *Annette et Lubin*, known as *Anyuta i Lyubim* in Russian and widely performed in the 1760s and 1770s both in versions set in France and in "adaptations for our customs") became as canonical for peasant heroines in comic opera as Sofiya was for young gentlewomen in serious comedy.

In the wake of successful productions of imported comic operas with texts by Favart and Sedaine and of *Anyuta*, Russian playwrights and poets took to writing comedies with music that reflected, with greater or lesser fidelity, the situation of the humbler classes of the time: peasants (both enserfed and free), artisans, lower ranks in the army and the navy, and, eventually, the merchant class and even the clergy. The comic opera was thus the dramatic genre that encompassed a social range broader than any other of its time.

VII. Song and Dance

A basic fact of Russian lower-class life of the time was the form of slavery known as serfdom. For all of her enlightenment and oft-reiterated opposition to tyranny, Catherine not only supported this archaic institution, but even extended it to areas where it did not previously exist, such as the Ukraine. When the popular successes by Favart that portrayed free peasant farmers in France were transplanted in Catherine's Russia, the result was the first full-scale portrayals on the Russian stage of serfs as protagonists. Now, criticism of mistreatment of serfs by their owners and of other abuses of serfdom was permitted and expected in that age to a degree that would seem unbelievable in the early nineteenth century. But it was permitted only provided that the abuses were attacked, not the institution itself. Catherine herself offered an example of such permissible criticism in her comedy *What Tricks Are These?*

Therefore no eyebrows were raised when Nikolai Nikolev (1758–1815) presented his "drama with voices" *Rozana and Lyubim* (premiered in Moscow in 1778 and regularly played in both capitals until the end of the century), with music composed by one of the members of the Kertselli (Kerzelli) family, either Ivan or Iosif. It was a comic opera about a peasant maiden, abducted by an amorous nobleman who eventually repents and returns her to her father so that she can marry the young fisherman she loves. Nikolev's libretto was a Russification of two of Favart's greatest successes: *Annette et Lubin* and *Ninette à la cour*. He followed these two texts with so much fidelity, in fact, that he anticipated by seven years Bertati's libretto for the Bianchi-Mozart *La villanella rapita*, which, had it not postdated Nikolev's effort, might have easily been mistaken for its model.

No one in the eighteenth century would have thought Nikolev's text incendiary, nor would the ruling classes (royalty and nobility), the principal audience of comic opera performances, ever have tolerated a work that they thought was directed against themselves or their interests. Both the authors of comic operas and the spectators considered the institution of serfdom a given of Russian life which, like all human institutions, was capable of being abused. In recent decades, however, an ahistorical interpretation of all this has prevailed in the Soviet Union, according to which such works as *Rozana and Lyubim* were denunciations of serfdom based not on Russifications of Favart and his contemporaries, but rather on the playwright's personal observations of concrete social realities.⁵ A mechanical binary oppositional system of classifying literary works as progressive or reactionary has forced scholars to classify all eighteenth-century comic operas that depict serfdom as one or the other, depending on whether or not the serf owners are attractively portrayed.

In this manner, *Rozana and Lyubim* and Yakov Knyazhnin's somewhat more original *Misfortune from a Coach*⁶ have become standard exhibits in Soviet textbooks, representing enlightened opposition to the upper classes and to slavery. Conversely, *The Village Feast, or Virtue Crowned* (*Derevenskii prazdnik, ili Uvenchannaia dobrodetel'*, 1777) by the poet Vasily Maikov (1728–78), with music by Mikhail Kertselli, has at times been assaulted as a reactionary, proserfdom tract, merely because it shows the relations between the serf owner and his serfs as amiable.⁷ One could

---

5   Berkov's *Istoriia russkoi komedii XVIII v.* is unique among the Soviet literary and musicological studies of the last three decades in denying that Nikolev's *Rozana and Lyubim* and similar works from its period (such as Knyazhnin's *Misfortune from a Coach* [see n. 6 below]) are antiserfdom tracts (190ff., 207ff.).

6   The playwright Yakov Knyazhnin (1742–91) is invariably remembered in posterity by the merciless epithet which Pushkin applied to him in *Evgeny Onegin*: *pereimchivyi* [imitational]. His neoclassical tragedies, much appreciated by his contemporaries, were transpositions into medieval Russia of the successful Italian (Pietro Metastasio, Scipione Maffei) or French (Racine, Voltaire) works of that genre. His lively verse comedies were a landmark in the development of Russian literary language.

   It is Knyazhnin's comic operas, however, that Pushkin's epithet most obviously fits. His two great successes in this genre were *Misfortune from a Coach* (*Neschast'e ot karety*, 1779; this title is often translated as *Accident with a Carriage* by commentators who are not familiar with the plot), with music by Vasily Pashkevich, and *The Hot-Mead Vendor* (*Sbitenshchik*, 1784), with a score composed by the Czech bassoonist Anton Bullandt. The first of these operas combines typical Favart features with some pointed commentary on the heartless custom of Russian noblemen selling their serfs into military service as a way of raising money for luxuries, in this case for an imported French coach. *The Hot-Mead Vendor* is a clever splicing together of characters and plots from well-known comedies by Molière, Sedaine, and Beaumarchais. The popularity of Knyazhnin's comic operas was second only to that of the Ablesimov and Matinsky works discussed here. Both *Misfortune from a Coach* and *The Hot-Mead Vendor* remained in the repertoire of Russian theater until the 1820s.

7   For example, B. N. Aseev, *Russkii dramaticheskii teatr XVII–XVIII vekov* (Moscow: Iskusstvo, 1958), 315 ("a typical example of a reactionary comic opera"; in the revised edition of the book, *Russkii dramaticheskii teatr ot ego istokov do kontsa XVIII veka* (Moscow: Iskusstvo, 1977), the adjective "reactionary" was changed to "pseudopopular"); and Keldysh, 259 ("a reactionary feudal idyll"). Because of this reputation, *The Village Feast* has been excluded from the collections of Maikov's poetry and plays that have appeared in postrevolutionary times. It can be found in *Sochineniia i perevody V. I. Maikova*, ed. L. N. Maikov (St. Petersburg: P. A. Efremov, 1867).

as easily turn this around and show that Maikov's portrayal of serfdom is far grimmer than Nikolev's.

Styled as "a pastoral drama with music in two acts," Maikov's play begins with the mannered wooing of a coy shepherdess by an eloquent shepherd. They seem to have stepped right off a delicate Sèvres teacup. These Rococo porcelain creatures are intended to represent Russian serfs living in the environs of Moscow. In the second act the lovers are duly betrothed, with the kindly aid of their owner. Other assembled serfs chant the praises of their wise master. An ideal relationship thus seems to exist between serfs and their owners. The benevolent squire expresses his concern for the welfare of his subjects to a visitor and in a vocal solo accompanied by a peasant chorus sings:

> If my peasants are pleased with me
> Then I am pleased with myself.
> If they are wealthy and free,
> Therein lies all my joy.

But the chieftain of a transient band of gypsies (who are treated in this play with the kind of racist contempt that late nineteenth-century Russian melodrama reserved for Jews, and Soviet drama of the late 1950s for Americans) gives the squire some sharp arguments. To his preaching of honor and virtue, the gypsy, in a tone reminiscent of Brecht's *Threepenny Opera*, rejoins with the following sung argument:

> He who has something in his pocket
> Will be honored even by the Heathen.
> But he whose pocket is empty
> Will buy nothing with his honor.
> He will be indeed vanquished by hunger
> And allowed to die among the Christians.

The gypsy's pretended astuteness at reading palms (which helps unite the lovers) so frightens the squire's bailiff that he confesses having instituted a system of bribes in the village, thereby bringing some serfs to the verge of ruin. And even though the virtuous serf owner promises to set everything right, the play's most striking point has been made: Maikov's happy peasants, who do not have to contend with the cruel voluptuary of *Rozana and Lyubim* and are not owned by the irresponsible and silly Gallomaniacs of Knyazhnin's *Misfortune from a Coach*, are still not protected from oppression and exploitation even though their owner happens to be a benevolent singing philosopher. It can thus be seen that *any* eighteenth-century comic opera can be used to demonstrate the inhumanity of slavery if one looks at it from the viewpoint of later, more enlightened times.

It is a measure of the freedom of Russian literature from censorship pressure in the reign of Catherine II prior to the French Revolution that the social issues raised by serfdom could be reflected in comic opera as openly as they were. Certainly the more outspoken examples of this genre could not have been published or performed in the reigns of Alexander I or Nicholas I half a century later. Yet in the 1770s and 1780s these works were produced at Catherine's court and in open public theaters and were performed by serf actors in the private theaters of wealthy magnates. Nor is there any indication that the empress and the upper hierarchy felt themselves indicted by the depiction of the abuses of serfdom in comic opera, any more than an American politician or banker today feels himself personally indicted by a portrayal of a corrupt politician or a dishonest banker in a Hollywood film.

The most popular Russian comic opera on a peasant subject, however, ignored serfdom altogether. It owed its huge and lasting success to the charm of its music and to the wit and gaiety of its dialogue, written in authentic-sounding peasant dialect. This was *The Miller Who Was a Wizard, a Cheat, and a Matchmaker* (*Mel'nik—koldun, obmanshchik i svat*)[8] by Aleksandr Ablesimov (1742–83), otherwise known as a minor journalist of the period and the author of several other, forgettable libretti. Initially performed in Moscow in 1779, *The Miller* had for a musical score

---

[8] This title is usually rendered into English with the four nouns separated by commas (e.g., D. S. Mirsky, *A History of Russian Literature* [New York: Alfred A. Knopf, 1958], 54). This creates the impression that the title refers to four characters: a miller, a wizard, a cheat, and a matchmaker. In the original Russian, the last three nouns serve as epithets, qualifying the miller. All four nouns refer to the same character.

a pastiche of Russian folk songs arranged by the violinist and conductor Mikhail Sokolovsky.⁹

One of the numerous progeny that Rousseau's *Le devin du village* engendered all over Europe (a not unillustrious lineage, since it also includes Mozart's *Bastien und Bastienne*),¹⁰ *The Miller* shows the unlikely predicament of a free peasant who is married to an impoverished noblewoman, and of their daughter, named of course Anyuta, who is in love with a neighboring farmer. Each of the parents wishes the daughter to marry into his or her own social class. The miller of the village, who moonlights as a quack magician, helps the young couple by convincing the parents that the young man is fatally predestined to be Anyuta's husband. The miller placates the parents' social prejudices with the argument that an independent farmer who owns his own homestead (*odnodvorets*) is a peasant and a nobleman at the same time.

The racy arguments among the characters and the abundance of popular peasant songs (including some that were taken from the traditional wedding ritual), plus such novelties as having a live horse onstage and real Russian balalaikas in the orchestra, all added up to an overwhelmingly

---

⁹ SK's original text included the then widely accepted information that Sokolovsky's score was "later revised by the composer Evstignei Fomin." Although the *Dramaticheskii slovar'*, a dictionary of drama published in Moscow in 1787, informed its readers that the score of *The Miller* "was arranged from old-Russian [*russkie*] songs by the contemporary Russian [*rossiiskii*] musician of the Moscow theater, Mr. Sokolovsky," his name did not appear either in the original printed libretto (Moscow, 1782) or in any surviving performance material; the music was attributed on account of its quality to Fomin, the most accomplished dramatic composer of the period, and first published under his name (vocal score, Moscow: Jurgenson, 1884). For a full clarification, see Aleksei Vasil'evich Finagin, "Evstignei Fomin: zhizn' i tvorchestvo," in A. V. Finagin et al., *Muzyka i muzykal'nyi byt staroi Rossii: materialy i issledovaniia* (Leningrad: Academia, 1927), 94–5.—Ed.

¹⁰ This obvious dependence of Ablesimov on Rousseau, recognized by prerevolutionary commentators and by Nikolai Findeizen (*Ocherki po istorii muzyki*, 2:213 and 216), has been either flatly denied in recent Soviet scholarship (Keldysh, 287–88), or else challenged. B. N. Aseev, *Russkii dramaticheskii teatr ot ego istokov do kontsa XVIII veka* (Moscow: Iskusstvo, 1977), 425–26, admits the similarities between Rousseau and Ablesimov, but denies that Ablesimov imitated his French predecessor: "The contrast between the natural and pure country life and the corrupting influence of the city, which is present in Rousseau's opera, is replaced in Ablesimov's play with the contrast between peasants and noblemen and, most importantly, with glorification of free peasant labor."

successful work. *The Miller* brought about a host of imitations, spread the renown of the genre of comic opera throughout Russia, and became a favorite for amateur theatricals (Vissarion Belinsky, the future critic, played the part of the father in an amateur student production in the late 1820s). It retained its popularity well into the nineteenth century and was occasionally revived in Soviet times.

The only other eighteenth-century Russian comic opera to enjoy a success comparable to *The Miller* was *The St. Petersburg Bazaar* (*Sanktpeterburgskii gostinyi dvor*)[11] by Mikhail Matinsky (1750–ca.1820). Matinsky was born a serf, possibly an illegitimate son of his owner. Aware of his intelligence and talents, the owner sent him to study in Italy (in this he followed a widespread custom during Catherine's reign; some of the best Russian painters and musicians of the period were Italian-schooled emancipated serfs). Upon returning to Russia, Matinsky was given his freedom and became a teacher of mathematics and geography at the exclusive boarding school for the daughters of the highest nobility, the Smolny Institute. His later writing efforts were devoted to textbooks on geography and geometry. It was during his stay in Italy that Matinsky wrote what is certainly the most original Russian comic opera of the eighteenth century. Matinsky was thought to have also composed the music for this piece. More recent research casts doubts on the assumption that Matinsky ever composed any music at all.[12]

The *St. Petersburg Bazaar* seems to owe less to a recognizable foreign model than does any other work of this genre. There is no young peasant heroine and, in fact, no love story at all. Matinsky turned his attention instead to the "dark kingdom" of the tradition-bound Russian merchant class. In so doing, he discovered an entirely new social and dra-

---

11 This work exists in two versions. The second version, revised by Matinsky and with its music rearranged by the court composer Vasily Pashkevich, was performed in 1792 under the title *You Shall Be Known by the Way You Live* (*Kak pozhivesh', tak i proslyvesh'*). The first version of the text remained the better known one, but the musical contributions of Pashkevich were incorporated into it in subsequent performances. The first version (i.e., *The St. Petersburg Bazaar*) is also the one found in various recent collections of eighteenth-century drama, for example the Berkov anthology and (in excerpts) in *Khrestomatiia po russkoi literature XVIII veka*, ed. A. V. Kokorev (Moscow: Gos. uchebno-pedagogicheskoe izd-vo, 1961). On the differences between the two versions of the play, see Findeizen, 2:224–30, and Keldysh, 315–24.

12 See Keldysh for a summary of this research.

matic dimension that nineteenth-century Russian drama was to explore and populate. The central character is the wealthy but miserly merchant Skvalygin (Mr. Tightwad), a greedy and unprincipled moneylender, who is shown both in his family life, with his doting, alcoholic wife and his stupid daughter, and in his various business practices.

Skvalygin forms an alliance with his prospective son-in-law, an equally corrupt civil servant named Kryuchkodei (Mr. Hook-and-Crook), who makes a practice of involving transient out-of-town peasants in horse-cart accidents and then extorting money from them for imaginary damages. Skvalygin and Kryuchkodei cook up a complicated financial swindle designed to victimize an army officer and two society ladies who had been careless about getting their dealings with Skvalygin certified and documented. In the second act, the victims invade Skvalygin's home during the engagement party (*posidelki*) for his daughter and Kryuchkodei, but can obtain no satisfaction. Owing to a clumsy blunder of the daughter, the two crooks believe themselves mutually betrayed and their misdeeds are exposed in the end.

From the very first two scenes, one showing Skvalygin putting the squeeze on the other merchants in the bazaar arcade and the other bringing in the two subsequently victimized noblewomen to bargain in a vocal sextet with four of the merchants, Matinsky displays a truly admirable grasp of the milieu and a profusion of dramatic invention. One original scene follows another throughout: the bargaining of the crafty merchants with their capricious customers; the indignant aria (in the northern *tsokanie* dialect) of the peasant[13] forced to pay damages for the accident he knows was caused on purpose; Skvalygin's stingy dispositions for the engagement party refreshments, clashing with the hospitable inclinations of his wife; the carousing of the previously prim and sedate merchants' wives who are briefly left alone with the liquor supply; and the complex and ingenious plot stratagem that brings the villains to justice.

All these scenes achieve a genuine dramatic impact. None of them seems to have any precedent in foreign or Russian comic traditions. Ma-

---

[13] I.e., a dialect in which words containing the sound denoted by the Russian letter ч, pronounced "ch," are modified by substitution of ц, pronounced "ts": thus *tselovek* for *chelovek* [person].—Ed.

tinsky managed to make even the moralizing scene between Skvalygin and his remonstrating virtuous nephew (an enlightened young merchant given to charitable works) interesting, lively, and believable. Musically, the work is also one of the finest of its kind, with very successful female choruses in the engagement party scene, pointing the way for future treatment of similar material by Glinka, Chaikovsky, and even Stravinsky (there are phrases in the betrothal scenes of both *The Miller* and *The St. Petersburg Bazaar* that have their exact counterparts in the text of *The Wedding*). Matinsky's use of an urban middle-class dialect for literary purposes was a pioneering event, leading in a direct line, via the merchant-class plays of Pyotr Plavilshchikov and Aleksandr Shakhovskoi, to Gogol's comedy *Marriage* and the plays of Aleksandr Ostrovsky.

The tendency of comic opera to depict a wide range of social groups led Russian playwrights of the period down some unusual paths. The prolific neoclassical poet and playwright Mikhail Kheraskov (1733–1807) tried his hand at comic opera with *The Good Soldiers* (*Dobrye soldaty*, 1780). The result was closer to sentimental drama than to comic opera. The heroine of the work is unjustly accused of theft while wandering about like Micaëla in search of her missing soldier-lover. There are a phenomenal number of scenes in which people find their long-lost relatives. The novelty of the piece was in its regimental milieu, for which the music by Hermann Raupach (the same composer who had, back in 1758, turned Aleksandr Sumarokov's *Alcestis* into one of the earliest Russian *opere serie*) provided an appropriately military background, with bugle calls and sung marches. One of these marches, "We Love You from the Heart" ("My vas liubim serdechno"), entered folklore; it became a favorite song of Russian soldiers in the nineteenth century and was still popular as late as World War I. The Russian equivalent of "For He's a Jolly Good Fellow," it was cited as such in a highly ironical context in Gogol's comedy *The Gamblers* (1842), where it is sung in honor of a stooge who is helping a band of confidence men swindle the protagonist out of his fortune.

Nikolai Lvov (1751–1803), a good minor poet of the period, an art critic, and a collector of folk songs (he collaborated in the famous Lvov-Pratsch collection of 1790), was responsible for *Postal Coachmen at the Relay* (*Iamshchiki na podstave*, 1788). It utilized the traditional musical lore of the drivers who transported travelers across the vast Russian plains and whose singing was to inspire so many of the later Russian poets, from Pushkin to Annensky. The musical score for this work, composed by Evstignei Fomin, is one of the most successful and attractive in the entire range of Russian comic opera.

An unexpected turn was taken by comic opera with the production of *The Candidate Priest* (*Stavlennik*), first performed by divinity students in the city of Yaroslavl, the "cradle of Russian theater," in 1780. The text was written by Yakov Sokolov, of whom nothing is known except that he was "a student of philosophy." Nor is anything known about the music, for the score has been lost. With *The Candidate Priest* comic opera invaded the realm of the Russian clergy, who were a separate caste in prerevolutionary times. The story deals with a competition for a job left vacant by the death of the parish priest. The leading candidate is Foma (Thomas), son of a wealthy priest, whose main qualifications for the job are a sonorous, low-pitched voice and a large supply of money his father has provided for bribes.

Other characters in the all-male cast are Foma's rival for the job, the poor bell-ringer's bright son Provor (an invented name, conveying the idea of agility and adroitness), whose family home has burned down and who needs the job desperately, but lacks funds for bribes; a nobleman at whose house Foma is a lodger and who fawns on and flatters the priest's son, his social inferior, so long as the latter provides the liquor; the mercenary secretary of the local administration; the incorruptible city official who has to judge at the candidates' competition; and a comical peasant who disrupts the examination scene when he mistakes Foma's voice for the lowing of his lost cow. The clumsy web of intrigue woven by Foma comes to naught when the well-prepared Provor bests him at reading and singing, but in defeat, Foma puts up a spirited defense for the right of the untalented and the unlearned to fend for themselves by whatever means they can.

Unlike other comic operas of the time that had prose dialogue between the sung numbers, *The Candidate Priest* follows the example of Popov's *Anyuta* in having its dialogue in iambic hexameter throughout. The writing is lively and witty, the characterization vivid, and the versification expertly done. There is no record of this work's performance in either of the capitals, but it did enjoy a lasting and deserved provincial success. There exists an account of an open-air performance of this piece staged in 1814 to celebrate Napoleon's defeat. Handwritten copies of the text were still circulated in Yaroslavl in the 1830s. What makes this work particularly interesting is its portrayal of members of an important social class that traditionally remained outside the scope of Russian literature until the late nineteenth century, when Nikolai Pomyalovsky, Nikolai Leskov, and Chekhov made the members of the clerical class the protagonists of some of their finer stories and novels.[14]

Before the eighteenth century was over, some 150 Russian comic operas had been written and performed. The popularity of this genre had its impact on the relaxation of the three classical unities, on the acceptance of Russian folk song as raw material for Western-style musical composition (a practice that became even more popular in the nineteenth and twentieth centuries), and on the mode of representing peasants and merchants on the Russian stage by later playwrights. Modern understanding of the historical importance of this genre began with Nikolai Findeizen's pioneering study published in 1928. But some of the more recent Soviet scholarship on comic opera, by saddling the form with anachronistic ideological content and ignoring its Western sources and parallels, has produced as much obfuscation as understanding.[15]

---

[14] The text of *The Candidate Priest* was published in *Russkaia starina* (St. Petersburg), June 1875, 277–300. The work was discussed in prerevolutionary histories of Russian drama. In Soviet times, because of its nonsatirical portrayal of clergy, it has usually been relegated to an occasional footnote; in fact, it was hardly mentioned at all until Berkov ventured a brief discussion of it in his *Istoriia russkoi komedii XVIII v.*, 208–11.

[15] This comment is not meant to minimize the useful information on Russian eighteenth-century comic opera that is to be found in the work of such literary historians as P. N. Berkov. Two musicological works dating from the ultrarepressive Zhdanov period offer a wealth of valuable documentation through the haze of their compulsory Stalinist clichés and falsifications: A. S. Rabinovich, *Russkaia opera do Glinki* (Moscow: Muzgiz, 1948), and T. Livanova, *Russkaia muzykal'naia kul'tura XVIII veka*, 2 vols. (Moscow: Muzgiz, 1953). A good presentation of the musical aspects of the topic in English is to be found in Gerald R. Seaman, *History of Russian Music* (New York and Washington: Praeger, 1967), vol. 1. The reader should be warned against the uninformed and factually unreliable treatment of Russian comic opera in Richard Anthony Leonard, *A History of Russian Music* (New York: Macmillan, 1957). James Bakst, in *A History of Russian-Soviet Music* (New York: Dodd, Mead, 1966), gives the subject an even more ideologically distorted and Stalinist slant than the official Soviet scholars.

VII. Song and Dance

* * *

On its original appearance this essay bore a prefatory note, stating: "This paper is based on the materials of my book in progress, *Russian Drama from Its Beginnings to the Age of Pushkin*. I am particularly grateful to Daniel Heartz and Marie-Hélène Huet for discussing eighteenth-century comic opera with me and for sharing their insights and expertise." The two informants named were distinguished colleagues on the faculty of the University of California, Berkeley (Prof. Huet then on the point of being abducted, in the spirit of comic opera, to Amherst College), in the departments of music and French, respectively. When the book was issued, this essay became its fifth chapter, augmented by the addition of a couple of sections that, departing from the contents of note 6 in the present version, more closely examined the work of Knyazhnin. The great significance of this essay is adumbrated, but done scant justice, in notes 4 and 15, which suggest the great miasma of misinformation and misinterpretation that had previously surrounded the subject of early Russian comic opera. SK is characteristically eager to expose the Soviet contribution to the mess, but Western accounts, inheriting the Romantic nationalist biases of the nineteenth century, were hardly less muddled, hardly less given to promoting the genre as autochthonous, and hardly less prone to draw a line, not forward to the genre from its French prototype, but backward to it from the nationalistic art of post-Napoleonic Russia, as exemplified in music primarily by the work of Glinka (or rather, by the myth of Glinka) and the *moguchaia kuchka*, or (as they are known in English) the Mighty Five, thus to prove that folkloric nationalism had always been an essential feature of Russian music. The 1961 Oxford dissertation by Gerald Seaman, "The Influence of Folk-Song on Russian Opera in the Eighteenth Century up to and including the Time of Glinka," one of the very first extended academic studies of Russian music in English, conveys the bias in its very title.

    The revolutionary aspect of SK's demonstration that Russian comic opera in the eighteenth century was a French import was its concomitant demonstration that folklore played a role in the early Russian operas comparable to the one it played in the French ones—that is, it was invoked to typify lower-class characters, not to characterize "the nation," or the national essence. Rather than denoting nationality or ethnicity, it connoted class. Just as the Romantic nationalism of the nineteenth century, although it found expression in a distinctively Russian sound, was a conceptual import from Germany, so the decorative nationalism (more accurately described as exoticism) of the eighteenth century was a generic import from France. SK spelled all of this out in that lapidary, crystalline style of his, and when one of us (RT) was given the task of supplying the Russian entries in the *New Grove Dictionary of Opera* (London: Macmillan, 1992), no effort was spared to publicize SK's views in the texts, and call attention to the present article, plus the chapter to which it led, in the bibliographies. Recent histories of opera (e.g., and most particularly, the most recent and best one, Carolyn Abbate and Roger Parker, *A History of Opera* [New York: Norton, 2012]) testify that Karlinskian thinking has infiltrated the general discourse of musicology.

Contralto:
Rossini, Gautier and Gumilyov[1]

> Contralto is a low sort of music that only ladies sing.
>
> —BONERS[2]

From its inception the art of opera admitted casting singers in roles that depicted characters of the opposite sex. In early operas by Monteverdi and Cavalli, it was usual to have tenors in women's garments portray nurses and other elderly women on the apparent assumption that female voices acquire a deeper pitch in old age. During the heyday of Alessandro Scarlatti in the late seventeenth century and of Handel in the early eighteenth, opera composers had at their disposal two kinds of male singers who could perform in the range usually associated with female voices: the highly popular soprano and alto castrati. These men, through surgery undergone in childhood, retained the soprano or alto voice of a little boy, reinforced with the power and resonance of adult male lungs.

The conventions of the eighteenth century allowed for casting of castrati in male roles, such as Orpheus or Julius Caesar. The audiences of the time were quite accustomed to seeing the heroine of the opera (almost invariably a female soprano) in love with a character who looked—more or less—like a man but sounded like a woman. In the last decades of the eighteenth century, castrato singers appeared primarily in *opera seria*, the musical equivalent of neoclassical tragedy, with texts that were often based on successful plays of that species. When the fourteen-year-old Mozart received a commission to compose his first *opera seria*, *Mitridate*,

---

[1] Originally published in *Language, Literature, Linguistics: In Honor of Francis J. Whitfield, on His Seventieth Birthday, March 25, 1986*, ed. M. S. Flier and S. Karlinsky (Berkeley: Berkeley Slavic Specialties, 1987), 128–41.

[2] BONERS. *Being a Collection of Schoolboy Wisdom. or Knowledge As It Is Sometimes Written, Compiled from Classrooms and Examination Papers by Alexander Abingdon, and Illustrated by Dr. Seuss* (New York: Viking Press, 1931), 32.

re di Ponto (after a tragedy by Racine), he had to tailor his music for a company whose four leading singers were two female sopranos and two castrati, one soprano and one alto.[3] But even in the works of his maturity in *opera seria* form, the magnificent *Idomeneo*, composed at twenty-five, and the last opera he wrote, *La clemenza di Tito*, the roles of romantic young lovers were scored for alto castrati, while the roles of father figures (Idomeneus and the Emperor Titus), which would have been basso parts in a mid-nineteenth-century opera, were entrusted to tenors.

Gioacchino Rossini was born three months after Mozart died. The genre of *opera seria* was still popular when Rossini began composing operas in 1808, at the age of sixteen, but the male sopranos and altos associated with this genre in Mozart's time were by then a vanishing breed. The last illustrious castrato singer, Giovanni Battista Velluti, made his debut in 1800. In 1813, Rossini composed for Velluti one of his less successful operas, *Aureliano in Palmira*. But earlier in that same year, Rossini produced the two operas that marked the beginning of his international fame, *Tancredi* and *L'italiana in Algeri*. In the first of these, an *opera seria* based on a neoclassical tragedy by Voltaire, Rossini assigned the role of the male protagonist, a heroic warrior, to a (female) contralto.[4] In the second one, even less conventionally, a contralto sang the leading female role in an *opera buffa*.

Contralto remained Rossini's preferred voice for his principal characters, either female or male. It seems safe to say that no other nineteenth- or twentieth-century composer wrote so many attractive contralto roles for

---

[3] Alfred Einstein, *Mozart: His Character, His Work*, trans. Arthur Mendel and Nathan Broder (New York: Oxford University Press, 1962), 398.

[4] The tradition of the *primo musico*, a woman (rather than a *primo uomo*) singing a leading male part such as would have been earlier assigned to a castrato, was a little older than SK here implies, and was not by any means peculiar to Rossini. The subject had not been extensively researched as of 1986, when SK was writing this, but has been since as part of the general burgeoning of interest in sexual and gender issues in theater and opera in response to what Heather Hadlock called "the 'first wave' of Anglo-American feminist opera studies," sparked by the appearance in English of Catherine Clément's *L'opéra; ou, La défaite des femmes* (Paris: B. Grasset, 1979), as *Opera, or, The Undoing of Women*, trans. Betsy Wing (Minneapolis: University of Minnesota Press, 1988). For an overview, see Hadlock's "Women Playing Men in Italian Opera, 1810–1835," in *Women's Voices across Musical Worlds*, ed. Jane A. Bernstein (Boston: Northeastern University Press, 2003), 285–307 (the quoted phrase is on p. 285).—Ed.

his heroines (Rosina in *Il barbiere di Siviglia*, sometimes transposed for a coloratura soprano in later times, but originally a contralto, and *La Cenerentola*, to name the two most popular ones) or for his romantic young heroes. Contraltos in "trouser roles" are of course familiar from later opera. Now and then we hear a contralto heroine, such as Donizetti's *La favorita* and, of course, Bizet's *Carmen*. But after Rossini's time, these were exceptional cases. In most nineteenth-century operas, contraltos were cast as mothers, the heroine's rivals, gypsies, seeresses, or attendants. Only Mikhail Glinka followed Rossini's example by casting contraltos as young men in both of his completed operas (Vanya in *A Life for the Tsar* and Ratmir in *Ruslan and Lyudmila*) and, what's more, he gave each of them one of the most attractive arias in their respective operas.[5]

One cause for Rossini's predilection for the contralto must have been the availability of a number of illustrious singers capable of performing brilliant coloratura passages in the lower range of a female voice (in the eighteenth century, the speciality of castrato altos). Among them were Adelaide Malanotte, the first Tancredi; Marietta Marcolini, who created contralto roles in four of Rossini's major operas; and Rosa Mariani, for whom he wrote the part of Arsace in his *Semiramide*. Yet when Rossini chose to marry an opera singer, it was not a contralto but a coloratura soprano, Isabella Colbran.[6] His younger contemporary, the French poet, novelist, and theater critic Théophile Gautier, who wrote a remarkable eulogy to the contralto voice in his poem "Contralto" (the subject of the present paper), came to appreciate that type of voice only gradually and for personal as well as artistic reasons.

In his capacity as journalist and critic, Gautier had occasion to praise repeatedly the talents of various members of the illustrious Italian clan of Grisi, specifically the celebrated soprano Giulia Grisi and her contralto

---

[5] Of the two Glinka roles adduced, only Ratmir belongs to the tradition under discussion. Women sopranos or altos singing boys' roles has lasted up to the present, and there are examples in many famous later operas, including Meyerbeer's *Les huguenots* (Page), Verdi's *Un ballo in maschera* (Oscar), Musorgsky's *Boris Godunov* (Tsarevich), Debussy's *Pelléas et Mélisande* (Yniold), and Strauss's *Der Rosenkavalier* (title role) and *Ariadne auf Naxos* (Composer), to mention a few.—Ed.

[6] On the singers of Rossini's time and his relationships with them, I used Richard N. Coe's extensive annotations and detailed index in his translation of Stendhal's *Life of Rossini* (New York: Orion Press, 1970) and Herbert Weinstock, *Rossini* (New York: Alfred A. Knopf, 1968).

sister, Giuditta. (It was for them that Vincenzo Bellini composed the parts of Juliet and Romeo in his opera *I Capuleti e i Montecchi*, in which they excelled; the sisters were also noted for portraying the two lovers in Rossini's *Bianca e Falerio*.)[7] Gautier praised the beauty of Giulia Grisi's face and body in several texts, most notably in the preface to his novel *Mademoiselle de Maupin*. But it was Giulia's and Giuditta's cousin, the ballerina Carlotta Grisi, who turned out to be possibly the greatest love of Gautier's life. It was for Carlotta Grisi that Gautier created the scenario for the ballet *Giselle* (1841), in which she acquired worldwide fame and which is one of the earliest ballets to retain its place in the repertory to this day. In 1843, Gautier provided Carlotta Grisi with her second greatest success, *La péri*, a work that was widely danced throughout Europe for the rest of the nineteenth century.

Yet, while the ballerina was grateful to Gautier for his ballet scenarios and for his worshipful reviews of her dancing, she insisted that they remain good friends and nothing more.[8] She was married to her choreographer and dancing partner Jules Perrot in what was apparently a marriage of convenience. When she was ready to move away from Perrot, it was not in the direction of Gautier that she went, but rather to Switzerland, where a wealthy member of the Radziwill family established her in a magnificent villa. Unable to reciprocate Gautier's passion, Carlotta Grisi did the next best thing: she introduced him to her younger sister Ernesta, a budding contralto who was later to become a noted specialist in trouser roles in Rossini's operas. Portraits of Ernesta Grisi show her as a shorter

---

[7] On the repertoire of Giulia and Giuditta Grisi, see *Teatral'naia entsiklopediia* (Moscow: Sovetskoe entsiklopediia, 1961–67), vol. 2, columns 146–47.

[8] The biographers of Carlotta Grisi (Serge Lifar, *Carlotta Grisi* [Paris: Albin Michel, 1941], 43) and of Gautier (Joanna Richardson, *Théophile Gautier: His Life and Times* [London: Max Reinhardt, 1958], 48–49 and *passim*) maintain that the relationship between the poet and the dancer was platonic. Edwin Binney 3rd, in his highly informative *Les ballets de Théophile Gautier* (Paris: Librairie Nizet, 1965), originally a Harvard dissertation, cites these and numerous other sources which all testify that Gautier's passion for Carlotta Grisi was not reciprocated except in terms of friendship (pp. 58–60). Binney nevertheless goes on to speculate that physical intimacy between them is within the realm of possibility, because "une ballerine de l'Opéra pleine d'ambition ne pouvait manquer de voir quel appui pouvait lui donner un critique influent" (p. 60). This kind of argument, based on the premise "it could have happened therefore it certainly did," reminiscent of recent conjectures about Chaikovsky's supposed suicide, is not otherwise typical of Binney's excellent book.

and stockier version of her dancing sister, to whom she bore an uncanny facial resemblance. In the spring of 1844, Théophile Gautier and Ernesta Grisi became lovers.

Gautier never married. His other love affairs, documented by his biographers, were more or less transient, ending after a year or two. But he and Ernesta Grisi were to stay together for twenty-two years. She was the mother of his daughters Judith and Estelle Gautier, who grew up to marry distinguished men of letters (Judith Gautier eventually became a noted writer in her own right). In Joanna Richardson's words, Ernesta provided Gautier with "the old domestic security, the pampering he had known as a boy."[9] While continuing her own musical career, she relieved the frequently impractical poet of household chores and financial worries by taking care of such matters herself. She was also reportedly a magnificent cook. It was shortly after the birth of their second daughter in November 1847 that Gautier expressed his love for Ernesta in the somewhat ambiguous eulogy to her voice, published in December of the same year and later included in his collection *Émaux et camées*.[10]

CONTRALTO

1 On voit dans le Musée antique,
    Sur un lit de marbre sculpté,
    Une statue énigmatique
    D'une inquiétante beauté.

2 Est-ce un jeune homme? est-ce une femme,
    Une déesse, ou bien un dieu?
    L'amour, ayant peur d'être infâme,
    Hésite et suspend son aveu.

3 Dans sa pose malicieuse,
    Elle s'étend, le dos tourné
    Devant la foule curieuse,
    Sur son coussin capitonné.

---

[9] Richardson, *Gautier*, 53–54.
[10] For the publication history of "Contralto," see the commentary by Claudine Gothot-Mersch in Théophile Gautier, *Émaux et camées*, ed. Claudine Gothot-Mersch (Paris: Gallimard, 1981), 236–38.

4   Pour faire sa beauté maudite,
    Chaque sexe apporta son don.
    Tout homme dit: C'est Aphrodite!
    Toute femme: C'est Cupidon!

5   Sexe douteux, grâce certaine,
    On dirait ce corps indécis
    Fondu, dans l'eau de la fontaine,
    Sous les baisers de Salmacis.

6   Chimère ardente, effort suprême
    De l'art et de la volupté,
    Monstre charmant, comme je t'aime
    Avec ta multiple beauté!

7   Bien qu'on défende ton approche,
    Sous la draperie aux plis droits
    Dont le bout à ton pied s'accroche,
    Mes yeux ont plongé bien des fois.

8   Rêve de poëte et d'artiste,
    Tu m'as bien des nuits occupé,
    Et mon caprice qui persiste
    Ne convient pas qu'il s'est trompé.

9   Mais seulement il se transpose,
    Et, passant de la forme au son,
    Trouve dans sa métamorphose
    La jeune fille et le garçon.

10 Que tu me plais, ô timbre étrange!
    Son double, homme et femme à la fois,
    Contralto, bizarre mélange,
    Hermaphrodite de la voix!

11 C'est Roméo, c'est Juliette,
    Chantant avec un seul gosier;
    Le pigeon rauque et la fauvette
    Perchés sur le même rosier;

VII. Song and Dance

12   C'est la châtelaine qui raille
       Son beau page parlant d'amour;
       L'amant au pied de la muraille,
       La dame au balcon de sa tour;

13   Le papillon, blanche étincelle,
       Qu'en ses détours et ses ébats
       Poursuit un papillon fidèle,
       L'un volant haut et l'autre bas;

14   L'ange qui descend et qui monte
       Sur l'escalier d'or voltigeant;
       La cloche mêlant dans sa fonte
       La voix d'airain, la voix d'argent;

15   La mélodie et l'harmonie,
       Le chant et l'accompagnement;
       A la grâce la force unie,
       La maîtresse embrassant l'amant!

16   Sur le pli de sa jupe assise,
       Ce soir, ce sera Cendrillon
       Causant près du feu qu'elle attise
       Avec son ami le grillon;

17   Demain le valeureux Arsace
       A son courroux donnant l'essor,
       Ou Tancrède avec sa cuirasse,
       Son épée et son casque d'or;

18   Desdemona chantant le Saule,
       Zerline bernant Mazetto,
       Ou Malcolm le plaid sur l'épaule;
       C'est toi que j'aime, ô contralto!

19   Nature charmante et bizarre
       Que Dieu d'un double attrait para,
       Toi qui pourrais, comme Gulnare,
       Être le Kaled d'un Lara,

> 20 Et dont la voix, dans sa caresse,
>   Réveillant le cœur endormi,
>   Mêle aux soupirs de la maîtresse
>   L'accent plus mâle de l'ami!

In the not entirely sympathetic preface to her excellently annotated edition of *Émaux et camées*, Claudine Gothot-Mersch wrote that "while woman is everywhere present [in this collection], love is nowhere to be found; what dominates is the madrigal."[11] In "Contralto," love is definitely present, though it is brought in through a tortuous path. His preference for the unconventional (or, perhaps, his horror of appearing conventional) led Gautier to filter the timbre of his life companion's voice and the cozy domesticity he enjoyed with her through the prism of French Romanticism's most daring theme, that of androgyny.[12] Gautier's contemporary Honoré de Balzac dealt with this theme in *Sarrazine* (1830) and *Séraphita* (1835) and Gautier himself touched on it in his novel *Mademoiselle de Maupin* in a somewhat gingerly manner. "Contralto" comes to grips with androgyny more boldly. In *Mademoiselle de Maupin* Gautier shielded himself by appealing to the authority of Shakespeare, unchallengeable for the Romantics. The most explicitly androgynous scenes of the novel take place during rehearsals of *As You Like It*, whose action these scenes parallel. The central theme and metaphor of "Contralto" is the sexual ambiguity of contralto in the operas of Rossini.

The entire poem is, in fact, an extended metaphorical equation between the ability of contralto singers in Rossini's operas to portray both female and male characters and the ancient myth of Hermaphroditus, the offspring of Hermes and Aphrodite, who possessed the sexual characteristics of both a man and a woman. But the components of this equation are presented in reversed order. The contralto voice which the poem eulogizes is first mentioned in the tenth of the poem's twenty stanzas. The first nine stanzas develop an idea which, were it stated in prose and not in Gautier's elegant verse, would find little agreement on the part of most readers. It is

---

[11] Ibid., 12.
[12] Gothot-Mersch calls the subject of hermaphroditism the "thème d'époque" (ibid., 237).

the assertion that depictions of hermaphroditism in the visual arts are erotically attractive for both men and women. Though it may be true that some female singers charm their audiences in trouser roles (the reverse disguise, male singers in female roles, has been relegated to broad comedy in nineteenth- and twentieth-century opera: the mother in Donizetti's *Convenzione e inconvenzione teatrale* or the cook in Prokofiev's *Love for Three Oranges*), what Gautier proclaims is the universal attractiveness of a *nude* hermaphroditic body. This declaration, deliberately paradoxical, can be backed by the poet with only one instance and even that one derived from mythology, the Ovidian myth of the nymph Salmacis who fell in love with Hermaphroditus and persuaded the gods to fuse their two bodies together. Gautier evokes this myth in the fifth stanza of his poem.

"Contralto" begins with a description of a concrete work of art, the ancient marble statue of the Sleeping Hermaphrodite at the Louvre Museum in Paris. In Gautier's time, as it still is today, this sculpture was placed in a corner with its back to the spectators and surrounded by railings which prevented them from seeing the front of the body.[13] This placement enables Gautier to speculate on the ambiguous fascination of the statue for both the male and the female visitors to the museum (stanzas two through four). Then, after the Ovidian reference, stanzas seven and eight tell of the poet's own love for the sculpture and for what it represents, an attraction that is intensified by the prohibition against seeing the whole of the statue and by the impossibility of giving any concrete expression to this love for a chimera ("chimère ardente, effort suprême / De l'art et de la volupté").

Stanza nine is the turning point of the entire poem, a pivot on which it revolves, making the preceding stanzas a metaphor for the stanzas that follow. This is achieved by use of synesthesia, a device favored by the Symbolist poets who followed Gautier and acknowledged him as their master, far more than by the Romantics to whose generation he belonged. Through synesthesia ("passant de la forme au son") the poet converts, in the tenth stanza, the visual charm of the statue of the hermaphrodite into its aural equivalent, a woman's contralto voice. This voice is something

---

[13] In a critical article published in 1839, Gautier advised the visitors at the Louvre Museum to wait until the guard's back is turned and then to examine the statue of the Sleeping Hermaphrodite ("this graceful chimera, a dream of antiquity") from all sides. Cited by Gothot-Mersch, ibid., 237.

a man may love without ambiguity. Therefore the negative epithets that were intermingled with eulogies in the first ten stanzas ("amour ... infâme," "pose malicieuse," "beauté maudite," "monstre charmant"), which all referred to the hermaphrodite, are absent in the last ten stanzas of the poem, devoted to the contralto voice.

The theme of operatic singing enters the poem in the eleventh stanza with a reference to a non-Rossinian opera. Romeo and Juliet in that stanza, "chantant avec un seul gosier," evoke a celebrated passage in Bellini's *I Capuleti e i Montecchi* which the soprano Juliet and the contralto Romeo sing in unison. This unison was much admired by Hector Berlioz and it was, according to Andrew Porter, obliterated in the twentieth-century performances of Bellini's opera prior to the 1970s, which transposed Romeo's music an octave down for a tenor voice, making the unison mentioned by Gautier impossible to perform.[14]

The four stanzas that follow this first operatic example enumerate a series of images or situations meant to illustrate the contralto's ability to sing in both the high and the low register: a raucous pigeon and a warbler perched on the same rosebush; a lover whose lady is above him on her balcony (Romeo and Juliet again); two butterflies, flying one above the other; an angel (apparently from Jacob's dream in the Old Testament) which descends and ascends a shimmering golden ladder; and, finally, a church bell that sounds "the voice of brass, the voice of silver." (Church bells and the alloys from which they are made were to interest Gautier during his visit to the Moscow Kremlin, some ten years after he wrote "Contralto.")

The vertical axis along which the imagery of stanzas eleven to fourteen is deployed serves to pay homage to the range and versatility of Ernesta Grisi's voice. In stanza fifteen there are no longer any contrasts. Instead, these four lines offer images of fusion between melody and harmony, singing and accompaniment, strength and grace, all culminating in a woman embracing the man she loves. The madrigal to Ernesta could have ended at this point. But Gautier preferred to make it more personal by enumerating the roles of the Rossinian repertoire in which she excelled (plus Zerlina in Mozart's *Don Giovanni*, a role that can be comfortably

---

14 Andrew Porter, *Music of Three Seasons: 1974–1977* (New York: Farrar, Straus and Giroux, 1978), 175–78.

sung by either a soprano or a mezzo): the protagonist of *La Cenerentola* and Desdemona in Rossini's *Otello* singing her song of the willow. Alongside these female roles of Cinderella, Desdemona and Zerlina, Gautier also lists three heroic male characters, whose music was scored by Rossini for the female contralto voice: Arsace in *Semiramide*, Tancredi, and Malcolm in *La donna del lago* (after Sir Walter Scott's poem *The Lady of the Lake*).[15] This enumeration is crowned by direct apostrophizing of the singer who performed all these roles: "C'est toi que j'aime, ô contralto!" Stanzas nineteen and twenty form a brief epilogue which alludes to two popular verse tales by Byron, *Lara*, in which the male protagonist's beloved was disguised as a young man, and *The Corsair*, in which she appeared in Turkish female garb. The final two lines of the poem neatly define Ernesta Grisi's function in Gautier's life: she was not only a woman who loved him, but one who, through her support, practicality, and lack of possessiveness, acted as a loyal male friend might have done.

After Gautier's death in 1872 and especially at the turn of the century, his literary reputation, so secure in his lifetime, suffered a precipitous decline in his native France.[16] This situation still continued in the first two decades of the twentieth century, at the time when Gautier's poetry came to be valued by poets of the English-speaking countries such as Ezra Pound and T. S. Eliot and by the Russian Acmeists, Nikolai Gumilyov above all.[17] In his 1911 essay on Gautier, Gumilyov argued that Gautier, because of the perfection of his form and his refusal to join any school or

---

[15] The roles of Tancredi, Arsace, and Malcolm were mentioned by Gautier in his article about the Paris debut of Pauline Viardot Garcia as the parts in which he would like to hear this singer. The article was published in 1839, five years before Gautier and Ernesta Grisi became lovers. Cited by Gothot-Mersch in Gautier, *Émaux*, 238.

[16] On the decline of Gautier's reputation at the end of the nineteenth century owing to dismissive attitudes of such utilitarian French critics as Émile Faguet and on the subsequent revival of Gautier's popularity in France by the middle of twentieth century, see René Jasinski, "Situation de Théophile Gautier," *Europe* (Paris), no. 601, a special issue devoted to Gautier (May 1979): 3–16.

[17] On the chronology of the enthusiasm for Gautier's poetry on the part of English and American poets and of the Russian Acmeists, see Serge Fauchereau, "Où Pound et Eliot rencontrent Goumilev, Mandelstam et Akhmatova," in the issue of *Europe* cited in the previous note, 57–73. In addition to literary phenomena, Gautier's impact on Russian culture of the early twentieth century can be seen from the fact that two of the ballets with which Sergei Diaghilev's company conquered Paris, *Le pavilion d'Armide* (1909) and *Le spectre de la rose* (1911), were based on texts by Gautier.

ideology, should be a model for Russian twentieth-century poets. In his Acmeist manifesto of 1913, Gumilyov placed Gautier's name next to those of Shakespeare, Rabelais and Villon.[18] In 1914 came his translation of *Émaux et camées*, including "Contralto."

КОНТРАЛЬТО

1. Въ музеѣ древняго познанья
   Лежитъ надъ мраморной скамьей
   Загадочное изваянье
   Съ тревожащею красотой.

2. То нѣжный юноша? Иль дѣва?
   Богиня, иль быть можетъ богъ?
   Любовь, страшась Господня гнѣва,
   Дрожитъ, удерживая вздохъ.

3. Такъ вызывающе-лукаво,
   Оно повернуто спиной,
   Лежитъ въ подушкахъ величаво,
   Предъ любопытною толпой.

4. Ахъ, красота его обида
   И каждый полъ въ него влюбленъ,
   Мужчины вѣрятъ: то Киприда!
   И женщины: то Купидонъ.

5. Невѣрный полъ, восторгъ безспорный,
   Сказали бъ, тѣло—кипарисъ
   Растаяло въ водѣ озерной
   Подъ поцѣлуемъ Салмасисъ.

6. Химера пламенная, диво
   Искусства и мечты больной,
   Люблю тебя я, звѣрь красивый,
   Съ твоей различной красотой.

---

[18] See Gumilyov's essays "Nasledie simvolizma i akmeizm" and "Teofil' Got'e" in N. Gumilev, *Sobranie sochinenii*, 4 vols. (Washington: Victor Kamkin, 1962–68), 4:171–76 and 386–96, respectively.

VII. Song and Dance

7   Хотя тебя ревниво скрыло
      Съ прямыми складками сукно,
      Ненужно, грубо и уныло,
      Тобой любуюсь я давно.

8   Мечта поэта и артиста,
      Я по ночамъ въ тебя влюбленъ,
      И мой восторгъ, пускай нечистый,
      Не долженъ обмануться онъ.

9   Онъ только терпитъ превращенье,
      Переходя изъ формы въ звукъ,
      Я вижу новое явленье —
      Красавица и съ нею другъ.

10   О какъ ты милъ мнѣ, тембръ чудесный,
      Гдѣ юноша съ женою слитъ,
      Контральто, выродокъ прелестный,
      Голосовой гермафродитъ!

11   То Ромео и то Джульета,
      Что голосомъ однимъ поютъ,
      Голубка съ голубемъ, до свѣта
      Одинъ нашедшіе пріютъ.

12   То передразниваетъ дама
      Въ нее влюбленнаго пажа,
      Любовникъ пѣснь ведетъ упрямо,
      На башнѣ вторитъ ей, дрожа.

13   То мотылекъ, что искрой бѣлой
      —Какъ летъ его неуловимъ—
      Спѣшитъ за бабочкой несмѣлой,
      Онъ наверху, она подъ нимъ.

14   То ангелъ сходитъ и восходитъ
      По лѣстницѣ, чей блескъ—добро;
      То колоколъ, что звукъ выводитъ,
      Смѣшавши мѣдь и серебро.

15 То связь гармоній и мелодій,
   То аккомпаниментъ и тонъ,
   То сила съ граціей въ природѣ,
   Любовницы томящій стонъ.

16 Сегодня это Сандрильона
   Передъ привѣтнымъ камелькомъ,
   Шутящая непринужденно
   Съ пріятелемъ своимъ сверчкомъ.

17 Потомъ Арзасъ великодушный,
   Не могшій удержать свой гнѣвъ,
   Или Танкредъ въ кольчугѣ душной,
   Схвативъ свой мечъ и шлемъ надѣвъ.

18 Поетъ Дездемона объ ивѣ,
   Малькольмъ закутался въ свой пледъ;
   Контральто, нѣтъ ни прихотливѣй
   Тебя, ни благороднѣй нѣтъ.

19 Твоя загадочная чара
   Сильна приманкою двойной
   Ты снова можешь, какъ Гюльнара,
   Для Лары нѣжнымъ быть слугой,

20 Въ чьей рѣчи слиты потаенно,
   Чтобъ страсть была всегда жива,
   И вздохи женщины влюбленной
   И друга твердыя слова.

Gumilyov used the last and most complete of the six editions of Gautier's collection that were published under the poet's supervision between 1852 and 1872.[19] Gumilyov's translation, *Emali i ka-*

---

[19] The publication history and the contents of the six different editions of *Émaux et camées* that appeared in Gautier's lifetime are outlined by Gothot-Mersch in her "Notice," Gautier, *Émaux*, 221–22.

mei,²⁰ could have served as a model of fidelity and empathy were it not marred by some spectacular misreadings. These begin in the prefatory sonnet, where the Persian word for hoopoe, "Hudhud" (apparently related etymologically to the Russian "udod"), cited by Gautier from Goethe's *West-östlicher Divan*, was mistaken by Gumilyov for a woman's proper name ("Nota le chant qu'Hudhud soupire" was rendered as "Pel o Gudut, zhivushchei siro"). But on the whole, Gumilyov's version of Gautier's collection shows both a profound affinity for the French poet and a great deal of technical resourcefulness. The French octosyllabic verse with cross rhymes that alternate feminine and masculine endings, in which the overwhelming majority of Gautier's poems is couched, is accurately conveyed by its Russian equivalent, quatrains of the familiar iambic tetrameter with an analogous rhyme scheme.

Gumilyov's version of "Contralto" is free of glaring misreadings of the kind cited above. There is a certain vagueness in a few lines, caused by lack of awareness of specific realia mentioned by Gautier. Thus, the collection of ancient art in the Louvre in the first line of the poem is rendered somewhat pompously as "In the museum of ancient cognition" ("V muzee drevniago poznan'ia"). The adjective "privetnyi," "cozy" or "affable," is not the right one for the fireplace that Rossini's Cenerentola is forced to tend by her brutish stepfather (sixteenth stanza). In the eighteenth stanza, Malcolm Graeme, about whom Scott's original poem said that "the belted plaid and tartan hose / Did ne'er more graceful limbs disclose," merely wore his plaid on his shoulder in Gautier. Gumilyov, however, mistaking the English and French "plaid" for the Russian "pled," which means a blanket or a lap-robe, has Malcolm disappear from view, limbs and all, by wrapping himself up in that blanket ("Mal'kol'm zakutalsia v svoi pled"). This eighteenth stanza is the one least faithfully rendered, because not only Malcolm vanishes, but so do the Mozartian reference to Zerlina and Masetto and Gautier's declaration of love for his mistress in the last line.

The greatest divergences between Gautier's and Gumilyov's texts occur in the first half of the poem, where the poet proclaims his attraction

---

[20] Teofil' Got'e, *Emali i kamei*, trans. N. Gumilev (St. Petersburg: M. V. Popov, 1914). I am grateful to the Houghton Library of Harvard University for making a copy of this rare edition available to me. [Gumilyov's translation can now be viewed through the Internet from a copy at the University of Wisconsin: http://babel.hathitrust.org/cgi/pt?id=wu.89010608297.—Ed.]

for the statue of the hermaphrodite, but qualifies this admission by a series of negative epithets. Gumilyov quite systematically intensifies the negativity. In stanza two, "peur d'être infâme" is "strashas' Gospodnia gneva" ("fearing the wrath of God") in Russian. Gautier says that the statue is a product "de l'art et de la volupté" (sixth stanza), but Gumilyov has "iskusstva i mechty bol'noi," "of art and of a sick [pathological] yearning." In the seventh stanza, where the poet admits to having stolen glances at the statue many times, Gumilyov adds three adverbs that do not correspond to anything in Gautier's text: "nenuzhno, grubo i unylo" ("uselessly, coarsely and despondently"). The next stanza continues describing the poet's attraction to the statue. Again Gumilyov adds a qualifier not present in Gautier: "puskai nechistyi" ("albeit impure"), which condemns the attraction far more strongly than the original text ever did. Worst of all, in the tenth stanza, where the subject of the poem has switched from the statue of the hermaphrodite to the contralto voice, which Gautier calls a "bizarre mélange," Gumilyov translates these words oxymoronically as "vyrodok prelestnyi" ("a charming degenerate").

All this intensification is especially strange when one remembers that the themes of androgyny and hermaphroditism were treated by Gumilyov in his own writings on at least six occasions and without condemnation.[21] There are other nits to pick in Gumilyov's translation if one is so inclined: the confusion between the two verse tales by Byron in the penultimate

---

[21] Androgynous situations or characters appear in his poems "Poedinok" [Single combat] (possibly inspired by the battle between Tancredi and Clorinda in Tasso) and "Androgin" [The androgyne], both included in his verse collection *Zhemchuga* [Pearls], 1907-10. An androgyne also appears in Gumilyov's short story "Puteshestvie v stranu efira" [Voyage to the land of ether]. Lesbianism is the theme of his poem "Zhestokoi" [To a cruel woman], and male homosexuality appears in the poem "Liubov'" [Love] and is alluded to in the dialogue between the poet Hafiz and his tame birds in the last scene of Gumilyov's puppet play *Ditia Allakha* [The child of Allah]. With the possible exception of "Liubov'," Gumilyov treated these topics in nonjudgmental or affirmative terms. See Gumilev, *Sobranie sochinenii*, 1:98-99, 111-12 and 174-76 for the poems cited above. The short story is in 4:68-80 and the play *Ditia Allakha* is in 3:95-135.

On the themes of androgyny and hermaphroditism in the poetry, fiction, and philosophy of the Russian Silver Age (the Symbolist and Postsymbolist periods), see Olga Matich, "Androgyny and the Russian Religious Renaissance," in *Western Philosophical Systems in Russian Literature: A Collection of Critical Studies*, ed. Anthony M. Mlikotin (Los Angeles: University of Southern California Press, 1979), 165-75; and "Androgyny and the Russian Silver Age," *Pacific Coast Philology* 14 (1979): 42-49.

stanza or the two occasions where new imagery was brought in so as to accommodate the rhyme: the body of Hermaphroditus is compared to cypress wood, "kiparis," so as to rhyme with Salmacis (fifth stanza); and the biblical angel's ladder in stanza fourteen is said to glitter with goodness, "dobro," so as to provide a rhyme with silver in the church bell, "serebro." There are also instances where Gumilyov took advantage of Russian grammatical gender, more strongly expressed than the French one, to improve Gautier's imagery. The pigeon and the warbler in stanza eleven are replaced by a more likely pair, male and female pigeons. The two butterflies in stanza thirteen also get to be sexually differentiated owing to the availability in Russian of two words for butterfly: "babochka," which is feminine, and "motylek," which is masculine.

And yet, despite these divergences from the original text, Gumilyov's translation is a masterful poem. Read as a whole, it does convey Gautier's elegance and his filigreed mastery of poetic craft. No rhymed translation can ever duplicate the original in toto. Gumilyov's version does the next best thing: it catches and reproduces the ardor, the ambiguity, and the deliberate perversity of this hymn to a particular timbre of the female voice, the contralto, which Rossini loved creatively, Gautier loved personally, and Gumilyov came to love through its reflection in his favorite poet's art.

A Cultural Educator of Genius[1]

The name of Sergei Diaghilev is linked with ballet in most people's minds, but it is not always clear in what capacity. After Diaghilev died in Venice on 12 August 1929 and was interred at that city's Orthodox cemetery, people in London and New York were reportedly heard to remark, "What a pity, I never saw him dance." Those better informed had long known that the bulky, heavyset Diaghilev was neither a dancer nor a choreographer. In 1951 a young art student named Jacqueline Lee Bouvier won an essay contest sponsored by *Vogue* magazine. In her essay, she described Diaghilev as an "alchemist unique in art history," whose specialty was achieving "an interaction of the arts, [and] an interaction of the cultures of East and West." The same essay cited Diaghilev's ability to get the best out of his composers, designers, and dancers, and to incorporate it into "a unified yet transient ballet masterpiece."[2]

This view is not wrong. But it is incomplete, only taking into account Diaghilev's activities from the period after 1909, when he was thirty-seven years old, when he was involved exclusively with ballet. In the West Sergei Diaghilev is remembered and honored as an impresario who exported Russian ballet to Europe and America, brought to the public view a galaxy

---

[1] Originally published in *The Art of Enchantment: Diaghilev's Ballets Russes, 1909–1919*, ed. Nancy Van Norman Baer (San Francisco: Fine Arts Museums of San Francisco/Universe Books, 1988), 14–25, the text included portions of SK's essay "Serge Diaghilev, Public and Private," which appeared in *Christopher Street*, March 1980, 48–54, repr. in *The "Christopher Street" Reader*, ed. Michael Denneny, Charles Ortleb, and Thomas Steele (New York: Coward-McCann, 1983), 265–73.

[2] Jacqueline Lee Bouvier, "People I Wish I Had Known," *The World in Vogue*, ed. Bryan Holme et al. (London: Secker and Warburg, 1963), 301. [The other subjects of this essay were Charles Baudelaire and Oscar Wilde. About a decade later, when the author was First Lady of the United States, she and her husband, John F. Kennedy, entertained Igor Stravinsky at the White House in honor of the composer's eightieth birthday. Toasting Stravinsky, President Kennedy recalled this essay and its subjects. Afterward, Stravinsky told Robert Craft, "I was afraid he was about to say his wife had made a study of homosexuality" (Igor Stravinsky and Robert Craft, *Dialogues and a Diary* [Garden City: Doubleday, 1963], 199).—Ed.]

VII. Song and Dance

of fine painters by commissioning them to do his sets, caused some of the greatest musical masterpieces of our century to be composed, and discovered or developed the talents of the best choreographers and dancers of his time. In Russian cultural history, however, Diaghilev was a central figure in the momentous cultural revival that began at the end of the 1890s, which affected the visual arts, philosophy, art history, literary criticism, and even the art of typography. To restrict the significance of Diaghilev to ballet alone[3] is to misunderstand the nature of his achievement and to diminish its scope.

Sergei Diaghilev was born on 19 March 1872 at Selishchev Barracks, a military settlement in the province of Novgorod where his father, Pavel, a military officer, was stationed. Sergei was an exceptionally large-headed baby and his birth cost his mother, Evgeniya (née Evreinova), her life. Two years later Pavel Diaghilev married Elena Panaeva, a cultivated woman and gifted amateur singer. This stepmother raised Sergei as though he were her own child. She supervised his early musical education, instilled a love of the arts, and was Diaghilev's closest confidante until her death in 1919.[4]

After graduating at the age of eighteen from *gimnaziia* (the equivalent of high school) in the provincial town of Perm, Diaghilev enrolled at the law school of St. Petersburg University. Law studies were a pretext, for his ambition at the time was to become a singer or a composer. He settled at the home of his father's older sister, Anna Filosofova, a veteran of the feminist movement of the 1860s who had helped to found the first women's college in Russia and secured better living conditions for women factory workers. The youngest of her five children, the tall and

---

[3] This was done in the two books in English published in 1979 to commemorate the fiftieth anniversary of Diaghilev's death: Richard Buckle, *Diaghilev* (New York: Atheneum, 1979), and John Percival, *The World of Diaghilev* (New York: Harmony Books, 1979).

[4] Diaghilev's voluminous correspondence with his stepmother and a "Chronicle of the Diaghilev Family," which she wrote in 1909, are now in the manuscript collection of the Institute of Russian Literature, Russian Academy of Sciences (Pushkin House) in St. Petersburg. Cited selectively by recent Soviet scholars, these documents should serve as a basic source for any future Diaghilev biography. [They have so served for the recent biography by the Dutch scholar Sjeng Scheijen, *Sergej Diaghilev: Een leven voor de kunst* (Amsterdam: Burt Bakker, 2009), available in English as *Diaghilev: A Life*, trans. Jane Hedley-Prôle and S. J. Leinbach (London: Profile Books, 2009).—Ed.]

strikingly handsome Dima (Dmitry), was the same age as Diaghilev and was also about to enter law school. To reward the two young men for finishing high school, their families sent them on a grand tour of Western Europe.

In Italy, during summer 1890, an intimate relationship developed between the two cousins. Lasting fourteen years, Diaghilev's love affair with his cousin Dima was the most durable and surely the most formative such relationship in his life. Through Dima, Diaghilev joined the intellectual coterie formed by Dima's classmates, who were later to form the nucleus of both the World of Art (*Mir iskusstva*) movement and the journal of that name that Diaghilev and his cousin were to edit. In this group were the future art historian and stage designer Aleksandr Benois; the dilettante musician Walter Nouvel, who was to remain Diaghilev's closest personal friend and who assisted him in his ballet enterprises; and Konstantin Somov, later a famous painter. About the same time Diaghilev joined the group, so did a Jewish art student, Lev Rosenberg, later known as the painter and stage designer Léon Bakst. Benois and Bakst were heterosexual; the rest were not. The artistic temperaments of all created a highly charged emotional atmosphere.

What had bonded these young men of diverse background was their love of the arts and their shared dissatisfaction with the way the arts were perceived and written about at that time. At the end of the 1880s and in the early 1890s cultural life in Russia was politically polarized and artistically provincialized. On one hand it was academically stagnant because of a taste for patriotic, storytelling painting, conventional, well-made plays with bourgeois morals, and Victorian novels. On the other hand, criticism was dominated by a school of critics who are now called revolutionary democrats in the Soviet Union, but who may more meaningfully be called radical utilitarians. Forerunners of twentieth-century Socialist Realism, the influential Russian critics of the end of the nineteenth century demanded that all art be socially relevant, address current problems, and be patriotic and strictly realistic in form. Their criteria entirely overlooked values such as originality or profundity. They preferred that the didactic message, which they saw as the aim of all art, be couched in familiar and accessible terms. Their insistence on topical relevance precluded any serious interest in the arts of earlier periods or of other cultures.

VII. Song and Dance

The young men around Diaghilev and Dima Filosofov in the World of Art group saw both of those approaches to art—official academic and countercultural revolutionary—as equally limiting, provincial, and philistine.[5] The aim of their association was mutual education and expansion of their cultural horizons. They quickly discovered large areas of important art ignored by the critics of their time: the Russian icons, church frescoes, and church architecture of the earlier centuries, held to be backward and superstitious, not beautiful; the eighteenth-century and early nineteenth-century Romantic painters, who supposedly lacked realism and social significance; and some Western phenomena, which also had been held to share these defects, such as the Pre-Raphaelites in England, the music of Wagner and his followers, and, after some hesitation, the French Impressionist painters, such as Degas and Monet. In literature, the World of Art group was among the first to realize that the great Russian writers of the nineteenth century—Gogol, Turgenev, Tolstoi, and Dostoevsky—were important not only as topical social commentators or indicters of the inequities of tsarist Russia, but also as magnificent and original literary artists, each of whom had his own vision of life that could not be fully explained by the catchall term *realism*. The rediscovery of the past and an interest in the new trends in the West, attitudes typical of the entire World of Art group, provided the background for the evolution and broadening of Sergei Diaghilev's tastes during the first half of the 1890s.

Diaghilev's musical ambitions led him to study singing with the famed Italian baritone Antonio Cotogni and composition with Nikolai Sokolov. In 1892 Diaghilev and Filosofov visited Lev Tolstoi and discussed social and moral issues with him. Tolstoi was so impressed that he entered into a brief correspondence with Diaghilev.[6] After this, the young Diaghilev made a constant practice of seeking out Russian and foreign celebrities, such as Chaikovsky, Aubrey Beardsley, and Oscar Wilde. He did this not out of vanity (as some memoirists have suggested), but in order to see what he could learn about art from these men. One does not always find

---

[5] This attitude is well illustrated in the unpublished diaries of Dima Filosofov, cited in Natalia Lapshina, *Mir iskusstva* [World of Art] (Moscow: Iskusstvo, 1977), 300–1.

[6] Diaghilev's encounters and correspondence with Tolstoi are in Il'ia Zil'bershtein and Vladimir Samkov, eds., *Sergei Diagilev i russkoe iskusstvo* [Sergei Diaghilev and Russian art] (Moscow: Izobrazitel'noe iskusstvo, 1982), 2:7–16.

the infallible taste of the later Diaghilev in the reports on these encounters in his letters to his stepmother.[7]

Thus, meeting Brahms and Verdi on his trips to Western Europe in 1893 and 1894, respectively, he thought both of them too aged and uninteresting. On the other hand, Emmanuel Chabrier, whose opera *Gwendoline* Diaghilev thought would be a new departure for French music, aroused his wild enthusiasm. Diaghilev's account of how he ingratiated himself with Chabrier and his wife in order to sit in their box at the premiere of *Gwendoline* already shows the mature Diaghilev's fabled ability to charm people and get them to do whatever he wanted.[8] His almost annual visits to Bayreuth opened for him the possibilities of the Wagnerian "unified work of art" (*Gesamtkunstwerk*), a synthesis of the musical, the visual, and the dramatic, which, though imperfectly realized at Bayreuth festivals, was basic to Diaghilev's later concept of ballet.

By 1894 some of Diaghilev's music had been played at private recitals and he had appeared as a singer at a public concert. But his musical ambitions suffered an irreparable blow in autumn of that year, when he showed his compositions to Nikolai Rimsky-Korsakov and asked to be taken on as a private pupil. As recorded in the journal of Rimsky's disciple Vasily Yastrebtsev, the composer told Diaghilev that he had no talent and that the pieces he had brought were absurd.[9] Despite Diaghilev's defiant response to this judgment,[10] he soon abandoned his music studies. The center of his interest during the next few years shifted from music to painting.

Diaghilev's involvement with painting was threefold. By dabbling in the stock market and investing in the new and unfamiliar commodity of electrical technology, he managed to increase the modest inheritance his

---

[7] A number of these reports are cited by Yury Novikov in "Sergei Diaghilev: The Early Years," ed. Joan Ross Acocella, trans. Roberta Reeder, forthcoming. I am grateful to Dr. Reeder for showing me an early draft of this still-incomplete manuscript. [Unfortunately, this study was never published.—Ed.]

[8] Cited by Novikov in "Sergei Diaghilev: The Early Years." [See previous note.—Ed.]

[9] Vasilii Iastrebtsev, *Nikolai Andreevich Rimskii-Korsakov: Vospominaniia* [Memoirs], *1886–1908*, ed. Aleksandr Ossovskii (Leningrad: Muzgiz, 1959), 1:207–8. A slightly garbled translation of this passage into English can be found in V. V. Yastrebtsev, *Reminiscences of Rimsky-Korsakov*, ed. and trans. Florence Jonas (New York: Columbia University Press, 1985), 90.

[10] Zil'bershtein and Samkov, 2:413–14. Yastrebtsev's memoirs and the sources cited here invalidate the frequent assertion that Diaghilev studied composition with Rimsky-Korsakov.

mother had left him to such an extent that he could start building a private art collection. Between 1896 and 1898 he published a number of critical articles on art in the periodical press, an activity that he later continued in his pathbreaking journal, *World of Art*. In 1897 and 1898 he organized a series of memorable art exhibits in St. Petersburg. The first of these featured English and German watercolor artists, the second showed Scandinavian art, and the third and most popular was devoted to contemporary Finnish and Russian painters.

In his art criticism, collecting, and exhibitions, Diaghilev's approach was consistent. He showed a keen interest in all forms of art manifesting the artist's individuality, and disdained art that was conventional or motivated either by ideological pieties or chauvinistic nationalism. By the second half of the 1890s, members of the World of Art group made a few disjointed attempts to bring this universalist aesthetic to public attention. Filosofov published some literary criticism. Benois and Somov exhibited paintings and watercolors of eighteenth-century scenes treated in a Modernist manner, and Diaghilev edited the yearbook of the Russian Imperial Theaters. The resulting book was a triumph of typographical art; it was one of Diaghilev's often-overlooked contributions to the appearance of books and journals, a contribution much recognized in the history of typography in Russia.

In 1898 Diaghilev put to use his fund-raising abilities, which were to serve him well during his later years as a ballet impresario, and persuaded the generous patroness of the arts Princess Mariya Tenisheva and the millionaire merchant Savva Mamontov to finance his journal, which he edited jointly with Filosofov, other members of the World of Art group serving as art critics, music critics, designers, or illustrators. *World of Art* was published for only five years, but historians of Russian literature, art, and culture—at least those in the West—see its appearance as triggering a major turning point in Russian cultural attitudes. D. S. Mirsky, the most authoritative historian of Russian literature, points out that between the 1860s and 1890s literature and the arts were valued in Russia only if they expressed ideas that were considered currently relevant. This explains, for example, why such a major literary figure as Anton Chekhov had difficulty getting recognition. The reigning radical ideologues thought Chekhov lacked topical relevance and therefore judged him politically harmful. However, by the end of the first decade of the twentieth century, Mirsky argues, Russian society was aesthetically one of the most sophisticated in Europe. He gives the main credit for this to Sergei Diaghilev.[11]

The two-pronged offensive against academicism and conformity on the one side, and the supposedly revolutionary insistence on the propagandistic and didactic aspects of art to the exclusion of everything else on the other, caused an enormous stir when *World of Art* began publication. Attacks came from diverse quarters, right and left alike. The patriarch of radical-utilitarian music and art criticism Vladimir Stasov, who had since 1847 championed realistic, nationalistic, and ideologically committed art, had earlier blasted Diaghilev's 1898 Russo-Finnish exhibit as "an orgy of depravity and insanity, with a few good, talented paintings that stand out like vivid and brilliant pieces of lovely fabric pinned to a tattered and dirty blanket." The paintings of the great visionary Mikhail Vrubel (whose work was later prominently featured in *World of Art*) were for Stasov "outrageous, ugly, and repulsive." The early issues of *World of Art* were greeted by vitriolic denunciations by Stasov, for whom the journal was "dominated by nonsense, ugliness, and filth," its editors were "inept, inexperienced, and lacking in all taste," and the art works reproduced in its illustrations (by Degas, Monet, Aubrey Beardsley, Bakst, Somov, and Benois, among others) looked like "the work of a three-year-old child holding a pencil for the first time." "If such art prevails," Stasov concluded in one of his articles, "humanity as a whole will have to be locked up in insane asylums."[12]

Simultaneously, Stasov's sworn enemy, the ultraconservative columnist Viktor Burenin, writing in the reactionary newspaper *New Times*,

---

11 D. S. Mirsky, *A History of Russian Literature*, ed. Francis J. Whitfield (New York: Alfred A. Knopf, 1958), 409–12.

12 V. V. Stasov, *Izbrannye sochineniia v trekh tomakh* [Selected writings in three volumes], vol. 3 (Moscow: Iskusstvo, 1952). The cited passages are drawn from articles "Vystavki" [Art exhibits] (1898), 215–28; "Nishchie dukhom" [The poor in spirit] (1899), 232–38; and "Podvor'e prokazhennykh" [The leper colony] (1899), 257–63. These articles were originally published in the newspaper *Stock Exchange News*.

Anton Chekhov, in a letter to his friend Aleksei Suvorin (the publisher of the conservative newspaper *New Times*), wrote that he was "physically repelled" by the abusive tone of the literary and art critics of his time, citing both Stasov and Burenin (see next note) as prime examples of what he meant. "That's not criticism or a world view; it's hate, insatiable animal spite," Chekhov wrote. "Why must they write in a tone fit for judging criminals rather than artists and writers? I just can't stand it. I simply can't" (Michael Henry Heim and Simon Karlinsky, eds., *Anton Chekhov's Life and Thought* (Berkeley: University of California Press, 1975), 250).

launched a series of equally bitter attacks on *World of Art*, characterized by the following passage:

> Of course the pretensions of *World of Art* or, more precisely, the pretensions of a Mr. Diaghilev who edits this journal, are not only astounding but also extraordinarily stupid.... I do not know whether Mr. Diaghilev belongs to the category of semiliterate adolescents or of fraudulent dilettantes. But there's no doubt that this upstart dilettante is the most comical and at the same time the most unbridled of modern self-appointed judges of art. It is none other than Mr. Diaghilev who preaches decadence and foments the mercenary self-promotion of artists.[13]

Both the far left and the far right sides of the political spectrum perceived Diaghilev's rejection of didacticism, realism, and nationalistic pride as a threat and strove to discredit the journal and the movement it represented by dubbing it "decadent," a label that stuck for many years.

World of Art and the annual art exhibitions it sponsored managed not only to change the course of Russian culture but also to lay the groundwork for all of its spectacular achievements during the first three decades of the twentieth century. As noted, artists and historians rediscovered the Russian icon, the architecture of churches and palaces of earlier centuries, and the beauty of the Baroque and Rococo periods. The French Impressionists and Postimpressionists were the journal's main blind spot—it began writing about them only in its last year of publication—but otherwise the journal informed its readers of the arts of the past and the present in a comprehensive way never before attempted by a Russian publication. The literary section of *World of Art*, edited by Filosofov, became the rallying point for the nascent Symbolist movement in Russian literature. The

---

[13] Quoted from Zil'bershtein and Samkov, 1:312. Burenin kept reviling *World of Art* in his columns for several years. Then, in 1900, his columns mentioned the "ultraswinish" personal relationship between Diaghilev and Dima Filosofov. According to the memoirs of Sergei Makovsky and Pyotr Pertsov (cited in Zil'bershtein and Samkov, 2:310, 506), the two cousins, after reading the column, put on their frock coats and top hats and went to Burenin's residence. Burenin himself opened the door, whereupon Diaghilev, without saying a word, put his large-sized hat on Burenin, pulled it over him down to his shoulders and departed. After this, Burenin never again mentioned Diaghilev in any of his writings.

journal opened its pages to major Symbolist poets, helping to assert their reputations, and it also published the work of an important group of religious philosophers, thus bringing back into Russian culture the dimensions of mysticism, metaphysics, and fantasy which had been banished by utilitarian critics.

It is often claimed in the West that World of Art (both the movement and its journal) represented an art-for-art's-sake aesthetic and that Diaghilev was opposed to socially committed art. Nothing could be more erroneous. Diaghilev's art criticism shows that he was fully aware of the social aspects of art. What he fought against was the enslavement of art and of the artist by simplistic political dogma. For much of the nineteenth century, the fate of art in Russia was decided by people who neither liked nor understood it, and for whom beauty and complexity were morally suspect. Everything about *World of Art*, from its philosophy to its outward appearance, was a refutation of that hegemony (which was, however, enthroned again after the Revolution). An auxiliary of *World of Art* was the concert series "Evenings of Contemporary Music" organized by group members Walter Nouvel and Alfred Nurok. It existed from 1900 to 1912 and introduced to the Russian public such composers as Debussy, Ravel, Schoenberg, and, in 1907, Stravinsky.

In 1903 there came an editorial crisis in *World of Art* that paralleled the crisis in the relationship between Diaghilev and Filosofov. Filosofov had joined some of the leading contributors to *World of Art* to start a religious journal called *The New Way*. Two of these contributors, the poet Zinaida Gippius and her husband, the novelist and critic Dmitry Merezhkovsky, set out to break up the relationship between Diaghilev and Filosofov, using as their lever Filosofov's ever-growing involvement in religious and revolutionary politics, a subject that held little interest for Diaghilev. The tug of war between Gippius and Diaghilev for Filosofov's affections lasted for three years, culminating in a victory for Gippius that left Diaghilev with deep emotional scars.[14]

In 1904 *World of Art* ceased publication. Its viewpoint and its mission were taken over and enhanced by several other important art journals

---

14 On the emotional triangle between Diaghilev, Filosofov, and Zinaida Gippius, see Vladimir Zlobin, *A Difficult Soul: Zinaida Gippius*, and my introductory essay to that book, "Who was Zinaida Gippius?" (Berkeley: University of California Press, 1980).

that appeared between 1904 and 1917.[15] After the demise of his journal, Diaghilev summed up its cultural policy by organizing the most grandiose and influential of his art exhibitions, the display of Russian portraits of the eighteenth and early nineteenth centuries that opened at the Tauris Palace in St. Petersburg in March 1905. Diaghilev traveled throughout Russia to locate 4,000 portraits, of which some 2,000 were exhibited. The result was the rediscovery of scores of fine Russian painters whose work had not been collected or studied in the nineteenth century because of its supposed deficiencies in psychological depth and social significance. It is because of Diaghilev that these paintings are today proudly displayed in Soviet museums and reproduced in scholarly monographs and on postcards. Art historians date from this exhibition a whole new attitude in Russian galleries and museums about methods of hanging and displaying paintings and sculptures.

With the end of both *World of Art* and his relationship with Filosofov, Diaghilev turned to Western Europe for his next projects. In 1906 he took an exhibition of Russian art ranging from ancient icons to Modernist paintings to Paris, Berlin, and Venice. In 1907 in Paris he arranged five historical concerts of Russian music from Glinka to Scriabin, with the appearances as conductors and soloists of Rimsky-Korsakov, Glazunov, Rachmaninoff, and Scriabin. In 1908 he brought to the Paris Opera an opulent production of Musorgsky's *Boris Godunov* with Fyodor Chaliapin. These performances consolidated the popularity of Russian nineteenth-century composers in the West. Diaghilev's next project was to take abroad a season of opera and ballet. The very idea of exporting Russian ballet to the West struck many of his contemporaries as outlandish.

In the early decades of the nineteenth century, ballet was a respected art in Russia. Choreographers, such as Charles Didelot and Adam Glushkovsky, were highly regarded by the intellectual community. Major writers, Pushkin and Gogol among them, wrote of the ballet with interest and enthusiasm. But at the end of the century this situation no longer existed. Even the choreographic genius of Marius Petipa could not rescue the ballet of the time from the absurdities that had become a part of its con-

---

[15] On important art journals, such as *The Golden Fleece, Apollon*, and others, which were all successors of *World of Art*, see Valentine Marcadé, *Le renouveau de l'art pictorial russe* (Lausanne: L'Age d'Homme, 1971).

vention: the convoluted plots about supernatural beings who expressed themselves in stilted pantomime, the low quality of most ballet music (the scores of Chaikovsky, Glazunov, and Riccardo Drigo were rare exceptions), sets and costumes inappropriate to the historical period depicted, and a corrupt star system that constantly sacrificed artistry and logic so that a prima ballerina who portrayed a beggar or a peasant girl was often allowed to appear in a pearl necklace and diamond tiara. Socially aware Russians of the turn of the century regarded ballet as a plaything of elderly lechers who liked watching legs in tights.

Aleksandr Benois and Walter Nouvel were rare instances of intellectuals who loved ballet and believed that it had the makings of a true art form. They at first had a hard time converting Diaghilev to this view. In October 1896 he complained in a letter to Benois that Nouvel's enthusiasm for ballet was "unendurable."[16] But in 1901, when he served briefly as an aide to the director of the Imperial Theaters, Prince Sergei Volkonsky, Diaghilev asked to be put in charge of a new production of *Sylvia* by Delibes. However, his plan to have the production designed by Bakst, Benois, and several other World of Art figures was vetoed and Diaghilev was dismissed from his position at the Imperial Theaters. Diaghilev made other attempts in the next few years to get access to the Imperial Theaters. His aim was to introduce into opera and possibly ballet productions an artistic synthesis of their component elements, the kind of synthesis that Wagner had dreamed of and that had been achieved in drama by Stanislavsky and Vladimir Nemirovich-Danchenko, whose Moscow Art Theater opened the same year that *World of Art* began publication.

By 1907, however, an innovative choreographer was working in Russia, trained at the Imperial Ballet School but interested in achieving a fusion between ballet and the nascent art of modern dance, as exemplified by Isadora Duncan. As Vera Krasovskaya has observed, Mikhail Fokine disliked the traditional ballet of the late nineteenth century as strongly as the World of Art group disliked the academicians and realist painters of the same period.[17] Much of Fokine's reform of ballet reflected the impact of the World of Art on the whole of Russian culture, and it was only natu-

---

16 Zil'bershtein and Samkov, 2:18.
17 Vera Krasovskaia, *Russkii baletnyi teatr nachala XX veka* [Russian ballet at the beginning of the twentieth century] (Leningrad: Iskusstvo, 1971–72), 2:158ff.

ral that he should make common cause with the artists of that group. It is, in fact, hard to think of a closer theatrical embodiment of the World of Art aesthetics of ca. 1895 than the ballet *Le pavillon d'Armide* (1907), with a libretto, scenery, and costumes by Benois and choreography by Fokine—an opulent glorification of the seventeenth and eighteenth centuries, with a story line taken from the Romantic poet Théophile Gautier.

Fokine had at his disposal an array of brilliant young dancers who believed in his ideas and were eager to appear in his ballets, among them Anna Pavlova, Tamara Karsavina, Sofya Fyodorova, Bronislava Nijinska, Vaslav Nijinsky, Adolph Bolm, and Georgy Rozai. So when Diaghilev's plan to bring to Paris several Russian operas in the spring of 1909 was cancelled because of insufficient financing, he and his associates decided to fill most of the season with Fokine ballets, most created earlier in St. Petersburg but in some cases revised for export. The enormous success of that first 1909 season, followed by the equally highly acclaimed one in 1910, led Diaghilev not to rely on dancers he borrowed from the Imperial Theaters in St. Petersburg and Moscow but to form his own company in 1911, Ballets Russes de Serge Diaghilev. Signaling his total commitment to ballet, this decision must have been reinforced by his personal alliance with Vaslav Nijinsky, whom he first met in 1908 and who became the object of his most intense emotional involvement since his break with Filosofov.

The early Paris seasons were a triumph for Diaghilev's dancers, for his designers (especially the friends of his youth, Benois and Bakst), and for Fokine's choreography. But in a larger sense, they were also a vindication of the positions for which the World of Art group had fought so hard during the 1890s. In *Les sylphides* Fokine went back to the *ballets blancs* of the age of Marie Taglioni, showing to what extent his reform was a return to the dance concepts of the age of Romanticism. Both *Les sylphides* and Schumann's *Carnaval* were rehabilitations of that very Romanticism that generations of Russian critics had rejected and reviled, beginning with Vissarion Belinsky in the 1840s.

The spectacular productions about love punished by death in an exotic setting (*Egyptian Nights*, renamed *Cleopatra* by Diaghilev, *Scheherazade*, and the later *Thamar*) all used this favorite theme of Russian Romantic poets such as Pushkin and Lermontov, a theme that was taken up in a big way by the senior Russian Symbolists Valery Bryusov and Fyodor Sologub, both of them valued contributors to *World of Art* around the turn of the century. The ballets that depicted ancient Greece perceived through a prism of Modernist sensibility (*Narcissus, Daphnis et Chloé, L'après-midi d'un faune*) represented another bridge between Russian Romantic poetry (ballads of Vasily Zhukovsky in the second decade of the nineteenth century) and the Symbolists (the plays of Innokenty Annensky in the first decade of the twentieth). And of course each of these Fokine ballets was a *Gesamtkunstwerk* of the kind that Diaghilev had dreamed of for years, with the harmony of all contributing elements. The exceptions were the divertissement ballets (*Le festin* and *Les Orientales*), which were medleys of composers and choreographers. But they were an aberration, not encountered in Diaghilev's subsequent seasons.

With *The Firebird* (1910) Diaghilev revealed to the world the genius of Igor Stravinsky, the composer closely associated with him for the rest of his life. Still in the repertory of many companies, the ballet is a masterpiece, but it also betrays the eclecticism inherent in the World of Art mentality. Fokine's choreography employs both the classical ballet techniques (the role of the Firebird) and a freer interpretive style (the Enchanted Princesses). Stravinsky's music draws on authentic folksongs from Rimsky-Korsakov's collection, but they are harmonized and orchestrated in the manner of French Impressionism. The libretto uses motifs from Russian folklore, but also includes elements taken from the Symbolist writers Aleksei Remizov and Sologub, and possibly even from *Swan Lake*.

In Russia, in the meantime, the Symbolism that inspired the early Diaghilev ballets was receding. The gates opened by World of Art had admitted a host of new schools of painting, which paralleled the rise of Cubism in the West. In literature the Symbolist movement was being challenged by such Futurist poets as Vladimir Mayakovsky and Velimir Khlebnikov, the latter specializing in ultra-Modernist and Primitivist portrayals of the Slavic Stone Age. Stravinsky's score for his next ballet for Diaghilev, *Petrushka* (1911), was, in its raucous modernity, a musical equivalent of these new developments, just as the theme of that ballet had clear analogies with Vsevolod Meyerhold's 1906 production of Aleksandr Blok's lyrical comedy *The Puppet Booth* (the play in which that great poet bade farewell to the Symbolist excesses of his youth). The angular beauty of Nijinsky's choreography for Debussy's *L'après-midi d'un faune*, one year after *Petrushka*, was likewise a step into the future and away from the

World of Art aesthetics. So was Nijinsky's *Jeux* (1913), the first Diaghilev ballet on a modern theme danced in modern dress.

The collaboration between Stravinsky and Nijinsky on *The Rite of Spring*, despite its archaic theme, was very much of a piece with the most recent advances in Russian literature and art of the time. Western audiences and critics, accustomed to the retrospective idealizations of the past in Fokine's ballets, were not ready for this breakthrough into Russian Futurism and they reacted with hostility. Stravinsky's music, initially rejected as vehemently as Nijinsky's choreography, went on to an independent career as a concert work and eventually won recognition as a great masterpiece in the history of music, but Nijinsky's choreography of *The Rite of Spring* was seen only a total of nine times and was never given the opportunity to win audiences through further exposure and greater familiarity.

Some contemporaries, including Benois and Fokine, have dismissed Nijinsky's choreography as inept and ugly, an opinion to which Stravinsky added a cachet by his utterances of the 1930s. But as Nijinsky's biographers Vera Krasovskaya and Richard Buckle have eloquently argued, as his sister Bronislava tried to demonstrate in her memoirs, and as Stravinsky himself came to recognize shortly before his death,[18] Vaslav Nijinsky was not only a great dancer, but also an innovative choreographer of remarkable vision and power. A study of photographs, drawings, and eyewitness accounts of his ballets will bear this out. But for once in his life, Diaghilev listened to the critics and the public. Influenced by them and, no doubt, by his rancor about Nijinsky's sudden marriage, which Diaghilev felt as a personal betrayal, he let both *Jeux* and *The Rite of Spring* lapse from the repertory.

Nijinsky's departure plunged Diaghilev into a period of uncertainty. After *Petrushka*, Fokine seems somehow to have lost his innovative touch. From about 1911 on, he could only repeat himself. Diaghilev had to learn that while he could go on presenting Fokine's earlier World of Art–style ballets (in the case of *Les sylphides* and *Scheherazade* almost ad infinitum), creating new specimens of this genre in the second decade of the twentieth

---

[18] On Stravinsky's changing attitude to Nijinsky's *Rite of Spring* choreography, see Pieter C. van den Toorn, *Stravinsky and "The Rite of Spring"* (Berkeley: University of California Press, 1987), 2, 6–8, 16. Millicent Hodson's reconstruction of that choreography, danced in 1987–88 by the Joffrey Ballet, confirms the unfairness of Fokine's and Stravinsky's hostile evaluations.

century was much harder. Not even all the glories of Ravel's music, which Diaghilev had commissioned, could save Fokine's *Daphnis et Chloé* (1912) from failure. Fokine's *The Legend of Joseph* and *Midas* (both 1914) were retreads of his earlier spectaculars, although *Le coq d'or* (1914) did contain some innovations dictated by its staging as a ballet-opera. Diaghilev was forced to turn to second-rate choreographers such as Boris Romanov and Adolph Bolm, and from 1915 on he fostered the choreographic abilities of his new discovery, Léonide Massine (in Russian, Leonid Myasin). A prolific dance maker, Massine never quite reached the level of originality and invention of Diaghilev's other major choreographers.

The liberal-democratic Revolution of February 1917, which overthrew the Romanov monarchy, was greeted ecstatically by the entire World of Art circle. This was the coming of the free and just society that Diaghilev had predicted and hailed in his oft-cited banquet speech at the time of the Revolution of 1905. He had Ivan Tsarevich carry a red flag in the finale of *The Firebird*, much to the consternation of the Parisian public, and he commissioned from Stravinsky an orchestration of "The Song of the Volga Boatmen" as a replacement for the old imperial anthem that used to be played at the beginnings of performances.[19] But the establishment of the Bolshevik dictatorship in October of the same year spelled the end of these sanguine hopes. Within a decade, the new regime began to impose on the arts the very restrictions that its nineteenth-century utilitarian precursors had advocated and which World of Art had struggled to depose. With very few exceptions (such as the dancers Aleksei Bulgakov and Mariya Piltz), almost everyone connected with the Diaghilev ballet and with Diaghilev's earlier enterprises joined the great exodus of 1918–22 and found themselves in the West.

The production in 1917 of Jean Cocteau's ballet *Parade* with choreography by Massine, music by Satie, and sets and costumes by Picasso marked the arrival of the international orientation that would become a hallmark of the Diaghilev ballets. He had used music by non-Russian composers almost from the beginning of his seasons, but after 1917 his

---

[19] The text of Diaghilev's speech welcoming the 1905 Revolution is reproduced in Buckle, *Diaghilev*, 87. Eyewitness accounts of the red flag in *The Firebird* are also cited there, 328–29. Like many people in the West, Buckle confuses and conflates the liberal-democratic Revolution of February 1917 with the Bolshevik-led October Revolution of the same year.

VII. Song and Dance

composers and designers were as likely as not to be foreigners. So were many of his dancers, even if they were given Russian-style stage names. Only his choreographers remained Russian-bred and -trained until the very end. The post-1917 Diaghilev repertory regularly included ballets on contemporary subjects, but he also kept alive many of the ballets from his early seasons and occasionally presented a nineteenth-century classic, such as a two-act version of *Swan Lake*.

In 1921 Diaghilev presented Europe with its first full-length Petipa ballet, *The Sleeping Beauty*, in which four exiled Russian ballerinas alternated in the leading part. But the production's English audience was not as enthusiastic for full-length ballets as it would be a half-century later. Financially, the production was a disaster.[20] Many commentators saw the presentation of the Chaikovsky classic by the same Diaghilev who had earlier given the world *The Rite of Spring* and *Parade* as a betrayal of his artistic principles, but in fact the production was very much in line with his usual practice of presenting innovative new ballets, while retaining in his repertory such earlier classics as *Swan Lake*.

After 1917 Diaghilev's umbilical connection to the World of Art aesthetics faded away. His principal Russian designers from 1914 on were the advanced Modernists Nataliya Goncharova and Mikhail Larionov, although he was to turn a few more times, for sentimental reasons, to his old associates Benois and Bakst. Beginning in 1917, he relied on Picasso, Braque, Matisse, Derain, Gris, and other painters from the School of Paris for his sets and costumes. The one World of Art trait that remained with Diaghilev until the very end was his devotion to ballets on eighteenth-century subjects, which began with *Le pavilion d'Armide* and continued through *The Good-Humored Ladies* (1917), *Pulcinella* (1920), and all the way to the visually arresting Massine–Nicolas Nabokov–Pavel Tchelitchew *Ode* of 1928.

In the 1920s Diaghilev discovered and promoted the talents of two strong and resourceful choreographers, Bronislava Nijinska and George Balanchine. They rewarded him with a half-dozen important ballets, four

---

[20] For more details about Diaghilev's reasons for staging *The Sleeping Beauty* and for the production's financial failure, see Boris Kochno, *Diaghilev and the Ballets Russes* (New York: Harper & Row, 1970), 168–75; and Nancy Van Norman Baer, *Bronislava Nijinska: A Dancer's Legacy*, exhibition catalogue ([San Francisco]: Fine Arts Museums of San Francisco, 1986), 27–28.

of which, Nijinska's *Les noces* and *Les biches* and Balanchine's *Apollo* and *The Prodigal Son*, are still in the repertory of various companies today.[21] While continuing his association with Stravinsky in the 1920s, Diaghilev also had ballets composed by his other Russian "musical sons," as he called them—Sergei Prokofiev (on three occasions), and also Nicolas Nabokov and Vladimir Dukelsky, later known as Vernon Duke of Broadway fame (on one occasion each). But he also relied on English, Italian, and especially French composers for his scores during this decade. In the last few years of his life Diaghilev watched closely the artistic developments in the Soviet Union and found some of them intriguing. The result of this interest was the ballet about Soviet life, *The Steel Leap* (this is a far closer translation of *Stal'noi skok* than the usual French *Le pas d'acier*), with a score by Prokofiev and design by the Soviet artist Georgy Yakulov.

Considering the various aspects of Diaghilev's heritage, one common denominator emerges—he was a cultural educator of genius. He brought his native culture out of narrow provincialism and taught his fellow countrymen to see and understand art, to broaden their literary and philosophical horizons, to publish beautiful journals, and to arrange art exhibitions. From the 1930s on, the Soviet regime did its best to undo his work, but an astounding amount of it survived and managed to prosper in post-Stalinist times. Outside of Russia Diaghilev revealed to the Western world the importance and beauty of Russian art and music. Ballet, when he turned his attention to it, was in a state of greater or lesser decline everywhere. He brought it to unprecedented new heights, reestablished its prestige as a major art form, and was ultimately responsible for its huge popularity in many countries where it was not previously known, such as Japan. In his last years, Diaghilev became a bibliophile and amassed an important collection of rare books and manuscripts, many of which have found their ways into the major university libraries of the Western world.

But if Diaghilev educated countries and societies, he was also a master educator of individual artists. Without his influence it would be hard to imagine the careers of Igor Stravinsky, Tamara Karsavina, Vaslav Nijinsky, Léonide Massine, Bronislava Nijinska, Aleksandra Danilova, George Balanchine, and Alicia Markova—a list by no means exhaustive. But even

---

21 See the section "His Legacy" in Percival, *The World of Diaghilev*, 125–40, on the fate of individual Diaghilev ballets in later decades.

artists who were fully formed when they began working with Diaghilev, such as Benois and Fokine, nonetheless had the finest moments of their careers during their association with him, moments that could not be duplicated after they had parted ways.

On a more personal level, there were his pedagogical relationships with the three young men with whom he was intimately involved during the 1920s—the dancer and choreographer Serge Lifar; the English dancer Patrick Healey-Kay, better known as Anton Dolin; and the composer and conductor Igor Markevich, who was Diaghilev's last love. All three were unknown and unformed artistically when they came to Diaghilev, and all went on to major careers in their respective fields.

Diaghilev was not an easy man to deal with, and the memoirs left by his associates reflect this. Alongside the intelligence and loyalty of Karsavina's recollections, we find hidden animosity (Benois), open hostility (Fokine), self-glorification (Lifar), and evasions combined with forgetfulness (Massine). But even the inexact memoirs add to the sum of our knowledge. The vast literature on Diaghilev and his era testifies that his life and achievement are of universal interest.

The publication in the Soviet Union of the two-volume collection of writings by and about Sergei Diaghilev, *Sergei Diagilev i russkoe iskusstvo*, in 1982, edited *con amore* by Ilya Zilbershtein and Vladimir Samkov, marked, despite certain evasions and distortions, the final rehabilitation of Diaghilev and his cause in the Soviet Union. In the current atmosphere of greater openness and relaxation of censorship, there is hope for publication of invaluable Diaghilev materials that are known to exist in here-to-fore inaccessible Soviet archives. Among them are private journals of Dima Filosofov, Filosofov's book-length manuscript on Aleksandr Benois, and the memoirs of Diaghilev's stepmother, Elena, and of Walter Nouvel.[22] Publication of these documents should make possible the future study of Diaghilev and his times with a depth of understanding and on a scale that has not been possible until now.

---

[22] These archival holdings were used by Nataliya Lapshina (see n. 5 above) and by Zilbershtein and Samkov.

Opera and Drama in Ravel[1]

*M*aurice Ravel's operatic works have not been fortunate. Anyone even slightly interested in music knows Ravel as the author of *Boléro*, the *Rapsodie espagnole* and *Daphnis et Chloé*. And yet his two astonishing operas, *L'heure espagnole* and *L'enfant et les sortilèges*, are still fairly obscure. They are shown very rarely in the theater, and were it not for recordings and radio broadcasts over the last decade, they might well have remained the sole property of musicologists. The lack of interest in these two masterpieces on the part of opera houses in the West is due in part to their technical difficulty. Though short, both operas require large expenditures and complicated props. The vocal parts demand virtuosos, but afford singers little opportunity to shine in full-blown, impressive arias. But the lack of interest can also be ascribed to the profound incomprehension, or rather the erroneous perceptions, of music critics. *L'heure espagnole* is usually put down as an amusing musical farce, *L'enfant et les sortilèges* as a fairy tale for children. In a small monograph on Ravel (subtitled "A Book for Young Readers"), published in Leningrad in 1964, Aleksandr Stupel, the author, rehearsing the usual dicta of French critics, actually calls *L'enfant et les sortilèges* a children's opera, which is like calling *Lolita* a children's novel just because the title character is a child.

The two operas were created nearly twenty years apart. They differ greatly in conception, in structure, and in the character of their music. But they do have a common denominator: the attempt to delineate the situation and personality of the characters not by musically illustrating the text (as in the operas of Richard Strauss), and not by combining text and music in one (as in Debussy's *Pelléas et Mélisande*), but through music that conveys a subjective, psychological quality (with reference to the characters singing) that seemingly contradicts the "objective" data of the libretto or the utterances of the characters themselves. The most telling example is the first

---

[1] Translated by Richard Taruskin. Originally published as "Opernaia dramaturgiia Ravelia" in *Novyi zhurnal*, no. 94 (1969): 115–25.

VII. Song and Dance

appearance of Concepcion, the heroine in *L'heure espagnole*. The everyday, prosaic recitative with which she addresses her husband the watchmaker is accompanied by a passionate, arching phrase from a solo cello. One English critic, probably Ernest Newman, thought that this seemingly unsuitable accompaniment was supposed to represent the ardent attachment of husband and wife. There is a simpler explanation. As it does throughout the opera, the musical commentary here conveys the subjective emotions of the character singing. In this case, Concepcion's whole being is suffused with anticipation of her coming rendezvous with her lover, the poet Gonzalve. That is what the cello is singing about, and the recitative the actual character sings—a reminder to her husband to wind the town clock—is just her outward prosaic manner, as it appears to the unobservant world.

The humorist and parodist who wrote under the pseudonym Franc-Nohain long wondered why Ravel thought his somewhat cynical comedy *L'heure espagnole*, written in a complicated variable meter and full of puns, was a fit libretto for an opera. Franc-Nohain's own conception was nothing like Ravel's opera. The bored wife of a watchmaker from Toledo has started up a romance with an affected, pretentious young poet. Having gotten her husband out of the house, Concepcion listens at length to the poet's passionate effusions, but it gradually dawns on her that for him the main thing in love is not love, but its literary possibilities. And yet Concepcion simply cannot let her chance of deceiving her husband go by! She has another admirer, the fat banker Don Inigo Gomez. But this stout banker, whom Concepcion has had brought to her room hidden inside a huge wall clock, has gotten stuck inside the clock and cannot take advantage of his unanticipated good fortune. The heroine weeps in frustration (and out of ungratified desire). But at the last minute she notices the muscular shoulders of the modest, bashful mule driver Ramiro, who throughout the action has been obediently fulfilling her whims, moving heavy clocks containing admirers from place to place. The mule driver has better luck than the poet or the banker. Or so the characters say, addressing the audience in the opera's epilogue: "Such is the moral of Boccaccio: The most able lover beats them all. In the game of love sooner or later it will be the driver's turn."[2]

---

[2] C'est la morale de Boccace:
Entre tous les amants, seul amant efficace,
Il arrive un moment, dans les déduits d'amour,
Où le muletier a son tour!

And that's it. As the author of the play himself observes in the epilogue, his characters are sketchy, one-dimensional puppets: the self-important banker, the precious poet, the dimwitted watchmaker of a husband, the naive simpleton Ramiro. But how these puppets come to life, take on depth, become human through Ravel's music! The male characters display a chivalry and idealism on which the author of the comedy surely never counted. Strange as it seems, the new dimensions introduced by the music do not contradict the text but reveal it from a new angle. The tenderness toward his wife and the affectionate turns of phrase in the watchmaker's part make the role more attractive and affecting than the stereotyped, mercilessly ridiculed cuckold portrayed by Franc-Nohain. The poet Gonzalve, in Ravel's musical incarnation, is truly seized with creative fervor. At the same time he is some sort of parodied reductio ad absurdum of Bryusov's Poet, for whom "this life of ours is just a thing / about which poets brightly sing."[3] His languid, super-Spanishy airs at once embody and parody his passion. But he so exhausts himself in these melodies, and with such rapture tries to turn them into literature, that there is nothing left of him for Concepcion. She has been nothing but a stimulus to engage his essential modus operandi, literature. The woman he loves hurls herself relentlessly into his embrace, but Gonzalve is already working on the poetic elaboration of the blissful moments he in fact has had no time to experience. Is this parody? Farce? Yes, of course, but on another level the operatic treatment has granted us a profound insight into the sources and nature of artistic creation.

The fat, funny banker has flirted with a saucy mistress and ended up looking a fool. What, you may ask, could be more trite? But even here, Ravel finds a way to infuse the part of the clock-stuck Inigo with all the tenderness and sympathy one could wish for. The orchestra accompanies the banker's singing with a sort of jingling, intoxicating waltz, pulverized by unexpected pauses. It is as though within the heavy, aging body of the banker an enraptured, romantic youth were imprisoned, unwilling to surrender, thirsting for something, dreaming of something. Once again, through music, a banal scene is transformed into a most compassionate commentary on youth and age. And, finally, the sympathetic, naive

---

[3] "Все в жизни лишь средство / Для ярко-певучих стихов" (Valery Bryusov, "Poetu").

driver (a dense bumpkin in Franc-Nohain's version) becomes, with the help of Ravel's music, the embodiment of gentle, manly benevolence and gallantry.

There remains, of course, Concepcion herself. Having humanized the male characters, Ravel seems not to have treated his heroine very kindly. And in truth, if in Franc-Nohain's comedy the distribution of forces was even—five amusing windup toys—in Ravel's opera we see four sympathetic idealists plus the same Concepcion as in the comedy, thinking of nothing except how to deceive her husband, no matter with whom. Her main aria is a despairing lament that fate has prevented her from fulfilling this plan, the composer making no concessions to her in the way of orchestral "extenuations." Can we therefore accuse Ravel of some kind of hidden misogyny and suspect him of harboring ideas about the essential nature of the female sex that were fashionable at the time of *L'heure espagnole*—ideas on the order of Przybyszewski or of certain plays by Leonid Andreev? Perhaps so, had Ravel not written an orchestral introduction to the opera that amounts in my view to a musical portrait of the heroine.

In the literature on Ravel, the introduction to *L'heure espagnole* is looked upon as an ingenious depiction of the watchmaker's shop. Critics have written a lot about the ticking pendulums, cuckoo clocks, music boxes, whirling toy ballerinas, and tweety birds virtuosically rendered by Ravel's orchestra. All of this is there in the music, but the sonic ornaments that have so delighted critics serve as but an adornment to the core of the introduction: a glum, monotonous five-bar phrase that runs through all the music at the beginning of the opera and that twice rises up into something like an outburst of despair. It would be hard to find in all of music a more perfect embodiment of ennui and tedium (the closest parallels: the introduction to Ravel's other opera, which depicts a bored child, and one of the *Véritables préludes flasques* by the musical humorist Erik Satie, where he wanted to convey the whimpering of a dog locked up in a house). But who is doing the whimpering and pining in the Toledo watchmaker's shop? Not the good-natured owner, who is always satisfied with his business, his clients and, to be sure, "himself, his dinner, and his wife."[4] The one languishing amid all this tinkling and ticking is the watchmaker's

---

[4] A. Pushkin, *Evgenii Onegin*, chap. 1, stanza 12 (lines that have become proverbial about cuckolds).—Ed.

wife, who in this reading of the introduction suddenly appears as a cousin of Katerina Izmailova in Shostakovich's opera. Only where Shostakovich has Leskov's bored heroine start love affairs, feed her father-in-law poisonous mushrooms, throttle a child,[5] drown her rival in the river, and end her own life in a suicide (and in addition to all of that, according to the composer's plan, indict all of tsarist Russia), Ravel's Spanish-French heroine is content with the first step—the affairs, without sacrificing anyone's life and without indulging in tragic finger-pointing. In this case Ravel's conception is of course the more true to life. If my interpretation of the introduction is correct, Concepcion's frivolity is explained and, in its way, justified by the orchestra, even before her first appearance on stage.

The bewitching melodies in *L'heure espagnole* are mainly assigned to the instruments of the orchestra. The poet Gonzalve is given a few passionate Spanish melodies, but they are obvious parodies of the pseudo-Spanish style in nineteenth-century operas. Only in the extended final quintet in habanera rhythm do the singers finally get a chance both to sing real tunes and to distinguish themselves with virtuoso coloratura ornaments while the orchestra is relegated to the role of rhythmic accompaniment. In building his whole opera on recitative singing with some rare individual melodic phrases that never receive any further development, Ravel was inspired, on his own admission, by *Marriage*, an unfinished and rather enigmatic opera fragment by Musorgsky, based on Gogol's comedy. What, exactly, Ravel might have taken from this fragment, besides the recitative principle (which was already available in both Dargomyzhsky and Debussy), is unclear. Neither in Ravel's correspondence nor in the accounts of memoirists are there any indications that Ravel was acquainted with Musorgsky's manuscript score. But *Marriage* had been published in an edition by Rimsky-Korsakov that monstrously distorted the composer's conception. Rimsky furnished his edition with notes on the supposedly "unperformable" and "hardly audible" rhythmic complications and "bad-sounding harmonies" in Musorgsky's manuscript, which he allegedly corrected (the way Turgenev corrected the meter in Tyutchev's "A Dream at Sea"). In the same notes, Rimsky gives examples of Musorgsky's rhythmic and harmonic finds, from which it is immediately clear that in this unfinished fragment, Musorgsky was trying to work out a rhyth-

---

5 Actually, Shostakovich omitted this episode from Leskov's story.—Ed.

mic design reminiscent of Stravinsky's *Les noces*, and that the harmonies that offended Rimsky-Korsakov, based on parallel seconds, came near to surpassing Béla Bartók. Rimsky made short work of all this "heresy," abbreviating and squeezing the rhythm into customary measures of three- or four-quarter time and turning the seconds into grace notes, following all the rules of textbook harmony. Thus, while it is tempting to trace the harmonic spice and the free rhythmic declamation in *L'heure espagnole* back to this evidently revolutionary bit of Musorgskian innovation, the simplified version to which Ravel had access, Rimsky's, does not support such a notion.

By the time Ravel returned to the operatic genre, about two decades after *L'heure espagnole*, his ideas about musical theater had changed fundamentally and he was attracted to altogether different tasks. In *L'enfant et les sortilèges*, the melodies are assigned to the human voices, with the orchestra given a more modest role—though even here Ravel's fabulous orchestra has brilliance and sparkle to spare. The libretto of Ravel's second opera was created in collaboration with the remarkable writer Colette. A subtle stylist, a profound student of the human heart, Colette was for some reason considered a boulevard *romancière* in prerevolutionary Russia. In Soviet journalism and criticism she is either ignored or hushed up, despite the wide popularity of her works in the West and the growing, tender love both for her books and her person among a very wide circle of readers in France as well as the USA, England, and especially Germany.

In the libretto she wrote for Ravel, Colette made use of the conventions and devices of French children's stories to create, in an ingenious form, an interesting and profound allegory of an eternal theme that has in recent years taken on a keen timeliness: the theme of the generation gap, of mutual incomprehension between "fathers and children,"[6] the unwillingness and incapacity of the younger generation to appreciate the spiritual, moral and social values of their "fathers." The bored little hero of the opera is a boy who has been sat down to do his homework, who is not allowed to run free, not allowed to torture animals for fun. During a short episode in which his mother admonishes him, the boy is silent.

---

[6] A reference to the title of Ivan Turgenev's famous novel *Ottsy i deti* (in English usually rendered as *Fathers and Sons* after Constance Garnett's nineteenth-century translation)—so famous that the author did not have to be named.—Ed.

To her received truths he makes no objection: he knows he will not be understood. Then comes an explosion: the child is left alone and, in order to feel free, gives himself up to an orgy of destruction and vandalism—he breaks dishes, douses the fire in the hearth, cuts the wallpaper, smashes the wall clock, tears his books and attacks his cat and pet squirrel, who run away in terror. All this is accompanied by a joyful cry: "Hurrah! To hell with homework! To hell with chores! I am free, free, bad but free!"

In *L'heure espagnole*, the action proceeded without interruption. Colette's libretto is built in a novel episodic form, an "opera with sliding drawers": in a long succession of individual episodes wherein the broken things and wounded animals pour out their feelings, the little hero gradually realizes the nature and consequences of his "revolt." In the first half of the opera, Colette somehow hit upon one of the themes of contemporaneous Russian poetry: the theme of "insurrection of things," the refusal of inanimate objects to serve the degraded purposes of mankind, as developed by Khlebnikov (*The Crane, Marquise des S.*), Mayakovsky, and Marina Tsvetaeva (*Poem of the Staircase*). The furniture refuses to hold the boy when he grows weary from destruction. The armchair and couch suddenly come to life in a cumbersome duet in the tempo of a sarabande. They announce their refusal to serve the little barbarian, while in the orchestra heavy chords in the piano and sliding trombone and cello glissandi create the impression that in the room the floor has tilted and all the furniture is threatening to slither off in some direction.

After the comically pompous furniture, the broken clock takes its turn—an aria for baritone. This is one of the most convincing examples of musical psychology in Ravel's operatic output. If in *L'heure espagnole* the composer was able to develop complicated psychological designs using Franc-Nohain's puppet-like characters, in his second opera, with the help of Colette, he imparts the same compelling humanity to inanimate objects, plants, and animals. The clock's part is an extended, and in its own way tragic, portrait of a certain type of functionary. Paramount in the life of this clock-man is order and utility. For long years the clock has honorably served humanity: it announced when it was time to get up, when to lie down, and when to receive one's nearest and dearest. The mechanical, swinging-pendulum rhythm of the aria gradually gives way to broad vocal lyricism—the clock's motives, you see, were altruistic; the clock wanted its ticking to accompany the boy into a bright and happy future. The same boy who went and broke the pendulum! The clock has come into collision with an irrational and destructive force, to which it reacts with outrage, grief, but mainly incomprehension ("but all I ever wanted was his happiness!"). In despair at running down, the clock stands itself in the corner to hide its shame and pain from the world, and the music illustrates its collapse with fitful rhythmic irregularities.

After the intricately devised episode with the clock (scarcely within a child's grasp), there follow episodes of a more diverting nature. The grotesque duet of broken dishes—a brash English porcelain teapot (a tenor, singing in a mixture of English and French) and an elegant Chinese teacup (a mezzo-soprano, holding forth in an arcane patois that is supposed to sound Chinese but that is based on guttural quasi-Japanese words like "hara-kiri" since, as the teacup notes, "either way it's incomprehensible")—is a colorfully orchestrated twenties-style foxtrot. The modish and sophisticated melody of the teacup (later repeated by the trombone in a stratospherically high register) distantly recalls the as-yet-unwritten *Boléro*. The monstrously difficult fioritura aria for the fire (coloratura soprano), enraged at having been doused by water from the teapot, recreates the brilliant cabalettas from the heyday of Italian bel canto. The chorus and dances of the separated shepherds and shepherdesses on the wallpaper the child has ripped are musically simple and ingenuous; yet if you listen closely to their delicate pastorale ("the naughty child has forever spoiled our tender tale"), you will find, unexpectedly, a lump in your throat.

Terrified by what he has seen and heard, the child seeks an answer in his books, from which he has just ripped out some pages. From a volume of German fairy tales arises a princess—his favorite heroine. She is in the clutches of an evil sorcerer, but the boy knows the tale by heart: to the aid of the princess leaps a valiant knight; in the orchestra the hoofbeats of his horse draw nigh, already the victory trumpets resound.... But at this point everything comes to a halt, because the pages describing the rescue of the princess have been destroyed. Now nothing can save her and in despair the little hero sees the shaggy paws of the sorcerer drawing her down beneath the earth, forever. And in his arithmetic workbook the tables with the answers have been destroyed and a chorus of nasty little numbers (children's voices) unloose on the child torrents of monstrous fractions, meaningless snatches from typical arithmetic examples ("so-

and-so bought such-and-such"), and obviously wrong calculations. The irrational evil in mankind is equally disastrous in the realm of dreams and fantasies (fairy tales) and in the logical world of applied mathematics.

The storm of numbers gives way to silence. The boy is stunned and staggered. The cat returns, and the child who had just been torturing it now throws himself upon this living being to unburden his soul. But the affronted tomcat has no time for its owner: he is now involved in a romance with a white kitty. If this episode is similar to a corresponding one in Chaikovsky's *Sleeping Beauty*, the music of this cacophonous catty duet, strangely enough, goes back to the slow movement of the "Pathétique" Symphony—the same faltering waltz-like pattern in five-beat measures.

The cats' duet serves as a transition to the second half of the opera. The action moves from the room into a garden, from a world of humanized objects to a world of humanized living creatures. The orchestral sonority immediately grows warmer as if receiving a blood transfusion, an effect achieved through a simple stroke of genius: the whole string section enters, having throughout the first half played only pizzicato, a few soloists apart. Against a background of long drawn-out phrases from the newly lyrical string orchestra, depicting a warm summer night, Ravel musically paints the chirping of crickets and the warbling of a nightingale. An offstage chorus, singing in an invented frog language (Colette's ways coinciding here with those of the Russian Futurists!), depicts distant croaking in a marsh. But now the child appears, showing that mankind treats nature no better than his own things. The trees (male chorus) drip resin from the wounds left by the boy's penknife, a dragonfly (contralto) laments a companion the boy has pinned, and a male bat despairingly rushes about feeding the young whose mother the child had killed with a well-aimed rap of his stick. A long ballet episode ("Dance of the Tree Frogs"), a sparkling waltz that develops and varies the melody of the pining dragonfly, ends in the scene of the boy's culminating epiphany.

A stupid tree frog (tenor buffo) hops beneath his feet, and the pet squirrel that escaped at the beginning of the opera warns it from the tree: "What about the cage? He'll put you in prison, just like me, you moron!" The shaken child tries to defend himself, saying that he kept the squirrel in a cage because he loved it and wanted to admire its agility. The squirrel's arioso in reply (mezzo-soprano) is the most remarkable page in the score for its depth, pathos, and expression. It is a terrible thing to introduce chaos and destruction into the constructive efforts of others (the episodes of the clock and the arithmetic workbook), terrible arbitrarily to separate lovers (shepherdesses on the wallpaper, the princess, the dragonflies), terrible to kill a living creature for fun (the bat, the trees). But the most shattering pages of this ostensibly amusing children's opera speak of one of the most horrible manifestations of our age: depriving others of their freedom under cover of humanitarian or progressive sentiments. One of the greatest composers of the nineteenth century had expressed this theme with the same zeal and clarity—Beethoven in *Fidelio*. The writer of these lines was present when a German journalist, listening to *L'enfant et les sortilèges* on a record with text in hand, having heard the squirrel's arioso in an excellent performance by the French singer Solange Michel, left the room, her lips trembling. "That's how it was with us under Hitler," she remarked later. It is unlikely that even the most detailed musical analysis could show exactly how Ravel achieved such a profound effect in this arioso, which lasts only about four pages in the score and conforms outwardly to the form of a slow Boston waltz.

In the opera's finale the little hero sums up what he has learned from the things and beasts. He binds the squirrel's injured paw and to the strains of a serenely glowing chorus slowly goes back home. Right before the curtain falls, he pronounces a single word, in which is expressed his whole understanding of the necessity of civilization, tradition, tolerance. That word is "Maman." Over the chorus the figures played by two oboes, which had depicted his boredom and disgust at the opera's beginning, now sound pleasant and attractive.

The operas of Ravel are brilliant in form, profound and humane in content. Their treatment of difficult and problematical aspects of human life in a glittering and seemingly playful tone is high artistry, artistry devoid of false pathos or pseudoprofundity, comparable to the similarly exalted yet sunny works of Goethe, Pushkin, and Mozart. And yet Ravel's operas are regarded by most opera houses as superfluous. On American television every year they show the utterly banal children's opera *Amahl and the Night Visitors* by Menotti; in Russian theaters they go on reviving *The Snow Maiden*, crude in music and libretto alike (a few individually delightful turns notwithstanding); and in Germany at yuletide the cozily philistine opera *Hänsel und Gretel* reigns—even though, whether in terms of artistic merit or in terms of musical beauty, these now traditional opuses are worlds beneath the fabulous second opera of Ravel. And needless to say, in terms of vocal and instrumental delights, *L'heure espagnole* far exceeds practically all the one-act operas in the established repertory, like *Pagliacci, Cavalleria rusticana,* or the melodramatic, tawdry *Salome* of Richard Strauss. What's the problem? Obviously, the problem is that their lightness of craft and playfulness of manner have prevented critics and public alike from sensing the full depth and significance of Ravel's operas. Just so, readers of Pushkin's time immediately went into ecstasies over *Boris Godunov,* while *The Bronze Horseman* and *The Little House in Kolomna* were for decades looked upon as unassuming trifles. Just so, the whole nineteenth century either never noticed or took offense at the most humane of Mozart's operas, *Così fan tutte,* and only in the twentieth did people understand that the libretto of this opera, which had offended Beethoven and Wagner with its "immorality," was in fact a polemical and humanitarian tract on behalf of tolerance and the rights of women. One can only hope that the recent radio broadcasts of Ravel's operas will lead to a reexamination of received ideas about these two most original and significant creations of the twentieth century. Just as a fresh reading of the *Così fan tutte* libretto led to a new appreciation of the opera's magnificent music (which had seemed to Wagner, blinded as he was by Victorian moralism, to be weak and ineffective), a deepened and freshened understanding of *L'heure espagnole* and *L'enfant et les sortilèges* must in the future reveal to listeners all the perfection and iridescent brilliance in these two scores by Ravel.

* * *

This lovely piece is SK's only Russian-language essay on music, and its allusions and choice of examples for comparison show him very much in the light of a Russian writer in exile writing for his peers. Among his papers that are now a part of the collections of the Bancroft Library at the University of California, Berkeley is a previous translation by a graduate student of his, Charty Bassett, from which we have adopted the delightful substitution, at the end of the first paragraph, of *Lolita* for Andrei Bely's *Kotik Letaev,* SK's original example of a work about—but not for—children. Some references that might be arcane for non-Russian readers have been clarified in footnotes.

Index of Names

Abbate, Carolyn 439
Ablesimov, Aleksandr Onisimovich 384n14, 429n6, 431, 432n10
Abraham, Gerald 351, 351n14n15
Achair [Gryzov], Aleksei 316, 316n13, 318
Acocella, Joan Ross 461n7
Adamovich, Georgy Viktorovich 62, 170, 256, 261, 263
Aeschylus 258
Afanasiev, Aleksandr Nikolaevich 388
Agenosov, Vladimir Veniaminovich 291n3
Aivazovsky, Ivan Konstantinovich 187
Akhmadulina, Bella Akhatovna 161, 161n12, 232n3, 234
Akhmatova, Anna Andreevna 24n22, 41, 55, 67n4, 86, 90, 96, 98, 103, 107, 111, 111n10, 125, 125n2, 126, 126n3, 127, 127n6, 130, 130n12, 135n8, 145, 149, 150, 183, 230, 234, 235, 240, 272, 306, 315n11, 318, 408, 408n3, 450n17
Aksakov, Sergei Timofeevich 62, 183
Aldanov, Mark [pseud. of Mark Aleksandrovich Landau] 263, 301
Alekseev, Mikhail Pavlovich 43
Alexander I (Tsar) 24, 431
Alexander III (Tsar) 324–28, 331, 348, 352, 373
Alexandra (Empress) 207
Alexis (Tsar) 378, 385
Alfeevskaya, Galina Sergeevna 373
Ambrose (Saint) 25
Anaximenes 259
Andersen, Larisa Nikolaevna 318, 319n17, 320
Andreev, Leonid Nikolaevich 313, 478
Andreev, Nikolai Efremovich 298
Andreevsky, Sergei Arkadievich 63, 133
Annensky, Innokenty Fyodorovich 10, 64, 86–92, 92n2, 93–96, 115, 126, 287, 436, 469
Antares, Nina 319n17
Apollinaire, Guillaume 222, 248
Appel, Alfred, Jr. 223n20, 242n1, 277n20, 294n8, 335n16
Apukhtin, Aleksei Nikolaevich 87, 324, 326, 333, 337, 344
Aragon, Louis 213
Argutinsky-Dolgorukov, Vladimir Nikolaevich 328
Ariosto, Ludovico 28, 148

Aristophanes 27, 289, 297, 306
Armstrong, Louis 290
Arndt, Walter 53, 53n5, 54, 55
Arnold, Denis 331n7
Arnoldson, Louise Parkinson 425n3
Arseniev, Vladimir Klavdievich 313n6
Asafiev, Boris Vladimirovich [Igor Glebov, pseud.] 361, 364, 365, 366, 385, 396n31
Aseev, Boris Nikolaevich 429n7, 432n10
Asimov, Isaac 289
Astaire, Fred 319
Auden, W. H. 61, 161, 161n12, 230, 238, 363
Azadovsky, Konstantin Markovich 187, 187n13
Bach, Johann Sebastian 58, 147, 264n23, 281
Baer, Nancy Van Norman 457n1, 472n20
Bagritsky, Eduard Georgievich 259
Baikov, Nikolai Apollonovich 315, 315n10
Bakhrakh, Aleksandr Vasilievich 154, 154n2n4, 155, 170, 174, 195
Bakhtin, Mikhail Mikhailovich 44, 45, 143
Bakst, James 437n15
Bakst, Léon [Lev Samoilovich Rozenberg] 97, 459, 463, 467, 468, 472
Balanchine, George 349, 472, 473
Ballanche, Pierre-Simon 15, 20
Balmont, Konstantin Dmitrievich 86, 88, 262, 269, 364
Balzac, Honoré de 147, 447
Balzamova, Mariya Parmenovna 208
Bank, Nataliya Borisovna 112n11
Bara, Theda 420
Baratynsky, Evgeny Abramovich 63, 64, 74, 76, 133, 183, 269
Barker, George 244
Barratt, Andrew 176n4
Bartók, Béla 480
Baryshnikov, Mikhail Nikolaevich 239, 240n8, 394n28
Bassett, Charty 265n25, 485
Batyushkov, Konstantin Nikolaevich 15, 63, 297
Baudelaire, Charles 88, 89, 91, 135, 136, 148, 222, 224n23, 226, 248, 457n2
Bayley, John 55
Bazanoff, Olga 265
Beardsley, Aubrey 460, 463
Beaumarchais, Pierre-Augustin Caron de 268, 429n6

Index of Names

Beckford, William Thomas 16, 33
Bédier, Joseph 20
Beerbohm, Henry Maximilian [Max] 143
Beethoven, Ludwig van 58, 117, 122, 147, 343, 362, 371, 484, 485
Belinsky, Vissarion Grigorievich 66, 73, 73n12, 74, 84n9, 133, 433, 468
Belkin, Anatoly Alekseevich 386, 386n17
Bellini, Vincenzo 58, 443, 449
Bely, Andrei [Boris Nikolaevich Bugaev] 50, 50n2, 92, 106, 112, 112n11, 114, 114n2, 115, 115n4n5, 116, 117, 117n7n8n9, 118, 119n13, 120, 122–24, 169, 180, 183, 218, 230, 237, 248n5, 262, 364, 418, 485
Bem, Alfred Lyudvigovich 18, 18n10, 169
Benediktov, Vladimir Grigorievich 74
Benny, Jack 243
Benois [Benua], Aleksandr Nikolaevich 138, 388, 388n20, 394n28, 459, 462, 463, 467, 468, 470, 472, 474
Bérard, Christian 244
Berberova, Nina Nikolaevna 240n8, 263, 263n16, 327, 327n11, 328, 329, 329n14, 332, 332n8, 337, 343, 345, 352, 352n17, 354
Berdyaev, Nikolai Aleksandrovich 99, 262
Berkov, Pavel Naumovich 426n4, 429n5, 433n11, 437n14n15
Berlin, Isaiah 60
Berlioz, Hector 60, 136, 138, 343, 449
Berman, Eugene 244, 248
Bernandt, Grigory Borisovich 59, 59n5
Bernardin de Saint-Pierre, Jacques-Henri 16
Bernstein, Jane A. 441n4
Bernstein, Leonard 308, 314
Bertati, Giovanni 424, 428
Bertenson, Lev Bernardovich 349
Bertenson, Vasily Bernardovich 349
Bertie-Delagard [Bertier de la Garde], Aleksandr Lvovich 32n5
Bestuzhev-Marlinsky, Aleksandr Aleksandrovich 23, 23n19, 73, 73n13, 77, 80
Bethea, David M. 73n13
Bianchi, Francesco 424, 428
Binney, Edwin, 3rd 443n8
Bird, Christopher 268n3
Bizet, Georges 442
Blacher, Boris 8
Blake, Patricia 229n1, 238
Blake, William 148, 240
Blazhkov, Igor Ivanovich 374n8
Blinov, Nikolai Orestovich 349

Blok, Aleksandr Aleksandrovich 86, 87, 89, 91, 92, 98, 99, 105, 105n1n2n3, 106, 106n4, 107, 108, 108n6, 109, 109n7, 110, 110n9, 111, 112, 112n12, 113, 123, 124, 126, 128, 129, 129n9, 130, 130n11, 133, 133n4, 134, 145, 146, 155n7, 165, 168, 181, 183, 209, 222, 244, 245, 248, 248n5, 256, 258, 258n12, 259, 269, 280, 285, 287, 469
Blok, Lyubov [Lyuba] Dmitrievna 108, 108n6
Blom, Eric 351n15
Boborykin, Pyotr Dmitrievich 279
Bochechkarov, Nikolai Lvovich 344
Bogdanovich, Ippolit Fyodorovich 35, 285
Bogomolov, Nikolai Alekseevich 101n5, 130n10
Bogoslovsky, A. 265n24
Boileau-Despréaux, Nicolas 135
Bokov, Viktor Fyodorovich 234
Bolm, Adolf Rudolfovich 468, 471
Boretskaya, Marfa Semyonovna 346
Boshnyak, Aleksandr Karlovich 29
Bosquet, Alain 259
Bossuet, Jacques-Bénigne 20, 22
Boucher, François 424
Bouis, Antonina W. 398n1
Bouryschkine. *See* Buryshkin
Bouvier, Jacqueline Lee 457, 457n2
Bouvier-Ajam, Maurice 135, 135n8n9
Bowen, Collyer 155n6
Boyer, Leonard 407
Brahms, Johannes 461
Braque, Georges 472
Brecht, Bertolt 430
Brendel, Erica 117n11
Bressler [Bresler], Boris Lvovich 314n6
Bretanitskaya, Alla Leonidovna 372n6
Breton, André 212, 213, 248, 266
Brett, Philip 330, 330n2
Brezhnev, Leonid Ilich 409
Brik, Lilya Yurievna 219, 219n14
Britten, Benjamin 330n2
Broder, Nathan 441n3
Brodsky, Joseph [Iosif Aleksandrovich] 229n1, 230, 234, 235, 237–40, 240n8
Brody, Ervin C. 43
Brown, Clarence 137, 137n12, 145n1, 150–53, 239
Brown, David 322n1, 324, 325, 325n5, 331, 331n6n7, 332, 332n9n10, 337, 338, 339n1, 340n4, 341–43, 343n6, 344, 345, 353, 353n19, 354, 354n20, 355, 355n24

Index of Names

Brown, Malcolm Hamrick 327, 327n11, 329, 329n14, 332, 332n10, 333n10, 341, 406n6n7
Browning, Elizabeth Barrett 306
Broyde, Steven 153, 153n4
Bruchnalski, Wilhelm Adolf 30n4
Brunetière, Ferdinand 136
Bryant, Anita 347
Bryusov, Valery Yakovlevich 88, 133, 176, 269, 468, 477, 477n3
Buckle, Richard 458n3, 470, 471n19
Budden, Julian 345, 345n9
Buffon, Georges Louis Leclerc, Comte de 277n19
Bulgakov, Aleksei Dmitrievich 471
Bulgakov, Mikhail Afanasievich 99, 413, 414
Bulgarin, Faddei Venediktovich 290
Bullandt, Anton 429n6
Bunge, Rudolf 202n16
Bunin, Ivan Alekseevich 162, 168, 177, 178, 301, 315, 418–20
Buñuel, Luis 213
Burago, Alla 145n1, 150, 151
Burenin, Viktor Petrovich 463, 463n12, 464n13
Burlyuk, David Davidovich 217
Burlyuk, Vladimir Davidovich 217
Buryshkin, Pavel Afanasievich [Paul Bouryschkine] 250, 250n6
Bush, George H. W. 346, 347
Byrd, William 330n2
Byron, George Gordon (Lord) 14–16, 16n7, 17, 17n8, 18, 18n11n12, 19–24, 24n21, 26, 28, 33–35, 66, 67, 69–71, 73, 77, 80, 185, 190, 450, 455
Calderón de la Barca, Pedro 66
Canudo, Ricciotto 366, 367, 368n14
Carleton, Peter 11
Carlisle, Olga Andreyev 161, 161n9, 264
Cartland, Barbara 345
Castro, Fidel 231
Catherine II [the Great] (Empress) 27, 423, 426, 428, 431, 433
Cavalli, Francesco 440
Celan, Paul 150
Chaadaev, Pyotr Yakovlevich 15, 31
Chabrier, Emmanuel 461
Chafe, Wallace 313n6
Chagall, Marc 248n5, 261, 381
Chaikovskaya, Aleksandra Ilinichna. *See* Davydova
Chaikovsky, Anatoly Ilich 323, 328, 335, 337, 350

Chaikovsky, Ilya Petrovich 323, 343
Chaikovsky, Ippolit Ilich 323, 333, 340, 350
Chaikovsky, Modest Ilich 323, 328, 334, 335, 342, 348–50, 350n10
Chaikovsky, Pyotr Ilich 8, 10, 12, 59, 89, 133, 248, 249, 322, 322n1, 323, 323n3, 324, 324n4, 325, 325n5n6, 326, 326n6n8, 327, 327n10n11, 328, 329n13n14, 330, 330n1n2n4, 331, 331n6n7, 332n8n9n10, 333, 333n10n11n12n13, 334, 334n15, 335–37, 339, 339n1n3, 340, 340n4n5n6, 341–43, 343n6n7, 344, 346n1, 347, 348, 348n4n5, 349, 349n7n8, 350, 350n9n10n11, 351, 351n12n13n14n15, 352, 352n16n17, 353, 353n18n19, 354, 354n20n21n22n 355, 355n23n24n25, 356, 356n26n27, 359, 359n3, 368, 373, 379, 412, 422, 435, 443n8, 460, 467, 472, 483
Chaliapin, Fyodor Ivanovich 12, 207, 314, 416, 416n1n2, 417, 418, 418n3, 419, 419n4, 420, 420n5, 421, 421n5n6n7, 422, 466
Chaliapina, Avdotya Mikhailovna 416
Charskaya, Lidiya Alekseevna 202
Chateaubriand, François-Auguste-René de 14, 15, 15n3n6, 16, 17, 17n8, 18, 18n10n11, 19, 19n13, 20–22, 22n18, 23, 23n20, 24–26, 26n24n25n28, 33, 67
Chateaubriand, Lucille de 23
Chauncey, George, Jr. 9n5, 347n3
Chebotarevskaya, Anastasiya Nikolaevna 403
Chekhov, Anton Pavlovich 8–10, 11n8, 48, 57, 71n7, 83, 91, 103, 133, 137, 162, 162n13, 182, 183, 201, 201n12, 233, 258, 258n12, 277, 278, 278n24, 285, 290, 310, 310n2, 437, 462, 463n12
Chelishchev. *See* Tchelitchew
Chénier, André-Marie de 19, 20, 272
Chernova-Kolbasina, Olga Eliseevna 180
Chernyshevsky, Nikolai Gavrilovich 133, 231, 370
Chicherin, Georgy Vasilievich 129
Chizhevsky, Dmitry Ivanovich 204n21
Chopin, Fryderyk 50, 164
Christoff, Boris 420
Chukovskaya, Lidiya Korneevna 125, 125n2, 126n3, 127, 408
Chukovsky, Kornei Ivanovich 86, 105, 105n2, 126
Chumina, Olga Nikolaevna 87
Churilin, Tikhon Vasilievich 212, 216–19, 219n11n14, 220, 220n16, 221, 221n17n18, 228, 260n14

Index of Names

Clark, Katerina 44
Clément, Catherine 441n4
Cocteau, Jean 471
Coe, Richard N. 442n6
Colbran, Isabella 442
Coleridge, Samuel Taylor 302
Colette, Sidonie-Gabrielle 480, 481, 483
Connolly, Julian W. 77n1
Constant, Benjamin 24, 24n21n22, 26, 67, 67n4
Conway, Frank 338n17
Copernicus, Nicolaus 283
Corneille, Pierre 46, 51n3
Cornwell, Neil 56n1, 57, 57n3, 59–61
Cotogni, Antonio 460
Coville, Lilian Grosvenor 312n5
Coward, Noel 244
Craft, Robert 358n1, 359, 359n4, 361–63, 364n7, 365, 366, 366n1, 367–69, 369n2, 370, 372, 374, 376n1, 386n16, 388n20, 389, 389n22, 390n23n24, 391n24n25, 392, 395, 396n30, 419n4, 457n2
Croce, Arlene 331
Cross, Anthony 79n3
Cuvier, Georges 25
Dal [Dahl], Vladimir Ivanovich 68n5, 391n24
Dalí, Salvador 213, 244
Daniels, Guy 413n8
Danilova, Aleksandra Dionisievna 473
Dante 42, 148, 275
Da Ponte, Lorenzo 424
Dargomyzhsky, Aleksandr Sergeevich 58, 386n16, 479
Darwin, Charles 267, 276, 277
Davis, Richard 186n10
Davison, R. M. 322n1
Davydov, Vladimir Lvovich [Bob] 337, 356
Davydova, Aleksandra Ilinichna [née Chaikovskaya] 323
Davydova, Lidiya Anatolievna 381n8
Debussy, Claude-Achille 442n5, 465, 469, 475, 479
Degas, Edgar 460, 463
Delibes, Léo 467
del Rio, Dolores 243
Delvig, Anton Antonovich 29, 37, 39, 288
Denisov, Edison Vasilievich 373
Denneny, Michael 457n1
Derain, André 472
Derzhanovsky, Vladimir Vladimirovich 366
Derzhavin, Gavrila Romanovich 115, 135, 269, 288

De Witte, Nikolai Petrovich 377n2
Diaghilev [Dyagilev], Pavel Pavlovich 458
Diaghilev, Sergei Pavlovich 10, 12, 81, 99, 104, 129, 133, 134, 138, 138n16, 324, 328, 335, 373, 393, 394n28, 419, 450n17, 457, 457n1, 458, 458n3n4, 459, 460, 460n6, 461, 461n7n8n10, 462–64, 464n13, 465, 465n14, 466–71, 471n19, 472, 472n20, 473, 473n21, 474
Diaghileva, Elena Valerianovna [née Panaeva] 458
Diaghileva, Evgeniya Nikolaevna [née Evreinova] 458
Dickinson, Emily 289
Didelot, Charles 466
Diderot, Denis 16, 425
Dietrich, Marlene 319n17
Diodorus 259
Dmitriev, Ivan Ivanovich 36
Dmitry (Tsarevich) 43, 44
Dmitry, False (Tsar) 43–47
Dmitry of Rostov (Saint) 66
Dobrolyubov, Nikolai Aleksandrovich 87
Dolin, Anton 474
Donizetti, Gaetano 94, 442, 448
Donne, John 235, 240
Dostoevsky, Fyodor Mikhailovich 10, 45, 47, 57, 60, 61, 84, 86, 97, 98, 104, 109, 222, 227, 239, 258, 260, 389, 460
Douglas, Alfred [Bosie] (Lord) 305
Drigo, Riccardo 467
Druskin, Mikhail Semyonovich 385, 396n31
Duberman, Martin Bauml 9n5, 347n3
Dubinsky, Rostislav Davidovich 410
Dubrovsky, George 420n5
Ducange, Victor 80
Ducis, Jean François 46
Duke, Vernon. See Dukelsky
Dukelsky, Vladimir Aleksandrovich 254, 473
Duncan, Isadora 205–7, 467
Duni, Egidio 425
Dyachkova, Lyudmila Sergeevna 369n1, 386n16, 388n20
Dymshits, Aleksandr Lvovich 145n2
Eckermann, J. P. 402
Eddy, Nelson 398
Efron, Ariadna Sergeevna [Alya] 171, 171n4, 175, 178, 180, 195
Efron, Georgy Sergeevich [Mur] 178–81, 196–99, 201
Efron, Sergei Yakovlevich 178–80, 195
Egorov, Boris Fyodorovich 56
Eikhenbaum, Boris Mikhailovich 84n9, 130

Index of Names

Einstein, Albert 45, 282
Einstein, Alfred 441n3
Eisenstein, Sergei Mikhailovich 149
Ekaterina Pavlovna (Grand Duchess) 24
Eliot, T. S. 135n8, 137, 138, 138n13, 152, 230, 234, 235, 239, 240, 363, 450, 450n17
Ellis, Henry Havelock 350
Éluard, Paul 212
Emerson, Caryl 43n1, 44–46, 46n2, 47, 47n2, 48
Emerson, Ralph Waldo 287
Erenburg [Ehrenburg], Ilya Grigorievich 165, 170, 282
Ermilov, Vladimir Vladimirovich 228
Ernst, Max 242
Ershov, Pyotr Pavlovich 73
Esenin, Sergei Aleksandrovich 103, 153, 205, 205n1, 206–9, 209n4, 210, 231, 269n4, 275
Estève, Edmond 16, 16n7, 18n11
Etkind, Efim Grigorievich 49, 193n21, 194n1
Evans, Edwin 351n15
Evdokimov, Valentin 317n14
Everson, William [Brother Antoninus] 306
Evtushenko, Evgeny Aleksandrovich 229, 229n1, 230, 231, 231n3, 232, 232n3, 234, 236, 237, 237n6, 290, 302, 409
Ezhov, Ivan Stepanovich 221, 221n17
Ezhov, Nikolai Ivanovich 269
Faguet, Émile 136, 137, 450n16
Fauchereau, Serge 135n8, 137, 138, 138n15, 450n17
Faulkner, William 289, 290
Favart, Charles Simon 423, 424, 424n2, 425, 426n4, 427, 428, 429n6
Fay, Laurel 405, 406n7, 414
Fedotov, Georgy Petrovich 169, 169n2, 170, 172, 174
Feinstein, Elaine 162, 163, 163n15
Fell, Marian 162
Fénelon, François 20
Fennell, John 52, 52n4, 53–55
Fet, Afanasy Afanasievich 133, 183, 276, 280, 288
Field, Andrew 98, 98n2, 155n6n7, 157n8, 160, 161n11, 229n1
Figner, Nikolai Nikolaevich and Medea 313
Filippov, Boris Andreevich 143, 143n25, 144n26, 145n2, 146, 147, 151, 216n7, 223n20, 296n11
Filosofov, Dmitry Vladimirovich 98–100, 102, 104, 459, 460, 460n5, 462, 464, 464n13, 465, 465n14, 466, 468, 474

Filosofova, Anna Pavlovna 98, 458
Finagin, Aleksei Vasilievich 432n9
Findeizen, Nikolai Fyodorovich 386, 386n16, 388, 426n4, 432n10, 433n11, 437
Fischel, Walter J. 35n8
Fischer-Dieskau, Dietrich 421
Fitzgerald, Edward 245n2
Flayderman, Philip S. 163n16
Fleishman, Lazar Solomonovich 108n6, 182n1, 187, 187n12, 298
Fletcher, John 43
Flier, Michael S. 10n6, 142n23, 440n1
Fofanov, Konstantin Mikhailovich 87
Fokine, Mikhail Mikhailovich 379, 387, 394n28, 467–70, 470n18, 471, 474
Fomin, Evstignei Ipatievich 432n9, 436
Fonvizin, Denis Ivanovich 135
Forster, E. M. 341
Franck, Harry A. 312n5
Franc-Nohain [Maurice Étienne Legrand] 476–78, 481
Freud, Sigmund 97, 212, 213, 353
Frick, David 11
Frost, Robert 281, 289
Froud, Nina 416n1, 417
Furtseva, Ekaterina Alekseevna 370
Fyodor (Tsar) 44
Fyodorov, Nikolai Fyodorovich 227
Fyodorova, Sofya Vasilievna [Sophie Federova] 468
Galanskov, Yury Timofeevich 237
Galilei, Galileo 283
García Lorca, Federico 148
Garden, Edward 333, 333n11n12n13, 337, 338, 340, 340n4, 342, 344, 352, 353, 353n18, 354, 355
Garnett, Constance 162, 480n6
Gascoyne, David 213, 213n4
Gasparov, Boris Mikhailovich 133n1
Gaucheron, Jacques 135n8, 136n10
Gautier, Estelle 444
Gautier, Judith 444
Gautier, Théophile 133, 133n1, 134, 135, 135n8, 136, 136n10, 137, 137n11, 138, 139, 139n20, 140, 140n21n22, 141, 142, 142n23, 143n24, 144, 440, 442, 443, 443n8, 444, 444n9n10, 447, 447n11n12, 448, 448n13, 449, 450, 450n15n16n17, 451, 453, 453n19, 454, 454n20, 455, 456, 468
Gee, John 352, 352n16
George, Stefan 305

Index of Names

Gernreich, Rudi 242
Gershtein, Emma Grigorievna 84n10
Gertsen. *See* Herzen
Gesualdo, Carlo 362
Ghiaurov, Nikolai 421
Gilbert, Stuart 93
Ginsberg, Allen 230
Ginzburg, Lidiya Yakovlevna 114n3
Gippius [Hippius], Zinaida Nikolaevna 10, 97, 97n1, 98–101, 101n3n4n5, 102, 102n6, 103, 104, 104n7, 106, 133, 134n5, 168, 178, 212, 212n2, 222, 230, 231n3, 263, 465, 465n14
Giroud, Vincent 332n8
Gladkov, Aleksandr Konstantinovich 402, 402n2
Glazunov, Aleksandr Konstantinovich 81, 328, 370, 401, 402, 406, 466, 467
Glebov, Igor. *See* Asafiev
Glinka, Fyodor Nikolaevich 377n2
Glinka, Mikhail Ivanovich 58, 343, 379, 386, 386n16, 435, 438, 442, 442n5, 466
Gluck, Christoph Willibald 31
Glushkovsky, Adam Pavlovich 466
Godunov, Boris (Tsar) 43, 43n1, 44–46, 46n2, 47, 65, 81, 420, 442n5, 466, 485
Goethe, Johann Wolfgang von 16, 32–36, 42, 66, 70, 70n6, 71, 139, 141, 143, 165, 179, 183, 287, 402, 454, 484
Gogh, Vincent van 91, 134
Gogol, Nikolai Vasilievich 8–10, 48, 56, 60, 73, 109, 118, 123, 214–16, 260, 277, 285, 290, 294, 412, 435, 460, 466, 479
Golovin, Aleksandr Yakovlevich 81, 393
Golovina, Alla Sergeevna 197n8, 198n10, 261
Gomolicki, Leon [Lev Nikolaevich Gomolitsky] 30n3, 36n9
Goncharova, Nataliya Nikolaevna 184
Goncharova, Nataliya Sergeevna 184n3, 219, 219n12n13, 364, 381, 472
Gorbachev, Mikhail Sergeevich 333, 354n22, 410
Gorky, Maksim [Aleksei Maksimovich Peshkov] 86, 90, 101, 103, 106, 134, 137, 168, 177, 290, 347, 362, 416n1, 417–21
Gorodetsky, Sergei Mitrofanovich 208, 306, 382
Gothot-Mersch, Claudine 136n10, 444n10, 447, 447n11n12, 448n13, 450n15, 453n19
Goujon, Jules 250
Goul. *See* Gul

Gramm, Donald 421
Grau, Shirley Ann 289
Green, Michael 131
Greene, Graham 363
Grétry, André 425
Griboedov, Aleksandr Sergeevich 56, 62, 81, 82, 133, 296, 299
Grieg, Edvard 386
Griffiths, Paul 345n8
Grigoriev, Apollon Aleksandrovich 133
Grimm (brothers) 379
Gris, Juan 472
Grisi, Carlotta 443, 443n8, 444
Grisi, Ernesta 142, 443, 444, 449, 450, 450n15
Grisi, Giuditta 443, 443n7
Grisi, Giulia 442, 443, 443n7
Grosheva, Elena Andreevna 417, 418, 418n3, 421n7
Grossman, Gregory 314n8
Grossman, Joan 11, 167n1
Grossman, Leonid Petrovich 41n16
Guicciolli, Teresa 18n11
Gul, Roman Borisovich 170, 174, 264
Gumilyov, Nikolai Stepanovich 48, 88, 95, 127, 127n4, 130, 133, 133n1, 134, 134n6, 135, 135n8, 136–38, 138n17n18, 139, 139n19n20, 140–42, 142n23, 143, 143n25, 144, 144n26, 145, 176, 216, 217, 218n9n10, 219, 220, 230, 231n3, 234, 269, 269n4, 272, 272n9, 275, 315n11, 318, 440, 450, 450n17, 451, 451n18, 453, 454, 454n20, 455, 455n21, 456
Guthrie, Maria 27
Hackel, Sergei 110, 110n9, 113
Hadlock, Heather 441n4
Hafiz of Shiraz 34, 35, 455n21
Haggerty, George 131, 207n2, 356n27
Halpern, Salomeya [Salomeya Nikolaevna Andronikova-Galpern] 175
Handel, George Frideric 440
Hanley, James 416n1, 417
Hanslick, Eduard 339
Hathaway, Mike 265
Haydn, Franz Joseph 58, 117, 345
Hayward, Max 145n1, 149, 163n15, 229n1, 238, 402n2
Hayworth, Rita 243
Healey-Kay, Patrick. *See* Dolin
Heartz, Daniel 438
Hedley-Prôle, Jane 458n4
Heim, Michael Henry 11n8, 310n2, 463n12
Heine, Heinrich 183

Index of Names

Heller [Geller], Leonid 193n21, 194n1
Hellman, Lillian 162, 162n13
Hemingway, Ernest 143
Henahan, Donal 326, 326n7, 329, 329n13, 331
Henri IV (King) 425
Henry, Pierre 93
Herodotus 28
Herzen, Aleksandr Ivanovich 84n9, 198
Hikmet, Nazim 137
Hinrichs, Jan Paul 310n1, 312, 312n5, 313, 314, 314n8, 315, 315n11
Hitler, Adolf 181, 399, 484
Hodson, Millicent 470n18
Hoffmann, E. T. A. 56
Holden, Anthony 356n26
Hollo, Anselm 229n1, 236, 237
Holme, Bryan 457n2
Holquist, Michael 44, 45
Homer 20, 129, 289, 292, 295, 296
Honegger, Arthur 7
Hopkins, William H. 79n4
Horace 27, 297
Huet, Marie-Hélène 438
Hughes, Robert P. 10n6, 114n1, 133n1
Hugo, Victor 33, 77, 134, 136, 227
Hulme, T. E. 137
Humperdinck, Engelbert 484
Iacuzzi, Alfred 424n2
Iarustovsky. See Yarustovsky
Ilina, Nataliya 320
Ilinsky, Oleg Pavlovich 118n12
Illichevsky, Aleksei Demianovich 40
Ioffe, Ieremiya Isaevich 244
Irving, Washington 379
Iskrenko, Nina Yurievna 298
Ivan IV [the Terrible] (Tsar) 43, 44
Ivanov, Georgy Vladimirovich 180, 209, 209n4, 216, 255, 263, 280, 294, 318
Ivanov, Vyacheslav Ivanovich 64, 86, 87, 106, 125, 127, 127n5, 230, 306
Ivask, Yury Pavlovich 169, 170, 174, 198n9, 204, 204n21, 264, 307, 307n5, 317n14
Ivnev, Ryurik [pseud. of Mikhail Aleksandrovich Kovalyov] 208
Izmailov, Nikolai Vasilievich 40, 40n16
Jakobson, Roman Osipovich 118
Jarrell, Randall 289
Jarrett, Emmett 265, 265n25
Jasinski, René 135n8, 137n11, 450n16
Jensen, Claudia R. 386n16
Johnson, Charles 50
Jonas, Florence 461n9
Joyce, James 93, 152, 263

Kael, Pauline 290
Kalmus, Edwin F. 367
Kamensky, Vasily Vasilievich 217
Kannegiser, Leonid Ioakimovich 208
Kapodistrias, Johannes (Count) 70
Karamzin, Nikolai Mikhailovich 14, 24, 28, 36, 44–47, 63, 67, 212, 217
Karlinsky, Simon [Semyon Arkadievich] [SK] 7, 7n1n2n3, 8, 8n4, 9, 9n5, 10, 10n6, 11, 11n8, 12, 41, 42, 42n19, 48, 48n3, 50n2n3, 51n3, 55, 56n1, 70n6, 73n13, 76, 96, 97n1, 101n3, 104, 104n7, 107n5, 109n7, 114n1n2, 131, 131n13, 132, 142n23, 143, 143n25, 144, 144n26, 145n2, 153, 161n9, 162–64, 164n18, 166n19, 173, 174n2, 176n4n5, 182n2, 186n8, 187n13, 207n2, 208n3, 209n4, 210, 211n6, 215n6, 230n2, 231n3, 236n5, 237n7, 238, 240n8, 242n1, 260n13n14, 264n22, 265, 265n25, 266, 266n26, 275n18, 277n20, 284n37, 291n2, 292n6, 294n8, 296n10, 302n2, 303n4, 308, 308n6, 310n2, 313n6, 317n14, 325n6, 327, 327n11, 329, 329n14, 335n16, 337, 338, 338n17, 344, 345, 346n1, 347n3, 348n6, 355, 356, 358n2, 363–68, 371, 391–94, 394n28, 395, 395n28, 396, 396n31, 404, 405, 405n5, 406, 407, 413, 414, 420n5, 422, 423n1, 432n9, 438, 439, 440n1, 441n4, 457n1, 463n12, 485
Karlstrom, Ann 395n28
Karpovich, Mikhail Mikhailovich 204n21
Karsavina, Tamara Platonovna 468, 473, 474
Karskaya, Ida Grigorievna 261
Kastalsky, Aleksandr Dmitrievich 373, 374, 387n18
Katenin, Pavel Andreevich 63n2
Kaufman, Abram Iosifovich 315n8, 316n13
Kayden, Eugene M. 163n16
Keldysh, Yury Vsevolodovich 426n4, 429n6, 432n17, 433n11n12
Kemball, Robin 193n21, 194n1
Kennedy, John F. 457n2
Kennedy, Michael 331n7
Kepler, Johannes 283
Kertselli [Kerzelli], Ivan Frantsevich 428
Kertselli [Kerzelli], Mikhail Frantsevich 429
Kertselli [Kerzelli], Iosif 428
Ketchian, Sonia I. 77n1
Kevorkian, Karen 395n28
Khachaturian, Aram Ilich 371, 371n5
Khaindrova, Lidiya Yulianovna 318

Index of Names

Khardzhiev, Nikolai Ivanovich 145n2
Kheraskov, Mikhail Matveevich 135, 435
Khin, Evgeniya Yurievna 56, 56n2
Khlebnikov, Velimir [Viktor] Vladimirovich 68, 96, 118, 121, 124, 126, 215, 215n6, 216, 217, 222, 227, 230, 232, 234, 244, 248n5, 259, 262, 269n4, 277, 281–83, 298, 381, 383, 469, 481
Khmarin [Kuznetsovas-Kuznetsov], Fyodor Grigorievich 319n17
Khmelnitskaya, Tamara Yurievna 112n11
Khmelnitsky, Nikolai Ivanovich 63
Khodasevich, Vladislav Felitsianovich 87, 96, 134, 134n7, 169, 174, 181, 195, 195n3, 222, 223, 223n20, 230, 238, 245, 263, 264n21, 306
Khomyakov, Aleksei Stepanovich 280, 294
Khrennikov, Tikhon Nikolaevich 371
Khrushchev, Nikita Sergeevich 209
King, Russell S. 135n8
Kireev, Sergei Aleksandrovich 350
Kireevsky, Ivan Vasilievich 72, 72n10
Kireevsky, Pyotr Vasilievich 384
Klaczko, Julian 35n7
Klein, Joachim 11, 166n19, 215n6, 266n26
Kleist, Heinrich von 164
Klimenko, Ivan Aleksandrovich 324
Klyuev, Nikolai Alekseevich 126, 132, 206, 207, 207n2, 208–10
Knapp, Lisa 11, 182n1
Knyazhnin, Yakov Borisovich 135, 429, 429n5n6, 431, 438
Kochno [Kokhno], Boris Evgenievich 138n16, 472n20
Koestenbaum, Wayne 338n18
Koestler, Arthur 283, 283n36
Kokorev, Aleksandr Vasilievich 433n11
Kokoshkin, Fyodor Fyodorovich 80
Kolosova, Marianna Ivanovna 318
Kolpakova, Nataliya Pavlovna 384n14
Komissarzhevskaya, Vera Fyodorovna 129, 313
Konstantin Pavlovich (Grand Duke) 27
Korkina, Elena Baurdzhanovna 187n13
Korolyova, Nina Valerianovna 64
Korovin, Konstantin Alekseevich 393
Koshansky-Olienikov, Olga 57n3
Kotek, Iosif Iosifovich 324, 344, 350
Koten, Bernard L. 229n1, 237
Kotzebue, August von 77, 78
Kowalewski, Joseph Étienne 36, 36n9
Kozlov, Ivan Ivanovich 40
Kozlovsky, Pyotr Borisovich (Prince) 15

Krasiński, Zygmunt 66
Krasovskaya, Vera Mikhailovna 467, 467n17, 470
Kriegsman, Alan M. 326, 326n8, 331, 331n5
Krishnamurti, Jiddu 262
Krivtsov, Nikolai Ivanovich 21
Kronberger, Maximilian [Maximin] 305
Kronenberger, Louis 42n19
Kruchyonykh, Aleksei Eliseevich 282
Kruzenshtern-Peterets, Yustina Vladimirovna 315n9
Krylov, Ivan Andreevich 63
Ktorova, Alla 301, 302
Küchelbecker [Kyukhelbeker], Wilhelm Karlovich 48, 62, 62n1, 64–66, 66n3, 67, 67n4, 68, 68n5, 69–71, 71n8n9, 72, 73, 73n11n13, 74, 75, 75n14, 76, 81, 81n5, 82
Küchelbecker, Yuliya Karlovna 72
Kudrova, Irma Viktorovna 188n15
Kukolnik, Nestor Vasilievich 82
Kuprin, Aleksandr Ivanovich 369
Kurosawa, Akira 313n6
Kuzmin, Mikhail Alekseevich 10, 48, 92, 106, 114, 124, 125, 125n1, 126, 127, 127n4n5n6, 128, 128n7n8, 129, 130, 130n10n12, 131, 132, 137, 176n4, 183, 230, 248n5, 307, 317, 317n15, 364
Kuznetsov, Anatoly Vasilievich 55
Laffitte, Sophie 261, 265
Laforgue, Jules 248
Lagerlöf, Selma 181
Lakond, Wladimir 340n5
Lamarck, Jean-Baptiste 25, 151, 277, 277n19
Lamartine, Alphonse de 16, 23, 134
Landor, Walter Savage 33
Lang, Paul Henry 339, 344, 351, 359n3
Lanson, Gustave 136
Lapshina, Nataliya Pavlovna 460n5, 474n22
Larionov, Mikhail Fyodorovich 472
La Rose, Rose 243
Lattimore, Owen 312n5
Lautréamont, Comte de [pseud. of Isidore-Lucien Ducasse] 213, 214, 222
Lavrov, Aleksandr Vasilievich 101n5
Lawless, Peter 264n21
Lecuona, Ernesto 319
Lednicki, Wacław 35n8, 40, 40n14n15, 41, 41n17
Legrand, Maurice Étienne. *See* Franc-Nohain
Leigh, Augusta 24
Leinbach, S. J. 458n4

Index of Names

Lelewel, Joachim 30, 39
Lemeshev, Sergei Yakovlevich 314
Lenau, Nikolaus 165
Lenin, Vladimir Ilich 100, 101, 110, 207, 232, 233, 276, 309, 371, 398, 399, 403, 406, 409, 421
Leonard, Richard Anthony 437n15
Leonardo da Vinci 97
Leoncavallo, Ruggiero 485
Leontiev, Konstantin Nikolaevich 307
Lermontov, Mikhail Yurievich 14, 41, 48, 56, 64, 69, 75, 75n14, 77–79, 79n2n4, 80, 81, 81n5, 82–84, 84n9n10, 90, 165, 183, 222, 237, 287, 468
Leskov, Nikolai Semyonovich 183, 411, 479, 479n5
Levertov, Denise 155, 155n6n7, 157, 157n1, 158, 160–62, 264
Leyland, Winston 131n13, 211n6
Lifar, Serge [Sergei Mikhailovich] 443n8, 474
Linnaeus [von Linné], Carl 277, 277n19
Liszt, Franz 60, 122
Livanova, Tamara Nikolaevna 437n15
Livingstone, Angela 163, 164, 187n13
Lobanov, Mikhail Evstafievich 19, 20
Lockspeiser, Edward 339, 351, 351n15, 355
Lomonosov, Mikhail Vasilievich 114, 277
Lomonosova, Raisa Nikolaevna 186, 186n10
London, George 420n5, 421n5
London, Nora 421n5
Lotman, Yury Mikhailovich 106n4
Louis XIV (King) 22, 68, 135
Lourie, Richard 265n25
Lowell, Robert 238
Lvov, Nikolai Aleksandrovich 435
Lyadov, Anatoly Konstantinovich 68n5
Lyubimov, Aleksei Borisovich 380
Macdonald, Hugh 343
MacDonald, Ian 408n1, 409–13, 413n7, 414
Macpherson, James [Ossian] 16, 17
Maeterlinck, Maurice 88
Maffei, Scipione 429n6
Magritte, René 214
Maikov, Apollon Nikolaevich 89
Maikov, Leonid Nikolaevich 429n7
Maikov, Vasily Ivanovich 429, 429n7, 430, 431
Mailer, Norman 400
Maimin, Evgeny Aleksandrovich 56
Makin, Michael 163, 163n17
Makovsky, Sergei Konstantinovich 464n13
Malamud, Bernard 289
Malanotte, Adelaide 442
Mallarmé, Stéphane 88, 91, 136
Malmstad, John E. 125n1, 128–30, 130n10n12, 291n1
Mamontov, Savva Ivanovich 462
Mandelstam, Nadezhda Yakovlevna 145n1, 149, 150, 150n3, 411
Mandelstam, Osip Emilievich 41, 84, 87–89, 96, 98, 105, 107, 126, 133, 135n8, 137, 145, 145n1n2, 146–53, 153n4, 162, 179, 209, 222, 230, 235, 238, 240, 276, 277, 277n19, 280, 288, 290, 296, 296n11, 297, 318, 450n17
Mandelstam, Yury Vladimirovich 373
Mann, Thomas 71, 235
Mansvetov, V. F. 169n2
Manzhelei, Olga Pavlovna 319n17
Mao Zedong 276, 303, 304, 314n8, 319
Marcadé, Jean-Claude 264, 264n22
Marcadé, Valentine [Valentina Dmitrievna] 466n15
Marchenko, Nikolai Nikolaevich. *See* Morshen
Marchenko, Nikolai Vladimirovich [Nikolai Narokov] 267, 268
Marcolini, Marietta 442
Mariani, Rosa 442
Markevich, Igor Borisovich 474
Markov, Vladimir Fyodorovich 114n1, 125n1, 127–30, 215n6, 220n15, 275, 291, 291n1, 294, 294n8, 298
Markova, Alicia 473
Marlowe, Christopher 8n4
Marshak, Samuil Yakovlevich 222
Marshall, Herbert 229n1, 236, 237, 237n7
Marx, Karl 10, 110, 172, 207, 212, 213, 276, 413
Mascagni, Pietro 485
Maslenikov, Oleg Aleksandrovich 117n9
Mass, Lawrence 330, 330n2
Massenet, Jules 421
Massine, Léonide [Leonid Fyodorovich Myasin] 398, 471–74
Matich, Olga Borisovna 97n1, 101–3, 455n21
Matinsky, Mikhail Alekseevich 384n14, 429n6, 433, 433n11, 434, 435
Matisse, Henri 472, 474
Matlaw, Ralph E. 57n3
Matveeva, Novella Nikolaevna 232n3, 234, 237
Maugham, Somerset 341
Maximin. *See* Kronberger

Mayakovsky, Vladimir Vladimirovich 86, 90, 96, 98, 103, 106, 118, 124, 129, 134, 145–47, 153, 165, 169, 172, 173, 193, 209, 212, 212n3, 215n6, 217, 218n10, 219, 219n4, 220, 229, 232, 237n7, 248n5, 281, 370, 371, 401, 402, 414, 421, 469, 481
McDowell, Edwin 55
McGinley, Phyllis 289
McLean, Hugh 11, 62n1, 436
McLean, Robert A. 150
McVay, Gordon 205n1, 206, 208–10, 210n5
Meck [Mekk], Galina Nikolaevna von 322
Meck, Nadezhda Filaretovna von 334, 351n15
Medovoi, M. I. 56n2
Meierkhold. *See* Meyerhold
Meller, Alex 242, 244, 245, 248, 249
Meller, Anna Semyonovna 242, 245
Mendel, Arthur 441n3
Mendeleev, Dmitry Ivanovich 108
Mendelssohn, Felix 58
Menegaldo, Elena [Hélène Paschutinsky] 265, 265n24
Menotti, Gian Carlo 484
Merezhkovsky, Dmitry Sergeevich 86, 88, 97–101, 101n4, 102, 104, 177, 178, 222, 257, 263, 279, 465
Mérimée, Prosper 360, 360n6, 392n25
Merrill, James 306
Merwin, W. S. 145n1, 150, 152
Meshchersky, Vladimir Petrovich (Prince) 326, 348
Mesmer, Anton 425
Metastasio, Pietro 429n6
Metner, Emily Karlovich [Emil Medtner] 115, 116
Meyer, Richard M. 202, 202n13
Meyerbeer, Giacomo 442n5
Meyerhold, Vsevolod Emilievich 81, 82, 82n6, 83, 83n7, 100, 129, 149, 399, 401, 418, 469
Meylan, Pierre 388n21, 389n21
Michel, Solange 484
Mickiewicz, Adam 27–30, 30n3n4, 31, 32, 32n5, 33–35, 35n7n8, 36, 36n9, 37–40, 40n14n15n16, 41, 41n16n17, 66
Mikhailovsky, Nikolai Konstantinovich 133, 137
Mikhail Pavlovich (Grand Duke) 72
Miller, Alex 105n1, 112, 113
Miller, Arthur 400
Mills, Belwin 367

Miłosz, Czesław 411
Milton, John 15, 19, 20
Milyukova [Chaikovskaya], Antonina Ivanovna 343
Minsky [Vilenkin], Nikolai Maksimovich 87
Mirkin, Boris 315n8
Mirsky, D. S. *See* Svyatopolk-Mirsky
Mitchinson, Paul 406n6
Mlikotin, Anthony M. 455n21
Mnukhin, Lev Abramovich 175n3
Mochulsky, Konstantin Vasilievich 256, 263
Molière [Jean-Baptiste Poquelin] 16, 51n3, 429n6
Molloy, Molly 10n6
Monet, Claude 460, 463
Monsigny, Pierre 425
Monteverdi, Claudio 362, 440
Montez, Maria 243
Moore, Marianne 230, 306
Moore, Thomas 34
Mooser, Robert-Aloys 426n4
Moreau, Gustave 91
Moreau, Jeanne 420
Morkovin, Vadim Vladimirovich 175
Morozova, Margarita Kirillovna 118, 122
Morris, Mitchell 338n18
Morshen, Nikolai [Nikolai Nikolaevich Marchenko] 10, 229n1, 230, 235, 236, 236n5, 267, 267n2, 268, 269, 269n5, 270, 270n6n7, 271, 271n8, 272, 272n9, 273, 273n10n11n12n13, 274, 274n14n15, 275, 275n16n17n18, 276, 277, 277n20n21, 278, 278n22n23, 279, 279n25n26n27, 280, 280n28n29n30n31, 281, 282, 282n34, 283, 283n35, 284, 284n37n38n39, 285, 285n40n41n42n43, 286, 286n44n45n46, 287, 287n47, 288, 288n48n49n50, 289, 289n51, 290, 291, 291n1n2n3, 292, 292n4n6, 293, 294, 294n9, 295, 296, 296n10, 297–300, 302
Morton, Lawrence 359, 359n3, 380, 380n7, 382, 383n12
Moss, Kevin 207n2, 308
Mozart, Wolfgang Amadeus 42, 58, 137, 150, 273, 362, 424, 425, 428, 432, 440, 441, 449, 454, 484, 485
Muhammad [Mahomet] 34
Muravyov-Apostol, Ivan Matveevich 27, 27n2, 28–30, 30n4, 34, 35, 35n7, 37, 37n11
Muravyov, Andrei Nikolaevich 19, 20
Muromtseva-Bunina, Vera Nikolaevna 177

Index of Names

Musorgsky, Modest Petrovich 44–47, 59, 419, 442n5, 466, 479, 480
Myasin. *See* Massine
Myaskovsky, Nikolai Yakovlevich 361, 380n6
Nabokov, Nicolas [Nikolai Dmitrievich] 208, 208n3, 472, 473
Nabokov, Vladimir Vladimirovich [Sirin] 9, 10, 26, 26n26, 50, 50n3, 51n3, 60, 71n7, 76, 76n15, 103, 105, 109, 109n8, 134, 140, 217n8, 223n20, 244, 245, 256n11, 263, 263n20, 264, 277, 301, 315, 318, 391n24
Nadson, Semyon Yakovlevich 87, 89
Naiman, Eric 11, 194n1
Napoleon I (Emperor) 46, 53, 141, 185, 190, 437, 438
Nash, Ogden 387
Nekrasov, Nikolai Alekseevich 231
Nemirovich-Danchenko, Vladimir Ivanovich 467
Nerval, Gérard de [pseud. of Gérard Labrunie] 135, 248
Nesmelov [Mitropolsky], Arseny Ivanovich 311, 316, 318, 320, 320n19
Nessler, Victor E. 202, 202n16
Newman, Ernest 476
Newmarch, Rosa 350
Nicholas I (Tsar) 27, 81, 83, 431
Nicholas II (Tsar) 201, 201n11, 324, 348, 420
Nichols, Johanna 313n6
Nietzsche, Friedrich 92, 93, 110
Nijinska, Bronislava [Bronislava Fominichna Nizhinskaya] 468, 472, 472n20, 473
Nijinsky, Vaslav [Vaslav Fomich Nizhinsky] 468–70, 470n18, 473
Nikisch, Arthur 117
Nikitin, Boris Semyonovich 355n23n25
Nikolai Pavlovich. *See* Nicholas I (Tsar)
Nikolev, Nikolai Petrovich 428, 429n5, 430
Nilender, Vladimir Ottonovich 190
Nilus, Evgeny Khrisanfovich 310n3
Nivat, Georges 198n13n14
Nouvel [Nuvel], Walter Fyodorovich 366, 459, 465, 467, 474
Novikov, Yury Vladimirovich 461n7n8
Nurok, Alfred Pavlovich 465
Oates, Joyce Carol 289
Obolensky, Dimitri Dimitrievich 161, 161n10, 214n5
O'Brien, Kevin 11, 174n1
Odoevsky, Vladimir Fyodorovich (Prince) 56, 56n1n2, 57, 57n3, 58, 59, 59n4n5, 60, 61, 63

Ogaryov, Nikolai Platonovich 198
Oistrakh, David Fyodorovich 371
Okudzhava, Bulat Shalvovich 229n1, 230, 232, 233, 235, 237, 238
Olcott, Anthony 265, 266
Oldani, Robert William 46, 46n2
Olesha, Yury Karlovich 413
Olizar, Gustaw (Count) 29
Omar Khayyám 245n2
Orléans, Charles d' 135
Orlov, Vladimir Nikolaevich 105n1, 106, 107, 111–13, 170n3, 171, 171n4, 172
Orlova, Aleksandra Anatolievna 322, 322n1, 323, 324, 324n4, 325, 325n6, 326, 327, 329, 331–33, 335, 337, 338, 341–44, 353, 354, 354n20n22, 355, 355n24
Ortleb, Charles 457n1
Osorgin, Mikhail Andreevich 172
Ossian. *See* Macpherson
Ossovsky, Aleksandr Vyacheslavovich 461n9
Ostrovsky, Aleksandr Nikolaevich 10, 48, 268, 435
Otsup, Nikolai Avdeevich 170, 222
Ovid [Publius Ovidius Naso] 289, 298, 448
Ozenfant, Amédée 91
Ozerov, Vladislav Aleksandrovich 63n2
Pachmuss, Temira 97, 97n1, 100, 102, 102n6, 103, 104, 104n7
Panaeva. *See* Diaghileva
Paperno, Irina Aronovna 11, 133n1
Parkau, Aleksandra Petrovna 310n3, 319
Parker, Roger 439
Parnok, Sofiya Yakovlevna 195
Parny, Évariste de 379
Parshchikov, Aleksei Maksimovich 298
Pascal, Blaise 20
Paschutinsky, Hélène. *See* Menegaldo
Pashkevich, Vasily Alekseevich 384n14, 429n6, 433n11
Pasler, Jann 376, 381n9
Pasternak, Boris Leonidovich 88, 91, 96, 99, 103, 107, 114, 114n3, 118, 146, 161–63, 163n16, 164–66, 168–70, 172, 173, 178, 182, 182n1, 183, 186, 186n11, 187, 187n12n13, 188–90, 190n16, 191, 192, 192n18n20, 193, 195, 197, 209, 215n6, 229, 230, 232, 235, 236, 244, 245, 248, 248n5, 259, 260, 273, 276, 278n23, 282, 298, 316, 318, 402n2, 404
Pasternak, Elena Vladimirovna 187, 187n13
Pasternak, Evgeny Borisovich 187, 187n13
Pasternak, Leonid Osipovich 165
Paulmann, Inge 108n6

Index of Names

Pavlova, Anna Pavlovna 239, 468
Pavlova, Karolina Karlovna 133
Pendergast, Sara 10n6, 308
Pendergast, Tom 10n6, 308
Percival, John 138n16, 458n3, 473n21
Pereleshin, Valery [pseud. of Valery
  Frantsevich Salatko-Petrishche] 7n1,
  10, 210, 284n37, 301, 302, 302n2, 303,
  303n3n4, 304–7, 307n5, 308, 310, 310n1,
  312, 315, 315n9n10n11, 316, 316n12n13,
  317, 317n14n15, 318, 318n16, 319, 320
Perrot, Jules 443
Perse, Saint-John 235
Pertsov, Pyotr Petrovich 464n13
Pertsov, Viktor Osipovich 192, 192n19
Peshkova, Katya 177
Peter I [the Great] (Tsar) 311
Petina, Irina [Irra] Stefanovna 314
Petipa, Marius [Ivanovich] 466, 472
Philidor, François-André Dancan 425
Piaf, Edith 319n17
Picasso, Pablo 471, 472
Pichot, Amédée 17, 18, 24n21
Pierre, André 418n3
Piltz, Mariya Yulievna 471
Pinza, Ezio 420
Pisarev, Dmitry Ivanovich 133, 134
Pisemsky, Aleksei Feofilaktovich 70n6
Pixérécourt, René-Charles Guilbert de 77
Plavilshchikov, Pyotr Alekseevich 435
Pleshcheev, Aleksei Nikolaevich 11n8
Pliny the Elder 25, 28
Poe, Edgar Allan 56, 147
Poggioli, Renato 128, 128n7
Pogodin, Aleksandr Lvovich 30n4
Polevoi, Nikolai Alekseevich 20
Poliak, Gregory 240n8
Poltoratsky, Nikolai Petrovich 174n1
Pomyalovsky, Nikolai Gerasimovich 437
Ponomaryov, A. 104n8
Poplavskaya, Nataliya Yulianovna 250, 251, 261
Poplavsky, Boris Yulianovich 7n2, 88, 89,
  109, 109n7, 180, 212, 215n6, 216, 217,
  217n8, 221–24, 224n23, 225, 225n25,
  226, 227, 227n29, 228, 242, 245,
  246, 246n3n4, 248, 248n5, 249–53,
  253n8, 254, 254n9, 255, 256, 256n11,
  257–60, 260n14, 261–63, 263n20, 264,
  264n21n22n23, 265, 265n24n25, 266,
  315n11, 318, 335
Poplavsky, Yulian Ignatievich 249–53,
  253n8, 257

Popov, Mikhail Ivanovich 426, 427, 436
Porter, Andrew 449, 449n14
Pound, Ezra 111, 135n8, 137, 138n13, 152,
  450, 450n17
Poznansky, Aleksandr Nikolaevich 325n6,
  326, 326n9, 327, 327n10, 330, 330n3n4,
  331, 332, 334n15, 337, 339n1, 343,
  343n7, 344, 345, 348, 348n1n2, 349, 350,
  354, 354n21
Pregel, Sofiya Yulievna 261
Pring, Samuel William 386n16
Proffer, Carl 55
Prokofiev, Sergei Sergeevich 361, 369, 371,
  380, 380n6, 400, 401, 418, 448, 473
Propp, Vladimir Yakovlevich 382, 382n10,
  387, 387n19, 390n24, 391n24
Proust, Marcel 29, 263
Prutkov, Kozma [collective pseud.] 70n6
Przhevalsky, Nikolai Mikhailovich 324, 344
Przybyszewski, Stanisław Feliks 478
Puccini, Giacomo 354
Pugachyov, Emelyan Ivanovich 184n4
Pushkin, Aleksandr Sergeevich 8, 10, 14,
  15, 17, 18, 18n9n10n12, 19, 19n13, 20,
  20n14, 21, 21n15n16n17, 22, 23, 23n19,
  24, 24n21n22, 25, 25n23, 26, 26n27,
  27–32, 32n5, 33–35, 35n7, 36–40,
  40n14n15n16, 41, 41n16n18, 42, 42n19,
  43–48, 48n3, 49, 49n1, 50, 50n2n3, 51,
  51n3, 52, 52n4, 53, 53n5, 54–56, 60,
  61, 63–65, 67, 67n4, 72, 73, 73n13, 74,
  76, 76n15, 77, 79, 79n3, 81, 83, 84, 88,
  105, 113, 118, 133, 135, 141, 145, 146,
  148, 163, 165, 166, 182, 182n1, 183,
  184, 184n3n4, 185, 185n5, 186, 186n8,
  187–91, 193, 194, 194n2, 216, 222, 227,
  233, 240, 244, 245, 268, 269, 273, 280,
  284, 286–88, 290, 294, 297, 360, 363,
  369, 376n2, 377, 379, 384, 390, 390n24,
  392n25, 414, 423n1, 429n6, 436, 438,
  466, 468, 478n4, 484, 485
Pyman, Avril 105n1, 106, 108, 111–13
Qu Yuan [Ch'u Yuan] 317, 317n15
Rabelais, François 45, 138, 451
Rabinovich, Aleksandr Semyonovich 437n15
Rachmaninoff, Sergei Vasilievich 12, 122,
  328, 370, 373, 418–20, 466
Racine, Jean-Baptiste 22, 31, 33, 46, 429n6,
  441
Radcliffe, Ann 16
Raevsky, Nikolai Nikolaevich 28
Raevsky-Hughes, Olga 11, 86n1, 186,
  186n11, 291n3

Index of Names

Raffel, Burton 145n1, 150, 151
Raft, George 243
Ramuz, Charles-Ferdinand 360n6, 385, 387, 388, 388n21, 389n21
Rannit, Alexis [Aleksei Konstantinovich Dolgoshev] 302, 303n3, 316n12
Rasputin, Grigory Efimovich 420
Raupach, Hermann 435
Ravel, Maurice 10, 362, 399, 419, 419n4, 465, 471, 475, 475n1, 476–81, 483–85
Reavey, George 229n1, 237
Rechy, John 306
Redzhi, Sofiya [S. A.] 319n17
Reeder, Roberta 461n7
Remizov, Aleksei Mikhailovich 68, 169, 181, 214, 263, 282, 298, 301, 364, 383, 389, 469
Repin, Ilya Efimovich 187
Reznikova, Nataliya Viktorovna 319
Riasanovsky, Nicholas [Nikolai Valentinovich] 41
Rice, James L. 346n1
Richardson, Joanna 443n8, 444, 444n9
Richardson, Samuel 16, 24
Rilke, Rainer Maria 147, 176, 178, 183, 187, 187n13, 189, 191, 192, 192n20, 195
Rimbaud, Arthur 88, 222, 248, 256, 262, 267, 305
Rimsky-Korsakov, Andrei Nikolaevich 374, 375
Rimsky-Korsakov, Nikolai Andreevich 59, 374, 375, 377n3, 379, 393, 419, 419n4, 461, 461n8n9n10, 466, 469, 479, 480, 484
Robbins Landon, H. C. 345, 345n9
Robeson, Paul 400
Rochester [Eddie Anderson] 243
Roditi, Edouard 259
Rodov, Semyon Abramovich 192n19
Rodriguez, Philippe 368n14
Rodzaevsky, Konstantin Vladimirovich 315n10
Roerich [Rerikh], Nikolai Konstantinovich 319, 362, 364, 383, 388, 388n20
Rogers, Ginger 319n17
Roland-Manuel, Alexis 366, 372n6
Rolland, Romain 137, 400
Romanov, Boris Georgievich 471
Ronsard, Pierre de 135
Rorem, Ned 356
Rosenthal, Harold 331n7
Roshchina-Insarova, Ekaterina Nikolaevna 314

Rossetti, Dante Gabriel 91, 306
Rossini, Gioachino 58, 379, 441, 441n4, 442, 442n6, 443, 447, 449, 450, 454, 456
Rostand, Edmond 187, 202
Rostropovich, Mstislav Leopoldovich 240n8
Rousseau, Jean-Jacques 16, 17n8, 22, 24, 322, 424, 425, 427, 432, 432n10
Rozai, Georgy Alfredovich 468
Rozanov, Vasily Vasilievich 222, 315n11, 324
Rozenberg, Lev Samoilovich. *See* Bakst
Rozhdestvensky, Gennady Nikolaevich 373
Rubinstein, Anton Grigorievich 386n16, 420, 421
Rubinstein, Nikolai Grigorievich 351n15
Rudinsky, Vladimir [Daniil Fyodorovich Petrov] 210
Rudnitsky, Konstantin Lazarevich 83n7
Russell, Robert 176n4
Ryleev, Kondraty Fyodorovich 287
Ryurik 60, 208
Rzewuski, Henryk (Count) 29
Rzhevsky, Leonid Denisovich 282, 282n33, 298, 298n12
Saadi 34, 35
Saakyants, Anna Aleksandrovna 171
Sachs, Hans 66
Sadie, Stanley 325n5
Sadovskaya, Mariya [M. A.] 319n17
Saint-Amant, Antoine Girard de 16, 135
Sainte-Beuve, Charles Augustin 25, 135
Sakharov, Andrei Dmitrievich 371n4, 400, 409
Sakulin, Pavel Nikitich 59, 59n4
Samkov, Vladimir Alekseevich 460n6, 461n10, 464n13, 467n16, 474, 474n22
Sapunov, Nikolai Nikolaevich 129
Satie, Erik 471, 478
Satovsky-Rzhevsky, Grigory [Harry], Jr. 318
Savenko, Svetlana Ilinichna 372n6
Scarlatti, Alessandro 440
Schaeffer, Pierre 93
Scheffel, Joseph Victor von 201, 202, 202n14n15, 203n17
Scheijen, Sjeng 458n4
Schelling, Friedrich Wilhelm Joseph von 57, 276
Schiller, Friedrich 77, 78, 82
Schnittke [Shnitke], Alfred Garrievich 374
Schoenberg, Arnold 116, 116n6, 465
Schopenhauer, Arthur 276
Schubert, Franz 117
Schumann, Robert 468
Schuvaloff, George 304

Index of Names

Scott, Sir Walter 24, 24n22, 77, 78, 81, 450, 454
Scriabin [Skryabin], Aleksandr Nikolaevich 244, 264n23, 466
Seaman, Gerald R. 437n15, 438
Sedaine, Michel-Jean 425, 425n3, 426n4, 427, 429n6
Selby, Elliott 352, 352n16
Selvinsky, Ilya [Karl] Lvovich 259
Sénancour, Étienne 67
Sénecé, Antoine Bauderon de 34
Senkovsky, Osip Ivanovich [Jósef Sękowski] 72, 73
Sergei Aleksandrovich (Grand Duke) 324, 348
Serov, Aleksandr Nikolaevich 58, 420
Serov, Boris 319n17
Setchkarev, Vsevolod Mikhailovich 77n1, 92n2, 265, 292
Severyanin, Igor [pseud. of Igor Vasilievich Lotaryov] 231, 290
Shakespeare, William 28, 42, 44, 46, 65, 69, 71, 72, 72n10, 80, 137, 148, 165, 305, 308, 346, 447, 451
Shakhovskaya, Zinaida Alekseevna 174
Shakhovskoi, Aleksandr Aleksandrovich 63, 63n2, 435
Shaliapin. See Chaliapin
Shamurin, Evgeny Ivanovich 221, 221n17
Shartse, Olga 105n1
Shaw, George Bernard 400
Shchedrin, Rodion Konstantinovich 372
Shchyogolev, Nikolai Aleksandrovich 318
Shchyogolev, Pavel Eliseevich 40
Shelley, Percy Bysshe 66, 70
Sherr, Barry P. 346n1
Shestov, Lev [pseud. of Lev Isaakovich Shvartsman] 99
Shevelenko, Irina Danielevna 187n13
Shklovsky, Viktor Borisovich 118, 130
Shokhman, Gennady Yakovlevich 355n23
Sholokhov, Mikhail Aleksandrovich 137
Shostakovich, Dmitry Dmitrievich 10, 75, 76, 336, 371, 371n4, 398, 398n1, 399–406, 406n6n7, 407, 408n1, 409–14, 422, 479, 479n5
Shostakovich, Irina Antonovna 371n4
Shostakovich, Maksim Dmitrievich 410
Shraibman, Dina Grigorievna 262
Shtein, Emmanuil 320n19
Shvarts, Evgeny Lvovich 68, 222
Simpich, Frederick 312n5
Sinyavsky, Andrei Donatovich 240n8

Sipovsky, Vasily Vasilievich 18, 18n9, 19, 19n13, 21–23
Sirin. See Nabokov, Vladimir
Skabichevsky, Aleksandr Mikhailovich 137
Škvorecký, Josef 409, 409n4
Slater, Lydia Pasternak [Lidiya Leonidovna Pasternak] 155n7, 161
Slonim, Mark [Marc] Lvovich 169
Słowacki, Juliusz 41
Sluchevsky, Konstantin Konstantinovich 216
Slutsky, Boris Abramovich 229
Smirnov, Valery Vasilievich 382, 383n12, 388n20
Smith, G. S. 292, 292n5
Sobańska, Karolina 29
Sofronov, Aleksei Ivanovich [Alyosha] 324, 335, 344, 350
Sokolov, Nikolai Aleksandrovich 460
Sokolov, Valery Solomonovich 349, 349n7
Sokolov, Yakov 436
Sokolovsky, Mikhail Matveevich 384n14, 432, 432n9
Solie, Ruth A. 338n18
Sologub, Fyodor [pseud. of Fyodor Kuzmich Teternikov] 88, 90, 317n14, 379, 389, 403, 468, 469
Soloukhin, Vladimir Alekseevich 293, 294, 294n7
Solovyov, Mikhail Sergeevich 118, 122
Solovyov, Sergei Mikhailovich 122
Solovyov, Vladimir Sergeevich 75n14, 87, 107, 118, 122–24, 133
Solzhenitsyn, Aleksandr Isaevich 10, 99, 274, 275, 275n16, 287, 301, 400, 409
Somov, Konstantin Andreevich 459, 462, 463
Sontag, Susan 240n8
Southey, Robert 33
Soutine, Chaim 261
Souzay, Gérard 8
Spiegelman, Joel 324, 324n4, 327
Sposobin, Igor Vladimirovich 122, 122n14
Staël, Madame de 21, 24n21n22, 25
Stakhovich, Aleksei Aleksandrovich 194
Stalin, Joseph 57, 59, 105, 146, 148, 149, 179, 213, 214n5, 229, 231n3, 232, 232n3, 238, 268, 269, 271, 307, 312, 318, 323, 324, 370, 398–402, 404, 405, 407–13, 418, 420, 422, 437n15, 473
Stanislavsky, Konstantin Sergeevich 467
Stasov, Vladimir Vasilievich 370, 463, 463n12
Steele, Thomas 457n1

Index of Names

Steiger [Shteiger], Anatoly Sergeevich 170, 174, 178, 191, 194–97, 197n8, 198, 198n9, 199, 200, 203, 204, 204n21, 303, 306, 307
Stein, Gertrude 143, 215
Steinberg [Shteinberg], Maksimilian Oseevich 375
Steiner, Rudolf 117
Stenbock-Fermor, Aleksandr Vladimirovich 325n6
Stenbock-Fermor, Ivan Ivanovich 326
Stenbock-Fermor, Vladimir (Count) 325n6
Stendhal [Marie-Henri Beyle] 442n6
Stephan, John J. 315n10
Sterne, Laurence 16
Sternfeld, Frederick W. 376n2
Stevens, Wallace 152, 244
Stilman, Leon 26, 26n27
Stokowski, Leopold 398
Strabo 28, 30, 37
Strachey, Lytton 341
Strauss, Richard 336, 419, 442n5, 475, 485
Stravinskaya, Kseniya Yurievna 369, 369n2
Stravinskaya, Tatyana Yurievna 369n2
Stravinskaya, Vera Arturovna [née de Bosset] 376n2, 389n22, 390n23
Stravinsky, Igor Fyodorovich 8, 10, 42, 59, 264n23, 358, 358n1, 359, 359n3n4, 360–64, 364n7, 365, 365n8n9n10, 366, 366n12, 367, 367n13, 368, 368n14, 369, 369n1n2, 370, 370n3, 371, 371n4, 372, 372n6, 373, 373n7, 374, 374n8, 375, 375n9, 376, 376n1n2, 377, 377n2n3, 378–80, 380n7, 381, 381n8n9, 382, 383n12, 384, 384n14, 385, 386, 386n16, 388, 388n20n21, 389, 389n22, 390, 390n23n24, 391, 391n24n25, 392, 392n25, 393, 393n26, 394, 395, 395n29, 396, 396n30n31, 402, 403, 405, 419, 419n4, 421, 421n7, 422, 435, 457n2, 465, 469, 470, 470n18, 471, 473, 480
Stravinsky, Sviatoslav [Soulima] 372n6, 393
Stravinsky, Yury Fyodorovich 369
Streisand, Barbra 399
Struve, Gleb Petrovich 8, 15n5, 40n14, 41, 114n1, 117n8, 143, 143n25, 144, 144n26, 145n2, 146, 147, 151, 187n14, 216n7, 223n20, 248n5, 256, 256n11, 296n11, 313
Struve, Nikita Alekseevich 187n14
Stuck, Franz von 91
Stupel, Aleksandr Dmitrievich 475
Sudeikin, Sergei Yurievich 129
Sukhovo-Kobylin, Aleksandr Vasilievich 70, 70n6

Sumarokov, Aleksandr Petrovich 46, 135, 435
Sumerkin, Aleksandr Evgenievich 182n2
Suvchinsky, Pyotr Petrovich 363, 366, 368, 372n6
Suvorin, Aleksei Sergeevich 201n12, 278, 310, 463n12
Svyatopolk-Mirsky, Dmitry Petrovich (Prince) 169, 172, 240, 256, 263, 431n8, 462, 463n11
Swedenborg, Emanuel 57
Szilard, Elena 117n9n10
Szulkin, Robert 229n1
Taglioni, Marie 468
Taranovsky, Kiril Fyodorovich 153
Taruskin, Richard 8, 46, 46n2, 47n2, 334n15, 339, 339n2, 351n12, 377n2, 380, 380n7, 381n9, 392, 395n29, 411, 411n6, 412, 413, 419n4, 439, 475n1
Tatishchev, Nikolai Dmitrievich 246, 246n3, 260–62, 264
Taupin, René 138, 138n13n18
Tchaikovsky. See Chaikovsky
Tchelitchew, Pavel Fyodorovich 242, 248, 261, 335, 472
Teilhard de Chardin, Pierre 235, 276, 283
Temple, Shirley 319n17
Tenisheva, Mariya Klavdievna (Princess) 462
Terapiano, Yury [Georgy] Konstantinovich 245, 263, 263n17
Teresa of Ávila (Saint) 227
Tereshkovich [Terechkovitch], Konstantin Andreevitch 261
Terras, Victor 12, 62n1, 81n5
Tesková, Anna 174, 175, 175n3, 176–81, 186, 186n9
Thomas, D. M. 49, 49n1, 51–55
Thomas, Dylan 244, 245
Thomson, Virgil 334n15, 403, 404n3
Tieck, Ludwig 71, 71n9, 72, 72n10
Tierney, Gene 243
Timenchik, Roman Davidovich 127n6
Titov, Nikolai Alekseevich 376n2, 377n2
Tkhorzhevsky, Ivan Ivanovich 245, 245n2
Tokarev, Dmitry Viktorovich 265n24
Tolstoi, Aleksei Konstantinovich 223n22, 273, 280, 294
Tolstoi, Lev Nikolaevich 8, 10, 14, 14n2, 48, 57, 60, 84, 84n9, 87, 92, 97, 109, 128, 133, 149, 179, 184, 201, 201n11, 206, 214, 237, 258, 277, 297, 328, 362, 363, 369, 460, 460n6
Tomashevsky, Boris Viktorovich 19, 19n13, 21, 24n22, 34, 34n6, 40n16

Index of Names

Toporov, Vladimir Nikolaevich 127n6
Toscanini, Arturo 401
Tovey, Donald Francis 339, 344, 351
Traugott, Elizabeth Closs 313n6
Trelawny, Edward John 70
Trifonov, Gennady Nikolaevich 10, 132
Trotsky, Leon [Lev Davidovich Bronshtein] 110, 399
Troyat, Henri 112
Tsiolkovsky, Konstantin Eduardovich 227
Tsivyan, Tatyana Vladimirovna 127n6
Tsvetaeva, Anastasiya [Asya] Ivanovna [A. Mein] 177, 185, 185n6, 190, 203
Tsvetaeva, Marina Ivanovna 8, 48, 84, 84n8, 88, 96, 103, 107, 124, 126, 129, 154, 154n1n2n3n4, 155, 155n5n6n7, 157–59, 161, 162, 162n14, 163, 163n15n17, 164, 167, 167n1, 168–70, 170n3, 171, 171n4, 172–74, 174n1n2, 175, 175n3, 176, 176n4n5, 177–82, 182n1n2, 183, 184, 184n3n4, 185, 185n5n7, 186, 186n9n10n11, 187, 187n13n14, 188, 188n15, 189, 190, 190n16, 191, 192, 192n20, 193, 193n21, 194, 194n1n2, 195, 195n3, 196, 197, 197n8, 198, 198n9, 199–202, 202n16, 203, 203n17n18, 204, 204n21, 209, 218, 219, 219n11n12n13, 220, 230, 232, 234, 237, 238, 240, 251, 251n7, 282, 283, 301, 306, 315, 318, 369, 381, 481
Tsvetaeva, Mariya Aleksandrovna [née Mein] 183
Tsvetaeva, Valeriya Ivanovna 183, 191
Tugendhold, Yakov Aleksandrovich 393
Tukhachevsky, Mikhail Nikolaevich 399, 401
Turgenev, Ivan Sergeevich 57, 294, 301, 460, 479, 480
Turgeneva, Anna [Asya] Alekseevna 117, 185n7
Turkov, Andrei Mikhailovich 216n7
Turyan, Marietta Andreevna 56n1
Tuwim, Julian 41, 41n18
Tynyanov, Yury Nikolaevich 62–64, 149
Tyutchev, Fyodor Ivanovich 89, 141, 152, 276, 479
Undset, Sigrid 181
Updike, John 240n8, 289
Ushinsky, Konstantin Dmitrievich 182, 183
Vaginov, Konstantin Konstantinovich 222
van den Toorn, Pieter C. 470n18
Varshavsky, Vladimir Sergeevich 245, 263, 263n18
Varunts, Victor Pavlovich 375n9

Vasilevskaya, Mara 319n17
Vaudoyer, Jean-Louis 138
Vega, Lope de 43
Vegesack, Siegfried von 268n3
Veidle. *See* Weidlé
Velimirović, Miloš 386n16
Velluti, Giovanni Battista 441
Verdi, Giuseppe 58, 345n9, 354, 362, 373, 442n5, 461
Vergil 28
Verhaeren, Émile 88
Verinovsky, Ivan Aleksandrovich 337
Verlaine, Paul 88, 114, 126, 136, 164, 305
Vershinina, Irina Yakovlevna 358n1, 360–62, 365, 377, 377n3, 379n4, 380, 380n6, 386n16, 387n18, 388n20
Vertinsky, Aleksandr Nikolaevich 260
Veselovsky, Aleksei Nikolaevich 17n8
Viau, Théophile de 16
Vicinus, Martha 9n5, 347n3
Victoria (Queen) 324
Vilchkovsky, Kirill Sergeevich 197, 198n9, 203, 203n19
Villa-Lobos, Heitor 314
Villon, François 126, 135, 147, 148, 151, 451
Vinokurov, Evgeny Mikhailovich 114n3, 234
Vishnevskaya, Galina Pavlovna 410, 413, 413n8
Vishnyak, Abram Grigorievich 195
Vitale, Serena 187n13
Vitins, Ieva 193n21
Vitkovsky, Evgeny Vladimirovich 304, 305
Vlad, Roman 364n7
Vladimir Svyatoslavich (Grand Prince) 381
Voinovich, Vladimir Nikolaevich 301
Voitov, Aleksandr 325, 354
Volin, Mikhail Nikolaevich 315n9
Volkoff, Vladimir [Vladimir Nikolaevich Volkov] 322
Volkonsky, Sergei Mikhailovich (Prince) 194, 467
Volkov, Solomon Moiseevich 349n8, 398, 398n1, 402, 402n2, 404–6, 406n7, 407, 410, 413, 414
Voloshin [Kirienko-Voloshin], Maksimilian Aleksandrovich 173, 248n5
Voltaire [François-Marie Arouet] 33, 35, 74, 137, 379, 429n6, 441
Voznesensky, Andrei Andreevich 229n1, 230, 232, 232n3, 235–38, 273n7
Vroon, Ronald 291n1
Vrubel, Mikhail Aleksandrovich 91, 463

Index of Names

Vsevolodsky-Gerngross, Vsevolod Nikolaevich 382, 382n11, 383n13, 384n15
Vyazemsky, Pyotr Andreevich (Prince) 15, 24n22, 29, 34, 36, 36n10, 39, 39n12n13, 40
Vyshinsky, Andrei Yanuarevich 414
Wagner, Richard 58, 60, 92, 93, 111, 114, 122, 150, 326, 331, 335, 362, 373, 460, 461, 467, 485
Walpole, Horace 16
Warner, Elizabeth A. 382, 382n11
Warrack, John 322, 331n7, 340, 340n4
Watteau, Jean-Antoine 424
Waugh, Evelyn 363
Weaver, Dennis 306, 309
Weber, Carl Maria von 58, 379
Webern, Anton 116, 116n6
Weidlé [Veidle], Vladimir Vasilievich 170, 256, 263, 281, 281n32, 283
Weinstock, Herbert 350n9, 352, 352n16, 442n6
Weintraub, Wiktor 30n4, 35n8
Weiss, Piero 334n15
Welty, Eudora 289
Werth, Alexander 234n4
White, Eric Walter 359, 364n7, 373, 373n7, 376, 376n2, 391n24
White, Hayden 345
Whitfield, Francis J. 142n23, 440n1, 463n11
Whitman, Walt 126, 230
Wilbur, Richard 238, 277n20, 281, 302
Wilde, Oscar 142, 230, 305, 324, 328, 347, 457n2, 460
Wilder, Billy 243
Wiley, Roland John 331n7, 340n3, 344
Wilson, Edmund 9, 50, 51n3, 105, 138
Wilson, Paul Robert 409n4
Wing, Betsy 441n4
Wolfe, Thomas 245
Wood, Ralph W. 351n15
Woodward, James B. 313n7
Wordsworth, Dorothy 24

Wordsworth, William 24
Yakulov, Georgy Bogdanovich 473
Yankovskaya, Viktoriya Yurievna 319
Yanovsky, Vasily Semyonovich 263, 263n19
Yarko, Sergei 257
Yarustovsky, Boris Mikhailovich 361, 365n8, 369n1, 386n16, 388n20, 403
Yastrebtsev, Vasily Vasilievich 461n9n10
Yates, Peter 404, 404n4
Yeats, W. B. 147, 152, 230
Yeltsin, Boris Nikolaevich 346, 347
Yulsky, Boris 315, 315n10
Zabolotsky, Nikolai Alekseevich 124, 212, 213, 214n5, 216, 216n7, 217, 221–23, 223n20n22, 224, 224n24, 225, 226, 226n26n27n28, 227, 228, 230, 235, 237, 238, 260n14, 276, 277
Zajaczkowski, Henry 340, 340n3, 344, 351n13
Zakharenko, Nina Gerasimovna 212n11
Zakovich, Boris 262
Zamyatin, Evgeny Ivanovich 177, 271, 389, 413, 414
Zelinsky, Kornely Lyutsianovich 223, 223n21
Zguta, Russell 386, 386n17, 387, 387n19
Zhdanov, Andrei Aleksandrovich 408, 408n2, 437n15
Zhdanov, Ivan 298
Zhirmunsky, Viktor Maksimovich 18, 18n12, 22
Zhivov, Mark Semyonovich 40
Zhukovsky, Vasily Andreevich 63, 227, 390n24, 469
Zilbershtein, Ilya Samoilovich 460n6, 461n10, 464n13, 467n16, 474
Zinovieva-Annibal, Lidiya Dmitrievna 127
Zlobin, Vladimir Ananievich 104, 104n7, 465n14
Zoshchenko, Mikhail Mikhailovich 226, 401, 402, 413
Zotov, Rafail Mikhailovich 80
Zozulya, Nataliya Vasilievna 270

www.ingramcontent.com/pod-product-compliance
Lightning Source LLC
Chambersburg PA
CBHW071354300426
44114CB00016B/2055